UPKAR'S

# Technical Trades RAILWAY ASSISTANT LOCO PILOT & TECHNICIAN (Grade-III) Examinations

*By*

*Sudhindra Pratap*

**Upkar Prakashan, Agra-2**

**Publishers**

**UPKAR PRAKASHAN**

2/11A, Swadeshi Bima Nagar, AGRA–282 002

**Phone :** 4053333, 2530966, 2531101

**Fax :** (0562) 4053330

**E-mail :** care@upkar.in, **Website :** www.upkar.in

**Branch Offices**

4845, Ansari Road, Daryaganj, **New Delhi**–110 002
**Phone :** 011–23251844/66

16-11-23/37, Moosarambagh, Teegan Guda Opp. RTA Office Main Road, Beside–Andhra Bank, **Hyderabad**–500 036 (TS)
**Phone :** 040–24557283

Paras Bhawan (First Floor), Khazanchi Road, **Patna**–800 004
**Phone. :** 0612–2303340

H-3, Block-B, Municipal Premises No. 15-2, Galiff Street, P.S. Shyampukur, **Kolkata**–700 003 (W.B.)
**Phone :** 033–25551510

B-33, Blunt Square, Kanpur Taxi Stand, Mawaiya, **Lucknow**–226 004 (U.P.)
**Phone :** 0522–4109080

8-310/1, A. K. House, Heeranagar, **Haldwani, Distt.–Nainital**–263139 (Uttarakhand)
**Mob. :** 7060421008

1461, Juni Shukrawari, Sakkardara Road, Opp. Hanuman Mandir, **Nagpur**–440 009
**Phone :** 0712–6564222

30-31, Jinsi Haat Maidan, Near Baba Ramdev Mandir, Malharganj, **Indore**–452 002 (M.P.)
**Phone :** 9203908088





ISBN : 978-93-5013-641-6

**Price :** ₹ 199.00
**(Rs. One Hundred Ninety Nine Only)**

**Code No. 1882**

**Printed at :** UPKAR PRAKASHAN (Printing Unit) Bye-pass, AGRA

# Contents

1. Refrigeration and Air-Conditioning ........ 3–15

2. Automobile Engineering ........ 16–28

3. Instrument Mechanical ........ 29–39

4. Thermodynamics ........ 40–53

5. Internal Combustion Engine (ICE) ........ 54–66

6. Fluid Mechanics ........ 67–82

7. Power Plant Engineering ........ 83–95

8. Turbomachinery ........ 96–106

9. Engineering Mechanics ........ 107–119

10. Strength of Materials ........ 120–133

11. Theory of Machines ........ 134–146

12. Vibration Analysis ........ 147–160

13. Materials Science ........ 161–171

14. Metal Forming ........ 172–182

15. Metal Casting ........ 183–193

16. Fabrication Process ........ 194–201

17. Metal Cutting ........ 202–212

18. Tool Engineering ........ 213–224

19. Metrology and Inspection ........ 225–234

20. Production Planning ........ 235–248

# Practice Sets
## Railway
## Assistant Loco Pilot
## &
## Technician (Grade-III) Exam.

# 1. Refrigeration and Air-Conditioning

- Refrigeration is a process in which work is done to move heat from one location to another. The work of heat transport is traditionally driven by mechanical work, but can also be driven by heat, magnetism, electricity, laser, or other means. Refrigeration has many applications, including, but not limited to: household refrigerators, industrial freezers, cryogenics, and air conditioning.
- Heat pumps may use the heat output of the refrigeration process, and also may be designed to be reversible, but are otherwise similar to refrigeration units.
- Refrigeration has had a large impact on industry, lifestyle, agriculture and settlement patterns. The idea of preserving food dates back to the ancient Roman and Chinese empires.
- However, refrigeration technology has rapidly evolved in the last century from ice harvesting to temperature controlled rail cars. The introduction of refrigerated rail cars contributed to the westward expansion of the United States, allowing settlement in areas that were not on main transport channels such as rivers, harbors, or valley trails.
- The history of artificial refrigeration began when Scottish professor William Cullen designed a small refrigerating machine in 1755. Cullen used a pump to create a partial vacuum over a container of diethyl ether, which then boiled, absorbing heat from the surrounding air. The experiment even created a small amount of ice, but had no practical application at that time.
- In 1758, Benjamin Franklin and John Hadley, professor of chemistry, collaborated on a project investigating the principle of evaporation as a means to rapidly cool an object at Cambridge University, England.
- They confirmed that the evaporation of highly volatile liquids, such as alcohol and ether, could be used to drive down the temperature of an object past the freezing point of water.
- They conducted their experiment with the bulb of a mercury thermometer as their object and with a bellows used to 'quicken' the evaporation; they lowered the temperature of the thermometer bulb down to 7 °F (−14°C), while the ambient temperature was 65 °F (18°C).
- They noted that soon after they passed the freezing point of water (32 °F), a thin film of ice formed on the surface of the thermometer's bulb and that the ice mass was about a quarter inch thick when they stopped the experiment upon reaching 7 °F (−14 °C).
- In 1805, American inventor Oliver Evans described a closed vapor-compression refrigeration cycle for the production of ice by ether under vacuum.
- In 1820, the English scientist Michael Faraday liquefied ammonia and other gases by using high pressures and low temperatures, and in 1834, an American expatriate to Great Britain, Jacob Perkins, built the first working vapor-compression refrigeration system in the world.
- In 1842, a similar attempt was made by American physician, John Gorrie, who built a working prototype, but it was a commercial failure. Like many of the medical experts during this time, Gorrie thought too much exposure to tropical heat led to mental and physical degeneration, as well as the spread of diseases such as malaria.
- He conceived the idea of using his refrigeration system to cool the air for comfort in homes and hospitals to prevent disease. American engineer Alexander Twining took out a British patent in 1850 for a vapor compression system that used ether.
- The first practical vapor compression refrigeration system was built by James Harrison, a British journalist who had emigrated to Australia. His 1856 patent was for a vapour compression system using ether, alcohol or ammonia.
- He built a mechanical ice-making machine in 1851 on the banks of the Barwon River at Rocky Point in Geelong, Victoria, and his first commercial ice-making machine followed in 1854.
- Harrison also introduced commercial vapour-compression refrigeration to breweries and meat packing houses, and by 1861, a dozen of his systems were in operation.
- The first gas absorption refrigeration system using gaseous ammonia dissolved in water was developed by Ferdinand Carré of France in 1859 and patented in 1860.
- Air conditioning is the process of altering the properties of air to more comfortable conditions, typically with the aim of distributing the conditioned air to an occupied space to improve thermal comfort and indoor air quality.
- The basic concept behind air conditioning is said to have been applied in ancient Egypt, where reeds were hung in windows and were moistened with trickling water.
- The evaporation of water cooled the air blowing through the window. This process also made the air more humid,

which can be beneficial in a dry desert climate. In Ancient Rome, water from aqueducts was circulated through the walls of certain houses to cool them.

- Other techniques in medieval Persia involved the use of cisternsand wind towers to cool buildings during the hot season.
- Modern air conditioning emerged from advances in chemistry during the 19th century, and the first large-scale electrical air conditioning was invented and used in 1902 by American inventor Willis Carrier.
- The introduction of residential air conditioning in the 1920s helped enable the great migration to the Sun Belt in the United States.
- Inductors or choke coils are made of iron core because large valued flux densities can be produced in iron cores and so inductances of large value can be had. Air-cored inductors become too much bulky to provide an inductance of a required value.
- An inductance draws instantaneous power but no average power. The power drawn by inductance during one quarter cycle is released in another quarter cycle, and so average power drawn by an inductance is zero.
- Power factor may be defined as the cosine of the phase angle between voltage and current. It may also be defined as the ratio of resistance to impedance or the ratio of true power to apparent power.
- The current component which is in phase with circuit voltage (i.e., $I \cos f$) and contributes to active or true power of the circuit is called the active (wattfull or in-phase) component of current.
- The current component which is in quadrature (or 90° out of phase) to the circuit voltage (*i.e.,* $I \sin \phi$) and contributes to reactive power of the circuit is called the reactive (or wattless) component of current.
- The power which is actually consumed or utilized in an ac circuit is called the true or active power of the circuit.
- Power is consumed only in resistance. It is given by the product of the circuit voltage $V$, current $I$ and power factor $\cos \phi$ i.e., $P = VI \cos \phi$. It is expressed in watts.
- A pure inductor and a pure capacitor do not consume any power, as in a quarter cycle whatsoever power is drawn from the supply source by these components, the same is returned to the supply source in the other quarter cycle. This power which flows back and forth (i.e., in both directions in the circuit) or reacts itself is called the reactive power. This is also known as wattless power.
- The reactive power of an ac circuit is given by the product of voltage $V$, current $I$ and sine of the phase anglef, i.e., Reactive power, $Q = VI \sin \phi$. It is expressed in reactive volt-amperes.
- In a purely capacitive circuit, current leads the applied voltage by 90° or $\pi/2$ radians.
- Inductive reactance of an inductor increases proportionately with the increase in supply frequency i.e., $X_L \propto f$.
- In 1758, Benjamin Franklin and John Hadley, a chemistry professor at Cambridge University, conducted an experiment to explore the principle of evaporation as a means to rapidly cool an object.
- Franklin and Hadley confirmed that evaporation of highly volatile liquids could be used to drive down the temperature of an object past the freezing point of water.
- They conducted their experiment with the bulb of a mercury thermometer as their object and with a bellows used to speed-up the evaporation. They lowered the temperature of the thermometer bulb down to −14°C (7°F) while the ambient temperature was 18°C (64 °F).
- In 1820, English scientist and inventor Michael Faraday discovered that compressing and liquefying ammonia could chill air when the liquefied ammonia was allowed to evaporate.
- In 1842, Florida physician John Gorrie used compressor technology to create ice, which he used to cool air for his patients in his hospital in Apalachicola, Florida.

# MULTIPLE CHOICE QUESTIONS

1. In a domestic refrigerator, a capillary tube controls the flow of refrigerant form the:
(a) expansion valve to the evaporator
(b) evaporator to the thermostat
(c) condenser to the expansion valve
(d) condenser to the evaporator

2. The coefficient of performance (COP) of a refrigerator working as a heat pump is given by:
(a) $(COP)_{heat\ pump} = (COP)_{refrigerator} + 2$
(b) $(COP)_{heat\ pump} = (COP)_{refrigerator} + 1$
(c) $(COP)_{heat\ pump} = (COP)_{refrigerator} - 1$
(d) $(COP)_{heat\ pump} = (COP)_{refrigerator}$

3. Consider the following steps:
1. Starting of compressor.
2. Starting of cooling tower pump
3. Starting of chiller water pump
4. Starting of blower motor of cooling coil
The correct sequence of these steps in the starting of a central air conditioning plant using chilled water cooling coil, is:
(a) 3, 1, 4, 2
(b) 1, 3, 2, 4
(c) 3, 2, 1 ,4
(d) 1, 3, 4, 2

4. Match List-I with List-II and select the correct answer using the codes given below the Lists:

| List-I | List-II |
|---|---|
| A. Freon 12 | 1. Centrifugal systems |
| B. Freon 22 | 2. Low temperature cold storage |
| C. Feron 11 | 3. Window type units |
| D. Ammonia | 4. Ice plants |

**Codes:**

| | **A** | **B** | **C** | **D** |
|---|---|---|---|---|
| (a) | 3 | 2 | 1 | 4 |
| (b) | 3 | 1 | 2 | 4 |
| (c) | 1 | 2 | 4 | 3 |
| (d) | 1 | 3 | 4 | 2 |

5. The equivalent diameter (D) of a circular duct corresponding to a rectangular duct having longer side '*a*' and shorter side '*b*' the same velocity and pressure drop is given by:
(a) $D = \frac{a+b}{ab}$ (b) $D = \frac{ab}{a+b}$
(c) $D = \frac{(a+b)}{2ab}$ (d) $D = \frac{2ab}{a+b}$

6. Consider the following statements: During sensible heating
1. moisture content increases
2. dry bulb temperature and wet bulb temperature increase.
3. dew point remains constant.
4. relative humidity increases.
Of these statements
(a) 1, 2 and 3 are correct
(b) 2, 3 and 4 are correct
(c) 2 and 3 are correct
(d) 1 and 2 are correct

7. Which of the following statements are correct?
1. The human body can lose heat even if temperature is less than the atmospheric temperature.
2. Relative humidity can be increased by cooling dehumidification.
3. Warm air increases the rate of radiation of heat from the human body.
4. Increase in air movement increases the evaporation from the human body.
Select the correct answer using the codes given below:
(a) 1 and 4 (b) 2 and 4
(c) 1 and 3 (d) 2 and 3

8. When the air is passed through an insulated chamber having sprays of water maintained at a temperature higher than the dew point temperature of entering air but lower than its dry bulb temperature, then the air is said to be:
(a) cooled and humidified
(b) cooled and dehumidified
(c) heated and humidified
(d) heated and dehumidified

9. The atmosphere air at dry bulb temperature of 15°C enters a heating coil maintained at 40°C. The air leaves the heating coil at 25°C. The bypass factor of the heating coil is:
(a) 0.376 (b) 0.476
(c) 0.6 (d) 0.67

10. If the specific heats of dry air and water vapour are 1.00 kJ/kg-K and 1.88 kJ/kg-K respectively and the humidity ratio is 0.011, then the specific heat of moist air at 25°C and 50% relative humidity will be
(a) 1.0207 kJ/kg – K
(b) 1.869 kJ/kg – K
(c) 1.891 kJ/kg– K
(d) 0.9793 kJ/kg –K

11. If a sample of moist air of 50% relative humidity at atmospheric pressure is isothermally compressed to a pressure of two atmospheres, then:
(a) its relative humidity will reduce to 25%
(b) its relative humidity will remain unchanged
(c) the sample of air will become saturated
(d) saturation pressure will increase to twice the value

12. Evaporative regulation of body temperature fails when the body temperature is:
(a) more than wet bulb temperature but less than dry bulb temperature
(b) more than dew point but less than wet bulb temperature
(c) more than dew point but less than dry bulb temperature
(d) less than dew point

13. Consider the following statements:
Effective temperature is not a true comfort index because
1. discomfort may be experienced at extremely high or low humidity.
2. the radiation effect of surrounding surfaces has not been taken into account.
3. it presumes the absence of drafts.
Of these statements:
(a) 1, 2 and 3 are correct (b) 1 and 2 arc correct
(c) 1 and 3 are correct (d) 2 and 3 arc correct

14. If wet bulb depression is equal to the sum of range and approach of a cooling tower, then the water:
(a) inlet temperature is equal to the wet bulb temperature of ambient air
(b) outlet temperature is equal to the wet bulb temperature of ambient air
(c) inlet temperature is equal to dry bulb temperature of ambient air
(d) outlet temperature is equal to dry bulb temperature of ambient air

15. Which of the following are the special features of a hermetically sealed compressor of a refrigerator?
1. The compressor may be reciprocating to rotary type.
2. No shaft seal is necessary.
3. More silent in operation.
4. COP is more than that of open compressor.
Select the correct answer using the codes given below:
(a) 2 and 4 (b) 1, 2 and 3
(c) 1, 3 and 4 (d) 2, 3 and 4

16. Consider the following statements.
The pressure in a capillary tube of a refrigerator decreases because:
1. tube wall offers frictional resistance.
2. refrigerant accelerates in the tube.
3. tube transfer the heat.
4. potential energy decreases
Of these statements:
(a) 1 and 2 are correct (b) 1, 2 and 3 are correct
(c) 2 and 4 are correct (d) 3 and 4 are correct

17. Consider the following statements:
High condenser pressure in a refrigeration system can occur because:
1. the water flow rate is lower than the desired value.
2. non-condensible gases are present in the system.
3. of accumulation of lubricating oil in condenser
4. of low charge of refrigerant in the system
Of these statements:
(a) 1, 3 and 4 are correct (b) 1, 2 and 3 are correct
(c) 1, 2 and 4 are correct (d) 2, 3 and 4 are correct

18. Consider the following statements:
Dry compression in reciprocating compressor is preferred because it:
1. prevents valve damage.
2. enables use of thermostatic exansion valve
3. minimizes irreversibilites in the compressor.
4. prevents washing out of the lubricating oil from cylinder walls.
Of these statements:
(a) 1 and 2 are correct (b) 2 and 3 are correct
(c) 1 and 4 are correct (d) 3 and 4 are correct

19. Match List-I with List-II and select the correct answer using the codes given below the lists:

| **List-I (Refrigerant)** | **List-II (Designation)** |
|---|---|
| A. Dichloro-difluoromethane | 1. R 718 |
| B. Water | 2. R 22 |
| C. Methyl chloride | 3. R 40 |
| D. Monochlorodi-fluoromethane | 4. R 12 |

**Codes:**

| | A | B | C | D |
|---|---|---|---|---|
| (a) | 1 | 4 | 2 | 3 |
| (b) | 1 | 4 | 3 | 2 |
| (c) | 4 | 1 | 3 | 2 |
| (d) | 4 | 1 | 2 | 3 |

20. Consider the following statements:
1. In Freon 22 system, moisture choking generally does not occur
2. Freon 11 is mainly used in large capacity air-conditioning plants with centrifugal compressors.
3. Presence of lubricating oil in evaporator will increase the heat transfer coefficient.
4. Refrigerants that are completely miscible with oil, do not cause oil choking.
Of these statements:
(a) 1, 2 and 3 are correct (b) 1, 2 and 4 are correct
(c) 2, 3 and 4 are correct (d) 1, 3 and 4 are correct

21. A carnot refrigerator works between the temperatures of 200 K and 300 K. If the refrigerator receives 1 kW of heat, the work requirement will be:
(a) 0.5 kW (b) 0.67 kW
(c) 1.5 kW (d) 3 kW

22. The refrigerant-12 (R-12) used in vapour compression refrigeration system is:
(a) $CHClF_2$ (b) $CCl_2F_2$
(c) $CHCl_2F$ (d) $CClF_2$

23. An expansion valve is not used for reducing pressure in the:
(a) vapour compression refrigeration cycle
(b) vapour absorption refrigeration cycle
(c) steam-jet refrigeration cycle
(d) gas refrigeration cycle

24. The function of a compressor in a vapour absorption system is performed by the:
(a) absorber
(b) absorber and pump
(c) pump and generator
(d) absorber, pump and generator

25. Consider the following statements:
In a reciprocating compressor, clearance volume is provided:
1. so that position does not hit and damage the valves
2. to account for differential thermal expansion of piston and cylinder
3. to account for machining tolerances
4. to achieve isentropic compression
Which of these statements are correct?
(a) 1, 2 and 3 (b) 1, 2 and 4
(c) 1, 3 and 4 (d) 2, 3 and 4

26. Replacing a water cooled condenser with an air-cooled one in a vapour compression refrigeration system with constant evaporator pressure result in:
(a) increase in condensation pressure
(b) decrease in pressure ratio
(c) increase in pressure ratio
(d) increase in condensation temperature

27. If the measured wet-bulb temperature and the thermodynamic wet-bulb temperature are equal, than the non-dimensional number with a value of unity is the:
(a) Lewis number (b) Prandtl number
(c) Schmidt number (d) Sherwood number

28. The ratio of weight of water vapour associated with unit weight of dry air to the weight of water vapour associated with unit weight of dry air saturated at the same dry-bulb temperature and pressure is known as:
(a) specific humidity (b) relative humidity
(c) absolute humidity (d) degree of saturation

29. Consider the following statements:
1. If air heated in a closed chamber, its dew point will increase
2. As relative humidity decreases the difference between the wet-bulb temperature and dew point will increase
3. In spray humidification process, the enthalpy of air will decrease
4. The dew-point temperature is always an indication of moisture content of the air
(a) 1 and 2 (b) 2 and 4
(c) 1 and 3 (d) 3 and 4

30. When moist air comes into contact with a waited surface whose temperature is less than the dry-bulb temperature but more than the wet-bulb temperature:
(a) sensible, latent and net heat transfers are from air to surface
(b) both sensible and net heat transfers arc from air to surface but latent neat transfer is from surface to air
(c) sensible heat transfer is from air to surface but both latent and net heat transfer are from surface to air
(d) sensible heat transfer is from surface to air but both latent and net heat transfers arc from air to surface

31. In a certain ideal refrigeration cycle, the COP of heat pump is 5. The cycle under identical conditions running as heat engine will efficiency as:
(a) Zero (b) 0.20
(c) 1.00 (d) 6.00

32. The power (kW) required per ton of refrigeration is $\frac{N}{COP}$, where COP is the coefficient of performance, then N is equal to:
(a) 2.75 (b) 3.50
(c) 4.75 (d) 5.25

33. Match List-I with List-II and select the correct answer using the codes given below the lists:

| **List-I** | **List-II** |
|---|---|
| A. Refrigerant 11 | 1. $CCl_2F_2$ |
| B. Refrigerant 12 | 2. $C_2Cl_2F_4$ |
| C. Refrigerant 22 | 3. $CCl_3F$ |
| D. Refrigerant 114 | 4. $CHClF_2$ |
| | 5. $CH_2ClF$ |

**Codes:**

| | A | B | C | D |
|---|---|---|---|---|
| (a) | 2 | 1 | 5 | 3 |
| (b) | 3 | 4 | 5 | 2 |
| (c) | 3 | 1 | 4 | 2 |
| (d) | 5 | 1 | 4 | 3 |

34. The expression, $\frac{0.622 p_v}{p_b - p_v}$ where $p_v$ = partial pressure of water vapour: $p_b$ = atmospheric barometric pressure, is used for calculating:
(a) relative humidity (b) degree of saturation
(c) humidity ratio (d) pressure of air

35. A cooling coil with a by pass factor of 0.1 and apparatus dew point (adp) of 12°C comes in contact with air having a dry-bulb temperature of 38°C and dew point of 9°C. Over the cooling coil, the air would undergo:
(a) sensible cooling
(b) cooling and humidification
(c) cooling and dehumidification
(d) adiabatic saturation

36. The main process which takes place in a desert-cooler is:
(a) sensible cooling
(b) dehumidification
(c) adiabatic saturation
(d) cooling and dehumidification

37. In a vapour compression cycle, the refrigerant, immediately after expansion valve is:
(a) saturated liquid (b) sub-cooled liquid
(c) dryvapour (d) wet vapour

38. Consider the following statements pertaining to a vapour compression type refrigerator:
1. The condenser rejects heat to the surroundings from the refrigerant.
2. The evaporator absorbs heat from the surroundings to be cooled.
3. Both the condenser and evaporator are heat exchangers with refrigerant as a common medium.
4 The amount of heat exchanged in condenser and evaporator are equal under steady conditions.

Which of the above statements are correct?
(a) 1 and 2 (b) 1, 2 and 3
(c) 1, 2 and 4 (d) 2, 3 and 4

39. The throttling device used in the domestic refrigerator is:
(a) internally equalized thermostatic expansion valve
(b) externally equalized thermostatic expansion valve
(c) automatic expansion valve
(d) capillary tube

40. In system A vapours are superheated by 10°C in the evaporator while in system B vapours are superheated by 10°C in a liquid vapour regenerative heat exchanger, other conditions being the same. Then:
(a) C.O.P of A = COP of B
(b) C.O.P. of both A and B > C.O.P. of Reversed Carnot Cycle
(c) C.O.P. of A > C.O.P. of B
(d) C.O.P. of A < C.O.P. of B

41. Match List-I (chemical formula of refrigerant) with List-II (Numerical Designation) and select the correct answer using the codes gives below the lists:

| **List-I (Chemical formula of refrigerant)** | **List-II (Numerical Designation)** |
|---|---|
| A. $NH_3$ | 1. 12 |
| B. $CCl_2F_2$ | 2. 22 |
| C. $CHClF_2$ | 3. 40 |
| D. $CCl_2FCClF_2$ | 4. 113 |
| | 5. 717 |

**Codes:**

| | A | B | C | D |
|---|---|---|---|---|
| (a) | 4 | 1 | 5 | 2 |
| (b) | 5 | 3 | 2 | 4 |
| (c) | 4 | 3 | 5 | 2 |
| (d) | 5 | 1 | 2 | 4 |

42. The efficiency of a carnot engine is given as 0.75. If the cycle directions is reversed, what will be the valve of C.O.P. for the carnot refrigerator?
(a) 0.27 (b) 0.33
(c) 1.27 (d) 2.33

43. In a regenerative cycle, steam with enthalpy of 3514 kJ/kg is expanded in h.p. turbine to a state corresponding to saturated enthalpy of water equal to 613 kJ/kg. If the pump work requirements in high pressure and low pressure zones are respectively 3 and 1 kJ/kg, amount of heat transferred in boiler is:
(a) 2897 kJ/kg
(b) 2898 kJ/kg
(c) 2904 kJ/kg
(d) 2905 kJ/kg

44. A refrigerator storage is supplied with 3600 kg of fish at a temperature of 27 °C. The fish has to be cooled to 23°C for preserving it for a long period without deterioration. The cooling takes place in 10 hours. The specific heat of fish is 2.0 kJ/kg K above freezing point of fish and 0.5 kJ/kg K below freezing point of fish, which is - 3°C. The latent heal of freezing is 230 kJ/kg. What is the power to drive the plant if the actual COP is half that of the ideal COP?
(a) 30 kW (b) 15 kW
(c) 12 kW (d) 6 kW.

45. Which one of the following is the most important function of thermostatic expansion valve?
(a) To control the degree of superheat
(b) To control the evaporator temperature
(c) To control the pressure drop
(d) To control the evaporator pressure

46. Which one of the following statements is correct?
(a) Dehumidifier coil surface temperature is above the dew point temperature but below the freezing point temperature
(b) Dehumidifier coil surface temperature is below the dew point temperature but above the freezing point temperature
(c) Dehumidifier coil surface temperature is below the dew point temperature and the freezing point temperature
(d) Dehumidifier coil surface temperature is above both the dew point temperature and the freezing point temperature

47. Consider the following statements:
If moist air is adiabatically saturated in an air washer then:
1. wet bulb temperature remains constant.
2. relative humidity increases.
3. dry bulb temperature decreases.
4. humidity ratio decreases.

Which of these statements are correct?
(a) 1, 2 and 3
(b) 1, 2 and 4
(c) 2, 3 and 4
(d) 1, 3 and 4

48. Which one of the following statements is true for effective temperature, ET?
(a) ET increases with increase in level of activity and it decreases with increase in air velocity
(b) ET decreases with increase in level of activity and it increases with increase in air velocity
(c) ET increases with increase in level of activity and it increases with increase in air velocity
(d) ET decreases with increase in level of activity and decreases with increase in air velocity

49. In on-off control refrigeration system, which one of the following expansion devices is used?
(a) Capillary tube
(b) Thermostat
(c) Automatic expansion valve
(d) Float valve

50. When does L.P. cut-off occur in a refrigeration system?
(a) If the ambient temperature is low
(b) If non-condensable gases are present in the condenser
(c) If refrigerant charge is low
(d) If lubricating oil gets accumulated-in the condenser

51. Moist air exists at a pressure of 1.01 bar. The partial pressure and saturation pressure of water vapour are 0.01 bar and 0.02 bar, respectively. What are the relative humidity and humidity ratio of the moist air, respectively?
(a) 50% and 0.00622 (b) 100% and 0.0126
(c) 50% and 0.0126 (d) 100% and 0.00622

52. In order to cool and dehumidify a stream of moist air, it must be passed over a coil at a temperature:
(a) which to lies between the dry bulb and wet bulb temperatures of the incoming stream
(b) which lies between the wet bulb and dew point temperatures of the incoming stream
(c) which is lower than the dew point temperature of the incoming stream
(d) of adiabatic saturation of incoming stream

53. Which of the features of expansion valves in the following lists are correctly matched?

| Expansion Device | | Feature |
|---|---|---|
| 1. Capillary tube | : | Chocking |
| 2. Thermostatic expansion valve | : | Constant temperature |
| 3. Automatic Expansion valve | : | Constant degree of superheat |
| 4. Float valve | : | Mass flow rate of refrigerant is proportional to load |

Select the correct answer using the codes given below.
**Codes:**
(a) 1 and 2 (b) 1 and 3
(c) 1 and 4 (d) 3 and 4

54. If moist air sensibly cooled above its dew point, which of the following statements are correct?
1. Relative humidity decreases
2. Wet bulb temperature decreases,
3. Wet bulb temperature increases
4. Humidity ratio remains constant.
Select the correct answer using the codes given below:
**Codes:**
(a) 1 and 2 (b) 1 and 3
(c) 3 and 4 (d) 2 and 4

55. Water in an insulated evaporative cooler evaporates at the rate of 0.003 kg/s. Air flow rate is 1 kg/s. What is the air temperature decrease if the specific heat of humid air is 1 kJ/kg. K and latent heat of water is 2500 kJ/kg?
(a) 2.5 °C (b) 3.0°C
(c) 7.5°C (d) 10°C

56. Match List-1 with List-II and select the correct answer using the codes given below the lists:

| List-I | List-II |
|---|---|
| A. Sulphur candle test | 1. Propane |
| B. Halide torch test | 2. Ammonia |
| C. Soap and water test | 3. Halocarbon refrigerants |
| D. Ammonia swab test | 4. Sulphur dioxide |

**Codes:**

| | A | B | C | D |
|---|---|---|---|---|
| (a) | 2 | 3 | 1 | 4 |
| (b) | 4 | 1 | 3 | 2 |
| (c) | 2 | 1 | 3 | 4 |
| (d) | 4 | 3 | 1 | 2 |

57. When a refrigeration plant is started, the evaporator temperature of the required value.
During this period, how does the compressor power requirement vary?
(a) It increases continuously .
(b) It decreases and then becomes constant
(c) It reaches a peak and then decreases.
(d) It remains constant

58. A Bell-Coleman air refrigeration system operates on which one of the following cycles?
(a) Reverse Diesel cycle
(b) Reverse Cannot cycle
(c) Reverse Brayton cycle
(d) Reverse Otto cycle

59. When the lower temperature is fixed, how can the C.O.P. of a refrigerating machine be improver:
(a) By raising the higher temperature
(b) By lowering the higher temperature
(c) By operating the machine at higher speeds
(d) By operating the machine at lower speeds

60. An electrolux system of refrigeration has:
(a) No liquid pump (b) One liquid pump
(c) Liquid pumps (d) Three liquid pumps

61. In a vapour compression refrigeration cycle, following data are obtained:

| | | |
|---|---|---|
| Ethalpy at suction to the compressor | : | 180 kJ/kg |
| Ethalpy at discharge from the compressor | : | 210kJ/kg |
| Enthalpy at exit from | : | 80 kJ/kg |

What is the C.O.P. of the cycle?
(a) 5.33 (b) 4.33
(c) 3.33 (d) 2.33

62. Consider the following statements pertaining to Room Sensible Heat Ratio (RSHR) line:
1. It is the line drawn on psychrometric chart through the room conditions.
2. Its slope is the ratio of sensible cooling load to room latent heat load.
3. The supply air condition must lie on this line for satisfactory performance.

Which of the statements given above are correct?
(a) 1, 2 and 3 (b) 1 and 2
(c) 1 and 3 (d) 2 and 3

63. When 40°C and 25 °C are the dry bulb temperatures of air entering and leaving a cooling coil, then the cooling coil temperature is 20°C. What is the bypass factor for the case of sensible cooling?
(a) 0.20 (b) 0.25
(c) 0.50 (d) 0.60

64. A water chiller with a capacity of 30 tons of refrigeration cools 20 $m^3$/hr of water entering at 12°C. What is the temperature of water leaving the chiller?
(a) 5°C (b) 6°C
(c) 7°C (d) 7.5°C

65. Consider the following refrigerants:
1. Ammonia
2. Carbon dioxide
3. Dichlorodifluoro methane
4. Tetrafluoromethane

Which one of the following is the correct order of their boiling points in the descending order?
(a) 1 – 2 – 3 – 4
(b) 4 – 3 – 1 – 2
(c) 3 – 1 – 2 – 4
(d) 2 – 4 – 1 – 3

66. Evaporator is used sometimes to dehumidify the air for conditioning purpose.
Which is one of the following is the correct statement?
In this situation the evaporator temperature should he kept:
(a) lower than the cooling fluid temperature
(b) more than the apparatus dew point temperature
(c) lower than the apparatus dew point temperature
(d) lower than the boiling temperature of fluid

67. In a Bell Coleman cycle refrigeration plant compression and expansion of air are isentropic. If the temperatures of air entering and leaving the expander are 300 K and 180 K respectively, what is the coefficient of performance of the plant?
(a) 1.5 (b) 2.0
(c) 2.5 (d) 3.0

68. Match List-I with List-II and select the correct answer using the code given below the lists:

| List-I | List-II |
|---|---|
| A. Bell Coleman refrigeration | 1. Expansion |
| B. Reversed Carnot cycle | 2. Heat Pump |
| C. Milk chilling plant | 3. Decreases COP |
| D. Superheating in refrigeration cycle | 4. Compressor |
| | 5. Brine |
| | 6. Vortex Refrigerator |
| | 7. Increases COP |

**Codes:**

| | A | B | C | D |
|---|---|---|---|---|
| (a) | 1 | 6 | 5 | 3 |
| (b) | 4 | 2 | 3 | 7 |
| (c) | 1 | 2 | 5 | 3 |
| (d) | 4 | 6 | 3 | 7 |

69. Which one of the following is the correct statement?
When moist air passes through a cooling tower, the process is:
(a) evaporative cooling
(b) adiabatic saturation
(c) cooling and dehumidification
(d) heating and humidification

70. Which one of the following is the correct statement?
During sensible cooling process for a moist air:
(a) specific humidity will decrease
(b) relative humidity will increase
(c) relative humidity will decrease
(d) specific humidity will increase

71. During a comfort air conditioning process, the moisture content of the air may start decreasing. Which one of the following is the correct statement?
In order to maintain the same level of comfort:
(a) WBT should be decreased
(b) DBT should be increased
(c) air velocity should be increased
(d) moisture content should be increased

72. The comfort air-conditioning can be obtained by innumerable combinations of DBT and relative humidity. Which one of the following combinations within the comfort zoom recommended to save the energy?
(a) Higher DBT and lower relative humidity
(b) Lower DBT and lower relative humidity
(c) Lower DBT and higher relative humidity
(d) Higher DBT and relative humidity

73. A refrigerating machine in heat pump mode has a C.O.P. of 4. If it is worked in refrigerating mode with a power input of 3 kW, what is the heat extracted from the food kept in a refrigerator?
(a) 180 kJ/min (b) 360 kJ/min
(c) 540 kJ/min (d) 720 kJ/min

74. To maintain comfort in an air conditioned space, how can a small increase in temperature be compensated?
(a) By humidification
(b) By ventilation
(c) By increasing air velocity
(d) By decreasing air velocity

75. Where is an oil separator in vapour compression refrigeration system installed?
(a) Between compressor and condenser
(b) Between expansion valve and receiver tank
(c) Inside compressor machinery
(d) Outside compressor machinery

76. Which one eco-friendly refrigerant out of the following is used in many domestical and a air-conditioners now-a-days?
(a) R – 22 (b) R – 113
(c) R – 123 (d) R – 134

77. Which one of the following is the correct statement? Adiabatic saturation process is moist air involves:
(a) cooling and humidification.
(b) cooling and dehumidification
(c) change in dew point temperature.
(d) constant relative humidity.

78. Which one of the following is the correct statement?
In domestic air conditioners air undergoes the process of:
(a) sensible cooling
(b) cooling and humidification.
(c) cooling and dehumidification
(d) dehumidification

79. Which one of the following is the correct statement?
Sensible heating of moist air will not affect the:
(a) relative humidity
(b) absolute humidity
(c) specific humidity
(d) wet bulb temperature

80. In an ideal refrigeration (reversed Carnot) cycle, the condenser and evaporator temperatures are 27°C and –13°C respectively. The COP of this cycle would be'
(a) 6.5 (b) 7.5
(c) 10.5 (d) 15.0

81. What is the process represented by the line 0 – 1 shown on the psychrometric chart (0 to 1)?
(a) Humidification and heating
(b) Humidification and cooling
(c) Dehumidification and cooling
(d) Dehumidification and heating

82. When are the wet bulb temperature and the temperature of adiabatic saturation equal?
(a) If Lewis number is equal to 1
(b) If Praridtl number is equal to 1
(c) If Schmidt number is equal to 1
(d) If Sherwood number is equal to 1

83. The cooling loads for a building are:
RSH = 100 kW (Room sensible heat)
RLH = 25 kW (Room latent heat)
OASH = 10 kW (Outside air sensible heat)
OALH = 10 kW (Outside air latent heat)
The bypass factor of the cooling coil is 0.15.
What are the values of the room sensible heat factor and external sensible heat factor respectively?
(a) 0.72 and 0.8 (b) 0.8 and 0.79
(c) 0.79 and 0.8 (d) 0.79 and 0.72

84. Which one of the following statements is correct?
Dew point temperature of a moist air sample remains constant during:
(a) a sensible heating or cooling process
(b) an adiabatic saturation process
(c) a dehumidification process
(d) a humidification process

85. Which one of the following statements is correct?
For a cooling and dehumidification process, the moist air has to be passed through a coil whose temperature is below the:
(a) dry-bulb temperature of the air
(b) wet-bulb temperature of the air
(c) dew-point temperature of the air
(d) critical temperature of the air

86. Which one of the following is the correct statement?
For a specified condenser temperature, the coefficient of performance of a refrigerator,
(a) increases with the increase in the evaporator temperature
(b) decreases with the increase in evaporator temperature
(c) is independent of the evaporator temperature
(d) is proportional to the square of the evaporator temperature

87. Match List-I with List-II and select the correct answer using the code given below the lists:

| **List-I (Commercial Name of Refrigerant** | **List-II (Chemical formula of Refrigerant)** |
|---|---|
| A. R 11 | 1. $CHClF_2$ |
| B. R 12 | 2. $CCl_2F_2$ |
| C. R 13 | 3. $CCl_3F$ |
| D. R 22 | 4. $ClF_3$ |

**Codes:**

| | **A** | **B** | **C** | **D** |
|---|---|---|---|---|
| (a) | 3 | 1 | 4 | 3 |
| (b) | 4 | 2 | 3 | 1 |
| (c) | 3 | 2 | 4 | 1 |
| (d) | 4 | 1 | 3 | 2 |

88. In a centralized air conditioning system, what is the power of a fan directly proportional to?
(a) Fan speed (b) $(\text{Fan speed})^2$
(c) $(\text{Fan speed})^3$ (d) $(\text{Fan speed})^4$

89. Which one of the following types of expansion valves is suitable for a refrigeration plant operating at constant load?
(a) Thermostatic expansion valve
(b) Automatic expansion valve
(c) Capillary tube
(d) None of the above

90. What is the cause of burn out of hermetically sealed refrigerant compressors?
(a) Phase to phase short because of worn insulation
(b) By prolonged overload operation
(c) By some mechanical failure
(d) All the above

91. Consider the following statements:
When a GSHF line is extended, it may strike the saturation curve at a point. This point is called:
1. effective surface temperature.
2. air saturation temperature.
3. water boiling temperature.
4. apparatus dew point.

92. Flash chamber is used in refrigeration for which one of the following?
(a) Decreasing the pressure during multistage compression
(b) Increasing the compressor pressure ratio
(c) Effective inter cooling medium for purpose of increasing COP
(d) Maintaining the same pressure and temperature

93. In order to substantially reduce of heat from atmosphere into cold refrigerant flowing in small diameter copper lindrically wrapped around the tubes, must be:
(a) Higher than critical radius of insulation
(b) Slightly lower than critical radius of insulation
(c) Equal to the critical radius of insulation
(d) Considerably higher than critical radius of insulation

94. A building in a cold climate is to be heated by a Carnot heat pump. The minimum outside temperature is –23°C. If the building is to he kept at 27°C and heat requirement is at the rate of 30 kW, what is the minimum power required for heat pump?
(a) 180 kW (b) 30 kW
(c) 6 kW (d) 5 kW

95. The deposition of frost on evaporator tubes of an air conditioner will result in:
(a) decrease in heat transfer
(b) increase in heat transfer
(c) no change in heat transfer
(d) increase in capacity of evaporator

96. A single-stage vapour compression refrigeration system cannot be used to produce ultralow temperatures because:
(a) refrigerants for ultra-low temperatures are not available
(b) lunbricants for ultra-low temperatures are not available
(c) volumetric efficiency will decrease considerably
(d) heat leakage into the system will be excessive

97. Fans used for mechanical draft (induced) cooling towers are:
(a) axial flow type
(b) radial flow type
(c) centrifugal type
(d) propeller type

98. When the lower temperature is fixed COP of a refrigerating machine can be improved by:
(a) operating the machine at higher speeds
(b) operating the machine at lower speeds
(c) raising the higher temperature
(d) lowering the higher temperature

99. The coefficient of performance of heat pump $[(COP)_{HP}]$ and that refrigerator $[(COP)_R]$
(a) $(COP)_{HP} = (COP)_R + 1$
(b) $(COP)_{HP} / (COP)_R 1$
(c) $(COP)_{HP} = (COP)_R - 1$
(d) $(COP)_{HP} < (COP)_R$

100. A good refrigerant should have:
(a) High latent heat of vaporization and low freezing point
(b) High operating pressure and low freezing point
(c) High specific volume and high latent heat of vaporization.
(d) Low COP and low freezing point.

101. Which of the following statements are true for Ammonia as a refrigerant?
1. It has higher compressor discharge temperature compared to fluororarbons.
2. It is toxic to mucous membranes.
3. It requires larger displacement per TR compared to fluorocarbons.
4. It reacts with copper and its alloys.
Select the correct answer using the codes given below:
(a) 1 and 2 (b) 1, 2 and 3
(c) 1, 2 and 4 (d) 2, 3 and 4

102. Vapour absorption refrigeration system works using the:
(a) ability of a substances to get easily condensed or evaporated
(b) ability of a vapour to get compressed or expanded
(c) affinity of a substance for another substance
(d) absorptivity of a substance.

103. Moist air is a mixture of dry air and water vapour. Hence, three independent intrinsic thermodynamic three independent intrinsic thermodynamic properties are required to fix its thermodynamic state. While using psychrometric chart, however, only two thermodynamic properties are needed since, psychrometric chart:
(a) is an approximation to actual properties
(b) assumes that both water vapour and dry air behave like perfect gases
(c) is drawn for actual properties of water vapour and dry air
(d) is drawn for a fixed pressure

104. In a saturated air-water vapour mixture, the
(a) dry bulb temperature is higher than the wet bulb temperature:
(b) dew point temperature is lower than the wet bulb temperature
(c) dry bulb, wet bulb and dew point temperatures are the same
(d) dry bulb temperature is higher than the dew point temperature

105. Effective temperature is that temperature of saturated air which gives the same degree of comfort as the air at given:
(a) DBT, WBT and incidental solar radiation
(b) WBT, incidental solar radiation and air flow rate
(c) DBT, sol-air temperature and air flow rate
(d) DBT, WBT and air flow rate

106. A human body feels comfortable when the heat produced by the metabolism of human body is equal to the:
(a) heat dissipated to the surroundings
(b) heat stored in the human body
(c) sum of (a) and (b)
(d) difference of (a) and (b)

107. In the case of sensible cooling of air, the coil efficiency is given by: (BPF = Bypass factor)
(a) BPF – 1 (b) 1 – BPF
(b) $\frac{1}{\text{BPF}}$ (d) 1+ BPF

108. In a spray washing system if the temperature of water is higher than the dry temperature of entering air, than the air is:
(a) heated and dehumidified
(b) heated and humidified
(c) cooled and humidified
(d) cooled and dehumidified

109. In a psychrometric process, the sensible heat added is 30 kJ/sec and the latent heat added is 20 kJ/sec. The sensible heat factor for the process will be:
(a) 0.3 (b) 0.5
(c) 0.67 (d) 1.5

110. The operating temperature of a cold storage is – 2°C, Heat leakage form the surrounding is 30 kW for the ambient temperature of 40°C. The actual COP of the refrigeration plant used is one fourth that of an ideal plant working between the same temperatures. The power required to drive the plant is:
(a) 1.86 kW (b) 3.72 kW
(c) 7.44 kW (d) 18.60 kW

111. Which of the following refrigerant has the maximum ozone depletion in the stratosphere?
(a) Ammonia
(b) Carbon dioxide
(c) Sulphur dioxide
(d) Fluorine

112. If air is passed through a solid chemical absorbent, the psychrometic process followed is:
(a) heating and dehumidification with the bulb temperature remaining fairly constant
(b) cooling and dehumidification
(c) dehumidification with sharp rise in wet bulb temperature
(d) dehumidification at constant dry bulb temperature.

113. A thermostatic expansion valve in a refrigeration system:
(a) ensures the evaporator completely filled with refrigerant of the load
(b) is suitable only for constant load system
(c) maintains different temperatures in evaporator
(d) none of the above.

114. By pass factor for a cooling coil:
(a) increases with increase in velocity of air passing through it
(b) decrease with increase in velocity of air passing through it
(c) remains unchanged with increase in velocity of air passing through it
(d) may increase or decrease with increase in velocity of air passing through it depending upon the condition of air entering

115. During sensible cooling:
(a) Relative humidity remains constant
(b) Wet bulb temperature increases
(c) Specific humidity increases
(d) Partial pressure of vapour remains constant

116. A heat pump working on a reversed carnot cycle has a COP of 5. If it works as a refrigerator taking 1 kW work input, the refrigerating effect will be:
(a) 1 kW (b) 2 kW
(c) 3 kW (d) 4 kW

117. A refrigerating system operating on reversed Brayton refrigeration cycle is used for maintaining 250 K. If the temperature at the exit of constant pressure cooling is 300 K and rise in the temperature of air in the refrigerator is so K, then the net work of compression will be (assume air as the working substance with $c_p$ = 1 kJ per kg per°C)
(a) 250 kJ/kg (b) 200 kJ/kg
(c) 50 kJ/kg (d) 25 kJ/kg

118. In a vapour compression refrigeration plant, the refrigerant leaves the evaporator at 195 kJ/kg and the condenser at 65 kJ/kg. For every kg of refrigerant the plant can supply per second a cooling load of:
(a) 70 kW (b) 100 kW
(c) 130 kW (d) 160 kW

119. While designing the refrigeration system of an aircraft prime consideration is that the:
(a) system has high COP
(b) H.P./ton is low
(c) weight of refrigerant circulated in the system is low
(d) weight of the refrigeration equipment is low

120. A valve which maintains a constant degree of superheat at the end of the evaporator coil, is called:
(d) automatic expansion valve
(b) high side float valve
(c) thermostatic expansion valve
(d) low side float valve

## ANSWERS WITH EXPLANATIONS

1. (d) 2. (b) 3. (c) 4. (a) 5. (d)
6. (c) 7. (a) 8. (a)

9. (c) $\text{BPF} = \dfrac{40-25}{40-15} = \dfrac{15}{25} = 0.6$

10. (a) $c_p$ of moist air = $c_p$ of dry air + humidity ratio × $c_p$ of water vapour

$$= 1.00 + 0.011 \times 1.88$$
$$= 1.0207 \text{ kJ/kg.K}$$

11. (c) 12. (c) 13. (a) 14. (c) 15. (b)
16. (a) 17. (d) 18. (c) 19. (d) 20. (a)

21. (a) $T_1 = 300 \text{ K}, T_2 = 200 \text{ K}$

$$\text{COP} = \frac{T_2}{T_1 - T_2} = \frac{200}{300-200} = \frac{200}{100} = 2$$

$$= \frac{Q}{W} = \frac{1}{W}$$

$$W = 0.5 \text{ kW}$$

22. (b) 23. (c) 24. (d) 25. (b) 26. (d)
27. (a) 28. (d) 29. (d) 30. (c)

31. (b) $(\text{COP})_{\text{HP}} = \dfrac{T_2}{T_1 - T_2} = 5$

$$\eta_{\text{H.E}} = \frac{T_1 - T_2}{T_1} = \frac{1}{5} = 0.2$$

32. (b) $\text{COP} = \dfrac{Q}{\text{COP}} = \dfrac{1\text{TR}}{W}$

$$W = \frac{1\text{TR}}{W}\frac{N}{\text{COP}}$$

$$\therefore N = 1\text{TR} = 350$$

33. (c) 34. (c)

35. (c) BPF = 0.1, ADP = 12°C, DBT = 38°C,

DPT = 90°C

$$\text{BPF for cooling coil} = \frac{t_{d2} - t_{d3}}{t_{d1} - t_{d3}}$$

$$1 = \frac{t_{d2} - 12}{38 - 12}$$

$$t_{d2} = 2.6 + 12 = 14.6°C > t_{d1}$$

Dehumidification takes place.

36. (c) 37. (d) 38. (b) 39. (d) 40. (c)
41. (d)

42. (b) $\eta_{\text{HE}} = 1 - = \dfrac{T_2}{T_1} = 0.75 \text{ or } \dfrac{T_2}{T_1} = 0.25$

$$(\text{COP})_{\text{Ref}} = \frac{T_2}{T_1 - T_2} = \frac{(T_2/T_1)}{1-(T_1/T_1)} = \frac{0.25}{1-0.25}$$

$$= \frac{0.25}{0.75} = \frac{1}{3} = 0.33$$

43. (a) $h_{\text{boiler}} = 3514 - (613 + 4) = 2897 \text{ kJ/kg}$

44. (c) $T_1 = 273 + 27 = 300 \text{ K}$

$$T_2 = 273 - 23 = 250 \text{ K}$$

$$(\text{COP})_{\text{Ref}} = \frac{T_2}{T_1 - T_2} = \frac{250}{300-250} = \frac{250}{50} = 5$$

$$Q = \frac{3600}{3600 \times 10}[2 \times (27+3) + 0.5(-3+23) + 230]$$

$$= 30 \text{ kJ/s}$$

$$\text{Actual COP} = \frac{5}{2} = 2.5$$

$$W = \frac{30}{2.5} = 12 \text{ kW}$$

45. (b) 46. (c) 47. (c) 48. (a) 49. (b)
50. (c)

51. (a) $p_a = 1.01 \text{ bar}, p_v = 0.01 \text{ bar}, p_s = 0.02 \text{ bar}$

$$\text{RH} = \frac{p_v}{p_s} = \frac{0.01}{0.02} \text{ or } 50\%$$

$$w = \frac{0.622 p_v}{p_a - p_v} = \frac{0.622 \times 0.01}{1.01 - 0.01} = 0.00622$$

52. (c) 53. (d) 54. (c)

55. (c) $m_w = 0.003 \text{ kg/s}, m_a = 1 \text{ kg/s},$

$$c_{pa} = 1\text{kJ/kg.K}, h_{fg} = 2500 \text{ kJ/kg},$$

$$m_a \times c_{pa} \times \Delta t = m_w \times h_{fg}$$

$$1 \times 1 \times \Delta. = 0.003 \times 2500$$

$$\Delta t = 7.5°C$$

56. (c) 57. (c) 58. (c) 59. (b) 60. (a)

61. (c) $\text{COP} = \dfrac{h_1 - h_4}{h_2 - h_1} = \dfrac{180-80}{210-180} = \dfrac{100}{30} = 3.33$

62. (c)

63. (b) $t_{d1} = 40d°C, t_{d2} = 25°C, t_{d3} = 20°C,$

$$\text{BPF} = \frac{t_{d2} - t_{d3}}{t_{d1} - t_{d3}} = \frac{25-20}{40-20} = \frac{5}{20} = 0.25$$

64. (d) $Q = 30 \times 3.5167 = 105.5 \text{ kW}$

$$m_w \times c_p(t_i - t_v) = Q$$

$$\frac{20 \times 1000}{3600} \times 4.187(12 - t_0) = 105.5$$

$$t_0 = 12 - 45 = 7.5°C$$

65. (b)

| **Refrigerant** | **B.P. (°C)** |
|---|---|
| 1. $NH_3(R-717)$ | − 33.3 |
| 2. $CO_2(R-744)$ | − 73.6 |
| 3. $CCl_2F_2(R-12)$ | − 29 |
| 4. $C_2Cl_2F_4(R-114)$ | − 3.6 |

66. (b)

67. (a) $T_3 = 300\text{ K}, T_4 = 180\text{ K}$

$$r_p = \frac{p_2}{p_1}\left(\frac{T_3}{T_4}\right)^{\frac{\gamma}{\gamma-1}} = \left(\frac{300}{180}\right)^{3.5} = 5.977$$

$$\text{COP} = \frac{1}{r_p^{\gamma-1/\gamma} - 1} = \frac{1}{(5.977)^{0.4/1.4} - 1} = 1.5$$

$$\text{COP} = \frac{1}{\frac{T_3}{T_4} - 1} = \frac{1}{\frac{300}{180} - 1} = 1.5$$

68. (c) 69. (a) 70. (a) 71. (d) 72. (c)

73. (c) $(\text{COP})_{HP} = 4$

$$(\text{COP})_{Ref} = (\text{COP})_{HP} - 1 = 4 - 1 = 3$$

$$\frac{Q}{W} = \frac{Q}{3}$$

$$Q = 9\text{ kW or } 540\text{ kJ/min}$$

74. (b) 75. (a) 76. (d) 77. (a) 78. (b)

79. (c)

80. (a) $\text{COP} = \frac{T_2}{T_1 - T_2} = \frac{260}{300 - 260} = \frac{260}{40} = 6.5$

81. (d) 82. (a)

83. (b) $\text{RSHF} = \frac{\text{RSH}}{\text{RSH} + \text{RLH}}$

$$= \frac{100}{100 + 25} = \frac{100}{125} = 0.8$$

$$\text{ESHF} = \frac{\text{RSHJ} + \text{OASH} + \text{BPF}}{(\text{RSH} + \text{OASH} \times \text{BPF}) + \text{RLH} + \text{OALH} + \text{BPF})}$$

$$= \frac{100 + 10 \times 0.15}{(100 + 25) + (10 + 10) \times 0.15}$$

$$= \frac{101.5}{128} = 0.79$$

84. (b) 85. (c) 86. (a) 87. (c) 88. (c)

89. (b) 90. (a) 91. (b) 92. (c) 93. (c)

94. (a) $T_1 = 273 + 27 = 300\text{ K}, T_2 = 273 - 23 = 250\text{ K}$

$$(\text{COP})_{HP} = \frac{T_1}{T_1 - T_2} = \frac{300}{300 - 250} = \frac{300}{50} = 6 = \frac{W}{Q}$$

$$W = 30 \times 6 = 180\text{ kW.}$$

95. (a) 96. (a) 97. (d) 98. (d) 99. (a)

100. (a) 101. (c) 102. (c) 103. (d) 104. (c)

105. (d) 106. (a) 107. (b) 108. (b)

109. (b) $\text{SHF} = \frac{\text{SH}}{\text{SH} + \text{LH}} = \frac{30}{30 + 20} = \frac{30}{50} = 0.5$

110. (d) $(\text{COP})_{th} = \frac{T_2}{T_1 - T_2} = \frac{271}{313 - 271} = 6.4524$

$$(\text{COP})_{act} = \frac{6.4524}{4} = 1.613$$

$$\text{Worked required } \frac{Q}{(\text{COP})_{act}} = \frac{30}{1.613} = 18.60\text{ kW}$$

111. (d) 112. (a) 113. (a) 114. (a) 115. (d)

116. (d) COP of heat pump $= \frac{Q_s}{W} = 5$

$$Q_r = 5W$$

$$Q_s = R + W$$

$$5W - W = R$$

$$R = 4W = 4 \times 1 = 4\text{ kW}$$

117. (d) Net work of compression for the reversed Brayton refrigeration cycle $= (h_2 - h_1) - (h_3 - h_4)$

Now, $\frac{T_2}{T_1} = \frac{T_3}{T_4}$

$$\therefore \quad T_2 = 250 \times \frac{300}{200} = 375\text{ K}$$

$$\text{Net work} = c_p[(T_2 - T_1) - (T_3 - T_4)]$$

$$= 0.1[(375 - 250) - (300 - 200)]$$

$$= 1[125 - 100 = 1 \times 25 = 25\text{ kJ/kg}]$$

118. (c) $h_1 = 195\text{ kJ/kg}, h_3 = h_4 = 65\text{ kJ/kg}$

Refrigeration effect $= h_1 - h_4 = 195 - 65$

$$= 130\text{ kJ/kg}$$

119. (d) 120. (c)

❑❑❑

# 2. Automobile Engineering

- Automobile engineering, incorporating elements of mechanical, electrical, electronic, software and safety engineering as applied to the design, manufacture and operation of motorcycles, automobiles, buses and trucks and their respective engineering subsystems.
- Some of the engineering attributes and disciplines that are of importance to the automotive engineer and many of the other aspects are included in it:
- **Safety engineering:** Safety engineering is the assessment of various crash scenarios and their impact on the vehicle occupants.
- **Fuel economy/emissions:** Fuel economy is the measured fuel efficiency of the vehicle in miles per gallon or kilometers per litre.
- **Vehicle dynamics:** Vehicle dynamics is the vehicle's response of the following attributes: ride, handling, steering, braking, comfort and traction.
- **NVH engineering:** NVH is the customer's feedback (both tactile [felt] and audible [heard]) from the vehicle. While sound can be interpreted as a rattle, squeal, or hoot; a tactile response can be seat vibration, or a buzz in the steering wheel.
- **Vehicle Electronics:** Automotive electronics is an increasingly important aspect of automotive engineering. Modern vehicles employ dozens of electronic systems.
- **Performance:** Performance is a measurable and testable value of a vehicles ability to perform in various conditions. Performance can be considered in a wide variety of tasks, but it's generally associated with how quickly a car can accelerate .
- **Shift quality:** Shift quality is the driver's perception of the vehicle to an automatic transmission shift event. This is influenced by the powertrain (engine, transmission), and the vehicle (driveline, suspension, engine and powertrain mounts, etc.) Shift feel is both a tactile (felt) and audible (heard) response of the vehicle. Durability/corrosion engineering: Durability and corrosion engineering is the evaluation testing of a vehicle for its useful life. Tests include mileage accumulation, severe driving conditions, and corrosive salt baths.
- Package / ergonomics engineering: Package engineering is a discipline that designs/analyzes the occupant accommodations (seat roominess), ingress/egress to the vehicle, and the driver's field of vision (gauges and windows). The package engineer is also responsible for other areas of the vehicle like the engine compartment, and the component to component placement.
- Ergonomics is the discipline that assesses the occupant's access to the steering wheel, pedals, and other driver/ passenger controls.
- **Climate control:** Climate control is the customer's impression of the cabin environment and level of comfort related to the temperature and humidity. From the windshield defrosting, to the heating and cooling capacity, all vehicle seating positions are evaluated to a certain level of comfort.
- **Drivability:** Drivability is the vehicle's response to general driving conditions. Cold starts and stalls, RPM dips, idle response, launch hesitations and stumbles, and performance levels.
- **Cost:** The cost of a vehicle program is typically split into the effect on the variable cost of the vehicle, and the up-front tooling and fixed costs associated with developing the vehicle. There are also costs associated with warranty reductions, and marketing.
- **Program timing:** To some extent programs are timed with respect to the market, and also to the production schedules of the assembly plants. Any new part in the design must support the development and manufacturing schedule of the model.
- **Assembly feasibility:** It is easy to design a module that is hard to assemble, either resulting in damaged units, or poor tolerances. The skilled product development engineer works with the assembly/manufacturing engineers so that the resulting design is easy and cheap to make and assemble, as well as delivering appropriate functionality and appearance.
- **Quality management:** Quality control is an important factor within the production process, as high quality is needed to meet customer requirements and to avoid expensive recall campaigns. The complexity of components involved in the production process requires a combination of different tools and techniques for quality control.
- Much like the Systems Engineer, the development engineer is concerned with the interactions of all systems in the complete automobile. While there are multiple components and systems in an automobile that have to function as designed, they must also work in harmony with the complete automobile.

- Another aspect of the development engineer's job is a trade-off process required to deliver all of the automobile attributes at a certain acceptable level.
- The development engineer is also responsible for organizing automobile level testing, validation, and certification. Components and systems are designed and tested individually by the Product Engineer. The final evaluation is to be conducted at the automobile level to evaluate system to system interactions.
- Manufacturing Engineers are responsible for ensuring proper production of the automotive components or complete vehicles. While the development engineers are responsible for the function of the vehicle, manufacturing engineers are responsible for the safe and effective production of the vehicle.
- In the rheostatic method of speed control for D.C., the shunt motor uses a resistance in series with the armature. This method will be unsuitable for changing loads.
- By the use of field diverter resistance in a D.C. series motor, we can obtain speed variations with load. Such speed variations will be above the normal speed.
- By using armature diverter resistance in a D.C. series motor we can obtain speed variations. Such speed variations will be below normal.
- With tapped field coils, speed variation can be obtained in a D.C. series motor. However the speed, when the setting is at full field will be below normal.
- A D.C. series motor uses a field diverter to control the speed. The field diverter is having 5 ohms resistance and carries 5 amps. The wattage rating of the field diverter will be 125 watts.
- In D.C. motors, by controlling the shunt field flux we get speeds above the rated speed.
- The speed of a D.C. motor, with the exception of that of a differentially compound motor, decreases with increase in load.
- The speed of a loaded D.C. shunt motor can be decreased below its rated speed by increasing the resistance in the armature circuit.
- When the speed of a D.C. shunt motor increases by field control, the back emf increases and the line current decreases.
- The tapped field control method is employed for controlling the speed of a D.C. series motor.
- Speed variation is possible by inserting a resistance in the series with supply. But this method is preferred only in a series motor.
- Varying the speed by inserting a resistance in the field circuit is possible both in shunt and compound motors.
- By using the field rheostatic control method in a D.C. shunt motor, the speed is approximately constant between no load and full load.
- While varying the speed of a D.C. shun motor through the field control method we get 15 to 30% above normal speed.
- For speed variation, the series resistance value of the shunt field rheostat will be equal to the shunt field current and the resistance will be equal to the shunt field resistance.
- As the load is increased, the speed of a D.C. shunt motor reduces slightly.
- The current drawn by a 220 V D.C. motor of armature resistance 0.5 ohm and back emf of 200 V will be 40 A.
- Locomotive application requires a high starting torque motors.
- In a loaded D.C. shunt motor when the flux approaches zero, then its speed will approach zero drawing heavy line current.
- The supply terminals of a D.C. shunt motor are reversed. There will be no effect on the motor operation. It will run normally.
- A D.C. shunt motor has an additional resistance $R_1$ in the shunt field and an additional resistance $R_2$ in the armature. For safe starting $R_1$ should be minimum and $R_2$ maximum.
- Which of the following type of D.C. motors, is least used differentially compound motor.
- In the automotive industry manufacturers are playing a larger role in the development stages of automotive components to ensure that the products are easy to manufacture. Design for Manufacturability in the automotive world is crucial to make certain whichever design is developed in the Research and Development Stage of automotive design.
- Other automotive engineers include those listed below:
  - Aerodynamics engineers will often give guidance to the styling studio so that the shapes they design are aerodynamic, as well as attractive.
  - Body engineers will also let the studio know if it is feasible to make the panels for their designs.
  - Change control engineers make sure that all of the design and manufacturing changes that occur are organized, managed and implemented.
  - Acoustics engineers are specific types of development engineers who do sound and aerodynamic testing to prevent loud cabin noises while the vehicle is on the road.

# MULTIPLE CHOICE QUESTIONS

1. The voltage-current characteristics of a DC generator for arc welding is a straight line between an open-circuit voltage of 80 V and short-circuit current of 300 A. The generator settings for maximum arc power will be:
(a) 80 V and 150 A (b) 40 V and 300 A
(c) 40 V and 150 V (d) V and 300 A

2. Which one of the following features improves the fatigue strength of a metallic material?
(a) increasing the temperature
(b) scratching the surface
(c) overstressing
(d) understressing.

3. Which one of the following pairs is correctly matched?
(a) Beauchamp tower first experiments on journal bearings
(b) Osborne reynolds antifriction bearings
(c) Sommerfeld number pivot and collar bearings
(d) Ball bearings hydrodynamic lubrication

4. Which of the following joining processes are best suited for manufacturing pipes to carry gas products?
1. Rivetting 2. Welding
3. Bolts and nuts
Select the correct answer using the codes given below:
**Codes:**
(a) 1 and 2 (b) 1 and 3
(c) 2 alone (d) 1, 2 and 3

5. The correct sequence of the given materials in ascending order of their weldability is:
(a) MS, copper, cast iron, aluminium
(b) Cast iron, MS, aluminium copper
(c) Copper, cast iron, MS, aluminium
(d) Aluminium, copper, cast iron, MS

6. A screw thread specified by M 20 × 25 C as per BIS thread system means:
(a) metric thread of 20 mm nominal diameter and 2.5 mm pitch having coarse tolerance
(b) metric thread of 20 mm root diameter and 2-5 mm pitch having coarse tolerance
(c) metric thread of fine class having 20 mm root diameter and 2.5 mm pitch
(d) metric thread of 20 mm shank diameter and 25 mm thread depth with coarse tolerance.

7. Which one of the following statements is correct?
(a) no flux is used in gas welding of mild steel
(b) borax is the commonly used flux coating on welding electrodes
(c) laser beam welding employs a vacuum chamber and thus avoids use of a shielding method
(d) AC can be used for GTAW process

8. Which one of the following statements with regard to belt drives is not correct?
(a) increase in the angle of wrap of the belt enables more power transmission
(b) maximum power is transmitted when the centrifugal tension is three times the tight side tension
(c) wide and thin belt is preferable for better life than a thick and narrow one
(d) crown is provided on the pulley to make the belt run centrally on the pulley

9. Angle of twist of a shaft of diameter d' is inversely proportional to:
(a) $d$ (b) $d^2$
(c) $d^3$ (d) $d^4$

10. Which one of the following sets of parameters should be monitored for determining safe operation of journal bearing?
(a) oil pressure, bearing metal temperature and bearing vibration
(b) bearing vibration, oil pressure and speed or shaft
(c) bearing metal temperature oil pressure
(d) oil pressure and bearing vibration.

11. The performance of a hydrodynamic journal bearing is a function of:
(a) Reynolds number (b) Sommerfield number
(c) Speed (d) Bearing modulus

12. Match List-I (Nature of Failure) with List-II (Nature of Member) and select the correct answer using the codes given below the lists:

| List-I (Nature of Failure) | List-II (Nature of Member) |
|---|---|
| A. Structural member fails in axial compression | 1. Knuckle Joint |
| B. A member fails along a 45° helical plane subjected to torsion | 2. Long column |
| C. A structural member bends and collapses under axial compression load | 3. Strut |
| D. A member fails in double shear for a joint | 4. Cast iron round bar subjected to torsion |

**Codes:**

| | A | B | C | D |
|---|---|---|---|---|
| (a) | 3 | 1 | 2 | 4 |
| (b) | 2 | 4 | 3 | 1 |
| (c) | 3 | 4 | 2 | 1 |
| (d) | 2 | 1 | 3 | 4 |

13. Which one of the following correctly relates the life of a roller bearing in millions of revolutions (L) the load P and the basic dynamic load rating for 1 million revolutions(C)?
(a) $L = (C/P)^3$ (b) $L = (C/P)^{10/3}$
(c) $L = (P/C)^3$ (d) $L = (C/P)^{1/3}$

14. Match List-I with List-II and select the correct answer using the codes given below the lists:

| List-I (Type of Thread) | List-II (Use) |
|---|---|
| A. Square thread | 1. Used in vice |
| B. Acme thread | 2. Used in lead screw |
| C. Buttress thread | 3. Used in screw jack |
| D. Trapezoidal thread | 4. Used in power transmission devices in machine tool |

**Codes:**

| | A | B | C | D |
|---|---|---|---|---|
| (a) | 2 | 3 | 4 | 1 |
| (b) | 2 | 3 | 1 | 4 |
| (c) | 3 | 2 | 1 | 4 |
| (d) | 3 | 2 | 4 | 1 |

15. The number of slots in a 25 mm castle nut are:
(a) 2 (b) 4
(c) 6 (d) 8

16. Which key is preferred for the condition where a large amount of impact torque is to betransmitted in both direction of rotation:
(a) Woodruff key
(b) Feather key
(c) Gib-head key
(d) Tangent key

17. Which of the following is true about following specifications: Hex Bolt M 16 NL-IS: 1363:
(a) 16 eye bolts used on electric motors
(b) a stress relieved blot for connecting rod
(c) a bolt with a nut
(d) a bolt with a nut and a lock nut

18. Which bearing is preferred for oscillating conditions?
(a) Double row roller hearing
(b) Angular contact single row ball bearing
(c) Taper roller bearing
(d) Needle roller hearing

19. Ball bearings are provided with a cage:
(a) to reduce friction
(b) to maintain the halls at a fixed distance apart
(c) to prevent the lubricant from flowing out
(d) to facilitate slipping of balls.

20. Thick steel plate cut with oxygen normally shows signs of cracking. This tendency for cracking can be minimized by:
(a) slow speed cutting
(b) cutting in two or more stages
(c) preheating the plate
(d) using oxy-acetylene flame

21. Jewel bearings are used in:
(a) contaminated atmosphere
(b) low-torque applications
(c) fully immersed in water condition
(d) high speed shafts

22. Match List-I with List-II and select the correct answer using the codes given below the lists:

| List-I (Type of joint) | List-II (Mode of joining members) |
|---|---|
| A. Cotter joint | 1. Connects two rods or bars permitting small amount of flexibility |
| B. Knuckle joint | 2. Rigidly connects two members |
| C. Turn buckle | 3. Connects two rods having threaded ends |
| D. Riveted joint | 4. Permanent fluid-tight joint between two plates. |
| | 5. Connects two shafts and transmits torque |

**Codes:**

| | A | B | C | D |
|---|---|---|---|---|
| (a) | 5 | 1 | 3 | 2 |
| (b) | 2 | 1 | 3 | 4 |
| (c) | 5 | 3 | 2 | 4 |
| (d) | 2 | 3 | 1 | 4 |

23. The most efficient riveted joint possible is one which would be as strong in tension, shear and bearing as the original plates to be joined. But this can never be achieved because:
(a) rivets cannot be made with the same material
(b) rivets are weak in compression
(c) there should be at least one hole in the plate reducing its strength
(d) clearance is present between the plate and the rivet

24. Which of the following stresses are associated with the tightening of a nut on a stud?
(a) Tensile stresses due to stretching of stud.
(b) Bending stresses of stud.
(c) Transverse shear stresses across threads.
(d) Torsional shear stresses in threads due to frictional resistance

25. The frictional torque for square thread at mean radius while raising load is given by (W= load, $R_0$ = Mean Radius, $\phi$ = Angle of friction, $\alpha$ = Helix angle):
(a) $WR_0 \tan(\phi - \alpha)$ (b) $WR_0 \tan(\phi + \alpha)$
(c) $WR_0 \tan \alpha$ (d) $WR_0 \tan \phi$

26. In a belt drive, if the pulley diameter is doubled keeping the tension and belt width constant, then it will be necessary to:
(a) increase the key length
(b) increase the key depth
(c) increase the key width
(d) decrease the key length

27. Consider the following statements:
    1. grinding
    2. coating
    3. hammer peening

    for improving the fatigue strength of steel.
    Of the above statements:
    (a) 1 and 2 are correct
    (b) 2 and 3 are correct
    (c) 1 and 3 are correct
    (d) 1, 2 and 3 are correct.

28. The following data refers to an open belt drive:

| | Pulley A | Pulley B |
|---|---|---|
| Purpose.... | Driving | Driven |
| Diameter.... | 450 mm | 750 mm |
| Angle of contact.... | $\theta_A = 150$ | $\theta_B = 210°$ |
| Coefficient of friction between belt and pulley | $f_A = 0.36$ | $f_B = 0.22$ |

The ratio of tensions may be calculated using the relation $(T_1/T_2) = \exp(z)$ where $z$ is:
(a) $f_A\theta_A$
(b) $f_B\theta_B$
(c) $(f_A + f_B)(\theta_A + \theta_B)/4$
(c) $(f_A\theta_A + f_B\theta_B)/2$

29. In a multiple V-belt drive, when angle belt is damaged, it is preferable to change the complete set to:
    (a) reduce vibration
    (b) reduce slip
    (c) ensure uniform loading
    (d) ensure proper alignment

30. Design of shafts made of brittle material is based on:
    (a) Guest's theory (b) Rankine's theory
    (c) St. Venant's theory (d) Von-Mises theory.

31. A motor car has wheel base of 280 cm and the pivot distance of front stub axles is 140 cm. When the outer wheel has turned through 30, the angle of turn of the inner frontwheel for correct steering will be:
    (a) 60° (b) $\cot^{-1} 2.23$
    (c) $\cot^{-1} 1.232$ (d) 30°

32. Match List-I with List-II and select answer using the codes given below the Lists:

| **List-I (Types of joints)** | **List-II (An element of the joint)** |
|---|---|
| A. Riveted joint | 1. Pin |
| B. Welded joint | 2. Strap |
| C. Bolted joint | 3. Lock washer |
| D. Knuckle joint | 4. Fillet |

**Codes:**

| | A | B | C | D |
|---|---|---|---|---|
| (a) | 4 | 3 | 2 | 1 |
| (b) | 2 | 3 | 4 | 1 |
| (c) | 2 | 4 | 3 | 1 |
| (d) | 2 | 4 | 1 | 3 |

33. Consider the following statements regarding power screws:
    1. The efficiency of a self-locking screw cannot be more than 50%
    2. If the friction angle is less than the helix angle of the screw, then the efficiency will be more than 50%
    3. The efficiency of ACME (trapezoidal) thread is less than that of square thread.

    Of these statements:
    (a) 1, 2 and 3-are correct (b) 2 and 3 are correct
    (c) 1 and 3 are correct (d) 1 and 2 are correct

34. Electron beam welding can be carried out in:
    (a) open air
    (b) a shielding gas environment
    (c) a pressurized inert gas chamber
    (d) vacuum

35. Given that $p$ = chain pitch
    C = centre distance
    N, $n$ = number of teeth on large and small sprocket respectively,
    The length of chain in terms of pitches can be approximated by:
    (a) $\frac{2C}{P}$
    (b) $\frac{2C}{P} + (N+n)/2$
    (c) $\frac{2C}{P} + \left[\frac{N+n}{2\pi}\right]\frac{p}{C}$
    (d) $\frac{2C}{P} + \frac{N+n}{2p} + \left[\frac{N-n}{2p}\right]^2 \frac{p}{C}$

36. When compared to a rod of the same diameter and material, a wire rope:
    (a) is less flexible
    (b) has a much smaller load carrying capacity
    (c) does not provide much warning before failure
    (d) provides much greater time for remedial action before failure

37. A shafts subjected to fluctuating loads for which the normal torque (T) and bending moment (M) are 1000 N-m add 500 N-m respectively. If the combined shock and fatigue factor for bending is 1.5 and combined shock and fatigue factor for torsion is 2, then the equivalent twisting moment for the shaft is:
    (a) 2000-N-m (b) 2050 N-m
    (c) 2100 N-m (d) 2136 N-m

38. The lead angle of a worm is 22.5°. Its helix angle will be:
    (a) 22.5° (b) 45°
    (c) 67.5° (d) 90°

39. Consider the following statements about anti-friction bearings:
    1. They have low starting and low running friction at moderate speeds

2. They have high resistance to shock loading.
3. They can carry both radial and thrust loads.
4. Their initial cost is high.
5. They can accommodated some amount of misalignment of shaft.

Of these statements:

(a) 1, 2, 3 and 4
(b) 1, 3 and 4 are correct
(c) 1, 4 and 5 are correct
(d) 1, 2, 3 and 5 are correct

40. The load cup of a screw jack is made separate from the head of the spindle to:
(a) enhance the load carrying capacity of the jack
(b) reduce the effort needed for lifting the working load
(c) reduce the value of frictional torque to be countered for lifting the load
(d) prevent the rotation of load being lifted

41. A bolt of uniform strength can be developed by:
(a) keeping the core diameter of threads equal to the diameter of unthreaded portion of the bolt.
(b) keeping the core diameter smaller than the diameter of the unthreaded portion.
(c) keeping the nominal diameter of threads equal the diameter of unthreaded portion of the bolt.
(d) one end fixed and the other end free.

42. Which designing a screw is a screw jack against buckling failure, the end conditions for the screw are taken as:
(a) both the ends fixed
(b) both the ends hinged
(c) one end fixed and other end hinged
(d) one end fixed and there end free

43. Match List-I with List-II and select the correct answer using the codes given below the list:

| List-I (Different types of detachable joints) | List-II (Specific use of these detachable joints) |
|---|---|
| A. Cotter joint | 1. Tie rod of a wall crane |
| B. Knuckle joint | 2. Suspension bridges |
| C. Suspension link joint | 3. Diagonal stays in boiler |
| D. Turn buckle (adjustable joint) | 4. Cross-head a steam engine |

**Codes:**

| | A | B | C | D |
|---|---|---|---|---|
| (a) | 4 | 2 | 3 | 1 |
| (b) | 4 | 3 | 2 | 1 |
| (c) | 3 | 2 | 1 | 4 |
| (d) | 2 | 1 | 4 | 3 |

44. A spur gear transmitting power is connected to the shaft with a key of rectangular section. The type (s) of stresses developed in the key is/are:
(a) shear stress alone
(b) hearing stress alone
(c) both shear and bearing stresses
(d) shearing, bearing and bending stresses.

45. The permissible stress in a filled weld is 100 N/mm. The fillet weld has equal leg lengths of 15 mm each. The allowable shearing load on weldment per cm length of the weld is:
(a) 225 kN (b) 15.0 kN
(c) 10.6 kN (d) 7.5 kN

46. Sources of power loss in a chain drive are given below:
1. Friction between chain and sprocket teeth.
2. Overcoming the chain stiffness.
3. Overcoming the friction in shaft bearing.
4. Frictional resistance of the motion of the chain in air or lubricant.

The correct sequence of descending order of power loss due to these sources is:
(a) 1, 2, 3, 4
(b) 1, 2, 4, 3
(c) 2, 1, 3, 4
(d) 2, 1, 4, 3

47. Consider the following design considerations:
1. Tensile failure
2. Creep failure
3. Bearing failure
4. Shearing failure
5. Bending failure

The design of the pin of a rocker arm of an I.C. engine is based on:
(a) 1, 2 and 4
(h) 1, 3 and .4
(c) 2, 3 and 5
(d) 3, 4 and 5

48. Which one of the following loadings is considered for design of axles?
(a) Bending moment only
(b) Twisting moment only
(c) Combined bending moment and torsion
(d) Combined action of bending moment, twisting moment and axial thrust.

49. Removal of metal particles from the raceway of a roiling contact bearing is a kind of failure of bearing known as:
(a) pitting
(b) wearing
(c) spalling
(d) scuffing

50. The design calculations of members subject to fluctuating loads with the same factor of safety yield the most conservative estimates when using:
(a) Gerber relation
(b) Soderberg relation
(c) Goodman relation
(d) none of the above

51. Match List-I with List-II and select the correct answer using the codes given below the lists:

| List-I | List-II |
|---|---|
| A. Crank shaft | 1. Supports the revolving parts and transmits torque. |
| B. Wire shaft | 2. Transmits motion between shafts where is not possible to effect a rigid coupling between them. |
| C. Axle | 3. Converts linear motion into rotary motion. |
| D. Plain shaft | 4. Supports only the revolving parts. |

**Codes:**

| | A | B | C | D |
|---|---|---|---|---|
| (a) | 3 | 2 | 1 | 4 |
| (b) | 4 | 2 | 3 | 1 |
| (c) | 3 | 2 | 4 | 1 |
| (d) | 1 | 4 | 2 | 3 |

52. Match List-I with List-II and select the correct answer using the codes given below the lists:

| List-I (Terminology) | List-II (Relevant terms) |
|---|---|
| A. Interference | 1. Arc of approach, arc of recess, circular pitch. |
| B. Dynamic load on tooth | 2. Lewis equation. |
| C. Static load | 3. Minimum number of teeth on pinion. |
| D. Contact ratio | 4. Inaccuracies in tooth profile |

**Codes:**

| | A | B | C | D |
|---|---|---|---|---|
| (a) | 3 | 4 | 1 | 2 |
| (b) | 1 | 2 | 3 | 4 |
| (c) | 4 | 3 | 2 | 1 |
| (d) | 3 | 4 | 2 | 1 |

53. Match List-I with List-II and select the correct answer using the codes given below the lists:

| List-I (Name) | List-II (Type) |
|---|---|
| A. Oldham coupling | 1. Joins collinear shafts and is rigid type. |
| B. Flange coupling | 2. Joins non-collinear shafts and is adjustable. |
| C. Universal coupling | 3. Joins collinear shafts and engages and disengages them during motion. |
| D. Friction coupling | 4. Compensates peripheral shafts, longitudinal and angular shifts of shafts. |

**Codes:**

| | A | B | C | D |
|---|---|---|---|---|
| (a) | 2 | 1 | 4 | 3 |
| (b) | 3 | 2 | 1 | 4 |
| (c) | 1 | 4 | 2 | 3 |
| (d) | 2 | 3 | 1 | 4 |

54. Match List-I with List-II and select the correct answer using the codes given below the lists:

| List-I (Requirement) | List-II (Type) |
|---|---|
| A. High temperature service. | 1. Teflon bearing. |
| B. High load | 2. Carbon bearing |
| C. No lubrication | 3. Hydrodynamic bearing |
| D. Bushings | 4. Sleeve bearing |

**Codes:**

| | A | B | C | D |
|---|---|---|---|---|
| (a) | 1 | 2 | 3 | 4 |
| (b) | 4 | 1 | 2 | 3 |
| (c) | 2 | 1 | 3 | 4 |
| (d) | 2 | 3 | 1 | 4 |

55. In the calculation of induced shear stress in helical springs, the Wahl's correction factor is used to take care of:
(a) combined effect of transverse shear stress and bending stress in the wire.
(b) combined effect of bending stress and curvature of the wire.
(c) combined effect of transverse shear stress and curvature of the wire.
(d) combined effect of torsional shear stress and transverse shear stress in the wire

56. Two rigid plates are clamped by means of bolt and nut with an initial force N. After tightening, a separating force P (P < N) is applied to the lower plate, which in turn ads on nut. The tension in the bolt after this is:
(a) (N + P) (b) (N – P)
(c) P (d) N

57. To ensure self-locking in a screw jack it is essential that helix angle is:
(a) larger than friction angle
(b) smaller than friction angle
(c) equal to friction angle
(d) such as to give maximum efficiency in lifting

58. A double fillet welded joint with parallel fillet weld of length L and leg B is subjected to a tensile force P. Assuming uniform stress distribution, the shear stress in distribution, the shear stress the weld is given by:
(a) $\frac{\sqrt{2}.P}{BL}$ (b) $\sigma_1 = \frac{P}{2hl}$
(c) $\frac{P}{\sqrt{2}.B.L}$ (d) $\frac{2P}{B.L}$

59. In flat belt drive, if the slip between the driver and the belt is 1%, that between belt and follower is 3% and driver and follower pulley diameters are equal, then the velocity ratio of the drive will be:
(a) 0.99 (b) 0.98
(c) 0.97 (d) 0.96

60. Effective stress in wire ropes during normal working is equal to the stress due to:
(a) axial load plus stress due to bending
(b) acceleration/retardation of masses plus stress due to bending
(c) axial load plus stress due to acceleration/ retardation
(d) bending plus stress due to acceleration/retardation

61. A transmission shaft subjected to bending loads must be designed on the basis of:
(a) maximum normal stress theory
(b) maximum shear stress theory
(c) maximum normal stress and maximum shear stress theories
(d) fatigue strength

62. Consider the following statements:
The form factor of a spur gear tooth depends upon the
1. number of teeth.
2. pressure angle.
3. addendum modification.
4. circular pitch.
Of these statements:
(a) 1 and 3 are correct
(b) 1 and 4 are correct
(c) 1, 2 and 3 are correct
(d) 1 and 4 are correct

63. When belt drive is transmitting maximum power:
(a) effective tension is equal to centrifugal tension
(b) effective tension is half of centrifugal tension
(c) driving tension on slack side is equal to the centrifugal tension
(d) driving tension on tight side is twice the centrifugal tension

64. Tapered roller bearing can take:
(a) radial load only
(b) axial load only
(c) both radial and axial loads and the ratio of these being less than unity
(d) both radial and axial loads and the ratio of these being greater than unity

65. In bearing characteristic number in a hydrodynamic bearing depends on:
(a) it is closer to real life situation
(b) it leads to a safer design
(c) it leads to cost effective design
(d) no other assumption is possible

66. The bearing characteristic number in a hydrodynamic bearing depends on:
(a) length, width and load
(b) length, width and speed
(c) viscosity, speed and load
(d) viscosity, speed and bearing pressure

67. Which one of the following welding processes uses non-consumable electrodes?
(a) TIG welding
(b) MIG welding
(c) Manual arc welding
(d) Submerged arc welding

68. Match List-I with List-II and Select the correct answer using the codes given below the Lists:

| **List-I (Filler)** | **List-II (Joining process)** |
|---|---|
| A. Cu, Zn, Ag alloy | 1. Braze welding |
| B. Cu, Sn alloy | 2. Brazing |
| C. Pb, Sb alloy | 3. Soldering |
| D. Iron oxide and aluminium powder | 4. TIG welding of aluminium. |

**Codes:**

| | A | B | C | D |
|---|---|---|---|---|
| (a) | 4 | 1 | 3 | 2 |
| (b) | 1 | 2 | 4 | 3 |
| (c) | 2 | 1 | 3 | 4 |
| (d) | 2 | 4 | 3 | 1 |

69. The maximum efficiency of a self-locking screw is:
(a) 50%
(b) 70%
(c) 75%
(d) 80%

70. Match List-I (Type of keys) with List-II (Characteristic) and select the correct answer using the codes given below the Lists:

| **List-I** | **List-II** |
|---|---|
| A. Woodruff key | 1. Loose fitting, light duty |
| B. Kennedy key | 2. Heavy duty |
| C. Feather key | 3. Self-aligning |
| D. Flat key | 4. Normal industrial use |

**Codes:**

| | A | B | C | D |
|---|---|---|---|---|
| (a) | 2 | 3 | 1 | 4 |
| (b) | 3 | 2 | 1 | 4 |
| (c) | 2 | 3 | 4 | 1 |
| (d) | 3 | 2 | 4 | 1 |

71. Consider the following statements:
MIG welding process uses
1. consumable electrode
2. non-consumable electrode
3. D. C power supply
4. A. C power supply.
Of these statements:
(a) 2 and 4 are correct
(b) 2 and 3 arc correct
(c) 1 and 4 are correct
(d) 1 and 3 are correct

72. In the case of a vertical belt pulley drive with $T_c$ as centrifugal tension and $T_0$ as the initial tension, the belt would tend to hang clear of the lower pulley when:
(a) $T_c < T_0$ (b) $T_c = T_0/3$
(c) $T_c > T_0$ (d) $T_c = T_0/2$

73. Given that $T_1$ and $T_2$ are the tensions on the tight and slack of the belt respectively, the initial tension of the belt taking centrifugal tension $T_c$ is equal to:
(a) $\frac{T_1+T_2+T_c}{3}$ (b) $\frac{T_1+T_2+2T_c}{2}$
(c) $\frac{T_1+T_2+3T_c}{2}$ (d) $\frac{T_1+T_2+4T_c}{3}$

74. Given that W = weight of load handled, $W_r$ = weight of rope, and $f$ = acceleration, the additional load in ropes of a hoist during starting is given by:
(a) $F_a = \left(\frac{W-W_r}{g}\right)f$ (b) $F_a = \left(\frac{W+W_r}{g}\right)f$
(c) $F_a = \left(\frac{W}{g}\right)f$ (d) $F_a = \left(\frac{W_r}{g}\right)f$

75. When a shaft transmits power through gears, the shaft experiences:
(a) torsional stresses alone
(b) bending stresses alone
(c) constant bending and varying torsional stresses
(d) varying bending and constant torsional stresses

76. The limiting wear load of spur gear is proportional to (where $E_p$ = Young's modulus of union material; $E_g$ = Young's modulus of gear material:
(a) $(E_p+E_g)^{-1}$ (b) $\left(\frac{E_p+E_s}{E_pE_s}\right)$
(c) $\left(1+\frac{E_p}{E_s}\right)$ (d) $\left(1+\frac{E_g}{E_B}\right)$

77. Which one of the following statements is not true of rolling contact bearing?
(a) The bearing characteristic number is given by $\frac{ZN}{p}$ where Z is the absolute viscosity of the lubricant, Nis the shaft speed and $p$ is the bearing pressure.
(b) Inner race of a radial ball bearing has an interference fit with the shaft and rotates along with it.
(c) Outer race of the hearing has in interference fit with bearing housing and does not rotate.
(d) In some cases, the inner race is stationary and outer race rotates.

78. In the multiple disc clutch, if there are 6 discs on the driving shaft and 5 discs on the driven shaft, then the number of pairs of contact surfaces will be equal to:
(a) 11 (b) 12
(c) 10 (d) 22

79. Match List-I with List-II and select the correct answer using the codes given below the lists:

| List-I (Bearing materials) | List-II (Properties) |
|---|---|
| A. Babbits | 1. Porous |
| B. Bronze | 2. Good emeddability |
| C. C.I. | 3. Suitable for high loads and low speeds |
| D. Sintered powdered metal | 4. Run well with C.I. journals |

**Codes:**

| | A | B | C | D |
|---|---|---|---|---|
| (a) | 2 | 3 | 4 | 1 |
| (b) | 3 | 2 | 1 | 4 |
| (c) | 2 | 3 | 1 | 4 |
| (d) | 3 | 2 | 4 | 1 |

80. Wahl stress factor takes into account:
(a) direct shear stress.
(b) torsional shear stress
(c) wire curvature effect
(d) direct shear and wire curvature effect.

81. Which of the following stresses are associated with the tightening of nut on a bolt?
(a) Tensile stress due to the stretching of bolt
(b) Bending stress due to the bending of bolt
(c) Crushing and shear stresses in threads
(d) Torsional shear stress due to frictional resistance between the nut and the bolt.
Select the correct answer using the codes given below:
(a) 1,2 and 4 (b) 1, 2 and 3
(c) 2, 3 and 4 (d) 1, 3 and 4

82. The shearing area of a key of length 'L' breadth '$b$' depth '$h$' is equal to:
(a) $b \times h$ (b) $L \times h$
(c) $L \times b$ (d) $L \times (h/2)$

83. Match List-I (Machine element) with List-II (Cause of failure) and select the correct answer using the codes given below the lists:

| List-I | List-II |
|---|---|
| A. Axle | 1. Shear stress |
| B. Cotter | 2. Tensile/ compressive stress |
| C. Connecting rod | 3. Wear |
| D. Journal bearing | 4. Bending stress |

**Codes:**

| | A | B | C | D |
|---|---|---|---|---|
| (a) | 1 | 4 | 2 | 3 |
| (b) | 4 | 1 | 2 | 3 |
| (c) | 4 | 1 | 3 | 2 |
| (d) | 1 | 4 | 3 | 2 |

84. In oxy-acetylene gas welding, for complete combustion, the volume of oxygen required per unit of acetylene is:
(a) 1 (b) 1.5
(c) 2 (d) 2.5

85. Consider the following statements. A splined shaft is used for
1. Transmitting power
2. Holding a flywheel rigidly in position
3. Moving axially the gear wheels mounted on it
4. Mounting V-belt pulleys on it.
Of these statements:
(a) 2 and 3 are correct
(b) 1 and 4 are correct
(c) 2 and 4 are correct
(d) 1 and 3 are correct

86. When two shafts are neither parallel nor intersecting, power can be transmitted by using:
(a) A pair of spur gears
(b) A pair of helical gears
(c) An Oldham's coupling
(d) A pair of spiral gears.

87. In the assembly design of shaft, pulley and key, the weakest members is:
(a) Pulley (b) Key
(c) Shaft (d) None

88. In the formulation of Lewis equation for toothed gearing, it is assumed that tangential tooth load $F_1$ acts on the:
(a) Pitch point
(b) Tip of the tooth
(c) Root of the tooth
(d) Whole face of the tooth

89. For a two-dimensional state $(\sigma_1, \sigma_2, \sigma_1 > 0, \sigma_2 < 0)$ the designed values are most conservative if which one of the following failure theories were used?
(a) maximum principal strain theory
(b) maximum distortion energy theory
(c) maximum shear stress theory
(d) maximum principal stress theory

90. Match List-I with List-II and select the correct answer using the codes given below the lists:

| **List-I** | **List-II** |
|---|---|
| A. Single-plate friction clutch | 1. Scooters clutch |
| B. Multi-plate friction clutch | 2. Rolling mills |
| C. Centrifugal clutch | 3. Trucks |
| D. Jaw clutch | 4. Mopeds |

**Codes:**

| | A | B | C | D |
|---|---|---|---|---|
| (a) | 1 | 3 | 4 | 2 |
| (b) | 1 | 3 | 2 | 4 |
| (c) | 3 | 1 | 2 | 4 |
| (d) | 3 | 1 | 4 | 2 |

91. Which of the following stresses are associated with the design of pins in hushed pin-type, flexible coupling?
1. Bearing stress
2. Bending stress
3. Axial tensile stress
3. Transverse shear stress
Select the correct answer using the codes given below:
(a) 1, 3 and 4 (b) 2, 3 and 4
(c) 1, 2 and 3 (d) 1, 2 and 4

92. The diameter of tommy bar for a screw jack is designed for:
(a) bending moment due to effort applied
(b) torque on the tommy bar due to effort applied
(c) a percentage of axial loads
(d) some axial loads coupled with transverse loads

93. Centrifugal tension in belts is:
(a) useful because it maintains some tension even when no power is transmitted
(b) not harmful because it does not take part in power transmission
(c) harmful because it increases belt tension and reduces the power transmitted
(d) a hypothetical phenomenon and does not actually exist in belts

94. In a single reduction, a large velocity ratio is required. The best transmission is:
(a) spur gear drive
(b) helical gear drive
(c) bevel gear drive
(d) worm gear drive

95. Which one of the following belts should not he used above 40°C?
(a) balata belt (b) rubber belt
(c) fabric belt (d) synthetic belt

96. Consider the following statements:
A nomenclature $\phi$ 50 H8/p8 denoted that
1. Hole diameter is 50 mm
2. It is a shaft base system
3. 8 indicates fundamental deviation.
Which of the statements given above is/are correct?
(a) 1, 2 and 3 (b) 1 and 2 only
(c) 1 and 3 only (d) 3 only

97. A certain minimum number of teeth is to be kept for a gear wheel:
(a) so that the gear is of a good size
(b) for better durability
(c) to avoid interference and undercutting
(d) for better strength.

98. In a single row deep groove ball-bearing, cages are needed to:
(a) separate the two races
(b) separate the balls from the inner race
(c) separate the outer race from the balls
(d) ensure that the balls do into cluster at one point and maintain proper relative angular positions.

99. Which one of the following types of bearings is employed in shafts of gearboxes of automobiles?
(a) hydrodynamic journal bearings
(b) multi-lobed journal hearings
(c) antifriction bearings
(d) hybrid journal bearings.

100. A hole is to be punched in a 15 mm thick plate having an ultimate shear strength of 3 $N\text{-}mm^{-2}$. If the allowable crushing stress in the punch is 6 $N\text{-}mm^{-2}$, the diameter of the smallest hole which can be punched is equal to:
(a) 15 mm (6) 30 mm
(c) 60 mm (d) 120 mm

101. The edge of a steel plate cut by oxygen cutting will get hardened when the carbon content is:
(a) less than 0.1 percent
(b) less than 0.3 percent
(c) more than 0.3 percent
(d) anywhere between 0.1 to 1.0 percent

102. The safe rim velocity of a flywheel is influenced by the
(a) centrifugal stresses (b) fluctuation of energy
(c) fluctuation of speed (d) mass of the flywheel

103. Match List-I (Bearings) with List-II (Applications) and select the correct answer using the codes given below the lists:

| **List-I** | **List-II** |
|---|---|
| A. Journal hearing | 1. Electric motors |
| B. Thrust bearing | 2. Watches |
| C. Conical pivot bearing | 3. Marine engines |
| D. Ball bearing | 4. Swivelling chairs |

**Codes:**

| | A | B | C | D |
|---|---|---|---|---|
| (a) | 3 | 4 | 1 | 2 |
| (b) | 4 | 2 | 1 | 3 |
| (c) | 3 | 4 | 2 | 1 |
| (d) | 4 | 2 | 3 | 1 |

104. Weld spatter occurs due to any of the following except:
(a) high welding current
(b) too small an electrode
(c) are
(d) wrong polarity

105. In a hydrodynamic journal bearing, there is:
(a) a very thin film of lubricant between the journal and the hearing such that there is contact between the journal and the bearing
(b) a thick film of lubricant between the journal and the bearing
(c) no lubricant between the journal and the bearing
(d) a forced lubricant between the journal and the bearing

106. Consider the following statements:
1. From design considerations, it is always advantageous to place cast iron ribs on the tension side rather than on the compression side.
2. Cast iron is an excellent choice for machine tool guides and frames
3. Cast iron parts have a low notch sensitivity.
Which of these statements are correct?
(a) 1, 2 and 3 (b) 2 and 3
(c) 1 and 3 (d) 1 and 2

107. Match List-I (Applications) with List-II (Choice of Bearings) and select the correct answer using the codes given below the lists:

| **List-I (Applications)** | **List-II (Choice of Bearings)** |
|---|---|
| A. Granite table of a coordinate measuring machine | 1. Hydrodynamic-bearing |
| B. Headstock spindle of a lathe | 2. Deep groove ball bearing |
| C. Crank shaft of a diesel engine | 3. Hydrostatic bearing |
| D. Armature of 0.5 kW induction motor | 4. Taper roller bearing |

**Codes:**

| | A | B | C | D |
|---|---|---|---|---|
| (a) | 1 | 4 | 3 | 2 |
| (b) | 3 | 2 | 1 | 4 |
| (c) | 1 | 2 | 3 | 4 |
| (d) | 3 | 4 | 1 | 2 |

108. If $k = 3$ for hail bearings and $k = 3.33$ for roller bearings, which one of the following correctly states the load (P) – Life (L) relationship for rolling contact bearings?
(a) $\frac{L_1}{L_2} = \left(\frac{P_1}{P_2}\right)^k$ (b) $\frac{L_1}{L_2} = \left(\frac{P_1}{P_2}\right)^{\frac{1}{(k-1)}}$
(c) $\frac{L_2}{L_1} = \left(\frac{P_1}{P_2}\right)^k$ (d) $\frac{L_2}{L_1} = \left(\frac{P_1}{P_2}\right)^{k-1}$

109. Consider the following statements regarding boundary lubrication conditions in hydrodynamic journal hearings:
1. It is an undesirable condition.
2. It always occurs during starting and stopping of the journal.
3. It necessitates frequent repair of the journal.
4. This condition can he completely eliminated by using high viscosity lubricant.
Which of the statements given above are correct?
(a) 1, 2 and 4 (b) 2, 3 and 4
(c) 1 and 2 (d) 3 and 4

110. When the lubricating oil is forced between the journal and bearing by external pressure, the bearing is known as:
(a) Zero film bearing
(b) Boundary lubricated bearing
(c) Hydrostatic bearing
(d) Hydrodynamic bearing

111. Intensity of radiation at a surface in perpendicular direction is equal to:
(a) product of emissivity of surface and $1/\pi$.
(b) product of emissivity of surface and $\pi$.
(c) product of emissive power of surface and $1/\pi$.
(d) product of emissive power of surface and $\pi$.

112. In a mass transfer process of diffusion of hot smoke in cold air in a power plant, the temperature profile and the concentration profile will become identical when:
(a) Prandtl No. = 1 (b) Nusselt No. = 1
(c) Lewis No. = 1 (d) Schemidt No. = 1

113. Which one of the following numbers represents the ratio of kinematic viscosity to the thermal diffusivity?
(a) Grashoff number
(b) Prandtl number
(c) Mach number
(d) Nusselt number.

114. After expansion from a gas turbine, the hot exhaust gases are used to heat the compressed air from a compressor with the help of a cross flow compact heat exchanger of 0.8 effectiveness. What is the number of transfer units of the heat exchanger?
(a) 2 (b) 4
(c) 8 (d) 16

115. A thin flat plate 2 m × 2 m is hanging freely in air. The temperature of the surrounding is 25°C. Solar radiation is falling on one side of the plate at the rate of 500 W/m$^2$. What should be the convective heat transfer coefficient in W/m$^2$ °C, if the temperature of the plate is to remain constant at 30°C?
(a) 25 (b) 50
(c) 100 (d) 200

116. In order to achieve maximum heat dissipation, the fin should be designed in such a way that:
(a) it should have maximum lateral surface at the root side of the fin
(b) it should have maximum lateral surface towards the tip side of the fin
(c) it should have maximum lateral surface near the centre of the fin
(d) it should have minimum lateral surface near the centre of the fin.

117. A composite hollow sphere with steady internal heating is made of 2 layers of materials of equal thickness with thermal conductivities in the ratio of 1:2 for inner to outer layers. Ratio of inside to outside diameter is 0.8. What is ratio of temperature drop across the inner and outer layers?
(a) 0.4 (b) 1.6
(c) 2 In 0.8 (d) 2.5

118. Upto the critical radius of insulation:
(a) added insulation increases heat loss.
(b) added insulation decreases heat loss.
(c) convection heat loss is less than conduction heat loss.
(d) heat flux decreases.

119. Match List-I (Governing Equations of Heat Transfer) with List-II (Specific Case of Heat Transfer) and select the correct answer using the code given below the lists:

| **List-I (Governing Equations of Heat Transfer)** | **List-II (Specific Cases of Heat Transfer)** |
|---|---|
| A. $\frac{d^2T}{dr^2}+\frac{2dT}{rdr}=0$ | 1. Pin fin 1-D case |
| B. $\frac{\partial^2 T}{\partial x^2}=\frac{1}{\alpha}\frac{\partial T}{\partial t}$ | 2. 1-D conduction in cylinder |
| C. $\frac{d^2T}{dr^2}+\frac{1}{r}\frac{dT}{dr}=0$ | 3. 1-D conduction in sphere |
| D. $\frac{d^2\theta}{dx^2}-m^2\theta=0$ | 4. Plane slab |

**Codes:**

| | A | B | C | D |
|---|---|---|---|---|
| (a) | 2 | 4 | 3 | 1 |
| (b) | 3 | 1 | 2 | 4 |
| (c) | 2 | 1 | 3 | 4 |
| (d) | 3 | 4 | 2 | 1 |

120. 6.0 kJ of conduction heat transfer has to take place in 10 minutes from one end to other end of a metallic cylinder of 10 cm cross-sectional area, length 1 metre and thermal conductivity as 100 W/m.K. What is the temperature difference between the two ends of the cylindrical bar?
(a) 80°C (b) 100°C
(c) 120°C (d) 160°C

## ANSWERS WITH EXPLANATIONS

1. (c) $V = V_0\left(1-\frac{I}{I_s}\right) = 80\left(1-\frac{I}{300}\right)$

For V = 40 V

$$40 = 80\left(1-\frac{I}{300}\right)$$

$$I = 150\text{ A}$$

2. (d) 3. (a) 4. (c) 5. (d) 6. (a)
7. (a) 8. (b)

9. (d) $\frac{T}{J}=\frac{G\theta}{l}$

$$\theta=\frac{Tl}{GJ}\propto\frac{1}{d^4}$$

10. (a) 11. (d) 12. (c) 13. (b) 14. (c)
15. (c) 16. (d) 17. (d) 18. (d) 19. (b)
20. (a) 21. (b) 22. (b) 23. (c) 24. (b)
25. (b) 26. (c) 27. (c) 28. (b) 29. (c)
30. (b)

31. (c) $l = 280$ cm, $b = 140$ cm, $\phi = 30°$

$$\cot\phi - \cot\theta = \frac{b}{l}$$

$$\cot 30° - \cot\theta = \frac{140}{280} = 0.5$$

$$\sqrt{3} - \cot\theta = 0.5$$

$$\theta = \cot^{-1}(1.232)$$

32. (c) 33. (a) 34. (d) 35. (d) 36. (d)

37. (d) $T_e = \sqrt{(K_M M)^2 + (K_T T)^2}$

$$= \sqrt{(1.5 \times 5000)^2 + (2 \times 1000)^2}$$

$= 2135$ N.m

38. (c) Helix angle, $\alpha = 90° -$ lead angle, $\gamma$
$90° - 22.5° = 67.5°$

39. (c) 40. (d) 41. (a) 42. (d) 43. (b)

44. (c)

45. (c) $P_s = 0.707\, h/\tau = 0.707 \times 15 \times 10 \times 100$
$= 10605$ N or 10.605 kN

46. (a) 47. (d) 48. (a) 49. (a) 50. (b)

51. (c) 52. (d) 53. (a) 54. (d) 55. (c)

56. (a) 57. (b)

58. (d) Shear stress in weld $= \dfrac{P}{\sqrt{BL}}$

59. (d) Total slip, $s = s_1 + s_2 = 1 + 3 = 4\%$

$$\frac{N_2}{N_1} = 1 = s = 1 - 0.04 = 0.96$$

60. (a) 61. (a) 62. (c) 63. (d) 64. (c)

65. (b) 66. (c) 67. (a) 68. (c) 69. (a)

70. (d) 71. (d) 72. (c) 73. (b) 74. (b)

75. (d) 76. (b) 77. (d)

78. (c) $n = n_1 + n_2 - 1 = 6 + 5 - 1 = 10$

79. (a) 80. (d) 81. (d) 82. (c) 83. (b)

84. (c) $C_2H_2 + O_2 = 2CO + H_2$
1 : 1

85. (d) 86. (d) 87. (b) 88. (b) 89. (d)

90. (d) 91. (d) 92. (a) 93. (c) 94. (d)

95. (b) 96. (c) 97. (c) 98. (d) 99. (c)

100. (b) $\pi d t \tau = \dfrac{\pi}{4} d^2 \sigma_c$

$$d = \frac{4t\tau}{\sigma_c} = \frac{4 \times 15 \times 3}{6} = 30 \text{ mm}$$

101. (c) 102. (a) 103. (c) 104. (d) 105. (a)

106. (b) 107. (b) 108. (c) 109. (a) 110. (c)

111. (c) Intensity of radiation, $I = E/\pi$

112. (d) The temperature profile and concentration profile will become identical when Schemidt number = 1

113. (b) Pradtl number, $Pr = \dfrac{\text{Kinetic viscosity}}{\text{Thermal diffusivity}}$

114. (b) Effectiveness, $\varepsilon = \dfrac{NTU}{1 + NTU}$

$$0.8 = \frac{NTU}{1 + NTU}$$

NTU = 4

115. (a) $Q = h_c\, A.dt$
$500 = h_c \times 2 \times 2\,(30 - 25)$

$$h_c = \frac{500}{20} = 25 \text{W/m}^2\text{C}$$

116. (a) The tin should have maximum lateral surface at the root side to achieve maximum heat dissipation.

117. (d) $t_1 - t_2 = Q\left[\dfrac{r_2 - r_1}{4\pi k_1 r_1 r_2}\right]$

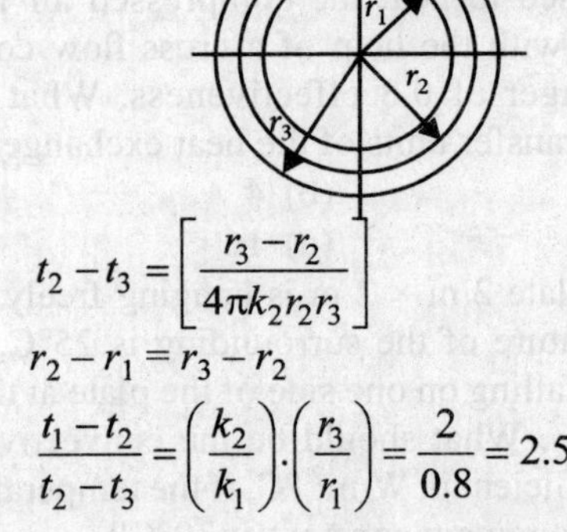


$$t_2 - t_3 = \left[\frac{r_3 - r_2}{4\pi k_2 r_2 r_3}\right]$$

$$r_2 - r_1 = r_3 - r_2$$

$$\frac{t_1 - t_2}{t_2 - t_3} = \left(\frac{k_2}{k_1}\right)\cdot\left(\frac{r_3}{r_1}\right) = \frac{2}{0.8} = 2.5$$

118. (c) $Q = \dfrac{2\pi L(t_1 - t_0)}{\left[\dfrac{\ln\left(\dfrac{r_2}{r_1}\right)}{k} + \dfrac{1}{h_0 r_2}\right]}$

Conductive thermal resistance increases with increasing $r_2$ and convective thermal resistance decreases with increasing $r_2$.

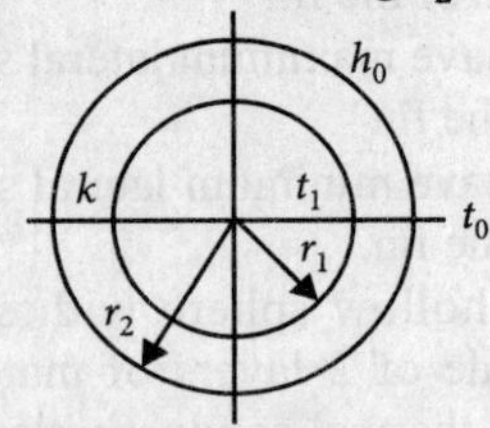


Thus $Q_{convective} < Q_{conductive}$

119. (d)

120. (b) $Q = kA\dfrac{(t_1 - t_2)}{L}$

$$t_1 - t_2 = \frac{QL}{kA} = \frac{6 \times 10^3}{100 \times 60 \times 100 \times 10 \times 10^{-4}}$$

$= 100°$ C

❑❑❑

# 3. Instrument Mechanical

- Instrumentation engineering is the engineering specialization focused on the principle and operation of measuring instruments that are used in design and configuration of automated systems in electrical, pneumatic domains etc.
- They typically work for industries with automated processes, such as chemical or manufacturing plants, with the goal of improving system productivity, reliability, safety, optimization, and stability.
- To control the parameters in a process or in a particular system, devices such as microprocessors, microcontrollers or PLCs are used, but their ultimate aim is to control the parameters of a system.
- Instrumentation engineering is loosely defined because the required tasks are very domain dependent. An expert in the biomedical instrumentation of laboratory rats has very different concerns than the expert in rocket instrumentation. Common concerns of both are the selection of appropriate sensors based on size, weight, cost, reliability, accuracy, longevity, environmental robustness and frequency response. Some sensors are literally fired in artillery shells. Others sense thermo-nuclear explosions until destroyed. Invariably sensor data must be recorded, transmitted or displayed. Recording rates and capacities vary enormously. Transmission can be trivial or can be clandestine, encrypted and low-power in the presence of jamming. Displays can be trivially simple or can require consultation with human factors experts. Control system design varies from trivial to a separate specialty.
- Instrumentation engineers are commonly responsible for integrating the sensors with the recorders, transmitters, displays or control systems. They may design or specify installation, wiring and signal conditioning. They may be responsible for calibration, testing and maintenance of the system.
- In a research environment it is common for subject matter experts to have substantial instrumentation system expertise. An astronomer knows the structure of the universe and a great deal about telescopes - optics, pointing and cameras (or other sensing elements). That often includes the hard-won knowledge of the operational procedures that provide the best results. For example, an astronomer is often knowledgeable of techniques to minimize temperature gradients that cause air turbulence within the telescope.
- Instrumentation is the use of measuring instruments to monitor and control a process.
- It is the art and science of measurement and control of process variables within a production, laboratory, or manufacturing area.
- An instrument is a device that measures a physical quantity such as flow, temperature, level, distance, angle, or pressure. Instruments may be as simple as direct reading thermometers or may be complex multi-variable process analyzers.
- Instruments are often part of a control system in refineries, factories, and vehicles. The control of processes is one of the main branches of applied instrumentation. Instrumentation can also refer to handheld devices that measure some desired variable.
- Diverse handheld instrumentation is common in laboratories, but can be found in the household as well. For example, a smoke detector is a common instrument found in most western homes.
- Instruments attached to a control system may provide signals used to operate solenoids, valves, regulators, circuit breakers, or relays. These devices control a desired output variable, and provide either remote or automated control capabilities.
- A Transmitter is a device that produces an output signal, often in the form of a 4–20 mA electrical current signal, although many other options using voltage, frequency, pressure, or ethernet are possible.
- Control instrumentation plays a significant role in both gathering information from the field and changing the field parameters, and as such are a key part of control loops.
- Elements of industrial instrumentation have long histories. Scales for comparing weights and simple pointers to indicate position are ancient technologies. Some of the earliest measurements were of time.
- In the early years of process control, process indicators and control elements such as valves were monitored by an operator that walked around the unit adjusting the valves to obtain the desired temperatures, pressures, and flows.
- As technology evolved pneumatic controllers were invented and mounted in the field that monitored the process and controlled the valves. This reduced the amount of time process operators were needed to monitor the process.
- The pneumatic and electronic signaling standards allowed centralized monitoring and control of a distributed process. The concept was limited by communication line lengths (perhaps 100 meters for

pneumatics). Each pipe or wire pair carried one signal.

- The next evolution of instrumentation came with the production of Distributed Control Systems (DCS) which allowed monitoring and control from multiple locations which could be widely separated.
- A process operator could sit in front of a screen (no longer a control board) and monitor thousands of points throughout a large complex. A closely related development was termed 'Supervisory Control and Data Acquisition' (SCADA).
- These technologies were supported by personal computers, networks and graphical user interfaces.
- A very simple example of an instrumentation system is a mechanical thermostat, used to control a household furnace and thus to control room temperature.
- A typical unit senses temperature with a bi-metallic strip. It displays temperature by a needle on the free end of the strip. It activates the furnace by a mercury switch.
- Any three phase load will be balanced when the loads (impedances) connected in three phases are same in magnitude as well as in phase.
- Any three phase load will be unbalanced if impedances in one or more phases differ from the impedance (s) of the remaining phase (s).
- Normally, unbalanced load is not employed on 3-phase, 3-wire ungrounded star-connected system because unbalanced loading may cause different voltage drops in lines. Consequently the three phase voltages are different (or unbalanced) in magnitude as well as in phase and it is quite possible that one phase voltage may exceed the line voltage. Such a condition is undesirable, since some loads may operate inefficiently due to lowering of the voltage and the other equipment may get damaged due to overvoltage.
- Phase sequence is the order or sequence in which the currents or voltages in different phases attain their maximum values one after the other.
  The given phase sequence can be reversed by interchanging any two terminals of the supply.
- Non-interlinked three phase system will require 6 wires while interconnected 3-phase system will require 3 or 4 wires. So non-interlinked system will be very complicated and expensive.
- In star-connected system similar (either start or finish) terminals of the three phases are connected together,to provide star or neutral point while in delta-connected system start terminal of one phase is connected to the finish terminal of the second phase and start terminal of second phase is connected to finish terminal of the third phase and so on to provide a closed circuit in 3-phase system.
- Neutral point of a star-connected system can be connected to earth, so relays and protective devices can be provided in star-connected system for protection of the system against ground faults and it is usually done in practice. These are the reasons that 3-phase alternators are usually star-connected.
- Delta-connected stem cannot provide 3-phase 4-wire system (*i.e.,* neutral wire cannot be carried) which is essential for supplying lighting as well as power loads.
- The most common motor control is the motor starter.
- The low voltage release tripped the motor. The motor can be restarted by pusing the 'ON' button when the potential difference returns to normal.
- Shading coil reduces vibration, chattering, noise, wear and heat in the armature of a starter magnetic core.
- When a contactor is in the open position, open positions, the armature is at its greatest distance from the core and the impedance of the coil is low.
- The 'ON' button of a starter should have at least on NO/ contact. (Normally Open contact)
- The 'OFF' button of a starter should have at least one N/C contact. (Normally Closed contact)
- Thermal overload relay is provided in a starter to protet the motor against excess current.
- Continuous chattering sound from the armature of an AC no-volt coil indicates open circuit in the shaded ring.
- In a 3-phase induction motor started by a D.O.L. starter, protection against the short circuit is given by the back-up fuses.
- Full load line current of a 3 HP, 3-phase, 415 volts. 50 Hz squirrel cage induction motor will be approximately 4.5 amps (1½ times the H.p.)
- Kitchen appliances use sensors for control.
- A refrigerator maintains a constant temperature by measuring the internal temperature.
- A microwave oven sometimes cooks via a heat-sense-heat-sense cycle until sensing done.
- An automatic ice machine makes ice until a limit switch is thrown.
- Pop-up bread toasters can operate by time or by heat measurements.
- Some ovens use a temperature probe to cook until a target internal food temperature is reached.
- A common toilet refills the water tank until a float closes the valve. The float is acting as a water level sensor.

# MULTIPLE CHOICE QUESTIONS

1. Cavitation damage in the turbine runner occurs near the:
   (a) inlet on the concave side of the blades
   (b) outlet on the concave side of the blades
   (c) outlet on the convex side of the blades
   (d) inlet on the convex side of the blades
2. In hydraulic power-generation systems, surge tanks are provided to prevent immediate damage to:
   (a) draft tube (b) turbine
   (c) tail race (d) penstocks.
3. The function of the draft tube in a reaction turbine is:
   (a) to enable the shaft of the turbine to be vertical
   (b) to transform a large part of pressure energy at turbine outlet into kinetic energy
   (c) to avoid whirl losses at the exit of the turbine
   (d) to transform a large part of kinetic energy at the turbine outlet into pressure energy.
4. Consider the following characteristics:
   1. The fluid enters the pump axially and is discharged radially.
   2. Maximum efficiency may be of the order of 90%.
   3. Development of a low head.
   4. A limited section capacity.

   Which of the above characteristics are possessed by axial flow pumps?
   (a) 1 and 2 (b) 2 and 3
   (c) 2 and 4 (d) 3 and 4
5. A centrifugal pump delivers water at the rate of 50 litres/s against a total head of 40 metres. Then the power required to drive the pump is:
   (a) 2 kW (b) 15.2 kW
   (c) 19.6 kW (d) 25.8 kW
6. Match List-I with List-II and select the correct answer using the codes given below the lists:

| List-I | List-II |
|---|---|
| A. Head race | 1. Channel, tunnel or pipes through which water is carried from reservoir to the turbine |
| B. Tail race | 2. Reservoir water level |
| C. Penstock | 3. Diverging tube discharging water from the turbine to the atmosphere |
| D. Draft tube | 4. The level at which water is discharged a atmospheric pressure |

**Codes:**

| | A | B | C | D |
|---|---|---|---|---|
| (a) | 1 | 3 | 2 | 4 |
| (b) | 2 | 4 | 1 | 3 |
| (c) | 1 | 4 | 2 | 3 |
| (d) | 2 | 3 | 1 | 4 |

7. Consider the following statements in respect of centrifugal pumps:
   1. Head developed is proportional to the square of the speed of rotation.
   2. Backward curved bladed impellers arc generally used in centrifugal pumps.
   3. These pumps generally do not require priming.
   4. Multistage pumps would give higher discharge proportional to the number of stages. Which of these statements are correct?

   (a) 1 and 2 (b) 2 and 3
   (c) 3 and 4 (d) 1 and 4
8. The relationship between overall efficiency ($\eta_0$), mechanical efficiency $\eta_{mech}$, and hydraulic efficiency ($\eta_{hyd}$) of a turbine is:
   (a) $\eta_0 = h_{mech} \times \eta_{hyd}$ (b) $\eta_0 = h_{mech}/\eta_{hyd}$
   (c) $\eta_0 = \eta_{hyd}/\eta_{mech}$ (d) $\eta_0 = \eta_{mech} - \eta_{hyd}$
9. Which one of the following correctly expresses the specific speed of a turbine and a pump, respectively?
   (a) $\frac{N\sqrt{Q}}{H^{3/4}}, \frac{N\sqrt{P}}{H^{5/4}}$ (b) $\frac{N\sqrt{P}}{H^{3/4}}, \frac{N\sqrt{Q}}{H^{5/4}}$
   (c) $\frac{N\sqrt{P}}{H^{5/4}}, \frac{N\sqrt{Q}}{H^{3/4}}$ (d) $\frac{N\sqrt{P}}{H^{7/4}}, \frac{N\sqrt{Q}}{H^{3/4}}$
10. Consider the following statements:
    In the thermoelectric refrigeration, the coefficient of performance is a function of:
    1. electrical conductivity of materials.
    2. peltier coefficient
    3. seebeck coefficient
    4. temperature at cold and hot functions
    5. thermal conductivity of materials.

    Of these statements:
    (a) 1, 3, 4 and 5 are correct
    (b) 1, 2, 3 and 5 correct
    (c) 1, 2, 4 and 5 correct
    (d) 2, 3, 4 and 5 correct
11. Which one of the following is not correct regarding both Kaplan and propeller turbines?
    (a) The runner is axial
    (b) The blades are wing type
    (c) There are four to eight blades
    (d) The blades can he adjusted.
12. Based on the direction of flow, which one of the following turbines is different from the other three?
    (a) Pelton turbine (b) Kaplan turbine
    (c) Dc Laval turbine (d) Parson's turbine
13. Which one of the following is an example of a pure (100%) reaction machine?
    (a) Pelton wheel (b) Francis turbine
    (c) Modern gas turbine (d) Lawn sprinkler

14. Consider the following statements:
1. A reverse jet protects Pelton turbine from over-speeding.
2. Runner blades of Francis turbine are adjustable.
3. Draft tube is used invariably in all reaction turbine installations.
4. Surge tank is a protective device on penstock.

Of these statements:
(a) 1 and 2 are correct (b) 2 and 3 are correct
(c) 3 and 4 are correct (d) 1 and 4 are correct.

15. Unit power $P_1$ is given by the expression:
(a) $p_1 = \frac{p}{\sqrt{H}}$ (b) $p_1 = \frac{p}{H^{3/2}}$
(c) $p_1 = \frac{p}{H^{3/4}}$ (d) $p_1 = \frac{p}{H^{3/5}}$

16. For discharge 'Q', the specific speed of a pump is '$N_s$'. For half discharge with the same head, the specific speed will be:
(a) $N_s$ (b) $\sqrt{2}N_s$
(c) $\frac{N_s}{\sqrt{2}}N_s$ (d) $2N_s$.

17. Which one of the following statements regarding ammonia absorption system is correct?
(a) a function of the temperature and pressure of the solution
(b) a function of the pressure of the solution irrespective of the temperature
(c) a function of the temperature of the solution alone
(d) independent of the temperature and pressure of the solution

18. For an impulse turbine with exit angle '$\phi$', the maximum hydraulic efficiency is:
(a) $\left(1-\frac{\cos\phi}{2}\right)$ (b) $\left(\frac{1}{2}+\cos\phi\right)$
(c) $\left(\frac{1+\cos\phi}{2}\right)$ (d) $\left(\frac{1-\cos\phi}{2}\right)$

19. The location of a surge tank in a high head hydraulic power plant would be:
(a) nearer to the dam
(b) at the powerhouse
(c) nearest to the powerhouse
(d) immaterial.

20. Match List-I with List-II and select the correct answer using the codes given below the lists:

| List-I (Water Turbines) | List-II (Application) |
|---|---|
| A. Pelton | 1. High head and low discharge |
| B. Francis | 2. High head and high discharge |
| C. Kaplan | 3. Medium head and medium discharge |
| | 4. Low head and high discharge |

**Codes:**

| | A | B | C |
|---|---|---|---|
| (a) | 1 | 3 | 2 |
| (b) | 1 | 3 | 4 |
| (c) | 2 | 4 | 3 |
| (d) | 3 | 2 | 4 |

21. Which one of the following helps in avoiding cavitation in centrifugal pumps?
(a) Low suction pressure (b) High delivery pressure
(c) Low delivery pressure (d) High suction pressure

22. Consider the following statements with regardto the specific speeds of different types of
1. High specific speed implies that it is a Pelton wheel
2. Medium specific speed implies that it is an axial flow turbine
3. Low specific speed implies that it is a Francis turbine
4. Which of these statements given above is/are correct?

(a) 1 only (b) 2 only
(c) 3 only (d) None

23. Which one of the following is the purpose of a surge tank in a Pelton turbine station?
(a) It acts as a temporary storage during load changes
(b) It prevents hydraulic jump
(c) It prevents surges at the transformer
(d) It prevents water hammer due to sudden reduction in load.

24. Match List-I (Type of Turbine) with List-II (Specific Speed) and select the correct answer using the code given below the lists:

| List-I (Type of Turbine) | List-II (Specific Speed) |
|---|---|
| A. Pelton | 1. 0.1 |
| B. Francis | 2. 3.0 |
| C. Propeller | 3. 4.0 |
| D. Kaplan | 5. 1.0 |

**Codes:**

| | A | B | C | D |
|---|---|---|---|---|
| (a) | 1 | 4 | 2 | 3 |
| (b) | 3 | 2 | 4 | 1 |
| (c) | 1 | 2 | 4 | 3 |
| (d) | 3 | 4 | 2 | 1 |

25. Consider the following statements: In hydraulic power plants
1. Pelton turbines are used for high heads.
2. Kaplan turbines are used for medium heads.
3. Francis turbines are used for low heads. Which of the above statements is/are correct?

(a) 1 only (b) 2 only
(c) 3 only (d) 1, 2 and 3

26. The speed ratio for Pelton wheel varies from:
(a) 0.45 – 0.50
(b) 0.6 – 0.7
(c) 0.30 – 0.40
(d) 0.8 – 0.9

27. Match List-I with List-II and select the correct answer using the codes given below the lists:

| List-I | List-II |
|---|---|
| A. Specific speed of pump | 1. $\left(\frac{N\sqrt{Q}}{H^{3/4}}\right)$ |
| B. Low specific speed of turbine. | 2. Screw pump |
| C. Pumping viscous oil | 3. Reaction turbine |
| D. Draft tube | 4. Turbine Pump |
| | 5. Very high specific speed |
| | 6. $\left(\frac{N\sqrt{P}}{H^{5/4}}\right)$ |
| | 7. Impulse turbine |

**Codes:**

| | A | B | C | D |
|---|---|---|---|---|
| (a) | 1 | 3 | 2 | 5 |
| (b) | 6 | 7 | 4 | 3 |
| (c) | 1 | 7 | 2 | 3 |
| (d) | 6 | 3 | 4 | 5 |

28. Match List-I with List-II and select the correct answer using the code given below the lists:

| List-I | List-II |
|---|---|
| A. Draft tube | 1. Impulse turbine |
| B. Surging | 2. Reciprocating pump |
| C. Air Vessel | 3. Reaction turbine |
| D. Nozzle | 4. Centrifugal pump |

**Codes:**

| | A | B | C | D |
|---|---|---|---|---|
| (a) | 1 | 2 | 4 | 3 |
| (b) | 3 | 4 | 2 | 1 |
| (c) | 1 | 4 | 2 | 3 |
| (d) | 3 | 2 | 4 | 1 |

29. A centrifugal pump was manufactured to couple directly to a 15 HP. electric motor running at 1950 rpm delivering 50 liters per minute against a total head of 20 m. It is desired to replace the pump. The head developed by pump is likely to be:

(a) 41.4 m
(b) 29.6 m
(c) 20 m
(d) 9.5 m

30. Which of the following statements are false regarding the relation Specific speed. $N_s\left(\frac{N\sqrt{Q}}{H^{5/4}}\right)$

(a) The relation is valid for both impulse as well as reaction turbines
(b) The value of specific speed depends on the system of units
(c) The value of specific speed for pelton wheel will be lower than that for Kaplan turbine for any system of units
(d) The dimensions of specific speed are: $(FLT^{-1})$.

31. Air vessel is used in a reciprocating pump to obtain:

(a) reduction of suction head
(b) rise in delivery head
(c) continuous supply of water at uniform rate
(d) increase in supply of water

32. Hydraulic transmission through fluid coupling is suitable for:

(a) Unsteady operation and increasing torque
(b) Unsteady operation and increasing speed
(c) Unsteady operation and low starting torque
(d) Increasing torque and low starting load

33. Match the following:

| List-I | List-II |
|---|---|
| A. Wicket gates | 1. Gradually converts the velocity head to pressure head |
| B. Volute tube | 2. Pressure head recovery |
| C. Draft tube | 3. High value of N and N |
| D. Axial flow | 4. Adjustable by governor pumps according to head |

**Codes:**

| | A | B | C | D |
|---|---|---|---|---|
| (a) | 4 | 1 | 2 | 3 |
| (b) | 1 | 3 | 2 | 4 |
| (c) | 2 | 3 | 4 | 1 |
| (d) | 2 | 3 | 1 | 4 |

34. Chances of occurrence of cavitation are high if the:

(a) local pressure becomes very high
(b) local temperature becomes low
(c) Thoma cavitation parameter exceeds a certain limit
(d) local pressure falls below the vapour pressure.

35. The specific speed of a hydraulic pump is the Speed of geometrically similar pump working against a unit head and:

(a) delivering unit quantity of water
(b) consuming unit power
(c) having unit velocity of flow
(d) having unit radial velocity

36. In the statement, "in a reaction turbine installation, the head of water is decreased and the rpm is also decreased at a certain condition of working. The effect of each of these changes will be to X power delivered due to decrease in head and to γ power delivered due to decrease in rpm". $\frac{N\sqrt{Q}}{H^{3/4}}$ X and Y stand respectively for:

(a) decrease and increase
(b) increase and increase
(c) decrease and decrease
(d) increase and decrease.

37. Specific speed of a pump and specific speed of a turbine are: (symbols have the usual meaning)

(a) $\frac{N\sqrt{Q}}{H^{3/4}}$ and $\frac{N\sqrt{P}}{H^{5/4}}$ respectively

(b) $\frac{N\sqrt{Q}}{H^{3/4}}$ and $\frac{N\sqrt{P}}{H^{3/4}}$ respectively

(c) $\frac{N\sqrt{Q}}{H^{5/4}}$ and $\frac{N\sqrt{P}}{H^{5/4}}$ respectively

(d) $\frac{N\sqrt{Q}}{H^{5/4}}$ and $\frac{N\sqrt{P}}{H^{3/4}}$ respectively

38. The following lists refer to fluid machinery Match List-I with List-II and select the correct answer using the codes given below the Lists:

| **List-I** | **List-II** |
|---|---|
| A. Draft tube | 1. Impulse turbine |
| B. Surging | 2. Reciprocating pump |
| C. Air Vessel | 3. Reaction turbine |
| D. Nozzle | 4. Centrifugal pump |

**Codes:**

| | A | B | C | D |
|---|---|---|---|---|
| (a) | 4 | 3 | 2 | 1 |
| (b) | 3 | 4 | 2 | 1 |
| (c) | 3 | 4 | 1 | 2 |
| (d) | 4 | 3 | 1 | 2 |

39. Match List-I with List-II and select the correct answer using the codes given below the Lists:

| **List-I (Tapes of turbines)** | **List-II (Characteristics of turbines)** |
|---|---|
| A. Propeller | 1. Inward flow reaction |
| B. Francis | 2. Tangential flow impulse |
| C. Kaplan | 3. Axial flow reaction with fixed vanes |
| D. Pelton | 4. Axial flow reaction with adjustable vanes |

**Codes:**

| | A | B | C | D |
|---|---|---|---|---|
| (a) | 2 | 4 | 1 | 3 |
| (b) | 3 | 4 | 1 | 2 |
| (c) | 2 | 1 | 4 | 3 |
| (d) | 3 | 1 | 4 | 2 |

40. Which of the following are the functions of a volute casing in a centrifugal pump?
1. To collect water from the periphery of the impeller and to transmits it to the delivery pipe at a constant velocity.
2. To increase the discharge of the pump.
3. To increase the efficiency of the pump.
4. To reduce the loss of head in discharge.

Select the correct answer from the codes given below:
(a) 1, 2 and 3
(b) 2, 3 and 4
(c) 1, 3 and 4
(d) 1 and 2

41. The movable wicket gates of a reaction turbine are used to:
(a) control the flow of water passing through the turbine
(b) control tile pressure under which the turbine is working.
(c) strengthen the casing of the turbine.
(d) reduce the size of the turbine.

42. Which of following are the beneficial effects of air vessel fitted to delivery side of a reciprocating pump?
1. Constant rate of discharge can be ensured
2. Power consumption can be reduced
3. Discharge can he increased
4. Constant velocity of the piston can he ensured.

Select the correct answer using the codes given below:
(a) 1 and 4 (b) 1 and 2
(c) 2 and 4 (d) 1 and 3

43. For attaining a non-overloading characteristic in centrifugal pumps:
(a) backward bent vanes are preferred over forward bent vanes.
(b) forward bent vanes are preferred over backward bent vanes.
(c) forward bent vanes are preferred over vanes radial at outlet.
(d) vanes radial at outlet are preferred over backward vanes.

44. Consider the following statements:
Cavitation in hydraulic machines occurs at the
1. exit of a pump
2. entry of the pump
3. exit of a turbine

Of these statements:
(a) 1 and 2 are correct (b) 1 and 3 are correct
(c) 1, 2 and 3 are correct (d) 2 and 3 are correct

45. Euler equation for water turbine is derived on the basis of:
(a) conservation of mass
(b) rate of change of linear momentum
(c) rate of change of angular momentum
(d) rate of change of velocity.

46. The Specific speed of a turbine is defined as the speed of a member of the same homologous series of such a size that it:
(a) delivers unit discharge at unit head.
(b) delivers unit discharge at unit power.
(c) delivers unit power at unit discharge.
(d) produces unit power under the unit head.

47. Match List-I with List-II and select the correct answer.

| List-I | List-II |
|---|---|
| A. Pelton wheel (single jet) | 1. Medium discharge, low head. |
| B. Francis Turbine | 2. High discharge, low head |
| C. Kaplan Turbine | 3. Medium discharge, medium head. |
| | 4. Low discharge, high head |

**Codes:**

| | A | B | C |
|---|---|---|---|
| (a) | 1 | 2 | 3 |
| (b) | 1 | 3 | 4 |
| (c) | 4 | 1 | 3 |
| (d) | 4 | 3 | 2 |

48. Consider the following statement:
If pump NFSH requirements are not satisfied, then
1. It will not develop sufficient head to raise water.
2. Its efficiency will be low.
3. It will deliver very low discharge.
4. It will be cavitated.

Of these statements:
(a) 1, 2 and 3 are correct
(b) 1 and 4 are correct
(c) 2, 3 and are 4 correct
(d) 1, 2, 3 and 4 are correct.

49. In reaction turbines, the draft tube is used:
(a) for the safety of the turbine.
(b) to convert the kinetic energy of flow by a gradual expansion of the flow cross-section.
(c) to destroy the undesirable eddies.
(d) for none of the above purposes.

50. Given that N = speed, P = Power, H = heat
The specific speed of a hydraulic turbine is given by:
(a) $\frac{N\sqrt{P}}{H^{4/5}}$ (b) $\frac{N\sqrt{P}}{H^{5/4}}$
(c) $\frac{P\sqrt{N}}{H^{4/5}}$ (d) $\frac{P\sqrt{N}}{H^{5/4}}$

51. As water flows through the runner of a reaction turbine, pressure acting on it would vary from:
(a) more than atmospheric pressure to vacuum
(b) less than atmospheric pressure to zero gauge pressure
(c) atmospheric pressure to more than atmospheric pressure
(d) atatmospheric pressure to vacuum.

52. Consider the following statements regarding torque converter:
1. It has a stationary set of blades in addition to the primary and secondary rotors.
2. It can be used for multiplication of torques.
3. The maximum efficiency of a inverter is less than that of a fluid coupling
4. In a converter designed to give a large increase of torque, the efficiency........speed ratio approaches unity.

Of these statements:
(a) 1, 2, 3 and 4 are correct
(b) 1, 2 and 3 are correct
(c) 1, 2 and 4 are correct
(d) 3 and 4 are correct

53. In contrast to fluid couplings, torque converters are operated:
(a) while completely filled with liquid
(b) while partially filled with liquid
(c) without liquid
(d) while completely filled with air.

54. Which one of the following statements regarding an impulse turbine is correct?
(a) There is no pressure variation in flow over the buckets and the fluid fills the passageway between the buckets
(b) There is no pressure variation in flow over the buckets and the fluid does not fill the passageway between the buckets
(c) There is pressure drop in flow over the buckets and the fluid fills the passageway between the buckets
(d) There is pressure drop in flow over the buckets and the fluid does not fill the passageway between the buckets.

55. A centrifugal pump is started with its delivery valve kept:
(a) fully open (b) fully closed
(c) partially open (d) 50% open.

56. Which one of the following forms of draft tube will NOT improve the hydraulic efficiency of the turbine?
(a) Straight cylindrical (b) Conical type
(c) Bell-mouthed (d) Bent tube.

57. Which one of the following turbines is used in underwater power stations?
(a) Pelton turbine
(b) Deriaz turbine
(c) Tubular turbine
(d) Turgo-impulse turbine.

58. A pelton wheel is ideally suited for:
(a) High head and low discharge
(b) High head and high discharge
(c) Low head and low discharge
(d) Medium head and medium discharge

59. Consider the following turbines:
1. Kaplan 2. Pelton wheel
3. Francis
The correct sequence in increasing order of the specific speeds of these turbines is:
(a) 2, 3, 1 (b) 2, 1, 3
(c) 3, 1, 2 (d) 1, 2, 3

60. Consider the following statements regarding the specific speed of a centrifugal pump:
1. Specific speed is defined as the speed of a geometrically similar pump developing unit power under unit head.
2. At the same specific speed, the efficiency is greater with larger capacity
3. The specific speed increases with increase in outer blade angle
4. The specific speed varies directly as the square root of the pump discharge.

Of these statements:
(a) 1 and 2 are correct
(b) 2 and 4 are correct
(c) 3 and 4 are correct
(d) 2 and 3 are correct

61. Which of the following purposes are served by the volute casing of a centrifugal pump?
1. Increase in the efficiency of the pump.
2. Conversion of part of the pressure head to velocity head.
3. Giving uniform flow of the fluid coming out of the impeller.

Select the correct answer using the codes given below:
(a) 1 and 2 (b) 1 and 3
(c) 2 and3 (d) 1, 2 and 3

62. Consider the following statements:
1. A draft tube may be fitted to the tail end of a Pelton head.
2. Kaplan turbine is an axial flow reaction turbine with adjustable vanes on the
3. Modern Francis turbine is a mixed flow reaction turbine.

Which of these statements are correct?
(a) 1, 2 and 3 (b) 1 and 2
(c) 2 and 3 (d) 1 and 3.

63. Consider the following data for the performance of a centrifugal pump: Speed: 1200 rpm, flow rate 30 $l$/s, head 5 kW
If the speed is increased to 1500 rpm, the power will be nearly equal to:
(a) 6.5 kW
(b) 8.7 kW
(c) 9.8 kW
(d) 10.9 kW

64. Consider the following pumps:
1. Centrifugal pump, single-stage
2. Centrifugal pump, multi-stage
3. Reciprocating pump
4. Jet pump

The pump (s) which can be used to lift water through a suction head of 12 m from a well would include:
(a) 2 alone
(b) 1, 3 and 4
(c) 4 alone
(d) 1 and 3

65. If $\omega_s$ and $\omega_p$ represent the angular velocities of driven and driving members of a fluid coupling respectively, then the slip is equal to:
(a) $1-\dfrac{\omega_s}{\omega_p}$ (b) $\dfrac{\omega_s}{\omega_p}$
(c) $\dfrac{\omega_p}{\omega_s}$ (d) $1-\dfrac{\omega_p}{\omega_s}$

66. Hydraulic ram is a pump which works on the principle of:
(a) Water hammer
(b) Centrifugal action
(c) Reciprocating action
(d) Hydraulic press

67. The correct sequence of the given hydraulic turbines in decreasing order of their specific speeds is:
(a) Pelton wheel, Francis turbine, Kaplan turbine
(b) Propeller turbine, Francis turbine, Pelton wheel
(c) Kaplan turbine, Pelton wheel, Francis turbine
(d) Francis turbine, Kaplan turbine, Pelton wheel.

68. Which one of the following pairs of formulae represents the specific speeds of turbine and pump respectively? *(Notations have their usual meanings),*
(a) $d\dfrac{NQ^{1/2}}{H^{3/4}}$ and $\dfrac{NP^{1/2}}{H^{5/4}}$ (b) $\dfrac{NQ^{1/2}}{H^{3/4}}$ and $\dfrac{NP^{1/2}}{H^{3/4}}$
(c) $\dfrac{NP^{1/2}}{H^{5/4}}$ and $\dfrac{NQ^{1/2}}{H^{5/4}}$ (d) $\dfrac{NP^{1/2}}{H^{3/4}}$ and $\dfrac{NQ^{1/2}}{H^{5/4}}$

69. Consider the following turbines/wheels:
1. Francis turbine
2. Pelton wheel with two or more jets
3. Pelton wheel with a single jet
4. Kaplan turbine.

The correct sequence of these turbines/wheels in increasing order of their specific speeds is:
(a) 2, 3, 1, 4 (b) 3, 2, 1 , 4
(c) 2, 3, 4, 1 (d) 3, 2, 4, 1

70. The gross head available to a hydraulic power plant is 100 m. The utilized head in the runner of the hydraulic turbine is 72 m. If the hydraulic efficiency of the turbine is 90%, the pipe friction head is estimated to be:
(a) 20 m (b) 18 m
(c) 16.2 m (d) 1.8 m

71. Air cooling is used for Freon compressors whereas water jacketing is adopted for cooling ammonia compressors. This is because
(a) latent heat of ammonia is higher than that of Freon
(b) thermal conductivity of water is higher than that of air
(c) specific heat of water is higher than that of air
(d) of the larger superheat from of ammonia compression cycle.

72. Consider the following statements regarding the volute casing of a centrifugal pump:
1. Loss of head due to change in velocity is eliminated.
2. Efficiency of the pump is increased.
3. Water from the periphery of the impeller is collected and transmitted to the delivery pipe at constant velocity.

Which of these statements are correct?
(a) 1, 2 and 3 (b) 1 and 2
(c) 2 and 3 (d) 1 and 3

73. The cavitation number of any fluid machineryis defined as $\sigma = \frac{p - p'}{pv^2/2}$ (p is absolute pressure, ρ is density and v is free stream velocity)
The symbol *p'* denotes:
(a) static pressure of fluid
(b) dynamic pressure of fluid
(c) vapour pressure of fluid
(d) shear stress of fluid.

74. Consider the following statements:
A water turbine governor
1. helps in starting and shutting down the turbo unit.
2. controls the speed of turbine set to match it with the hydroelectric system.
3. sets the amount of load which a turbine unit has to carry

Which of these statements are correct?
(a) 1, 2 and 3 (b) 1 and 2
(c) 2 and 3 (d) 1 and 3

75. Consider the following statements regarding a torque converter:
1. Its maximum efficiency is less than that of the fluid coupling
2. It has two runners and a set of stationary vanes interposed between them.
3. It has two runners.
4. The ratio of secondary to primary torque is zero for the zero value of angular velocity of secondary.

Which of these statements are correct?
(a) 1 and 2 (b) 3 and 4
(c) 1 and 4 (d) 2 and 4

76. Consider the specific speed ranges of the following types of turbines:
1. Francis 2. Kaplan
3. Pelton The sequence of their specific speed in increasing order is:
(a) 1, 2, 3 (b) 3, 1, 2
(c) 3, 2, 1 (d) 2, 3, 1.

77. In a PERT network, expected project duration in found to be 36 days from the start of the project. The variance is four days. The probability that the project will be completed in 36 days is?
(a) zero (b) 34%
(c) 50% (d) 84%

78. The variance ($V_1$) for critical path $a \rightarrow b = 4$ time units, $b \rightarrow c = 16$ units, $c \rightarrow d = 4$ time units, $d \rightarrow e = 1$ time unit.
The standard deviation of the critical path $a \rightarrow e$ is:
(a) 3 (b) 4
(c) 5 (d) 6

79. Estimated time T, and variance of the activities 'V on the critical path in a PERT new work are given in the following table:

| Activity | $T_e$ (days) | V (days)$^2$ |
|---|---|---|
| *a* | 17 | 4 |
| *b* | 15 | 4 |
| *c* | 8 | 1 |

The probability of completing the project in 43 days is:
(a) 15.6% (b) 50.0%
(c) 81.4% (d) 90.0%

80. The earliest occurrence time for event 'I' is 8 weeks and the latest occurrence time for events 'I' is 26 weeks. The earliest occurrence time for evens '2' is 32 weeks and the latest occurrence time for events '2' is 37 weeks. If the activity time is 11 weeks, then the total float will be:
(a) 11 (b) 13
(c) 18 (d) 24

81. Consider the following statements:
Thermal stress is induced in a component in general, when
1. a temperature gradient exists in the component.
2. the component is free from any restraint.
3. it is restrained to expand or contract freely.

Which of the above statements is/are correct?
(a) 1 and 2 (b) 2 and 3
(c) 3 alone (d) 2 alone.

82. Consider the following statements in case of beams:
1. Rate of change of shear force is equal to the rate of loading at a particular section.
2. Rate of change of bending moment is equal to the shear force at a particular section.
3. Maximum shear force in a beam occurs at a point where bending moment is either zero or bending moment changes sign.

Which of the above statement is/are correct'?
(a) 1 alone
(b) 2 alone
(c) 1 and 2
(d) 1, 2 and 3.

83. Which of the following are fabricated using engineering plastics?
1. Surface plate
2. Gears
3. Guide ways for machine tools
4. Foundary patterns.

Select the correct answer using the codes given below:

**Codes:**

(a) 1, 2 and 3 (b) 1
(c) 2, 3 and 4 (d) 1, 2, 3 and 4.

84. Consider the following statements:
Polytetrafluoroethane is
1. a thermoplastic material.
2. having high friction co-efficient.
3. a thermosetting material.
4. having low friction co-efficient.
5. an electric insulator.
6. non-sticking to surfaces.

Which of the above statements are correct?

(a) 1, 2 and 5 (b) 2, 3 and 6
(c) 3, 4 and 5 (d) 3, 2 and 5.

85. Which of the following fibre materials are used for reinforcement in composite materials:
1. Glass 2. Boron carbide
3. Graphite

Select the correct answer using the codes given below:

**Codes:**

(a) 1 and 2 (b) 1 and 3
(c) 2 and 3 (d) 1, 2 and 3.

86. Consider the following statements:
The strength of a single point cutting tool depends upon
1. rake angle
2. clearance angle
3. lip angle.

Which of these statements are correct?

(a) 1 and 3 (b) 2 and 3
(c) 1 and 2 (d) 1, 2 and 3.

87. Which of the following materials are used in Grinding wheel?
1. aluminium oxide
2. cubic boron nitride
3. silicon carbide.

Select the correct answer using the codes given below:

**Codes:**

(a) 1, 2 and 3 (b) 1 and 2
(c) 2 and 3 (d) 1 and 3.

88. Consider the following statements related to piereing and blanking:
1. Shear on the punch reduces the maximum cutting force.
2. Shear increases the capacity of the press needed.
3. Shear increases the life of the punch.
4. The total energy needed to make the cut remains unaltered due to provision of shear.

Which of the above statements are correct?

(a) 1 and 2 (b) 1 and 4
(c) 2 and 3 (d) 3 and 4.

89. Consider the following steps involved in hammer forging a connecting rod from bar stock:
1. Blocking 2. Trimming
3. Finishing 4. Fullering.
5. Edging

Which of the following is the correct sequence of operations?

(a) 1, 4, 3, 2 and 5 (b) 4, 5, 1, 3 and 2
(c) 5, 4, 3, 2 and 1 (d) 5, 1, 4, 2 and 3

90. The graph shows the results of various quality levels for a component

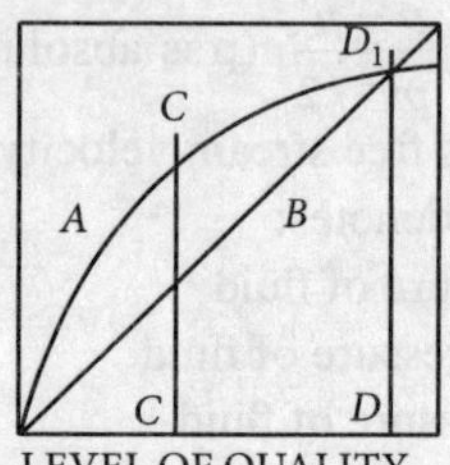


Consider the following statements:
1. Curve A shows the variation of value of component.
2. Curve B shows the variation of cost of the component.
3. Graph is called as fish bone diagram.
4. The preferred level of quality is given by line CC.
5. The preferred level of quality is given by line DD.

Which of the above statements are correct?

(a) 1, 2 and 5 (b) 1, 3 and 4
(c) 2, 3 and 4 (d) 1, 2 and 3

## ANSWERS WITH EXPLANATIONS

1. (b) 2. (d) 3. (d) 4. (d)

5. (c) $Q = 50\times10^{-3}\,m^3/s$, $H = 40$ m

$Q = 50\times10^{-3}\,m^{-3}/s$, $H = 40$ m

$$P = \frac{\gamma QH}{10^3} = \frac{9-81\times10^3\times50\times10^{-3}\times40}{10^3}$$

$= 19.62$ km

6. (b) 7. (a) 8. (a) 9. (c) 10. (b)

11. (d) The blades of propeller turbine are fixed.

12. (b) 13. (b) 14. (c) 15. (b)

16. (b) For a pump, $N_s = \frac{N\sqrt{Q}}{H^{3/4}}$

$N_s \propto \sqrt{Q}$

$$\frac{N_{s2}}{N_{s1}} = \frac{\sqrt{\frac{Q}{2}}}{Q}$$

$$N_{s2} = N_{s2}\frac{N_s}{\sqrt{2}}$$

17. (a) 18. (c) 19. (c) 20. (b) 21. (d)
22. (c) 23. (a) 24. (a) 25. (a) 26. (a)
27. (c) 28. (b)

29. (c) N = 1950 rpm, Q = 50 1 pm or $50 \times 10^{-3}\ m^3/min, H = 20m$

30. (d) 31. (a) 32. (c) 33. (a) 34. (d)
35. (a)

36. (a) For a reaction turbine, $P \alpha H^{3/2}$. Thus decrease of head would result in decrease of power developed.

$N \alpha \frac{1}{\sqrt{P}}$ or $P \alpha \frac{1}{N^2}$. Thus decrease in speed will result in increase in power.

37. (a) 38. (b) 39. (d) 40. (c) 41. (a)
42. (b) 43. (a) 44. (b) 45. (b) 46. (d)
47. (d) 48. (d) 49. (b) 50. (b) 51. (a)
52. (b) 53. (a) 54. (a) 55. (b) 56. (a)
57. (c) 58. (a) 59. (a) 60. (b) 61. (d)
62. (c)

63. (c) $P \alpha N^3 . P_2 = P_1 \left(\frac{N_2}{N_1}\right)^3 = 5\left(\frac{1500}{1200}\right)^3$

$= 9.8$ kW

64. (c) 65. (a) 66. (a) 67. (b) 68. (c)
69. (b)

70. (b) Frictional head lost,

$H_L = \eta_{hyd} \times H - H_u = 0.9 \times 100 - 72 = 18\,m$

71. (a) 72. (a) 73. (c) 74. (c) 75. (d)
76. (b)

77. (c) $T_e = 36$ days, $\sigma = \sqrt{4} = 2$ days, $T_s = 36$ days

$z = \frac{T_s - T_c}{\sigma} = \frac{36-36}{2} = 0$

For z = 0, P = 50%

78. (c) $\sigma = \sqrt{\sum \text{variance}}$

$= \sqrt{4+16+4+1} = \sqrt{25} = 5$

79. (c) $\sum T_e = 17 + 15 + 8 = 40$ days

$\sum V = 4 + 4 + 1 = 9$

$\sigma = \sqrt{\sum V} = \sqrt{9} = 3$

$T_s = 43$ days

$z = \frac{T_s - T_e}{\sigma} = \frac{43-40}{3} = 1$

For $z = 1$, P = 0.8143 or 81.43%

80. (c) Total float,

$FT = [(TL)_d - (TE)_i] - t_{ij} = (37 - 8) - 11$

$= 18$ weeks

81. (c) Thermal stress is induced in a component when it is restrained to expand or contract freely.

82. (c)

83. (c) Engineering plastics can be used for (i) gears, (ii) guideways for machine tools, and (iii) foundry patterns.

84. (a)

85. (a) Glass and Boron Carbide is used for reinforcement in composite materials.

86. (d) The strength of a single point cutting tool depends upon (i) rake angle, (ii) clearance angle, and (iii) lip angle.

87. (a) $Al_2O_3$, BN and SiC are used in grinding wheels.

88. (b)

89. (b) The sequence of operations in hammer forging a connecting rod are:

Fullering → Edging → Blocking → Finishing → Trimming

90. (d)

❑❑❑

# 4. Thermodynamics

- Thermodynamics is a branch of physics concerned with heat and temperature and their relation to energy and work. It defines macroscopic variables, such as internal energy, entropy, and pressure, that partly describe a body of matter or radiation.
- It states that the behavior of those variables is subject to general constraints, that are common to all materials, not the peculiar properties of particular materials. These general constraints are expressed in the four laws of thermodynamics.
- Thermodynamics describes the bulk behavior of the body, not the microscopic behaviors of the very large numbers of its microscopic constituents, such as molecules.
- Its laws are explained by statistical mechanics, in terms of the microscopic constituents.
- Thermodynamics applies to a wide variety of topics in science and engineering.
- Thermo-dynamics is the subject of the relation of heat to forces acting between contiguous parts of bodies, and the relation of heat to electrical agency.
- Initially, thermodynamics, as applied to heat engines, was concerned with the thermal properties of their 'working materials' such as steam, in an effort to increase the efficiency and power output of engines.
- The plain term 'thermodynamics' refers to a macroscopic description of bodies and processes.
- Thermodynamics arose from the study of two distinct kinds of transfer of energy, as heat and as work, and the relation of those to the system's macroscopic variables of volume, pressure and temperature. Transfers of matter are also studied in thermodynamics.
- Thermodynamic equilibrium is one of the most important concepts for thermodynamics. The temperature of a thermodynamic system is well defined, and is perhaps the most characteristic quantity of thermodynamics.
- In engineering practice, thermodynamic calculations deal effectively with such systems provided the equilibrium thermodynamic variables are nearly enough well-defined.
- Central to thermodynamic analysis are the definitions of the system, which is of interest, and of its surroundings. The surroundings of a thermodynamic system consist of physical devices and of other thermodynamic systems that can interact with it.
- An example of a thermodynamic surrounding is a heat bath, which is held at a prescribed temperature, regardless of how much heat might be drawn from it.
- There are four fundamental kinds of physical entities in thermodynamics, states of a system, walls of a system, thermodynamic processes of a system, and thermodynamic operations.
- A thermodynamic system can be defined in terms of its states. In this way, a thermodynamic system is a macroscopic physical object, explicitly specified in terms of macroscopic physical and chemical variables that describe its macroscopic properties.
- A thermodynamic operation is an artificial physical manipulation that changes the definition of a system or its surroundings. Usually it is a change of the permeability or some other feature of a wall of the system that allows energy (as heat or work) or matter (mass) to be exchanged with the environment.
- A thermodynamic system can also be defined in terms of the cyclic processes that it can undergo.
- A cyclic process is a cyclic sequence of thermodynamic operations and processes that can be repeated indefinitely often without changing the final state of the system.
- For thermodynamics and statistical thermodynamics to apply to a physical system, it is necessary that its internal atomic mechanisms fall into one of two classes:
- those so rapid that, in the time frame of the process of interest, the atomic states rapidly bring system to its own state of internal thermodynamic equilibrium; and
- those so slow that, in the time frame of the process of interest, they leave the system unchanged.
- Thermodynamic facts can often be explained by viewing macroscopic objects as assemblies of very many microscopic oratomic objects that obey Hamiltonian dynamics.
- The microscopic or atomic objects exist in species, the objects of each species being all alike. Because of this likeness, statistical methods can be used to account for the macroscopic properties of the thermodynamic system in terms of the properties of the microscopic species.
- Thermodynamics states a set of four laws that are valid for all systems that fall within the constraints implied by each. In the various theoretical descriptions of thermodynamics these laws may be expressed in seemingly differing forms, but the most prominent formulations are the following:
- Zeroth law of thermodynamics: If two systems are each in thermal equilibrium with a third, they are also in thermal equilibrium with each other.
- First law of thermodynamics: The increase in internal

energy of a closed system is equal to the difference of the heat supplied to the system and the work done by it: $\Delta U = Q - W$ (Note that due to the ambiguity of what constitutes positive work, some sources state that $\Delta U = Q + W$, in which case work done on the system is positive.)

- The first law of thermodynamics asserts the existence of a state variable for a system, the internal energy, and tells how it changes in thermodynamic processes.
- The law allows a given internal energy of a system to be reached by any combination of heat and work. It is important that internal energy is a variable of state of the system whereas heat and work are variables that describe processes or changes of the state of systems.
- The first law observes that the internal energy of an isolated system obeys the principle of conservation of energy, which states that energy can be transformed (changed from one form to another), but cannot be created or destroyed.
- Second law of thermodynamics: Heat cannot spontaneously flow from a colder location to a hotter location.
- The second law of thermodynamics is an expression of the universal principle of dissipation of kinetic and potential energy observable in nature.
- The second law is an observation of the fact that over time, differences in temperature, pressure, and chemical potential tend to even out in a physical system that is isolated from the outside world.
- Entropy is a measure of how much this process has progressed. The entropy of an isolated system that is not in equilibrium tends to increase over time, approaching a maximum value at equilibrium.
- In classical thermodynamics, the second law is a basic postulate applicable to any system involving heat energy transfer; in statistical thermodynamics, the second law is a consequence of the assumed randomness of molecular chaos
- Third law of thermodynamics: As a system approaches absolute zero the entropy of the system approaches a minimum value.
- The third law of thermodynamics is a statistical law of nature regarding entropy and the impossibility of reaching absolute zero of temperature.
- This law provides an absolute reference point for the determination of entropy. The entropy determined relative to this point is the absolute entropy.
- Thermodynamics distinguishes classes of systems by their boundary sectors.
- AC magnets are made of laminated iron to reduce the heating effect.
- The purpose of overload protection in a motor circuit is to protect the motor from sustained over-currents.
- If an operator pushes the start-button of the three-phase induction motor starter and the motor start to hum, but does not run, the propable trouble is one fuse is blown and the motor is of single phasing.
- When the reset button does not reestablish the control circuit after an overload, the probable cause is the overload trip has not cooled sufficiently.
- Operation of a thermal overload relay depends on ambient temperature and temperature due to load current.
- Line voltage of star-connected, 3-phase circuit is 415 V. The phase voltage will be 230 V.
- The line voltage of a delta-connected, 3-phase circuit is 415 V. The phase voltage will be 415 V.
- The phase current of a star-connected, 3-phase circuit is 100 amps. The line current will be 100 amps.
- The appropriate fusing current of 35 SWG copper wire is 5 amps.
- The approximate full load current of a 3-phase delta connected 3 HP motor is 4.5 amps.
- An open system has a boundary sector that is permeable to matter; such a sector is usually permeable also to energy, but the energy that passes cannot in general be uniquely sorted into heat and work components. Open system boundaries may be either actually restrictive, or else non-restrictive.
- A closed system has no boundary sector that is permeable to matter, but in general its boundary is permeable to energy. For closed systems, boundaries are totally prohibitive of matter transfer.
- An adiabatically isolated system has only adiabatic boundary sectors. Energy can be transferred as work, but transfers of matter and of energy as heat are prohibited.
- A purely diathermic ally isolated system has only boundary sectors permeable only to heat; it is sometimes said to be a dynamically isolated and closed to matter transfer. A process in which no work is transferred is sometimes called a dynamic.
- An isolated system has only isolating boundary sectors. Nothing can be transferred into or out of it.

# MULTIPLE CHOICE QUESTIONS

1. A reversible engine receives heat from a reservoir at 700°C and rejects heat at a temperature $T_2$. A second reversible engine operating on Carnot cycle receives heat rejected by the first engine and rejects heat to a sink at 37°C. If work output from each of the engines is equal, what is the value of temperature $T_2$?
   (a) 641.5 K (b) 537 K
   (c) 516 K (d) 498.5 K
2. According to the Maxwell relation, which of the following is/arc correct?
   (a) $\left(\frac{\partial v}{\partial T}\right)_p = -\left(\frac{\partial s}{\partial p}\right)_T$ (b) $\left(\frac{\partial s}{\partial v}\right)_p = \left(\frac{\partial p}{\partial T}\right)_v$
   (c) $\left(\frac{\partial P}{\partial T}\right)_v = \left(\frac{\partial p}{\partial s}\right)_v$ (d) All of the above
3. Which one of the following relationships defines Gibbs' free energy G?
   (a) G = H + TS
   (b) G = H – TS
   (c) G =U + 7S
   (d) G = U –TS
4. Consider the following statements:
   1. Two reversible adiabatics can never intersect each other.
   2. For a thermodynamic process $\frac{dQ}{T} + 1 \geq 0$, where I is the measure of irreversibility.

   Which of the statements given above is/are correct?
   (a) 1 only
   (b) 2 only
   (c) Both 1 and 2
   (d) Neither 1 nor 2
5. Constant pressure lines in the superheated region of the Mother diagram have what type of slope?
   (a) A positive slope
   (b) A negative slope
   (c) Zero slope
   (d) May have either positive or negative slope.
6. Which one of the following is the extensive property of a thermodynamic system?
   (a) Volume
   (b) Pressure
   (c) Temperature
   (d) Density
7. Which one of the following is the correct statement? Steam is said to be superheated when the
   (a) actual volume is greater than volume of saturated steam
   (b) actual volume is less than volume of saturated steam
   (c) actual volume is equal to volume of saturated steam
   (d) None of the above
8. If $M_1, M_2, M_3$ be molecular weight of constituent gases and $m_1, m_2, m_3, \ldots$ their corresponding mass fractions, then what is the molecular weight M of the mixture equal to?
   (a) $m_1 M_1 + m_2 M_2 + m_3 M_3 + \ldots$
   (b) $\frac{1}{m_1 M_1 + m_2 M_2 + m_3 M_3 + \ldots}$
   (c) $\frac{1}{m_1 M_1} + \frac{1}{m_2 M_2} + \frac{1}{m_3 M_3} + \ldots$
   (d) $\frac{1}{\left(\frac{m_1}{M_1}\right) + \left(\frac{m_2}{M_2}\right) + \left(\frac{m_3}{M_3}\right) + \ldots}$
9. If a gas obeys van-der Waals' equation at the critical point, then $\frac{RT_c}{p_c v_c}$ is equal to which one of the following?
   (a) 0 (b) 1
   (c) 1.5 (d) 2.67
10. Which one of the following is the correct statement? Two adiabatics will
    (a) intersect at absolute zero temperature
    (b) never intersect
    (c) become orthogonal at absolute zero temperature
    (d) become parallel at absolute zero temperature
11. Match List-I with List-II and select the correct answer using the codes given below the lists:

| List-I | List-II |
|---|---|
| A. Irreversibility | 1. Mechanical equivalent |
| B. Joule-Thomson experiment | 2. Thermodynamic temperature scale |
| C. Joule's experiment | 3. Throttling process |
| D. Reversible engine | 4. Loss of availability |

**Codes:**

| | A | B | C | D |
|---|---|---|---|---|
| (a) | 1 | 2 | 3 | 4 |
| (b) | 1 | 2 | 4 | 3 |
| (c) | 4 | 3 | 2 | 1 |
| (d) | 4 | 3 | 1 | 2 |

12. For air standard Brayton cycle, increase in the maximum temperature of the cycle, while keeping the pressure ratio the same, would result in:
    (a) increase in air standard efficiency
    (b) decrease in air standard efficiency
    (c) no change in air standard efficiency
    (d) increase in the efficiency but reduction in net work
13. Which one of the following cycles working within the same temperature limits has the highest work ratio?
    (a) Carnot cycle (b) Joule cycle
    (c) Otto cycle (d) Rankine cycle.

14. The equation of state $pv = RT(1 + B/v + C/v^2 + D/v^3 + ..)$ is known as:
(a) Van der Waals equation
(b) Benedict-Webb-Rubin equation
(c) Gibbs equation
(d) Virial equation.

15. What is the ratio of the slopes for p—v curves for an adiabatic process and an isothermal process?
(a) $1/\gamma$ (b) $\gamma+1$
(c) $\gamma$ (d) $\frac{1}{\gamma+1}$

16. Match List-I (Thermodynamic system/prime mover) with List-II (Thermodynamic cycle) and select the correct answer using the codes given below the lists:

| **List-I** | **List-II** |
|---|---|
| A. Air liquefaction plant | 1. Atkinson cycle |
| B. Gas turbine with multistage compression and multistage expansion | 2. Brayton cycle |
| C. Free piston engine/ compressor with a gas turbine | 3. Ericsson cycle |
| D. Pulse jet | 4. Reversed Stirling cycle |
| | 5. Lenoir cycle |

**Codes:**

| | A | B | C | D |
|---|---|---|---|---|
| (a) | 1 | 2 | 4 | 3 |
| (b) | 1 | 2 | 3 | 4 |
| (c) | 4 | 3 | 1 | 5 |
| (d) | 4 | 3 | 5 | 1 |

17. What is the molecular weight (approximate) for the gas whose specific heats are as follows?
$c_p = 1.967$ kJ/kg K ; $c_v = 1.507$ kJ/kg K
(a) 17 (b) 18
(c) 19 (d) 20

18. Consider the following statements:
The maximum temperature produced by the combustion of a unit mass of fuel depends upon
1. L.C.V. 2. Ash content
3. Mass of air supplied 4. Pressure in the furnace
Of these statements,
(a) 1 alone is correct (b) 1 and 3 are correct
(c) 2 and 4 are correct (d) 3 and 4 are correct

19. The critical pressure ratio $\left(\frac{p_2}{p_1}\right)$ for maximum discharge through a nozzle is:
(a) $\left(\frac{2}{n+1}\right)^{\left(\frac{n-1}{n}\right)}$ (b) $\left(\frac{2}{n+1}\right)^{\left(\frac{n}{n-1}\right)}$
(c) $\left(\frac{2}{n-1}\right)^{\left(\frac{n}{n+1}\right)}$ (d) $\left(\frac{2}{n-1}\right)^{\left(\frac{n+1}{n}\right)}$

20. Match List-I with List-II and select the correct answer using the codes given below the lists:

| **List-I (Parameter)** | **List-II (Property)** |
|---|---|
| A. Volume | 1. Path function |
| B. Density | 2. Intensive property |
| C. Pressure | 3. Extensive property |
| D. Work | 4. Point function |

**Codes:**

| | A | B | C | D |
|---|---|---|---|---|
| (a) | 3 | 2 | 4 | 1 |
| (b) | 3 | 2 | 1 | 4 |
| (c) | 2 | 3 | 4 | 1 |
| (d) | 2 | 3 | 1 | 4 |

21. Ratio of specific heats for an ideal gas is given by: (symbols have the usual meanings)
(a) $\frac{1}{1-\frac{R}{c_p}}$ (b) $\frac{1}{1-\frac{c_p}{R}}$
(c) $\frac{1}{1+\frac{c_p}{R}}$ (d) $\frac{1}{1+\frac{R}{c_p}}$

22. For a Carnot engine $T_1 > T_2$. When $T_2$ is decreased by $\Delta T$ with $T_1$ remaining same then efficiency is $\eta_1$, and when $T_1$ is increased by $\Delta T$ with $T_2$ remaining same, efficiency is $\eta_2$. Which one of the following is the correct expression for $(\eta_1 - \eta_2)$?
(a) $\frac{(T_2-T_1)\Delta T+(\Delta T)^2}{T_2(T_2+\Delta T)}$ (b) $\frac{(T_2-T_1)\Delta T+(\Delta T)^2}{T_1(T_1+\Delta T)}$
(c) $\frac{(T_1-T_2)\Delta T+(\Delta T)^2}{T_1(T_1+\Delta T)}$ (d) $\frac{(T_1-T_2)\Delta T+(\Delta T)^2}{T_1(T_1+\Delta T)}$

23. The heat transferred in a thermodynamic cycle of a system consisting of four processes are successively 0, 8, 6 and -4 units. The net change in the internal energy of the system will be:
(a) – 8 (b) zero
(c) 10 (d) – 10

24. If a system undergoes an irreversible adiabatic process, then (symbols have usual meanings:
(a) $\int\frac{dQ}{T} = 0$ and $\Delta S > 0$ (b) $\int\frac{dQ}{T} = 0$ and $\Delta S = 0$
(c) $\int\frac{dQ}{T} > 0$ and $\Delta S = 0$ (d) $\int\frac{dQ}{T} < 0$ and $\Delta S < 0$

25. During a process with heat and work interactions, the internal energy of a system increases by 30 kJ. The amounts of heat and work interactions are respectively:
(a) – 50 kJ and – 80 kJ
(b) –50 kJ and 80 KJ
(c) 50 kJ and 80 kJ
(d) 50 kJ and – 80 kJ

26. The mathematical conditions at the critical point for a pure substance would be:

(a) $\frac{\partial p}{\partial v} < 0; \frac{\partial^2 p}{\partial v^2} = 0$ and $\frac{\partial^3 p}{\partial v^3} = 0$

(b) $\frac{\partial p}{\partial v} = 0; \frac{\partial^2 p}{\partial v^2} < 0$ and $\frac{\partial^3 p}{\partial v^3} = 0$

(c) $\frac{\partial p}{\partial v} = 0; \frac{\partial^2 p}{\partial v^2} = 0$ and $\frac{\partial^3 p}{\partial v^3} < 0$

(d) $\frac{\partial p}{\partial v} = 0; \frac{\partial^2 p}{\partial v^2} = 0$ and $\frac{\partial^3 p}{\partial v^3} = 0$

27. What is the value of slope for an isothermal process on *p–v* diagram for an ideal gas?
(a) $-p/v$ (b) – v/p
(c) $-1/(pv)$ (d) $-pv$

28. Forced draught fans of a large steam generator have:
(a) Backward curved blades
(b) Forward curved blades
(c) Straight or radial blades
(d) Double curved blades

29. Air from a reservoir is to be passed through a supersonic nozzle so that the jet will have a Mach number of 2. If the static temperature of the jet is not to be less than 27°C, the minimum temperature of air in the reservoir should be:
(a) 48.6°C
(b) 167°C
(c) 267°C
(d) 367°C

30. The air standard efficiency of Diesel cycle will be less than that of Otto cycle in the case of:
(a) same compression ratio and same heat input
(b) same maximum pressure and same heat input
(c) same maximum pressure and same output
(d) same maximum pressure and same maximum temperature

31. A section diverging in the direction of flow can be used as which of the following?
1. Subsonic nozzle
2. Supersonic nozzle
3. Subsonic diffuser
4. Supersonic diffuser

Select the correct answer using the code given below:
(a) 1 only (b) 2 and 3
(c) 1 and 4 (d) 3 only

32. Air is compressed adiabatically in a steady flow process with negligible change in potential and kinetic energy. The work done in the process is given by:

(a) $-\int p\,dv$ (b) $+\int p\,dv$

(c) $-\int v\,dp$ (d) $+\int v\,dp$

33. Which one of the following properties remains unchanged for a real gas during Joule-Thomson process?
(a) Temperature
(b) Enthalpy
(c) Entropy
(d) Pressure

34. In respect of a closed system, when an ideal gas undergoes a reversible isothermal process:
(a) heat transfer is zero
(b) change in internal energy is equal to work transfer
(c) work transfer is zero
(d) heat transfer is equal to work transfer.

35. The volumetric air content of a tyre at 27°C and at 2 bar is 30 litres. If one morning the temperature dips to – 3°C, then the air pressure in the tyre would be:
(a) 1.8 bar
(b) 11 bar
(c) 0.8 bar
(d) the same as at 27°C

36. One kg of a perfect gas is compressed from pressure $p_1$ to pressure $p_2$ by
1. isothermal process
2. adiabatic process
3. the law $pv^{1.1}$ = constant

The correct sequence of these processes in increasing order of their work requirement is:
(a) 1, 2, 3 (b) 1, 3, 2
(c) 2, 3, 1 (d) 3, 1, 2.

37. Triple point temperature of water is:
(a) 273 K
(b) 273.14 K
(c) 273.15 K
(d) 273.16 K.

38. In a test of a water-jacketed compressor, the shaft work required is 90 kN-m/kg of air compressed. During compression, increase in enthalpy of air is 30 kJ /kg of air and increase in enthalpy of circulating cooling water is 40 kJ/kg of air. The change in velocity is negligible. The amount of heat lost to the atmosphere from the compressor per kg of air is:
(a) 20 kJ (b) 60 kJ
(c) 80 kJ (d) 120 kJ

39. Match List-I with List-II and select the correct answer using the codes given below the lists:

| List-I | List-II |
|---|---|
| A. The entropy of a pure crystalline substance is zero at absolute zero temperature | 1. First law of thermodynamics |
| B. Spontaneous processes occur in a certain direction | 2. Second law of thermodynamics |

| | | | |
|---|---|---|---|
| C. If two bodies are in thermal equilibrium with a third body, then they are also in thermal equilibrium with each other | | 3. Third law of thermodynamics | |
| | | 4. Zeroth law of thermodynamics | |
| D. The law of conservation of energy | | | |

**Codes:**

| | A | B | C | D |
|---|---|---|---|---|
| (a) | 2 | 3 | 4 | 1 |
| (b) | 3 | 2 | 1 | 4 |
| (c) | 3 | 2 | 4 | 1 |
| (d) | 2 | 3 | 1 | 4 |

40. 1600 kJ of energy is transferred from a heat reservoir at 800 K to another heat reservoir at 400 K. The amount of entropy generated during the process would be:
(a) 6 kJ/K (b) 4 kJ/K
(c) 2 kJ/K (d) zero.

41. For a compression or heating process, what is the expression for effectiveness ε?
(a) $\varepsilon = \dfrac{\text{Increase of availability of the surroundings}}{\text{Loss of availability of the system}}$
(b) $\varepsilon = \dfrac{\text{Increase of availability of the system}}{\text{Loss of availability of the surroundings}}$
(c) $\varepsilon = \dfrac{\text{Loss of availability of the surroundings}}{\text{Increase of availability of the system}}$
(d) $\varepsilon = \dfrac{\text{Loss of availability of the system}}{\text{Increase of availability of the surroundings}}$

42. Match List-I (Cycle) with List-II (Process) and select the correct answer using the codes given below the lists:

| **List-I (Cycle)** | **List-II (Process)** |
|---|---|
| A. Otto | 1. Two isothermal and two constant volume |
| B. Stirling | 2. Two isothermal and two isobar |
| C. Ericsson | 3. Two isentropic and two isobar |
| D. Brayton | 4. Two isentropic and two constant volume |
| | 5. Two isentropic and two isothermal |

**Codes:**

| | A | B | C | D |
|---|---|---|---|---|
| (a) | 4 | 1 | 2 | 3 |
| (b) | 4 | 1 | 3 | 5 |
| (c) | 1 | 4 | 2 | 5 |
| (d) | 1 | 4 | 5 | 3 |

43. The specific heat $c_p$ is given by:
(a) $T\left(\dfrac{\partial v}{\partial T}\right)_p$ (b) $T\left(\dfrac{\partial v}{\partial S}\right)_p$
(c) $T\left(\dfrac{\partial S}{\partial T}\right)_p$ (d) $T\left(\dfrac{\partial T}{\partial v}\right)_p$

44. In free expansion of a gas between two equilibrium states, the work transfer involved:
(a) can be calculated by joining the two states on $p - v$ coordinates by any path and estimating the area below
(b) can be calculated by joining the two states by a quasi-static path and then finding the area below
(c) is zero
(d) is equal to heat generated by friction during expansion

45. Consider the following statements:
(1) The Second Law analysis can be applied to thermodynamic cycles only and not to individual processes.
(2) The Second Law analysis clearly gives an idea about the irreversibilities in the heat exchangers whereas no idea is obtained from the First Law analysis.
Which of the statements given above is/are correct?
(a) 1 only (b) 2 only
(c) Both 1 and 2 (b) Neither 1 nor 2

46. Which of the following statements are associated with second law of thermodynamics
1. When a system executes a cyclic process, network transfer is equal to net heat transfer.
2. It is impossible to construct an engine, that operating in a cycle will produce no other effect than the extraction of heat from a reservoir and performance of an equivalent amount of work.
3. It is impossible by any procedure, no matter how idealized, to reduce any system the absolute zero of temperature in a finite number of operations
4. It is impossible to construct a device that operating in a cycle will produce no effect other than transfer of heat from a cooler to hotter body.
Select the correct answer using the codes given below:
(a) 1, 2 and 4 (b) 2 and 4
(c) 2, 3, and 4 (d) 2 and 3

47. Clausius inequality is stated as:
(a) $\oint \delta Q < 0$ (b) $\oint \delta Q = 0$
(c) $\oint \dfrac{\delta Q}{T} > 0$ (d) $\oint \dfrac{\delta Q}{T} \leq 0$

48. A heat engine working on Carnot cycle receives heat at the rate of 40 kW from a source at 1200 K and rejects it to a sink at 300 K. The heat rejected is:
(a) 30 kW (b) 20 kW
(c) 10 kW (d) 5 kW

49. An electric power generating station produces 400 MW. If the coal releases $36\times10^8$ kJ/h of energy, the rate of rejection of heat from the power plant is:
(a) 200 MW (b) 400 MW
(c) 600 MW (d) 800 MW

50. An ideal gas with initial volume, pressure and temperature of 0.1 m$^3$, 1 bar and 27°C respectively is compressed in a cylinder by a piston such that its final volume and pressure are 0.04 m3 and 5 bar respectively, then its final temperature will be:
(a) – 123°C (b) 54°C
(c) 327°C (d) 600°C

51. A cyclic heat engine receives 600 kJ of heat from a 1000 K source and rejects 450 kJ to a300 K sink. The quantity $\oint \frac{\delta Q}{T}$ and efficiencyof the engine are respectively:
(a) 2.1 kJ/K and 70% (b) – 0.9 kJ/K and 25%
(c) + 0.9 kJ/K and 70% (d) – 2.1 kJ/K and 50%

52. Which of the following symptoms show that the combustion in air is necessarily complete:
(a) Absence of oxygen in exhaust
(b) Absence of nitrogen in exhaust
(c) Absence of free carbon in exhaust
(d) Absence of carbon monoxide in exhaust

53. Orsat gas analyzer determines volumetric composition of the flue gases in respect of:
(a) $O_2$ and $N_2$ (b) $O_2$ and $CO_2$
(c) $CO_2$, CO and $N_2$ (d) $N_2$, $O_2$, $CO_2$ and CO

54. In isentropic flow between two points:
(a) the stagnation pressure decreases in the direction of flow
(b) the stagnation temperature and stagnation pressure decrease with increase in the velocity
(c) the stagnation temperature and stagnation pressure may vary
(d) the stagnation temperature and stagnation pressure remain constant

55. Work done in a free expansion process is:
(a) positive (b) negative
(c) zero (d) maximum

56. Match List-I (Quantity) with List-II (Measuring Device) and select the correct answer using the codes given below the lists:

| List-I (Quantity) | List-II (Measuring Device) |
|---|---|
| A. Engine speed | 1. Manometer |
| B. Fuel heating value | 2. Tachometer |
| C. Air velocity | 3. Hydrometer |
| D. Relative humidity of air | 4. Calorimeter |
| | 5. Hygrometer |

**Codes:**

| | A | B | C | D |
|---|---|---|---|---|
| (a) | 2 | 5 | 1 | 4 |
| (b) | 1 | 5 | 3 | 4 |
| (c) | 2 | 4 | 1 | 5 |
| (d) | 1 | 4 | 3 | 5 |

57. For the expression $\int p\,dv$ to represent the work,which of the following conditions should apply?
(a) The system is closed one and process takes place in non-flow system.
(b) The process is non-quasi-static.
(c) The boundary of the system should not move in order that work may be transferred.
(d) If the system is open one, it should be non-reversible

58. Variation of pressure and volume at constant temperature are correlated through:
(a) Charles' law (b) Boyle's law
(c) Joule's law (d) Gay Lussac's law

59. The velocity of sound in an ideal gas does not depend on:
(a) the specific heat ratio of the gas
(b) the molecular weight of the gas
(c) the temperature of the gas
(d) the density of the gas

60. Match List-I with List-II and select the correct answer using the codes given below the lists:

| List-I | List-II |
|---|---|
| A. Joule-Thomson coefficient | 1. 5/2 R |
| B. $c_p$ for monoatomic gas | 2. $c_v$ |
| C. $c_p - c_v$ for diatomic gas | 3. R |
| D. $\left(\frac{\partial U}{\partial T}\right)_v$ | 4. $\left(\frac{\partial T}{\partial p}\right)_h$ |

**Codes:**

| | A | B | C | D |
|---|---|---|---|---|
| (a) | 3 | 2 | 4 | 1 |
| (b) | 4 | 1 | 3 | 2 |
| (c) | 3 | 1 | 4 | 2 |
| (d) | 4 | 2 | 3 | 1 |

61. An inventor claims that heat engine has the following specifications:
Power developed = 50 kW,
Fuel burned per hour = 3 kg
Heating value of fuel = 75,000 kJ per kg
Temperature limits = 627°C and 27°C
Cost of fuel = Rs. 30/kg.
Value of po\ er = Rs. 5/kWh,
The performance of his engine is:
(a) possible (b) not possible
(c) economical (d) uneconomical

62. In a normal shock wave in one-dimensional flow:
(a) pressure, density and temperature increase
(b) velocity, temperature and density increase
(c) pressure, density and temperature decrease
(d) velocity, pressure and density decrease

63. Identify the process of change of a closed system in which the work transfer is maximum:
(a) Isothermal (b) Isochoric
(c) Isentropic (d) Polytropic

64. A system executes a cycle during which there are four heat transfers:
$Q_{12} = 220$ kJ, $Q_{23} = -25$ kJ, $Q_{34} = -180$ kJ, $Q_{41} = 50$ kJ.
The work during three of the processes is:
$W_{12} = 15$ kJ, $W_{23} = -10$ kJ, $W_{34} = 60$ kJ. The work during the process 4 – 1 is :
(a) – 230 kJ (b) 0 kJ
(c) 230 kJ (d) 130 kJ

65. Which one of the following statements is not correct?
(a) Change in entropy during a reversible adiabatic process is zero.
(b) Entropy increases with the addition of heat.
(c) Throttling is a constant entropy expansion process.
(d) Change in entropy when a gas is heated under constant pressure is given by
$$s_2 - s_1 = mc_p \log_e \frac{T_2}{T_1}$$

66. If *u, t, v, s, h* and *p* refer to internal energy, temperature, volume, entropy, enthalpy and pressure respectively; and subscript 0 refers to environment conditions, availability function for a closed system is given by:
(a) $u + p_0 v - T_0 s$ (b) $u - p_0 v + T_0 s$
(c) $h + p_0 v + T_0 s$ (d) $h - p_0 v + T_0 s$

67. If *h, p,* T and *v* refer to enthalpy, pressure, temperature and specific volume respectively; and subscripts *g* and *f* refer to saturation conditions of vapour and liquid respectively, then Clausius-Clapeyron equation applied to change of phase from liquid to vapour states is:
(a) $\frac{dp}{dt} = \frac{(h_g - h_f)}{(v_g - v_f)}$ (b) $\frac{dp}{dt} = \frac{(h_g - h_f)}{T(v_g - v_f)}$
(c) $\frac{dp}{dt} = \frac{(h_g - h_f)}{T}$ (d) $\frac{dp}{dt} = \frac{(v_g - v_f)T}{(h_g - h_f)}$

68. A gas turbine cycle with infinitely large number of stages during compression and expansion approaches:
(a) Stirling cycle (b) Atkinson cycle
(c) Ericsson cycle (d) Brayton cycle

69. The COP of a refrigerator on a reversed Carnot cycle is 5. The ratio of higher absolute temperature to the lower temperature (*i.e.*, $T_2/T_1$) is:
(a) 1.25 (b) 1.3
(c) 1.4 (d) 1.2

70. For an ideal gas, the expression $\left[T\left(\frac{\partial s}{\partial T}\right)_p - T\left(\frac{\partial s}{\partial T}\right)_v\right]$ is equal to:
(a) zero (b) $c_p / c_v$
(c) R (d) RT

71. For a non-flow constant pressure process, the heat exchange is equal to:
(a) zero
(b) the work done
(c) the change in internal energy
(d) the change in enthalpy

72. For a real thermodynamic cycle:
(a) $\oint \frac{dQ}{T} >$ but $< \infty$ (b) $\oint \frac{dQ}{T} < 0$
(c) $\oint \frac{dQ}{T} = 0$ (d) $\oint \frac{dQ}{T} = \infty$

73. A higher value of Van der Waals constant for a gas indicates that the:
(a) molecules of the gas have smaller diameter
(b) gas can be easily liquified
(c) gas has higher molecular weight
(d) gas has lower molecular weight

74. Total enthalpy of steam at the inlet of a nozzle is 2800 kJ while static enthalpy at the exit is 2555 kJ. What is the steam velocity at the exit if expansion is isentropic?
(a) 70 m/s (b) 245 m/s
(c) 450 m/s (d) 700 m/s

75. In an adiabatic process 6000 J of work is performed on a system. In the non-adiabatic process by which the system returns to its original state, 1000 J of heat is added to the system. What is the work done during non-adiabatic process?
(a) +7000 J (b) – 7000 J
(c) +5000 J (d) – 5000 J

76. Heat flows between two reservoirs having temperatures 1000 K and 500 K, respectively. If the entropy change of the cold reservoir is 10 kJ/K, then what is the entropy change for the hot reservoir?
(a) –10 kJ/K
(b) – 5 kJ/K
(c) 5 kJ/K
(d) 10 kJ/K

77. Match List-I with List-II and select the correct answer using the codes given below the lists:

| **List-I** | **List-II** |
|---|---|
| A. Bottle filling of gas | 1. Absolute zero temperature |
| B. Nernst-Simon statement | 2. Variable flow |
| C. Joule-Thomson effect | 3. Quasi-static path |
| D. $\int p\,dv$ | 4. Isenthalpic process |
| | 5. Dissipative effect |
| | 6. Low grade energy |
| | 7. Pressure and temperature during phase change |

**Codes:**

| | A | B | C | D |
|---|---|---|---|---|
| (a) | 6 | 5 | 4 | 3 |
| (b) | 2 | 1 | 4 | 3 |
| (c) | 2 | 5 | 7 | 4 |
| (d) | 6 | 1 | 7 | 4 |

78. $M_1$ kg of water at $T_1$ is isobarically and adiabatically mixed with $M_2$ kg of water at $T_2$ ($T_1 > T_2$). The entropy change of the universe is:
(a) Necessarily positive
(b) Necessarily negative
(c) Always zero
(d) Negative or positive but not zero

79. A heat engine using lake water at 12°C as source and the surrounding atmosphere at 2°C as sink executes 1080 cycles per minute. If amount of heat supplied per cycle is 57 J, what is the output of the engine?
(a) 66 W
(b) 56 W
(c) 46 W
(d) 36 W

80. A reversible heat engine runs between high temperature $T_1$ and low temperature $T_2$. The work output of this heat engine is used to run a reversible refrigeration cycle absorbing heat at temperature $T_3$ and rejecting at temperature $T_2$. What is the COP of the combined system?
(a) $\left(\frac{T_1 - T_2}{T_1}\right)\left(\frac{T_3}{T_2 - T_3}\right)$ (b) $\left(\frac{T_2}{T_1 - T_2}\right)\left(\frac{T_2 - T_3}{T_3}\right)$
(c) $\left(\frac{T_1}{T_1 - T_2}\right)\left(\frac{T_3}{T_2 - T_3}\right)$ (d) $\left(\frac{T_3}{T_1 - T_3}\right)\left(\frac{T_1}{T_2 - T_1}\right)$

81. Match List-I with List-II and select the correct answer using the codes given below the lists:

| List-I | List-II |
|---|---|
| A. Reversible cycle | 1. Measurement of temperature |
| B. Mechanical work | 2. Clapeyron equation |
| | 3. Clausius Theorem |
| C. Zeroth Law | 4. High grade energy |
| D. Heat | 5. 3rd law of thermodynamics |
| | 6. In exact differential |

**Codes:**

| | A | B | C | D |
|---|---|---|---|---|
| (a) | 3 | 4 | 1 | 6 |
| (b) | 2 | 6 | 1 | 3 |
| (c) | 3 | 1 | 5 | 6 |
| (d) | 1 | 4 | 5 | 2 |

82. A. closed thermodynamic system is one in which:
(a) There is no energy or mass transfer across the boundary
(b) There is no mass transfer, but energy transfer exists
(c) There is no energy transfer, but mass transfer exists
(d) Both energy and mass transfer take place across the boundary, but the mass transfer is controlled by valves

83. A refrigerating machine working on reversed Carnot cycle takes out 2 kW of heal from the system at 200 K while working between temperature limits of 300 K and 200 K. COP and power consumed by the cycle will respectively, be:
(a) 1 and 1 kW (b) 1 and 2 kW
(c) 2 and 1 kW (d) 2 and 2 kW

84. If a gas obeys Van-der Waals equation at the critical point, then what does $\frac{RT_c}{p_c V_c}$ equal to?
(a) zero (b) unity
(c) 1.50 (d) 2.67

85. For a gas, pressure p, volume v and temperature T are dependent on each other. Then which one of the following *p-v-*T relationships will be-obeyed?
(a) $\left(\frac{\partial p}{\partial T}\right)_v \left(\frac{\partial v}{\partial T}\right)_p \left(\frac{\partial v}{\partial p}\right)_T = -1$
(b) $\left(\frac{\partial p}{\partial T}\right)_v \left(\frac{\partial T}{\partial v}\right)_p \left(\frac{\partial v}{\partial p}\right)_T = -1$
(c) $\left(\frac{\partial p}{\partial T}\right)_v \left(\frac{\partial v}{\partial T}\right)_p \left(\frac{\partial p}{\partial v}\right)_T = -1$
(d) $\left(\frac{\partial p}{\partial T}\right)_v = \left(\frac{\partial T}{\partial v}\right)_p \left(\frac{\partial p}{\partial v}\right)_T$

86. A battery is used to light a bulb, run a fan and heat an electric iron in case of a power failure. If each of the above systems has 100 W rating and is run for 15 minutes, what are the work done (W) and heat transferred (Q) by the battery'?
(a) W = 90 kJ and Q = 90 kJ
(b) W = 180 kJ and Q =0
(c) W = 270 kJ and Q = 0
(d) W = 90 kJ and Q = 180 kJ

87. Match List-I with List-II and select the correct answer using the codes given below the lists:

| List-I | List-II |
|---|---|
| A. Heat | 1. PMM-2 |
| B. Engine | 2. High grade energy |
| C. Stirring work | 3. variable flow |
| D. Mechanical work | 4. Nernst-Simon statement |
| | 5. Dissipative |
| | 6. Inexact differential |
| | 7. PMM-1 |

**Codes:**

| | A | B | C | D |
|---|---|---|---|---|
| (a) | 2 | 5 | 4 | 3 |
| (b) | 2 | 1 | 5 | 7 |
| (c) | 6 | 5 | 4 | 2 |
| (d) | 6 | 1 | 5 | 2 |

88. A system undergoes a change of state during which 100 kJ of heat is transferred to it and it does 50 kJ of work. The system is brought back to its original state through a process during which 120 kJ of heat is transferred to it. What is the work done by the system?
(a) 50 kJ (b) 70 kJ
(c) 120 kJ (d) 170 kJ

89. A reversible engine exchanges heat from three thermal reservoirs A, B and C at 1000 K, 800 K and 200 K respectively. If the engine receives 500 kJ from .A and 400 kJ from B, then what is the heat exchanged from thermal reservoir C?
(a) 450 kJ rejected to thermal reservoir C
(b) 350 kJ rejected to thermal reservoir C
(c) 250 kJ rejected to thermal reservoir C
(d) 200 kJ rejected to thermal reservoir C

90. A 100Q resistor carrying a constant current of 0.5 A is kept at a constant temperature of 300 K by a stream of cooling water. In a time interval of 30 minutes, what are the changes in entropy for the resistor and that of the universe, respectively?
(a) 0 and 150 J/K (b) 150 J/K and 0
(c) 300 J/K and 0 (d) 0 and 300 J/K

91. A system of 100 kg mass undergoes a process in which its specific entropy increase's from 0.30 kJ/kg K to 0.35 kJ/kg K. At the same time, the entropy of the surroundings decreases from 80 kJ/K to 75 kJ/K. What is the type of this process?
(a) Reversible
(b) Irreversible
(c) Impossible
(d) Not identifiable with the data given

92. Two reversible engines are working in series between a high temperature reservoir at 1000 K and a low temperature reservoir at 300 K in such a way that the heat rejected by the preceding engine is completely absorbed by the succeeding engine and both the engines develop the same amount of work per cycle. What is the intermediate temperature between first and second engines?
(a) 700 K
(b) 650 K
(c) 350 K
(d) Not possible to be estimated with the given data

93. Which one of the following is the correct statement?
(a) The Mach number is less than 1 at a point where the entropy is maximum whether it is Rayleigh or Fanno line.
(b) A normal shock can appear in subsonic flow.
(c) The downstream Mach number across a normal shock is mate than one.
(d) The stagnation pressure across a normal shock decreases.

94. What is/are the effect (s) of supersaturation in nozzle flow?
1. It increases the mass flow.
2. It increases friction in the nozzle.
3. It increases exit velocity.
4. It reduces dryness fraction of steam.
Select the correct answer using the code given below:
(a) 1 only (b) 1 and 3
(c) 1, 2 and 4 (d) 3 only

95. Consider the following statements:
A tube section diverging in the direction of fluid flow can be used as
1. supersonic nozzle
2. subsonic nozzle
3. supersonic diffuser
4. subsonic diffuser
Which of the statements given above is/are correct?
(a) 1 only (b) 1 and 4
(c) 3 only (d) 2 and 3

96. Which one of the following is the shock that occurs for an airplane travelling at supersonic speed?
(a) Normal shock
(b) Oblique shock
(c) Bow shock
(d) Air shock

97. What does choked flow through a steam nozzle mean?
1. Discharge is maximum
2. Discharge is zero
3. Throat velocity is sonic
4. Exit pressure is less than or equal to critical pressure
Select the correct answer using the code given below:
(a) 1 only (b) 2 only
(c) 1 and 3 only (d) 1, 3 and 4

98. When a convergent-divergent nozzle is subjected to a pressure ratio $p_2 / p_1$ greater than the critical pressure ratio, what does the divergent section exhibit?
(a) Decreasing pressure (b) Flow separation
(c) Normal shock (d) Increasing pressure

99. What are the properties of a thermodynamic system, whose value for the entire system is equal to the sum of their values for individual parts of the system?
(a) Thermodynamic properties
(b) Extensive properties
(c) Intensive properties
(d) None of the above

100. A new temperature scale in degrees N is to be defined. The boiling and freezing points of water on this scale are 400°N and 100°N respectively. What will be the reading on new scale corresponding to 60°C?
(a) 110° N (b) 180° N
(c) 210° N (d) 280° N

101. Which of the following thermodynamic properties relate to the Clausius-Clapeyron equation?
1. Pressure 2. Temperature
3. Entropy 4. Specific volume
5. Enthalpy 6. Internal energy
Select the correct answer using the code given below:
(a) 1, 2, 6, 5 (b) 4, 2, 3, 5
(c) 6, 4, 1 (d) 4, 5, 2, 1

102. Which one of the following is heat absorbed or rejected during a polytropic process?
(a) $\left(\frac{\gamma-n}{\gamma-1}\right)\times$ work done
(b) $\left(\frac{\gamma-n}{\gamma-1}\right)^2\times$ work done
(c) $\left(\frac{\gamma-n}{\gamma-1}\right)^3\times$ work done
(d) $\left(\frac{\gamma-n}{1-n}\right)\times$ work done

103. During a cycle comprising four processes, the heat transfers during three processes are +45 kJ, – 30 kJ, – 25 kJ. What should be the heat transfer during the fourth process so that the network done during the cycle is zero?
(a) Zero (b) +10 kJ
(c) – 10 kJ (d) – 20 kJ

104. Which thermometer is independent of the substance or material used in its construction?
(a) Mercury thermometer
(b) Alcohol thermometer
(c) Ideal gas thermometer
(d) Resistance thermometer

105. A closed system undergoes a process during which 150 kJ of heat is added to it. The system is then restored to its initial state. If the heat transfer and work transfer for the second process are – 50 kJ and +75 kJ respectively, what is the work transfer for the first process?
(a) 25 kJ (b) 50 kJ
(c) 75 kJ (d) 100 kJ

106. A heat engine in a thermodynamic cycle draws 500 kJ of heat energy from a source at 1000 K per cycle and rejects certain amount of heat energy at 300 K per cycle. Then, which one of the following is correct?
(a) The amount of heat energy rejected must be 150 kJ
(b) The amount of heat energy rejected must be less than 150 kJ
(c) The amount of heat energy rejected must be greater than 150 kJ
(d) It is not possible to make any statement regarding the amount of heat energy rejected per cycle from the data given

107. An ideal heat pump and an ideal refrigerator, which are reversible in operation, operate between same upper and lower temperature limits. If the coefficient of performance of the refrigerator is 4.5, then what is the coefficient of performance of the heat pump?
(a) 3.5 (b) 5.5
(c) 2.5 (d) 6.5

108. Air standard diesel cycle has a compression ratio of 14 and cut-off takes place at 6% of the stroke. What is the cut-off ratio?
(a) 0.60 (b) 0.78
(c) 1.78 (d) None of the above

109. The thermal efficiency of the Carnot engine is 0.5. If the engine is operated as refrigerator, what is the COP of the refrigerator?
(a) 0.5 (b) 1.0
(c) 2.0 (d) 25

110. In a reversible isothermal expansion process, the fluid expands, from 10 bar and 2m$^3$ to 2 bar and 10 m$^3$. During the process the heat supplied is at the rate of 100 kW. What is the rate of work done during the process?
(a) 20 kW (b) 35 kW
(c) 80 kW (d) 100 kW

111. A system undergoes a change of state during which 80 kJ of heat is transferred to it and it does 60 kJ of work. The system is brought hack to its original slate through a process during which 100 kJ of heat is transferred to it. The work done by the system is:
(a) 40 kJ (b) 60 KJ
(c) 120 kJ (d) 180 kJ

112. Thermodynamic work is the product of:
(a) two intensive properties
(b) two extensive properties
(c) an intensive property and change in an extensive property
(d) an extensive property and change in an intensive property

113. A reversible heat engine operating between hot and cold reservoirs delivers a work output of 54 kJ white it rejects a heat of 66 kJ. The efficiency of this engine is:
(a) 0.45 (b) 0.66
(c) 0.75 (d) 0.82

114. Which one of the following expressions for *Tds* is true for a simple compressible substance? (Notations have the usual meaning).
(a) $dh - vdp$ (b) $dh + vdp$
(c) $dh - pdv$ (d) $dh + pdv$

115. If a pure substance contained in a rigid vessel passes through the critical state on heating, its initial state should be:
(a) subcooled water
(b) saturated water
(c) wet steam
(d) saturated steam

116. Which one of the following is the correct expression for change in the internal energy for a small temperature change $\Delta T$ for an ideal gas?
(a) $\Delta u = c_v \times \Delta T$
(b) $\Delta u = c_p \times \Delta T$
(c) $\Delta u = \frac{c_p}{c_v} \times \Delta T$
(d) $\Delta u = (c_p - c_v)\Delta T$

117. Which of the following are pure substances?
1. Steam and water mixture in a container
2. Atomospheric air
3. Air and liquid air in a container
4. Gaseous combustion products
Select the correct answer using the codes given below:
**Codes:**
(a) 1, 2 and 3 and 4
(b) 2, 3 and 4
(c) 1, 3, and 4
(d) 1, 2 and 4

118. The entropy of a mixture of pure gases is the sum of the entropies of constituents evaluated at:
(a) temperature and pressure of the mixture
(b) temperature of the mixture and the partial pressure of the constituents
(c) temperature and volume of the mixture
(d) pressure and volume of the mixture

119. The Gibbs free-energy function is a property comprising:
(a) pressure, volume and temperature
(b) enthalpy, temperature and entropy
(c) temperature, pressure and enthalpy
(d) volume, enthalpy and entropy

120. An electric motor of 5 kW is subjected to a braking test for 1 hour. The heat generated by the frictional forces in the process is transferred to the surroundings at 20°C. The resulting entropy change will be:
(a) 22.1 kJ/K
(b) 30.2 kJ/K
(c) 61.4 kJ/K
(d) 82.1 kJ/K

## ANSWERS WITH EXPLANATIONS

1. (a) 2. (a) 3. (b) 4. (a) 5. (a)
6. (a) 7. (a) 8. (d) 9. (d) 10. (b
11. (d)

12. (c) $\eta = 1 - \frac{1}{r_p^{(\gamma-1)/\gamma}}, r_p = \frac{p_2}{p_1}$

Efficiency of Brayton does not depend on maximum temperature.

13. (a) $\text{Work ratio} = \frac{\text{Work of Expansion} - \text{Work of compression}}{\text{Work of expansion}}$

Carnot: $R_w = 1 - \frac{T_2}{T_1}$

Joule: $R_w = 1 - \frac{1}{\left(\frac{T_2}{T_1}\right)^{\frac{\gamma}{\gamma-1}}}$

Otto: $R_w = 1 - \frac{1}{\left(\frac{T_2}{T_1}\right)^{\frac{1}{\gamma-1}}}$

Rankine: $R_w = \frac{w_t - w_p}{w_t} = \frac{(h_1 - h_2) - (h_{f4} - h_{f3})}{h_1 - h_{f4}}$

14. (d)

15. (c) Adiabatic process $pv^\gamma = c$ or $p = \frac{c}{v^\gamma}$

Slope, $\frac{dp}{dv} = c\left[-\gamma v^{-\gamma-1}\right] = pv^\gamma\left[-rv^{-\gamma-1}\right]$

$= -p\gamma v^{-1}$

Isothermal process, $pv = c$ or $p = \frac{c}{v}$

Slope; $\frac{dp}{dv} = -cv^{-2} = -pv \times v^{-2} = -pv^{-1}$

$\frac{(dp/dv)_{\text{adb}}}{(dp/dv)_{\text{iso}}} = \frac{-p\gamma v^{-1}}{-pv^{-1}} = \gamma$

16. (b)

17. (b) $R = c_p - c_v = 1.967 - 1.507 = 0.46$

Molecular weight, $M = \frac{R_u}{R} = \frac{8.314}{0.46} = 18$

18. (b) 19. (b) 20. (a)

21. (a) $\frac{c_p}{c_v} = \gamma$ and $c_p - c_v = R$

$\frac{c_p}{c_v} - 1 = \frac{R}{c_v}$

$\frac{c_p}{c_v} = 1 + \frac{R}{c_v}$ and $1 - \frac{c_v}{c_p} = \frac{R}{c_p}$

$\frac{c_v}{c_p} = 1 - \frac{R}{c_p}$

$\frac{c_p}{c_v} = 1 - \frac{1}{1 - \frac{R}{c_p}}$

22. (c) $\eta_{\text{Carnot}} = 1 - \frac{T_2}{T_1}$

$\eta_1 = 1 - \frac{T_2 - \Delta T}{T_1}$

$\eta_2 = 1 - \frac{T_2}{T_1 + \Delta T}$

$\eta_1 - \eta_2 = \frac{T_2}{T_1 + \Delta T} - \frac{T_2 + \Delta T}{T_1}$

$= \frac{T_1T_2 - (T_1 + \Delta T)(T_2 - \Delta T)}{T_1(T_1 + \Delta T)}$

$= \frac{T_1T_2 - (T_1T_2 + T_2.\Delta T - T_1.\Delta T - (\Delta T)^2)}{T_1(T_1 + \Delta T)}$

$= \frac{(T_1 - T_2)\Delta T + (\Delta T)^2)}{T_1(T_1 + \Delta T)}$

23. (c) $\delta Q = dU + \delta W$

$\delta Q_1 = dU_1 + \delta W_1$

$0 = dU_1 + \delta W_1$

Similarly $8 = dU_2 + \delta W_2$

$6 = dU_3 + \delta W_3 \quad -4 = dU_4 + \delta W_4$

$$0+8+6-4 = (dU_1 + dU_2 + dU_3 + dU_4) + (\delta W_1 + \delta W_2 + \delta W_3 + \delta W_4)$$

$10 = \sum dU + 0$

$\therefore \sum dU = 10$ units.

24. (d) For irreversible process, $\int \frac{dQ}{T} < 0$ and $\Delta S < 0$

25. (a) $\delta Q = \delta W + dU$

$dU = \delta Q - \delta W = 30$

$dU = -50 + 80 = 30$ kJ

26. (b) At the critical point,

$$\frac{\partial p}{\partial v} = 0, \frac{\partial^2 p}{\partial v^2} < 0 \text{ and } \frac{\partial^3 p}{\partial v^3} = 0$$

as the c. p. the value of $p$-$v$ curve is maximum.

27. (a) 28. (a) 29. (a) 30. (a) 31. (b)
32. (c) 33. (b) 34. (d)

35. (a) $p_2 = \frac{p_1 T_2}{T_1} = \frac{2 \times 270}{300} = 1.8$ bar

36. (a) 37. (d)

38. (d) $w_{shaft} = 90$ kN.m/kg or 90 kJ/kg

$(\Delta h)_{air} = +30$ kJ/kg

$(\Delta h)_{water} = -40$ kJ/kg

$q = w_{shaft} + (\Delta h)_{air} + (\Delta h)_{water}$

$= 90 + 30 - 40 = 80$ kJ/kg or air

39. (c)

40. (c) $(\Delta s)_{gen} = Q\left(\frac{1}{T_2} - \frac{1}{T_1}\right)$

$= 1600\left(\frac{1}{400} - \frac{1}{800}\right) = 2$kJ/K

41. (b) 42. (a) 43. (c) 44. (c) 45. (c)
46. (c) 47. (d)

48. (c) $T_1 = 1200$ K, $T_2 = 300$ K, $Q_1 = 40$ kW

$$\frac{Q_1}{T_1} = \frac{Q_2}{T_2}, Q_2 = 40 \times \frac{300}{1200} = 10 \text{ kW}$$

49. (c) $Q_1 = \frac{36 \times 10^8}{3600 \times 10^3} = 1000$ MW

W = 400 MW

$Q_1 - Q_2 = W$

$Q_2 = 1000 - 400 = 600$ MW

50. (c) $V_1 = 0.1\text{m}^3, p_1 = 1\text{bar}, T_1 = 27 + 273 = 300$ K,

$V_2 = 0.04$ m$^3$, $p_2 = 5$bar

$$\frac{p_1 V_1}{T_1} = \frac{p_2 V_2}{T_2}$$

$$T_2 = T_1 \frac{p_2}{p_1} \times \frac{V_2}{V_1} = 300 \times \frac{5}{1} \times \frac{0.04}{0.1} = 600 \text{ K}$$

or $t_1 = 600 - 273 = 327$°C

51. (b) $\oint \frac{dQ}{T} = \frac{Q_1}{T_1} - \frac{Q_2}{T_2} = \frac{600}{1000} - \frac{450}{300} = -0.9$kJ/K

$$\eta = 1 - \frac{Q_2}{Q_1} = 1 - \frac{450}{600} = 0.25 \text{ or } 25\%$$

52. (c) 53. (d) 54. (c) 55. (c) 56. (c)
57. (a) 58. (b) 59. (b) 60. (b) 61. (b)
62. (a) 63. (d)

64. (b) $\Sigma Q = 220 - 25 - 180 + 50 = 65$ kJ

$\Sigma W = 15 - 120 + 60 + W_{4-1} = 65\text{kJ} + W_{4-1}$

According to the first law thermodynamics,

$\Sigma W = \Sigma Q$

$65 + W_{4-1} = 65$

$W_{4-1} = 0$ kJ

65. (c) 66. (a) 67. (b) 68. (b)

69. (d) $(COP)_{Ref} = \frac{T_2}{T_1 - T_2} = \frac{1}{\frac{T_1}{T_2} - 1} = 5$

$5\frac{T_1}{T_2} - 5 = 1$

$\frac{T_1}{T_2} = \frac{6}{5} = 1.2$

70. (c) 71. (d) 72. (c) 73. (d)

74. (d) $v = \sqrt{2(2800 - 2555) \times 10^3}$

$= 700$ m/s

75. (a) W = – 600 J, Q = + 1000 J

In an adiabatic process, Q = 0

$Q_{1-2} = W_{1-2} + U_{1-2}$

$0 = -6000 + U_{1-2}$

$U_{1-2} = 6000 \text{ J}, U_{2-1} = -6000$ J

In a non-adiabatic process,

$Q_{2-1} = W_{2-1} + U_{2-1}$

$1000 = W_{2-1} - 6000$

$W_{2-1} = +7000$ J

76. (d) $\frac{Q_1}{T_1} = \frac{Q_2}{T_2}$

$\frac{Q_1}{1000} = \frac{Q_2}{5000}$

$Q_1 = 2Q_2$

Now $\frac{Q_2}{T_2} = 10, Q_2 = 500 \times 10 = 5000$ kJ

$\therefore\ Q_1 = 2 \times 5000 = 10{,}000$ kJ

$$\Delta S_1 = \frac{Q_1}{T_1} = \frac{10{,}000}{1{,}000} = 10 \text{ kJ/K}$$

77. (b) 78. (a)

79. (d) $T_1 = 273 + 12 = 285$ K, $T_2 = 273 + 2 = 275$ K

$$Q_1 = 57 \text{ J/cycle} = 57 \times \frac{1080}{60} = 1026 \text{ W}$$

$$\eta = 1 - \frac{T_2}{T_1} = 1 - \frac{275}{285} = 0.035 = \frac{W}{Q_1}$$

$$W = 1026 \times 0.025 = 36 \text{ W}$$

80. (a) 81. (b) 82. (b)

83. (c) $T_1 = 300$ K, $T_2 = 200$ K

$$COP = \frac{T_2}{T_1 - T_2} = \frac{200}{300 - 200} = \frac{200}{100} = 2$$

$$\text{Power consumed} = \frac{Q}{COP} = \frac{2}{2} = 1 \text{kW}$$

84. (d) $\dfrac{RT_c}{p_c v_c} = \dfrac{8}{3} = 2.67$

85. (b)

86. (a) $W = \dfrac{100 \times 15 \times 60}{10^3} = 90$ kJ

$$Q = W = 90 \text{ kJ}$$

87. (d)

88. (d) $Q_{1-2} = +100$ kJ, $W_{1-2} = +50$ kJ

$$Q_{1-2} = W_{1-2} + U_{1-2}$$

$$U_{1-2} = 100 - 50 = 50 \text{ kJ}$$

$$Q_{2-1} = W_{2-1} + U_{2-1}$$

$$120 = W_{2-1} - 50$$

$$W_{2-1} = 170 \text{ kJ}$$

89. (d)

90. (a) $Q = I^2 Rt = (0.5)^2 \times 100 \times 30 \times 60 \times 10^{-3} = 45$ kJ

$$(\Delta S)_{\text{universe}} = \frac{Q}{T} = \frac{45 \times 1000}{300} = 150 \text{ J/K}$$

$$(\Delta S)_{\text{resistor}} = 0$$

91. (a) 92. (b) 93. (a) 94. (c) 95. (b)

96. (a) 97. (c) 98. (a) 99. (c)

100. (d) Let $t = a_x + b$

$$400 = ax_s + b$$

$$100 = ax_i + b$$

$$a = \frac{300}{x_s - x_i}, b = 100 - \frac{300x_i}{x_s - x_i}$$

$$t°N = \left(\frac{300}{x_s - x_i}\right)x + 100 - \frac{300x_i}{x_s - x_i}$$

$$= \left(\frac{300}{x_s - x_i}\right)(x - x_i) + 100$$

Also $t°C = \left(\dfrac{x - x_i}{x_s - x_i}\right) \times 100$

$$t°N = 3t°C + 100 = 3 \times 60 + 100 = 280°N$$

101. (d) 102. (a) 103. (b) 104. (c)

105. (d) $Q_{1-2} = +150$ kJ, $Q_{2-1} = -50$ kJ,

$$Q_{2-1} = +75 \text{ kJ}$$

$$Q_{1-2} = W_{1-2} + U_{1-2}$$

$$150 = W_{1-2} + U_{1-2}$$

$$U_{1-2} = 150 - W_{1-2}$$

$$Q_{2-1} = W_{2-1} + U_{2-1} \quad -50 = +75 - (150 - W_{1-2})$$

$$W_{1-2} = 25 \text{ kJ}$$

106. (a)

107. (b) $(COP)_{\text{Ref}} = \dfrac{T_2}{T_1 - T_2} = 4.5$

$$(COP)_{\text{pump}} = 1 + (COP)_{\text{ref}} = 1 + 4.5 = 5.5$$

108. (c)

109. (b) $\eta_{\text{Carnot}} = 1 - \dfrac{T_2}{T_1} = 0.5$

$$\frac{T_2}{T_1} = 0.5$$

$$(COP)_{\text{Ref}} = \frac{T_2}{T_1 - T_2} = \frac{1}{\frac{T_1}{T_2} - 1} = \frac{1}{2 - 1} = 1.0$$

110. (d)

111. (c) $Q_{1-2} = +80$ kJ, $W_{1-2} = +60$ kJ

$$Q_{1-2} = W_{1-2} + U_{12}$$

$$U_{12} = 80 - 60 = 20 \text{kJ}$$

$$Q_{2-1} = W_{2-1} + U_{21}$$

$$100 = W_{2-1} - 20$$

$$W_{2-1} = 100 + 20 = 120 \text{ kJ}$$

112. (c)

113. (a) $W = +54$ kJ, $Q_2 = -66$ kJ

$$Q_1 = W - Q_2 = 54 + 66 = 120 \text{kJ}$$

$$\text{Efficiency, } \eta = \frac{W}{Q_1} = \frac{54}{120} = 0.45$$

114. (a) $h = u + pv$

$$dh = d(u + pv) = (du + p.dv) + v.dp$$

$$= T.ds + vdp$$

$$T.s\ dh - v.dp$$

115. (d) 116. (a) 117. (a) 118. (a)

119. (b)

120. (c) $h = T.\ ds$

$$5 \times 3600 = (273 + 20).ds$$

$$ds = \frac{5 \times 3600}{293} = 61.4 \text{ kJ/K}$$

❑❑❑

# 5. Internal Combustion Engine (ICE)

- An internal combustion engine (ICE) is an engine where the combustion of a fuel occurs with an oxidizer (usually air) in a combustion chamber that is an integral part of the working fluid flow circuit.
- In an internal combustion engine the expansion of the high-temperature and high-pressure gases produced by combustion apply direct force to some component of the engine.
- The force is applied typically to pistons, turbine blades, or a nozzle. This force moves the component over a distance, transforming chemical energy into useful mechanical energy. The first commercially successful internal combustion engine was created by Étienne Lenoir around 1859.
- The term internal combustion engine usually refers to an engine in which combustion is intermittent, such as the more familiar four-stroke and two-stroke piston engines, along with variants, such as the six-stroke piston engine and the Wankel rotary engine.
- Internal combustion engines are quite different from external combustion engines, such as steam or Stirling engines, in which the energy is delivered to a working fluid not consisting of, mixed with, or contaminated by combustion products.
- Working fluids can be air, hot water, pressurized water or even liquid sodium, heated in a boiler. ICEs are usually powered by energy-dense fuels such as gasoline or diesel, liquids derived from fossil fuels. While there are many stationary applications, most ICEs are used in mobile applications and are the dominant power supply for cars, aircraft, and boats.
- Typically an ICE is fed with fossil fuels like natural gas or petroleum products such as gasoline, diesel fuel or fuel oil. There's a growing usage of renewable fuels like biodiesel for compression ignition engines and bioethanol for spark ignition engines. Hydrogen is sometimes used, and can be made from either fossil fuels or renewable energy.
- Although various forms of internal combustion engines were developed before the 19th century, their use was hindered until the commercial drilling and production of petroleum began in the mid-1850s. By the late 19th century, engineering advances led to their widespread adoption in a variety of applications.
- Early internal combustion engines were started by hand cranking. Various types of starter motor were later developed. These included:
  - An auxiliary petrol engine for starting a larger petrol or diesel engine. The Hucks starter is an example
  - Cartridge starters, such as the Coffman engine starter, which used a device like a blank shotgun cartridge. These were popular for aircraft engines
  - Pneumatic starters
  - Hydraulic starters
  - Electric starters
- Electric starters are now almost universal for small and medium-sized engines, while pneumatic starters are used for large engines.
- The first piston engines did not have compression, but ran on an air-fuel mixture sucked or blown in during the first part of the intake stroke. The most significant distinction between modern internal combustion engines and the early designs is the use of compression and, in particular, in-cylinder compression.
- The base of a reciprocating internal combustion engine is the engine block which is typically made of cast iron or aluminum.
- he engine block contains the cylinders. In engines with more than 1 cylinder they're usually arranged either in 1 row (straight engine) or 2 rows (boxer engine or V engine); 3 rows are occasionally used (W engine) in contemporary engines, and other engine configurations are possible and have been used.
- Single cylinder engines are common for motorcycles and in small engines of machinery. Water cooled engines contain passages in the engine block where cooling fluid circulate (the water jacket).
- Some small engines are air cooled, and instead of having a water jacket the cylinder block has fins protruding away from it to cool by directly transferring heat to the air.
- The cylinder walls are usually finished by honing to obtain a cross hatch which is better able to retain the oil. A too rough surface would quickly harm the engine by excessive wear on the piston.
- The pistons are short cylindrical parts which seal one end of the cylinder from the high pressure of the compressed air and combustion products and slide continuously within it while the engine is in operation.
- The top wall of the piston is termed its crown and is typically flat or concave. Some two stroke engines use pistons with a deflector head. Pistons are open at the bottom and hollow except for an integral reinforcement structure (the piston web).

- When an engine is working the gas pressure in the combustion chamber exerts a force on the piston crown which is transferred through its web to a gudgeon pin. Each piston has rings fitted around its circumference that mostly prevent the gases from leaking into the crankcase or the oil into the combustion chamber.
- In two stroke gasoline engines the crankcase is part of the air–fuel path and due to the continuous flow of it they do not need a separate crankcase ventilation system.
- The cylinder head is attached to the engine block by numerous bolts or studs. It has several functions. The cylinder head seals the cylinders on the side opposite to the pistons; it contains short ducts (the ports) for intake and exhaust and the associated intake valves that open to let the cylinder be filled with fresh air and exhaust valves that open to allow the combustion gases to escape.
- However, 2-stroke crankcase scavenged engines connect the gas ports directly to the cylinder wall without poppet valves; the piston controls their opening and occlusion instead. The cylinder head also holds the spark plug in the case of spark ignition engines and the injector for engines that use direct injection.
- All CI engines use fuel injection, usually direct injection but some engines instead use indirect injection. SI engines can use acarburetor or fuel injection as port injection or direct injection. Most SI engines have a single spark plug per cylinder but some have 2. A head gasket prevents the gas from leaking between the cylinder head and the engine block.
- The opening and closing of the valves is controlled by one or several camshafts and springs—or in some engines—a desmodromic mechanism that uses no springs. The camshaft may press directly the stem of the valve or may act upon a rocker arm, again, either directly or through a pushrod.
- The crankcase is sealed at the bottom with a sump that collects the falling oil during normal operation to be cycled again. The cavity created between the cylinder block and the sump houses a crankshaft that converts the reciprocating motion of the pistons to rotational motion.
- The crankshaft is held in place relative to the engine block by main bearings, which allow it to rotate. Bulkheads in the crankcase form a half of every main bearing; the other half is a detachable cap. In some cases a single main bearing deck is used rather than several smaller caps.
- A rod is connected to offset sections of the crankshaft (the crankpins) in one end and to the piston in the other end through the dudgeon pin and thus transfers the force and translates the reciprocating motion of the pistons to the circular motion of the crankshaft.
- Usually eddy current damping is used in PMMC instruments.
- Moving coil instruments are preferred measurement of dc voltages only because of their inherent advantages such as low power consumption, no hysteresis loss, very effective and reliable eddy current damping, high torque-weight ratio, no effect of stray magnetic field etc. and incapability of measuring ac voltages as explained below:
- The dynamometer type instruments are suitable both for dc and ac measurements because they have square-law response.
- As the electrodynamic type instruments have the same accuracy on dc and ac both, they are called the transfer instruments.
- Thermocouple and electrostatic type instruments also fall in this category.
- Dynamometer type instruments are usually not used for dc measurements as these instruments have higher cost, higher power consumption, low torque-weight ratio, non-uniform scale and other several drawbacks in comparison to PMMC instruments.
- The end of the connecting rod attached to the dudgeon pin is called its small end, and the other end, where it is connected to the crankshaft, the big end. The big end has a detachable half to allow assembly around the crankshaft. It is kept together to the connecting rod by removable bolts.
- The cylinder head has attached an intake manifold and an exhaust manifold to the corresponding ports. The intake manifold connects to the air filter directly, or to a carburetor when one is present, which is then connected to the air filter.
- It distributes the air incoming from these devices to the individual cylinders. The exhaust manifold is the first component in the exhaust system. It collects the exhaust gases from the cylinders and drives it to the following component in the path.

# MULTIPLE CHOICE QUESTIONS

1. Consider the following statements regarding the advantages of fuel injection over carburetion in S.I. engines:
   1. Higher power output and increased volumetric efficiency.
   2. Simple and inexpensive injection equipment.
   3. Longer life of injection equipment.
   4. Less knocking and reduced tendency for back-fire.

   Select the correct answer using the codes given below:

   **Codes:**

   (a) 1, 2 and 3 (b) 1, 2 and 4

   (c) 2 and 3 (d) 1 and 4

2. Match List I with List II and select the correct answer using the codes given below the lists:

| **List-I (Elements of a complete carburettor)** | **List-II (Rich-mixture requirement)** |
|---|---|
| A. Idling system | 1. To compensate for dilution of charge |
| B. Economiser | 2. For cold starting |
| C. Acceleration pump | 3. For meeting maximum power range of operation |
| D. Choke | 4. For meeting rapid opening of throttle |

**Codes:**

| | A | B | C | D |
|---|---|---|---|---|
| (a) | 1 | 2 | 3 | 4 |
| (b) | 1 | 3 | 4 | 2 |
| (c) | 2 | 3 | 4 | 1 |
| (d) | 4 | 1 | 2 | 3 |

3. Match List I with List II and select the correct answer using the codes given below the lists:

| **List-I (S.I. Engine Problem)** | **List-II (Characteristic of fuel responsible for the problem)** |
|---|---|
| A. Cold starting | 1. Front end volatility |
| B. Carburettor icing | 2. Mid-range volatility |
| C. Crankcase dilutions | 3. Tail end volatility |

**Codes:**

| | A | B | C |
|---|---|---|---|
| (a) | 1 | 2 | 3 |
| (b) | 1 | 3 | 2 |
| (c) | 2 | 3 | 1 |
| (d) | 3 | 1 | 2 |

4. Besides mean effective pressure, the data needed for determining the indicated power of an engine would include:

   (a) piston diameter, length of stroke and calorific value of fuel

   (b) piston diameter, specific fuel consumption and calorific value of fuel

   (c) piston diameter, length of stroke and speed of rotation

   (d) specific fuel consumption, speed of rotation and torque

5. For a typical automobile C.I engine, for conditions of increasing engine speed match List I with List II and select the correct answer using codes given below the lists:

| **List-I (Performance parameter)** | **List-II (Tendency, qualitatively)** |
|---|---|
| A. Power output | 1. Increasing and then decreasing |
| B. Torque | 2. Decreasing and then increasing |
| C. Brake specific fuel consumption | 3. Increasing throughout the range |
| | 4. Decreasing throughout the range |

**Codes:**

| | A | B | C |
|---|---|---|---|
| (a) | 1 | 2 | 3 |
| (b) | 1 | 4 | 3 |
| (c) | 2 | 3 | 4 |
| (d) | 3 | 1 | 2 |

6. Consider the following statements:

   I. The performance of an S.I. engine can be improved by increasing the compression ratio.

   II. Fuels of higher octane number can be employed at higher compression ratio.

   Of theses statements

   (a) both I and II are true (b) both I and II are false

   (c) I is true but II is false (d) I is false but II is true

7. Match List I with List II and select the correct answer using the codes given below the lists:

| **List-I (Name of propellant)** | **List-II (Type of propellant)** |
|---|---|
| A. Nitric acid | 1. Fuel |
| B. Hydrogen | 2. Monopropellant |
| C. Fuming nitric acid hydrazine | 3. Oxidizer |
| D. Methyl nitrate-methyl alcohol | 4. Compounded liquid mono propellant |
| | 5. Hypergolic propellant |

**Codes:**

| | A | B | C | D |
|---|---|---|---|---|
| (a) | 2 | 1 | 4 | 5 |
| (b) | 1 | 2 | 5 | 4 |
| (c) | 3 | 1 | 5 | 4 |
| (d) | 3 | 1 | 4 | 5 |

8. The object of providing masked inlet valve in the air passage of compression-ignition engines is to
(a) enhance flow rate
(b) control air flow
(c) induce primary swirl
(d) induce secondary turbulence

9. Which one of the following events would reduce the volumetric, efficiency of a vertical compression ignition engine?
(a) Intel valve closing after bottom head centre
(b) Inlet valve closing before bottom dead centre
(c) Inlet valve opening top dead centre
(d) Exhaust valve closing after top dead centre

10. As compared to air standard cycle, in actual working, the effect of variation in specific heats is to:
(a) increase maximum pressure and maximum temperature.
(b) reduce maximum pressure and maximum temperature.
(c) increase maximum pressure and decrease maximum temperature.
(d) decrease maximum pressure and Increase maximum temperature.

11. For the same maximum pressure and heat input:
(a) the exhaust temperature of petrol engine is more than that of diesel engine
(b) the exhaust temperature of diesel engine is more than that of petrol engine
(c) the exhaust temperature of dual cycle engine is less than that of diesel engine
(d) the exhaust temperature of dual cycle engine is more than that of petrol engine

12. In Orsat apparatus:
(a) Carbon dioxide is absorbed in cuprous chloride
(b) Carbon monoxide is absorbed in caustic potash solution
(c) Oxygen is absorbed in pyrogallic acid
(d) Nitrogen is absorbed in hot nickel chrome compound

13. In solid propellants rockets, ammonium picrate is usually added as:
(a) an additive (b) an inhibitor
(c) a darkening agent (d) a plasticizer

14. A turbo prop is preferred to turbo jet because:
(a) it has high propulsive efficiency at high speeds
(b) it can fly at supersonic speeds
(c) it can fly at high elevations
(d) it has high power for take off

15. The air fuel ratio for idling speed of an automobile petrol engine is closer to:
(a) 10 : 1 (b) 15 : 1
(c) 17 : 1 (d) 21 : 1

16. Which of the following statements is "true"?
(a) The term "KNOCK" is used for on identical phenomenon in a spark ignition and compression ignition engine
(b) "KNOCK" is a term associated with a phenomeno a taking place in the early part of combustion in a spark ignition engine and the later part of combustion in a spark ignition engine
(c) "KNOCK" is a term associated with a phenomenon taking place in the early part of combustion in a spark ignition engine and the later part of combustion in a compression ignition engine
(d) None of the above

17. The essential function of the carburettor in a spark ignition engine is to:
(a) meter the fuel into air stream and amount dictated by the load and speed
(b) bring about mixing of air and fuel to get a homogeneous mixture
(c) vaporize the fuel
(d) distribute fuel uniformly to all cylinders in a multicylinder engine and also vaporize it.

18. Match List I with List II and select the correct answer using the codes given below the lists:

| **List-I** | **List-II** |
|---|---|
| A. Pre-combustion chamber | 1. Compression swirl |
| B. Turbulent chamber | 2. Masked inlet valve |
| C. Open combustion chamber | 3. Spark ignition |
| D. F-head combustion chamber | 4. Combustion induced swirl |
| | 5. M-chamber |

**Codes:**

| | A | B | C | D |
|---|---|---|---|---|
| (a) | 4 | 5 | 3 | 2 |
| (b) | 1 | 3 | 5 | 2 |
| (c) | 2 | 3 | 1 | 5 |
| (d) | 4 | 1 | 2 | 3 |

19. Consider the following statements comparing I.C. engines and gas turbines:
1. Gas turbines are simple, compact and light in weight.
2. Complete expansion of working substance is possible in I.C. engines and not in gas turbines.
3. There is flexibility in the design of different components of gas turbines as different processes take place in different components.
4. Even low grade fuels can be burnt in gas turbines.

Of these statement:
(a) 1, 2 and 3 are correct (b) 1, 3 and 4 and correct
(c) 2, 3 and 4 are correct (d) 1, 2 and 4 are correct

20. Which of the following factors increase detonation in the SI engine?
1. Increase spark advance.
2. Increased speed.
3. Increased air-fuel ratio beyond stoichiometric strength.
4. Increased compression ratio.

Select the correct answer using the codes given below:

**Codes:**

(a) 1 and 3 (b) 2 and 4
(c) 1, 2 and 4 (d) 1 and 4

21. Reference fuels for knock rating of SI engine fuels would include:
(a) iso-octane and alpha-methyl naphthalene.
(b) normal octane and aniline
(c) iso-octane and n-hexane
(d) *n*-heptane and is-octane

22. Consider the following measures:
1. Increasing the compression ratio.
2. Increasing the intake air temperature.
3. Increasing the length to diameter ratio of the cylinder.
4. Increasing the engine speed.

The measures necessary to reduce the tendency to knock in CI engines would include:
(a) 1, 2 and 3 (b) 1, 2 and 4
(c) 1, 3 and 4 (d) 2, 3 and 4

23. Match List I with List II and select the correct answer using the codes given below the Lists:

| List-I (Operating condition) | List-II (Approximate air fuel ratio) |
|---|---|
| A. Idling | 1. 16 |
| B. Part load operation | 2. 10 |
| C. Full load | 3. 12.5 |
| D. Cold start | 4. 3 |

**Codes:**

| | A | B | C | D |
|---|---|---|---|---|
| (a) | 2 | 1 | 3 | 4 |
| (b) | 1 | 2 | 4 | 3 |
| (c) | 2 | 1 | 4 | 3 |
| (d) | 1 | 2 | 3 | 4 |

24. Generally, in Bosch type fuel injection pumps, the quantity of fuel is increased or decreased with change in load, due to change in:
(a) timing of start of fuel injection
(b) timing of end fuel injection
(c) injection pressure of fuel
(d) velocity of flow of fuel

25. If the approximate average mean pressures during induction, compression, power and exhaust strokes of an internal combustion engine are respectively 15 kN/m$^2$ below atomosphere, 200 kN/m above atmosphere, 1000 kN/m$^2$ above atmosphere and 20 N/m2 above atmosphere, then the resultant mean effective pressure, in kN/m$^2$, is:
(a) 765 (b) 795
(c) 800 (d) 805

26. An automatic expansion valve is required to maintain constant:
(a) pressure in the evaporator
(b) temperature in the freezer
(c) pressure in the liquid line
(d) temperature in the condenser

27. Which one of following quantities is assumed constant for an internal combustion engine while estimating its friction power by extrapolation through Willan's line?
(a) Brake thermal efficiency
(b) Indicated thermal efficiency
(c) Mechanical efficiency
(d) Volumetric efficiency

28. Excessive pressure drop in liquid line in a refrigerating system causes:
(a) high condenser pressure
(b) flashing of the liquid refrigerant
(c) higher evaporator pressure
(d) under cooling of the liquid refrigerant

29. If V is the jet velocity Vo is the Vehicle velocity, the propulsive efficiency of a rocket is given by:

(a) $\dfrac{2(V_0/V_1)}{1+\left(\dfrac{V_0}{V_1}\right)}$ (b) $\dfrac{(V_0/V_1)}{1+\left(\dfrac{V_0}{V_1}\right)^2}$

(C) $\dfrac{V_0}{V_0+V_1}$ (D) $\dfrac{V_1}{V_0+V_1}$

30. Match List I with List II in respect of a chemical rocket engine and select the correct answer using the codes given below the List:

| List-I | List-II |
|---|---|
| A. Ethyl alcohol | 1. Liquid oxidiser |
| B. Nitrocellulose | 2. Liquid fuel |
| C. Ammonium perchlorate | 3. Solid oxidizer |
| D. Hydrogen peroxide | 4. Solid fuel |

**Codes:**

| | A | B | C | D |
|---|---|---|---|---|
| (a) | 1 | 3 | 2 | 4 |
| (b) | 2 | 3 | 4 | 1 |
| (c) | 2 | 4 | 3 | 1 |
| (d) | 4 | 1 | 2 | 3 |

31. Match List I with List II and select the correct answer using the codes given below the lists:

| List-I (Operating mode of SI engine) | List-II (Appropriate air-fuel ratio) |
|---|---|
| A. Idling | 1. 125 |
| B. Cold starting | 2. 9.0 |
| C. Cruising | 3. 16.0 |
| D. Maximum power | 4. 22.0 |
| | 5. 3.0 |

**Codes:**

| | A | B | C | D |
|---|---|---|---|---|
| (a) | 2 | 4 | 5 | 1 |
| (b) | 1 | 3 | 4 | 2 |
| (c) | 5 | 2 | 1 | 3 |
| (d) | 2 | 5 | 3 | 1 |

32. A gas engine has a swept volume of 300 cc and clearance volume of 25 cc. Its volumetric efficiency is 0.88 and mechanical efficiency is 0.90. What is the volume of the mixture taken in per stroke?
(a) 248 cc (b) 252 cc
(c) 264 cc (d) 286 cc

33. Knocking in the SI engine decreases in which one of the following orders of combustion chamber designs?
(a) F head, L head, I head
(b) T head, L head, F head
(c) I head, T head, F head
(d) F head, I head, T head.

34. The two reference fuels used for cetane rating are:
(a) cetane and isooctane
(b) cetane and tetraethyl lead
(c) cetane and *n*-heptane
(d) cetane and α-methyl naphthalene.

35. Match List I with List II, in respect of SI engines, and select the correct answer by using given below the lists:

| List-I | List-II |
|---|---|
| A. Highest useful compression ratio | 1. Ignitable mixture |
| B. Dopes | 2. Knock rating, of fuels |
| C. Limiting mixture strength | 3. Detonation |
| D. Delay period | 4. Chain of chemical reactions in combustion chamber |

**Codes:**

| | A | B | C | D |
|---|---|---|---|---|
| (a) | 2 | 3 | 1 | 4 |
| (b) | 3 | 2 | 1 | 4 |
| (c) | 2 | 3 | 4 | 1 |
| (d) | 3 | 4 | 2 | 1 |

36. By higher octane number of SI fuel, it is meant that the fuel has:
(a) higher heating value (b) higher flash point
(c) lower volatility (d) longer ignition delay

37. Which of the following factors would increase the probability of knock in the CI engines?
1. Long ignition delay of fuel
2. Low self ignition temperature of fuel
3. Low volatility of fuel
Select the correct answer using the codes given below:
**Codes:**
(a) 1, 2 and 3 (b) 1 and 2
(c) 1 and 3 (d) 2 and 3

38. Use of hermetically sealed compressor in a vapour compression refrigeration system results in:
(a) decrease in energy consumption
(b) increase in energy consumption
(c) increase in COP
(d) increase in pressure ratio

39. The correct sequence of the decreasing order of brake thermal efficiency of the three given basic type of IC engines is:
(a) 4 stroke CI engine, 4 stroke SI engine. 2 stroke SI engine
(b) 4 stroke SI engine, 4 stroke CI engine, 2 stroke SI engine
(c) 4 stroke CI engine, 2 stroke SI engine. 4 stroke SI engine
(d) 2 stroke SI engine, 4 stroke SI engine, 4 stroke CI engine.

40. Keeping other parameters constant brake power diesel engine can he increased by:
(a) decreasing the density of intake air
(b) increasing the temperature of intake air
(c) increasing the pressure of intake air
(d) decreasing the pressure of intake air.

41. The method of determination of indicated power of multi-cylinder SI engine is by the use of:
(a) Morse test (b) Prony brake test
(c) Motorist test (d) Heat balance test

42. Consider the following statements: As compared to turboprop, a turbojet
1. can operate at higher altitudes
2. can operate at higher flight velocities
3. is more fuel efficient at lower speeds
Of these statements:
(a) 1, 2 and 3 are correct
(b) 1 and 2 are correct
(c) 2 and 3 are correct
(d) 1 and 3 are correct.

43. Propulsion efficiency of a jet engine is given by (where *u* is flight velocity and V is jet velocity relative to aircraft):
(a) $2u/(V - u)$ (b) $(V + u)/2u$
(c) $2u/(V + u)$ (d) $(V - u)/2u$

44. In the Orsat flue gas analyser, ammoniacal cuprous chloride is used to absorb:
(a) $CO_2$ (b) CO
(c) $O_2$ (d) $N_2$

45. List I gives the different terms related to combustion while List II gives the outcome of the events that follow. Match List 1 with List II and select the correct answer.

| List-I | List-II |
|---|---|
| A. Association | 1. Pseudo shock |
| B. Dissociation | 2. Knock |
| C. Flame front | 3. Endothermic |
| D. Abnormal combustion | 4. Exothermic |

**Codes:**

| | A | B | C | D |
|---|---|---|---|---|
| (a) | 3 | 4 | 1 | 2 |
| (b) | 4 | 3 | 1 | 2 |
| (c) | 3 | 4 | 2 | 1 |
| (d) | 4 | 3 | 2 | 1 |

46. Which one of the following engines will have heavier flywheel than the remaining ones?
(a) 40 HP. four-stroke petrol engine running at 1500 ramp.
(b) 40 H.P. two-stroke petrol engine running at 1500 rmp.
(c) 40 H.P. two-stroke diesel engine running at 750 rmp.
(d) 40 H.P. four-stroke diesel engine running at 750 rmp.

47. Consider the following statements: Knock in the SI engine can be reduced by
1. supercharging
2. retarding the spark.
3. using a fuel of long straight chain structure.
4. increasing the engine speed.
Of these statement:
(a) 1 and 2 are correct (b) 2 and 3 are correct
(c) 1, 3 and 4 are collect (d) 2 and 4 are correct

48. Consider the following statements: The injector nozzle of a CI engine is required to inject fuel at a sufficiently high pressure in order to
1. be able to inject fuel in a chamber of high pressure at the end of the compression stroke.
2. inject fuel at high velocity to facilitate atomization.
3. ensure that penetration is not high.
Of the above statements
(a) 1 and 2 are correct (b) 1 and 3 are correct
(c) 2 and 3 are correct (d) 1, 2 and 4 are correct

49. Match List I with List II select the correct answer

| List-I (SI engine operating mode) | List-II (Desired air-fuel ratio) |
|---|---|
| A. Idling | 1. 13.0 |
| B. Cold starting | 2. 4.0 |
| C. Cruising | 3. 16.0 |
| D. Full throttle | 4. 9.0 |

**Codes:**

| | A | B | C | D |
|---|---|---|---|---|
| (a) | 4 | 3 | 2 | 1 |
| (b) | 2 | 4 | 1 | 3 |
| (c) | 4 | 2 | 1 | 3 |
| (d) | 2 | 4 | 3 | 1 |

50. Compensating jet in carburettor supplies almost constant amount of petrol at all speeds because:
(a) the jet area is automatically varied depending on the suction.
(b) the flow from the main jet is diverted to the compensating jet with increase in speed.
(c) the diameter of the jet is constant and the discharge coefficient is invariant.
(d) the flow is produced due to the static head in the float Chamber.

51. In the context of performance evaluation of I.C. Engine, match List I with List II and select the correct answer

| List-I (Parameter) | List-II (Equipment for measurement) |
|---|---|
| A. Brake power (B.H.P.) | 1. Bomb calorimeter |
| B. Engine speed | 2. Electrical techometer |
| C. Calorific value of fuel | 3. Hydraulic dynamometer |
| D. Exhaust emissions | 4. Flame ionisation detector |

**Codes:**

| | A | B | C | D |
|---|---|---|---|---|
| (a) | 3 | | 2 | 4 |
| (b) | 4 | 2 | 1 | 3 |
| (c) | 3 | 2 | 1 | 4 |
| (d) | 2 | 3 | 4 | 1 |

52. Consider the following statements:
In open cycle turbo jet engines used in military aircraft, reheating the exhaust gas from the turbine by burning more fuel is used to increase.
1. thrust.
2. the efficiency of engine.
3. the range of aircraft.
Of these statements:
(a) 1 and 3 are correct
(b) 1 and 2 are correct
(c) 2 and 3 are correct
(d) 1, 2 and 3 are correct.

53. In a turbo-jet engine, subsequent to heat addition to compressed air, to get the power output, the working substance is expanded in:
(a) turbine blades, which is essentially an isentropic process.
(b) turbine blades, which is polytropic process.
(c) exit nozzle, which is essentially an isentropic process.
(d) exit nozzle, which is a constant volume process.

54. Consider the following statements relating to rocket engines:
1. The combustion chamber in a rocket engine is directly analogous to the reservoir of a supersonic wind tunnel.
2. Stagnation conditions exist at the combustion chamber.
3. The exit velocities of exhaust gases are much higher than those in jet engines.
4. Efficiency of rocket engines is higher than that of jet engines.
Of these statements:
(a) 1, 3 and 4 are correct
(b) 1, 3 and 4 are correct
(c) 1, 2 and 3 are correct
(d) 1 and 4 are correct

55. Only rocket engines can be propelled to 'SPACE' because:
(a) they can generate very high thrust.
(b) they have high propulsion efficiency.
(c) these engines can work on several fuels.
(d) they are not air-breathing engines.

56. Items given in List I and List II pertain to gas analysis. Match List I with List II and select the correct answer.

| **List-I** | **List-II** |
|---|---|
| A. $CO_2$ | 1. Alkaline pyrogallol |
| B. Orsat apparatus | 2. KOH solution |
| C. CO | 3. Wet analysis |
| D. $O_2$ | 4. Ammoniacalcurprous chloride |
| | 5. Dry analysis |

**Codes:**

| | A | B | C | D |
|---|---|---|---|---|
| (a) | 2 | 3 | 1 | 4 |
| (b) | 1 | 3 | 2 | 4 |
| (c) | 1 | 5 | 4 | 2 |
| (d) | 2 | 5 | 4 | 1 |

57. Which of the following factors are responsible formation of $NO_X$ in spark ignition engine combustion:
1. Incomplete combustion
2. High temperature
3. Availability of answer.
(a) 2 and 3
(b) 1 and 2
(c) 1 and 3
(d) 1, 2 and 3

58. The presence of nitrogen in the products of combustion ensures that:
(a) complete combustion of fuel takes place
(b) incomplete combustion of fuel occurs
(c) dry products of combustion are analysed
(d) air is used for the combustion

59. For maximum specific output of a constant volume cycle (Otto cycle):
(a) the working fluid should he air
(b) the speed should he high
(c) suction temperature should be high
(d) temperature of the working fluid at the end of compression and expansion should be equal

60. A two-stroke engine has a speed of 750 rpm. A four stroke engine having an identical cylinder size runs at 1500 rpm. The theoretical output of the two-stroke engine will:
(a) be twice that of the four-stroke engine
(b) be half that of the four-stroke engine
(c) be the same as that of the four-stroke
(d) depend upon whether it is a C.I. or S.I. engine

61. For same power output and same compression ratio, as compared to two-stroke engines, four-stroke S.I. engines have:
(a) higher fuel consumption
(b) lower thermal efficiency
(c) higher exhaust temperatures
(d) higher thermal efficiency

62. In a SI Engine, which one of the following is the correct order of the fuels with increasing detonation tendency?
(a) Paraffins, Olefins,Naphthenes, Aeromatics
(b) Aeromatics, Naphthenes, Paraffins,Olefins
(c) Naphthenes, Olefins, Aeromatics, Paraffins
(d) Aeromatics, Naphthenes, Olefins, Paraffins

63. Consider the following statements: Detonation in the S.I. engine can be suppressed by
1. retarding the spark timing
2. increasing the engine speed.
3. using 10% rich mixture.
Of these statements:
(a) 1 and 3 are correct (b) 2 and 3 are correct
(c) 1, 2 and 3 are correct (d) 1 and 2 are correct

64. The pipes and fittings in an ammonia refrigeration system should be made of:
(a) cast street or wrought iron
(b) aluminium
(c) naval brass
(d) copper

65. A sample of moist air is at a temperature T and relative humidity 50%. A part of the moisture is removed adiabatically by using an absorbent. If the heat of adsorption is negligible, the resulting air will have the same:
(a) dry bulb temperature but a lower wet bulb temperature
(b) wet bulb temperature but a higher dry bulb temperature
(c) dry bulb temperature but a higher dry bulb temperature
(d) wet bulb temperature but a lower dry bulb temperature

66. Consider the following statements:
1. Volumetric efficiency of diesel engines is higher than that of SI engines
2. When a SI engine is throttled; its mechanical efficiency decreases.
3. Specific fuel consumption increases as the power capacity of the engine increases.
4. Inspite of higher compression ratios, the exhaust temperature in diesel engines is much lower than that in SI engines.
Of these statements:
(a) 1, 2, 3 and 4 are correct
(b) 1, 2 and 3 are correct
(c) 3 and 4 are correct
(d) 1, 2 and 4 are correct

67. Consider the following statements about a rocket engine:
    1. It is a very simple in construction and operation.
    2. It can attain very high vehicle velocity.
    3. It can operate for very long duration.

    Of these statements:
    (a) 1 and 3 are correct (b) 1 and 2 are correct
    (c) 2 and 3 are correct (d) 1, 2 and 3 are correct
68. In summer air-conditioning, the conditioned air passing through the space undergoes a process of:
    (a) sensible cooling
    (b) sensible heating
    (c) cooling and dehumidification
    (d) heating and humidification
69. Which of the following are the assumptions involved in the auto-ignition theory put forth for the onset of knock in SI engines?
    1. Flame velocity is normal before the onset of auto ignition.
    2. A number of end-gas elements auto ignite simultaneously.
    3. Preflame reactions are responsible for preparing the end-gas to ignite.

    Select the correct answer using the codes given below:
    (a) 1 and 2 (b) 1 and 3
    (c) 2 and 3 (d) 1, 2 and 3
70. Suppose, the mean body surface temperature of a certain unclothed person is 30°C, the mean temperature of surrounding surfaces is 21°C and the air within the room is at 32°C, 90 per cent RH, then the person will lose maximum body heat by:
    (a) convection
    (b) radiation
    (c) mass transfer
    (d) convection, radiation mass transfer
71. In some carburettors, meter rod and economiser device is used for:
    (a) cold starting (b) idling
    (c) power enrichment (d) acceleration
72. Which of the following pairs of engine and performance/characteristic is/are correctly matched?
    1. Turbojet: Efficiency increases with flight speed
    2. SI engine: Lowest specific fuel consumption
    3. Turboprop: Suitable for low flight speeds

    Select the correct answer using the codes given below:
    **Codes:**
    (a) 1 and 2 (b) 2 and 3
    (c) 1 and 3 (d) 2 alone
73. Which one of the following is the correct sequence of the position of the given components in a turboprop?
    (a) Propeller, Compressor, Turbine, Burner
    (b) Compressor, Propeller, Burner, Turbine
    (c) Propeller, Compressor, Burner, Turbine
    (d) Compressor, propeller, Turbine, Burner
74. Consider the following statements: The thrust of rocket engine depends upon:
    1. Effective jet velocity
    2. Weight of the rocket
    3. Rate of propellant consumption

    Of these statements:
    (a) 1 and 2 are correct (b) 1 and 3 are correct
    (c) 2 and 3 are correct (d) 1, 2 and 3 are correct
75. Consider the following statements: In a turbojet engine, thrust may be increased by:
    1. Increasing the jet velocity
    2. Increasing the mass flow rate of air.
    3. After burning of the fuel.

    Of these statements:
    (a) 1 and 2 are correct
    (b) 2 and 3 are correct
    (c) 1 and 3 are correct
    (d) 1, 2 and 3 are correct
76. The effective jet exit velocity from a rocket is 2700 m/s. The forward flight velocity is 1350 m/s. The propulsive efficiency of the unit is:
    (a) 200% (b) 100%
    (c) 66.666% (d) 33.333%
77. Consider the following emission of an IC engine:
    (1) CO (2) HC
    (3) $NO_x$ (4) Particulates

    Which of these emissions cause photochemical smog?
    (a) 1 and 4 (b) 1 and 2
    (c) 2 and 3 (d) 3 and 4
78. Velocity of flame propagation in the SI engine is maximum for a fuel-air mixture which is:
    (a) 10% richer than stocihiometric
    (b) Equal to stoichiometric
    (c) More than 10% richer than stocihiometric
    (d) 10% leaner than stoichiometric
79. Divided chamber diesel engines use lower injection pressures compared to open chamber engines because:
    (a) Pintle nozzles cannot withstand high injection pressures
    (b) High air swirl does not require high injection pressures for atomization
    (c) High injection pressures may cause over penetration
    (d) High injection pressure causes leakage of the fuel at the pintle
80. In a variable speed S.I. Engine, the maximum torque occurs at the maximum:
    (a) Speed
    (b) Brake power
    (c) Indicated power
    (d) Volumetric efficiency

81. In a domestic refrigerator, a capillary tube controls the flow of refrigerant form the:
(a) expansion valve to the evaporator
(b) evaporator to the thermostat
(c) condenser to the expansion valve
(d) condenser to the evaporator

82. The coefficient of performance (COP) of a refrigerator working as a heat pump is given by:
(a) $(COP)_{heat\ pump} = (COP)_{refrigerator} + 2$
(b) $(COP)_{heat\ pump} = (COP)_{refrigerator} + 1$
(c) $(COP)_{heat\ pump} = (COP)_{refrigerator} - 1$
(d) $(COP)_{heat\ pump} = (COP)_{refrigerator}$

83. Consider the following steps:
(a) Starting of compressor.
(b) Starting of cooling tower pump
(c) Starting of chiller water pump
(d) Starting of blower motor of cooling coil
The correct sequence of these steps in the starting of a central air conditioning plant using chilled water cooling coil, is:
(a) 3, 1, 4, 2
(b) 1, 3, 2, 4
(c) 3, 2, 1 ,4
(d) 1, 3, 4, 2

84. Match List-I with List-II and select the correct answer using the codes given below the Lists:

| List-I | List-II |
|---|---|
| A. Freon 12 | 1. Centrifugal systems |
| B. Freon 22 | 2. Low temperature cold storage |
| C. Feron 11 | 3. Window type units |
| D. Ammonia | 4. Ice plants |

**Codes:**

| | A | B | C | D |
|---|---|---|---|---|
| (a) | 3 | 2 | 1 | 4 |
| (b) | 3 | 1 | 2 | 4 |
| (c) | 1 | 2 | 4 | 3 |
| (d) | 1 | 3 | 4 | 2 |

85. The equivalent diameter (D) of a circular duct corresponding to a rectangular duct having longer side '*a*' and shorter side '*b*' the same velocity and pressure drop is given by:
(a) $D = \frac{a+b}{ab}$
(b) $D = \frac{ab}{a+b}$
(c) $D = \frac{(a+b)}{2ab}$
(d) $D = \frac{2ab}{a+b}$

86. Consider the following statements: During sensible heating
1. moisture content increases
2. dry bulb temperature and wet bulb temperature increase.
3. dew point remains constant.
4. relative humidity increases.
Of these statements
(a) 1, 2 and 3 are correct
(b) 2, 3 and 4 are correct
(c) 2 and 3 are correct
(d) 1 and 2 are correct

87. Which of the following statements are correct?
1. The human body can lose heat even if temperature is less than the atmospheric temperature.
2. Relative humidity can be increased by cooling dehumidification.
3. Warm air increases the rate of radiation of heat from the human body.
4. Increase in air movement increases the evaporation from the human body.
Select the correct answer using the codes given below:
(a) 1 and 4
(b) 2 and 4
(c) 1 and 3
(d) 2 and 3

88. When the air is passed through an insulated chamber having sprays of water maintained at a temperature higher than the dew point temperature of entering air but lower than its dry bulb temperature, then the air is said to be:
(a) cooled and humidified
(b) cooled and dehumidified
(c) heated and humidified
(d) heated and dehumidified

89. The atmosphere air at dry bulb temperature of 15°C enters a heating coil maintained at 40°C. The air leaves the heating coil at 25°C. The bypass factor of the heating coil is:
(a) 0.376
(b) 0.476
(c) 0.6
(d) 0.67

90. If the specific heats of dry air and water vapour are 1.00 kJ/kg-K and 1.88 kJ/kg-K respectively and the humidity ratio is 0.011, then the specific heat of moist air at 25°C and 50% relative humidity will be
(a) 1.0207 kJ/kg – K
(b) 1.869 kJ/kg – K
(c) 1.891 kJ/kg– K
(d) 0.9793 kJ/kg –K

91. Consider the following factors:
(a) Wind velocity
(b) Type of a activity
(c) Indoor design conditions
(d) Door openings
Occupancy load in cooling load calculation depends upon:
(a) 1 and 2
(b) 1 and 3
(c) 1 and 4
(d) 2 and 3

92. Match List-I (Basic components of Aqua ammonia refrigeration system) with List-II functions of the components in the system and select the correct Answer using the codes given below the lists:

| List-I | List-II |
|---|---|
| A. Generator | 1. Dehydration |
| B. Analyser | 2. Removal of vapour from strong aqua-ammonia solution |
| C. Rectifier | 3. Producing dry ammonia vapour by removing traces for water particles completely |
| D. Receiver | 4. Storage of high pressure liquid ammonia |
| | 5. Formation of liquid ammonia from high pressure vapours. |

**Codes:**

| | A | B | C | D |
|---|---|---|---|---|
| (a) | 3 | 1 | 2 | 5 |
| (b) | 5 | 3 | 4 | 2 |
| (c) | 1 | 3 | 2 | 5 |
| (d) | 2 | 1 | 3 | 4 |

93. A condenser of refrigeration system rejects heat at rate of 120 kW.While its compressor consumes a power of 30 kW. The coefficient of performance of the system would be:
(a) 1/4 (b) 1/3
(d) 3 (d) 4

94. Waste heat can be effectively used in which one of the following refrigeration system?
(a) Vapour compression cycle
(b) Vapour absorption cycle
(c) Air refrigeration cycle
(d) Vortex refrigeration system

95. In aircraft, air-refrigeration cycle is used because of:
(a) low unit weight per tonne of refrigeration
(b) high heat transfer rate
(c) lower temperature at high-altitudes
(d) higher coefficient of performance

96. A pressure gauge on discharge side of a refrigerant compressor reads too high. The reason could be:
1. Lack cooling water
2. water temperature being high
3. Dirty condenser surface
4. Refrigerant temperature being too high
Of these reasons:
(a) 1, 2 and 4 are valid (b) 1, 2 and 3 are valid
(c) 2, 3 and 4 are valid (d) 1, 2 and 4 are valid.

97. Consider the following statements:
A decrease in evaporator temperature of a vapour compression machine lead to:
1. an increase in refrigerating effect
2. an increase in specific volume of vapour
3. a decrease in volumetric efficiency of compressor
4. an increase in compressor work.
Of these statements:
(a) 1, 3 and 4 are correct (b) 1, 2 and 3 are correct
(c) 2, 3 and 4 are correct (d) 2 and 4 are correct.

98. Match List-I with Li.st-II and select the correct answer using the codes given below the lists:

| List-I | List-II |
|---|---|
| A. Air | 1. Direct contact freezing of food |
| B. Ammonia | 2. Centrifugil compressor system |
| C. Carbon dioxide | 3. Large industrial temperature installation |
| D. Refrigerant-11 | 4. Automotive air-conditioners. |
| | 5. Aircraft refrigeration |

**Codes:**

| | A | B | C | D |
|---|---|---|---|---|
| (a) | 4 | 3 | 1 | 2 |
| (b) | 5 | 3 | 1 | 2 |
| (c) | 2 | 4 | 3 | 5 |
| (d) | 5 | 3 | 2 | 1 |

99. Consider the following statements:
In psychrometry, wet-bulb temperature is a measure enthalpy of moist air, so that in the psychrometric chart:
1. the constant enthalpy lines are also constant wet bulb temperature lines.
2. the wet-bulb and dry bulb temperature are same at any condition
3. the wet-bulb and dry-bulb temperature are equal at saturation condition.
Of these statements:
(a) 1 alone is correct
(b) 1 and 2 are correct
(c) 1 and 3 are correct
(d) 2 and 3 are correct

100. At 100% relative humidity, the wet bulb temperature is:
(a) more than dew point temperature
(b) same as dew point temperature
(c) less than dew point temperature
(d) equal to ambient temperature.

101. During the adiabatic cooling of moist-air:
(a) DBT remains constant
(b) Specific humidity remains constant
(c) relative humidity remains constant
(d) WBT remains constant

102. When a stream of moist air is passed over a cold and dry cooling coil such that no condensation takes place, then the air stream will get cooled along the line of
(a) constant wet bulb temperature
(b) constant dew point temperature
(c) constant relative humidity
(d) constant enthalpy

103. For large tonnage (more than 200 tons) air-conditioning applications, which one of the following types of compressors is recommended?
(a) Reciprocating (b) Rotating
(c) Centrifugal (d) Screw

104. In a cooling tower, "approach" is the temperature difference between the:
(a) hot inlet water and cold outlet water
(b) hot inlet water and WBT
(c) cold outlet water and WBT
(d) DBT and WBT.

105. When the discharge pressure is too high in refrigeration system, high pressure control is installed to:
(a) stop the cooling fan.
(b) stop the water circulating pump
(c) regulate the flow of cooling water
(d) stop the compressor.

106. Consider the following statements:
In the case of a vapour compression machine, if the condensing temperature of the refrigerant is closer to the critical temperature, then there will be:
1. excessive power consumption
2. high compression
3. large volume flow
Of these statements:
(a) 1, 2 and 3 are correct (b) 1 and 2 are correct
(c) 2 and 3 are correct (d) 1 and 3 are correct

107. Hydrogen is essential in an electrolux refrigeration system, because:
(a) it acts as a catalyst in the evaporator
(b) the reaction between hydrogen and ammonia is endothermic in evaporator and exothermic in absorber
(c) the cooled hydrogen leaving the heat exchanger cools the refrigerant entering the evaporator
(d) it helps in maintaining a low partial pressure for the evaporating ammonia

108. In an ideal refrigeration (reversed Carnot) cycle, the condenser and evaporator temperatures are 27°C and –13°C respectively. The COP of this cycle would be'
(a) 6.5 (b) 7.5
(c) 10.5 (d) 15.0

109. A single-stage vapour compression refrigeration system cannot be used to produce ultralow temperatures because:
(a) refrigerants for ultra-low temperatures are not available
(b) lunbricants for ultra-low temperatures are not available
(c) volumetric efficiency will decrease considerably
(d) heat leakage into the system will be excessive

110. Vapour absorption refrigeration system works using the:
(a) ability of a substances to get easily condensed or evaporated
(b) ability of a vapour to get compressed or expanded
(c) affinity of a substance for another substance
(d) absorptivity of a substance.

111. Two summer air-conditioning systems with non-zero by pass factor are proposed for a room with a known sensible and latent heat load.. System A operates with ventilation but system B operates without ventilation. Then the:
(a) bypass factor of system A must be less than the bypass factor of system B
(b) bypass factor of system A must be more than the bypass factor of system B
(c) apparatus dew point for system A must be lower than the apparatus dew point for system B.
(d) apparatus dew point for system A must be higher than the apparatus dew point for system B.

112. Evaporative air-cooler used effectively when:
(a) dry-bulb temperature is very close to the wet bulb temperature
(b) dry-bulb temperature is high and relative humidity is high
(c) dry-bulb temperature is low and relative humidity is high
(d) dry-bulb temperature is high and the relative humidity is low.

113. The minimum temperature to which water can be cooled in a cooling tower is:
(a) the dew point temperature of air
(b) the wet-bulb temperature of air
(c) the dry bulb temperature of air
(d) the ambient air temperature

114. In a vapour compression refrigeration system, throttle valve is used in place of an expander because:
(a) It considerably reduces the system weight.
(b) It improves the COP, as the condenser is small.
(c) The positive work in isentropic expansion of liquid is very small.
(d) It leads to significant cost reduction.

115. 2000 cc. of air takes 1½ minutes to pass through a standard Specimen of sand (5.08 cm high and 5.08 cm in dia.). The manometer indicates pressure as 5 g/cm$^2$. In this case the permeability number is:
(a) 30 (b) 42
(c) 51 (d) 67

116. A spherical drop of molten metal of radius 2 mm was found to solidify in 10 seconds. A similar drop of radius 4 mm would solidify in:
(a) 14.14 second (b) 20 seconds
(c) 18.30 second (d) 40 seconds

117. The voltage-current characteristics of a DC generator for arc welding is a straight line between an open-circuit voltage of 80 V and short-circuit current of 300 A. The generator settings for maximum arc power will be:
(a) 80 V and 150 A (b) 40 V and 300 A
(c) 40 V and 150 V (d) V and 300 A

118. Consider the following statements:
1. Practically all common refrigerants have approximately the same COP and power requirement.
2. Ammonia mixes freely with lubricating oil and this helps lubrication of compressors.
3. Dielectric strength of refrigerants is an important property in hermetically sealed compressor units.
4. Leakage of ammonia can detected by halide torch method.

Of these statements
(a) 1, 2, and 4 are correct (b) 2 and 4 are correct
(c) 1, 3 and 4 are correct (d) 1 and 3 are correct

119. The most commonly used method for the design of duct size is the:
(a) velocity reduction method
(b) equal friction method
(c) static regain method.
(d) dual or double dust method.

120. The refrigerant used for absorption refrigerators working heat from solar collectors is mixture of water and:
(a) Carbon dioxide (b) Sulphur dioxide
(c) Lithium bromide (d) Freon 12

## ANSWERS WITH EXPLANATIONS

1. (b) 2. (b) 3. (a) 4. (c) 5. (d)
6. (d) 7. (c) 8. (a) 9. (b) 10. (b)
11. (a) 12. (c) 13. (a) 14. (d) 15. (a)
16. (a) 17. (a) 18. (a) 19. (a) 20. (d)
21. (d) 22. (b) 23. (a) 24. (b)

25. (a) Resultant m.e.p. = 1000 – 200 – (15 + 20)
$$= 765 \text{ kN/M}^2$$

26. (d) 27. (b) 28. (d) 29. (a) 30. (c)
31. (d)

32. (c) $\eta_{vol} = 1 + \dfrac{V_c}{V_s} = 0.88$

$$V_c + V_s = 0.88\ V_s = 0.88 \times 300 = 264 \text{ c.c.}$$

33. (a) 34. (d) 35. (b) 36. (d) 37. (b)
38. (a) 39. (a) 40. (c) 41. (a) 42. (b)
43. (c) 44. (b) 45. (d) 46. (d) 47. (d)
48. (a) 49. (a) 50. (b) 51. (c) 52. (b)
53. (a) 54. (c) 55. (d) 56. (d) 57. (a)
58. (d) 59. (a) 60. (c) 61. (d) 62. (d)
63. (d) 64. (a) 65. (c) 66. (a) 67. (b)
68. (b) 69. (d) 70. (d) 71. (b) 72. (c)
73. (c) 74. (b) 75. (a)

76. (c) Propulsive efficiency,
$$\eta_P = \frac{2v_f}{v_g + v_f} = \frac{2 \times 1350}{2700 + 1350} = \frac{2}{3} = 66.666\%$$

77. (c) 78. (a) 79. (b) 80. (c) 81. (d)
82. (b) 83. (c) 84. (a) 85. (d) 86. (c)
87. (a) 88. (a)

89. (c) $\text{BPF} = \dfrac{40 - 25}{40 - 15} = \dfrac{15}{25} = 0.6$

90. (a) $c_p$ of moist air = $c_p$ of dry air + humidity ratio × $c_p$ of water vapour
$$= 1.00 + 0.011 \times 1.88$$
$$= 1.0207 \text{ kJ/kg.K}$$

91. (d) 92. (d)

93. (d) $Q_r = 120$ kW, $W_c = 30$ kW,
$$\text{COP} = \frac{Q_r}{W_c} = \frac{120}{30} = 4$$

94. (b) 95. (a) 96. (b) 97. (a) 98. (b)
99. (c) 100. (c) 101. (d) 102. (b) 103. (c)
104. (b) 105. (c) 106. (c) 107. (d)

108. (a) $\text{COP} = \dfrac{T_2}{T_1 - T_2} = \dfrac{260}{300 - 260} = \dfrac{260}{40} = 6.5$

109. (a) 110. (c) 111. (c) 112. (d) 113. (a)
114. (c)

115. (d) Permeability number, $P = \dfrac{Vh}{pAt}$

$V = 2000$ c.c., $t = 1.5$ min, $h = 5.08$ cm, $d = 5.08$ cm, $p = 5 \text{ g/cm}^2$
$$P = \frac{2000 \times 5.08}{5 \times \frac{\pi}{4}(5.08)^2 \times 1.5} = 66.83 = 67$$

116. (d) Solidification time for a sphere,
$$t \alpha \left(\frac{V}{A}\right)^2$$
$$\frac{V}{A} = \frac{\left(\frac{4}{3}\pi r^3\right)}{4\pi r^2} = \frac{r}{3}$$
$$t \propto r^2$$
$$\frac{t_2}{t_1} = \left(\frac{4}{3}\right)^2 = 4$$
$$t_2 = 4 \times 10 = 40 \text{ s}$$

117. (c) $V = V_0\left(1 - \dfrac{I}{I_s}\right) = 80\left(1 - \dfrac{I}{300}\right)$

For V = 40 V
$$40 = 80\left(1 - \frac{I}{300}\right)$$
$$I = 150 \text{ A}$$

118. (d) 119. (a) 120. (c)

❑❑❑

# 6. Fluid Mechanics

- Fluid mechanics is the branch of physics which involves the study of fluids and the forces on them. Fluid mechanics can be divided into fluid statics, the study of fluids at rest; and fluid dynamics, the study of the effect of forces on fluid motion.
- It is a branch of continuum mechanics, a subject which models matter without using the information that it is made out of atoms; that is, it models matter from a macroscopic viewpoint rather than from microscopic.
- Fluid mechanics, especially fluid dynamics, is an active field of research with many problems that are partly or wholly unsolved.
- Fluid mechanics can be mathematically complex, and can best be solved bynumerical methods, typically using computers. A modern discipline, called computational fluid dynamics (CFD), is devoted to this approach to solving fluid mechanics problems.
- Particle image velocimetry, an experimental method for visualizing and analyzing fluid flow, also takes advantage of the highly visual nature of fluid flow.
- The study of fluid mechanics goes back at least to the days of ancient Greece, when Archimedes investigated fluid statics and buoyancy and formulated his famous law known now as the Archimedes' principle, which was published in his work On Floating Bodies - generally considered to be the first major work on fluid mechanics.
- Fluid statics or hydrostatics is the branch of fluid mechanics that studies fluids at rest. It embraces the study of the conditions under which fluids are at rest in stable equilibrium; and is contrasted with fluid dynamics, the study of fluids in motion.
- Hydrostatics is fundamental to hydraulics, the engineering of equipment for storing, transporting and using fluids. It is also relevant to geophysics and astrophysics to meteorology, to medicine and many other fields.
- Hydrostatics offers physical explanations for many phenomena of everyday life, such as why atmospheric pressure changes with altitude, why wood and oil float on water, and why the surface of water is always flat and horizontal whatever the shape of its container.
- Fluid dynamics is a subdiscipline of fluid mechanics that deals with fluid flow—the natural science of fluids in motion.
- It has several sub disciplines itself, including aerodynamics and hydrodynamics . Fluid dynamics has a wide range of applications, including calculating forces and moments on aircraft, determining the mass flow rate of petroleum through pipelines, predicting weather patterns, understanding nebulae in interstellar space and modelling fission weapon detonation.
- Some of its principles are even used in traffic engineering, where traffic is treated as a continuous fluid, and crowd dynamics.
- Fluid dynamics offers a systematic structure—which underlies these practical disciplines—that embraces empirical and semi-empirical laws derived from flow measurement and used to solve practical problems.
- The solution to a fluid dynamics problem typically involves calculating various properties of the fluid, such as velocity, pressure, density, and temperature, as functions of space and time.
- Like any mathematical model of the real world, fluid mechanics makes some basic assumptions about the materials being studied. These assumptions are turned into equations that must be satisfied if the assumptions are to be held true.
- Fluid mechanics assumes that every fluid obeys the following:

  – Conservation of mass
  – Conservation of energy
  – Conservation of momentum
- Further, it is often useful (at subsonic conditions) to assume a fluid is incompressible – that is, the density of the fluid does not change.
- Similarly, it can sometimes be assumed that the viscosity of the fluid is zero (the fluid is inviscid). Gases can often be assumed to be inviscid. If a fluid is viscous, and its flow contained in some way (e.g. in a pipe), then the flow at the boundary must have zero velocity.
- Fluids are composed of molecules that collide with one another and solid objects. The continuum assumption, however, considers fluids to be continuous. That is, properties such as density, pressure, temperature, and velocity are taken to be well-defined at "infinitely" small points, defining a REV (Reference Element of Volume), at the geometric order of the distance between two adjacent molecules of fluid.
- Properties are assumed to vary continuously from one point to another, and are averaged values in the REV. The fact that the fluid is made up of discrete molecules is ignored.
- The continuum hypothesis is basically an approximation, in the same way planets are approximated by point particles when dealing with celestial mechanics, and therefore results in approximate solutions.

- Consequently, assumption of the continuum hypothesis can lead to results which are not of desired accuracy. However, under the right circumstances, the continuum hypothesis produces extremely accurate results.
- Those problems for which the continuum hypothesis does not allow solutions of desired accuracy are solved using statistical mechanics. To determine whether or not to use conventional fluid dynamics or statistical mechanics, the Knudsen number is evaluated for the problem.
- The Knudsen number is defined as the ratio of the molecular mean free path length to a certain representative physical length scale.
- This length scale could be, for example, the radius of a body in a fluid. Problems with Knudsen numbers at or above one are best evaluated using statistical mechanics for reliable solutions.
- The Navier–Stokes equations are the set of equations that describe the motion of fluid substances such as liquids and gases.
- These equations state that changes in momentum(force) of fluid particles depend only on the external pressure and internal viscous forces (similar to friction) acting on the fluid.
- Thus, the Navier–Stokes equations describe the balance of forces acting at any given region of the fluid.
- The Navier–Stokes equations are differential equations which describe the motion of a fluid. Such equations establish relations among the rates of change of the variables of interest.
- This means that solutions of the Navier–Stokes equations for a given physical problem must be sought with the help of calculus. In practical terms only the simplest cases can be solved exactly in this way.
- These cases generally involve non-turbulent, steady flow (flow does not change with time) in which the Reynolds number is small.
- A wattmeter is essentially an inherent combination of an ammeter and a voltmeter and, therefore, consists of two coils known as current coil (CC) and potential coil (PC).
- Power in ac circuit is given by $P = VI\cos\phi$ where $V$ and I are rms values of voltage and current respectively and $f$ is the phase angle between $V$ and $I$. The fact that the power factor ($\cos\phi$) is involved in the expression for power, we cannot measure power in ac circuits by using an ammeter and a voltmeter.
- Since deflecting torque in a dynamometer type wattmeter is directly proportional to true power in both cases dc and ac and the instrument is spring controlled, the scale of the instrument is uniform.
- In order to cause the resultant flux in shunt magnet to lag in phase by exactly 90° behind the applied voltage, one or more copper rings, known as copper shading bands, are provided on one limb of the shunt magnet.
- In the two wattmeter method of measurement of power in a 3-phase circuit the readings of two wattmeters depends upon the pf of load. One of the wattmeter gives negative reading when the phase angle f of the load varies from 60° to 90°
- One of the two wattmeters, in a two wattmeter method of measuring power in a balanced 3-phase circuit, will keep showing zero as the load is varied if and only if the power factor of the load remains constant at 0.5. The reading of other wattmeter will vary with the variation in load.
- Wattmeter reading for inductive loads are given as

  $$W_1 = V_L I_L \cos(30^\circ - \phi)$$
  $$W_2 = V_L I_L \cos(30^\circ + \phi)$$

  For unity pf load, both wattmeters give equal readings, each equal to half the total power of the circuit.

  For pf of load 0.5 (lagging). Wattmeter $W_1$ will give total power of load and wattmeter $W_2$ gives zero reading.

  For zero pf load. The readings of two wattmeters are equal but of opposite sign.

  So wattmeter $W_2$ gives – ve reading when phase angle $\phi$ varies from 60° to 90°. For obtaining the reading of wattmeter$W_2$ either the connection of current coil or pressure coil should be changed and readings obtained after the reversal of connections should be subtracted from the other wattmeter reading in order to get the total power.
- The essential difference between an energy meter and a wattmeter is that the former is fitted with some type of registration mechanism whereby all the instantaneous readings of power are summed over a definite period of time whereas the latter indicates the value of power at particular instant when it is read.
- The rotating system of the energy meter is made as small as possible so that frictional torque is reduced to the minimum.
- An aluminium disc is usually preferred to a copper disc in order to have resistance per unit weight smaller.
- The number of revolutions made by the aluminium disc for 1 kWh of energy consumption is called the meter constant of an energy meter.
- In some energy meters, the disc continues rotating when the potential coils are excited but with no load current flow. This defect is known as creeping.
- Creeping error can be avoided by either cutting two holes (or slots) in the disc on the opposite sides of the spindle or attaching a small piece of iron wire to the edge of the disc.
- The disc rotates continuously in the series magnetic field under load conditions and so there is a dynamically induced emf in the disc which induces eddy currents. Due to interaction of eddy currents with the field of series magnet a braking torque proportional to the square of the energizing current is developed. The braking torque so developed is called the self-braking torque.

# MULTIPLE CHOICE QUESTIONS

1. Hydrodynamic and thermal boundary layer thickness are equal for Prandtl number:
(a) equal to zero
(b) less than 1
(c) equal to 1
(d) more than 1
2. In a rotameter as the flow rate increases, the float:
(a) rotates at higher speed
(b) rotates at lower speed
(c) rises in the tube
(d) drops in the tube
3. A two-dimensional fluid flow is described by the velocity components $u = 5x^3, v = -15x^2 y$. The stream function at point will be:
(a) $2 \text{ m}^2/\text{s}$ (b) $2 \text{ m}^3/\text{s}$
(c) $10 \text{ m}^3/\text{s}$ (b) $20 \text{ m}^3/\text{s}$
4. Match the following:

| List-I | List-II |
|---|---|
| A. Circular sewer maximum discharge | 1. $y = 0.938$ D |
| B. Maximum velocity in circular sewer | 2. $y = 0.81$ D |
| C. Triangular Channel | 3. $y_c = \frac{4}{5}\text{E}, \frac{v_c^2}{2g} = \frac{y_c}{4}$ |
| D. Bourdon gauge | 4. $y_c = \frac{2}{3}\text{E}, \frac{v_c^2}{2g} = \frac{y_c}{4}$ |

**Codes:**

| | A | B | C | D |
|---|---|---|---|---|
| (a) | 4 | 3 | 2 | 1 |
| (b) | 3 | 4 | 1 | 2 |
| (c) | 2 | 3 | 1 | 4 |
| (d) | 1 | 4 | 2 | 3 |

5. Aging of pipe implies:
(a) pipe becoming smoother with time
(b) relative roughness decreasing periodically
(c) increase in absolute roughness periodically with time
(d) increase in absolute roughness linearly with time
6. A nozzle has velocity head at outlet of 10m. If it is kept vertical the height reached by the stream is:
(a) 100 m (b) 10 m
(c) $\sqrt{10}$ m (d) $\frac{1}{\sqrt{10}}$
7. Laminar sub-layer may develop during flow over a flat-plate. It exists in:
(a) laminar zone
(b) transition zone
(c) turbulent zone
(d) laminar and transition zone
8. The velocity components for a two dimensional incompressible flow of a fluid are $u = x - 4y$ and $v = -y - 4x$. It can be concluded that:
(a) the flow does not satisfy the continuity equation
(b) the flow is rotational
(c) the flow is irrotational
(d) none of the above
9. A $\frac{1}{25}$ model of a ship it to be tested for estimating the wave drag. If the speed of the prototype is 1.0 m/s, then the speed at which the model must be tested is:
(a) 0.04 m/s (b) 0.2 m/s
(c) 5.0 m/s (d) 25.0 m/s
10. In which of the following cases frictional drag is predominating?
1. Tennis ball 2. Parachute
3. Arrow 4. Cyclist
(a) 1 and 2 only (b) 2 and 3
(c) 2, 3 and 4 only (d) 1, 2 and 3 only.
11. Match the following:

| List-I | List-II |
|---|---|
| A. Wave drage of a ship | 1. Cavitation in pumps and turbines |
| B. Pressure coefficient | 2. $\rho r.rL^3 r$ |
| C. Thoma numbers | 3. Re = 0.1 |
| D. Stokes Law | 4. $\frac{\Delta p}{\rho V^2/2}$ |

**Codes:**

| | A | B | C | D |
|---|---|---|---|---|
| (a) | 1 | 2 | 4 | 3 |
| (b) | 4 | 3 | 1 | 2 |
| (c) | 1 | 3 | 4 | 2 |
| (d) | 2 | 4 | 1 | 3 |

12. The terminal velocity of small sphere falling in a viscous fluid is:
(a) proportional to the diameter of the sphere
(b) inversely proportional to the viscosity of the fluid
(c) inversely proportional to the diameter of the sphere
(d) proportional to the density of the fluid.
13. Which of the following statement is true?
(a) For an ideal fluid $\mu = 0$. $\rho = 0$ constant, K = 0
(b) A floating body is in stable, unstable or neutral equilibrium according to as the metacentric height is zero, positive or negative.
(c) The exact analysis of viscous flow problems can be made by Euler's equation
(d) The most economical diameter of a pipe is the one for which the annual fixed cost and annual power cost (to overcome friction) are minimum.

14. Which of the following statements is false?
(a) The lift force (per unit length) on a body depends on the density of the fluid
(b) For laminar flow through a pipe, the loss of head is directly proportional to velocity as well as viscosity of fluid
(c) A hydraulic jump occurs when a supercritical flow comes across sub critical flow
(d) At the stall point for the airfoil, the lift is minimum and the drag decreases sharply beyond it.

15. Which of the following is not a dimensionless group?
(a) $\frac{\Delta p}{\rho N^2 D^2}$ (b) $\frac{gH}{N^2 D^2}$
(c) $\frac{\rho \omega D^2}{\mu}$ (d) $\frac{\Delta p}{\rho V^3}$

16. For a real fluid moving with uniform velocity, the pressure:
(a) Depends upon depth and orientation
(b) is independent of depth but depends upon orientation
(c) is independent of orientation but depends upon depth
(d) is independent of both depth and orientation

17. Consider the following assumptions:
1. Steady flow
2. Inviscid flow
3. Flow along a stream line
4. Conservative force field
For an ideal fluid, which of the statements are correct?
(a) 1 and 2 (b) 1, 2 and 4
(c) 2, 3 and 4 (d) 1, 3 and 4

18. The vertical component of force on a curved surface submerged in a static liquid is to the:
(a) mass of the liquid above the curved surface
(b) weight of the liquid above curved surface
(c) product of pressure at C.G. multiplied by the area of the curved surface
(d) product of pressure at C.G. multiplied by the projected area of the curved surface

19. A pipe friction test shows that, over the range of speeds used for the test, the non-dimensional friction factor '*f*' varies inversely with Reynolds Number. From this, one can conclude that the:
(a) fluid must be compressible
(b) fluid must be ideal
(c) pipe must be smooth
(d) flow must be laminar

20. Chezy's formula is given by (*m, i,* C and V are, respectively, the hydraulic mean depth, slope of the channel, Chezy's constant and average velocity of flow)
(a) $V = i\sqrt{mC}$ (b) $V = C\sqrt{im}$
(c) $V = m\sqrt{iC}$ (d) $V = \sqrt{miC}$

21. The standard sea level atmospheric pressure is equivalent to:
(a) 10.2 m of freshwater of $\rho = 998$ kg/m$^3$
(b) 10.2 m of salt water $\rho = 1025$ kg/m$^3$
(c) 25.5 m of kerosene of $\rho = 800$ kg/m$^3$
(d) 6.4 m of carbon tetrachloride of $\rho = 1590$ kg/m$^3$

22. Which one of the following represents equilibrium of a static fluid? (Symbols have the usual meaning)
(a) $\frac{dp}{dz} = -\frac{\rho}{g}$ (b) $\frac{dp}{g} = -\frac{dz}{\rho}$
(c) $\rho\, dp = -\frac{dz}{g}$ (c) $\frac{dp}{\rho} = -g\, dz$

23. A tank with four equal vertical faces of width/ and depth *h* is filled up with a liquid. If the force on any vertical side is equal to the forceat the bottom, then value of $\frac{h}{l}$ will be:
(a) 2 (b) $\sqrt{2}$
(c) 1 (d) $\frac{1}{2}$

24. Match. List-I (Physical properties of fluid) with List-II (Dimension/Definitions) and select the correct answer using codes given below the Lists:

| **List-I** | **List-II** |
|---|---|
| A. Absolute viscosity | 1. $\frac{du}{dy}$ is constant |
| B. Kinematic viscosity | 2. Newton per metre |
| C. Newtonian fluid | 3. Poise |
| D. Surface tension | 4. $\frac{\text{Stress}}{\text{Strain}}$ constant |
| | 5. Strokes |

**Codes:**

| | A | B | C | D |
|---|---|---|---|---|
| (a) | 5 | 3 | 2 | 1 |
| (b) | 3 | 5 | 2 | 4 |
| (c) | 5 | 3 | 4 | 2 |
| (d) | 3 | 5 | 1 | 2 |

25. If the governing equation for a flow field is given by $\nabla^2\phi = 0$ and the velocity is given by $\vec{V} = \nabla\phi$, the:
(a) $\nabla \times \vec{V} = 0$ (b) $\nabla \times \vec{V} = 1$
(c) $\nabla^2 \times \vec{V} = 1$ (d) $(\vec{V}.\nabla)\vec{V} = \frac{\partial \vec{V}}{\partial t}$

26. Which one of the following equations represents the continuity equation for steady compressible fluid flow?
(a) $\nabla.\rho\overline{V} + \frac{\partial \rho}{\partial t} = 0$ (b) $\nabla.\rho\overline{V} + \frac{\partial \rho}{\partial t} = 0$
(c) $\nabla.\overline{V} = 0$ (d) $\nabla.\rho\overline{V} = 0$

27. A liquid of specific gravity 0.82 flows with a velocity 4.4 m/s. Its velocity head is:
(a) 0.82 m
(b) 4.43 m
(c) 1 m
(d) 19.6 m

28. Match List-I with List-II and select the correct answer using the codes given below the Lists:

| List-I | List-II |
|---|---|
| A. Orifice meter | 1. Measurement of flow in a channel |
| B. Broad creasted weir | 2. Measurement of velocity in a pipe/ channel |
| C. Pitol tube | 3. Measurement of flow in a pipe of may inclination |
| D. Rotameter | 4. Measurement of upward flow in a vertical pipe |

**Codes:**

| | A | B | C | D |
|---|---|---|---|---|
| (a) | 3 | 1 | 4 | 2 |
| (b) | 1 | 3 | 2 | 4 |
| (c) | 3 | 1 | 2 | 4 |
| (d) | 1 | 3 | 4 | 2 |

29. Decrease in temperature, in general, results in:
(a) an increase in viscosities of both gases and liquids
(b) a decrease in the viscosity of liquids and gases
(c) an increase in the viscosity of liquids and an decrease in that of gases
(d) a decrease in the viscosity of liquids and an increase in that of gases

30. Consider the following statements:
(a) Streak line indicates instantaneous position of particles of fluid passing through a point.
(b) Streamlines are paths traced by a fluid particle with constant velocity.
(c) Fluid particles cornot cross streamlines irrespective of the type of flow.
(d) Streamlines converge as the fluid is accelerated, and diverge when retarded.
Which of these statements are correct?
(a) 1 and 4
(b) 1, 3 and 4
(c) 1, 2, and 4
(d) 2 and 3

31. If the diameter of a capillary tube is doubled, the capillary-rise will become:
(a) $\sqrt{2}$ times less
(b) double
(c) half
(d) $\sqrt{2}$ times more

32. A stepped pipeline with four different cross-sections discharges water at the rate of 2 litres per second. Match List-I (Areas of pipe is sq. cm) with List-II (velocities of water in cm/s) and select the correct answer using the codes given below the list:

| List-I | List-II |
|---|---|
| A. 500 | 1. 4 |
| B. 100 | 2. 5 |
| C. 400 | 3. 10 |
| D. 200 | 4. 15 |
| | 5. 20 |

**Codes:**

| | A | B | C | D |
|---|---|---|---|---|
| (a) | 5 | 1 | 2 | 3 |
| (b) | 1 | 4 | 2 | 3 |
| (c) | 1 | 4 | 3 | 4 |
| (d) | 3 | 2 | 5 | 1 |

33. Fluid flow rate Q, can be measured easily with the help of a venturi tube, in which the difference of two pressures, ΔP, measured at an upstream point and at the smallest cross-section of the tube, is used. If a relation $\Delta P \propto Q^n$ exists, then n is equal to:
(a) $\frac{1}{3}$ (b) $\frac{1}{2}$
(c) 1 (d) 2

34. The drag force D on a certain object in a certain flow is a function of the coefficient of viscosity p, the flow speed, V and the body dimension L (for geometrically similar objects); then D is proportional to:
(a) $L\mu V$ (b) $\frac{\mu^2 V^2}{L^2}$
(c) $\mu^2 V^2 L^2$ (d) $\frac{\mu L}{V}$

35. A metallic piece weighs 80 N in air and 60 N in water. The relative density of the metallic piece is about:
(a) 8 (b) 6
(c) 4 (d) 2

36. Match List-I (Nature of equilibrium of floating body) with List-II (Conditions for equilibrium) and selectthe correct answer using the codes given below the lists:

| List-I (Nature of equilibrium of floating body | List-II (Conditions for equilibrium |
|---|---|
| A. Unstable equilibrium | 1. $\overline{MG} = 0$ |
| B. Netutral equilibrium | 2. M is above G |
| C. Stable equilibrium | M is below G |
| | 4. $\overline{BG} = 0$ |

where M, G and B are metacentre, centre of gravity and centre of buoyancy respectively.

**Codes:**

| | A | B | C |
|---|---|---|---|
| (a) | 1 | 3 | 2 |
| (b) | 3 | 1 | 2 |
| (c) | 1 | 3 | 4 |
| (d) | 4 | 2 | 3 |

37. The velocity potential function in a two dimensional flow fluid is given by $\phi = x^2 - y^2$. The magnitude of velocity at the point (1, 1) as:
(a) 2
(b) 4
(c) $2\sqrt{2}$
(d) $4\sqrt{2}$

38. The relations between shear stress (τ) and velocity gradient for ideal fluids, Newtonian fluids and non-Newtonian fluids are given below. Select the correct combination:

(a) $\tau = 0; \tau = \mu\left(\frac{du}{dy}\right)^2; \tau = \mu\left(\frac{du}{dv}\right)^3$

(b) $\tau = 0; \tau = \mu\left(\frac{du}{dy}\right)^2; \tau = \mu\left(\frac{du}{dy}\right)^2$

(c) $\tau = \mu\left(\frac{du}{dy}\right); \tau = \mu\left(\frac{du}{dy}\right)^2; \tau = \mu\left(\frac{du}{dy}\right)^3$

(d) $\tau = \mu\left(\frac{du}{dy}\right); \tau = \mu\left(\frac{du}{dy}\right)^2; \tau = 0$

39. Consider the following statements:
1. For stream function to exist, the flow should be irrotational.
2. Potential functions are possible even though continuity is not satisfied.
3. Stremlines diverge where the flow is accelerated.
4. Bernoulli's equation will be satisfied for flow across a cross-section.

Which of the above statements is/are correct?
(a) 1, 2 3 and 4 (b) 1, 3 and 4
(c) 3 and 4 (d) 2 only

40. Match List-I (Device) with List-II (Use) and select the correct answer using the codes given below the lists:

| List-I (Device) | List-II (Use) |
|---|---|
| A. Picot tube | 1. Boundary shear stress |
| B. Preston tube | 2. Turbuleny velocity fluctuations |
| C. Flow Nozzle | 3. The total head |
| D. Hot wire anemometer | 4. Flow rate |

**Codes:**

| | A | B | C | D |
|---|---|---|---|---|
| (a) | 4 | 2 | 3 | 1 |
| (b) | 3 | 1 | 4 | 2 |
| (c) | 4 | 1 | 3 | 2 |
| (d) | 3 | 2 | 4 | 1 |

41. Flow separation is caused by:
(a) thinning of boundary layer thickness to zero
(b) a negative pressure gradient
(c) a positive pressure gradient
(d) reduction of pressure to local vapour pressure

42. A laminar flow is taking place in a pipe. Match List-I (Term) with List-II (Expression) and select the correct answer using the codes given below the lists:

| List-I (Term) | List-II (Expression) |
|---|---|
| A. Discharge, Q | 1. $\frac{16\mu}{\rho VD}$ |
| B. Pressure drop, $\frac{\Delta P}{L}$ | 2. $\frac{\pi d^3 \Delta p}{128\mu L}$ |
| C. Friction factor, $f$ | 3. $\frac{32\mu V}{D^2}$ |
| | 4. $\frac{\pi d^4 \Delta p}{128\mu L}$ |

**Codes:**

| | A | B | C |
|---|---|---|---|
| (a) | 2 | 3 | 4 |
| (b) | 4 | 3 | 1 |
| (c) | 4 | 1 | 3 |
| (d) | 1 | 4 | 2 |

43. The magnus effect is defined as:
(a) the generation of lift per unit drage force
(b) the circulation induced in an aircraft wing
(c) the separation of boundary layer near the trailing edge of a slender body
(d) the generation of lift on a rotating cylinder in a uniform flow.

44. A $\frac{1}{25}$ model of a ship is to be tested for estimating the wave drag. If the speed of the ship is 1 m/s, then the speed at which the model must be tested is:
(a) 0.04 m/s (b) 0.2 m/s
(c) 5.0 m/s (d) 25.0 m/s

45. Consider the following statements for a two-dimensional potential flow:
1. Laplace equation for stream function must be satisfied.
2. Laplace equation for velocity potential must be satisfied.
3. Stremlines and equipotential lines are mutually perpendicular.
4. Streamlines can intersect each other in very high speed flows.

Which of the above statement s are correct?
(a) 1 and 4 (b) 2 and 4
(c) 1, 2 and 3 (d) 2, 3 and 4

46. Which of the following equations are forms of continuity equations?
($\vec{V}$ is the velocity and ∀ is volume)

1. $A_1\vec{V}_1 = A_2\vec{V}_2$ 2. $1\frac{du}{\partial x} + \frac{dv}{\partial y} = 0$

3. $\int_S \rho\vec{V}.dA + \int_\forall \rho\, d\forall = 0$ 4. $\frac{1}{r}\frac{\partial(rv_r)}{\partial r} + \frac{\partial v_z}{\partial z} = 0$

Select the correct answer using the codes below:

**Codes:**

(a) 1, 2, 3 and 4 (b) 1 and 2
(c) 3 and 4 (d) 2, 3 and 4

47. A solid P floats with half of its volume immersed in water and solid Q floats with two-thirds of the volume immersed in water. The densities of solider P and Q are in ratio:
(a) 1 : 2 (b) 1:3
(c) 2:3 (d) 3:4

48. The Bernoulli's equation refers to conservation of:
(a) mass (b) linear momentum
(c) angular momentum (d) energy

49. The continuity equation in a differential form is:
(a) $\frac{dA}{A} + \frac{dV}{V} + \frac{dp}{\rho} = \text{constant}$
(b) $\frac{A}{dA} + \frac{V}{dV} + \frac{\rho}{dp} = \text{constant}$
(c) $\frac{dA}{A} + \frac{dV}{V} + \frac{dp}{\rho} = 0$
(d) $AdA + VdV + p\,d\rho = 0$

50. Velocity defect in boundary layer theory is defined as:
(a) the error in the measurement of velocity at any point in the boundary layer
(b) the difference between the velocity at a point within the boundary layer and the free stream velocity
(c) the difference between the velocity at any point within the boundary layer and the velocity nearer the boundary
(d) the ratio between the velocity at a point in the boundary layer and the free stream velocity.

51. The drage coefficient for laminar flow varies with Reynolds number (Re) as:
(a) $Re^{1/2}$ (b) Re
(c) $Re^{-1}$ (d) $Re^{-1/2}$

52. Match List-I (Basic Ideal Flow) with List-II (Example) and select the correct answer using the codes given below the lists:

| List-I (Basic Ideal Flow) | List-II (Example) |
|---|---|
| A. Superposition of a uniform flow over a doublet | 1. Flow over a half Rankine body |
| B. Superposition of a uniform flow over a source and sink | 2. Flow over a Rankine oval |
| C. Superposition of a uniform flow over a source | 3. Flow over a rotating body |
| D. Superposition of a free vortex flow along with a uniform flow over a doublet | 4. Flow over a stationary body |

**Codes:**

| | A | B | C | D |
|---|---|---|---|---|
| (a) | 4 | 1 | 2 | 3 |
| (b) | 3 | 2 | 1 | 4 |
| (c) | 4 | 2 | 1 | 3 |
| (d) | 3 | 1 | 2 | 4 |

53. The square root of the ratio of inertia force to gravity force is called:
(a) Reynolds number (b) Froude number
(c) Mach number (d) Euler number

54. The thickness of turbulent boundary layer at a distance $x$ from the leading edge over a flat plate varies as:
(a) $x^{4/5}$ (b) $x^{1/2}$
(c) $x^{1/5}$ (d) $x^{3/5}$

55. For two-dimensionaly fluid element in $x$-$y$ plane the rotational component is given by:
(a) $\omega_z = \frac{1}{2}\left(\frac{\partial u}{\partial x} - \frac{\partial v}{\partial y}\right)$
(b) $\omega_z = \frac{1}{2}\left(\frac{\partial u}{\partial x} + \frac{\partial v}{\partial y}\right)$
(c) $\omega_z = \frac{1}{2}\left(\frac{\partial v}{\partial x} - \frac{\partial u}{\partial y}\right)$
(d) $\omega_z = \frac{1}{2}\left(\frac{\partial v}{\partial x} - \frac{\partial u}{\partial y}\right)$

56. Which of the following relations must hold for an irrotational two-dimensional flow in the $x - y$ plane:
(a) $\frac{\partial v}{\partial y} - \frac{\partial u}{\partial x} = 0$ (b) $\frac{\partial u}{\partial z} - \frac{\partial v}{\partial x} = 0$
(c) $\frac{\partial w}{\partial y} - \frac{\partial v}{\partial z} = 0$ (d) $\frac{\partial v}{\partial x} - \frac{\partial u}{\partial y} = 0$

57. The coefficient of friction $f$ in terms of shear stress $\tau_0$ is given by:
(a) $f = \frac{\rho v^2}{2\tau_0}$ (b) $f = \frac{\tau_0}{\rho v^2}$
(c) $f = \frac{2\tau_0}{\rho v^2}$ (d) $\frac{2\rho v_0}{\tau_0}$

58. Velocity distribution in a turbulent boundary layer follows:
(a) Logarithmic law (b) Parabolic law
(c) Linear law (d) Cubic law

59. What is the discharge for laminar flow through a pipe of diameter 40 mm having centre line velocity of 1.5 m/s?
(a) $\frac{3\pi}{59}\,\text{m}^3/\text{s}$ (b) $\frac{3\pi}{2,500}\,\text{m}^3/\text{s}$
(c) $\frac{3\pi}{5000}\,\text{m}^3/\text{s}$ (d) $\frac{3\pi}{10000}\,\text{m}^3/\text{s}$

60. Which one of the following is the expression for momentum thickness θ of a boundary layer?

(a) $\theta = \int_0^\delta \left[1 - \frac{U}{U_0}\right]^2 dy$

(b) $\theta = \int_0^\delta \left[1 - \frac{U}{U_0}\right]^2 dy$

(c) $\theta = \int_0^\delta \frac{U}{U_0}\left[1 - \frac{U}{U_0}\right] dy$

(d) $\theta = \int_0^\delta \frac{U}{U_0}\left[1 - \left(\frac{U}{U_0}\right)^2\right] dy$

61. The displacement thickness at section, for an air stream ($\rho = 1.2 kg/m^3$) moving with a velocity of 10 m/s over a flat plate is 0.5 mm. What is the loss of mass rate of flow of air due to boundary layer formation in kg per meter width of plate per second?

(a) $6\times10^{-3}$ (b) $6\times10^{-5}$

(c) $3\times10^{-3}$ (d) $2\times10^{-3}$

62. In a laminar boundary layer over a flat plate, what would be the ratio of wall shear stresses $\tau_1$ and $\tau_2$ at the two sections which lie at distances $x_1 = 30$ cm and $x_2 = 90$ cm from the leading edge of the plate?

(a) $\frac{\tau_1}{\tau_2} = 3.0$ (b) $\frac{\tau_1}{\tau_2} = \frac{1}{3}$

(c) $\frac{\tau_1}{\tau_2} = (3.0)^{1/2}$ (d) $\frac{\tau_1}{\tau_2} = (3.0)$

63. Which one of the following is caused by the occurrence of a normal shock in the diverging section of a convergent-divergent nozzle?

1. Velocity jump 2. Pressure jump
3. Velocity drop 4. Pressure drop

Select the correct answer using the codes given below:

(a) 1 only (b) 1 and 2

(c) 2 and 3 (d) 1 and 4

64. A circular plate of 1.5 m diameter is submerged in water with its greatest and least depths below the water surface being 2 m and 0.75 m respectively. When is the approximate magnitude of the total thrust on one face of the plate?

(a) 24 kN (b) 28 kN

(c) 12 kN (d) 16 kN

65. Which one of the following statements is correct?
A steady flow of diverging straight steam lines:

(a) is a uniform flow with local acceleration
(b) has convective normal acceleration
(c) has convective tangential acceleration
(d) has both convective normal and tangential accelerations.

66. Which one of the following is the expression of the rotational component for a two-dimensional fluid element in $x - y$ plane?

(a) $\omega_z = \frac{1}{2}\left(\frac{\partial v}{\partial x} - \frac{\partial u}{\partial y}\right)$ (b) $\omega_z = \frac{1}{2}\left(\frac{\partial v}{\partial x} - \frac{\partial u}{\partial y}\right)$

(c) $\omega_z = \frac{1}{2}\left(\frac{\partial v}{\partial x} - \frac{\partial v}{\partial y}\right)$ (d) $\omega_z = \frac{1}{2}\left(\frac{\partial u}{\partial x} + \frac{\partial v}{\partial y}\right)$

67. What is the percentage error in the estimation of the discharge due to an error of 2% in the measurement of the reading of a differential manometer connected to an orifice meter?

(a) 4 (b) 3

(c) 2 (d) 1

68. Which one of the following is the characteristics of a fully developed laminar:

(a) The pressure drop in the flow direction is zero
(b) The velocity profile changes uniformly in the flow direction
(c) The velocity profile does not change in the flow direction
(d) The Reynolds number for the flow is critical.

69. Which one of the following is the correct relationship between the boundary layer thickness δ, displacement thickness δ* and the momentum thickness θ?

(a) $\delta < \delta^* > \theta$
(b) $\delta^* > \theta > \delta$
(c) $\theta > \delta > \delta^*$
(d) $\theta > \delta^* > \delta$

70. The thickness of turbulent boundary layer at a distance $x$ from the leading edge on a flat plate varies as:

(a) $x^{4/5}$ (b) $x^{3/5}$

(c) $x^{1/2}$ (d) $x^{1/5}$

71. When a falt plate of 0.1 m² area is pulled at a constant velocity of 30 cm/s parallel to another stationary plate pocaled at a distance 0.01 cm from it and the space in between filled with a fluid of dynamic viscosity = 0.01 Ns/m², the force required to be applied is

(a) 0.3 N (b) 3 N

(c) 10 N (d) 16 N

72. Which one of the following is the continuity equation in differential form?

(The symbols have usual meanings)

(a) $\frac{dA}{A} + \frac{dV}{V} + \frac{d\rho}{\rho} = \text{constant}$

(b) $\frac{dA}{A} + \frac{dV}{V} + \frac{d\rho}{\rho} = 0$

(c) $\frac{A}{dA} + \frac{V}{dV} + \frac{\rho}{d\rho} = \text{constant}$

(d) $AdA + VdA + \rho d\rho = 0$

73. What will be the maximum efficiency of the pipeline if one-third of the available head in flow through the pipeline is consumed by friction?
(a) 33.33% (b) 50.00%
(c) 66.66% (d) 75.00%

74. Which one of the following is satisfied if the flow is irrotational for a two-dimensional fluid element in the $x$–$y$ plane?
(a) $\frac{\partial v}{\partial x} = \frac{\partial u}{\partial y}$ (b) $\frac{\partial v}{\partial x} = \frac{\partial u}{\partial y}$
(c) $\frac{\partial u}{\partial x} = \frac{\partial v}{\partial y}$ (d) $\frac{\partial u}{\partial x} = \frac{\partial v}{\partial y}$

75. The velocity distributions in laminar boundary layer is given by the relation $u/u_\infty = y/\delta$. What is the momentum thickness for the boundary layer?
(a) δ/2 (b) δ/3
(c) δ/4 (d) δ/6

76. How is the Von-Karman momentum integral equation expressed (θ is momentum thickness)?
(a) $\frac{\tau_0}{\frac{1}{2}\rho U_\infty^2} = \frac{\partial\theta}{\partial x}$ (b) $\frac{\tau_0}{2\rho U_\infty^2} = \frac{\partial\theta}{\partial x}$
(c) $\frac{\tau_0}{\rho U_\infty^2} = \frac{\partial\theta}{\partial x}$ (d) $\frac{\tau_0}{\frac{1}{3}\rho U_\infty^2} = \frac{\partial\theta}{\partial x}$

77. Air (kinematic viscosity $= 15 \times 10^{-6}$ m$^2$/s) with a free stream velocity of 10 m/s flows over a smooth two-dimensional flat plate. If the critical Reynolds number is 5 × 10, what is the maximum distance from the leading edge up to which laminar boundary layer exists?
(a) 30 cm (b) 75 cm
(c) 150 cm (d) 300 cm

78. Using the Prandtl's mixing length concept, how is the turbulent shear stress expressed?
(a) $\rho l \frac{du}{dy}$ (b) $\rho l^2 \frac{du}{dy}$
(c) $\rho l \left(\frac{du}{dy}\right)^2$ (d) $\rho l^2 \left(\frac{du}{dy}\right)^2$

79. Consider the following statements:
The state of stress in a fluid consists of normal pressure only if the fluid:
1. is at rest
2. is in uniform motion
3. has non-uniform velocity profile
4. has zero viscosity.
Which of the statements given above are correct?
(a) 1, 2 and 3
(b) 1, 2 and 4
(c) 1, 3 and 4
(d) 2, 3 and 4

80. Darcy-Weisback equation for the head loss in a flow through a pipe is given by $h_1 = 4flv^2$ (2gd) (the symbols have the usual meaning). For the laminar flow through a circular pipe, how does the friction factor $f$ vary with the Reynolds number (Re):
(a) $f$ = 8/Re (b) $f$ = 16/Re
(c) $f$= 32/Re (d) $f$ = 64/Re

81. The velocity distribution in laminar boundary layer is given by the relation $u/u_x = y/\delta$.
What is the displacement thickness for the boundary layer?
(a) δ (b) δ/2
(c) δ/3 (d) δ/4

82. Which one of the following equations gives the velocity distribution across a circular pipe having a viscous flow?
(a) $u = u_{max}[1-(r/R)^2]$ (b) $u = u_{max}[R^2 - r^2]$
(c) $u = u_{max}[1-(r/R)]^2$ (d) $u = u_{max}[1+(r/R)]^2$

83. In a two-dimensional fluid flow, $u = 6x + xy$. Which one of the following gives the component of the velocity to satisfy the continuity equation?
(a) $6x + xy$ (b) $6 + xy$
(c) $-(6x + xy)$ (d) $-\left(6y + \frac{1}{2}y^2\right)$

84. If $u = ax$ and $v = -ay$ give the velocity distribution for a two-dimensional flow, what is the equation of a stream line passing through the point (3, 1)?
(a) $xy = 3$ (b) $x + y = 4$
(c) $x + 3y = 6$ (d) $x^2y = 9$

85. Consider the following statements:
1. Boundary-layer thickness in laminar flow is greater than that of turbulent flow.
2. Boundary-layer thickness of turbulent flow is greater than that of laminar flow.
3. Velocity distributes uniformly in a turbulent boundary-layer.
4. Velocity has a gradual variation in a laminar boundary layer. Which of the statements given above are correct?
(a) 1, 3 and 4 only (b) 1, 2, 3 and 4
(c) 1 and 2 only (d) 2 3 and 4, only

86. Motion economy is better achieved by
(a) method study
(b) time study
(c) work space design
(d) process planning.

87. Which one of the following is the correct statement?
The velocity profiles for fully developed laminar and turbulent flow, respectively, in a pipe are:
(a) parabolic and parabolic
(b) parabolic and elliptic
(c) linear and 1/7 power law
(d) parabolic and 1/7 power law

88. Which one of the following is the correct statement?

For the case of laminar flow between two fixed parallel plates, the shear stress is

(a) constant across the passage
(b) maximum at the centre and zero at the boundary
(c) zero all through the passage
(d) maximum at the boundary and zero at the centre

89. Consider the following statements:

The coefficient of discharge $C_d$ of a venturimeter takes into account.

1. the effect of roughness of the surface
2. non-uniform velocity distributions at inlet and throat section.
3. Reynolds number of flow
4. discharge
5. length of throat
6. diameter of throat
7. diameter ratio

Which of the statements given above are correct?

(a) 1, 2, 4 and 5 (b) 1, 4, 5 and 6
(c) 1, 2, 3 and 7 (d) 2, 6 and 7

90. Which one of the following expresses the error in discharge due to error in the measurement of head over a triangular notch?

(a) $\frac{dQ}{Q} = \frac{5dH}{2H}$ (b) $\frac{dQ}{Q} = \frac{3dH}{2H}$

(c) $\frac{dQ}{Q} = \frac{7dH}{2H}$ (d) $\frac{dQ}{Q} = \frac{1dH}{2H}$

91. Which one of the following is the correct statement?

A differential manometer connected to a pitotstatic tube used for measuring fluid velocity gives:

(a) static pressure
(b) total pressure
(c) dynamic pressure
(d) difference between total pressure and dynamic pressure.

92. Which one of the following correctly represents the shear stress distribution across a section of a circular pipe having a viscous flow?

(a) $\tau = \frac{\partial pr^2}{\partial x}$ (b) $\tau = \frac{\partial p(r/2)}{\partial x}$

(c) $\tau = -\frac{\partial p(r/2)}{\partial x}$ (d) $\tau = \frac{\partial p(r)}{\partial x}$

93. A pipe of diameter (D) conveying a discharge Q is to be replaced by parallel pipes of smaller diameter (d) to discharge the same quantity.

What will be the ratio of $\frac{D}{d}$?

($f$ is same for all pipes)

(a) $\frac{D}{d} = 2$ (b) $\frac{D}{d} = \sqrt{2}$

(c) $\frac{D}{d} = 4^{1/5}$ (d) $\frac{D}{d} = 4^{1/3}$

94. Match List-I (Forms of Bernouli'sEquation ) with List-II (Units of these forms) and select the correct answer using codes given below the lists:

| List-I (Forms of Bernouli's Equation | List-II (Units of these forms) |
|---|---|
| A. $p + wz + \frac{\rho V^2}{2}$ | 1. total energy per unit volume |
| B. $\frac{p}{A} + gz + \frac{V^2}{2}$ | 2. total energy per unit mass |
| C. $\frac{p}{w} + z + \frac{V^2}{2g}$ | 3. total energy per unit weight |

**Codes:**

| | A | B | C |
|---|---|---|---|
| (a) | 1 | 2 | 3 |
| (b) | 1 | 3 | 2 |
| (c) | 2 | 1 | 3 |
| (d) | 2 | 3 | 1 |

95. Which one of the following is the correct statement?

A frictionless, incompressible fluid flows steadily through a convergent nozzle, then its.

(a) energy must decrease
(b) velocity must decrease
(c) pressure must decrease
(d) momentum must decrease

96. Which one of the following statements is correct? For stability of a floating body:

(a) M should lie between G and B (in that order)
(b) M should lie above B and G (in that order)
(c) M should lie below B and G (in that order)
(d) M should coincide with B and G

97. Consider the following statements:

A rectangular block of wood of size L × B × H will float in water in such a way that:

(a) the longest dimension is vertical
(b) the longest dimension is horizontal
(c) the metacentre is above centre of gravity
(d) the centre of buoyancy is above the centre of gravity

Which of the statements given above is/are correct?

(a) 1 only
(b) 2 only 3, only
(c) 2, 3 and 4
(d) 1, 3 and 4

98. Bernoulli's equation is derived by making which one of the following assumptions?
(a) The flow is steady only
(b) The flow is uniform and incompressible
(c) The flow is non-viscous, uniform and steady
(d) The flow is steady, non-viscous, incompressible and irrotational.

99. A skater weighing 1000 N skates at a speed of 20 m/s on ice maintained at 0°C. The average skating area supporting the skater is 0.001 $m^2$and the coefficient of friction between the skatesandice is 0.02. What will be the average thickness of a film of water existing at the interface between the skater and ice? (Take dynamic viscosity of water as 0.001 $Ns/m^2$)
(a) $10^{-5m}$
(b) $10^{-6}$
(c) $10^{-2}$
(d) Not possible to estimate since there cannot be a possibility, of formation of a thin film of water at interface

100. Flow separation is likely to take place when the pressure gradient in the direction of flow is:
(a) zero
(b) adverse
(c) slightly favourable
(d) strongly favourable

101. The vertical component of the hydrostatic force on a submerged curved surface is the:
(a) mass of liquid vertically above it
(b) weight of the liquid vertically above it
(c) force on a vertical projection of the surface
(d) product of pressure at the centroid and the surface area

102. If a hydraulic press has a ram of 12.5 cm diameter and plunger of 1.25 cm diameter, what force would be required on the plunger to raise a mass of 1 tonne on the ram?
(a) 981 N (b) 98.1 N
(c) 9.81 N (d) 0.98 N

103. A liquid mass readjusts itself and undergoes a rigid body type of motion when it is subjected to a:
(a) constant angular velocity
(b) constant angular acceleration
(c) linearly varying velocity
(d) linearly varying acceleration

104. In a two-dimensional flow, where $u$ is the $x$-component and $v$ is the $y$-component of velocity, the equation of streamline is given by:
(a) $udx – vdy = 0$ (b) $vdx – udy = 0$
(c) $uv\,dx – dy = 0$ (d) $udx + vdy = 0$

105. The continuity equation $\frac{\partial u}{\partial x}+\frac{\partial v}{\partial y}+\frac{\partial w}{\partial z}=0$ is valid only for:
(a) ideal fluid flow
(b) incompressible fluid whether the flow is steady or not
(c) steady flow, whether is compressible or not
(c) steady flow and compressible fluids

106. From a reservoir, water is drained through two pipes of 10 cm and 20 cm diameter respectively. If the frictional head loss in both the pipes is same, then the ratio of discharge through the larger pipe to that through the smaller pipe will be:
(a) $\sqrt{2}$ (b) $2\sqrt{2}$
(c) 4 (d) $4\sqrt{2}$

107. While water passes through a given pipe at a mean velocity 'V, the flow is found to change from laminar to turbulent. If another fluid of specific gravity 0.8 and coefficient of viscosity 20% of that of water, is passed through the same pipe, the transition of flow from laminar to turbulent is expected if the flow velocity is:
(a) 2V (b) V
(c) V/2 (d) V/4

108. A hydraulic jump is formed in a 5.0 wide rectangular channel with sequent depths of 0.2 m and 0.8 m. The discharge in the channel, in $m^3/s$. is:
(a) 2.43 (b) 3.45
(c) 4.43 (d) 5.00

109. If the velocity distribution in a turbulent boundary layer is given by $\frac{u}{u_\infty}=\left(\frac{y}{\delta}\right)^{1/9}$ then the ratio of displacement thickness to nominal boundary layer thickness will be:
(a) 1.0 (b) 0.6
(c) 0.3 (d) 0.1

110. The barometric pressure at the base of mountain is 750 mm Hg and at the top 600 mm Hg. If the average air density is 1 $kg/m^3$, the height of the mountain is approximately:
(a) 2000 m (b) 3000 m
(c) 4000 m (d) 5000 m

111. At the interface of a liquid and a gas at rest, the pressure is:
(a) higher on the concave side compared to that on the convex side
(b) higher on the convex side compared to that on the concave side
(c) equal on both sides
(d) equal to surface tension divided by radius of curvature on both sides

112. A rectangular tank of base size 3 m × 3 m contains oil of specific gravity 0.8 upto a height of 8 m. When it is accelerated at 2.45 $m/s^2$ vertically upwards, the force on the base of the tank will be:
(a) 29400 N
(b) 38240 N
(c) 78400 N
(d) 49050 N

113. Match List-I with List-II and select the correct answer using the codes given below the lists:

| List-I (Device) | List-II (Use) |
|---|---|
| A. Barometer | 1. Gauge pressure |
| B. Hydrometer | 2. Local atmospheric pressure |
| C. U-tube manometer | 3. Relative density |
| D. Bourden gauge | 4. Pressure differential |

**Codes:**

| | A | B | C | D |
|---|---|---|---|---|
| (a) | 2 | 3 | 1 | 4 |
| (b) | 3 | 2 | 1 | 4 |
| (c) | 3 | 2 | 4 | 1 |
| (d) | 2 | 3 | 4 | 1 |

114. The continuity equation for 3-dimensional flow $\frac{\partial u}{\partial x}+\frac{\partial v}{\partial y}+\frac{\partial w}{\partial z}=0$ is applicable to:
(symbols have usual meanings)
(a) steady flow
(b) uniform flow
(c) ideal fluid flow
(d) ideal as well as viscous fluid flow

115. Bernoulli's equation $\frac{p}{\rho}+\frac{v^2}{2}=gh=$ constant is applicable for:
(a) steady, frictionless and incompressible flow along a streamline
(b) uniform and frictionless flow along a streamline when ρ is a function $p$
(c) steady and frictionless flow along a stremline when ρ is a function of $p$
(d) steady, uniform and incomperssible flow along a streamline.

116. Two identical pipes of length 'L', diameter '$d$' and friction factor $f$ are connected is parallel between two points For the same total volume flow rate with pipe of same diameter '$d$' and same friction factor '$f$', the single length of the pipe will be:
(a) $\frac{L}{2}$ (b) $\frac{L}{\sqrt{2}}$
(c) $\sqrt{2}L$ (d) $\frac{L}{4}$

117. Two venturimeters of different area ration are connected at different locations of a pipeline to measure discharge. Similar manometers are used across the two venturimeters to register the head differences. The first venturimeter of area ratio 2 registers a head difference '$h$' while the second venturimeter registers '$5h$'. The area ratio for the second venturimeter is:
(a) 3 (b) 4
(c) 5 (d) 6

118. The thickness of laminar boundary layer at a distance 'X' from the leading edge over a flat plate varies as:
(a) X (b) $X^{1/2}$
(c) $X^{1/5}$ (d) $X^{4/5}$

119. Consider the following coefficients:
(Re = Reynold number)
1. $1.328\,Re^{-(0.5)}$ for laminar flow
2. $0.72\,Re^{-(0.2)}$ for turbulent flow
3. $0.072\,Re^{-(0.2)}$ for turbulent flow
4. $1.028\,Re^{-(0.5)}$ for laminar flow.

The Coefficients for drag for a flat plate would include:
(a) 1 and 2 (b) 2 and 4
(c) 1 and 3 (d) 3 and 4

120. Consider the following statements:
1. Gases are considered incompressible when Mach number is less than 0.2
2. A Newtonian fluid is incompressible and non-viscous
3. An ideal fluid has negligible surface tension

Which of these statements (s) is/are correct?
(a) 2 and 3 (b) 2 alone
(c) 1 alone (d) 1 and 3

## ANSWERS WITH EXPLANATIONS

1. (c) 2 (c)

3. (a) $u=5x^3, v=-15x^2yu=\frac{\partial\psi}{\partial y}=5x^3$

$y=5x^3y+c_1$

$v=\frac{\partial\psi}{\partial y}=-15x^2y$

$\psi=5x^3y+c_2$

Taking $c_1=c_2=0$

$\psi=5\times1\times2=10\,m^3/s$

4. (d) 5. (b)

6. (b) Velocity head, $\frac{v^2}{2g}=h=10$ m

7. (c)

8. (c) $u=x-4v, v=-y-4x$

$\frac{\partial u}{\partial x}=1, \frac{\partial u}{\partial y}=-4$

$\frac{\partial v}{\partial x}=-4, \frac{\partial v}{\partial y}=-1$

Continuity equation is: $\frac{\partial u}{\partial x}+\frac{\partial v}{\partial y}=1-1=0$

Hence continuity equation is satisfied.

For the flow to be irrotational, $\frac{\partial u}{\partial x}=\frac{\partial v}{\partial y}$

i.e., – 4 = – 4. Hence the flow is irroratIonal

9. (b) $\dfrac{v_m}{v_p} = \sqrt{\dfrac{1_m}{1_p}}, v_m = 1.0\sqrt{\dfrac{1}{25}} = 0.2$ m/s

10. (d) 11. (d)

12. (b) Terminal velocity of a small sphere falling in a viscous fluid,

$$v = \frac{d_2(y_s - y_f)}{18\mu}$$

13. (d) 14. (d)

15. (d) $\dfrac{\Delta p}{pv^3} = \dfrac{mL^{-1}T^{-2}}{[ML^{-3}][LT^{-1}]} = M^{1-1}L^{-1+3+3}T^{-2+3}$

$= L^{-1}T$, which is non-dimensional

16. (d) 17. (a) 18. (b)

19. (c) If $f \alpha \dfrac{1}{\text{Re}}$, then the pipe must be smooth.

20. (b)

21. (b) At sea level, $h = 760$ mm of Hg

(a) $\dfrac{760 \times 10^{-3} \times 13.6 \times 9.81 \times 10^3}{9.81 \times 998} = 10.35$ m

(b) $\dfrac{760 \times 10^{-3} \times 13.6 \times 10^3}{1025} = 10.08\text{m} = 10.1\text{m}$

(c) $760 \times 10^{-3} \times 13.6 / 0.8 = 12.92$m

(d) $760 \times 10^{-3} \times 13.6 / 1.590 = 6.5$m

22. (d) Bernoulli's equation is:

$$\frac{v^2}{2g} + \frac{p}{\rho g} + z = \text{const}$$

For $v = 0, \dfrac{p}{\rho g} + z = \text{const}$

$$\frac{p}{\rho g} + z = \text{const}$$

$$dp/\rho + gdz = 0 \text{ or } \frac{dp}{\rho} = -gdz$$

23. (a) Force on the bottom, $F_b = h\gamma l^2$

Force on the sides $F_s = 0.5\gamma lh^2$

For $F_s = F_b$

$0.5\gamma lh^2 = \gamma hl^2$

$\therefore \dfrac{h}{l} = 2$

24. (d) 25. (a) 26. (a)

27. (c) Velocity head $= \dfrac{v^2}{2g} = \dfrac{(4.4)^2}{2 \times 9.81} = 0.987 = 1$m

28. (c) 29. (c) 30. (c)

31. (c) Capillary rise, $h \propto \dfrac{1}{d}$

32. (b) $Q = A_v = 2000$ cm$^3$/s

33. (d) $Q \propto \sqrt{h}$ or $h \propto Q^2$

34. (a) $L\mu V = \dfrac{m \times kg}{m \times s} \times \dfrac{m}{s} = \text{kg.m/s}^2 = \text{N}$

35. (d) Relative density $= \dfrac{\text{weight in air}}{\text{weight is water}}$

$= \dfrac{80}{60} = 1.33 = 2$

36. (b)

37. (c) $\phi = x^2 - y^2$

$u = \dfrac{\partial \phi}{\partial x} = -2x$

$v = -\dfrac{\partial \phi}{\partial y} = +2y$

$v = \sqrt{u^2 + v^2} = \sqrt{4x^2 + 4y^2}$

$v_{(1,1)} = \sqrt{8} = 2\sqrt{2}$

38. (b) 39. (b) 40. (b) 41. (c) 42. (b)

43. (d)

44. (b) $v_p = v_m\sqrt{\dfrac{l_p}{l_m}}$

$1 = v_m\sqrt{25} = 5v_m$

$v_m = \dfrac{1}{5} = 0.2$ m/s

45. (c) 46. (b)

47. (d) Weight of solid P, $W_P$ = weight of water displaced

$= \dfrac{1}{2}V_p \times 10^3 \times 9.81$N

Weight of solid Q, $W_Q = \dfrac{1}{2}V_Q \times 10^3 \times 9.81$N

$\rho_P = \dfrac{W_p}{9.81V_p} = \dfrac{1}{2} \times 10^3$

$\rho_Q = \dfrac{W_Q}{9.81V_p} = \dfrac{1}{2} \times 10^3$

$\dfrac{\rho_p}{\rho_Q} = \dfrac{1}{2} \times \dfrac{3}{2} = \dfrac{3}{4}$ or 3 : 4

48. (d)

49. (d) $Q = A_{\rho v}$ = const

Taking in of both sides

$\ln A + \ln \rho + \ln v = \ln$ const

Taking differential, we have

$$\frac{dA}{A} + \frac{d\rho}{\rho} + \frac{dv}{v} = 0$$

50. (c) 51. (d) 52. (c)

53. (a) $\frac{\delta}{x} = \frac{0.37}{(\text{Re}_x)^{1/5}} = \frac{0.37}{\left(\frac{U_x}{v}\right)^{1/5}} \propto x^{-1/5}$ or $\delta \propto x^{4/5}$

54. (a) 55. (d) 56. (d) 57. (c) 58. (d)

59. (c) $Q = A_v = \frac{\pi}{4}(0.04)^2 \times 1.5 = \frac{3\pi}{5000} \text{ m}^3/\text{s}$

60. (c)

61. (a) $\delta^* = 0.5 \text{ mm}, \rho = 1.2 \text{ kg/m}^3, u = 10 \text{ m/s}$

Loss of mass rate of flow of air $= \delta^* \rho u$

$= 0.5 \times 10^{-3} \times 1.2 \times 10 = 6 \times 10^{-3}$ kg/m

62. (c) Boundary shear stress $\propto \frac{1}{\sqrt{\text{Re}_x}} \propto \frac{1}{\sqrt{x}}$

$$\frac{\tau_1}{\tau_2} = \sqrt{\frac{x_2}{x_1}} = \sqrt{\frac{90}{30}} = \sqrt{3}$$

63. (d) 64. (a) 65. (d) 66. (a)

67. (d) For an orificemeter $Q \propto \sqrt{H}$ or $Q = K\sqrt{H}$,

where, K = a constant

$$\ln Q = \ln K + \frac{1}{2} \ln H$$

$$\frac{dQ}{Q} = 0 + \frac{1}{2}, \frac{dH}{H} = \frac{1}{2} \times 2 = 1\%$$

68. (b) 69. (a) 70. (a)

71. (b) $A = 0.1\text{m}^2, U = 30 \text{cm/s}, b = 0.01 \text{cm}, \mu = 0.01 \text{N.s/m}^2$

$$\tau = \frac{\mu U}{b} - \frac{1}{2}\frac{dp}{dx}(b - 2y)$$

$$q = \frac{Ub}{2} - \frac{b^3}{12\mu}.\frac{dp}{dx}$$

For $q = 0, \frac{dp}{dx} = \frac{6\mu U}{b^2}$

$$\tau = \frac{\mu U}{b} - \frac{1}{2} \times \frac{6\mu U}{b^2}(b - 2y)$$

$$\tau = \frac{\mu U}{b} - \frac{3\mu U}{b^2}(b - 2y)$$

Average shear stress

$$\tau_{\text{avg}} = \frac{1}{b}\int_0^b \left[\frac{\mu U}{b} - \frac{3\mu U}{b^2}(b - 2y)\right] dy$$

$$= \frac{1}{b}\left[\frac{\mu U y}{b} = \frac{3\mu U}{b^2}(by - y^2)\right]_0^b$$

$$= \frac{1}{b}\left[\mu U - 3\mu U(b^2 - b^2)\right]^0 = \frac{\mu U}{b}$$

$$= \frac{0.01 \times 0.3}{0.01 \times 10^{-2}} = 30 \text{ N/m}^2$$

Force required $= t_{\text{avg}} \times A = 30 \times 0.1 = 3\text{N}$

72. (b) 73. (c) 74. (a)

75. (d) $\frac{U}{U_\infty} = \frac{y}{\delta}$

Momentum thickness,

$$\theta = \int_0^\delta \frac{u}{U_\infty}\left(1 - \frac{u}{U_\infty}\right) dy = \int_0^\delta \frac{y}{\delta}\left(1 - \frac{y}{\delta}\right) dy$$

$$= \left|\frac{y^2}{2\delta} - \frac{y^3}{3\delta^2}\right|_0^\delta = \frac{\delta}{2} - \frac{\delta}{3} = \frac{\delta}{6}$$

76. (c)

77. (b) $v = 15 \times 10^{-6} \text{m}^2/\text{s}, U^\infty = 10 \text{ m/s}$

$$\text{Re}_c = 5 \times 10^5$$

$$\text{Re}_c = \frac{U_\infty x}{v}$$

$$x = \frac{5 \times 10^5 \times 15 \times 10^{-6}}{10} = 0.75 \text{m or } 75 \text{ cm}$$

78. (d) 79. (b) 80. (d)

81. (c) $\delta^* = \int_0^\delta \left(1 - \frac{u}{U_\infty}\right) dy$

$$= \int_0^\delta \left(1 - \frac{y}{,}\right) dy = \left|y - \frac{y^2}{2'}\right| = \delta - \frac{\delta}{2} = \frac{\delta}{2}$$

82. (a)

83. (d) $u = 6x + xy$

Continuity equation in two-dimension is:

$$\frac{\partial u}{\partial x} + \frac{\partial v}{\partial y} = 0$$

$$u = \frac{\partial \phi}{\partial x}, v = \frac{\partial \phi}{\partial y}$$

$$\frac{\partial v}{\partial y} = 6 + y$$

(a) $\frac{\partial v}{\partial y} = x\frac{\partial}{+1}$

$6 + y + x \neq 0$

(b) $\frac{\partial v}{\partial y} = x, 6 + y + x \neq 0$

(c) $\frac{\partial v}{\partial y} = -(6 + x) = -(6 + x)$

$6 + y - 6 - 6x \neq 0$

$(6 + y) - (6 + y) = 0)$

84. (a) The equation of stream line is:

$$\frac{dx}{u} = \frac{dy}{v}$$

$$\frac{dx}{ax} = \frac{dy}{-av}$$

$$\frac{1}{a}\ln x = -\frac{1}{a}\ln y + c$$

The stream line passes through point (3, 1)

$$\frac{1}{a}\ln 3 = -\frac{1}{a}\ln + c = 0 + c$$

$$c = \frac{1}{a}\ln 3$$

$$\frac{1}{a}\ln x = -\frac{1}{a}\ln y + \frac{1}{a}\ln 3$$

or $\ln x = -\ln y + \ln 3$

$$\ln x + \ln y = \ln 3$$

$$\ln xy = \ln 3$$

$$xy = 3$$

85. (a) Pressure inside a soap bubble,

$$p = \frac{8\sigma}{d}$$

$$\sigma = \frac{pd}{8} = \frac{25 \times 50 \times 10^{-3}}{8} = 0.156\ \text{N/m}$$

86. (a) 87. (d) 88. (d) 89. (a)

90. (a) For a triangular notch.

$$Q \propto H^{5/2}$$

$$\ln Q = \frac{5}{2}\ln H$$

$$\frac{dQ}{Q} = \frac{5}{2} = \frac{dH}{H}$$

91. (c) 92. (c)

93. (c) $Q = Q_1 + Q_2$

Since $d_1 = d_2 = d$

$\therefore$ $Q_1 = Q_2$

$\therefore$ $Q = 2Q_1$

$$D^2 v = 2d^2 v_1 \qquad ...1$$

Also $\frac{fLv^2}{2gD} = \frac{flv^2}{2gd_1}$

$$\frac{v^2}{D} = \frac{v_1^2}{d^{11}}$$

$$\left(\frac{v}{v^1}\right)^2 = \frac{D}{d_1} = \frac{D}{d}$$

from eq. 1., $\frac{v}{v^1} = 2\left(\frac{d}{D}\right)^2$

$$\left(\frac{v}{v_1}\right)^2 = 4\left(\frac{d}{D}\right)^4$$

$$\therefore \quad \frac{D}{d} = 4\left(\frac{d}{D}\right)^4$$

$$\frac{D}{d} \times 4\left(\frac{d}{D}\right)^4 = 4$$

$$\left(\frac{D}{d}\right)^5 = 4$$

$$\frac{D}{d} = 4^{1/5}$$

94. (a) 95. (c) 96. (b) 97. (b) 98. (d)

99. (a) 100. (c) 101. (b)

102. (b) $\frac{F}{\left(\frac{\pi}{4}\times(1.25)^2\right)} = \frac{1000\times 9.81}{\frac{\pi}{4}\times(12.5)^2}$

$$F = \left(\frac{1.25}{1.25}\right)^2 \times 1000 \times 9.81 = 98.1\ \text{N}$$

103. (a)

104. (b) Equation of a stream line is: $\frac{dx}{u} = \frac{dy}{v}$

or $udx - udy = 0$

105. (a) Continuity equation is applicable for incompressible fluids and steady motion.

106. (d) Frictional head loss in a pipe

$$h_f = \frac{4flv^2}{2gd}$$

$$Q = \frac{\pi}{4}d^2 v \text{ or } v = \frac{4Q}{\pi d^2}$$

$$\therefore\ h_f = \frac{4fl}{2gd} \times \frac{16Q^2}{\pi^2 d^4} = \left(\frac{32fl}{\pi^2 g}\right) \times \frac{Q^2}{d^5} \propto \frac{Q^2}{d^5}$$

For $h_{f1} = h_{f2}$

$$\frac{Q_1^2}{d_1^5} = \frac{Q_2^2}{d_2^5}$$

$$\frac{Q_2}{d_1} = \left(\frac{d_2}{d_1}\right)^{5/2} = \left(\frac{20}{10}\right)^{5/2} \quad 2^{5/2} = \sqrt{32} = 4\sqrt{2}$$

107. (d) $Re = \frac{vd}{v}$

$$v = \frac{\mu}{\rho}, v_2 = \frac{0.2\mu}{0.8\rho} = \frac{\mu}{4\rho} = \frac{v}{4}$$

$$\frac{vd}{v} = \frac{4v_2 d}{v}$$

$$v_2 = \frac{v}{4}$$

108. (c) $y_1 = 0.2\text{m}, y_2 = 0.8\text{m}$,

$$\frac{y_2}{y_1} = \frac{1}{2}\left[\sqrt{1+8F_1^2} - 1\right]$$

$$\frac{0.8}{y_1} = \frac{1}{2}\left[\sqrt{1+8F_1^2} - 1\right]$$

$$8 = \sqrt{1+8F_1^2} - 1$$

$$1+8F_1^2 = 9^2 = 81$$

$$8F_1^2 = 80$$

$$F_1^2 = 80$$

$$F_1 = 3.16$$

$$F_1^2 = \frac{v_1^2}{gy_1}$$

$$10 = \frac{v_1^2}{9.81\times 0.2}, v_1^2 = 19.62$$

$$v_1 = 4.429 \text{ m/s}$$

$$Q = by_1v_1 = 5\times 0.2\times 4.429\times 4.43 \text{ m}^3\text{/s}$$

109. (d) Displacement thickness,

$$\delta' = \int_0^\delta \left(1-\frac{u}{U_x}\right)dy = \int_0^\delta \left[1-\left(\frac{y}{\delta}\right)^{1/9}\right]dy$$

$$= \left| y - \frac{1}{\delta^{1/9}}.y^{10/9}\times\frac{9}{10}\right|_0^\delta = \delta = \frac{9}{10}\delta = \frac{\delta}{10}$$

$$\frac{\delta'}{\delta} = \frac{1}{10} = 0.1$$

110. (a) 111. (d)

112. (d) Hydrostatic force

$= 0.8\times 10^3\times 9.80\times 8 = 62720\text{ N}\downarrow$

Accelerating force $= 3\times 3\times 8\times 0.8\times 10^3\times 2.45$

$= 141120\text{ N}\uparrow$

Force on the base of the tank $= 141120 - 62720$

$= 78400\text{ N}\uparrow$

113. (d) 114. (c) 115. (a)

116. (a) $Q = Q_1 + Q_2$

$$v_1 = \frac{4Q_1}{\pi d_1^2}, v_2 = \frac{4Q_2}{\pi d_2^2}$$

$$\frac{Q_1}{Q_2} = \frac{A_1v_1}{A_2v_2} = \frac{\frac{\pi}{4}d_1^2v_1}{\frac{\pi}{4}d_2^2v_2} = \left(\frac{d_1}{d_2}\right)^2\left(\frac{v_1}{v_2}\right)$$

For $d_1 = d_2 = d$

$$\frac{Q_1}{Q_2} = \frac{v_1}{v_2}$$

Frictional head loss, $h_f = \dfrac{4flv^2}{2gd}$

$$Q_1 = \frac{\pi}{4}d^2v, v = \frac{4Q}{\pi d^2} \text{ or } v \propto Q$$

$$\frac{4fL_ev^2}{2gd} = \frac{4fL_ev_1^2}{2gd} + \frac{4fLv_2^2}{2gd}$$

$$L_ev^2 = Lv_1^2 + Lv_2^2$$

$$L_eQ^2 = LQ_1^2 + LQ_2^2$$

$$Q_1 = Q_2 = \frac{Q}{2} \text{ for same } d$$

$$L_eQ^2 = \frac{LQ^2}{4} + L\frac{Q^2}{4} = \frac{LQ^2}{2}$$

$$L_e = \frac{L}{2}$$

117. (b) For venturimeter,

$$Q = C_d\left[\frac{A_1A_2}{A_1^2 - A_1^2}\right]\times\left[2g\left(\frac{s_2}{s_1}-1\right)h\right]^{1/2}$$

$$\alpha \propto \frac{A_1}{\sqrt{\left(\frac{A_1}{A_2}\right)^2 - 1}}\sqrt{h}$$

For $\dfrac{A_1}{A_2} = 2$

$$Q_1 \propto \sqrt{\frac{h}{3}}$$

$$Q_1 \propto \frac{\sqrt{5h}}{\sqrt{\left(\frac{A_1}{A_2}\right)^2 - 1}}$$

For $Q_1 = Q_2$

$$\sqrt{\frac{h}{3}} = \frac{\sqrt{5h}}{\left[\left(\frac{A_1}{A_2}\right)^2 - 1\right]^{1/2}}$$

$$\sqrt{\left(\frac{A_1}{A_2}\right)^2 - 1} = \sqrt{5\times 3}$$

$$\left(\frac{A_1}{A_2}\right)^2 - 1 = 15$$

$$\left(\frac{A_1}{A_2}\right)^2 = 16$$

$$\frac{A_1}{A_2} = 4$$

118. (b) Thickness of laminar boundary layer over a flat plate,

$$\delta = \frac{5x}{\sqrt{Re_x}} = \frac{5x}{\sqrt{\frac{vx}{v}}} \propto x^{1/2}$$

119. (c) 120. (b)

❑❑❑

# 7. Power Plant Engineering

- Power engineering is a subfield of energy engineering that deals with the generation, transmission, distribution andutilization of electric power and the electrical devices connected to such systems including generators, motors and transformers.
- Although much of the field is concerned with the problems of three-phase AC power – the standard for large-scale power transmission and distribution across the modern world – a significant fraction of the field is concerned with the conversion between AC and DC power and the development of specialized power systems such as those used in aircraft or for electric railway networks.
- It was a subfield of electrical engineering before the emergence of energy engineering.
- Electricity became a subject of scientific interest in the late 17th century with the work of William Gilbert.
- Over the next two centuries a number of important discoveries were made including the incandescent light bulb and the voltaic pile. Probably the greatest discovery with respect to power engineering came from Michael Faraday who in 1831 discovered that a change in magnetic flux induces an electromotive force in a loop of wire—a principle known as electromagnetic induction that helps explain how generators and transformers work.
- In 1881 two electricians built the world's first power station at Godalming in England.
- The Edison Electric Light Company, developed the first steam-powered electric power station on Pearl Street in New York City.
- In 1885 the Italian physicist and electrical engineer Galileo Ferraris demonstrated an induction motor and in 1887 and 1888 the Serbian-American engineer Nikola Tesla filed a range of patents related to power systems including one for a practical two-phase induction motor which Westinghouse licensed for his AC system
- By 1890 the power industry had flourished and power companies had built literally thousands of power systems (both direct and alternating current) in the United States and Europe – these networks were effectively dedicated to providing electric lighting.
- In 1891, Westinghouse installed the first major power system that was designed to drive an electric motor and not just provide electric lighting. The installation powered a 100 horsepower (75 kW) synchronous motor at Telluride, Colorado with the motor being started by a Tesla induction motor.
- Although the 1880s and 1890s were seminal decades in the field, developments in power engineering continued throughout the 20th and 21st century. In 1936 the first commercial high-voltage direct current (HVDC) line using mercury-arc valves was built between Schenectady and Mechanicville, New York.
- In 1957 Siemens demonstrated the first solid-state rectifier however it was not until the early 1970s that this technology was used in commercial power systems.
- In 1959 Westinghouse demonstrated the first circuit breaker that used SF6 as the interrupting medium. SF6 is a far superior dielectric to air and, in recent times, its use has been extended to produce far more compact switching equipment and transformers.
- Many important developments also came from extending innovations in the ICT field to the power engineering field. For example, the development of computers meant load flow studies could be run more efficiently allowing for much better planning of power systems. Advances in information technology and telecommunication also allowed for much better remote control of the power system's switchgear and generators.
- There are currently 56,000 power engineers currently employed in the province of Ontario. Electric power is the mathematical product of two quantities: current andvoltage. These two quantities can vary with respect to time (AC power) or can be kept at constant levels (DC power).
- Most refrigerators, air conditioners, pumps and industrial machinery use AC power whereas computers and digital equipment use DC power (the digital devices you plug into the mains typically have an internal or external power adapter to convert from AC to DC power).
- AC power has the advantage of being easy to transform between voltages and is able to be generated and utilized by brushless machinery.
- DC power remains the only practical choice in digital systems and can be more economical to transmit over long distances at very high voltages (see HVDC).
- The ability to easily transform the voltage of AC power is important for two reasons: Firstly, power can be transmitted over long distances with less loss at higher voltages. So in power networks where generation is distant from the load, it is desirable to step-up the voltage of power at the generation point and then step-down the voltage near the load.

- Secondly, it is often more economical to install turbines that produce higher voltages than would be used by most appliances, so the ability to easily transform voltages means this mismatch between voltages can be easily managed.
- Solid state devices, which are products of the semiconductor revolution, make it possible to transform DC power to different voltages, build brushless DC machines and convert between AC and DC power.
- Power Engineering deals with the generation, transmission, distribution andutilization of electricity as well as the design of a range of related devices. These include transformers, electric generators, electric motors and power electronics.
- The power grid is an electrical network that connects a variety of electric generators to the users of electric power. Users purchase electricity from the grid so that they do not need to generate their own.
- Power engineers may work on the design and maintenance of the power grid as well as the power systems that connect to it.
- Such systems are called on-grid power systems and may supply the grid with additional power, draw power from the grid or do both. The grid is designed and managed using software that performs simulations of power flows.
- Power engineers may also work on systems that do not connect to the grid. These systems are called off-grid power systems and may be used in preference to on-grid systems for a variety of reasons.
- Today, most grids adopt three-phase electric power with alternating current. This choice can be partly attributed to the ease with which this type of power can be generated, transformed and used.
- However, many larger industries and organizations still prefer to receive the three-phase power directly because it can be used to drive highly efficient electric motors such as three-phase induction motors.
- Transformers play an important role in power transmission because they allow power to be converted to and from higher voltages. This is important because higher voltages suffer less power loss during transmission.
- This is because higher voltages allow for lower current to deliver the same amount of power, as power is the product of the two. Thus, as the voltage steps up, the current steps down. It is the current flowing through the components that result in both the losses and the subsequent heating.
- These losses, appearing in the form of heat, are equal to the current squared times the electrical resistance through which the current flows, so as the voltage goes up the losses are dramatically reduced.
- For these reasons, electrical substations exist throughout power grids to convert power to higher voltages before transmission and to lower voltages suitable for appliances after transmission.
- Generation of electrical power is a process whereby energy is transformed into an electrical form. There are several different transformation processes, among which are chemical, photo-voltaic, and electromechanical.
- Electromechanical energy conversion is used in converting energy from coal, petroleum, natural gas, uranium into electrical energy. Of these, all except the wind energy conversion process take advantage of the synchronous AC generator coupled to a steam, gas or hydro turbine such that the turbine converts steam, gas, or water flow into rotational energy, and the synchronous generator then converts the rotational energy of the turbine into electrical energy.
- It is the turbine-generator conversion process that is by far most economical and consequently most common in the industry today.
- The AC synchronous machine is the most common technology for generating electrical energy. It is called synchronous because the composite magnetic field produced by the three stator windings rotate at the same speed as the magnetic field produced by the field winding on the rotor.
- A simplified circuit model is used to analyze steady-state operating conditions for a synchronous machine. The phasor diagram is an effective tool for visualizing the relationships between internal voltage, armature current, and terminal voltage.
- The excitation control system is used on synchronous machines to regulate terminal voltage, and the turbine-governor system is used to regulate the speed of the machine. However, in highly interconnected systems, such as the "Western system", the "Texas system" and the "Eastern system", one machine will usually be assigned as the so-called "swing machine", and which generation may be increased or decreased to compensate for small changes in load, thereby maintaining the system frequency at precisely 60 Hz.
- The operating costs of generating electrical energy is determined by the fuel cost and the efficiency of the power station. The efficiency depends on generation level and can be obtained from the heat rate curve.
- We may also obtain the incremental cost curve from the heat rate curve. Economic dispatch is the process of allocating the required load demand between the available generation units such that the cost of operation is minimized.
- Emission dispatch is the process of allocating the required load demand between the available generation units such that air pollution occurring from operation is minimized. In large systems, particularly in the West, a combination of economic and emission dispatch may be used.

- The electricity is transported to load locations from a power station to a transmission subsystem. Therefore we may think of the transmission system as providing the medium of transportation for electric energy.
- The transmission system may be subdivided into the bulk transmission system and the sub-transmission system. The functions of the bulk transmission are to interconnect generators, to interconnect various areas of the network, and to transfer electrical energy from the generators to the major load centers.
- This portion of the system is called "bulk" because it delivers energy only to so-called bulk loads such as the distribution system of a town, city, or large industrial plant. The function of the sub-transmission system is to interconnect the bulk power system with the distribution system.
- Transmission circuits may be built either underground or overhead. Underground cables are used predominantly in urban areas where acquisition of overhead rights of way are costly or not possible.
- They are also used for transmission under rivers, lakes and bays. Overhead transmission is used otherwise because, for a given voltage level, overhead conductors are much less expensive than underground cables.
- The transmission system is a highly integrated system. It is referred to as the substation equipment and transmission lines. The substation equipment contain the transformers, relays, and circuit breakers.
- Transformers are important static devices which transfer electrical energy from one circuit to another in the transmission subsystem. Transformers are used to step up the voltage on the transmission line to reduce the power loss which is dissipated on the way.
- A relay is functionally a level-detector; they perform a switching action when the input voltage (or current) meets or exceeds a specific and adjustable value. A circuit breaker is an automatically operated electrical switch designed to protect an electrical circuit from damage caused by overload or short circuit.
- A change in the status of any one component can significantly affect the operation of the entire system. Without adequate contact protection, the occurrence of undesired electric arcing causes significant degradation of the contacts, which suffer serious damage.
- There are three possible causes for power flow limitations to a transmission line. These causes are thermal overload, voltage instability, and rotor angle instability. Thermal overload is caused by excessive current flow in a circuit causing overheating.
- Voltage instability is said to occur when the power required to maintain voltages at or above acceptable levels exceeds the available power.
- Rotor angle instability is a dynamic problem that may occur following faults, such as short circuit, in the transmission system. It may also occur tens of seconds after a fault due to poorly damped or undamped oscillatory response of the rotor motion.
- The distribution system transports the power from the transmission system/substation to the customer. Distribution feeders can be radial or networked in an open loop configuration with a single or multiple alternate sources.
- Rural systems tend to be of the former and urban systems the latter. The equipment associated with the distribution system usually begins downstream of the distribution feeder circuit breaker.
- The transformer and circuit breaker are usually under the jurisdiction of a "substations department". The distribution feeders consist of combinations of overhead and underground conductor, 3 phase and single phase switches with load break and non-loadbreak ability, relayed protective devices, fuses, transformers (to utilization voltage), surge arresters, voltage regulators and capacitors.
- Slip-ring induction motors are usually started with full-line voltage across the stator terminals and by introducing variable resistor in each phase of the rotor circuit. The external resistances introduced in each phase of the rotor circuit not only reduces the current at the starting instant but increases the starting torque also due to improvement in pf.
- Squirrel cage induction motor is suitable for constant speed industrial drives of small power where speed control is not required and where starting torque requirements are of medium or low value, such as for printing machinery, flour mills and other shaft drives of small power.
- Wound rotor (or slip-ring) induction motors are used for loads requiring severe starting conditions or for loads requiring speed control such as for driving line shafts, lifts, pumps, generators, winding machines, cranes, hoists, elevators, compressors, small electric excavators, printing presses, turn tables, strokers, large ventilating fans, crushers etc.
- An induction motor derives its name from the fact that the current in the rotor conductors is induced by the motion of rotor conductors relative to the magnetic field developed by the stator currents.
- Two types of 3-phase induction motors are (i) squirrel cage and (ii) wound rotor or slip-ring induction motors. Squirrel cage induction motor is generally preferred.

# MULTIPLE CHOICE QUESTIONS

1. In the bottoming cycle of cogeneration, low grade waste heat is used for:
(a) processing (b) power generation
(c) feed water heating (d) none of the above
2. The main aim of compounding steam turbine is to:
(a) improve efficiency
(b) reduce steam consumption
(c) reduce motor speed
(d) reduce turbine size
3. A throttle governed steam develops 201. H.P. with 281 kg/hr of steam and 50 IHP with 521 kg/hr of steam. The steam consumption in kg/hr when developing 15 IHP will be nearly:
(a) 150 kg/hr (b) 156 kg/hr
(c) 241 kg/hr (d) 290 kg/hr
4. Governing of steam turbines can be done by the following:
1. Nozzle control
2. Throttle control
3. Providing additional valve and passage
The correct answer will be:
(a) 1, 2 and 3
(b) 1 and 2 only
(c) 2 and 3 only
(d) 1 and 3 only
5. In a steam power plant, feed water heater is a heat exchanger to preheat feed water by:
(a) live steam from steam generator
(b) hot flue gases coming out of the boiler furnace
(c) hot air from air preheater
(d) extracting steam from turbine
6. Economizer is generally placed between:
(a) last superheater/reheater and air preheater
(b) air preheater and chimney
(c) electrostatic precipitators
(d) induced draft fan and forced draft fan.
7. Attempting is:
(a) reduction of steam pressure
(b) reduction of steam temperature
(c) discharge of flue gases at certain height
(d) conditioning of disposable fluids for minimum pollution
8. In Fluidized bed combustion velocity of fluid is proportion of ($r$ = radius of the particle) as:
(a) $\frac{1}{r}$ (b) $\frac{1}{\sqrt{r}}$
(c) $\sqrt{r}$ (d) $r$
9. Match the following:

| List-I | List-II |
|---|---|
| A. Moderator | 1. Graphite |
| B. Control rod | 2. Boron |
| C. Poison | 3. Concrete |
| D. Shield Material | 4. Hafmium |

Codes:

| | A | B | C | D |
|---|---|---|---|---|
| (a) | 1 | 4 | 3 | 2 |
| (b) | 3 | 1 | 2 | 4 |
| (c) | 4 | 3 | 2 | 1 |
| (d) | 1 | 4 | 2 | 3 |

10. Which one of the following factors has the maximum effect of the equivalent evaporation of a boiler?
(a) Steam generator pressure
(b) Feed water inlet temperature
(c) Heating surface of the boiler
(d) Quality of steam produced.
11. Consider the following statements:
1. Safety valve in boilers will operate as soon as the pressure reaches the rated value.
2. Two safety valves are provided for quick release of pressure.
3. Blow down valve is operated regularly to remove sediments if any.
4. Water level is monitored electrically in all large boilers
Of these statements:
(a) 1 and 2 are correct (b) 2 and 3 are correct
(c) 3 and 4 are correct (d) 1 and 4 are correct
12. The average number of fast neutrons produced in the fission of an U-235 atom is nearly:
(a) 1.23 (b) 2.46
(c) 3.69 (d) 4.92
13. In an ideal steam power cycle with the same inlet pressure, the low dryness fraction of steam in the last stage of expansion process can be avoided by:
(a) providing regeneration
(b) providing reheating
(c) reducing the superheat
(d) lowering the condenser pressure.
14. Match List-I with List-II in respect of nuclear reactor and select the correct answer using the codes given below the lists:

| List-I | List-II |
|---|---|
| A. Poison | 1. Hafnium |
| B. Moderator | 2. Graphite |
| C. Cladding | 3. Zirconium |
| D. Fission Product | 4. Strontium-90 |

Codes:

| | A | B | C | D |
|---|---|---|---|---|
| (a) | 2 | 1 | 4 | 3 |
| (b) | 2 | 1 | 3 | 4 |
| (c) | 1 | 2 | 3 | 4 |
| (d) | 1 | 2 | 4 | 3 |

15. Consider the following statements:
Uranium oxide is chosen as fuel element in the nuclear reactors, because Uranium oxide
1. is more stable than Uranium.

2. does not corrode easily.
3. is more brittle.
4. has dimensional stability.

Among these statements:
(a) 1, 2 and 4 are correct
(b) 1, 2 and 3 are correct
(c) 1 2, 3 and 4 are correct
(d) 3 and 4 are correct

16. Energy released by the fission of one U-235 atom is nearly:
(a) 2000 MeV (b) 1000 MeV
(c) 200 MeV (d) 20 MeV

17. Match List-I (Component) with List-II (Properties) in the context of nuclear reactors and select the correct answer using the codes given below the lists:

| **List-I** | **List –II** |
|---|---|
| A. Coolant | 1. Low neutron absorption |
| B. Moderator | 2. Low radiation damage |
| C. Fuel | 3. High heal transfer coefficient |
| D. Shield | 4. High absorption of radiation. |

**Codes:**

| | A | B | C | D |
|---|---|---|---|---|
| (a) | 3 | 1 | 4 | 2 |
| (b) | 3 | 1 | 2 | 4 |
| (c) | 1 | 4 | 4 | 2 |
| (d) | 1 | 3 | 2 | 4 |

18. Consider the following statements:
1. Pulverised fuel gives high and controlled burning rate.
2. Insufficient air causes excessive smoking of exhaust.
3. Excess air is provided to control the flue gas temperature
4. Effect of sulphur in fuel is to give high heat transfer rate.

Which of these statements are correct?
(a) 3 and 4 (b) 2 and 3
(c) 1 and 2 (d) 1 and 4

19. Consider the following:
1. Safety valve
2. Fusible plug
3. Feed water pump
4. Pressure gauge

The essential boiler mountings would include.
(a) 1, 3 and 4 (b) 3 and 4
(c) 1, 2 and 3 (d) 1, 2 and 4

20. Which one of the following gaseous fuels does not have different higher and lower calorific values?
(a) Methane (b) Ethane
(c) Carbon monoxide (d) Hydrogen

21. Consider the following statements regarding an impulse turbine:
1. Relative velocity at the inlet and exit of the rotor blades are the same.
2. Absolute velocity at the inlet and exit of the rotor blades are the same.
3. Static pressure within the rotor blade channel is constant.
4. Total pressure within the blade channel is constant.

Of these statements
(a) 1 and 4 arc correct (b) 2 and 3 arc correct
(c) 1 and 3 arc correct (d) 2 and 4 are correct

22. The circulation ratio for once through steam generators is:
(a) 1 (b) 2
(c) 2.5 (d) 5

23. Consider the following accessories:
1. Superheater 2. Air pre-heater
3. Economizer

The correct sequence of the position of these accessories along the flow of flue gas in a steam power plant is:
(a) 3, 1, 2 (b) 1, 2, 3
(c) 1, 3, 2 (d) 2, 1, 3

24. Inside a large power boiler, the flue gas pressure will be above the atmospheric pressure:
(a) at the furnace
(b) nearsuperheater region
(c) at the base of the chimney
(d) after the forced draught fan

25. Steam enters a diffuser at Mach number 2.5 and exits at Mach number 1.8. The shape of the diffuser is:
(a) divergent (b) convergent
(c) convergent-divergent (d) divergent-convergent

26. Shock waves in nozzles would occur while turbines arc operating:
(a) at overload conditions
(b) at part load conditions
(c) above critical pressure ratio
(d) at all off-design conditions

27. Steam enters the rotor of a reaction turbine with an absolute velocity of 236 m/s and relative velocity of 132 m/s. It leaves the rotor with a relative velocity of 232 m/s and absolute velocity of 126 m/s. The specific work output is:
(a) 36.3 kW (b) 40.1 kW
(c) 43.8 kW (d) 47.4 kW

28. The work output from a reaction turbine stage is 280 kW per kg/s of steam. If the nozzle efficiency is 0.92 and rotor efficiency is 0.90, the isentropic static enthalpy drop will be:
(a) 352 kW (b) 347 kW
(c) 338 kW (d) 332 kW

29. In a steam turbine, the enthalpy drops in the fixed blade and moving blade are 48 kJ and 32 kJ respectively. The degree of reaction is:
(a) 40% (b) 55%
(c) 60% (d) 66.6%

30. When the water level in the boiler falls to an unsafe limit, safety is ensured by the:
(a) stop valve
(b) safety valve
(c) fusible valve
(d) blow-off cock

31. Large temperature rise of boiler feed water in the economiser should be avoided because:
(a) the economiser efficiency will reduce
(b) the overall steam generator efficiency will reduce
(c) effectiveness of regenerator will he lower
(d) flue gas will cool to dew point

32. Consider the following statements:
The erosion of steam turbine blades increases with the increase of
1. moisture in the steam
2. blade speed
Which of these statement (s) is/are correct?
(a) 1 alone
(b) 2 alone
(c) 1 and 2
(d) Neither 1 nor 2

33. Consider the following statements:
Steam turbines are suitable for use as prime movers for large steam power plants because
1. a single steam turbine can be designed for a capacity of 1000 MW or more
2. much higher speed may he possible as compared to a reciprocating engine
3. they are more compact when compared to a gas turbine power plant
4. the maintenance cost and running cost maynot increase with years of service.
Which of these statements are correct?
(a) 1, 2 and 3
(b) 2, 3 and 4
(c) 1, 2 and 4
(d) 1, 3 and 4

34. Which one of the following types of nuclear reactor does not require a heat exchanger?
(a) Boiling water
(b) Pressurized water
(c) Sodium-cooled
(d) Gas-cooled

35. Consider the following statements regarding nuclear reactors:
1. A mixture of radioactive materials is used as fuel
2. Spent fuel is reprocessed to recover thorium/plutonium
3. Control rods are made of zirconium
4. Spent fuel is fully disposed of safely, as waste.
Which of these statements are correct?
(a) 1 and 2 (b) 3 and 4
(c) 1 and 3 (d) 1, 3 and 4

36. Match List-I with List-I1 regarding nuclear reactors and select the correct answer using the codes given below the lists:

| List-I | List-II |
|---|---|
| A. Moderator | 1. U-233 |
| B. Biological shield | 2. Hafnium |
| C. Poison | 3. Beryllium |
| D. Nuclear fuel | 4. Sodium |
| | 5. Lead |

**Codes:**

| | A | B | C | D |
|---|---|---|---|---|
| (a) | 3 | 2 | 5 | 1 |
| (b) | 4 | 5 | 2 | 3 |
| (c) | 3 | 5 | 2 | 1 |
| (d) | 4 | 2 | 1 | 3 |

37. Dryness fraction of steam means the mass ratio of:
(a) wet steam to dry steam
(b) dry steam to water particles in steam
(c) water particles to total steam
(d) dry steam to total steam.

38. A nucleus $_{92}A^{235}$ emits alpha and beta particles and is converted to the nucleus $_{82}$Bu. The total number of alpha and beta particles emitted in the reaction is 11. Their respective numbers are:
(a) 5 and 6 (b) 7 and 4
(c) 4 and 7 (d) 6 and 5

39. Amount of oxygen needed to completely burn 1 kg of methane $(CH_4)$ is:
(a) 2 kg (b) 4 kg
(c) 16 kg (d) 22 kg

40. There is no steam drum in:
(a) La Mont boiler (b) Loeffler boiler
(c) Benson boiler (d) Velox boiler

41. Match List-I (Equipments) with List-II (Types) and select the correct answer using the codes given below the lists:

| List-I | List-II |
|---|---|
| A. Steam trap | 1. Fire tube type |
| B. Water-level indicator | 2. Boiler mounting |
| C. Cornish boiler | 3. Drumless type |
| D. Benson boiler | 4. Boiler accessory |
| | 5. Indirectly heated |

**Codes:**

| | A | B | C | D |
|---|---|---|---|---|
| (a) | 2 | 4 | 3 | 5 |
| (b) | 2 | 4 | 5 | 3 |
| (c) | 4 | 2 | 1 | 5 |
| (d) | 4 | 2 | 1 | 3 |

42. The function of an economizer in a steam power plant is to:
(a) increase the temperature of air supplied to a boiler
(b) increase the enthalpy of feed water

(c) condense the exhaust steam from the turbine
(d) heat the fuel before combustion.

43. Consider the following statements:
A tube, with the section diverging in the direction of flow, can be used as
1. supersonic nozzle 2. subsonic nozzle
3. supersonic diffuser 4. subsonic diffuser
Select the correct answer using the codes given below:
(a) 1 alone (b) 3 alone
(c) 1 and 4 (d) 2 and 3

44. A nozzle is discharging steam through critical pressure ratio. When the back pressure is further decreased, the nozzle flow rate will:
(a) decrease
(b) increase
(c) remain unaltered
(d) first increase to maximum and then will decrease

45. The half life of radioactive radon is 3.8 days. The time at the end of which 1/20th of the Radon sample will remain undecayed will be:
(a) 3.8 days (b) 16.5 days
(c) 33 days (d) 76 days

46. Ratio of enthalpy drop in moving blades to the total enthalpy drop in the fixed and moving blades is called:
(a) Reheat factor (b) Blade efficiency
(c) Degree of reaction (d) Internal efficiency

47. Maximum blade efficiency of a Parson's turbine is given by: ($\alpha$ is nozzle angle)
(a) $\frac{\cos^2 \alpha}{1+2\cos^2 \alpha}$ (b) $\frac{\cos \alpha}{1+2\cos^2 \alpha}$
(c) $\frac{2\sin^2 \alpha}{1+2\sin^2 \alpha}$ (d) $\frac{2\cos^2 \alpha}{1+2\cos^2 \alpha}$

48. The most efficient ideal regenerative steam power cycle is:
(a) Rankine cycle (b) Carnot cycle
(c) Brayton cycle (d) Joule cycle

49. In modem steam plants using pulverized fuel firing, the flue gases:
(a) first pass through air preheaters and then through economizer
(b) first pass through economizer and then through air preheaters
(c) pass simultaneously through air preheaters and economizer which are connected in parallel
(d) pass through economizer only.

50. Consider the following statements:
The purpose of reheating the steam in a steam turbine power plant is to
1. increase specific output
2. increase turbine efficiency
3. reduce the turbine speed
4. reduce specific steam consumption.
Which of the statements are correct?
(a) 2 and 4 (b) 1 and 3
(c) 1, 2 and 4 (d) 1, 3 and 4

51. A sodium graphite reactor uses sodium:
(a) as coolant and graphite as moderator
(b) as moderator and graphite as coolant
(c) with graphite as moderator and water as coolant
(d) as moderator and sodium, graphite and water together as coolant.

52. Purpose of moderator in nuclear reactor is to:
(a) slow down the neutrons produced in fission
(b) reduce nuclear pollution
(c) control the reactor temperature so that protons produced are less
(d) moderate the steam pressure to slow down the chain reaction.

53. In Fast Breeder Reactor:
(a) the moderator used is water
(b) the moderator used is graphite
(c) the moderator used is carbon dioxide
(d) no moderator is used.

54. If the enthalpies at the entry and exit of a nozzle are 3450 kJ/kg and 2800 kJ/kg and the initial velocity is negligible, then the velocity at the exit is:
(a) 806.2 m/s (b) 25.5 m/s
(c) 36 m/s (d) 1140.2 m/s

55. A nozzle is said to have choked flow when
1. discharge is maximum.
2. throat velocity is sonic.
3. nozzle exit pressure is more than the critical pressure.
4. discharge is zero
Select the correct answer using the codes given below:
(a) 1 only (b) 1 and 2
(c) 4 only (d) 1, 2 and 3

56. Consider the following characteristics:
1. High steam and blade velocities
2. Low steam and blade velocities
3. Low speeds of rotation
4. High carry-over loss
Which of these characteristics are possessed by a simple impulse turbine?
(a) 1 and 2 (b) 2 and 3
(c) 1 and 4 (d) 3 and 4

57. In a simple impulse turbine, the nozzle angle at the entrance is 30°. What will be the blade-speed ratio for maximum diagram efficiency?
(a) 0.433 (b) 0.25
(c) 0.5 (d) 0.75

58. In a two-row Curtis stage with symmetrical blading:
(a) work done by both rows of moving blades are equal
(b) work done by the first row of moving blades is double of the work done by second row of moving blades
(c) work done by the first row of moving blades is three times the work done by second row of moving blades

59. In reaction turbines, with reduction of inlet pressure:
(a) the blade heights increase as the specific volume of steam decrease.
(b) the blade heights increase as the specific volume of steam increases
(c) the blade heights decrease as the specific volume of steam increases
(d) the blade heights decrease as the specific volume of the steam decreases.

60. If the enthalpy drops of moving blade and fixed blade of a stage in a reaction turbine are 9 and 11 kJ/kg respectively, then degree of reaction of stage is:
(a) 0.1 (b) 0.45
(c) 0.55 (d) 1.0

61. Which of the following combustion systems requires maximum excess air?
(a) Pulverized coal combustion
(b) Oil burners
(c) Gas burners
(d) Chain grate stoker

62. Match List-I with List-II and select the correct answer using the codes given below the lists:

| **List-I** | **List-II** |
|---|---|
| A. Fuel | 1. Graphite |
| B. Cladding | 2. Natural Uranium |
| C. Coolant | 3. Magnox |
| D. Moderator | 4. $CO_2$ |

**Codes:**

| | A | B | C | D |
|---|---|---|---|---|
| (a) | 1 | 4 | 3 | 2 |
| (b) | 2 | 4 | 4 | 1 |
| (c) | 1 | 3 | 4 | 2 |
| (d) | 2 | 4 | 3 | 1 |

63. If $k$ is the ratio of the rate of production of neutrons to the rate of loss of neutrons, the reactor is called a critical reactor, when:
(a) $k = 0$ (b) $0 < k < 1$
(c) $k = 1$ (d) $k > 1$

64. The most commonly used moderator in nuclear power plants is:
(a) heavy water (b) concrete and bricks
(c) steel (d) graphite

65. Consider an actual regenerative Rankine cycle with one open feed water heater. For each kg steam entering the turbine, $m$ kg steam with a specific enthalpy of $h_1$ is bled from the turbine. Specific enthalpy of water entering the heater is $h_2$. The specific enthalpy saturated liquid leaving the heater is equal to:
(a) $mh_1 - (h_2 - h_1)$ (b) $h_1 - m(h_2 - h_2)$
(c) $h_2 - m(h_2 - h_1)$ (d) $mh_2 - (h_2 - h_1)$

66. In the case of supersaturated steam flow through a nozzle, which of the following statements are correct?
1. Availability increases
2. Mass flow coefficient is greater than unity.
3. Nozzle velocity coefficient is less than unity.

Select the correct answer using the codes given below:

**Codes:**
(a) 1, 2 and 3 (b) 1 and 2
(c) 2 and 3 (d) 1 and 3

67. Which of the following thermal power plants will have the highest overall thermal efficiency?
(a) Steam power plant
(b) Gas turbine power plant
(c) Combined gas and steam power plant
(d) Diesel power plant

68. The function of the moderator in nuclear reactor is to:
(a) stop chain reaction
(b) reduce the speed of the neutrons
(c) absorb neutrons
(d) reduce temperature

69. Match List-I (Feature) with List-II (Turbine/ Staging) and select the correct answer using the codes given below the lists:

| **List-I (Feature)** | **List-II (Turbine/Staging)** |
|---|---|
| A. Single stage impulse turbine | 1. Person's turbine |
| B. Pressure compounding | 2. de Laval turbine |
| C. Velocity compounding | 3. Rateau staging |
| D. Reaction turbine | 4. Curtis staging |

**Codes:**

| | A | B | C | D |
|---|---|---|---|---|
| (a) | 4 | 1 | 2 | 3 |
| (b) | 2 | 3 | 4 | 1 |
| (c) | 4 | 3 | 2 | 1 |
| (d) | 2 | 1 | 4 | 3 |

70. In steam and other vapour cycles, the process of removing non-condensable is called:
(a) Scavenging process
(b) Depuration process
(c) Exhaust process
(d) Condensation process

71. Which of the following are fertile materials?
(a) $U^{33}$ and $Pu^{239}$ (b) $U^{238}$ and $Th^{239}$
(c) $U^{238}$ and $Th^{232}$ (d) $U^{235}$ and $Pu^{236}$ 72

72. S.I unit for radioactivity is:
(a) joule
(b) amu
(c) Curie
(d) Becquerel

73. Which one of the following is the purpose of blow-down in a boiler?
(a) To control drum level
(b) To control solid concentration in the boiler water
(c) To increase the steam temperature
(d) To lower the steam temperature

74. Steam flows at the rate of 10 kg/s through a supersonic nozzle. Throat diameter is 50 mm. Density ratio and velocity ratio with reference to throat and exit are respectively 2.45 and 0.8. What is the diameter at the exit'?
(a) 122.5 mm (b) 58 mm
(c) 70 mm (d) 62.5 mm

75. An attemparator is used in some utility boilers:
(a) ahead of super heater for initial superheating.
(b) for optimizing steam output from the generator
(c) to regulate steam pressure
(d) to control degree of superheat.

76. What is the purpose of moderator in a nuclear reactor?
(a) Moderate the fission temperature
(b) Reduce the speed of fast moving neutrons
(c) Reduce β and γ rays
(d) Absorb excess neutrons in the reactor

77. What is the efficiency of an ideal regenerative Rankine cycle power plant using saturated steam at 327°C and pressure 135 bar at the inlet to the turbine, and condensing temperature of 27°C (corresponding saturation pressure of 3.6 kPa)?
(a) 92% (b) 33%
(c) 50% (d) 42%

78. In a coupled separating and throttling calorimeter, 0.9 is the dryness fraction of steam in the separating unit and 0.95 is the dryness fraction in the throttling unit. What is the approximate value of the dryness fraction of the steam sample?
(a) 0.855 (b) 0.925
(c) 0.947 (d) 0.950

79. Consider the following statements:
1. Fusible plug is a device used to put off fire in the furnace of the boiler when the level of water in the boiler falls to an unsafe limit.
2. Superheater is a device used to increase the temperature of saturated steam without raising its pressure.
3. An economizer decreases the steam raising capacity of boiler

Which of the above statements is/are correct?
(a) 1 and 2
(b) 2 and 3
(c) 1 only
(d) 1, 2 and 3

80. What is the cause of reheat factor in a steam turbine?
(a) Reheating (b) Superheating
(c) Supersaturation (d) Blade friction

81. In a simple turbine, the nozzle angle at the entrance is 30°. What is the blade speed ratio for maximum diagram efficiency?
(a) 0.25 (b) 0.5
(c) 0.433 (d) 0.125

82. Match List-I (Reactor) with List-II (Characteristic) and select the correct answer using the code given below the lists:

| List-I (Rector) | List-II (Characteristic) |
|---|---|
| A. Heterogeneous reactor | 1. May not need moderator |
| B. Candu reactor | 2. Natural uranium fuelled and heavy water cooled |
| C. Boiling water reactor | 3. Fuel and moderator are at different phases |
| D. Fast breeder reactor | 4. Coolant water boils in the case of the reactor |

**Codes:**

| | A | B | C | D |
|---|---|---|---|---|
| (a) | 3 | 4 | 2 | 1 |
| (b) | 1 | 2 | 4 | 3 |
| (c) | 3 | 2 | 4 | 1 |
| (d) | 1 | 4 | 2 | 3 |

83. Match List-I (Name of Boiler) with List-II (Type) and select the correct answer using the rode given below the lists:

| List-I (Name of Boiler) | List-II (Type) |
|---|---|
| A. Stirling | 1. Bent water tube |
| B. Cochran | 2. Once through flow |
| C. Lancashire | 3. Vertical fire tube |
| D. Benson | 4. Incline water tube |
| | 5. Horizontal fire tube |

**Codes:**

| | A | B | C | D |
|---|---|---|---|---|
| (a) | 2 | 5 | 4 | 1 |
| (b) | 1 | 3 | 5 | 2 |
| (c) | 2 | 3 | 5 | 1 |
| (d) | 1 | 5 | 4 | 2 |

84. In a steam power plant what is the outcome of regenerative feed heating?
1. Increase in specific output
2. Increase in cycle efficiency
3. Improved quality of exhaust steam
4. Reduced condenser load

Select the correct answer using the code given below:
(a) 1 and 3 only (b) 2 only
(c) 2 and 4 (d) 1, 2 and 3

85. Consider the following statements in the context of high pressure boilers:
1. The tendency of scale formation is eliminated due to high velocity of water through tubes.
2. The heat transfer coefficient is increased by increasing the velocity of water through tubes.
3. The steam can he raised quickly to meet the variable load.

Which of the statements given above are correct?
(a) 1 and 2 only (b) 2 and 3 only
(c) 1 and 3 only (d) 1, 2 and 3

86. Why is enriched Uranium required as fuel when ordinary water is used as a moderator?
(a) Ordinary water has low moderating efficiency
(b) Ordinary water has high moderating absorption
(c) Ordinary water has high moderating efficiency
(d) Ordinary water has low neutron absorption.

87. Which one of the following gases is normally not used as a coolant in nuclear reactor?
(a) Hydrogen (b) Helium
(c) Carbon dioxide (d) Nitrogen

88. Which one of the following is correct?
De Laval turbine is a
(a) simple reaction turbine
(b) simple impulse turbine
(c) velocity compounded impulse turbine
(d) pressure compounded impulse turbine

89. Which one of the following is the correct statement?
Reheating of steam under ideal conditions takes place at constant
(a) entropy (b) enthalpy
(c) pressure (d) temperature

90. Consider the following statements about reactors:
1. Candu reactor is a natural uranium fuelled, heavy water cooled and moderated reactor.
2. In a pressurized water reactor the coolant water boils in the core of the reactor
3. Liquid metal is preferred as a coolant in case of a homogeneous reactor.

Which of the statements given above is/are correct?
(a) 1 only (b) 2 only
(c) 1 and 3 only (d) 1, 2 and 3

91. What is the material of thick walled canisters in which nuclear waste is buried deep?
(a) Zirconium (b) Lead
(c) Stainless steel (d) Tin

92. An isentropic nozzle is discharging steam at the critical pressure ratio. When the back pressure is further decreased, which one of the following will take place?
(a) Nozzle flow decreases
(b) Nozzle flow increases
(c) Nozzle flow will first increase, reach a maximum and then decrease
(d) Nozzle flow will remain unaltered.

93. How does entropy change when the supersaturation occurs in a steam nozzle?
(a) The entropy decreases
(b) The entropy increases
(c) The entropy decreases and then increases
(d) The entropy increases and then decreases.

94. Consider the following statements in respect of nozzles:
1. The nozzle efficiency is defined as the ratio of the actual enthalpy drop to the isentropic enthalpy drop between the same pressures.
2. Velocity coefficient is defined as the ratio of exit velocity when the flow is isentropic, to the actual velocity.
3. The included angle of divergence is usually kept more than 20°.

Which of the statements given above is/are correct?
(a) 1 only (b) 1 and 2 only
(c) 3 only (d) 1, 2 and 3

95. In a convergent-divergent steam nozzle, the flow is supersonic at which location?
(a) Entrance of the nozzle
(b) Throat
(c) Converging portion of the nozzle
(d) Diverging portion of the nozzle

96. A fast breeder reactor uses which one of the following as fuel?
(a) Thorium (b) $U^{235}$
(c) Plutonium (d) Enriched uranium

97. Consider the following statements:
1. Heat is generated in a nuclear reactor by fission of U-235 by neutron.
2. Percentage of U-238 in natural Uranium is around 0.71.
3. Plutonium is not a naturally occurring nuclear fuel.

Which of the statements given above is/are correct?
(a) 1 only (b) 2 and 3 only
(c) 1 and 3 only (d) 1, 2 and 3

98. Match List-I with List-II and select the correct answer using the code given below the lists:

| List-I (Turbine Performance Factor) | List-II (Definition) |
|---|---|
| A. Reheat factor | 1. $\frac{\text{Adiabatic heat drop}}{\text{heat supplied}}$ |
| B. Internal efficiency | 2. $\frac{\text{Total work done on the motor}}{\text{Total adiabatic heat}}$ |
| C. Degree or reaction | 3. $\frac{\text{Cumulative heat drop of all stages}}{\text{Total adiabatic heatdrop}}$ |
| D. Rankine efficiency | 4. $\frac{\text{Enthalpy drop in moving blades}}{\text{Enthalpy drop in the stage}}$ |

**Codes:**

| | A | B | C | D |
|---|---|---|---|---|
| (a) | 3 | 2 | 4 | 1 |
| (b) | 4 | 1 | 3 | 2 |
| (c) | 4 | 2 | 3 | 1 |
| (d) | 3 | 1 | 4 | 2 |

99. The enthalpy of steam entering a, turbine in a Rankine cycle is 3200 kJ/kg. The enthalpy after isentropic expansion is 2400 kJ/kg and the enthalpy at the end of actual expansion is 2560 kJ/kg. What is the turbine efficiency?
(a) 75% (b) 80%
(c) 85% (d) 90%

100. For a steam jet angle of 30° (from the tangential direction) at the entrance, what is the maximum blade efficiency (approximate) of a Parson's turbine?
(a) 0.85 (b) 0.49
(c) 0.4 (d) 0.3

101. In a reaction turbine enthalpy drop per stage is 60 unit while the enthalpy drop in the moving blade is 32 unit. What is the degree of reaction?
(a) 0.28 (b) 0.46
(c) 0.53 (d) 1.87

102. Where is shock effect felt in a nozzle?
(a) Divergent portion (b) Entrance
(d) Convergent portion (d) Throat

103. What is the value of the Mach number in the convergent portion of a steam nozzle?
(a) one (b) zero
(c) > 1 (d) > 1(≠ 0)

104. Consider the following statements:
1. In a nozzle, if the fluid velocity is greater than the local sound velocity, the duct must converge.
2. In a diffuser, if the fluid velocity is greater than the local sound velocity, then the duct must converge.

Which of the statements given above is/are correct?
(a) 1 only (b) 2 only
(c) Both 1 and 2 (d) Neither 1 nor 2

105. For a convergent nozzle, what is the correct expression for the critical pressure, if the inlet pressure is $P_1$ ?

(a) $p_1\left(\frac{2}{\gamma+1}\right)^{\gamma/\gamma-1}$ (b) $p_1\left(\frac{\gamma+1}{2}\right)^{\gamma/\gamma-1}$

(c) $p_1\left(\frac{2}{\gamma+1}\right)^{\gamma-1/\gamma}$ (d) $p_1\left(\frac{\gamma+1}{2}\right)^{2\gamma/\gamma-1}$

106. Which of the following are the advantages of a surface condenser?
1. Less quantity of make up water is required.
2. It is suitable for higher capacity plants.
3. Power requirements of circulating pump and air pump are much less.

Select the correct answer using the code given below:
(a) 1 and 2 only (b) 2 and 3 only
(c) 1 and 3 only (d) 1, 2 and 3

107. Consider the following statements:
1. Reheating in a steam power plant leads to increased condenser requirement.
2. The efficiency of regenerative cycle in a steam power plan is maximum when the temperature of bled steam is equal to the geometric mean of the extreme temperatures of the primary flow cycle.

Which of the statements given above is/are correct?
(a) 1 only (b) 2 only
(c) Both 1 and 2 (d) Neither 1 nor 2

108. Consider the following statements:
1. In a steam power plan, the volume flow at the low pressure end is considerably reduced by bleeding.
2. Theoretically, the efficiency of a steam power plant increases with the increasing number of feed heaters but the gain is in diminishing return.

Which of the statements given above is/are correct?
(a) 1 only (b) 2 only
(c) Both 1 and 2 (d) Neither 1 nor 2

109. Entropy of a saturated liquid at 227 °C is 2.6 kJ/kg K. Its latent heat of vaporization is 1800kJ/kg: then the entropy of saturated vapor at 227°C would be:
(a) 2.88 kJ/kg K (b) 6.2 kJ/kg K
(c) 7.93 kJ/kg K (d) 10.53 kJ/kg K

110. Which of the following statements are true about CANDU reactors?
1. Fuel elements contain natural-uranium dioxide
2. Pressurized heavy-water coolant is used
3. Horizontal pressure tube is used

(a) 1 and 2 only (b) 1 and 3 only
(c) 2 and 3 only (d) 1, 2 and 3

111. When inspection doors on the wails of boilers are opened, flame does not leap out because:
(a) these holes are small
(b) pressure inside is negative
(c) flame travels always in the direction of flow
(d) these holes are located beyond the furnace

112. An induced draft fan is normally located at the:
(a) outlet of the steam generator before the dust collector
(b) outlet of the steam generator after the dust collector
(c) inlet of the steam generator before the air heater
(d) inlet of the steam generator after the air heater

113. The boiler used in the Nuclear Station at Tarapor is of the:
(a) pressurized water type
(b) boiling water type
(c) gas cooled type
(d) liquid metal cooled type

114. Consider the following statements:
1. Breeder reactor produces more plutonium than what it consumes.
2. Zirconium is used as a shield material.
3. Lead is the commonly used moderator.

Of these, the ones which are not correct will include:
(a) 1, 2 and 3 (b) 1 and 2
(c) 2 and 3 (d) 1 and 3

115. Which one of the following groups of devices are used for part recovery of heat from the flue gases leaving the tube banks in a water tube boiler?
(a) Drum internals, super heaters and economiser
(b) Economiser, air preheater and electrostatic precipitator
(c) Water wall, drum internals and super heaters
(d) Super heaters, economiser and air preheater

116. In large power boilers, soot blowers are used at regular intervals for cleaning the tubes. What is the fluid used for the same?
(a) Low pressure steam (b) Hot gases
(c) Hot air (d) Boiling water

117. In high pressure water tube boilers, the tube bundles are:
(a) hung from top girders
(b) supported on brick walls
(c) bolted on steel structures
(d) firmly fixed on any structure

118. Consider the following statements:
1. Actual mass flow rate of steam will be less than the theoretical value in all cases of flow through a nozzle
2. Mass flow of steam cannot be increased beyond a certain value in the case of flow through a nozzle.
3. Actual velocity of steam at the exit of a nozzle will always be less than the theoretical value.

Of these statements:
(a) 1, 2 and 3 are correct
(b) 1 and 2 are correct
(c) 2 and 3 are correct
(d) 1 and 4 are correct

119. If in an impulse turbine designed for free vortex flow, the tangential velocity of steam at the root radius of 250 mm is 430 m/s and the Made height is 100 mm, then the tangential velocity of steam at the tip will be:
(a) 602 m/s (b) 504 m/s
(c) 409 m/s (d) 307 m/s

120. If in a steam turbine stage, heat drop in moving blade ring is 40 kJ/kg and that in the fixed blade ring is 60 kJ/kg, then the degree of reaction is:
(a) 20% (b) 40%
(c) 68% (d) 70%

121. High energy rate forming process used for forming components from thin metal sheets or deform thin tubes is:
(a) Petro-forming
(b) Magnetic pulse forming
(c) Explosive forming
(d) Electro-hydraulic forming

122. In the 3-2-1 principle of fixture design, 3 refers to number of:
(a) Set ups possible
(b) Clamps required
(c) Positions on primary face
(d) Locating positions

123. The optimum cutting speed is one which should have:
1. High metal removal rate
2. High cutting tool life
3. Balance the metal removal rate and cutting tool life.

(a) 2 and 3 (b) 1 and 2 only
(c) 2 and 3 only (d) 3 only

124. Satellite is a non-ferrous cast alloy composed of:
(a) Cobalt, chromium and tungsten
(b) Tungsten, vanadium and chromium
(c) Molybdenum, tungsten and chromium
(d) Tungsten, molybdenum, chromium and vanadium

125. External threads can be produced by:
1. Rolling 2. Grinding
3. Milling

(a) 1 and 3 only (b) 1 and 2 only
(c) 2 and 3 only (d) 1, 2 and 3

## ANSWERS WITH EXPLANATIONS

| | | | | |
|---|---|---|---|---|
| 1. (b) | 2. (c) | 3. (c) | 4. (a) | 5. (d) |
| 6. (a) | 7. (b) | 8. (c) | 9. (d) | 10. (a) |
| 11. (d) | 12. (b) | 13. (a) | 14. (c) | 15. (c) |
| 16. (c) | 17. (b) | 18. (c) | 19. (d) | 20. (c) |
| 21. (a) | 22. (a) | 23. (c) | 24. (d) | 25. (a) |
| 26. (c) | | | | |

27. (a) For reaction turbine, $v_{f1} = v_{f2} = v_f$

$$\sin\alpha_1 = \frac{v_f}{236}, \sin\beta_2 = \frac{v_f}{232} \therefore \alpha_1 = \beta_2$$

$$\sin\alpha_2 = \frac{v_f}{126}, \sin\beta_1 = \frac{v_f}{132} \therefore \alpha_1 = \beta_2$$

$$R_d = 0.5$$

Now $R_d = \dfrac{v_{r2}^2 - v^2}{2u(v_{\omega 1} + v_{\omega 2})}$ and $w = u(v_{w1} + v_{w2})$

$$= \frac{v_{r2}^2 - v_{r1}^2}{2R_d} = \frac{232^2 - 132^2}{2 \times 0.5}$$

$$= 36.4 = 36.3 \text{ kW}$$

28. (c) $(\Delta h)_{\text{isen}} = \dfrac{w}{\eta_n \times \eta_r} = \dfrac{280}{0.92 \times 0.90} = 338\text{kW}$

29. (c) $R_d = \dfrac{(\Delta h)_m}{(\Delta h)_m + (\Delta h)_f} = \dfrac{48}{48+32}$

$$= \frac{48}{80} = 0.60 \text{ or } 60\%$$

| | | | | |
|---|---|---|---|---|
| 30. (c) | 31. (c) | 32. (c) | 33. (c) | 34. (c) |
| 35. (c) | 36. (c) | 37. (d) | 38. (b) | |

39. (a) $CH_4 + 2O_2 = CO_2 + 2H_2O$

| | | | | |
|---|---|---|---|---|
| 40. (c) | 41. (d) | 42. (b) | 43. (c) | 44. (c) |
| 45. (b) | 46. (c) | 47. (d) | 48. (b) | 49. (b) |

50. (c) 51. (a) 52. (a) 53. (d)

54. (d) $v_e = \sqrt{2(h_1 - h_2)}$

$$= \sqrt{2(3450 - 2800) \times 10^3} = 1140.2 \text{ m/s}$$

55. (b) 56. (c)

57. (a) $\rho = \dfrac{\cos \alpha_1}{2}$ for $(\eta_b)_{max}$

$$\frac{\cos 30°}{2} = \frac{0.866}{2} = 0.433$$

58. (a) 59. (a)

60. (b) $R_d = \dfrac{9}{9+11} = \dfrac{9}{20} = 0.45$

61. (d) 62. (b) 63. (c) 64. (d) 65. (c)
66. (b) 67. (c) 68. (b) 69. (b) 70. (a)
71. (c) 72. (d) 73. (b)
74. (c)

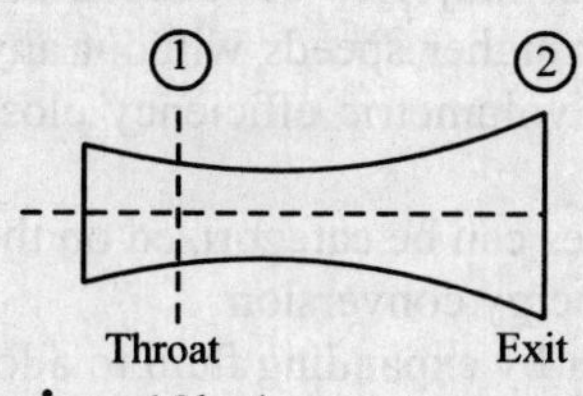


$$\dot{m}_s = 10 \text{kg/s},$$

$$d_1 = 50\text{mm}, \frac{\rho_1}{\rho_2} = 2.45,$$

$$\frac{c_1}{c_2} = 0.8$$

$$A_1 c_1 \rho_1 = A_2 c_2 \rho_2$$

$$A_2 = \frac{A_1}{A_2} = \frac{c_1 \rho_1}{c_2 \rho_2} = 0.8 \times 2.45 = 1.96$$

$$d_2 = d_1 d_2 = d_1 \sqrt{1.96} = 50$$

$$50\sqrt{1.96} = 70 \text{ mm}$$

75. (a) 76. (b)

77. (c) $\eta = 1 - \dfrac{T_2}{T_1} = 1 = \dfrac{300}{600}$

$$= 1 = 1 - 0.5 = 0.5 \text{ or } 50\%$$

78. (a) $x = x_1, x_2 = 0.9 \times 0.95 = 0.855$

79. (a) 80. (d)

81. (c) $P = p\dfrac{\cos \alpha_1}{2} = \dfrac{\cos 30°}{2} = 0.433$

82. (c) 83. (b) 84. (c) 85. (c) 86. (b)
87. (a) 88. (b) 89. (a) 90. (d) 91. (c)
92. (d) 93. (a) 94. (d) 95. (b) 96. (c)
97. (c) 98. (a)

99. (b) $h_1 = 3200$ kJ/kg, $h_2 = 2300$ kJ/kg,
$h_2 = 2560$ kJ/kg

$$\eta_1 = \frac{h_1 - h_2}{h_1 - h_2} = \frac{3200 - 2560}{3200 - 2400}$$

$$\frac{640}{800} = 0.8 \text{ or } 80\%$$

100. (b) $\alpha_1 = 30°$,

$$(\eta b)_{max} = \frac{2\cos^2 \alpha_1}{1 + \cos^2 \alpha_1}$$

$$= \frac{2\cos^2 30°}{1 + \cos^2 30°}$$

$$= 0.857$$

101. (a) $R_d = \dfrac{32}{60} = 0.53$

102. (a) 103. (c) 104. (c) 105. (a) 106. (b)
107. (c) 108. (c) 109. (b) 110. (a) 111. (c)
112. (c) 113. (a) 114. (a) 115. (d) 116. (a)
117. (c) 118. (a)

119. (d) $v_1 r_1 = v_2 r_2$

$$v_2 = \frac{430 \times 250}{350} = 307 \text{ m/s}$$

120. (b) Degree of reaction $= \dfrac{40}{40+60} = 0.4$ or 40%

121. (d) **Electro-hydraulic forming is used for forming components from thin metal sheets or deform thin tubes.**

122. (d) **In the 3 – 2 – 1 principle of fixture design, 3 refers to locating positions.**

123. (d) **The optimum cutting speed is one which should balance the metal removal rate and cutting tool life.**

124. (d) **Stellite is a non-ferrous cast alloy composed of Co. Cr and W.**

125. (d) **External threads can be produced by rolling, grinding and milling.**

❑❑❑

# 8. Turbomachinery

- Turbo machinery, in mechanical engineering, describes machines that transfer energy between a rotor and a fluid, including both turbines and compressors.
- While a turbine transfers energy from a fluid to a rotor, a compressor transfers energy from a rotor to a fluid. The two types of machines are governed by the same basic relationships including Newton's second Law of Motion and equation for compressible fluids.
- Centrifugal pumps are also turbo machines that transfer energy from a rotor to a fluid, usually a liquid, while turbines and compressors usually work with a gas.
- In general, the two kinds of turbo machines encountered in practice are open and closed turbo machines.
- Open machines such as propellers, windmills, and enshrouded fans act on an infinite extent of fluid, whereas, closed machines operate on a finite quantity of fluid as it passes through a housing or casing.
- Turbo machines are also categorized according to the type of flow. When the flow is parallel to the axis of rotation, they are called axial flow machines, and when flow is perpendicular to the axis of rotation, they are referred to as radial (or centrifugal) flow machines.
- There is also a third category, called mixed flow machines, where both radial and axial flow velocity components are present.
- Turbo machines may be further classified into two additional categories: those that absorb energy to increase the fluid pressure, i.e. pumps, fans, and compressors, and those that produce energy such as turbines by expanding flow to lower pressures.
- Certainly there are significant differences between these machines and between the types of analysis that are typically applied to specific cases. This does not negate the fact that they are unified by the same underlying physics of fluid dynamics, gas dynamics, aerodynamics, hydrodynamics, and thermodynamics.
  - Radial turbine
  - Axial compressor
  - Axial fan
  - Centrifugal compressor
  - Centrifugal fan
  - Centrifugal pump
  - Francis turbine
  - Gas turbine
  - Industrial fans
  - Jet engine
  - Mechanical fan
  - Mixed flow compressor
  - Steam turbine
  - Turbocharger
  - Turboexpander
  - Turbofans
  - Turbojet
  - Turboprop
  - Turbopump
  - Turboshaft
  - Turbines
  - Water turbine
- Any devices that extracts energy from or imparts energy to a continuously moving stream of fluid (liquid or gas) can be called a Turbo machine.
- Elaborating, a turbo machine is a power or head generating machine which employs the dynamic action of a rotating element, the rotor; the action of the rotor changes the energy level of the continuously flowing fluid through the machine. Turbines, compressors and fans are all members of this family of machines.
- In contrast to Positive displacement machines especially of the reciprocating type which are low speed machines based on the mechanical and volumetric efficiency considerations, majority of turbo machines run at comparatively higher speeds without any mechanical problems and volumetric efficiency close to hundred per cent.
- Turbo machines can be categorized on the basis of the direction of energy conversion:
- Produce power by expanding fluid to a lower pressure or head (hydraulic, steam and gas turbines).
- Axial flow turbo machines - When the path of the through-flow is wholly or mainly parallel to the axis of rotation, the device is termed an axial flow turbo machine.
- Radial flow turbo machines - When the path of the through-flow is wholly or mainly in a plane perpendicular to the rotation axis, the device is termed a radial flow turbo machine. Ex Centrifugal pump.
- Therefore, the change of radius between the entry and the exit is finite. A Radial turbo machine can be inward or outward flow type depending on the purpose that needs to be served.
- Outward flow type increases the energy level of the fluid and vice-versa. Due to continuous change in direction, several radial stages can't be used (mostly around 3 stages).
- Impulse Turbo machines - There is no pressure change of the fluid or gas in the turbine blades (the moving blades) e.g. Pelton turbine. Do not require a pressure casement around the rotor since the fluid jet is created by the nozzle prior to reaching the blading on the rotor.
- Reaction Turbo machines - Reaction turbines develop torque by reacting to the gas or fluid's pressure or mass. The pressure of the gas or fluid changes as it passes through the turbine rotor blades.
- A pressure casement is needed to contain the working fluid e.g. Francis turbines and most steam turbines. For compressible working fluids, multiple turbine stages are usually used to harness the expanding gas efficiently. Newton's third law describes the transfer of energy for reaction turbines.

# MULTIPLE CHOICE QUESTIONS

1. Optimum pressure ratio for maximum specific output for ideal gas turbine plant operating at initial temperature of 300 K and maximum temperature of 1000 K is closer to:
(a) 4 (b) 8
(c) 12 (d) 16

2. In a parallel flow gas turbine recuperator, the maximum effectiveness is:
(a) 100%
(b) 75%
(c) 50%
(d) between 25% and 45%

3. When the outlet angle from the rotor of a centrifugal compressor is more than 90°, then the blades are said to be:
(a) forward curved
(b) backward curved
(c) radial
(d) either backward or forward curved.

4. According to fan laws, which of the following relation is valid?
(Q – discharge, N – speed, D – diameter) Subscripts 1 and 2 for two sets of conditions):
(a) $\left(\frac{Q_1}{Q_2}\right)=\left(\frac{N_1}{N_2}\right)^2$ (b) $\left(\frac{Q_1}{Q_2}\right)=\left(\frac{N_1}{N_2}\right)^3$
(c) $\left(\frac{Q_1}{Q_2}\right)=\left(\frac{D_1}{D_2}\right)^2$ (d) $\left(\frac{Q_1}{Q_2}\right)=\left(\frac{D_1}{D_2}\right)^3$

5. The Mach number at inlet of gas turbine diffuser is 0.3. The shape of the diffuser would be:
(a) converging (b) diverging I
(c) stagnation enthalpy (d) stagnation pressure

6. For two-stage compressor in which index of compression for low pressure stage is *m* and for high pressure stage is *n*. The load sharing with perfect intercooling is expressed as:
(a) $\frac{W_1}{W_2}=\frac{m(n-1)}{n(m-1)}$ (b) $\frac{W_1}{W_2}=\frac{n(n-1)}{m(m-1)}$
(c) $\frac{W_1}{W_2}=\frac{n}{m}$ (d) $\frac{W_1}{W_2}=\frac{m}{n}$

7. The degree of reaction of a turbomachine is defined as the ratio of the:
(a) static pressure change in the rotor to that in the stator.
(b) static pressure change in the rotor to that is the stage.
(c) static pressure change in the stator to that is the rotor.
(d) total pressure change in the rotor to that in the stage.

8. Consider the following statements:
1. Reciprocating compressors are best suited for high pressure and low volume
2. The effect of clearance volume on power consumption is negligible for the same volume of discharge.
3. While the compressor is idling, the delivery valve is kept open by the control
4. Intercooling of air between the stages of compression helps to minimize losses.
Of these statements:
(a) 1 and 2 are correct
(b) 1 and 3 are correct
(c) 2 and 4 are correct
(d) 3 alone is correct

9. Consider the following statements:
The typical air velocities in the ducts of air-conditioning systems are:
1. lower in residential buildings as compared to those of public buildings
2. higher in residential buildings as compared to those of public buildings
3. higher in industrial buildings has compared to those of public buildings
4. equal in all types of buildings
Which of these statements is/are correct?
(a) 1 alone
(b) 1 and 3
(c) 2 and 3
(d) 4 alone

10. A multistage compressor is to be designed for a given flow rate pressure ratio. If the compressor consists of axial flow stages followed by centrifugal instead of only axial flow-stages, then the:
(a) overall diameter would be decreased
(b) overall diameter would be increased
(c) axial length of the compressor would be increased
(d) axial length of the compressor would be decreased.

11. The clearance volume of a reciprocating compressor directly affects:
(a) piston speed
(b) noise level
(c) volumetric efficiency
(d) temperature of air after compression.

12. In an axial flow gas turbine, the hot gases approach the rotor inlet with an absolute velocity of 600 m/s in a direction 30° from the wheel tangent. The gases leave the rotor axially. If the blade speed is 300 m/s, then the theoretical power output per kg/s of gas flow will be approximately:
(a) 132 kW (b) 156 kW
(c) 172 kW (d) 205 kW.

13. The difference between the comfort air-conditioning and industrial air-conditioning lies in the:
(a) equipment used (b) process adopted
(c) indoor requirements (d) ambient conditions
14. The state of air supplied by a cooling coil with a by-pass factor 'X' lies on the psychrometric chart at the:
(a) intersection of RSHF line with saturation curve
(b) Intersection of GSHF line with saturation curve
(c) point which divides RSHF line in proportion to 'X' and (1 – X)
(d) point which divides ESHF line in proportion to 'X' and (1 – X)
15. Performance of a reciprocating compressor is expressed by:
(a) $\frac{\text{Isothermal work}}{\text{Indicated work}}$ (b) $\frac{\text{Indicated work}}{\text{Isothermal work}}$
(c) $\frac{\text{Adiabatic work}}{\text{Indicated work}}$ (d) $\frac{\text{Indicated work}}{\text{Adiabatic work}}$
16. In a simple gas turbine power plant operating on standard Brayton cycle power needed to drive the compressor is 175 kW, rate of heat supplied during constant pressure heat addition process is 675 kW. Turbine output obtained during expansion is 425 kW. What is the rate of heat rejection during constant pressure heat rejection?
(a) 75 kW (b) 425 kW
(c) 500 kW (d) 925 kW
17. Which one of the following is the correct statement?
(a) Both work ratio and thermal efficiency improve.
(b) Work ratio improves but thermal efficiency decreases.
(c) Thermal efficiency improves but work ratio decreases.
(d) Both work ratio and thermal efficiency decrease.
18. A gas turbine cycle with infinitely large number of stages during compression and expansion leads to which one of the following?
(a) Stirling cycle
(b) Atkinson cycle
(c) Ericsson cycle
(d) Brayton cycle
19. Pulse jet engine operation can be idealized/approximated to follow which one of the following?
(a) Brayton cycle (b) Ericsson cycle
(c) Lenoir cycle (d) Stirling cycle
20. Consider the following statements:
For a single-stage water cooled air compressor,
1. the volumetric efficiency decreases as the pressure ratio is increased.
2. shaft power/m$^3$/min of free air increases as the pressure ratio is increased.
Which of the statements given above is/are correct?
(a) 1 only (b) 2 only
(c) Both 1 and 2 (d) Neither 1 nor 2
21. In aircraft gas turbines, the axial flow compressor is preferred because:
(a) of high pressure rise
(b) it is stall free
(c) of low frontal area
(d) of higher thrust
22. In axial flow compressor, exit flow angle deviation from the blade angle is a function of:
(a) blade camber
(b) space-chord ratio
(c) both blade camber and space-chord ratio
(d) blade camber and incidence angle
23. The thrust of a jet propulsion power unit can be increased by:
(a) injecting water into compressor
(b) burning fuel after gas turbine
(c) injecting ammonia into the combustion chamber
(d) all of the above.
24. In a gas turbine cycle with two stages of rehearing, working between maximum pressure $p_1$ and minimum pressure $p_4$, the optimum reheat pressure would be:
(a) $(p_1 p_4)^{1/3}$ and $(p_1 p_2)^{2/3}$
(b) $(p_1^2 p_4)^{2/3}$ and $(p_1 p_4^2)^{1/2}$
(c) $\sqrt{p_1 p_4}$ and $p_1 \sqrt{p_4}$
(d) $(p_1 p_4)^{1/2}$ and $(p_1 p_4)^{2/3}$
25. Intercooling in gas turbines:
(a) decreases net output but increases thermal efficiency
(b) increases net output but decreases thermal efficiency
(c) decreases both net output and thermal efficiency
(d) increases both net output and thermal efficiency.
26. For a two-stage reciprocating compressor, compression from pressure $p_1$ to $p_3$ is with perfect intercooling and no pressure losses. If compression in both cylinders follows the same polytropic process and the atmospheric pressure is $p_a$, then the intermediate pressure $p_2$ is given by:
(a) $p_2 = (p_1 + p_3)/2$ (b) $p_2 = \sqrt{p_1 \cdot p_3}$
(c) $p_2 = p_a \frac{p_3}{p_1}$ (d) $p_2 = p_a \cdot \sqrt{p_3 / p_1}$
27. If (to geometrically similar impellers of a centrifugal compressor are operated at the. same speed, then their head discharge and power will vary with their diameter ratio:
(a) $d$, $d^2$ and $d^3$ respectively
(b) $d$, $d^3$ and $d^5$ respectively
(c) $d$, $d^3$ and $d^5$ respectively
(d) $d^2$, $d$ and $d^3$ respectively

28. High positive incidence in an axial compressor blade raw leads to:
(a) suppression of separation of flow on the blade
(b) choking of the flow
(c) separation of flow on the pressure side of the blade
(d) separation of flow on the suction side of the blade.

29. Consider the following statements about modifications gas turbine power plant working en a simple Brayton cycle:
1. Incorporation of regeneration process increases specific work output as well as thermal efficiency.
2. Incorporation of regeneration process increases thermal efficiency but specific work output remains unchanged.
3. Incorporation of intercooling process in a multi-stage compression increases specificwork output but the heat input also increases.
4. incorporation of intercooling process in a multi-stage compression system increases specific work output, but the heat addition remains unchanged.

Which of the above statements are correct?
(a) 1 and 3 (b) 1 and 4
(c) 2 and 3 (d) 2 and 4

30. This stagnation pressure rise in a centrifugal compressor stage takes place:
(a) only in the diffuser
(b) in the diffuser and impeller
(c) only in the impeller
(d) only in the inlet guide vanes.

31. Consider the following statements:
1. Intercooling is effective only at lower pressure ratios and high turbine inlet temperatures.
2. There is very little gain in thermal efficiency when intercooling is used without the benefit of regeneration.
3. With higher value of '$y$' and $c_p$ of the working fluid, will net power output of Brayton cycle will increase.

Of these statements:
(a) 1, 2 and 3 are correct (b) 1 and 2 are correct
(c) 1 and 3 are correct (d) 2 and 3 are correct

32. Large clearance volume in reciprocating compressor results in
(a) reduced volume flow rate
(b) increased volume flow rate
(c) lower suction pressure
(d) lower delivery pressure

33. In a reciprocating air compressor the compression work per kg of air
(a) increases as clearance volume increases
(b) decreases as clearance volume increases
(c) is independent of clearance volume
(d) increases with clearance volume only of multi-stage compressor

34. Consider the following statements:
When air is to be compressed to reasonably high pressure, it is usually carried out by multistage compressor with an intercooler between the stages because
1. work supplied is saved
2. weight of compressor is reduced.
3. more uniform torque is obtained leading to the reduction in the size of flywheel.
4. volumetric efficiency

Of the four statements listed above:
(a) 1 alone is correct
(b) 2 and 4 are correct
(c) 1, 2 and 3 are correct
(d) 1, 2, 3 and 4 are correct

35. Shielding in a nuclear reactor is generally done to protect against:
(a) excess electrons
(b) X-rays
(c) α-and β-rays
(d) neutron and gamma rays

36. In a centrifugal compressor assuming the same overall dimensions, blade inlet angle and rotational speeds, which of the following bladings will give the maximum pressure rise?
(a) Forward curved blades
(b) Backward curved blades
(c) Radial blades
(d) All three types of bladings have the same pressure rise.

37. Under which one of the following sets of conditions will a supersonic compressor have the highest efficiency?
(a) Rotor inlet velocity is supersonic and exit velocity subsonic; stator inlet velocity is subsonic and exit velocity is subsonic.
(b) Rotor inlet velocity is supersonic and exit velocity subsonic; stator inlet velocity is supersonic and exit velocity is subsonic.
(c) Rotor inlet velocity is supersonic and exit velocity supersonic; stator inlet is supersonic and exit velocity is subsonic.
(d) Rotor inlet velocity is supersonic and exit velocity supersonic; stator inlet velocity is subsonic and exit velocity is Subsonic

38. The energy released in the fission of one U-235 nucleus approximately:
(a) 100 MeV (b) 200 MeV
(c) 300 MeV (d) 400 MeV

39. The critical value of Mach number for a subsonic airfoil is associated with sharp increase in drag due to local shock formation and its interaction with the boundary layer. A typical value of tills critical Mach number is of the order of
(a) 0.4 to 0.5 (b) 0.75 to 0.85
(c) 1.1 to 1.3 (d) 1.5 to 2.0

40. Consider the following statements:
Blowdown is necessary on boilers, because
1. the boiler water level is lowered rapidly in case it accidentally rises too high.
2. the precipitated sediment or sludge is removed while the boiler is in service.
3. the concentration of suspended solids in the boiler is controlled.
Of these statements:
(a) 1, 2 and 3 are correct (b) 1 and 2 are correct
(c) 3 alone is correct (d) 1 and 3 are correct

41. In a centrifugal compressor, the highest Mach number leading to shockwave in the fluid flow occurs at:
(a) diffuser inlet radius
(b) diffuser outlet radius
(c) impeller inlet radius
(d) impeller outlet radius

42. A double acting steam engine with a cylinder diameter of 19 cm and a stroke of 30 cm has a cut-off of 0.35. The expansion ratio for this engine is nearly:
(a) 1.05 (b) 2.85
(c) 6.65 (d) 10.05

43. For a multistage compressor, the polytropic efficiency is:
(a) the efficiency of all stages combined together
(b) the efficiency of one stage
(c) constant throughout for all the stages.
(d) a direct consequence of the pressure ratio.

44. Which one of the following is the effect of blade shape on performance of centrifugal compressor?
(a) Backward curved blade has poor efficiency
(b) Forward curved blades has higher efficiency
(c) Backward curved blades lead to stable performance
(d) Forward curved blades produce lower pressure ratio.

45. Surging basically implies:
(a) unsteady, periodic and reversed flow
(b) forward motion of air at a speed above sonic velocity
(c) the surging action due to the blast of blade shape on in a compressor.
(d) forward movement of aircraft.

46. Which one of the following types of compressors is mostly used for supercharging of I.C. engines?
(a) Radial flow compressor
(b) Axial flow compressor
(c) Roots blower
(d) Reciprocating compressor

47. Phenomenon of choking in compressor means:
(a) no flow of air.
(b) fixed mass flow rate regardless of pressure ratio.
(c) reducing mass flow rate with increase in pressure ratio
(d) increased inclination of the chord with air steam.

48. The optimum intermediate pressure $p_i$ for a gas turbine plant operating between pressure limits $p_l$ and $P_2$ with perfect intercolling between the two stages of compression (with identical isentropic efficiency) is given by:
(a) $p_1 = p_2 - p_1$ (b) $p_i = p_i = \frac{1}{2}(p_1 + p_2)$
(c) $p_i = \sqrt{p_1 \cdot p_2}$ (d) $p_i = \sqrt{p_2^2 \cdot p_1^2}$

49. Once through boiler is named as such because:
(a) flue gas passes only in one direction
(b) there is no recirculation of water
(c) air as sent through the same direction
(d) steam is sent out only in one direction

50. Centrifugal compressors are suitable for large discharge and wider mass flow range, but at a relatively low discharge pressure of the order of 10 bars, because of:
(a) low pressure ratio
(b) limitation of size of receiver
(c) large speeds
(d) high compression index

51. Given: $v_{w2}$ = velocity of whirl at outlet
$u_2$ = peripheral velocity of the blade tips
The degree of reaction in a centrifugal compressor is equal to:
(a) $1 - \frac{v_{w2}}{2u_2}$ (b) $1 - \frac{u_2}{2v_{w2}}$
(c) $1 - \frac{2v_{w2}}{u_2}$ (d) $1 - \frac{v_{w2}}{u_2}$

52. Match List-I with List-II (pertaining to blower performance) and select the correct answer using the codes given below the lists:

| List-I | List-II |
|---|---|
| A. Slip | 1. Reduction of whirl velocity |
| B. Stall | 2. Fixed mass flow rate regardless of pressure ratio |
| C. Choking | 3. Flow separation |
| | 4. Flow area separation |

Codes:

| | A | B | C |
|---|---|---|---|
| (a) | 4 | 3 | 2 |
| (b) | 1 | 3 | 2 |
| (c) | 4 | 1 | 3 |
| (d) | 2 | 3 | 4 |

53. In a gas turbine cycle, the turbine output is 600 kJ/kg, the compressor work is 400 kJ/kg and the heat supplied is 1000 k/kg. The thermal efficiency of this cycle is:
(a) 80% (b) 60%
(c) 40% (d) 20%

54. In a single-stage open-cycle gas turbine, the mass flow through the turbine is higher than the mass flows through compressor, because:
(a) the specific volume of air increases by use of intercooler
(b) the temperature of air increases in the reheater
(c) the combustion of fuel takes place in the combustion chamber
(d) specific heats at constant pressure for incoming air and exhaust gases are different

55 Reaction turbine discharges 3 m/s of water under a head of 10 m with an overall efficiency of 92%. The power developed is:
(a) 295.2 kW (b) 237.0 kW
(c) 271.0 kW (d) 265.2 kW

56. In steam turbine terminology, diaphragm refers to:
(a) separating wall between rotors carrying nozzles
(b) the ring of guide blades between rotors
(c) a partition between low and high pressure dies
(d) the flange connecting the turbine exit to the condenser

57. Gas turbine develops 120 kJ of work while the compressor absorbed 60 kJ of work and the heat supplied is 200 kJ. If regenerator which would recover 40% of the heat in the exhaust were used, then the increase in the overall thermal efficiency would be:
(a) 10.2% (b) 8.6%
(c) 6.9% (d) 5.7%

58. In a two-stage compressor with ideal intercooling, for the work requirement to be minimum, the intermediate pressure $p_i$ in terms of condenser and evaporator pressure $p_c$ and $p_e$ respectively is:
(a) $pi = p_c p_e$ (b) $pi = P_i = \sqrt{P_a P_e}$
(c) $p_i = P_i = \sqrt{P_a / P_e}$ (d) $p_i = p_c / p_e$

59. A four-stage compressor with perfect intercooling between stages compresses air from 1 bar to 16 bar. The optimum pressure in the last intercooler will be:
(a) 6 bar (b) 8 bar
(c) 10 bar (d) 12 bar

60. In the centrifugal air compressor design practice, the value of polytropic exponent of compression is generally taken as:
(a) 1.2 (b) 1.3
(c) 1.4 (d) 1.5

61. The turb machine used to circulate refrigerant in large refrigeration plant is:
(a) a centrifugal compressor
(b) a radial turbine
(c) an axial compressor
(d) an axial turbine

62. The energy transfer process is:
(a) continuous in a reciprocating compressor and intermittent in an axial compressor
(b) continuous in an axial compressor and intermittent in a reciprocating compressor
(c) continuous in both reciprocating and axial compressors
(d) intermittent in both reciprocating and axial compressors.

63. In an axial flow co impresser stage, air enters and leaves the stage axially. If the whirl component of the air leaving the rotor is half the mean peripheral velocity of the rotor Wades, then the degree of reaction will be:
(a) 1.00 (b) 0.75
(c) 0.50 (d) 0.25

64. If an axial flow compressor is designed for a constant velocity through all stages, then the area of annulus of the succeeding stages will:
(a) remain the same
(b) progressively decrease
(c) progressively increase
(d) depend upon the number of stages.

65. What will be the shape of the velocity triangle at the exit of a radial bladed centrifugal impeller, taking into account slip?
(a) Right-angled
(b) Isosceles
(c) All angles less than 90°
(d) One angle greater than 90°

66. In a De Laval nozzle expanding superheated steam from 10 bar to 0.1 bar, the pressure as the minimum cross-section will be:
(a) 3.3 bar
(b) 5.46 bar
(c) 8.2 bar
(d) 9.9 bar

67. Which one of the following statements is the?
(a) In a multi-stage compressor, adiabatic efficiency less than stage efficiency
(b) In a multi-stage turbine; adiabatic efficiency is less than the stage efficiency
(c) Preheat factor for a multistage compressor is greater than one
(d) Preheat factor does not effect the multistage compressor performance

68. At constant efficiency, the horse power of a fan is:
(a) proportional to rpm
(b) proportional to $(\text{rpm})^2$
(c) proportional to $(\text{rpm})^3$
(d) a polynomial function of rpm

69. At the eye tip of a centrifugal impeller, blade velocity is 200 m/s while the uniform axial velocity at the inlet is 150 m/s. If the sonic velocity is 300 m/s, then the inlet Mach number of the flow will be:
(a) 0.50 (b) 0.66
(c) 0.83 (d) 0.87

70. A gas turbine works on which one of the following cycles?
(a) Brayton (b) Rankine
(c) Stirling (d) Otto

71. Reheating in a gas turbine:
(a) increases the compressor work
(b) decreases the compressor work
(c) increases the turbine work
(d) decreases the turbine work

72. A 3-stage reciprocating compressor has suction pressure of 1 bar delivery pressure of 27 bar. For minimum work of compression, the delivery pressure of 1st stage is:
(a 14 bar (b) 9 bar
(c) 5.196 bar (d) 3 bar

73. Consider the following factors:
1. Cylinder size
2. Clearance ratio
3. Delivery pressure
4. Compressor shaft power.
The factors which affect the volumetric efficiency of a single-stage reciprocating air compressor would include:
(a) 1 and 2 (b) 3 and 4
(c) 2 and 3 (d) 1 and 4

74. A three-stage Rateau turbine is designed in such a manner that the first two stages develop equal power with identical velocity diagram while the third one develops more with higher blade speed. In such a multistage turbine the blade ring diameter:
(a) is the same for all the three stages
(b) gradually increases from the first to the third
(c) of the third stage is greater than that of the first two stages,
(d) of the third stage is less than that of the first two stages.

75. In Centrifugal compressor terminology, vaneless space refers to the space between:
(a) the inlet and blade inlet edge
(b) blades in the impeller
(c) diffuser exit and volute casing
(d) impeller tip and diffuser inlet edge

76. If the static temperature rise in the rotor and stator respectively are $\Delta T_A$ and $\Delta T$,B then degree of reaction in an axial flow compressor is given by:
(a) $\frac{\Delta T_A}{\Delta T_B}$ (b) $\frac{\Delta T_A}{\Delta T_A + \Delta T_B}$
(c) $\frac{\Delta T_B}{\Delta T_a + \Delta T_B}$ (d) $\frac{\Delta T_B}{\Delta T_A}$

77. Consider the following statements relating to a closed gas turbine cycle:
1. The cycle can employ monatomic gas like helium instead of air to increase the cycle efficiency if other conditions are the same.
2. The efficiency of heat exchanger increases with the use of helium
3. The turbine blades suffer higher corrosion damages.
4. Higher output can be obtained for the same size.
Which of these statements are correct?
(a) 1, 2 and 3 (b) 1, 2 and 4
(c) 2, 3 and 4 (d) 1, 3 and 4

78. The capacity of an air compressor is specified as 10 $m^3$/min. It means that the compressor is capable of:
(a) supplying 3 $m^3$ of compressed air per minute
(b) compressing 3 $m^3$ of free air per minute
(c) supplying 3 $m^3$ of compressed air at NTP
(d) compressing 3 $m^3$ of standard air per minute

79. A two-stage compressor takes in air at 1.1 bars and, discharges at 20 bars. For maximum efficiency, the intermediate pressure is:
(a) 10.55 bars (b) 7.33 bars
(c) 5.5 bars (d) 4.7 bars

80. Which one of the following pairs of features and compressors type is not correctly matched?
(a) Intake and delivery ports compression is attainedby back flow and internal compression cylindrical rotor set to eccentric casing : Vane compressor
(b) Intermittent discharge requires receiver, produces compressor high pressure, slow speed and lubrication problems : Reciprocating Compressor
(c) Continuous flow, radial flow, handles large volume, much higher speed and fitted into design of aero-engines : Centrifugal compressor
(d) Successive pressure drops through contracting compressor passages, blades are formed from a number of circular arcs, axial flow : Axial compressor

81. Consider the following statements:
The volumetric efficiency of a reciprocating compressor can be enhanced by
1. heating the intake air
2. decreasing the clearance volume
3. cooling the intake air
Which of these statements is/are correct?
(a) 1 alone
(b) 1 and 2
(c) 2 and 3
(d) 3 alone

82. Reciprocating compressors are provided with:
(a) simple disc/plate valve
(b) poppet valve
(c) spring-loaded disc valve
(d) solenoid valve

83. Consider the following statements:
In centrifugal compressors, there is a tendency of increasing surge when
1. the number of diffuser vanes is less than the number of impeller vanes
2. the number of diffuser vanes is greater than the number of impeller vanes
3. the number of diffuser vanes is equal to the number of impeller vanes
4. mass flow is greatly in excess of that corresponding to Lbs design mass flow

Which of these statements is/are correct?
(a) 1 and 4 (b) 2 alone
(c) 3 and 4 (d) 2 and 1

84. In an axial flow compressor design, velocity diagrams are constructed from the experimental data of aerofoil cascades. Which one of the, following statements in this regard is correct?
(a) Incidence angle of the approaching air is measured from the trailing edge of the blade
(b) δ is the deviation angle between the angle of incidence and tangent to the amber line
(c) The deflection of the gas steam while passing through the cascade is given by $\varepsilon = \alpha_1 - \alpha_2$
(d) ε is the sum of the angle of incidence and camber less any deviation angle, i.e. $\varepsilon = i + \theta - \delta$

85. The efficiency of a simple gas turbine can be improved by using a regenerator, because the:
(a) work of compression is reduced
(b) heat required to be supplied is reduced
(c) work output of the turbine is increased
(d) heat rejected is increased.

86. Consider the following statements: The reheat cycle helps to reduce
1. fuel consumption
2. steam flow
3. the condenser size

Which of these statements are correct?
(a) 1 and 2 (b) 1 and 3
(c) 2 and 3 (d) 1, 2 and 3

87. For a two-stage reciprocating air compressor, the suction pressure is 1.5 bar and the delivery pressure is 54 bar. What is the value of the ideal intercooler pressure?
(a) 6 bar (b) 9 bar
(c) 27.75 bar (d) $\frac{9}{\sqrt{12}}$ bar

88. If n the polytropic index of compressor and $\frac{p_2}{p_1}$ is the pressure ratio for a three-stage compressor with ideal intercoolling, the on total work of three stage is:
(a) $\frac{3n}{(n-1)} p_1 v_1 \left\{ \left( \frac{p_2}{p_1} \right)^{(n-1)/n} - 1 \right\}$
(b) $\frac{n}{(n-1)} p_1 v_1 \left\{ \left( \frac{p_2}{p_1} \right)^{(n-1)/n3} - 1 \right\}$
(c) $\frac{n}{(n-1)} p_1 v_1 \left\{ \left( \frac{p_2}{p_1} \right)^{(n-1)/n} - 1 \right\}$
(d) $\frac{3n}{(n-1)} p_1 v_1 \left\{ \left( \frac{p_2}{p_1} \right)^{(n-1)/3n} - 1 \right\}$

89. The flow in the vaneless space between the impeller exit and diffuser inlet of a centrifugal compressor can be assumed as:
(a) free vortex
(b) forced vortex
(c) solid body rotation
(d) logarithmic spiral

90. The effect of friction on flow of steam through a nozzle is to:
(a) decrease the mass flow rate and to increase the wetness at the exit
(b) increase the mass flow rate and to increase the exit temperature
(c) decrease the mass flow rate and to decrease the wetness of the steam
(d) increase the exit temperature, without any effect on the mass flow rate.

91. Consider the following statements regarding the axial flow in an air compressor :
1. Surging is a local phenomenon while stalling affects the entire compressor.
2. Stalling is a local phenomenon while surging affects the entire compressor.
3. The pressure ratio of an axial compressor stage is smaller than that of a centrifugal compressor stage.

Of these statements:
(a) 1, 2 and 3 are correct (b) 1 and 2 are correct
(c) 2 and 3 are correct (d) 1 and 3 are correct.

92. The thermal efficiency of a gas turbine cycle with regeneration in terms of $T_3$ (maximum temperature), $T_1$ (minimum temperature)$r_p$ (pressure ratio) and $k - \left( \frac{c_p}{c_v} \right)$ is given by:
(a) $1 - \frac{T_1}{T_3} r_p^{\left(\frac{k}{k-1}\right)}$ (b) $1 - \frac{T_1}{T_3} r_p^{\left(\frac{k}{k-1}\right)}$
(c) $1 - \frac{T_3}{T_1} r_p^{\left(\frac{k-1}{k}\right)}$ (d) $1 - \frac{T_1}{T_3} r_p^{\left(\frac{k-1}{k}\right)}$

93. The pressure rise in the impeller of centrifugal compressor is achieved by:
(a) the decrease in volume and diffusion action the
(b) centrifugal action and decrease in volume

(c) the centrifugal and diffusion action
(d) the centrifugal and push-pull action.

94. Compared to axial compressors centrifugal compressors are more suitable for:
(a) high head, low How rate
(b) low head, low flow rate
(c) low head, high How rate
(d) high head, high flow rate

95. Stalling of blades in axial-flow compressor is the phenomenon of:
(a) air stream blocking the passage
(b) motion of air at sonic velocity
(c) unsteady, periodic and reversed flow
(d) air stream not able to follow the blade contour
(e) the same turbine can be used for both plants

96. What is the ratio of the static enthalpy rise in the rotor to the static enthalpy rise in the stage of an axial flow compressor defined as?
(a) Power input factor
(b) Flow coefficient
(c) Temperature coefficient
(d) Degree of reaction

97. A gas turbine plant working on Joule cycle produces 4000 kW of power. If its work ratio is 40%, what is the power consumed by the compressor?
(a) 2400 kW (b) 4000 kW
(c) 6000 kW (d) 8000 kW

98. The suction pressure is 1 bar and delivery pressure is 125 bar. What is the ideal intermediate pressure at the end of first stage for a 3-stage air compressor?
(a) 25 bar (b) 5 bar
(c) 10 bar (d) 20 bar

99. Which one of the following is correct?
In a gas turbine cycle with regeneration
(a) pressure output increases
(b) work output decreases
(c) thermal efficiency increases
(d) heat input increases

100. A centrifugal compressor is suitable for which of the following?
(a) High pressure ratio, low mass flow
(b) Low pressure ratio, low mass flow
(c) High pressure ratio, high mass flow
(d) Low pressure ratio, high mass flow

101. Which one of the following types of impeller vanes are most commonly used in centrifugal type compressors?
(a) Forward curved (b) Radial
(c) Backward curved (d) Tangential

102. Given:
$\eta_s$ = Stage efficiency, $\eta_n$ = Nozzle efficiency,
$\eta_s$ = Blade efficiency,
which one of the following is correct?
(a) $\eta_n = \eta_b = \eta_s$ (b) $\eta_b = \eta_s \eta_n$
(c) $\eta_s \times \eta_n \times \eta_s = 1$ (d) $\eta_s = \eta_s \eta_n$

103. Which one of the following is correct?
For incompressible flow a diverging section acts as a diffuser for upstream flow which is:
(a) subsonic only
(b) supersonic only
(c) body subsonic and supersonic
(d) sonic

104. Roots blower is an example of:
(a) Reciprocating (positive displacement) compressor
(b) Rotary (positive displacement) compressor
(c) Centrifugal compressor
(d) Axial compressor

105. Irrotational flow occurs when:
(a) Flow takes place in a duct of uniform cross-section at constant mass flow rate
(b) Streamlines are curved
(c) There is no net rotation of the fluid element about its mass centre.
(d) Fluid element does not undergo any change in size or shape.

106. A single-stage impulse with a diameter of 120 cm runs at 3000 rpm. If the blade speed ratio is 0.42, then the inlet velocity of steam will be:
(a) 79 m/s (b) 188 m/s
(c) 45° m/s (d) 900 m/s

107. In an ideal impulse turbine, the:
(a) absolute velocity at the inlet of moving blade is equal to that at the outlet
(b) relative velocity at the inlet of the moving blade is equal to that at the outlet
(c) axial velocity at the inlet is equal to that at the outlet
(d) whirl velocity at the inlet is equal to that at the outlet.

108. For a Parson's reaction turbine if a, and $\alpha_2$ are fixed angles at inlet and exit respectively and $\beta_1$ and $\beta_2$ are the moving blade angles at entrance and exit respectively, then:
(a) $\alpha_1 = \alpha_2$ and $\beta_1 = \beta_2$ (b) $\alpha_1 = \alpha_1$ and $\alpha_2 = \beta_2$
(c) $\alpha_1 < \beta_1$ and $\alpha_2 = \beta_2$ (d) $\alpha_1 = \beta_2$ and $\beta_1 = \alpha_2$

109. The isentropic enthalpy drop in moving blade is two-thirds of the isentropic enthalpy drop in fixed blades of a turbine. The degree of reaction will be:
(a) 0.4 (b) 0.6
(c) 0.66 (d) 1.66

110. In a fully trubulent flow through a rough pipe, the friction factor '*f*' is (Re is the Reynolds number and $\xi_s / D$ is relative roughness):
(a) A function of Re
(b) A function of Re and $\xi_s / D$
(c) A function of $\xi_s / D$
(d) independent of Re and $\xi_s / D$

111. In a boundary layer developed along the flow, the pressure decreases in the downstream direction. The boundary layer thickness would:
(a) Tend to decrease
(b) Remain constant
(c) Increase rapidly
(d) Increase gradually

112. Which one of the following statements is true of flow around a submerged body?
(a) For subsonic, non-viscous flow, the drag is zero
(b) For supersonic flow the drag coefficient is dependent equally on Mach number and Reynolds number
(c) The lift and drag coefficient of an aerofoil is independent of Reynolds number
(d) For incompressible flow around an aerofoil, the profile drag is the sum of form drag and skin friction drag.

113. If '$n$' variables in a physical phenomenon contained '$m$' fundamental dimensions, then the variables can be arranged into:
(a) $n$ dimensionless terms
(b) $m$ dimensionless terms
(c) $(n–m)$ dimensionless terms
(d) $(n + m)$ dimensionless terms

114. Given power 'P' of a pump, the head 'H' and the discharge 'Q' and the specific weight 'ω' of the liquid, dimensional analysis would lead to the result that 'P' is proportional to:
(a) $H^{1/2} Q^2 w$ (b) $H^{1/2} Qw$
(c) $HQ^{1/2} w$ (d) $HQw$

115. A 1 : 20 model of a spillway dissipates 0.25 hp. The corresponding prototype horsepower dissipated will be:
(a) 0.25 (b) 5.00
(c) 447.20 (d) 8944.30

116. If the stream function is given by $\psi = 3xy$, then the velocity at a point (2, 3) will be:
(a) 7.21 unit (b) 10.82 unit
(c) 18 unit (d) 54 unit

117. Efficiency of nozzle governed turbines is affected mainly by losses due to:
(a) partial admission
(b) throttling
(c) interstage pressure drop
(d) condensation in last stages.

118. Stability of a freely floating object is assured if its centre of:
(a) Buoyancy lies below its centre of gravity
(b) Gravity coincides with its centre of buoyancy
(c) Gravity lies below its metacenter
(d) Buoyancy lies below its metacenter

119. A vertical sluice gate, 2.5 m wide and weighing 500 kg is held in position due to horizontal force of water on one side and associated friction force. When the water level drops down to 2 m above the bottom of the gate, the gate just starts sliding down. The coefficient of friction between the gate and the supporting structure is:
(a) 0.20 (b) 0.10
(c) 0.05 (d) 0.02

120. The reheat cycle in steam power plant is mainly adopted to
(a) improve thermal efficiency
(b) decrease the moisture content in low pressure stages to a safe value
(c) decrease the capacity of condenser
(d) recover the waste heat of toiler

## ANSWERS WITH EXPLANATIONS

1. (b) Maximum possible pressure ratio,

$$r_p = \left(\frac{T_2}{T_1}\right)^{\frac{\gamma}{\gamma-1}} = \left(\frac{1000}{300}\right)^{3.5} = 67.62$$

Pressure ratio for maximum output $= \sqrt{r_p}$

$$= \sqrt{67.62} = 8.22 = 8$$

| | | | | |
|---|---|---|---|---|
| 2. (c) | 3. (a) | 4. (d) | 5. (b) | 6. (a) |
| 7. (b) | 8. (b) | 9. (b) | 10. (b) | 11. (c) |

12. (d) $v_{w1} = va_1 \cos\alpha_1 = 600\cos 30° = 519.615$ m/s

$v_{w2} = 0,\ u = 300$ m/s

Power output per kg/s of gas flow,

$$P = \frac{v_{w1} \times u}{10^3} = \frac{519.615 \times 300}{10^3} = 155.9 = 156 \text{ kW}$$

| | | | | |
|---|---|---|---|---|
| 13. (c) | 14. (d) | 15. (a) | 16. (b) | 17. (b) |
| 18. (c) | 19. (c) | 20. (c) | 21. (c) | 22. (c) |
| 23. (a) | 24. (a) | 25. (b) | 26. (b) | 27. (d) |
| 28. (a) | 29. (d) | 30. (b) | 31. (d) | 32. (d) |
| 33. (a) | 34. (a) | 35. (c) | 36. (a) | 37. (c) |
| 38. (b) | 39. (c) | 40. (c) | 41. (b) | |

42. (b) Expansion ratio $= \dfrac{1}{\text{cut off}} = \dfrac{1}{0.35} = 2.85$

| | | | | |
|---|---|---|---|---|
| 43. (c) | 44. (c) | 45. (a) | 46. (b) | 47. (b) |
| 48. (c) | 49. (b) | 50. (a) | 51. (a) | 52. (b) |

53. (d) $\eta_{th} = \dfrac{w_t - w_c}{q_s} = \dfrac{600-400}{1000} = \dfrac{200}{1000} = 0.2$ or 20%

54. (c)

55. (c) $p = \gamma\, QH\, \eta_0 = \dfrac{9.81 \times 1000 \times 30 \times 10 \times 0.92}{10^3}$

$= 270.76 = 271$ kW

56. (a)

57. (d) $y_{th} \dfrac{W_t - W_c}{Q_s} = \dfrac{120-60}{200} = \dfrac{60}{200} = 0.3$ or 30%

Heat in exhaust gases

$= Q_s - W_t = 200 - 120 = 80$ kJ

Heat recovered in regenerator

$= 0.4 \times 30 = 32$ kJ

Heat supplied $= 200 - 32 - 168$ kJ

New efficiency $= \dfrac{120-60}{168} = 35.7\%$

Increase in efficiency $= -35.7 - 30.0 = 5.7$

58. (b)
59. (b) Optimum pressure in the last intercooler

$$= \left(\frac{p_s}{P_1}\right)^{3/4} (16)^{3/4} = 8 \text{ bar}$$

60. (c) 61. (c) 62. (c)
63. (d) $R_d = \dfrac{v_f}{2u}(\tan\beta_1 + \tan\beta_2)$

$$\frac{v_f}{u} = \frac{1}{2}, \tan\beta_1 = \tan\beta_2 = \frac{1}{2}$$

$$R_d = \frac{1}{4}\left(\frac{1}{2} + \frac{1}{2}\right) = 0.25$$

64. (a) 65. (c)
66. (b) Throat pressure,

$$p_2 = p_1 p_1 \left[\frac{2}{n+1}\right]^{\frac{n}{n-1}}$$

$$= 10\left[\frac{2}{2.3}\right]^{\frac{13}{0.3}} = 5.46 \text{ bar}$$

67. (c) 68. (b)
69. (c) Mach number,

$$M = \frac{\text{axial velocity at inlet}}{\text{sonic velocity}}$$

$$= \frac{150}{300} = 0.5$$

70. (a) 71. (c)
72. (d) $p_2 = (p_1 p_3)^{1/3} - (27 \times 1)^{1/3} - 3$ bar
73. (a) 74. (b) 75. (d) 76. (b) 77. (b)
78. (c)
79. (d) $p_1 = \sqrt{p_1 p_2} = \sqrt{1.1 \times 20}$

$= 4.69 = 4.7$ bar

80. (c) 81. (c) 82. (a) 83. (d) 84. (a)
85. (b) 86. (a)
87. (a) $p_i = \sqrt{1.5 \times 54} = 9$ bar
88. (d) 89. (b) 90. (c) 91. (d) 92. (d)
93. (d) 94. (c) 95. (a) 96. (d)
97. (a) Work ratio $= \dfrac{W_t - W_c}{W_t}$

$$0.4 = \frac{4000 - W_c}{4000}$$

$W_c = 2400$ kW

98. (b) $p_i = \left(\dfrac{p_3}{p_1}\right)^{1/3}$

$$= \left(\frac{125}{1}\right)^{1/3} = 5 \text{ bar}$$

99. (c) 100. (d) 101. (c) 102. (d) 103. (a)
104. (b) 105. (c)
106. (c) $u = \dfrac{\pi DN}{60} = \dfrac{\pi \times 1.2 \times 300}{60} = 188.5$ m/s

$$\rho = \frac{u}{v_{a1}}$$

$$v_{a1} = \frac{188.5}{0.42} = 4488 = 45° \text{ m/s}$$

107. (b) 108. (d)
109. (a) $R_d = \dfrac{(\Delta h)_m}{(\Delta h)_m (\Delta h)_f} = \dfrac{\frac{2}{3}(\Delta h)_f}{\frac{2}{3}(\Delta h)_f + (\Delta h)_f}$

$$= \frac{\frac{2}{3}}{\frac{2}{3}+1} = \frac{2}{5} = 0.4$$

110. (b) 111. (d) 112. (b) 113. (c) 114. (d)
115. (d) Power, P $\propto$ (model ratio)$^{7/2} \propto 20^{7/2}$

$$P_p = P_m \times 20^{7/2} = 0.25 \times 20^{7/2}$$

$= 8944.30$ HP

116. (b) $\psi = 3xy$

$$u = \frac{\delta\psi}{\delta y} = 3x, v - \frac{\delta\psi}{\partial} = -3y$$

Resultant velocity,

$$v = \sqrt{u^2 + v^2} \quad = \sqrt{9x^2 + 9y^2}$$

$$= \sqrt{9 \times 4 + 9 \times 9} = \sqrt{117} = 10.82 \text{ unit}$$

117. (a) 118. (c)
119. (b) Area of gate at sliding, $A = 2 \times 2.5 = 5 \text{ m}^2$

Force, on upstream of gate, $P = \dfrac{1}{2}\rho g h A$

$$= \frac{1}{2} \times 10^3 \times 9.81 \times 2 = 49050\text{N}$$

Frictional force, $F = \mu P$

$$500 \times 9.81 = \mu \times 49050$$

$$\mu = 0.10$$

120. (a)

❑❑❑

# 9. Engineering Mechanics

- Engineering mechanics is the application of mechanics to solve problems involving common engineering elements.
- The goal of this Engineering Mechanics course is to expose students to problems in mechanics as applied to plausibly real-world scenarios.
- Dynamics all which are all highly applicable in engineering. but the most important part of them is statics (study of body at rest) which is not only a base for all others, but also have the highest engineering application.
- Physics also involve optics, waves, quantum, and relativity theory, which have no fundamental engineering application yet.
- Forces act along the members, and there are no shear forces or moments. A truss is therefore defined as a system composed entirely of two-force members, which only carry axial loads.
- The ends of a truss are pinned, so that they don't carry moments. The only reactions at the ends of a truss member are forces. External forces on trusses act only on the end points.
- Truss problems are solved by the method of sections, where an imaginary cut is made through the member(s) of interest, and global equilibrium of forces and moments are used to determine the forces in the members, or by the method of joints, in which a single joint is isolated and analyzed and the resulting forces (not necessarily with a numerical value) are transferred to adjacent joints, where the process is repeated.
- Applied mechanics is a branch of the physical sciences and the practical application of mechanics.
- Applied mechanics examines the response of bodies (solids and fluids) or systems of bodies to external forces. Some examples of mechanical systems include the flow of a liquid under pressure, the fracture of a solid from an applied force, or the vibration of an ear in response to sound.
- A practitioner of the discipline is known as a mechanician.
- Applied mechanics, as its name suggests, bridges the gap between physical theory and its application to technology.
- As such, applied mechanics is used in many fields of engineering, especially mechanical engineering. In this context, it is commonly referred to as engineering mechanics.
- Much of modern engineering mechanics is based on Isaac Newton's laws of motion while the modern practice of their application can be traced back to Stephen Timoshenko, who is said to be the father of modern engineering mechanics.
- Within the theoretical sciences, applied mechanics is useful in formulating new ideas and theories, discovering and interpreting phenomena, and developing experimental and computational tools.
- In the application of the natural sciences, mechanics was said to be complemented by thermodynamics by physical chemists Gilbert N. Lewis and Merle Randall, the study of heat and more generally energy, and electro mechanics, the study of electricity and magnetism.
- The current carrying wire wound spirally in the form of helix is known as solenoid or coil.
- When a current carrying conductor is placed at right angle to the direction of magnetic field, a mechanical force is experienced on the conductor in a direction perpendicular to both the direction of magnetic field and flow of current. The direction of this force can be determined by Fleming's left hand rule.
- According to Fleming's left hand rule if the thumb, forefinger and middlefinger of the left hand are stretched in such a way that they are at right angles to each other mutually and forefinger points towards the direction of the magnetic field, middle finger towards the direction of the flow of current then thumb will point the direction of force acting on the conductor.
- The magnitude of dynamically induced emf in a conductor moving at right angles to a uniform magnetic field is given as $e = Blv$ volts. If the conductor moves at an angle $\theta$ to the magnetic field, then $e = Blv \sin \theta$ volts

  The direction of dynamically induced emf is given by Fleming's right hand rule. According to Fleming's right hand rule:

  If the thumb, forefinger and middle finger of right hand are held mutually perpendicular to each other, forefinger pointing into the direction of the field and thumb in the direction of motion of conductor then the middle finger will point in the direction of the induced emf.
- The direction of flow of electrons is opposite to that of conventional current.
- The steady flow of electrons in one direction caused by the applied electric field constitutes electric current, called the drift current.
- EMF (electromotive force) is the force that causes a current to flow in an electric circuit while the potential difference between any two points in an electric circuit is that difference in their electrical state which tends to cause flow of electricity from one point to the other.

# MULTIPLE CHOICE QUESTIONS

1. Enriched uranium is required as fuel in a nuclear reactor, if light water is used as moderator and coolant, because light water has:
(a) high neutron absorption cross-section
(b) low moderating efficiency
(c) high neutron scatter cross-section
(d) low neutron absorption cross-section

2. An elevator weighing 100 kN attains an upward velocity of 4 *m/s* in two seconds with uniform acceleration. The tension in the cable will be approximately:
(a) 30 kN
(b) 100 kN
(c) 120 kN
(d) 200 kN.

3. Electric lift is moving downwards with an acceleration of *g*/3 the vertical force between a passenger in the lift and its floor is equal to:
(a) 2/3$^{rd}$ of the passenger's weight
(b) 3/4$^{th}$ of the passenger's weight
(c) passenger's weight
(d) 4/3 times the passenger's weight

4. A spring of stiffness *k* is compressed by a length 'A'and a ball is placed on the top of it. When the spring is released the ball is seen to rise through a height *h*. When two such springs are kept one over the other, and the combination is compressed by same length X what is the height reached by the ball, kept on the combined springs when released?
(a) *h*/2 (b) *h*
(c) $\sqrt{2}h$ (d) 2*h*

5. Which one of the following principles laws converts a dynamics problems to an equivalent statics problem?
(a) Newton's second law of motion
(b) D' Alembert's principle
(c) Principle of conservation of energy
(d) Principle of conservation of momentum

6. Match List-1 with List-II and select the correct answer using the codes given below the lists: (these pertain to nuclear reactors)

| **List-I** | **List-II** |
|---|---|
| A. Coolant | 1. Carbon dioxide |
| B. Control | 2. Zirconium |
| C. Poison | 3. Cadmium |
| D. Cladding | 4. Graphite |
| | 5. Hafnium |

**Codes:**

| | A | B | C | D |
|---|---|---|---|---|
| (a) | 5 | 2 | 3 | 4 |
| (b) | 5 | 1 | 3 | 4 |
| (c) | 1 | 3 | 5 | 2 |
| (d) | 1 | 2 | 5 | 3 |

7. Which one of the following principles cannot be used to solve problems involving friction?
(a) D' Alembert's principle
(b) Equations of Motion
(c) Principle of work and energy
(d) Conservation of energy

8. The length of the chest-expander spring when it is unstretched, is 0.6 m and its stiffness is 10 N/mm. The work done in stretching it to 1 m will be:
(a) 800 J (b) 1600 J
(c) 3200 J (d) 6400 J

9. Crushed ore is dropped on a conveyor belt at the rate of 300 kg/s. The belt moves, it speed of 2 m/s. The net force acting on the belt that keeps it moving at the same speed is:
(a) 30 N (b) 60N
(c) 300 N/m (d) 600 A

10. Two pieces of steel and brass weighing 20 N and 10 N respectively fall freely under the action of gravity from a tower. For the two pieces which one of the following will be equal after falling and equal distance?
(a) Acceleration (b) Momentum
(c) Potential energy (d) Kinetic energy

11. If tension in the rope of a lift while moving up is double the tension when moving down, the acceleration of lift is:
(a) *g*/2 (b) *g*/3
(c) *g*/4 (d) *g*/5

12. A rectangular block of width *ft* and height *h* is resting on a rough horizontal floor.A horizontal pull is to be applied at any height on the block. In order to avoid overturning, *b/h* should be:
(a) less than μ (b) more than μ
(c) less than 2μ (d) more than 2μ

13. Two bodies of weight 100 N and 200 N are resting on two smooth inclined planes. The bodies are connected by a rope passing over a pulley at the junction of the planes. If inclination of planes is 30° and 45°, then the tension in the rope will be:
(a) 80 N (b) 100 N
(c) 200 N (d) 300 N

14. At what height from the base of a pillar must the end of a rope of length*l* be fixed so that a man standing on the ground and pulling it at the other end may have the greatest tendency to overturn the pillar:
(a) *l*/2 (b) *l*/3
(c) $l/\sqrt{2}$ (d) 3*l*/4

15. A man wishes to move a heavy block resting on a rough floor. How he can do it with minimum effort?
(a) by pulling with a rope
(b) by pushing
(c) by tipping it over
(d) impossible to move

16. D Alemberts principle is used to:
(a) solve static problems
(b) solve kinematics problems
(c) convert dynamic problems into equivalent static problems
(d) solve elasticity problems

17. An elevator weighing 10 kN attains an upward velocity of 5 m/s in 2*s* with uniform acceleration. The tension in the supporting rope is:
(a) 3.75 kN
(b) 625 kN
(c) 7.45 kN
(d) 1, 2.55 kN

18. The first law of motion provides the definition of:
(a) momentum
(b) force
(c) acceleration
(d) energy

19. A mass m is initially in the rest position. A constant force is applied on it. The velocity acquired by it in a given displacement will he directly proportional to:
(a) $\sqrt{m}$ (b) $1/\sqrt{m}$
(c) $m$ (d) $1m$

20. Consider the following statements:
1. Forced circulation is always used in high pressure power boilers.
2. Soot blowers are used for cleaning tube surfaces at regular intervals.
3. Electrostatic precipitator is used to remove fly ash from flue gases.

Which of these statements are correct?
(a) 1, 2 and 3 (b) 2 and 3
(c) 1 and 3 (d) 1 and 2

21. Which one of the following statements is correct?
(a) Energy and work are scalars
(b) Force and work are vectors
(c) Energy, momentum and velocity are vectors
(d) Force, momentum and velocity are scalars.

22. A block of weight 2 N falls from a height of 1 m on the top of a spring. If the spring gets compressed by 0.1 m to bring the weight momentarily to rest, then the spring constant would be:
(a) 50 N/m (b) 100 N/m
(c) 200 N/m (d) 400 N/m

23. A person, carrying on his head a jewellery box of weight W jumped down from the third story of a building. Before touching the ground, he will feel a load of magnitude:
(a) zero (b) $\frac{W}{2}$
(c) W (d) infinity

24. A box rests in the rear of a truck moving with a deceleration of 2 m/s$^2$. To prevent the box from sliding, the approximate value of static coefficient of friction between the box and the bed of the truck should be:
(a) 0.1 (b) 0.2
(c) 0.3 (d) 0.4

25. Two particles of same mass are moving with same speed on circular paths of radii $r$, and $r_2$. The ratio of their centripetal forces would be:
(a) $r_2 / r_1$ (b) $\sqrt{(r_2 / r_1)}$
(c) $(r_2 / r_1)^2$ (d) $(r_1 / r_2)^2$

26. A wheel of mass $m$ and radius $r$ is in accelerated rolling motion without slip under a steady axle torque T. If the coefficient of kinetic friction is $m$, the friction from the ground on the wheel is:
(a) μmg
(b) T/*r*
(c) zero
(d) None of the above

27. The centripetal force on a vehicle rounding a curve on a level track is provided by:
(a) gravity
(b) friction between the tress and the track
(c) the torque applied to its steering wheel
(d) its brakes

28. A stone of mass m at the end of a string of length *l* is whirled in a vertical circle at a constant speed. The tension in the string will be maximum when the stone is:
(a) at the top of the circle
(b) half way down from the top
(c) quarter way down from the top
(d) at the bottom of the circle

29. The output of a boiler is normally stated as:
(a) evaporative capacity in tonnes of steamthat can he produced from and at 100°C
(b) weight of steam actually produced at rated pressure in tonnes per hour
(c) boiler horse power
(d) weight of steam produced per kg of fuel

30. Match List-I with List-11 and select the correct answer using the codes given below the lists.

| List-I | List-II |
|---|---|
| A. Bin system | 1. Dust collection |
| B. lone furnace | 2. High turbulence |
| C. Tangential burners | 3. Highslag recovery |
| D. Scrubber | 4. Pulverised fuel |

**Codes:**

| | A | B | C | D |
|---|---|---|---|---|
| (a) | 4 | 3 | 1 | 2 |
| (b) | 4 | 3 | 2 | 1 |
| (c) | 3 | 4 | 1 | 2 |
| (d) | 3 | 4 | 2 | 1 |

31. Match List-I (turbines) with List-II (classification) and select the correct answerusing the codes given below the list:

| List-I | List-II |
|---|---|
| A. Parson's | 1. Pressure compounded |
| B. De Laval | 2. Reaction |
| C. Rateau | 3. Simple impulse |
| D. Curtis | 4. Velocity compounded |

**Codes:**

| | A | B | C | D |
|---|---|---|---|---|
| (a) | 3 | 2 | 1 | 4 |
| (b) | 2 | 3 | 4 | 1 |
| (c) | 2 | 3 | 1 | 4 |
| (d) | 3 | 2 | 4 | 1 |

32. A thin circular ring of mass M and radius R is rotating about it axis with a constant angular velocity ω. Two objects each of mass m are Attached gently to the opposite ends of a diameter of the ring. The wheel now rotates with an angular velocity of:

(a) $\frac{\omega M}{M+m}$ (b) $\frac{\omega (M+2M)}{M}$

(c) $\frac{\omega (M+2m)}{M+2m}$ (d) $\frac{\omega M}{M+2m}$

33. A ballet of mass 1 kg is fired with a velocity of $u$ m/s from a gun of mass 10 kg. The ratio of kinetic energies of bullet and gun is:

(a) 10 (b) 11
(c) 1.1 (d) 0.1

34. Two masses, 2 kg and 8 kg, are moving with equal kinetic energy. The ratio of magnitudes of their momentum is:

(a) 0.25 (b) 0.50
(c) 0.625 (d) 1.00

35. A mass M is moving with a constant velocity parallel to *jr*-axis. It angular momentum with respect to the origin:

(a) is zero (b) remains constant
(c) goes on increasing (d) goes on decreasing.

36. A bullet hits and gets embedded in a solid block resting on a horizontal frictionless table. What is conserved?

(a) momentum alone
(b) kinetic energy along
(c) momentum and kinetic energy both
(d) none of these

37. Two balls at same temperature collide. What is conserved?

(a) temperature (b) velocity
(c) kinetic energy (d) momentum

38. For perfectly elastic bodies the value of the coefficient of restitution is:

(a) zero (b) 0.372
(c) 0.500 (d) 1.000

39. A jet engine works on the principle of:

(a) conservation of energy
(b) conservation of linear momentum
(c) conservation of mass
(d) conservation of mass and momentum.

40. A ball falls from a height of 1 m, hits the ground and rebounds with half its velocity just before impact. Then after rising it falls and hits the ground and again rebounds with half its velocity just before impact, and so on. The total distance travelled by the ball till it comes to rest on the ground is:

(a) 2 m (b) 5/3 m
(c) 4/3 m (d) 5/4 m

41. A ball A of mass m falls under gravity from a height h and strikes another ball B of mass m which is supported at rest on a spring of stiffness *k*. Assume perfectly elastic impact. Immediately after the impact:

(a) the velocity of ball A is $(1/2)\sqrt{2}\,gh$
(b) the velocity of ball A is zero
(c) the velocity of both balls is $(1/2)\sqrt{2}\,gh$
(d) none of the above.

42. A bullet enters a plank of 30 mm thickness with a velocity of 100 m/s and emerges out from the plank with a velocity of 50 m/s. What is the minimum thickness of the plank so that the bullet remains embedded in the plank:

(a) 100 mm (b) 80 mm
(c) 60 mm (d) 40 mm

43. The outward radial flow turbine in which there are two rotors rotating in opposite directions is known as:

(a) 50% reaction radial turbine
(b) cantilever turbine
(c) Lungstrom turbine
(d) pass-out turbine

44. A train of weight 200 × $10^4$ N is running on a horizontal track at a constant speed of 10 m/s, overcoming a constant frictional force of 20 × 10 N. What is the power of the engine drinking the train?

(a) 800 kW
(b) 1200 kW
(c) 200 kW
(d) 400 kW

45. The power required by a machine having an efficiency of 80% for raising a load of 24 N through a distance of 36 m in 1 minutes is:

(a) 12 W (b) 18 W
(c) 50 W (d) 450 W

46. A car of mass 2000 kg is traveling at a constant speed of 50 m/s. The car has to resist a wind drag $F_D = 10v$ (N), where $v$ is the velocity of the car in m/s. The power required by the engine is:

(a) 5 kW (b) 10 kW
(c) 25 kW (d) 30 kW

47. When compared to stable flow, for supersaturated flow of steam through a nozzle the available enthalpy drop:
(a) remains the same (b) increases
(c) decreases (d) is unpredictable.

48. A man is pulling a bucket of water up to the roof of a building of 6 m height. The total weight of the rope is 20 N and the weight of the bucket with water is 100 N. The work done by the man is:
(a) 720 N-m (b) 420 N-m
(c) 660 N-m (d) 600 N-m

49. A train of weight 5000 kN is pulled on a level track with a constant speed of 10 m/s. The frictional force is 75 kN. The power of the engine is:
(a) 375 kW (b) 750 kW
(c) 1875 kW (d) 3000 kW

50. A mechanical system can be said to be conservative if the:
(a) potential energy of the system remains constant
(b) kinetic energy of the system remains constant
(c) sum of the kinetic and potential energies remains constant
(d) linear momentum remains constant

51. If the kinetic energy of the body becomes four times its initial value then the new:
(a) three times its initial value
(b) four times its initial value
(c) twice the initial value
(d) unchanged

52. A man throws bricks to a height of 12 m where they reach with a speed of 12 m/s. If he throws the bricks such that they just reach that height. What percentage of energy will he save?
(a) 19% (b) 26%
(c) 38% (d) 57%

53. A cord is used to lower vertically a block of mass M a distance d at a constant downward acceleration of g/4. Then the work done by the cord on the block is:
(a) Mgd/4 (b) 3Mgd/4
(c) – 3Mgd/4 (d) Mgd

54. A uniform chain of length L and mass M lying on a smooth table such that one third of its length is hanging vertically down over the edge of the table. If *g* is the acceleration due to gravity, the work required to pull the hanging part on to the table is:
(a) MgL (b) MgL/3
(c) MgL/9 (d) MgL/18

55. A cage with a parrot sitting in it is suspended from a spring balance. The parrot starts flying. The reading of the spring balance will:
(a) increase (b) decrease
(c) no change (d) be zero

56. The principle of conservation of energy cannot be applied in case of:
(a) a particle moving in gravitational field
(b) flow of heat through a metal
(c) ideal flow of water in a pipe
(d) sliding of a particle along inclined plane with friction.

57. The law of conservation of mechanical energy is valid:
(a) irrespective of the nature of force held
(b) in gravitational field
(c) only if the total work done by the particle in moving around in a closed trajectory is zero
(d) only if the force is tangential to the trajectory.

58. A wound watch spring possesses energy stored in the form of:
(a) kinetic energy
(b) potential energy
(c) mechanical potential energy
(d) mechanical kinetic energy

59. The total energy of a stone thrown up will be maximum at:
(a) the ground level (b) the highest point
(c) middle of the path (d) all heights

60. Which of the following cannot be increased by using an appropriate machine?
(a) force (b) torque
(c) velocity (d) work

61. When two bodies stick together after collision, the collision is said to be:
(a) perfectly elastic (b) partially elastic
(c) completely inelastic (d) plastic

62. A particle of mass *m* has momentum *p*. Its kinetic energy is:
(a) $mp$ (b) $p^2m$
(c) $p^2/m$ (d) $p^2/(2m)$

63. When a mass is rotating in a plane about a fixed point, its angular momentum is directed along:
(a) the radius
(b) the tangent to the orbit
(c) a line perpendicular to the plane of rotation
(d) none of the above.

64. A body moves down a smooth inclined plane and if same body is dropped vertically down from the same height as that of the inclined plane top, then following parameters on reaching the ground will be same:
(a) Velocity
(b) momentum
(c) kinetic energy
(d) all of the above

65. What is the work done if a bucket of water weighing 10 N is pulled up from a well 20 m deep by a rope weighing 1 N/m?
(a) 200 N-m (b) 400 N-m
(c) 500 N-m (d) 600 N-m

66. In the case of a flywheel of mass moment of intertia 'I' rotating at an angular velocity ω the expression $\frac{1}{2}I\omega^2$ represents the:
(a) centrifugal force (b) angular momentum
(c) torque (d) kinetic energy

67. Which of the following statements are correct?
(1) Impulse turbine rotor blades are thick at the centre.
(2) Rateau turbine is more efficient than Curtis turbine.
(3) Blade velocity coefficient for an impulse turbine is of the order of 60%.
Select the correct answer using the codes given below:
(a) 1, 2 and 3 (b) 1 and 2
(c) 1 and 3 (d) 2 and 3

68. A circular disc rolls without slip on an inclined plane. The ratio of its rotational kinetic energy to the total energy is:
(a) $\frac{1}{4}$ (b) $\frac{1}{2}$
(c) $\frac{1}{3}$ (d) $\frac{2}{3}$

69. A tapering bar (diameters of end sections being $d_1$ and $d_2$) and a bar of uniform cross-section '$d$' have the same length and are subjected to the same axial pull. Both the bars will have the same extension if '$d$' is equal to:
(a) $\frac{d_2+d_2}{2}$ (b) $\sqrt{d_1 d_2}$
(c) $\sqrt{\frac{d_1 d_2}{2}}$ (d) $\sqrt{\frac{d_1+d_2}{2}}$

70. The number of independent elastic constants required to express the stress strain relationship for a linearly elastic isotropic materials is:
(a) One (b) Two
(c) Three (d) Four

71. The deformation of a bar under its own weight as compared to that when subjected to a direct axial load equal to its own weight will be:
(a) The same (b) One-fourth
(c) Half (d) Double

72. The critical pressure ratios for flow of dry saturated and superheated steam through a nozzle are respectively:
(a) 0.5279 and 0.550
(b) 0577 and 0.550
(c) 0.577 and 0.546
(d) 0.5279 and 0.546

73. Given that $a$ = nozzle angle, $n$ = number of rows of moving blades in a velocity compounded. Impulse turbine, the optimum blade speed ratio is:
(a) $2\cos\alpha_1 n$ (b) $\frac{n\cos\alpha_1}{2}$
(c) $\frac{\cos\alpha_1}{2(n+1)}$ (d) $\frac{\cos\alpha_1}{2n}$

74. In a Parson's turbine stage, blade velocity is 320 m/s at the mean radius and the rotor blade exit angle is 30″. For minimum kinetic energy of the steam leaving the stage, the steam velocity at the exit of the stator will be:
(a) $640/\sqrt{3}$ m/s (b) 640 m/s
(c) $320/\sqrt{3}$ m/s (d) $160/\sqrt{3}$ m/s

75. For a free vortex design of blade in the rotor of *a* reaction axial turbine, the specific work along the blade height is:
(a) higher at the blade hub and lower at the blade tip
(b) constant from huh to tip
(c) lower at the hub and tip but different from the mean section
(d) same at the hub and tip but different from the mean section.

76. Two hollow shafts of the same material have the same length and outside diameter. Shaft 1 has internal diameter equal to one-third of the outer diameter and shaft 2 has internal diameter equal to half of the outer diameter. If both the shafts are subject to the same torque, the ratio of their twists $\theta_1/\theta_2$ will be equal to:
(a) 16/81
(b) 8/27
(c) 19/27
(d) 243/256

77. A simply supported beam of constant flexural rigidity and length 2 L carries a concentrated load 'P' at its mid-span and the deflection under that load is δ. If a cantilever beam of the same flexural rigidity and length is subjected to load 'P' at its free end, them the deflection at the free end will be:
(a) 1/2δ (b) δ
(c) 2δ (d) 4δ

78. A solid shaft of diameter 100 mm, length 1000 mm is subjected to a twisting moment 'T'. The maximum shear stress developed in the shaft is 60 N/mm. A hole of 50 mm diameter is now drilled throughout the length of shaft. To develop a maximum shear stress of 60 N/ mm in the hollow shaft, the torque 'T' must he reduced by:
(a) T/4 (b) T/8
(c) T/12 (d) T/16

79. A circular shaft is subjected to the combined action of bending, twisting and direct axial loading. The maximum bending stress σ maximum shearing stress $\sqrt{3}\sigma$ and a uniform axial stress σ(compressive) are produced. The σ maximum compressive normal stress produced in the shaft will be:
(a) 3 σ (b) 2 σ
(c) σ (d) Zero

80. Two closed-coil springs are made from the same small diameter wire, one wound on 2.5 cm diameter core and the other on 1.25 cm diameter core. If each spring has V coils, then the ratio of their spring constants would be:

(a) 1/16 (b) 1/8
(c) 1/4 (d) 1/2

81. A reaction turbine stage has angles *a*, α, β, γ as nozzle angle, inlet blade and outlet blade angle respectively. The expression for maximum efficiency of the turbine is given by:

(a) $\frac{2\cos^2\beta}{1+\cos^2\beta}$ (b) $\frac{2\cos^2\gamma}{1+\cos^2\gamma}$

(c) $\frac{2\cos^2\alpha}{1+\cos^2\alpha}$ (d) $\frac{\cos(\alpha+\beta)}{\cos^2\gamma}$

82. Consider the following
1. Safety valve. 2. Steam trap
3. Steam separator 4. Economiser.
Among these the boiler accessories would include:

(a) 1, 2 and 3 (b) 2, 3 and 4
(c) 1 and 4 (d) 1, 2, 3 and 4

83. Circumferential stress in a cylindrical steel boiler shell under internal pressure is 80 MPa, Young's modulus of elasticity and Poisson's ratio are respectively $2 \times 10^5$ MPa and 0.28.
The magnitude of circumferential strain in the boiler shell will be:

(a) $3.44\times10^{-4}$ (b) $3.84\times10^{-4}$
(c) $4\times10^{-4}$ (d) $4.56\times10^{-4}$

84. The state of plane stress in a plate of 100 mm thickness is given as
$\sigma_{xx} = 100\ \text{N/mm}^2, \sigma_{xy} = 200\ \text{N/mm}^2$
Young's modulus = 300 N/mm²
Poission's ratio = 0.3
The stress developed in the direction of thickness is:

(a) zero (b) 90 N/mm²
(c) 100 N/mm² (d) 200 N/mm²

85. The number of elastic constants for a completely anisotropic elastic material which follows Hooks laws is

(a) 3 (b) 4
(c) 21 (d) 25

86. The bending moment equation, as a function of distance *x* measured from the left end, for a simply supported beam of span. L m carrying a uniformly distributed load of intensity *w* N/m will be given by:

(a) $M = wL/2(L-x) - W/2(L-x)N.m$
(b) $M = wL/2x - wx^2/2 - N.m$
(c) $M = wL/2(L-x)^2 - w/2(L-x)N.m$
(d) $M = wx^2/2 - wL\,x/2N.m$

87. A rod of material with E = 200 × 10³ MPa and $\propto = 10^{-3}$ mm/mm°C is fixed at both the ends. It is uniformly heated such that the increase in temperature is 30°C. The stress, developed in the rod is:

(a) 6000 N/mm² (tensile)
(b) 6000 N/mm² (compressive)
(c) 2000 N/mm² (tensile)
(d) 2000 N/mm² (compressive)

88. Two beams of equal cross-sectional area arc subjected to equal bending moment. If one beam has square cross-section and the other has circular section, then

(a) Both beams will be equally strong
(b) Circular section beam will be stronger
(c) Square section beam will be stronger
(d) The strength of the beam will depend on the nature of loading

89. A cantilever beam of rectangular cross-section is subjected to a load W at its free end. If the depth of the beam is doubled and the load is halved, the deflection of the free end as compared to original deflection will be:

(a) Half (b) One-eighth
(c) One-sixteenth (d) Double

90. The degree of reaction of a turbine is defined as the ratio of:

(a) static pressure drop to total energy transfer
(b) total energy transfer to static pressure drop.
(c) change of velocity energy across the turbine to the total energy transfer.
(d) velocity energy to pressure energy.

91. A solid circular shaft is subjected to pure torsion. The ratio of maximum shear stress to maximum normal stress at any point would be

(a) 1 : 1 (b) 1 : 2
(c) 2 : 1 (d) 2 : 3

92. A short column of external diameter D and internal diameter *d* carries an eccentric load *d*. The greatest eccentricity which the load can have without producing tension on the cross-section of the column would be

(a) $\frac{d+D}{8}$ (b) $\frac{d^2+D^2}{8d}$

(c) $\frac{d^2+D^2}{8D}$ (d) $\sqrt{\frac{d^2+D^2}{8}}$

93. A bar of length L and of uniform cross-section area A and second moment of area *I* is subjected to a pull P. If Young's modulus of elasticity of the bar material is E, the expression for strain energy stored in the bar will be:

(a) $\frac{P^2L}{2AE}$ (b) $\frac{PL^2}{2EI}$

(c) $\frac{PL^2}{AE}$ (d) $\frac{P^2L}{AE}$

94. If a thick cylindrical shell is subjected to internal pressure, then hoop stress, radial stress and longitudinal stress at a point in the thickness will be:
(a) Tensile, compressive and tensile respectively
(b) All compressive
(c) All tensile
(d) Tensile, compressive and compressive respectively.

95. A thin cylinder with both ends closed is subjected to internal pressure *p*. The longitudinal stress at the surface has been calculated as $\sigma_0$. Maximum shear stress at the surface will be equal to:
(a) $2\sigma_0$ (b) $1{,}5\sigma_0$
(c) $\sigma_0$ (d) $0.5\sigma_0$

96. The maximum shear occurs on the outermost fibres of a circular shaft under torsion. In a close coiled helical spring, the maximum shear stress occurs on the:
(a) Outermost fibres
(b) Fibres at mean diameter
(c) Innermost fibres
(d) End coils

97. A circular solid shaft is subjected to a bending moment of 400 kN.m and a twisting moment of 300 kN.m. On the basis of the maximum principal stress theory, the direct stress is σ and according to the maximum shear stress theory, the shear stress is *t* The ratio σ/*t* is:
(a) $\frac{1}{5}$ (b) $\frac{3}{4}$
(c) $\frac{9}{5}$ (d) $\frac{11}{6}$

98. Which one of the following pairs is not correctly matched?
(a) Fertile material…….U-233
(b) Atomic number……..Number of protons.
(c) Mass defect………Binding energy
(d) Cross-section ……..Scattering

99. The energy released during the fission of one atom of Uranium-235 in million electron vote is about:
(a) 100 (b) 200
(c) 300 (d) 400

100. For the same internal diameter, wall thickness, material and internal pressure, the ratio of maximum stress, induced in a thin cylindrical and in a thin spherical pressure vessel will be:
(a) 2 (b) $\frac{1}{2}$
(c) 4 (d) $\frac{1}{4}$

101. A company sells 14,000 units of its product. It has a variable cost of ₹ 15 per unit. Fixed cost is ₹ 47,000 and the required profit is ₹ 23,000.Per unit product price (in ₹) will be:
(a) 60 (b) 40
(c) 30 (d) 20

102. The inventory carrying cost includes:
(a) expenditure incurred for payment of bills
(b) placing an order
(c) receiving and inspecting
(d) obsolescence and depreciation.

103. For a product, the direct labour cost is ₹ 5 and direct materials cost is ₹ 10. The annual cost of direct materials is expected to be ₹ 2,00,000 and the annual overhead to be absorbed is ₹ 1,20,000. The total cost of the product will be:
(a) ₹ 16 (b) ₹ 18
(c) ₹ 19 (d) ₹ 21

104. If Break-even point = Total fixed cost $\left(1-\frac{\text{Variable cost per unit}}{X}\right)$, then X is the:
(a) overheads (b) price per unit
(c) direct cost (d) materials cost

105. In the EOQ model, if the unit ordering cost is doubled, the EOQ:
(a) is halved
(b) is doubled
(c) Increase 1.414 times
(d) Decrease 1.414 times.

106. Which one of the following does not form a part of the direct cost of a component?
(a) Cost of special tooling used
(b) Cost of material used
(c) Cost of material wasted
(d) Wages of the labour actually involved.

107. Match List-I (Cost Element) with List-II (Type of Cost and select the correct answer using the codes given below the lists:

| **List-I (Cost Element)** | **List-II (Type of Cost)** |
|---|---|
| A. Discount | 1. Ordering cost |
| B. Preparation of the machine for a product | 2. Material cost |
| C. Negotiations with vendors | 3. Set-up cost |
| D. Rent for the warehouse | 4. Carrying cost |

**Codes:**

| | A | B | C | D |
|---|---|---|---|---|
| (a) | 2 | 1 | 3 | 4 |
| (b) | 4 | 3 | 1 | 2 |
| (c) | 2 | 3 | 1 | 4 |
| (d) | 4 | 1 | 3 | 2 |

108. Which one of the following correctly represent the average inventory turnover ratio for raw materials?
(a) Annual sales/annual inventory
(b) Average working process volume/total production volume
(c) Annual consumption average inventory
(d) Volume of spare parts/total annual sale

109. Dry flue gases with a composition of $CO_2$ = 10.4%, $O_2$ = 9.6 and $N_2$ = 80%, indicate that:
(a) excess air is used
(b) air is insufficient
(c) hydrogen is not present in the coal
(d) air is just sufficient

110. Which one of the following analysis is not associated with inventory management?
(a) ABC (b) EOQ
(c) AOQ (d) VED

111. Out of the following listed below, which two items would you consider under category (c) under ABC analysis:
Annual Usage of items

| Items No. | Annual usage X 1000 | Unit cost ₹ |
|---|---|---|
| A | 30 | 0.10 |
| B | 300 | 0.15 |
| C | 2 | 200.00 |
| D | 60 | 0.10 |
| E | 5 | 0.30 |
| F | 300 | 0.10 |
| G | 10 | 0.05 |
| H | 7 | 0.10 |
| I | 20 | 0.10 |
| J | 5 | 0.20 |

(a) B and F (b) C and E
(c) E and J (d) G and H.

112. Match List-I with List-II and select the correct answer using the codes given below the Lists:

| List-I (Elements of cost) | List-II (nature of Cost) |
|---|---|
| A. Interest on capital | 1. Variable |
| B. Direct labour | 2. Semi-variable |
| C. Water and electricity | 3. Fixed |

**Codes:**

| | A | B | C |
|---|---|---|---|
| (a) | 3 | 1 | 2 |
| (b) | 2 | 1 | 3 |
| (c) | 3 | 2 | 1 |
| (d) | 2 | 3 | 1 |

113. There are two products A and B with the following characteristics:

| Product | Demand | Ordercost (in ₹/order) | Holdingcost (in ₹/unit) |
|---|---|---|---|
| A | 100 | 100 | 4 |
| B | 400 | 100 | 1 |

The economic order quantities (EOQ) of product A and B will be in the ratio of:
(a) 1 : 1 (b) 1 : 2
(c) 1 · 4 (d) 1 : 8

114. Classifying items in A, B and C categories for selective control in inventory managements is done by arranging items in the decreasing order of:
(a) total inventory costs (b) item value
(c) annual usage value (d) item demand

115. In inventory contorl theory, to economic order quantity (E.O.Q.) is:
(a) average level of inventory
(b) optimum lot size
(c) lot size corresponding to break-even analysis
(d) capacity of a warehouse.

116. Consider the following statements:
1. ABC analysis is based on Pareto's principal
2. FIFO and LIFO policies can be used for material valuation in materials management.
3. Simulation can be used for inventory control.
4. EOQ (Economic Order Quantity) formula ignores variations in demand pattern.

Of these statements:
(a) 1 alone is correct (b) 2 and 3 are correct
(c) 2, 3 and 4 are correct (d) 1, 2, 3 and 4 are correct

117. Given that, θ = procurement cost per order, D = number of units demanded per year, H = holding cost per unit per year, $i$ = rate of interest, $p$ = purchase prices per unit. The procurement quantity per order (Q) is given by:
(a) $Q = \dfrac{2.\theta.D}{H + iP}$ (b) $Q = \sqrt{\dfrac{2.\theta.D}{iH + P}}$
(c) $Q = \sqrt{\dfrac{2.\theta.D}{H + iP}}$ (d) $Q = \sqrt{\dfrac{2.\theta}{D(H + iP)}}$

118. Annual demand for a product costing ₹100 Per piece is ₹900. Ordering cost per order is ₹100 and inventory holding cost is ₹2 per unit per year. The economic size is:
(a) 200 (b) 300
(c) 400 (d) 500

119. Which of the following cost elements are considered while determining the Economic Lot Size for purchase?
1. Inventory carrying cost
2. Procurement cost
3. Set up cost.

Select the correct answer using the codes given below:
(a) 1, 2 and 3 (b) 1 and 2
(c) 2 and 3 (d) 1 and 3

120. Consider the following costs:
1. Cost of inspection and return of goods
2. Cost of obsolescence
3. Cost of scrap
4. Cost of insurance
5. Cost of negotiation with suppliers.

Which of these costs are related to inventory carrying cost?
(a) 1, 2 and 3 (b) 1, 3 and 4
(c) 2, 3 and 4 (d) 2, 4 and 5

## ANSWERS WITH EXPLANATIONS

1. (c)
2. (a) $T = W\left(1 - \frac{a}{g}\right)$

$$T = W\left(1 - \frac{2}{9.81}\right) = 79.61 = 80N$$

3. (a) $a = \frac{g}{3}$

$$T = W\left(1 - \frac{a}{g}\right) = W\left(1 - \frac{1}{3}\right) = \frac{2}{3}W$$

4. (a) $W = k\delta$

$$U = \frac{1}{2}k\delta \times \delta = \frac{1}{2}k\delta^2 = mgh$$

$$m = \frac{k\delta^2}{gh}$$

For two springs in series, $k_e = \frac{k}{2}$

$$U = \frac{1}{2} \times \frac{k}{2} \times \delta^2 = \frac{k\delta^2}{4} = mgh_1$$

$$h_1 = \frac{k\delta^2}{4mg} = \frac{k\delta^2}{4 \times \frac{k\delta^2}{2h}} = \frac{h}{2}$$

5. (b) 6. (c) 7. (b)
8. (a) $\delta = 1 - 0.6 = 0.4$ m

$$\text{Work done} = \frac{1}{2}k\delta = \frac{1}{2} \times 10 \times \frac{400^2}{10^3} = 800 \text{ J}$$

9. (d) $F = ma = 300 \times 2 = 600$ N
10. (c)
11. (b) $1 + a/g = 2\,(1 - a/g)$

$a = g/3$

12. (d) $P = \mu W$

$W \times b/2 > \mu R h$

$b/h > 2\mu$

13. (a) $200a/g = W_2 \sin 45° - T = 100\sqrt{2} - T$

$100a/g = T - W_1 \sin 30° = T - 50$

Comparing, we get T = 80 N

14. (c) $M = T\cos(l^2 - h^2)^{1/2}.h = Th(l^2 - h^2)^{1/2}$

$dM/dh = 0$ gives $h = l/\sqrt{2}$

15. (c) 16. (c)
17. (d) $T = w\,(1 = a/g)$

$= 10\,(1 + 2.5/9.8) = 12.55$ KN

18. (b)
19. (b) $a = \frac{F}{m}$

$$v^2 - u^2 = 2as$$

$$v^2 = 2as = 2as\frac{2Fs}{m}$$

$$v \alpha \frac{1}{\sqrt{m}}$$

20. (b) 21. (b) 22. (d) 23. (a)
24. (b) $\mu W = \frac{Wa}{g}$

$$\mu = \frac{a}{g} = \frac{2}{9.81} = 0.2$$

25. (d) 26. (a) 27. (b) 28. (d) 29. (b)
30. (b) 31. (c)
32. (a) $MR^2\omega = (M + 2m)R^2\omega_1$

$$\omega_1 = (M\omega/[M + 2m]$$

33. (a) $1 \times u = 10 \times v$

$$v = \frac{u}{10}$$

$$\text{Ratio of kinetic energies} = \frac{\frac{1}{2} \times 1 \times u^2}{\frac{1}{2} \times 10 \times \frac{u^2}{100}} = 10$$

34. (b) $\frac{1}{2} \times 2u^2 = \frac{1}{2} \times 8 \times v^2$

$$u = 2v$$

$$\text{Ratio of momentum} = \frac{m_1 u}{m_2 v} = \frac{2 \times 2v}{8 \times v} = \frac{1}{2} = 0.5$$

35. (b) 36. (a) 37. (d) 38. (d) 39. (b)
40. (b) $s = h(1 + 2c^2 + 2c^4 + ...)$

$$= h\left(1 + 2c^2 \times \frac{4}{3}\right)$$

$$= \left[1 + 2 \times \left(\frac{1}{2}\right)^2 \times \frac{4}{3}\right] = \frac{5}{3} \text{ m}$$

41. (b)
42. (c) $m_1 v_1 x_1 = m_2 v_2 x_2$

$m_1 = m_2$

$100 \times 30 = 50 \times x_2$

$x_2 = 60$ mm

43. (c)
44. (c) Power of the engine = Frictional force × speed

$$= \frac{20 \times 10^3 \times 10}{10^3} = 200 \text{ kW}$$

45. (b) $\text{Power} = \frac{24 \times 36}{60 \times 0.8} = 18\text{W}$
46. (c) Wind drag, $F = 10v = 10 \times 50 = 500$ N

$$\text{Power required} = \frac{Fv}{10^3} = \frac{500 \times 50}{10^3} = 25 \text{ kW}$$

47. (c)
48. (c) $\text{Total work done} = 100 \times 6 + \frac{1}{2} \times 20 \times 6$

$= 660$ Nm

49. (b) Power of engine $75 \times 10 = 750$ kW

50. (c)

51. (c) $E_1 = \frac{1}{2}mv_2^1, E_2 = \frac{1}{2}mv_2^2$

$\frac{1}{2}mv_2^2 = 4 \times \frac{1}{2}mv_1^2$

$v_2 = 2v_1$

$mv_2 = 2mv_1$

52. (c) $E_1 = \frac{1}{2}mv_2^2 + mgh = 72\text{ m} + 12\text{ mg}$

$E_2 = \text{mgh} = 12\text{ mg}$

$E_1 - E_2 = 72\text{ mg}$

$\text{Percentage saving} = \left(\frac{E_1 - E_2}{E_1}\right) \times 100$

$= \frac{72\text{ m} \times 9.81 \times 100}{(72\text{ m} + 12 \times 9.81 \times m)}$

$= 38\%$

53. (c) T = M$g$, F = M$a$ = M$g$/4
Net force = M$g$/4 – M$g$ = – 3 M$g$/4
Work done = – 3 M$g$ $d$/4

54. (d) Work done = (M$g$/6) × L/3 = M$g$ L/18

55. (b) 56. (d) 57. (c) 58. (c) 59. (d)

60. (d) 61. (c)

62. (b) $p = mv$

$v = \frac{P}{m}$

$\text{K.E} = \frac{1}{2}mv^2 = \frac{1}{2}m \times \frac{p^2}{m^2} = \frac{p^2}{2m}$

63. (d) 64. (d)

65. (b) Total work done = Work done to pull the bucket + work done to pull the rope

$= 10 \times 20 + \frac{1}{2} \times 20 \times 1 \times 20 = 400\text{ N.m}$

66. (d) 67. (b)

68. (c) Translation kinetic energy, $K_1 = \frac{1}{2}mv^2$

$= \frac{1}{2}mr^2 \times \omega^2$

Rational kinetic energy, $K_2 = \frac{1}{2}\text{ I}\,\omega^2$

$= \frac{1}{2} \times \frac{1}{2}mr^2\ \omega^2 = \frac{1}{2}mr^2\,\omega^2$

Total kinetic energy, $K = \frac{3}{4}mr^2\omega^2$

$\frac{K_2}{K} = \frac{1}{4} \times \frac{4}{3} = \frac{1}{3}$

69. (b) $\frac{4Pl}{\pi E d_1 d_2} = \frac{4Pl}{\pi E d^2}$

$\therefore\ d = \sqrt{d_1 d_2}$

70. (b) 71. (c)

72. (c) $\frac{p_2}{p_1} = \left(\frac{2}{n+1}\right)^{\frac{n}{n-1}}$,

$n$ = 1.135 for dry saturated steam and 1.3 for superheated steam

$= \left(\frac{2}{2.135}\right)^{\frac{1.135}{0.135}} = 0.577 = \left(\frac{2}{2.3}\right)^{\frac{1.3}{0.3}}$

73. (d)

74. (c) Steam velocity at exit of stator = 320 tan 30°

$= \frac{320}{\sqrt{3}}$ m/s

75. (a) For a free vortex, $\upsilon_w \propto \frac{1}{r}$

76. (d) $G_1 = G_2, l_1 = l_2, D_1 = D_2, d_1 = \frac{1}{3}D_1$

$d_2 = \frac{1}{2}D_2, T_1 = T_2 = T$

$\frac{T}{J} = \frac{G,}{l}$

G, $l$ and T being same for both the shafts,

$\theta = \propto \frac{1}{J}$

$\frac{\theta_1}{\theta_2} = \frac{J_2}{J_1} = \frac{\frac{\pi}{32}D_2^4\left[1 - \left(\frac{d_2}{D_2}\right)^4\right]}{\frac{\pi}{32}D_1^4\left[1 - \left(\frac{d_1}{D_1}\right)^4\right]}$

$\frac{\left[1 - \left(\frac{1}{2}\right)^4\right]}{\left[1 - \left(\frac{1}{3}\right)^4\right]} = \frac{\left(\frac{15}{16}\right)}{\left(\frac{80}{81}\right)} = \frac{243}{256}$

77. (c) Simply supported beam,

$\delta_1 = \frac{PL^3}{3EI} = \frac{P(2L)^3}{48EI} = \frac{PL^3}{6EI}$

Cantilever beam,

$\delta_1 = \frac{PL^3}{3EI}$

$\delta_2 = 2\delta_1 = 2\delta$

78. (d) $d$ = 100 mm, $l$ = 1000 mm

$\tau_{max} = \frac{16T}{\pi d^3} = 60\text{ N/mm}^2$

$T = T_s = \frac{\pi d^3}{16} \times 60$

For the hollow shaft,

$\tau_{max} = \frac{16T}{\pi d^3(1 - k^4)} = \frac{16T}{\pi d^3\left[1 - \left(\frac{50}{100}\right)^4\right]}$

$$= \frac{16}{15} \times \frac{16T}{\pi d^3}$$

$$T = \frac{16}{15} \times \frac{\pi d^3}{16 \times 60} = \frac{15}{16} T_s = \frac{15}{16} T$$

$$\text{Reduction in torque} = T\left(1 - \frac{15}{16}\right) = \frac{T}{16}$$

79. (b) $\sigma_{1,2} = \frac{1}{2}(\sigma_d + \sigma_b) \pm \frac{1}{2}\sqrt{(\sigma_d - \sigma_b)^2 + 4\tau^2}$

$$= \frac{1}{2}(-\sigma + \sigma) \pm \frac{1}{2}\sqrt{(-\sigma - \sigma)^2 + 4 \times 3\sigma^2}$$

$$= 0 \pm \frac{1}{2}\sqrt{4\sigma^2 + 12\sigma^2}$$

$$= \pm\, 2\sigma$$

Maximum compressive stress = $2\sigma$

80. (b) $G_1 = G_2, d_1 = d_2, D_1 = 2.5$ cm,

$D_2 = 1.25$ cm, $n_1 = n_2 = n$,

Spring constant, $k = \frac{Gd^4}{8D^3 n}$

$G$, $d$ and $n$ being value

$$k \propto \frac{1}{D^3}$$

$$\frac{k_1}{k_2} = \left(\frac{D_2}{D_1}\right)^3 = \left(\frac{1.25}{2.5}\right)^3 = \frac{1}{8}$$

81. (c) 82. (b)

83. (a) $\sigma_\theta = 80\text{MPa}, E = 2 \times 10^5 \text{MPa}, n = 0.28$

$$\sigma_1 = \frac{\sigma_\theta}{2} = 40\text{MPa}$$

$$\varepsilon_\theta = \frac{1}{E}[\sigma_\theta - v\sigma_1]$$

$$= \frac{\sigma_\theta}{E}[1 - 0.5v]$$

$$= \frac{80}{2 \times 10^5}[1 - 0.5 \times 0.28] = 3.44 \times 10^{-4}$$

84. (b) 85. (c) 86. (b) 87. (b)

88. (c) $A_s = A_C = A$

Let $a$ = side of square

$d$ = diameter of circle

Then $a^2 = A$ or $a = \sqrt{A}$

$\frac{\pi}{4} d^2 = A$ or $d = \sqrt{\frac{4A}{\pi}}$

Moment of resistance, $M_r = \sigma z$

For same $\sigma$, $M_r \propto Z$

$$z_s = \frac{a^3}{6} = \frac{1}{6} A^{3/2}$$

$$z_C = \frac{\pi d^3}{32} = \frac{\pi}{32}\left(\frac{4A}{32}\right)^{3/2} = \frac{1}{7} A^{3/2}$$

$\therefore$ Square beam is stronger than circular beam

89. (a) $\delta = \frac{WL^3}{3EI}$

$$\delta \propto \frac{W}{I}$$

$$\delta_1 \propto \frac{12W}{bh^3}$$

$$\delta_2 \propto \frac{12 \times \frac{W}{2}}{b \times (2h)^3} = \frac{6W}{8bh^3} = \frac{3}{4} = \frac{W}{bh^3}$$

$$\frac{\delta_2}{\delta_1} = \frac{3}{4} \times \frac{1}{12} = \frac{1}{16}$$

90. (a)

91. (a) $\tau_{max} = \frac{16T}{\pi d^3}$

$\sigma_{max} = \tau_{max}$ for $\theta = 45°$

92. (b) Tensile stress $= -\frac{P}{A} + \frac{Pe}{l} + \frac{D}{2} = 0$

$$\therefore \frac{1}{A} = \frac{eD}{2l}$$

$$\frac{4}{\pi(D^2 - d^2)} = \frac{eD \times 64}{2 \times \pi(D^4 - d^4)}$$

$$e = \frac{8\pi(D^4 - d^4)}{64 \times \pi \times D(D^2 - d^2)}$$

$$= \frac{D^2 + d^2}{8D}$$

93. (d) $U = \frac{1}{2} \times \text{stress} \times \text{strain} \times \text{Volume}$

$$= \frac{1}{2} \times \frac{P}{A} \times \frac{P}{AE} \times AL$$

$$= \frac{1}{2} \times \frac{P^2 L}{AE}$$

94. (d)

95. (d) $\sigma_1 = \sigma_0$ then $\sigma_\theta = 2\sigma_0$

Maximum shear stress,

$$\tau_{max} = \frac{\sigma_0 - \sigma_1}{2}$$

$$= \frac{2\sigma_0 - \sigma_0}{2} = \frac{\sigma_0}{2}$$

96. (c)

97. (c) $M_e = \frac{1}{2}\left[M + \sqrt{M^2 + T^2}\right]$

$$= \frac{1}{2}\left[400 + \sqrt{400^2 + 300^2}\right]$$

$= 450$ k.N.m

$$\sigma_b = \frac{32M}{\pi d^3} = \frac{32}{\pi d^3} \times 450$$

$$T_e = \sqrt{M^2 + T^2} = 500 \text{ kN.m}$$

$$\tau = \frac{16T}{\pi d^3} = \frac{16}{\pi d^3} \times 500$$

$$\frac{\sigma_b}{\tau} = \frac{2 \times 450}{500} = \frac{9}{5} = 1.8$$

98. (a) 99. (b)

100. (a) $(\sigma_\theta)_{cyl} = \frac{pd}{2t}$

$(\sigma_\theta)_{cyl} = \frac{pd}{4t}$

$\frac{(\sigma_\theta)_{cyl}}{(\sigma_\theta)_{sph}} = 2$

101. (d) Total sale price = Fixed cost + Variable cost + Profit

= 47,000 + 15 × 14,000 + 23,000

= 280,000

Profit price = $\frac{280,00}{14,00}$ = Rs. 21

102. (d)

103. (d) Number of products made annualy

$\frac{\text{Annual cost of direct materials}}{\text{Direct material cost}} = 2,00,000/10$

= 20,000

Total cost of product = Direct labour cost + direct materials cost + overhead cost per unit

$= 5 + 10 + \frac{1,20,000}{20,000}$

= 5 + 10 + 6 = Rs. 21

104. (b) Fixed cost + variable cost = Sales income

$$\text{BEP} = \frac{\text{Fixed cost}}{1 - \frac{\text{Variable cost}}{\text{Selling price}}}$$

105. (c) $Q^* = \sqrt{\frac{2DC_0}{C_c}}$

$Q^* \propto \sqrt{C_0}$

$\frac{Q_2^*}{Q_1^*} = \sqrt{\frac{C_{02}}{C_{01}}} = \sqrt{\frac{1}{2}} = 1.4.14$

106. (a) 107. (c) 108. (c) 109. (c) 110. (c)

111. (d)

| Item No. | Annual usage × 1000 | Unit cost ₹ | Annual x unit cost |
|---|---|---|---|
| A | 30 | 0.10 | 3 |
| B | 300 | 0.15 | 4 |
| C | 2 | 200.00 | 400 |
| D | 60 | 0.10 | 6 |
| E | 5 | 0.30 | 1.5 |
| F | 300 | 0.10 | 30 |
| G | 10 | 0.05 | 0 |
| H | 7 | 0.10 | 0.7 |
| I | 20 | 0.10 | 2 |
| J | 5 | 020 | 1 |

**The minimum product of annual usage and unit cost is that of items G and H.**

112. (d)

113. (c) $\text{EOQ} = \sqrt{\frac{2DC_0}{C_c}}$

$Q^*_A = \sqrt{\frac{2 \times 100 \times 100}{1}} = 50\sqrt{2}$

$Q^*_B = \sqrt{\frac{2 \times 40 \times 100}{1}} = 200\sqrt{2}$

$Q^*_A / Q^*_B = 50/100 = 1:4$

114. (c) 115. (b) 116. (d) 117. (c)

118. (d) D = 900 $C_0$ = ₹ 100/order,

$C_c$ = ₹ 2/unit per year,

$\text{EOQ} = \sqrt{\frac{2DC_0}{C_c}}$

$= \sqrt{\frac{2 \times 900 \times 100}{2}} = 300$

119. (b) 120. (c)

❑❑❑

# 10. Strength of Materials

- Strength of materials, is a subject which deals with the behavior of solid objects subject to stresses and strains.
- The complete theory began with the consideration of the behavior of one and two dimensional members of structures, whose states of stress can be approximated as two dimensional, and was then generalized to three dimensions to develop a more complete theory of the elastic and plastic behavior of materials.
- An important founding pioneer in mechanics of materials was Stephen Timoshenko.
- The study of strength of materials often refers to various methods of calculating the stresses and strains in structural members, such as beams, columns, and shafts.
- The methods employed to predict the response of a structure under loading and its susceptibility to various failure modes takes into account the properties of the materials such as its yield strength, ultimate strength, Young's modulus, and Poisson's ratio; in addition the mechanical element's macroscopic properties (geometric properties), such as it length, width, thickness, boundary constraints and abrupt changes in geometry such as holes are considered.
- In materials science, the strength of a material is its ability to withstand an applied load without failure. The field of strength of materials deals with forces and deformations that result from their acting on a material.
- A load applied to a mechanical member will induce internal forces within the member called stresses when those forces are expressed on a unit basis. The stresses acting on the material cause deformation of the material in various manner.
- Deformation of the material is called strain when those deformations too are placed on a unit basis. The applied loads may be axial (tensile or compressive), or shear. The stresses and strains that develop within a mechanical member must be calculated in order to assess the load capacity of that member.
- This requires a complete description of the geometry of the member, its constraints, the loads applied to the member and the properties of the material of which the member is composed. With a complete description of the loading and the geometry of the member, the state of stress and of state of strain at any point within the member can be calculated.
- Once the state of stress and strain within the member is known, the strength (load carrying capacity) of that member, its deformations (stiffness qualities), and its stability (ability to maintain its original configuration) can be calculated.
- The calculated stresses may then be compared to some measure of the strength of the member such as its material yield or ultimate strength. The calculated deflection of the member may be compared to a deflection criteria that is based on the member's use.
- The calculated buckling load of the member may be compared to the applied load. The calculated stiffness and mass distribution of the member may be used to calculate the member's dynamic response and then compared to the acoustic environment in which it will be used.
- Material strength refers to the point on the engineering stress–strain curve (yield stress) beyond which the material experiences deformations that will not be completely reversed upon removal of the loading and as a result the member will have a permanent deflection.
- The ultimate strength refers to the point on the engineering stress–strain curve corresponding to the stress that produces fracture.
- Transverse loading - Forces applied perpendicular to the longitudinal axis of a member. Transverse loading causes the member to bend and deflect from its original position, with internal tensile and compressive strains accompanying the change in curvature of the member. Transverse loading also induces shear forces that cause shear deformation of the material and increase the transverse deflection of the member.
- Axial loading - The applied forces are collinear with the longitudinal axis of the member. The forces cause the member to either stretch or shorten.
- Torsional loading - Twisting action caused by a pair of externally applied equal and oppositely directed force couples acting on parallel planes or by a single external couple applied to a member that has one end fixed against rotation.
- Compressive stress is the stress state caused by an applied load that acts to reduce the length of the material along the axis of the applied load, it is in other words a stress state that causes a squeezing of the material. A simple case of compression is the uniaxial compression induced by the action of opposite, pushing forces.
- Compressive strength for materials is generally higher than their tensile strength. However, structures loaded

in compression are subject to additional failure modes, such as buckling, that are dependent on the member's geometry.

- Tensile stress is the stress state caused by an applied load that tends to elongate the material along the axis of the applied load, in other words the stress caused by pulling the material. The strength of structures of equal cross sectional area loaded in tension is independent of shape of the cross section. Materials loaded in tension are susceptible to stress concentrations such as material defects or abrupt changes in geometry.
- Shear stress is the stress state caused by the combined energy of a pair of opposing forces acting along parallel lines of action through the material, in other words the stress caused by faces of the material sliding relative to one another.
- Yield strength its the lowest stress that produces a permanent deformation in a material. In some materials, like aluminum alloys, the point of yielding is difficult to identify, thus it is usually defined as the stress required to cause 0.2% plastic strain. This is called a 0.2% proof stress.
- Compressive strength is a limit state of compressive stress that leads to failure in a material in the manner of ductile failure (infinite theoretical yield) or brittle failure (rupture as the result of crack propagation, or sliding along a weak plane - see shear strength).
- Tensile strength or ultimate tensile strength is a limit state of tensile stress that leads to tensile failure in the manner of ductile failure (yield as the first stage of that failure, some hardening in the second stage and breakage after a possible "neck" formation) or brittle failure (sudden breaking in two or more pieces at a low stress state). Tensile strength can be quoted as either true stress or engineering stress, but engineering stress is the most commonly used.
- Fatigue strength is a measure of the strength of a material or a component under cyclic loading, and is usually more difficult to assess than the static strength measures. Fatigue strength is quoted as stress amplitude or stress range ($\Delta\sigma = \sigma_{max} - \sigma_{min}$), usually at zero mean stress, along with the number of cycles to failure under that condition of stress.
- Impact strength, is the capability of the material to withstand a suddenly applied load and is expressed in terms of energy. Often measured with the Izod impact strength test or Charpy impact test, both of which measure the impact energy required to fracture a sample.
- Deformation of the material is the change in geometry created when stress is applied .Deformation is expressed by the displacement field of the material.
- Strain or reduced deformation is a mathematical term that expresses the trend of the deformation change among the material field. Strain is the deformation per unit length. Deflection is a term to describe the magnitude to which a structural element is displaced when subject to an applied load.
- Elasticity is the ability of a material to return to its previous shape after stress is released. In many materials, the relation between applied stress is directly proportional to the resulting strain (up to a certain limit), and a graph representing those two quantities is a straight line.
- The slope of this line is known as Young's modulus, or the "modulus of elasticity." The modulus of elasticity can be used to determine the stress–strain relationship in the linear-elastic portion of the stress–strain curve.
- The linear-elastic region is either below the yield point, or if a yield point is not easily identified on the stress–strain plot it is defined to be between 0 and 0.2% strain, and is defined as the region of strain in which no yielding (permanent deformation) occurs.
- Plasticity or plastic deformation is the opposite of elastic deformation and is defined as unrecoverable strain. Plastic deformation is retained after the release of the applied stress. Most materials in the linear-elastic category are usually capable of plastic deformation.
- Brittle materials, like ceramics, do not experience any plastic deformation and will fracture under relatively low stress. Materials such as metals usually experience a small amount of plastic deformation before failure while ductile metals such as copper and lead or polymers will plastically deform much more.
- Ultimate strength is an attribute related to a material, rather than just a specific specimen made of the material, and as such it is quoted as the force per unit of cross section area (N/m2).
- The ultimate strength is the maximum stress that a material can withstand before it breaks or weakens.
- A Factor of safety is a design criteria that an engineered component or structure must achieve. FS = UTS/R, where FS: the factor of safety, R: The applied stress, and UTS: ultimate stress (psi or N/m2)
- Margin of Safety is also sometimes used to as design criteria. It is defined MS = Failure Load/(Factor of Safety * Predicted Load) - 1
- Design stresses that have been determined from the ultimate or yield point values of the materials give safe and reliable results only for the case of static loading.
- Many machine parts fail when subjected to a non-steady and continuously varying loads even though the developed stresses are below the yield point. Such failures are called fatigue failure.
- The failure is by a fracture that appears to be brittle with little or no visible evidence of yielding. However, when the stress is kept below "fatigue stress" or "endurance limit stress", the part will endure indefinitely.
- A purely reversing or cyclic stress is one that alternates between equal positive and negative peak stresses during each cycle of operation. In a purely cyclic stress, the average stress is zero.

# MULTIPLE CHOICE QUESTIONS

1. A tapering bar (diameters of end sections being $d_1$ and $d_2$) and a bar of uniform cross-section '*d*' have the same length and are subjected to the same axial pull. Both the bars will have the same extension if '*d*' is equal to
   (a) $\frac{d_2+d_2}{2}$ (b) $\sqrt{d_1 d_2}$
   (c) $\sqrt{\frac{d_1 d_2}{2}}$ (d) $\sqrt{\frac{d_1+d_2}{2}}$
2. Which of the following is true (μ= Poisson's ratio):
   (a) $0<\mu<-1/2$ (b) $1<\mu<0$
   (c) $1<\mu<-1$ (d) $\infty<\mu<-\infty$
3. For most brittle materials, the ultimate strength in compression is much larger than the ultimate strength is tension. That is mainly due to:
   (a) presence of flaws and microscopic cracks or cavities
   (b) necking in tension
   (c) severity of tensile stress as compared to compressive stress
   (d) non-linearity of stress-strain diagram.
4. Bending moment M and torque T is applied on a solid circular shaft. If the maximum bending stress equals to maximum shear stress developed, then M is equal to:
   (a) $\frac{T}{2}$ (b) T
   (c) 2T (d) 4T
5. When bending moment M and torque T is applied on a shaft then equivalent torque is:
   (a) M + T (b) $\sqrt{M^2+T^2}$
   (c) $\frac{1}{2}\sqrt{M^2+T^2}$ (d) $\frac{1}{2}\left(m+\sqrt{M^2+T^2}\right)$
6. A helical spring has N turns of coil of diameter D, and a second spring, made of same wire diameter and of same material, has N/2 turns of coil of diameter 2D. If the stiffness of the first spring is k, then the stiffness of the second spring will be:
   (a) k/4 (b) k/2
   (c) 2k (d) 4k
7. If a prismatic bar be subjected to an axial tensile stress σ then shear stress induced on a plane inclined at θ with the axis will be:
   (a) $\frac{\sigma}{2}\sin 2\theta$ (b) $\frac{\sigma}{2}\cos 2\theta$
   (c) $\frac{\sigma}{2}\cos^2\theta$ (d) $\frac{\sigma}{2}\sin^2\theta$
8. Select the proper sequence
   1. Proportional Limit 2. Elastic limit
   3. Yielding 4. Failure
   (a) 2, 3, 1, 4 (b) 2, 1, 3, 4
   (c) 1, 3, 2, 4 (d) 1, 2, 3, 4
9. The relationship between constants E. G and K is given by:
   (a) $E=\frac{G+3K}{9KG}$ (b) $E=\frac{3G+K}{9KG}$
   (c) $E=\frac{9KG}{G+3K}$ (d) $E=\frac{9KG}{3G+K}$
10. For the two shafts in parallel, find which statements is true?
    (a) Torque in each shaft is the same
    (b) Shear stress in each shaft is the same
    (c) Angle of twist of each shaft is the same
    (d) Torsional stiffness of each shaft is the same
11. A vertical hanging bar of length L and weighing w N/unit length carries a load W at the bottom. The tensile force in the bar at a distance *y* from the support will be given by:
    (a) W + *w*L (b) W + *w* (L – *y*)
    (c) (W + *w*) *y*/L (d) $W+\frac{W}{w}(L-y)$
12. In the case of bi-axial state of normal stress, the normal stress on 45° plane is equal to:
    (a) the sum of the normal stresses
    (b) difference of the normal stresses
    (c) half the sum of the normal stresses
    (d) half the difference of the normal stresses
13. The temperature stress is a function of
    1. Coefficient of linear expansion
    2. Temperature rise
    3. Modulus of elasticity

    The correct answer is:
    (a) 1 and 2 only (b) 1 and 3 only
    (c) 2 and 3 only (d) 1, 2 and 3
14. When two springs of equal length are arranged to form a cluster spring then which of the following statements are true:
    1. Angle of twist in both the springs will he equal
    2. Deflection of both the springs will be equal
    3. Load taken by each spring will be half the total load
    4. Shear stress in each spring will be equal.

    (a) 1 and 2 only (b) 2 and 3 only
    (c) 2 and 4 only (d) 1, 2 and 4 only
15. When σ and Young's Modulus of Elasticity E remains constant, the energy-absorbing capacity of part subject to dynamic forces, is a function of its.
    (a) length (b) cross-section
    (c) volume (d) none of the above

16. Principal stresses at a point in plane stressed element are $\sigma_x = \sigma_y = 500$ kg/cm$^2$. Normal stress on the plane inclined at 45° to $x$-axis will be:
(a) 0 (b) 500 kg/cm$^2$
(c) 707 kg/cm$^2$ (d) 1000 kg/cm$^2$

17. Two coiled springs, each having stiffness K, are placed in parallel. The stiffness of the combination will be:
(a) 4K (b) 2K
(c) $\frac{K}{2}$ (d) $\frac{K}{4}$

18. A steel rod of 1 sq. cm. cross sectional area is 100 cm long and has a Young's modulus of elasticity $2 \times 10^6$ kg/cm$^2$. It is subjected to an axial pull of 2000 kgf. The elongation of the rod will be:
(a) 0.05 cm (b) 0.1 cm
(c) 0.15 cm (d) 0.20 cm

19. If the area of cross-section of a wire is circular and if the radius of this circle decreases to half its original value due to the stretch of the wire by a load, then the modulus of elasticity of the wire will be:
(a) one-fourth of its original value
(b) halved
(c) doubled
(d) unaffected

20. Match List-I with List-II and select the correct answer using the codes' giver below the lists:

| List-I | List-II |
|---|---|
| A. Ductility | 1. Impac test |
| B. Toughness | 2. Fatigue test |
| C. Endurance limit | 3. Tension test |
| D. Resistance to penetration | 4. Hardness test |

**Codes:**

| | A | B | C | D |
|---|---|---|---|---|
| (a) | 3 | 2 | 1 | 4 |
| (b) | 4 | 2 | 1 | 3 |
| (c) | 3 | 1 | 2 | 4 |
| (d) | 4 | 1 | 2 | 3 |

21. If a material had a modulus of elasticity of $2.1 \times 10^6$ kgf/cm$^2$ and a modulus of rigidity of $0.8 \times 10^6$ kgf/cm$^2$ then the approximate value of the Poisson's ratio of the material would be:
(a) 0.26 (b) 0.31
(c) 0.47 (d) 05

22. A long slender bar having uniform rectangular cross-section 'B×H' is acted upon by an axial compressive force. The sides B and H are paralled to $x$-and $y$-axes respectively. The ends of the bar are fixed such that they behave as pinpointed when the bar buckles in a plane normal to $x$-axis, and they behave as built-in when the bar buckles in a plane normal to $y$-axis. If load capacity in either mode of buckling is same, then the value of $\frac{H}{B}$ will be B:
(a) 2 (b) 4
(c) 8 (d) 16

23. Match List-I with List-II and select correct answer using the codes given below the lists:

| List I (Condition of beam) | List II (Bending moment diagram) |
|---|---|
| A. Subjected to bending moment at the end of a cantilever. | 1. Triangle |
| B. Cantilever carrying uniformly distributed load over the whole length. | 2. Cubic parabola |
| C. Cantilever carrying linearly varying load from zero at the fixed end to maximum at the support. | 3. Parabola |
| D. A beam having load at the centre and supported at the ends. | 4. Rectangle |

**Codes:**

| | A | B | C | D |
|---|---|---|---|---|
| (a) | 4 | 1 | 2 | 3 |
| (b) | 4 | 3 | 2 | 1 |
| (c) | 3 | 4 | 2 | 1 |
| (d) | 3 | 4 | 1 | 2 |

24. The number of independent elastic constants required to express the stress strain relationship for a linearly elastic isotropic materials is
(a) One (b) Two
(c) Three (d) Four

25. A simply supported beam of rectangular section 4 cm by 6 cm carries a mid-span concentrated load such that the 6 cm side lies parallel to line of action of loading; deflection under the load is δ. If the beam is now supported with the 4cm side parallel to line of action of loading, the deflection under the load will be:
(a) 0.44 δ (b) 0.67 δ
(c) 1.5 δ (d) 2.25 δ

26. A shaft was initially subjected to bending moment and then was subjected to torsion. If the magnitude of bending moment is found to be the same as that of the torque, then the ratio of maximum bending stress to shear stress would be:
(a) 0.25 (b) 0.50
(c) 2.0 (d) 4.0

27. A horizontal beam with square cross-section is simply supported with sides of the square horizontal and vertical and carries a distributed loading that produces maximum bending stress σ in the beam. When the beam is placed with one of the diagonals horizontal the maximum bending stress will be:
(a) $\frac{1}{\sqrt{2}}\sigma$ (b) σ
(c) $\sqrt{2}\sigma$ (d) 2σ

28. The property by which an amount of energy is absorbed by a material without plastic deformation, is called:
(a) toughness (b) impact strength
(c) ductility (d) resilience

29. In the assembly of pulley, key and shaft:
(a) pulley is made the weakest
(b) key is made the weakest
(c) key is made the strongest
(d) all the three are designed for equal strength

30. Circumferential and longitudinal strains in cylindrical boiler under internal steam pressure, are $\varepsilon_1$ and $\varepsilon_2$ respectively. Change in volume of the boiler cylinder per unit volume will be:
(a) $\varepsilon_1 + 2\varepsilon_2$ (b) $\varepsilon_1 + \varepsilon_2^2$
(c) $2\varepsilon_1 + \varepsilon_2$ (d) $\varepsilon_1^2 + \varepsilon_2$

31. A metal pipe of 1 *m* diameter contains a fluid having a pressure of 10 kgf/cm$^2$. If the permissible tensile stress in the metal is 200 kgf/cm$^2$ then the thickness of the metal required for making the pipe would be:
(a) 5 mm (b) 10 mm
(c) 20 mm (d) 25 mm

32. A length of 10 mm diameter steel wire is coiled to a close coiled helical spring having 8 coils of 75 mm mean diameter, and the spring has a stiffness k. If the same length of wire is coiled to 10 coils of 60 mm mean diameter, then the spring stiffness will be:
(a) *k* (b) 1.25 k
(c) 1.56 k (d) 1.95 k

33. The buckling load will he maximum for a column, if:
(a) one end of the column is clamped and the other end is free
(b) both ends of the column are clamped
(c) both ends of the column are hinged
(d) one end of the column is hinged and the other end is free

34. If the principal stresses corresponding to a two-dimensional state of stress are $\sigma_1$ and $\sigma_2$. If $\sigma_1$ is greater than $\sigma_2$ and both are tensile, then which one of the following would be the correct criterion for failure by yielding, according to the maximum shear stress criterion?
(a) $(\sigma_1 + \sigma_2)/2 = \pm\, \sigma_{yp}/2$
(b) $\sigma_1/2 = \pm\, \sigma_{yp}/2$
(c) $\sigma_2/2 = \pm\, \sigma_{yp}/2$
(d) $\sigma_1 = \pm\, \sigma_{yp}$

35. A state of pure shear in a biaxial stress is given by:
(a) $\begin{bmatrix} \sigma_1 & \sigma_1 \\ 0 & \sigma_2 \end{bmatrix}$ (b) $\begin{bmatrix} \sigma_1 & 0 \\ 0 & -\sigma_2 \end{bmatrix}$
(c) $\begin{bmatrix} \sigma_x & \tau_{xy} \\ 0 & -\sigma_Y \end{bmatrix}$ (d) none of the above

36. The number of strain readings (using strain gauges) needed on a plane surface to determine the principal strains and their direction is:
(a) 1 (b) 2
(c) 3 (d) 4

37. When two mutually perpendicular principal stresses are unequal but alike, the maximum shear stress is represented by:
(a) the diameter of the Mohr's circle
(b) half the diameter of the Mohr's circle
(c) one-third the diameter of the Mohr's circle
(d) one-fourth the diameter of the Mohr's circle

38. If the value of Poisson's ratio is zero, then it means that:
(a) the material is rigid
(b) there is no longitudinal strain in the material
(c) the material is perfectly plastic
(d) the longitudinal strain in the material is infinite

39. The deformation of a bar under its own weight as compared to that when subjected to a direct axial load equal to its own weight will be
(a) The same (b) One-fourth
(c) Half (d) Double

40. When a weight of 100 N falls on a spring of stiffness 1 kN/m from a height of 2m, the deflection caused in the first fall is:
(a) equal to 0.1 m (b) between 0.1 and 0.2 m
(c) equal to 0.2 m (d) more than 0.2 m

41. Two hollow shafts of the same material have the same length and outside diameter. Shaft 1 has internal diameter equal to one-third of the outer diameter and shaft 2 has internal diameter equal to half of the outer diameter. If both the shafts are subject to the same torque, the ratio of their twists $\theta_1/\theta_2$ will be equal to
(a) 16/81 (b) 8/27
(c) 19/27 (d) 243/256

42. A solid shaft of diameter 'D' caries a twisting moment that develops maximum shear stress $\tau$. If the shaft is replaced by a hollow one of outside diameter 'D' and inside diameter D/2, then the maximum shear stress will be:
(a) $1.067\tau$ (b) $1.143\tau$
(c) $1.333\tau$ (d) $2\tau$

43. A circular shaft can transmit a torque of 5 kNm. If the torque is reduced to 4 kNm then the maximum value of bending moment that can be applied to the shaft is:
(a) 1 kNm (b) 2 kNm
(c) 3 kNm (d) 4 kNm

44. A thin cylinder contains fluid at a pressure of 500 N/m$^2$, the internal diameter of the shell is 0.6 m and the tensile stress in the material is to be limited to 9000 N/m$^2$. The shell must have a minimum wall thickness of nearly:
(a) 9 mm (h) 11 mm
(c) 17 mm (d) 21mm

45. A steel hub of 100 mm internal diameter and uniform thickness of 10 mm was heated to a temperature 300°C to shrink-fit on a shaft. On cooling, a crack developed parallel to the direction of the length of the hub. Consider the following factors in this
1. Tensile hoop stress
2. Tensile radial stress
3. Compressive hoop stress
4. Compressive radial stress

The cause of failure is attributable to:
(a) 1 alone (b) 1 and 3
(c) 1, 2 and 4 (d) 2, 3 and 4

46. A compound cylinder with inner radius 5 cm and outer radius 7 cm is made by shrinking one cylinder on to the other cylinder. The junction radius is 6 cm and the junction pressure is 11 kg/cm$^2$. The maximum hoop stress developed in the inner cylinder is:
(a) 36 kgf/cm$^2$ compression
(b) 36 kgf/cm$^2$ tension
(c) 72 kgf/cm$^2$ compression
(d) 72 kgf/cm$^2$tension

47. Cracks in helical springs used in railway carriages usually start on the inner side of the coil because of the fact that:
(a) it is subjected to a higher stress than the outer side
(b) it is subjected to a higher cyclic loading than the outer side
(c) it is more stretched than the outer side during the manufacturing process
(d) it has a lower curvature than the outer side

48. Two helical springs of the same material and of equal circular cross-section and length and number of turns, but having radii 90 mm and 40 mm, kept concentrically (smaller radius spring within the larger radius spring), arc compressed between two parallel planes with a load P. The inner spring will carry a load equal to:

(a) $\frac{P}{2}$ (b) $\frac{P}{3}$

(c) $\frac{P}{1.088}$ (d) $\frac{P}{2.088}$

49. Rankine-Gordon formula for buckling is valid for:
(a) long column
(b) short column
(c) short and long column
(d) very long column

50. If failure in shear along 45° planes is.to be avoided then a material subjected to uniaxial tension should have its shear strength equal to at least:
(a) tensile strength
(b) compressive strength
(c) half the difference between the tensile and compressive strengths
(d) half the tensile strength

51. A shaft is subjected to a maximum bending stress of 80 N/mm$^2$ and maximum shearing stress equal to 30 N/mm$^2$ at a particular section. If the yield point in tension of the material is 280 N/mm$^2$, and maximum shear stress theory of failure is used, then the factor of safety obtained will be:
(a) 2.5 (b) 2.8
(c) 3.0 (d) 3.5

52. If $\sigma_y$ is the yield strength of a particular material, then the distortion energy theory is expressed as:
(a) $(\sigma_1-\sigma_2)^2+(\sigma_2-\sigma_3)^2+(\sigma_3-\sigma)^2=2s_y^2$
(b) $(\sigma_1^2+\sigma_2+\sigma_3)-2v(\sigma_1\sigma_2+\sigma_2\sigma_3+\sigma_3\sigma_1)=\sigma_y^2$
(c) $(\sigma_1-\sigma_2^2)+(\sigma_2-\sigma_3)^2+(\sigma_3-\sigma_1)^2=3\sigma_y^2$
(d) $(1-2v)(\sigma_1+\sigma_2+\sigma_3)^2=2(1+v)\sigma_y$

53. Hoop stress and longitudinal stress in a boiler shell under internal pressure are 100 MN/ m$^2$ and 50,MN/ m$^2$ respectively. Young's modulus of elasticity and Poisson's ratio of the shell material are 200 GN/m$^2$ and 0.3 respectively. The hoop strain in boiler shell is:
(a) $0.425 \times 10^{-3}$
(b) $0.5 \times 10^{-3}$
(c) $0.585 \times 10^{-3}$
(d) $0.75 \times 10^{-3}$

54. The stretch in a steel rod of circular section, having a length '*l*' subjected to a tensile load 'P' and tapering uniformly from a diameter $d_1$ at one end to a diameter $d_2$ at the other end, is given:
(a) $Pl/4Ed_1d_2$ (b) $Pl\pi/Ed_1d_2$
(c) $Pl/4E(d_1.d_2)$ (d) $4P.l/\pi.E.d_1.d_2$

55. A simply supported beam of constant flexural rigidity and length 2 L carries a concentrated load 'P' at its mid-span and the deflection under that load is δ. If a cantilever beam of the same flexural rigidity and length is subjected to load 'P' at its free end, them the deflection at the free end will be
(a) 1/2δ (b) δ
(c) 2δ (d) 4δ

56. If Poisson's ratio for a material is 0.5, then the elastic modulus for the material is:
(a) three times its shear modulus
(b) four times its shear modulus
(c) equal to its shear modulus
(d) indeterminate.

57. From a tension test, the yield strength of steel is found to be 200 N/mm$^2$. Using a factor of safety of 2 and applying maximum principal stress theory of failure, the permissible stress in the steel shaft subjected to torque will be:
(a) 50 N/mm$^2$
(b) 57.7 N/mm$^2$
(c) 86.6 N/mm$^2$
(d) 100 N/m m$^2$

58. A solid shaft of diameter 100 mm, length 1000 mm is subjected to a twisting moment 'T'. The maximum shear stress developed in the shaft is 60 N/mm. A hole of 50 mm diameter is now drilled throughout the length of shaft. To develop a maximum shear stress of 60 N/ mm in the hollow shaft, the torque 'T' must he reduced by
(a) T/4 (b) T/8
(c) T/12 (d) T/16

59. A rectangular section beam subjected to a bending moment M varying along its length is required to develop same maximum bending stress at any cross-section. If the depth of the section is constant, then its width will vary as:
(a) M (b) $\sqrt{M}$
(c) $M_2$ (d) 1/M

60. Consider the following statements:
If at section distant from one of the ends of the beam, M represents the bending moment, V the shear force and w the intensity of loading, then
1. $dM/dx = V$
2. $dV/dx = w$
3. $dw/dx = y$ (the deflection of the beam at the section)

Of these statements:
(a) 1 and 3 are correct
(b) 1 and 2 are correct
(c) 2 and 3 are correct
(d) 1, 2 and 3 are correct

61. A cantilever beam having 5 m length is so loaded that it develops a shearing force of 20 T and a bending moment of 20 T-m at a section 2m from the free end. Maximum shearing force and maximum, bending moment developed in the beam under this load, are respectively 50 T and 125 T-m. The load on the beam is:
(a) 25 T concentrated load at free end.
(b) 20 T concentrated load at free end.
(c) 5 T concentrated load at free end and 2 T/m load over entire length.
(d) 10 T/mudl over entire length

62. Consider the following statements:
State of stress in two dimensions at a point in a loaded component can be completely specified by indicating the normal and shear stresses on
1. A plane containing the point
2. Any two planes passing through the point
3. Two mutually perpendicular planes passing through the point

Of these statements
(a) 1 and 3 arc correct (b) 2 alone is correct
(c) 1 alone is correct (d) 3 alone is correct

63. Which one of the following properties is more sensitive to increase in strain rate?
(a) Yield strength (b) Proportional limit
(c) Elastic limit (d) Tensile strength

64. A simply supported beam carrying a concentrated load W at mid-span deflects by $\delta_1$ under the load. If the same beam carries the load W such that it is distributed uniformly over entire length and undergoes a deflection $\delta_2$ at the mid span. The ratio, $\delta_1 : \delta_2$ is:
(a) 2 : 1 (b) $\sqrt{2}$ :1
(c) 1.6 : 1 (d) 1 : 2

65. Match List-I with List-II and select the correct answer using the codes given below the lists:

| **List I (End conditions of columns)** | **List-II (Lowest critical load)** |
|---|---|
| A. Column with both ends hinged | 1. $(\pi^2EI)/L^2$ |
| B. Column with both ends fixed | 2. $(2\pi^2EI)/L^2$ |
| C. Column with one end fixed and the other end hinged: | 3. $(\pi^2EI)/L^2$ |
| D. Column with one end fixed and the other end free | 4. $(\pi^2EI)/4L^2$ |

*(E is the young's modulus of elasticity of column material, L is the length and I is the second moment of area of cross-section of the column).*

**Codes:**

| | A | B | C | D |
|---|---|---|---|---|
| (a) | 1 | 2 | 3 | 4 |
| (b) | 3 | 2 | 1 | 4 |
| (c) | 1 | 3 | 2 | 4 |
| (d) | 2 | 4 | 3 | 1 |

66. Euler's formula can be used for obtaining crippling load for a M.S. column with hinged ends. Which one of the following conditions for the slenderness ratio $l/k$ is to be satisfied?
(a) $5 < \frac{l}{k} < 8$ (b) $9 < \frac{l}{k} < 8$
(c) $19 < \frac{l}{k} < 40$ (d) $\frac{l}{k} \geq 80$

67. A 3-meter long steel cylindrical shaft is rigidly held at its two ends. A pulley is mounted on the shaft at 1 meter from one end; the shaft is twisted by applying torque on the pulley.
The maximum shearing stresses developed in $1m$ and $2m$ lengths are respectively $\tau_1$ and $\tau_2$. The ratio $\tau_2$, $\tau_1$ is:
(a) 1/2 (b) 1
(c) 2 (d) 4

68. A closely-coiled helical spring is acted upon by an axial force. The maximum shear stress developed in the spring is *t*. Half of the length of spring is cut off and the remaining spring is acted upon by the same axial force. The maximum shear stress in the spring in the new condition will be:
(a) 1/2 τ (b) τ
(c) 2τ (d) 4τ

69. A circular shaft is subjected to the combined action of bending, twisting and direct axial loading. The maximum bending stress σ maximum shearing stress $\sqrt{3}\sigma$ and a uniform axial stress σ(compressive) are produced. The σ maximum compressive normal stress produced in the shaft will be
(a) 3 σ (b) 2 σ
(c) σ (d) Zero

70. Permissible bending moment in a circular shaft under pure bending is M according to maximum principal stress theory of failure.According to maximum shear stress theory of failure, the permissible bending moment in the same shaft is:
(a) 1/2M (b) M
(c) $\sqrt{M}$ (d) 2M

71. A long helical spring having a spring-stiffness of 12 kN/m and number of turns 20, breaks into two equal parts. The resultant spring stiffness will be:
(a) 6 kN/m (b) 12 kN/m
(c) 24 kN/m (d) 30 kN/m

72. Consider the following statements.
State of stress at a point when completely specified, enables one to determine the
1. Principal stresses at the point.
2. Maximum shearing stress at the point
3. Stress components on any arbitrary plane containing the point

Of these statements:
(a) 1, 2 and 3 are correct (b) 1 and 3 are correct
(c) 2 and 3 arc correct (d) 1 and 2 are correct

73. Match List-I (End conditions of columns) with List-II (Equivalent length in terms of length of hinged-hinged column) and select the correct answer using the codes given below the lists:

| List-I | List-II |
|---|---|
| A. Both ends hinged | 1. L |
| B. One end fixed and other end free | 2. $L/\sqrt{2}$ |
| C. One end fixed and the other pin-jointed | 3. $\frac{L}{2}$ |
| D. Both ends fixed | 4. 2L |

**Codes:**

| | A | B | C | D |
|---|---|---|---|---|
| (a) | 1 | 4 | 3 | 2 |
| (b) | 1 | 4 | 2 | 3 |
| (c) | 3 | 1 | 2 | 4 |
| (d) | 3 | 1 | 4 | 2 |

74. Two closed-coil springs are made from the same small diameter wire, one wound on 2.5 cm diameter core and the other on 1.25 cm diameter core. If each spring has V coils, then the ratio of their spring constants would be
(a) 1/16 (b) 1/8
(c) 1/4 (d) 1/2

75. The maximum bending moment in a simply supported beam of length L loaded by a concentrated load W at the midpoint is given by:
(a) WL (b) $\frac{WL}{2}$
(c) $\frac{WL}{4}$ (d) $\frac{WL}{8}$

76. Match List-I with List-II and select the correct answer using the codes given below the list:

| List-I | List-II |
|---|---|
| A. Bending moment is constant | 1. Point of contra-flexure |
| B. Bending moment is maximum or minimum | 2. Shear force changes sign |
| C. Bending moment is zero | 3. Slope of shear force diagram is zero over the portion of the beam |
| D. Loading is constant | 4. Shear force is zero over the portion of the beam. |

**Codes:**

| | A | B | C | D |
|---|---|---|---|---|
| (a) | 4 | 1 | 2 | 3 |
| (b) | 1 | 4 | 2 | 3 |
| (c) | 3 | 1 | 2 | 4 |
| (d) | 3 | 1 | 4 | 2 |

77. If the shear force acting at every section of a beam is of the same magnitude and of the same direction then it represents a:
(a) Simply supported beam with a concentrated load at the centre
(b) Overhung beam having equal overhang at both supports and carrying equal concentrated loads acting in the same direction at the free ends
(c) Cantilever subjected to concentrated load at the free end
(d) Simply supported beam having concentrated loads of equal magnitude and in the same direction acting at equal distances from the supports

78. A cantilever beam carries a load W uniformly distributed over its entire length. If the same load is placed at the free and of the same cantilever, then the ratio of maximum deflection in the first case to that in the second case will be:
(a) 3/8 (b) 8/3
(c) 5/8 (d) 8/5

79. Circumferential stress in a cylindrical steel boiler shell under internal pressure is 80 MPa, Young's modulus of elasticity and Poisson's ratio are respectively $2 \times 10^5$ MPa and 0.28.
The magnitude of circumferential strain in the boiler shell will be
(a) $3.44 \times 10^{-4}$ (b) $3.84 \times 10^{-4}$
(c) $4 \times 10^{-4}$ (d) $4.56 \times 10^{-4}$

80. For a cantilever beam of length 'L' flexural rigidity E*l* and loaded at its free end by a concentrated load 'M' match list-I with list-II and select the correct answer:

| List-I | List-II |
|---|---|
| A. maximum bending moment. | 1. WL |
| B. Strain energy | 2. $WL^2/2EI$ |
| C. Maximum slope | 3. $WL^3/2EI$ |
| D. Maximum deflection | 4. $W^2L^2/6EI$ |

**Codes:**

| | A | B | C | D |
|---|---|---|---|---|
| (a) | 1 | 4 | 3 | 2 |
| (b) | 1 | 4 | 2 | 3 |
| (c) | 4 | 2 | 1 | 3 |
| (d) | 4 | 3 | 1 | 2 |

81. At a certain section at a distance '*x*' from one of the supports of a simply supported beam, the intensity of loading, bending moment and shear force are $W_x$, $M_x$, and $V_x$, respectively, if the intensity of loading is varying continuously along the length of the beam, them the invalid relation is:
(a) Slop, $Q_x = \frac{Mx}{Vx}$ (b) $V_x = \frac{dMx}{dx}$
(c) $W_x = \frac{d^2Mx}{dx^2}$ (d) $W_x = \frac{dV_x}{dx}$

82. The equivalent bending moment under combined action of bending moment M and torque T is:
(a) $\sqrt{M^2+T^2}$ (b) $\frac{1}{2}\sqrt{M^2+T^2}$
(c) $\frac{1}{2}\sqrt{M^3+T^2}$ (d) $\frac{1}{2}\left(M+\sqrt{M^2+T^2}\right)$

83. The bending moment (M) is constant over a length segment *l* of a beam. The shearing force will also be constant over this length and is given by:
(a) M/*l* (b) M/2*l*
(c) M/4*l* (d) none of the above

84. In a thick cylinder, subjected to internal and external pressures, let $r_1$ and $r_2$ be the internal and external radii respectively. Let *u* be the radial displacement of a material element at radius $r, r_2 \geq r \geq r_1$. Identifying the cylinder axis as *z* axis, the radial strain component $\varepsilon_r$ is:
(a) *u/r* (b) *u*/θ
(c) *du/dr* (d) *du/d*θ

85. Auto-frettage is the method of:
(a) joining thick cylinders
(b) calculating stresses in thick cylinders
(c) prestressing thick cylinders
(d) increasing the life of thick cylinders

86. Given that
*d* = diameter of spring.
R = mean radius of coils.
*n* = number of coils, and
G = modulus of rigidity.
The stiffness of the close-coiled helical spring subject to an axial load W is equal to:
(a) $\frac{Gd^4}{64R^3n}$ (b) $\frac{Gd^3}{64R^3n}$
(c) $\frac{Gd^4}{32R^3n}$ (d) $\frac{Gd^4}{64R^3n}$

87. When a close-coiled helical spring is subjected to a couple about its axis, the stress induced in the wire material of the spring is:
(a) bending stress only
(b) direct shear stress only
(c) a combination of torsional shear stress and bending stress
(d) a combination of bending stress and direct shear stress

88. If a shaft made from ductile material is subjected to combined bending and twisting moments, calculations based on which one of the following failure theories would give the most conservative value?
(a) Maximum principal stress theory
(b) Maximum shear stress theory
(c) Maximum strain energy theory
(d) Maximum distortion energy theory

89. During tensile-testing of a specimen using Universal Testing Machine, the parameters actually measured include:
(a) true stress and true strain
(b) Poisson's ratio and Young's modulus
(c) engineering stress and engineering strain
(d) load and elongation

90. The state of plane stress in a plate of 100 mm thickness is given as
$\sigma_{xx} = 100\ \text{N/mm}^2, \sigma_{xy} = 200\ \text{N/mm}^2$
Young's modulus = 300 N/mm$^2$
Poission's ratio = 0.3
The stress developed in the direction of thickness is
(a) zero
(b) 90 N/mm$^2$
(c) 100 N/mm$^2$
(d) 200 N/mm$^2$

91. A plane stressed clement is subjected to the state of stress given by $\sigma_x = \tau_{xy} = 10\ \text{kgf/cm}^2$ and $\sigma_x = 0$. Maximum shear stress in the element is equal to:
(a) $50\sqrt{3}$ kgf cm$^2$ (b) 100 kgf/cm$^2$
(c) $50\sqrt{5}$ kgf/cm$^2$ (d) 150 kgf/cm$^2$

92. Match List-I (Elastic properties of an isotropic elastic material) with List-II (Nature of strain produced) and select the correct answer using the codes given below the Lists:

| List-I | List-II |
|---|---|
| A. Young's modulus | 1. Shear strain |
| B. Modulus of rigidity | 2. Normal strain |

C. Bulk modulus 3. Transverse strain
D. Poisson's ratio 4. Volumetric strain

**Codes:**

| | A | B | C | D |
|---|---|---|---|---|
| (a) | 2 | 1 | 3 | 4 |
| (b) | 2 | 1 | 4 | 3 |
| (c) | 3 | 4 | 1 | 2 |
| (d) | 4 | 3 | 1 | 2 |

93. The relationship between the Lame's constant 'λ'. Young's modulus 'E' and the Poisson's ratio '$v$' is:

(a) $\lambda = \frac{Ev}{(1+v)(1-2y)}$ (b) $\lambda = \frac{Ev}{(1+2v)(1-v)}$

(c) $\lambda = \frac{Ev}{(1+v)}$ (d) $\lambda = \frac{Ev}{(1-v)}$

94. A 10 cm long and 5 cm diameter steel rod fits snugly between two rigid walls 10 cm apart at room temperature. Young's modulus of elasticity and coefficient of linear expansion of steel are $2 \times 10^6$ kg/cm$^2$ and $12 \times 10^{-6}$ per °C respectively. The stress developed in rod due to a 100°C rise in temperature will be:

(a) $6 \times 10^{-10}$ kg/cm$^2$ (b) $6 \times 10^{-10}$ kg/cm$^2$
(c) $2.4 \times 10^3$ kg/cm$^2$ (d) $2.4 \times 10^4$ kg/cm$^2$

95. The number of elastic constants for a completely anisotropic elastic material which follows Hooks laws is

(a) 3 (b) 4
(c) 21 (d) 25

96. The bending moment equation, as a function of distance $x$ measured from the left end, for a simply supported beam of span. L m carrying a uniformly distributed load of intensity $w$ N/m will be given by

(a) $M = wL/2(L-x) - W/2(L-x)N.m$

(b) $M = wL/2x - wx^2/2 - N.m$

(c) $M = wL/2(L-x)^2 - w/2(L-x)N.m$

(d) $M = wx^2/2 - wL\,x/2N.m$

97. If a beam is subjected to a constant bending moment along its length, then the shear force will:

(a) also have a constant value everywhere along its length
(b) be zero at all sections along the beam
(c) be maximum at the centre and zero at the ends
(d) zero at the centre and maximum at the ends

98. A simply supported beam with width '$b$' and depth '$d$' carries a central load Wand undergoes deflection 8 at the centre. If the width and depth are interchanged, the deflection at the centre of the beam would attain the value:

(a) $\frac{d}{b}\delta$ (b) $\left(\frac{d}{b}\right)^2 \delta$

(c) $\left(\frac{d}{b}\right)^3 \delta$ (d) $\left(\frac{d}{b}\right)^{3/2} \delta$

99. For a composite consisting of a bar enclosed inside a tube of another material when compressed under a load 'W' as a whole through rigid collars at the end of the bar. The equation of compatibility is given by (suffixes 1 and 2) refer to bar and tube respectively:

(a) $W_1 + W_2 = W$ (b) $W_1 + W_2 = \text{constant}$

(c) $\frac{W_1}{A_1E_1} = \frac{W_2}{A_2E_2}$ (d) $\frac{W_2}{A_2E_1} = \frac{W_2}{A_1E_2}$

100. A rod of material with E = 200 × 10$^3$ MPa and $\propto = 10^{-3}$ mm/mm°C is fixed at both the ends. It is uniformly heated such that the increase in temperature is 30°C. The stress, developed in the rod is

(a) 6000 N/mm$^2$ (tensile)
(b) 6000 N/mm$^2$ (compressive)
(c) 2000 N/mm$^2$ (tensile)
(d) 2000 N/mm$^2$ (compressive)

101. A wooden beam of rectangular cross-section 10 cm deep by 5 cm wide carries maximum shear force of 2000 kg. Shear stress at neutral axis of the beam section is:

(a) zero (b) 40 kgf/cm$^2$
(c) 60 kgf/cm$^2$ (d) 80 kgf/cm$^2$

102. Two beams of equal cross-sectional area arc subjected to equal bending moment. If one beam has square cross-section and the other has circular section, then

(a) Both beams will be equally strong
(b) Circular section beam will be stronger
(c) Square section beam will be stronger
(d) The strength of the beam will depend on the nature of loading

103. A cantilever beam of rectangular cross-section is subjected to a load W at its free end. If the depth of the beam is doubled and the load is halved, the deflection of the free end as compared to original deflection will be

(a) Half (b) One-eighth
(c) One-sixteenth (d) Double

104. The ratio of the compressive critical load for a long column fixed at both the ends and a column with one end fixed and the other end free is:

(a) 2 : 1 (b) 4:1
(c) 8 : 1 (d) 16 : 1

105. Maximum shear stress in a solid shaft of diameter D and length L twisted through an angle θ is τ. A hollow shaft of same material and length having outside and inside diameters of D and D/2 respectively is also twisted through the same angle of twist θ. The value of maximum shear stress in the hollow shaft will be.

(a) $\frac{16}{15}\tau$ (b) $\frac{8}{7}\tau$

(c) $\frac{4}{3}\tau$ (d) $\tau$

106. From design point of view, spherical pressure vessels are preferred over cylindrical pressure vessels because they:
(a) are cost effective in fabrication
(b) have uniform higher circumferential stress
(c) uniform lower circumferential stress
(d) have a larger volume for the same quantity of material used

107. A solid circular shaft is subjected to pure torsion. The ratio of maximum shear stress to maximum normal stress at any point would be
(a) 1 : 1 (b) 1 : 2
(c) 2 : 1 (d) 2 : 3

108. Which one of the following gives the correct expression for strain energy stored in a beam of length L and of uniform cross-section having moment of inertia I and subjected to constant bending moment M?
(a) $\frac{ML}{EI}$ (b) $\frac{ML}{2EI}$
(c) $\frac{M^2L}{EI}$ (d) $\frac{M^2L}{2EI}$

109. Plane stress at a point in a body is defined by principal stresses 3σ and σ.The ratio of the maximum normal stress to the maximum shear stress on the plane of maximum shear stress is:
(a) 1 (b) 2
(c) 3 (d) 4

110. A cylindrical vessel with flat bottom can be deep drawn by:
(a) shallow drawing
(b) single action deep drawing
(c) double action deep drawing
(d) triple action deep drawing.

111. A short column of external diameter D and internal diameter *d* carries an eccentric load *d*. The greatest eccentricity which the load can have without producing tension on the cross-section of the column would be
(a) $\frac{d+D}{8}$ (b) $\frac{d^2+D^2}{8d}$
(c) $\frac{d^2+D^2}{8D}$ (d) $\sqrt{\frac{d^2+D^2}{8}}$

112. A bar of length L and of uniform cross-section area A and second moment of area *I* is subjected to a pull P. If Young's modulus of elasticity of the bar material is E, the expression for strain energy stored in the bar will be
(a) $\frac{P^2L}{2AE}$ (b) $\frac{PL^2}{2EI}$
(c) $\frac{PL^2}{AE}$ (d) $\frac{P^2L}{AE}$

113. If a thick cylindrical shell is subjected to internal pressure, then hoop stress, radial stress and longitudinal stress at a point in the thickness will be
(a) Tensile, compressive and tensile respectively
(b) All compressive
(c) All tensile
(d) Tensile, compressive and compressive respectively.

114. A thin cylinder with both ends closed is subjected to internal pressure *p*. The longitudinal stress at the surface has been calculated as $\sigma_0$. Maximum shear stress at the surface will be equal to
(a) $2\sigma_0$ (b) $1{,}5\sigma_0$
(c) $\sigma_0$ (d) $0.5\sigma_0$

115. The maximum shear occurs on the outermost fibres of a circular shaft under torsion. In a close coiled helical spring, the maximum shear stress occurs on the
(a) Outermost fibres
(b) Fibres at mean diameter
(c) Innermost fibres
(d) End coils

116. A circular solid shaft is subjected to a bending moment of 400 kN.m and a twisting moment of 300 kN.m. On the basis of the maximum principal stress theory, the direct stress is σ and according to the maximum shear stress theory, the shear stress is *t* The ratio σ/*t* is
(a) $\frac{1}{5}$ (b) $\frac{3}{4}$
(c) $\frac{9}{5}$ (d) $\frac{11}{6}$

117. According to the maximum shear stress theory of failure, permissible twisting moment in a circular shaft is T. The permissible twisting moment in the same shaft as per the maximum principal stress theory of failure will be
(a) T/2 (b) T
(c) $\sqrt{2T}$ (d) 2T

118. The state of plane stress at a point is described by $\sigma_x = \sigma_y$ and $\tau_{xy} = 0$. The normal stress on the plane inclined at 45° to the *x*-plane will be
(a) σ (b) $\sqrt{2\sigma}$
(c) $\sqrt{3\sigma}$ (d) 2σ

119. Consider the following statements:
State of stress in two dimensions at a point in a loaded component can be completely specified by indicating the normal and shear stresses on
1. A plane containing the point
2. Any two planes passing through the point
3. Two mutually perpendicular planes passing through the point

Of these statements
(a) 1 and 3 arc correct (b) 2 alone is correct
(c) 1 alone is correct (d) 3 alone is correct

120. For a composite consisting of a bar enclosed inside a tube of another material when compressed under a load 'W' as a whole through rigid collars at the end of the bar. The equation of compatibility is given by (suffixes 1 and 2) refer to bar and tube respectively

(a) $W_1 + W_2 = W$ (b) $W_1 + W_2 =$ constant

(c) $\frac{W_1}{A_1E_1} = \frac{W_2}{A_2E_2}$ (d) $\frac{W_2}{A_2E_1} = \frac{W_2}{A_1E_2}$

## ANSWERS WITH EXPLANATIONS

1. (b)
2. (a) Poisson's ratio lies between zero and 0.5
3. (a)
4. (a) Maximum bending stress, $\sigma_{max} = \frac{32M}{\pi d^2}$

Maximum shear stress $\tau_{max} = \frac{16T}{\pi d^3}$

For $\sigma_{max} = \tau_{max}$

$$M = \frac{T}{2}$$

5. (b)
6. (a) $n_1 = N, D_1 = D, d_1 = d; d_2 = d,$

$G_1 = G_2, n_2 = N/2, D_2 = 2D$

Stiffness, $k = \frac{Dd^4}{8D^3n}$

For same G and $d$, $k \propto \frac{1}{D^3n}$

$$\frac{k_1}{k_2} = \left(\frac{D_2}{D_1}\right)^3 \times \left(\frac{n_2}{n_1}\right)$$

$$= \left(\frac{2D}{D}\right)^3 \times \left(\frac{N}{2N}\right) = 4$$

$$k_2 = \frac{k}{4}$$

7. (a) 8. (d) 9. (c) 10. (c) 11. (a)
12. (c) Normal stress on oblique plane under biaxial loading,

$$\sigma_n = \frac{1}{2}(\sigma_x + \sigma_y) + \frac{1}{2}(\sigma_x - \sigma_y)\cos 2\theta$$

For $\theta = 45°$

$$\sigma_n = \frac{1}{2}(\sigma_x + \sigma_y)$$

13. (d) Temperature stress, $\sigma_t = E\alpha.\Delta\theta$
14. (c) 15. (c)
16. (b) $\sigma_n = \frac{1}{2}(\sigma_x + \sigma_y) + \frac{1}{2}(\sigma_x - \sigma_y)\cos\theta$

For $\theta = 45°$

$$\sigma_n = \frac{1}{2}(\sigma_x + \sigma_y) + \frac{1}{2}(500 + 500) = 500 \text{ kg/cm}^2$$

17. (b)
18. (b) $A = 1$ cm$^2$, $l = 100$ cm, $E = 2 \times 10^6$ kgf/cm$^2$

W = 2000 kgf

$$dt = \frac{Wl}{AE} = \frac{2000 \times 100}{1 \times 2 \times 10^6} = 0.1\text{cm}$$

19. (d) Modulus of elasticity of wire does not depend on wire diameter.
20. (c) 21. (b)
22. (a) $P_x = \frac{\pi^2 EI_x}{L^2} = \frac{\pi^2 EBH^3}{12L^2}$

$$P_y = \frac{4\pi^2 EI_y}{L^2} = \frac{4\pi^2 EBH^3}{12L^2}$$

For $P_x = P_y$

$$\frac{\pi^2 EBH^3}{12L^2} = \frac{4\pi^2 EBH^3}{12L^2}$$

or $H^2 = 4B^2$

$$\frac{H}{B} = 2$$

23. (b) 24. (b)
25. (d) Mid-span deflection of a simply supported beam carrying concentrated load at the centre,

$$\delta = \frac{WL^3}{48EI}$$

$$\delta \propto \frac{1}{l}$$

$$\frac{\delta_2}{\delta_1} = \frac{I_1}{I_2}$$

$$\frac{\delta_2}{\delta} = \frac{\left(\frac{4 \times 6^2}{12}\right)}{\left(\frac{6 \times 4^3}{12}\right)} = \left(\frac{6}{4}\right)^2$$

$$\delta_2 = 2.25\delta$$

26. (d) Bending stress, $\sigma = \frac{32M}{\pi d^3}$

Shear stress, $\tau = \frac{16T}{\pi d^3}$

For M = T, $= \frac{\sigma}{\tau} = 2$

27. (c) 28.(a) 29. (b)
30. (c) $\varepsilon_\theta = \frac{1}{E}(\varepsilon_\theta - v\sigma_1) = \varepsilon_1$

$$\varepsilon_2 = \frac{1}{E}(\sigma_1 - v\sigma_\theta) = \varepsilon_2$$

$$V = \pi dl$$

$\ln V = \ln \pi + 2\ln d + \ln l$

$\frac{\delta V}{V} = 2\frac{\delta d}{d} + \frac{\delta l}{l}$

$\varepsilon_0 = 2\varepsilon_1 + \varepsilon_2$

31. (d) $\sigma_\theta = \frac{pd}{2t}$

$t = \frac{10 \times 100}{2 \times 200} = 2.5$ cm or 25 mm

32. (c) $d = 10$ mm, $n_1 = 8, D_{m1} = 75$ mm

$n_2 = 10, D_{m2} = 60$ mm

Spring stiffness, $k = \frac{Gd^4}{8D_m^3 n}$

$\therefore k \propto \frac{1}{D_m^3 n}$

$\frac{k_2}{k_1} = \frac{D_{m1}^3 n_1}{D_{m2}^3 n_2} = \left(\frac{75}{60}\right)^3 \times \frac{8}{10}$

$k_2 = 1.5625$ k

33. (b)

34. (a) According to maximum shear stress theory

$\frac{\sigma_1 + \sigma_2}{2} = \frac{\sigma_{yp}}{2}$

35. (d) 36. (c) 37. (b) 38. (a) 39. (c)

40. (d) $W(h + \delta) = \frac{1}{2}k\delta^2$

$100(2 + \delta) = \frac{1}{2} \times 1000 \times \delta^2$

$= 5\delta^2 - \delta - 2 = 0$

$\delta = \frac{1 \pm \sqrt{1 + 40}}{10} = 0.74 \text{ m} > 0.2 \text{ m}$

41. (d)

42. (a) $\tau_s = \frac{16T}{\pi D^3}$

$\tau_h = \frac{16T}{\pi D^2(1 - k^4)} = \frac{16T}{\pi D^3\left(1 - \frac{1}{16}\right)} = \frac{16}{15}\tau_s$

$= 1.067\tau$

43. (c) Equivalent torque, $T_e = \sqrt{M^2 + T^2}$

$5 = \sqrt{M^2 + 16}$

$M = 3$ kN.m

44. (c) $\sigma_\theta = \frac{pd}{2t}$

$t = \frac{500 \times 0.6}{2 \times 9000} = 16.66 = 17$ mm

45. (a)

46. (c) Maximum hoop stress in the inner cylinder

$(\sigma_\theta)i = \frac{2r_3^2 p_s}{\left(r_3^2 - r_q^2\right)}$

$= \frac{2 \times 6^2 \times 11}{(6^2 - 5^2)} = -72$

47. (d)

48. (c) $G_1 = G_2, d_1 = d_2$

$D_{wl} = 180$ mm, D

$\frac{8W_1 D_{m2}^3 n_1}{G_1 d_1^4} = \frac{8W_2 D_{m2}^3 n_2}{G_2 d_2^4}$

$\frac{W_1}{W_2} = \left(\frac{Dm_2}{Dm_1}\right)^3 = \left(\frac{80}{180}\right)^3 = \frac{1}{11.39}$

$W_1 + W_2 = P$

$W_1(1 + 11.39) = P$

$W_1 = \frac{1139}{1.088} \times P = \frac{P}{1.088}$

49. (a) 50. (d)

51. (b) $\sigma = 80 \text{ N/mm}^2$, $\tau = 30 \text{ N/mm}^2$, $\sigma = 280 \text{ N/mm}^2$

$\sigma_y = 280 \text{ N/mm}^2$

According to maximum shear stress theory, yield stress in shear,

$\tau_y = \frac{\sigma_y}{2} = \frac{280}{2} = 140 \text{ N/mm}^2$

Maximum shear stress induced,

$\tau_y = \frac{1}{2}\sqrt{\sigma^2 + 4\tau^2} = 50 \text{ N/mm}^2$

$= \frac{1}{2}\sqrt{\sigma^2 + 4\tau^2}$

$= \frac{1}{2}\sqrt{80^2 + 4 + 30^2}$

Factor of safety $= \frac{\tau_y}{\tau_{max}} = \frac{140}{50} = 2.8$

52. (a)

53. (a) $\sigma_\theta = 100\text{MN/m}^2, \sigma_t = 50\text{GN/m}^2, E = 200 \text{ MN/m}^2, v = 0.3$

$E_\theta = \frac{1}{E}[\sigma_\theta - v\sigma_1]$

$= \frac{1}{200 \times 10^3}[100 - 0.3 \times 50]$

$= 42.5 \times 10^{-5}$ or $0.425 \times 10^{-3}$

54. (d) 55. (c)

56. (d) $G = \frac{E}{2(1 + v)} = \frac{E}{2(1 + 0.5)} = \frac{E}{3}$

or $E = 3G$

57. (d) $\sigma_y = 200\text{N/mm}^2$, FOS = 2

Allowable stress,

$$\sigma_y = \frac{\sigma_y}{\text{FOS}} = \frac{200}{2} = 100 \text{ N/mm}^2$$

According to maximum principal stress theory,

$$\sigma_1 = \sigma_y$$

Under torsion, maximum principal stress,

$$\sigma_1 = \tau$$

Permissible stress = 100 N/mm$^2$

58. (d)

59. (a) Bending stress, $\sigma = \frac{M}{z}$

For $\sigma$ to remain constant,

$$z \propto M$$

For a rectangular beam of width $b$ and depth $h$.

$$z = \frac{bh^2}{6}$$

$$\therefore \quad bh^2 \propto M$$

For $h$ = constant, $b \alpha$ M

60. (b) 61. (d) 62. (d) 63. (c)

64. (c) $\delta_1 = \frac{Wl^3}{48 \text{ EI}}$

$$\delta_1 = \frac{5}{348}\frac{wL^4}{\text{EI}} = \frac{5}{348}\frac{\text{WL}^3}{\text{EI}}$$

$$\delta_1 : \delta_2 :: \frac{1}{48} : \frac{5}{348}$$

$$::1 : \frac{5}{8} :: 1.6 : 1$$

65. (c) 66. (d) 67. (a)

68. (b) Shear stress in helical spring,

$$\tau = \frac{8\text{WD}_m}{\pi d^3}$$

Shear stress does not depend on length of the spring.

$$\tau_2 = \tau_1 = \tau$$

69. (b) 70. (b)

71. (c) Spring stiffness, $k = \frac{Gd^4}{8\text{D}_m^3 n}$

$$\therefore \quad k \propto \frac{1}{n}$$

$$k_2 = 2k_1 = 24\text{N/M}$$

72. (a) 73. (b) 74. (b) 75. (c) 76. (c)

77. (c)

78. (a) End deflection of a cantilever carrying *udl,*

$$\delta_1 = \frac{\text{WL}^3}{8\text{EI}}$$

End deflection of a cantilever carrying concentrated load at the free end,

$$\delta_2 = \frac{\text{WL}^3}{3\text{EI}}$$

$$\frac{\delta_1}{\delta_2} = \frac{3}{8}$$

79. (a) 80. (b) 81. (a) 82. (d) 83. (a)

84. (c) 85. (c) 86. (a) 87. (a) 88. (b)

89. (d) 90. (b)

91. (c) $\tau_{\max} = \frac{1}{2}\sqrt{(\sigma_x - \sigma_y)^2 + 4\tau^2_{xy}}$

$$= \frac{1}{2}\sqrt{(100-0)^2 + 4\times 100^2}$$

$$= 50\sqrt{5} \text{ kgf/cm}^2$$

92. (b) 93. (a)

94. (c) $\sigma_t = \text{E}\ \alpha.\Delta\theta$

$$= 2\times 10^6 \times 12\times 10^{-6} \times 100$$

$$= 2.4\times 10^3 \text{ kg/cm}^2$$

95. (c) 96. (b) 97. (b) 98. (b) 99. (c)

100. (b)

101. (c) $\tau_{\text{N.A}} = \frac{3}{2}\tau_{\text{mean}} = \frac{3}{2}\times\frac{2000}{10\times 5}$

$$= 60 \text{ kgf/cm}^2$$

102. (c) 103. (c) 104. (d) 105. (b)

106. (c) $\frac{(\sigma_\theta)_{\text{sphere}}}{(\sigma_\theta)_{\text{cylinder}}} = \frac{pd}{4t}\times\frac{2t}{pd} = \frac{1}{2}$

107. (a) 108. (d)

109. (c) $\sigma_1 = 3\sigma, \sigma_2 = 0$

$$\tau_{\max} = \frac{\sigma_1 - \sigma_2}{2} = \frac{3\sigma - \sigma}{2} = \sigma$$

$$\frac{\sigma_1}{\tau_{\max}} = \frac{3\sigma}{\sigma} = 3$$

110. (c) 111. (b) 112. (a) 113. (d) 114. (d)

115. (c) 116. (c)

117. (d) According to the maximum shear stress theory,

$$\tau_{\max} = \frac{\sigma_1 - \sigma_2}{2} = \tau_y = \frac{\sigma_y}{2}$$

$$\frac{16\text{T}}{\pi d^3} = \frac{\sigma_y}{2}$$

$$\therefore \quad \sigma_y = \frac{32\text{T}}{rd^3}$$

According to maximum principal stress theory,

$$\sigma_1 = \sigma_y\ \frac{32\text{T}}{rd^3} = 2\left(\frac{16\text{T}}{\pi d^3}\right)$$

Hence, permissible torque = 2T

118. (a) $\sigma_1 = \frac{1}{2}(\sigma_x + \sigma_y) + \frac{1}{2}(\sigma_x - \sigma_y)\cos 2\theta$

At $\theta = 45°$

$$\sigma_1 = \frac{1}{2}(\sigma + \sigma) + \frac{1}{2}(\sigma - \sigma) = \sigma$$

119. (d) 120. (c) ❑❑❑

# 11. Theory of Machines

- The subject Theory of Machines may be defined as that branch of Engineering - Science, which deals with the study of relative motion between the various parts of machine, and forces which act on them. The knowledge of this subject is very essential for an engineer in designing the various parts of a machine.
- Kinematics -It is that branch of Theory of Machines which deals with the relative motion between the various parts of the machines with out forces applying to it.
- Dynamics- It is that branch of Theory of Machines which deals with the forces and their effects, while acting upon the machine parts in motion.
- Kinetics- It is that branch of Theory of Machines which deals with the inertia forces which arise from the combined effect of the mass and motion of the machine parts.
- Statics- It is that branch of Theory of Machines which deals with the forces and their effects while the machine parts are at rest. The mass of the parts is assumed to be negligible.
- Kinematics is the branch of mechanics concerned with the motions of objects without being concerned with the forces that cause the motion. In this latter respect it differs from dynamics, which is concerned with the forces that affect motion.
- There are three basic concepts in kinematics - speed, velocity and acceleration.
- Whether it's finishing a 5K race or a marathon, completing a sprint triathlon or an Ironman, doing a century ride or a stage race, simply getting back into shape or competing at the highest level in any sport, our goal is to deliver healthy athletes to the starting line, physically and mentally prepared to meet the challenge.
- Your Kinetic Motion experience begins with a complete evaluation to catch bio-mechanical imbalances before they become injuries. For triathletes, the next step is a video-taped session in the pool with our swim coach.
- Then we do thorough testing to establish the plateau from which we launch your comprehensive coaching plan. Finally, we provide full-service travel planning to get you to the finest national and international racing venues. We want to take you from the beginning of your journey to the finish line of your dreams.
- In mechanics and physics, simple harmonic motion is a type of periodic motion where the restoring force is directly proportional to the displacement. It can serve as a mathematical model of a variety of motions, such as the oscillation of a spring.
- In addition, other phenomena can be approximated by simple harmonic motion, including the motion of a simple pendulum as well as molecular vibration.
- Simple harmonic motion is typified by the motion of a mass on a spring when it is subject to the linear elastic restoring force given by Hooke's Law. The motion is sinusoidal in time and demonstrates a single resonant frequency.
- In order for simple harmonic motion to take place, the net force of the object at the end of the pendulum must be proportional to the displacement.
- Simple harmonic motion provides a basis for the characterization of more complicated motions through the techniques of Fourier analysis.
- Velocity and acceleration analysis of mechanisms can be performed vectorially using the relative velocity and acceleration concept. Usually we start with the given values and work through the mechanism by way of series of points A, B, C, etc.
- Friction is resistance to motion. which also resist the other body from its motion in particular direction.
- It is the co which may be parralel or non parralel depending on type of drive usedmponents which is used for the motion transfer or power transmission from one s. Belts are flexible made of rubber,fibers etc.
- Chains are made of metals which are positive drive meands that no slip occurs.Rope are used where centre distancedistancedistance is very large.ropes are madeof fibers and metal wires depending on load conditions.
- If the centre of gravity of a body of mass M has a linear acceleration a, then the resultant of the external forces acting on the body must be Ma.
- Inertia is the resistance of any physical object to a change in its state of motion or rest, or the tendency of an object to resist any change in its motion. It is proportional to an object's mass.
- Centre of gravity is the point in or near a body at which the gravitational potential energy of the body is equal to that of a single particle of the same mass located at that point, and through which the resultant of the gravitational forces on the component particles of the body acts.
- of gravity is the point in or near a body at which the gravitational potential energy of the body is equal to that of a single particle of the same mass located at that point, and through which the resultant of the gravitational forces on the component particles of the body acts.

- A force is any influence that causes a free body to undergo a change in speed, a change in direction, or a change in shape. Force can also be described by intuitive concepts such as a push or pull that can cause an object with mass to change its velocity, i.e., to accelerate, or which can cause a flexible object to deform.
- This latter force is called the Inertia Force and it is numerically equal to the product of mass and acceleration of the centre of gravity. It acts in the opposite direction to the acceleration.
- The system of external forces and inertia forces is treated as if in statical equilibrium. Note that the use of centrifugal force in governor problems is a particular example of this principle.
- Using boiling water to produce mechanical motion goes back about 2,000 years, but early devices were not practical. Since the late 1700s steam engines have become a major source of mechanical power.
- The first applications were removing water from mines. In 1781 James Watt patented a steam engine that produced continuous rotative motion.
- These 10hp engines enabled a wide range of manufacturing machinery to be powered. The engines could be sited anywhere that water and coal or wood fuel could be obtained. Within a century,in 1883, engines that could provide 10,000 hp were feasible.
- Steam engines could also be applied to vehicles such as traction engines and the railway locomotives which are commonly just called steam engines outside America.
- The stationary steam engine was an important component of the Industrial Revolution, overcoming the limitations imposed by shortage of sites suitable for water mill and allowing factories to locate where water power was unavailable.
- Governor is a devise used for control the quantity of fuel according to the speed so control the variation of speed due to varying load. These are generally applied on IC engines but it also applied some time on steam turbines and gas turbines.
- A dynamometer or "dyno" for short, is a device for measuring force, moment of force (torque), or power. For example, the power produced by an engine, motor or other rotating prime mover can be calculated by simultaneously measuring torque and rotational speed (RPM).
- A dynamometer can also be used to determine the torque and power required to operate a driven machine such as a pump. In that case, a motoring or driving dynamometer is used.
- A dynamometer that is designed to be driven is called an absorption or passive dynamometer. A dynamometer that can either drive or absorb is called a universal or active dynamometer.
- In addition to being used to determine the torque or power characteristics of a machine under test (MUT), dynamometers are employed in a number of other roles.
- In standard emissions testing cycles such as those defined by the United States Environmental Protection Agency (US EPA), dynamometers are used to provide simulated road loading of either the engine (using an engine dynamometer) or full powertrain (using a chassis dynamometer).
- In fact, beyond simple power and torque measurements, dynamometers can be used as part of a test bed for a variety of engine development activities, such as the calibration of engine management controllers, detailed investigations into combustion behavior, and tribology.
- In the medical terminology, hand-held dynamometers are used for routine screening of grip and hand strength, and the initial and ongoing evaluation of patients with hand trauma or dysfunction. They are also used to measure grip strength in patients where compromise of the cervical nerve roots or peripheral nerves is suspected.
- In the rehabilitation, kinesiology, and ergonomics realms, force dynamometers are used for measuring the back, grip, arm, and/or leg strength of athletes, patients, and workers to evaluate physical status, performance, and task demands.
- Typically the force applied to a lever or through a cable is measured and then converted to a moment of force by multiplying by the perpendicular distance from the force to the axis of the level

# MULTIPLE CHOICE QUESTIONS

1. Scotch yoke mechanism is used to generate:
(a) sine functions (b) square roots
(c) logarithms (d) inversions

2. In full depth $14\frac{1}{2}$ degree involute system, the smallest number of teeth in a pinion which meshes with rack without interference is:
(a) 12 (b) 16
(c) 25 (d) 32

3. Inversion of a mechanism is:
(a) changing of a higher pair to lower pair
(b) obtained by fixing different links in a kinematic chain
(c) turning it upside down
(d) obtained by reversing the input and output motion

4. The sense of coriolis component 2 *vw* is the same as that of the relative velocity vector *v* rotated:
(a) 45° in the direction of rotation of the link containing the path
(b) 45° in the direction opposite to the rotation of the link containing the path
(c) 90° in the direction of rotation of the link containing the path
(d) 180° in the direction opposite to the rotation of the link containing the path

5. Match the following $14\frac{1}{2}$ degree composite system of gears

| List-I | List-II |
|---|---|
| A. Dedendum | 1. $\frac{2}{P}$ |
| B. Clearance | 2. $\frac{0.157}{P}$ |
| C. Working depth | 3. $\frac{1.157}{P}$ |
| D. Addendum | 4. $\frac{1}{P}$ |

**Codes:**

| | A | B | C | D |
|---|---|---|---|---|
| (a) | 1 | 2 | 3 | 4 |
| (b) | 4 | 3 | 2 | 1 |
| (c) | 3 | 2 | 1 | 4 |
| (d) | 3 | 1 | 2 | 4 |

6. Certain machine requires a torque of (500 + 50 sin 2θ) kN.m to drive it where θ is the angle of rotation of shaft measured from certain datum. The machine is directly coupled to an engine which produces a troque (500 + 50 sin θ) kN.m in a cycle. How many times the value of torque of machine and engine will be identical?
(a) 1 (b) 2
(c) 4 (d) 8

7. Which of the following are inversions of a double slider crank chain?
1. Whitworth return motion.
2. Scotch Yoke,
3. Oldham's Coupling.
4. Rotary engine.
Select correct answer using the codes given below:
**Codes:**
(a) 1 and 2
(b) 1, 3 and 4
(c) 2 and 3
(d) 2, 3 and 4

8. Match List-I with List-II and select the correct answer using the codes given below the lists.

| List-I | List-II |
|---|---|
| A. Governor | 1. Pantograph device |
| B. Automobile differential | 2. Feed-back control |
| C. Dynamic Absorber | 3. Epicyclic train |
| D. Engine Indicator | 4. Two-mass oscillator |

**Codes:**

| | A | B | C | D |
|---|---|---|---|---|
| (a) | 1 | 2 | 3 | 4 |
| (b) | 4 | 1 | 2 | 3 |
| (c) | 2 | 3 | 4 | 1 |
| (d) | 4 | 3 | 2 | 1 |

9. Consider the following statements:
Coriolis component of acceleration depends on
1. velocity of slider.
2. angular velocity of the link.
3. acceleration of slider.
4. angular acceleration of link.
Of these statements:
(a) 1 and 2 are correct
(b) 1 and 3 are correct
(c) 2 and 4 are correct
(d) 1 and 4 are correct

10. Which one of the following sets of accelerations is involved in the motion of the piston inside the cylinder of a uniform rotating cylinder mechanism?
(a) Coriolis and radial acceleration
(b) Radial and tangential acceleration
(c) Coriolis and gyroscopic acceleration
(d) Gyroscopic and tangential acceleration

11. If the rotating mass of a rim type flywheel is distributed on another rim type flywheel whose mean radius is half the mean radius of the former, then energy stored in the latter at the same speed will be:
(a) four times the first one
(b) same as the first one
(c) one-fourth of the first one
(d) one and a half times the first one

12. Match List-I with List-II and select the correct answer using the codes given below the lists:

| List-I | List-II |
|---|---|
| A. Quadric cycle chain | 1. Elliptic trammel |
| B. Single slider crank chain | 2. Rapsons slide |
| | 3. Ackerman steering |
| C. Double slider crank chain | 4. Eccentric mechanism |
| D. Crossed slider crank chain | 5. Pendulum pump |

**Codes:**

| | A | B | C | D |
|---|---|---|---|---|
| (a) | 5 | 4 | 2 | 1 |
| (b) | 3 | 1 | 5 | 4 |
| (c) | 5 | 3 | 4 | 2 |
| (d) | 3 | 5 | 1 | 2 |

13. A flywheel is fitted to the crankshaft of an engine having 'E' amount of indicated work per revolution and permissible limits of coefficients of fluctuation of energy and speed as $K_e$ and $K_s$ respectively. The kinetic energy of the flywheel is then given by:
(a) $\frac{2K_eE}{K_s}$ (b) $\frac{K_eE}{2K_s}$
(c) $\frac{K_eE}{K_s}$ (d) $\frac{K_sE}{2K_e}$

14. A Hartnell governor has its controlling force F given by $F = p + qr$, where $r$ is the radius of the balls and $p$ and $q$ are constants. The governor becomes isochronous when:
(a) $p = 0$ and q is positive
(b) $p$ is positive and $q = 0$
(c) $p$ is negative and $q$ is positive
(d) $p$ is positive and $q$ is also positive

15. A system in dynamic balance implies that:
(a) the system is critically damped
(b) there is no critical speed in the system
(c) the system is also statically balanced
(d) there will be absolutely no wear of bearings

16. Which one of the following can completely balance several masses revolving in different planes on a shaft?
(a) A single mass in one of the planes of the revolving masses
(b) A single mass in a different plane
(c) Two masses in any two planes
(d) Two equal masses in any two planes

17. A thin circular disc is rolling with a uniform linear speed along a straight path on a plane surface. Consider the following statements in this regard:
1. All points of the disc have the same velocity.
2. The centre of the disc has zero acceleration.
3. The centre of the disc has centrifugal acceleration.
4. The point on the disc making contact with the plane surface has zero acceleration.

Of these statements:
(a) 1 and 4 are correct (b) 3 and 4 are correct
(c) 3 alone is correct (d) 2 is alone is correct

18. An electric lift is moving downwards with an acceleration of $\frac{g}{3}$. The vertical force between a passenger in the lift and its floor is equal to:
(a) $\frac{2}{3}$ of the passenger's weight
(b) $\frac{3}{4}$ of the passenger's weight
(c) passenger's weight
(d) $\frac{4}{3}$ of the passenger's weight

19. In a circular arc cam with roller follower, the acceleration in any position of the lift would depend only upon:
(a) total lift, total angle of lift, minimum radius of cam and cam speed
(b) radius of circular arc cam, speed, location of centre of circular arc and roller diameter
(c) weight of cam follower linkage, spring stiffness and cam speed
(d) total lift, centre of gravity of the cam and cam speed

20. The Klain's method of construction for reciprocating engine mechanism:
(a) is a simplified version of instantaneous centre method
(b) utilizes a quadrilateral similar to the diagram of mechanism for reciprocating engine
(c) enables determination of Corioli's component
(d) is based on the acceleration diagram

21. Two co-axial rotors having moments of inertia $I_1$, $I_2$ and angular speeds $\omega_1$ and $\omega_2$ respectively are engaged together. The loss of energy during engagement is equal to:
(a) $\frac{I_1I_2(\omega_1-\omega_2)^2}{2(I_1+I_2)}$ (b) $\frac{I_1I_2(\omega_1^2-\omega_2^2)^2}{2(I_1+I_2)}$
(c) $\frac{2I_1I_2(\omega_1-\omega_2)^2}{(I_1+I_2)}$ (d) $\frac{I_1\omega_1^2-I_2\omega_2^2}{(I_1+I_2)}$

22. A spring controlled governor is found unstable. It can be made stable by:
(a) increasing the spring stiffness
(b) decreasing the spring stiffness
(c) increasing the ball weight
(d) decreasing the ball weight

23. If a number of forces act on a rigid body, each force may he replaced by an equal and parallel force acting through a Fixed point, together with a couple. For the rigid body to be in equilibrium:
(a) the resultant force at the fixed point must be zero

(b) the resultant couple on the body must be zero
(c) both resultant force and couple must be zero
(d) none of the above need be zero

24. A rotor which is balanced statically but not dynamically is supported on two ball bearings L apart and at high speed of the rotor, reaction of the left bearing is R. The right side of the bearing is shifted to a new position 2L apart from the left bearing: At the same rotor speed, dynamic reaction on the left bearing in the new arrangement will:
(a) remain same as before
(b) become equal to 2R
(c) become equal to $\frac{1}{2}$R
(d) become equal to $\frac{1}{4}$R

25. Consider the following statements regarding a high speed in-line engine with identical reciprocating parts with cranks spaced to give equal firing intervals:
1. All harmonic forces, except those which are multiples of half the number of cylinders, are balanced.
2. Couples are balanced if the engine is symmetrical about a plane normal to the axis of the cranks shaft.
3. In a four cylinder in-line engine, second and fourth harmonic forces are unbalanced whereas in a six cylinder in-line engine, second fourth and sixth harmonic forces are unbalanced.
Of these statements:
(a) 1, 2 and 3 are correct (b) 1 and 3 are correct
(c) 1 and 2 are correct (d) 2 and 3 are correct

26. Consider the following statements regarding the differential of an automobile:
1. The speed of the crown wheel will always be the mean of the speeds of the two road wheels.
2. The road wheel speeds are independent of the number of teeth on the planets.
3. The difference between the speed of the road wheels depends on the number of teeth on the planets.
4. The ratio of speeds of the road wheels depends upon the number of teeth on the gear wheels attached to them and on the crown wheel.
Of these statements:
(a) 1 and 2 are correct (b) 3 and 4 are correct
(c) 1 and 3 are correct (d) 2 and 4 are correct

27. The instantaneous centre of rotation of a rigid thin disc rolling on a plane rigid surface is located at:
(a) the centre of the disc
(b) an infinite distance on the plane surface
(c) the point of contact
(d) the point on the circumference situated vertically opposite to the contact point

28. Consider the following statements:
1. Round bar in a round hole forms a turning pair.
2. A square bar in a square hole forms a sliding pair.
3. A vertical shaft in a foot-step bearing forms a successful constraint.
Which of these statements are correct?
(a) 1 and 3
(b) 1 and 2
(c) 2 and 3
(d) 1, 2 and 3

29. For a spring controlled governor to be stable, the controlling force (F) is related to the radius ($r$) by the equation:
(a) $F = ar - b$ (b) $F = ar + b$
(c) $F = ar$ (d) $F = a/r + b$

30. Which one of the following is an Open Pair?
(a) Ball and socket joint (b) Journal bearing
(c) Lead screw and nut (d) Cam and follower

31. In a 4-stroke I.C engine, the turning moment during the compression stroke is:
(a) positive throughout
(b) negative throughout
(c) positive during major portion of the stroke
(d) negative during major portion of the stroke

32. Match List-I (Applications) with List-II (drive element) and select the correct answer using the codes given below the lists:

| **List-I** | **List-II** |
|---|---|
| A. Automobile differential | 1. Flat belt |
| B. Bicycle | 2. V-belt |
| C. Planning machine | 3. Chain drive |
| D. Radiator fan of automobile motion | 4. Gear drive |

**Codes:**

| | A | B | C | D |
|---|---|---|---|---|
| (a) | 4 | 3 | 1 | 2 |
| (b) | 1 | 3 | 4 | 2 |
| (c) | 4 | 2 | 1 | 3 |
| (d) | 1 | 2 | 4 | 3 |

33. Which of the following statements hold good for a multi-collar thrust bearing carrying an axial thrust of W unit?
1. Friction moment is independent of the number of collars.
2. The intensity of pressure is affected by the number of collars.
3. Coefficient of friction of the bearing surface is affected by the number of collars.
(a) 1 and 2 (b) 1 and 3
(c) 2 and 3 (d) 1, 2 and 3

34. The centre of gravity of the coupler link in a 4-bar mechanism would experience:
(a) no acceleration
(b) only linear acceleration
(c) only angular acceleration
(d) both linear and angular accelerations

35. Which of the following statements regarding laws governing the friction between dry surfaces are correct?
   1. The friction force is dependent on the velocity of sliding.
   2. The friction force is directly proportional to the normal force.
   3. The friction force is dependent on the materials of the contact surfaces.
   4. The friction force is dependent on the area of contact surfaces.

   (a) 2, 3 and 4 (b) 1 and 3
   (c) 2 and 4 (d) 1, 2, 3 and 4

36. Which of the following statements are correct?
   1. For constant velocity ratio transmission between two gears, the common normal at the point of contact must always pass through a fixed point on the line joining the centres of rotation of the gears.
   2. For involute gears the pressure angle changes with change in centre distance between gears.
   3. The velocity ratio of compound gear train depends upon the number of teeth of the input and output gears only.
   4. Epicyclic gear trains involve rotation of at least one gear axis about some other gear axis.

   (a) 1, 2 and 3 (b) 1 and 3
   (c) 1, 2 and 4 (d) 2, 3 and 4

37. Match list-1 with list-II and select the correct answer using the codes given below the lists:

| List-I | List-II |
|---|---|
| A. Hunting | 1. One radius of rotation for each speed. |
| B. Isochronism | 2. Too sensitive |
| C. Stability | 3. Mean force exerted at the sleeve during change of speed |
| D. Effort | 4. Constant equilibrium speed for various radii of rotation |

**Codes:**

| | A | B | C | D |
|---|---|---|---|---|
| (a) | 2 | 4 | 1 | 3 |
| (b) | 3 | 1 | 4 | 3 |
| (c) | 2 | 1 | 4 | 3 |
| (d) | 2 | 1 | 3 | 4 |

38. A system of masses rotating in different parallel planes is in dynamic balance if the resultant:
   (a) force is equal to zero
   (b) couple is equal to zero
   (c) force and the resultant couple are both equal to zero
   (d) force is numerically equal to the resultant couple, but neither of them need necessarily be zero

39. A fixed gear having 200 teeth is in mesh with another gear having 50 teeth. The two gears are connected by an arm. The number of turns made by the smaller gear for one revolution of arm about the centre of the bigger gear is:

   (a) $\frac{2}{4}$ (b) 3
   (c) 4 (d) 5

40. An involute pinion and gear are in mesh. If both have the same size of addendum, then there will be an interference between the:
   (a) tip of the gear tooth and flank of pinion
   (b) tip of the pinion and flank of gear
   (c) flanks of both gear and pinion
   (d) tips of both gear and pinion

41. Given $\theta$ = angle through which the axis of the outer forward wheel turns

   $\phi$ = angle through which the axis of the inner forward wheel turns

   $a$ = distance between the pivots of front axle and

   $b$ = wheel base

   For correct steering, centre lines of the axes of four wheels of an automobile should meet at a common point. This condition will be satisfied if:

   (a) $\cos\theta - \cos\phi = \frac{a}{b}$ (b) $\cot\theta - \cot\phi = \frac{a}{b}$

   (c) $\cos\theta + \cos\phi = \frac{a}{b}$ (d) $\tan\theta + \tan\phi = \frac{b}{a}$

42. If air resistance is neglected while it is executing small oscillations, the acceleration of the bob of a simple pendulum at the midpoint of its swing will be:
   (a) zero
   (b) a minimum but not equal to zero
   (c) a maximum
   (d) not determinable unless the length of the pendulum and the mass of the bob arc known

43. In order to draw the acceleration diagram. it is necessary to determine the Coriolis component of acceleration in the case of:
   (a) crank and slotted lever quick return mechanism
   (b) slider-crank mechanism
   (c) four-bar mechanism
   (d) pantograph

44. What is the correct sequence of the following steps in engine analysis?
   1. Vibration analysis
   2. Inertia force analysis
   3. Balancing analysis
   4. Velocity and Acceleration analysis

   Select the correct answer using the codes given below:

   (a) 2, 4, 1, 3 (b) 2, 4, 3, 1
   (c) 4, 2, 1, 3 (d) 4, 2, 3, 1

45. If μ is the actual coefficient of friction in a belt moving in grooved pulley, the groove angle being 2α, the virtual coefficient of friction will be:

(a) $\frac{\mu}{\sin\alpha}$ (b) $\frac{\mu}{\cos\alpha}$

(c) $\mu\sin\alpha$ (d) $\mu\cos\alpha$

46. Match List-I (positioning of two shafts) with List-II (possible connection) and select the correct answer using the codes given below the Lists:

| List-I | List-II |
|---|---|
| A. Parallel shafts with slight offset | 1. Hooke's joint |
| B. Parallel shafts at a reasonable distance | 2. Worm and wheel |
| C. Perpendicular shafts | 3. Oldham coupling |
| D. Intersecting shafts | 4. Belt and pulley |

**Codes:**

| | A | B | C | D |
|---|---|---|---|---|
| (a) | 4 | 3 | 2 | 1 |
| (b) | 4 | 3 | 1 | 2 |
| (c) | 3 | 4 | 1 | 2 |
| (d) | 3 | 4 | 2 | 1 |

47. Match List-I with List-II and select the correct answer using the codes given below the Lists:

| List-I | List-II |
|---|---|
| A. Quadric cycle chain | 1. Rapson's slide |
| B. Single slider crank chain | 2. Oscillating cylinder engine mechanism |
| C. Double slider crank chain | 3. Ackermann steering mechanism |
| D. Crossed slider crank chain | 4. Oldham coupling |

**Codes:**

| | A | B | C | D |
|---|---|---|---|---|
| (a) | 1 | 2 | 4 | 3 |
| (b) | 4 | 3 | 2 | 1 |
| (c) | 3 | 4 | 1 | 2 |
| (d) | 3 | 2 | 4 | 1 |

48. Match List-I with List-II and select the correct answer using the codes given below the Lists:

| List-I | List-II |
|---|---|
| A. Flywheel | 1. Dunkerley Method |
| B. Governor | 2. Turning Moment |
| C. Critical speed | 3. d' Alembert's Principle |
| D. Inertia Force | 4. Speed control on bar with load. |

**Codes:**

| | A | B | C | D |
|---|---|---|---|---|
| (a) | 4 | 2 | 3 | 1 |
| (b) | 4 | 2 | 1 | 3 |
| (c) | 2 | 4 | 3 | 1 |
| (d) | 2 | 4 | 1 | 3 |

49. The sensitivity of an isochronous governor is:

(a) zero (b) one

(c) two (d) infinity

50. When the primary direct crank of a reciprocating engine is positioned at 30°clockwise, the secondary reverse crank for balancing will be at:

(a) 30° anticlockwise (b) 60° anticlockwise

(c) 30° clockwise (d) 60° clockwise

51. A reverted gear train is one in which the output shaft and input shaft:

(a) rotate in opposite directions

(b) are co-axial

(c) are at right angles to each other

(d) are at an angle to each other

52. In the case of an involute toothed gear, involute starts from:

(a) addendum circle (b) dedundum circle

(c) pitch circle (d) base circle

53. Two geared shafts A and B having moments of inertia $I_a$ and $I_b$ and angular acceleration$\alpha_a$and$\alpha_b$ respectively arc meshed together. B rotates at G times the speed or A. If the gearing efficiency of the two shafts is η, then is order to accelerate B, the torque which must be applied to A will be:

(a) $I_a\alpha_a + G^2 I_b \frac{\alpha_a}{\eta}$ (b) $G^2 I_a \frac{\alpha_b}{\eta}$

(c) $G^2 I_a \frac{\alpha_a}{\eta}$ (d) $G^2 I_b \frac{\alpha_b}{\eta}$

54. Which of the following pair (s) is/are correctly matched?

I. Four-bar chain ....Oscillating-oscillating converter

II. Inertia governor ...Rate of change of engine speed

III. Hammer blow ...Reciprocating unbalance

Select the correct answer using the codes given below:

(a) I alone (b) I, II and III

(c) II and III (d) land III

55. The pitching of a ship in the ocean is an oscillatory periodic motion. A ship is pitching 6° above and 6° below with a period of 20s from its horizontal plane. Consider the following statements in this regard:

1. The motion has a frequency of oscillation (i.e. pitching) of 3 cycles/minute.
2. The motion has an angular frequency of 3.14 rad/s
3. The angular velocity of precession of ship's rotor is $\frac{\pi}{300}$ rad/s
4. The amplitude of pitching is $\frac{\pi}{30}$ rad

Which of these statements are correct?

(a) 1 and 2 (b) 1, 2 and 4

(c) 2, 3 and 4 (d) 1, 3 and 4

56. Which of the following pairs are correctly matched? Select the correct answer using the codes given below the pairs.

| Mechanism | Chain from which derived |
|---|---|
| 1. Whitworth quick return motion | Single slider crank chain |
| 2. Oldham's coupling | Four-bar chain |
| 3. Scotch Yoke | Double slider crank chain |

**Codes:**
(a) 1 and 2 (b) 1, 2 and 3
(c) 1 and 3 (d) 2 and 3

57. In S.H.M. with respect to the displacement vector, the positions of Velocity vector and Acceleration vector will he respectively:
(a) 180° and 90°
(b) 90° and 180°
(c) 0° and 90°
(d) 90° and 0°

58. When a slider moves with a velocity V on a link rotating at an angular speed of ω, the Corioli's component of acceleration is given by:
(a) $\sqrt{2v\omega}$ (b) $v\omega$
(c) $\frac{v\omega}{2}$ (d) $2v\omega$

59. The total number of instantaneous centres for a mechanism consisting of '*n*' links is:
(a) $\frac{n}{2}$ (b) $n$
(c) $\frac{n-1}{2}$ (d) $\frac{n(n-1)}{2}$

60. Two links OA and OB are connected by a pin joint at 'O'. The link OA turns with angular velocity $\omega_1$radians per second in the clockwise direction and the link OB turns with angular velocity $\omega_2$ radians per second in the anticlockwise direction. If the radius of the pin at 'O' is '*r*' then the rubbing velocity at the pin joint 'O' will be:
(a) $\omega_1.\omega_2.r$ (b) $(\omega_1 - \omega_2)r$
(c) $(\omega_1 + \omega_2)r$ (d) $(\omega_1 + \omega_2)2r$

61. In a cam drive, it is essential to offset the axis of a follower to:
(a) decrease the side thrust between the follower and guide
(b) decrease the wear between follower and cam surface
(c) take care of space limitation
(d) reduce the cost

62. The working surface above the pitch surface of the gear tooth is termed as:
(a) Addendum (b) Dedendum
(c) Flank (d) Face

63. In the case of a flywheel, the maximum fluctuation of energy is the:
(a) sum of maximum and minimum energies
(b) difference between the maximum and minimum energies
(c) ratio of the maximum and minimum energy
(d) ratio of the minimum and maximum energy

64. Match List-I with List-II and select the correct answer using the codes given below the Lists:

| List-I | List-II |
|---|---|
| A. Compound train | 1. Hart mechanism |
| B. Quick return mechanism | 2. Coriolis force |
| C. Exact straight line motion | 3. Transmission of motion around bends and corners |
| D. Approximate straight line motion | 4. Watt mechanism |

**Codes:**

| | A | B | C | D |
|---|---|---|---|---|
| (a) | 1 | 2 | 3 | 4 |
| (b) | 3 | 2 | 1 | 4 |
| (c) | 3 | 4 | 1 | 2 |
| (d) | 1 | 4 | 3 | 2 |

65. Given that
$m$ = mass of the ball of the governor,
ω = angular velocity of the governor and
$g$ = accelerate due to gravity,
The height of Watt's governor is given by:
(a) $\frac{g}{2\omega^2}$ (b) $\frac{g}{\omega^2}$
(c) $\frac{\sqrt{2g}}{\omega^2}$ (d) $\frac{g}{\omega^2}$

66. Match List-I with List-II and select the correct answer using the codes given below the lists:

| List-I | List-II |
|---|---|
| A. End thrust | 1. Plain bearing |
| B. No cage | 2. Ball bearing |
| C. More accurate centering | 3. Needle bearing |
| D. Can be overloade | 4. Tapered roller bearing |

**Codes:**

| | A | B | C | D |
|---|---|---|---|---|
| (a) | 3 | 4 | 2 | 1 |
| (b) | 4 | 3 | 1 | 2 |
| (c) | 3 | 4 | 1 | 2 |
| (d) | 4 | 3 | 2 | 1 |

67. For a given fractional change of speed, if the displacement of the sleeve is high, then the governor is said to be:
(a) Hunting (b) Isochronous
(c) Sensitive (d) Stable

68. In a multi-cylinder in-line internal combustion engine, even number of cylinders is chosen so that:
(a) uniform firing order is obtained
(b) the couples are balanced
(c) primary forces are balanced
(d) secondary forces arc balanced

69. Match List-I with List-II and select the correct answer using the codes given below the Lists:

| List-I | List-II |
|---|---|
| A. 4 links, 4 turning pairs | 1. Complete constraint |
| B. 3 links, 3 turning pairs | 2. successful constraint |
| C. 5 links, 5 turning pairs | 3. Rigid Frame |
| D. Footstep bearing | 4. Incomplete constant |

**Codes:**

| | A | B | C | D |
|---|---|---|---|---|
| (a) | 3 | 1 | 4 | 2 |
| (b) | 1 | 3 | 2 | 4 |
| (c) | 3 | 1 | 2 | 4 |
| (d) | 1 | 3 | 4 | 2 |

70. The relative acceleration of two points which are at variable distance apart on a moving link can he determined by using the:
(a) threecentres in line theorem
(b) instantaneous centre of rotation method
(c) Coriolis component of acceleration method
(d) Klein's construction

71. Which one of the following pairs is correctly matched?
(a) Governors....Interference
(b) Gears....Hunting
(c) Klein's construction....Acceleration at piston
(d) Cam....Pinion

72. The primary disturbing force due to inertia of reciprocating parts of mass $m$ at radius $r$ moving with an angular velocity $\omega$ is given by:
(a) $m\omega^2 r \sin\theta$ (b) $m\omega^2 r \cos\theta$
(c) $m\omega^2 r \frac{\sin 2\theta}{n}$ (d) $m\omega^2 r \frac{\cos 2\theta}{n}$

73. Consider the following statements:
A pinion of $14\frac{1°}{2}$ pressure angle and 48 involute teeth has a pitch circle diameter of 28.8 cm. It has
1. Module of 6 mm
2. Circular pitch of 18 mm
3. Addendum of 6 mm
4. Diametral pitch of $\frac{11}{113}$
Which of these statements are correct?
(a) 2 and 3 (b) 1 and 3
(c) 1 and 4 (d) 2 and 4

74. For a given lift of the follower in a given angular motion of the cam, the acceleration/ retardation of the follower will be the least when the profile of the cam during the rise portion is:
(a) Such that the follower motion is simple harmonic
(b) Such that the follower motion has a constant velocity from start to end
(c) A straight line, it being a tangent cam
(d) Such that the follower velocity increases linearly for half the rise portion and then decreases linearly for the remaining half of the rise portion

75. Consider the following statements regarding the choice of conjugate teeth for the profile of mating gears:
1. They will transmit the desired motion.
2. They are difficult to manufacture.
3. Standardization is not possible.
4. The cost of production is low.
Which of these statements are correct?
(a) 1, 2 and 3 (b) 1, 2 and 4
(c) 2, 3 and 4 (d) 1, 3 and 4

76. The motion transmitted between the teeth of two spur gears in mesh is generally:
(a) Sliding
(b) Rolling
(c) Rotary
(d) Partly sliding and partly rolling

77. In a single slider four-bar linkage, when the slider is fixed, it forms a mechanism of:
(a) Hand pump
(b) Rolling
(c) Quick return
(d) Oscillating cylinder

78. Consider the following parameters:
1. Limit of peripheral speed
2. Limit of centrifugal stress
3. Coefficient of fluctuation of speed
4. Weight of the rim
Which of these parameters are used in the calculation of the diameter of flywheel rim?
(a) 1, 3 and 4 (b) 2, 3 and 4
(c) 1, 2 and 3 (d) 1, 2 and 4

79. Consider the following speed governors:
1. Porter governor 2. Hartnell governor
3. Watt governor 4. Proell governor.
The correct sequence of development of these governors is:
(a) 1, 3, 2 ,4 (b) 3, 1, 4, 2
(c) 3, ,1 ,2, 4 (d) 1, 3, 4, 2

80. If a two-mass system is dynamically equivalent to a rigid body, then the system will not satisfy the condition that the:
(a) Sum of the two masses must be equal to that of the rigid body

(b) Polar moment of inertia of the system should be equal to that of the rigid body
(c) Centre of gravity (e.g.) of the system should coincide with that of the rigid body
(d) Total moment of inertia about the axis through e.g. must be equal to that of the rigid body

81. A rigid shaft when laid on horizontal parallel ways will not roll if the:
(a) Centre of gravity falls parallel to shaft axis
(b) Centre of gravity lies on the shaft axis
(c) Horizontal moments are large
(d) Vertical moments are large

82. If the ratio of the length of connecting rod to the crank radius increases, then:
(a) Primary unbalanced forces will increase
(b) Primary unbalanced forces-will decrease
(c) Secondary unbalanced forces will increase
(d) Secondary unbalanced forces will decrease

83. Match List-I with List-II and select the correct answer using the codes given below the Lists:

| **List-I** | **List-II** |
|---|---|
| A. Quick return mechanism | 1. Lathe |
| B. Apron mechanism | 2. Milling machine |
| C. Indexing mechanism | 3. Shaper |
| D. Regulating wheel | 4. Centreless grinding |

**Codes:**

| | A | B | C | D |
|---|---|---|---|---|
| (a) | 3 | 2 | 1 | 4 |
| (b) | 2 | 3 | 4 | 1 |
| (c) | 4 | 2 | 3 | 1 |
| (d) | 3 | 1 | 2 | 4 |

84. A point on a link connecting a double slider crank chain-will trace a:
(a) straight line (b) circle
(c) parabola (d) ellipse

85. A wheel is rolling on a straight level track with a uniform velocity '*v*'. The instantaneous velocity of a point on the wheel lying at the mid-point of a radius:
(a) varies between $3\frac{v}{2}$ and $-\frac{v}{2}$
(b) varies between $\frac{v}{2}$ and $-\frac{v}{2}$
(c) varies between 3 $3\frac{v}{2}$ and $-\frac{v}{2}$
(d) does not vary and is equal to $v$

86. A four-bar chain has:
(a) all turning pairs
(b) one turning pair and the others are sliding pairs
(c) one sliding pair and the others are turning pairs
(d) all sliding pairs

87. Sensitiveness of a governor is defined as:
(a) $\dfrac{\text{Range of speed}}{2\times\text{Mean speed}}$
(b) $\dfrac{2\times\text{Mean speed}}{\text{Range of speed}}$
(c) Mean speed × Range of speed
(d) $\dfrac{\text{Range of speed}}{\text{Mean speed}}$

88. The velocity ratio in the case of the compound train of wheels is equal to:
(a) $\dfrac{\text{No. of teeth on first drivers}}{\text{No. of teeth on last follower}}$
(b) $\dfrac{\text{No. of teeth on last follower}}{\text{No. of teeth on first drivers}}$
(c) $\dfrac{\text{Product of teeth on the drivers}}{\text{Product of teeth on the follower}}$
(d) $\dfrac{\text{Product of teeth on the follower}}{\text{Product of teeth on the drivers}}$

89. Consider the following pairs of parts:
1. Pair of gear in mesh
2. Belt and pulley
3. Cylinder and piston.
4. Cam and follower

Among these, the higher pairs are:
(a) 1 and 4 (b) 2 and 4
(c) 1, 2 and 3 (d) 1, 2 and 4

89. A Kaplan turbine is a:
(a) Outward flow reaction turbine
(b) Inward flow impulse turbine
(c) Low head axial flow turbine
(d) High head mixed flow turbine

90. Which of the following hydraulic turbines are reaction turbines?
1. Francis
2. Kaplan
3. Propeller

(a) 1, 2 and 3 (b) 1 and 2 only
(c) 2 and 3 only (d) 1 and 3 only

91. In modern steam generator, the correct path of gases from boiler furnace to chimney is:
(a) Boiler furnace, Economizer, Air preheater, Superheater and Chimney
(b) Boiler furnace, Superheater, Air preheater, Economizer and Chimney
(c) Boiler furnace, Air preheater, Superheater, Economizer and Chimney
(d) Boiler furnace, Superheater, Economizer, Air preheater and Chimney

92. Clapeyron's equation is used for finding out the:
(a) 'Dryness fraction of steam only
(b) Entropy of superheated vapour only
(c) Specific volume at any temperature and pressure
(d) Total heat of superheated steam only

93. In a locomotive boiler, the draught is produced by:
(a) Chimney (b) ID fan
(c) FD fan (d) Steam jet

94. Out of the following impurities generally found in water, which one requires special consideration in case of very high pressure boilers?
(a) Hydrogen (b) Ammonia
(b) Silica (c) Dissolved salts

95. Willans line represents:
(a) Total steam consumption vs. power output with throttle governing
(b) Total steam consumption vs. power output with cutoff governing
(c) Behaviour of supersaturated steam through nozzles
(d) Condensation of steam while flowing through the turbine

96. Consider the following statements for an incompressible fluid flowing through a convergent-divergent duct:
1. The convergent part acts as a nozzle.
2. The divergent part acts as a diffuser.
3. The maximum limiting speed of the fluid is the sonic velocity.
Which of these statements are correct?
(a) 1, 2 and 3 (b) 1 and 2 only
(c) 2 and 3 only (d) 1 and 3 only

97. An isentropic nozzle is discharging steam through critical pressure ratio. If the back pressure is further decreased, the discharge will:
(a) Decrease
(b) Increase
(c) Remain unaffected
(d) Come to a dead stop due to shock waves

98. State of a wet vapour cannot be specified only by:
(a) Pressure and temperature
(b) Pressure and dryness fraction
(c) Temperature and dryness fraction
(d) Pressure and volume

99. Pertaining to a steam boiler, which of the following statements is correct?
(a) Primary boiler heat transfer surface Includes evaporator section, economizer and air preheater
(b) Primary boiler heat transfer surface includes evaporator section, economizer and superheater section
(c) Secondary boiler heat transfer surface includes superheater, economizer and air preheater
(d) Primary boiler heat transfer surface includes evaporator section, superheater section and reheat section

100. Which of the following statements is not correct for the volumetric efficiency of a reciprocating air compressor?
(a) It decreases with increase in ambient temperature
(b) It increases with decrease in pressure ratio
(c) It increases with decrease in clearance ratio
(d) It decreases with increase in delivery pressure

101. In a single stage reciprocating air compressor, the work done on air to compress it from suction pressure to delivery pressure will be minimum when the compression is:
(a) Isothermal process
(b) Adiabatic process
(c) Polytropic process
(d) Constant pressure process

102. In an axial flow compressor, stalling is the phenomenon of:
(a) Air motion at sonic velocity
(b) Air stream blocking the passage
(c) Reversed flow of air
(d) Air stream not following the blade contour

103. In Rayleigh flow at subsonic Mach numbers, heat addition:
(a) Decreases static pressure
(b) Decreases enthalpy
(c) Increases static pressure
(d) Decreases static temperature

104. The function of economizer in a boiler is to:
(a) Superheat the steam
(b) Reduce fuel consumption
(c) Increase steam pressure
(d) Maintain saturation temperature

105. In which modification of simple gas turbine cycle, is work ratio increased?
1. Regenerative gas turbine cycle
2. Gas turbine cycle with reheating
(a) Both 1 and 2 (b) 1 only
(c) 2 only (d) Neither 1 only 2

106. Reheat between multi-stage expansions Joule cycle increases
1. Overall work output
2. The work ratio
3. The thermal efficiency
Which of the above are correct?
(a) 1, 2 and 3
(b) 1 and 2 only
(c) 2 and 3 only
(d) 1 and 3 only

107. For a given discharge in a channel at critical depth:
(a) The specific energy is minimum
(b) The specific energy is maximum
(c) The total energy is minimum
(d) The total energy is maximum

108. Flow takes place at Reynolds number of 1500 in two different pipes with relative roughness of 0001 and 0002. The friction factor:
(a) Will be higher in case of pipe with relative roughness of 0001
(b) Will be higher in case of pipe with relative roughness of 0.002
(c) Will be same in both pipes
(d) In the two pipes cannot be compared on the basis of data given

109. Weber number is ratio of square root of inertia force to:
(a) Surface force (b) Gravity force
(c) Pressure force (d) Viscous force

110. What is the correct statement regarding normal shock wave in a gas?
(a) Normal shock is reversible
(b) The downstream flow as well as upstream flow is supersonic
(c) The entropy increases across the shock
(d) The entropy remains constant

111. Across a normal shock:
(a) The pressure and temperature rise
(b) The density and temperature decrease
(c) The velocity and pressure increase
(d) The velocity and pressure decrease

## ANSWERS WITH EXPLANATIONS

1. (a)

2. (d) $z_{min} = \frac{2}{\sin^2 14.5°} = 32$

3. (b) 4. (c) 5. (c)

6. (b) $500 + 50 \sin 2\theta = 500 + 50 \sin \theta$

$\sin 2\theta = \sin \theta$

or $\sin 2\theta = \sin \theta = 0$

$2 \sin \theta \cos \theta - \sin \theta = 0$

Either $\sin \theta = 0$ giving $\theta = 0°, 180°, 360°$

or $\cos \theta = \frac{1}{2}$, giving $\theta = 60°, 300°$

$\theta = 0°, 60°, 180°, 300° = 4$ times

7. (c) 8. (c) 9. (a) 10. (d) 11. (d)

12. (c) $E \alpha I, I \alpha R^2$

$\frac{E_2}{E1}\left(\frac{R_2^1}{R_1}\right) = \left(\frac{1}{2}\right)^2 = \frac{1}{4}$

13. (b) 14. (a) 15. (c) 16. (a) 17. (d)

18. (a) $W - T = \frac{W}{3}$

$T = \frac{2}{3}W$

19. (b) 20. (d)

21. (a) $\Delta KE = \frac{1}{2}(I_1\omega_1^2 - I_2\omega_2^2) - \frac{1}{2}(I_1\omega_1'^2 - I_2\omega_2'^2)$

For momentum balance,

$I_1\omega_1 + I_2\omega_2 = I_1\omega'_1 + I_2\omega'_2$

$= \omega'_1 = \omega'_2 = \frac{I_1\omega_1 + I_2\omega_2}{I_1 + I_2}$

$\Delta KE = \frac{I_1 I_2}{2(I_1 + I_2)}(\omega_1 - \omega_2)^2$

22. (b) 23. (c)

24. (a) $R_1 = \frac{W}{2}$, $W = 2R_1$

$R_2 \times 2L = 2R_1 \times L$

$R_2 = R_1$

25. (a) 26. (d) 27. (c) 28. (d) 29. (a)
30. (d) 31. (d) 32. (a) 33. (a) 34. (d)
35. (d) 36. (c) 37. (a) 38. (c) 39. (d)
40. (a) 41. (b) 42. (a) 43. (a) 44. (c)
45. (a) 46. (a) 47. (d) 48. (d)

49. (a) $\text{Sensitivity} = \frac{2(N_1 - N_2)}{(N_1 + N_2)}$

For isochronous governor, $N_1 = N_2$

$\therefore$ Sensitivity = zero

50. (d) $\theta$ for secondary reverse crank = $2\theta$for primary direct frank in the same direction

51. (b) 52. (d) 53. (a) 54. (c)

55. (c) Frequency of oscillation $= \frac{60}{20} = 3$ cpm

Angular velocity of precession

$= \frac{2\pi}{20} \times \frac{\pi}{30} = \frac{\pi^2}{300}$ rad/s

Amplitude of pitching $= \frac{6\pi}{180} = \frac{\pi}{30}$ rad

56. (c)

57. (b) Let $x = A \sin \omega t$

$x = A\omega \cos \omega t$

$\ddot{x} = -A\omega^2 \sin \omega t = A\omega^2 \sin(180° + \omega t)$

58. (d) 59. (d)

60. (c) $v_r = r(\omega_1 - (-\omega_2)] = r(\omega_1 + \omega_2)$

61. (b) 62. (c) 63. (b) 64. (b) 65. (b)
66. (d) 67. (c) 68. (a) 69. (d) 70. (b)
71. (c) 72. (b)

73. (b) $m = \frac{d}{z} = \frac{288}{48} = 6$ mm

$p = m = \pi \times 6 = 18.84$ mm

$h_a = 1m = 6$ mm

$P = \frac{1}{m} = \frac{1}{6}$

74. (b) 75. (b) 76. (d) 77. (a) 78. (a)
79. (b) 80. (d) 81. (b) 82. (d)
83. (d) 84. (d)

85. (b) $v \alpha r, v_A = \pm\frac{v}{2}$

86. (a) 87. (c) 88. (c) 89. (d)

89. (c) Kaplan turbine is a low head axial flow turbine.

90. (a) The reaction turbine are:
Francis, Kaplan, Propeller.

91. (d) In a modern steam generator, the path of gases from boiler furnance to chimney is:
Boiler furnance → Super heater → Economizer → Air preheater → Chimney

92. (c) Clapayron's equation is used to find out the specific volume at any temperature and pressure.

93. (d) In a locomotive boiler, the draught is produced by steam jet.

94. (c) In case of very high pressure boiler, impurities of silica in water require special consideration.

95. (a) William's line represents total steam consumption v's power output with throttle governing.

96. (b) For an incompressible fluid flowing through a convergent-divergent duct, the convergent part acts as a nozzle and the divergent part acts as a diffuser.

97. (c) If the back pressure in an isentropic nozzle discharging steam through critical pressure ratio is further decreased, the discharge will remain unaffected.

98. (a) State of wet vapour cannot be specified only by pressure and temperature.

99. (d) Primary boiler heat transfer surface includes evaporator section, economizer and air-preheater.

100. (d) $\eta_v = 1 + c - c\left(\frac{p_2}{p_1}\right)^{\frac{1}{n}} = \frac{p_1 T_0}{p_0 T_1}\left[1 + c - c\left(\frac{p_2}{p_1}\right)^{\frac{1}{\eta}}\right]$

$\eta_v$ decreases as $\left(\frac{p_2}{p_1}\right)$ ratio increass.

101. (a) The work done on single stage reciprocating compressor is minimum when the compression is isothermal process.

102. (d) In an axial flow compressor, stalling is the phenomenon of air stream not following the blade contour.

103. (a) In Rayleigh flow at subsonic Mach numbers, heat addition decreases static pressure.

104. (b) The function of economizer in a boiler is to reduce fuel consumption.

105. (c) In a simple gas turbine cycle, work ratio increases with reheating.

106. (b) Reheat between multi-stage expansions in Joule cycle increases overall work output and work ratio.

107. (a) For a given discharge in a channel at critical depth, the specific energy is minimum.

108. (c) Re = 1500, Frication factor for a pipe
$f = \frac{64}{\text{Re}}$. Hence $F_1 = F_2$

109. (a) Weber number $= \left(\frac{\text{Inertia force}}{\text{Surface tension force}}\right)^{1/2}$

110. (c) The entropy increases across the normal shock wave in a gas.

111. (a) Across a normal shock the pressure and temperature rise.

❑❑❑

# 12. Vibration Analysis

- Vibration is a mechanical phenomenon whereby oscillations occur about an equilibrium point. The oscillations may be periodic such as the motion of a pendulum or random such as the movement of a tire on a gravel road.
- Vibration is occasionally "desirable". For example, the motion of a tuning fork, the reed in a woodwind instrument or harmonica, or mobile phones or the cone of a loudspeaker is desirable vibration, necessary for the correct functioning of the various devices.
- More often, vibration is undesirable, wasting energy and creating unwanted sound – noise. For example, the vibrational motions of engines, electric motors, or any mechanical device in operation are typically unwanted.
- Such vibrations can be caused by imbalances in the rotating parts, uneven friction, the meshing of gear teeth, etc. Careful designs usually minimize unwanted vibrations.
- The study of sound and vibration are closely related. Sound, or "pressure waves", are generated by vibrating structures, these pressure waves can also induce the vibration of structures . Hence, when trying to reduce noise it is often a problem in trying to reduce vibration.
- Free vibration occurs when a mechanical system is set off with an initial input and then allowed to vibrate freely. Examples of this type of vibration are pulling a child back on a swing and then letting go or hitting a tuning fork and letting it ring.
- The mechanical system will then vibrate at one or more of its "natural frequency" and damp down to zero.
- Forced vibration is when a time-varying disturbance is applied to a mechanical system. The disturbance can be a periodic, steady-state input, a transient input, or a random input.
- The periodic input can be a harmonic or a non-harmonic disturbance. Examples of these types of vibration include a shaking washing machine due to an imbalance, transportation vibration .or the vibration of a building during an earthquake.
- For linear systems, the frequency of the steady-state vibration response resulting from the application of a periodic, harmonic input is equal to the frequency of the applied force or motion, with the response magnitude being dependent on the actual mechanical system.
- Vibration testing is accomplished by introducing a forcing function into a structure, usually with some type of shaker. Alternately, a DUT (device under test) is attached to the "table" of a shaker. Vibration testing is performed to examine the response of a device under test (DUT) to a defined vibration environment.
- The measured response may be fatigue life, resonant frequencies or squeak and rattle sound output (NVH). Squeak and rattle testing is performed with a special type of quiet shaker that produces very low sound levels while under operation.
- For relatively low frequency forcing, servo hydraulic (electrohydraulic) shakers are used. For higher frequencies, electro dynamic shakers are used. Generally, one or more "input" or "control" points located on the DUT-side of a fixture is kept at a specified acceleration.
- Other "response" points experience maximum vibration level (resonance) or minimum vibration level (anti-resonance). It is often desirable to achieve anti-resonance in order to keep a system from becoming too noisy, or to reduce strain on certain parts of a system due to vibration modes caused by specific frequencies of vibration.
- The most common types of vibration testing services conducted by vibration test labs are Sinusoidal and Random. Sine (one-frequency-at-a-time) tests are performed to survey the structural response of the device under test (DUT).
- A random (all frequencies at once) test is generally considered to more closely replicate a real world environment, such as road inputs to a moving automobile.
- Most vibration testing is conducted in a 'single DUT axis' at a time, even though most real-world vibration occurs in various axes simultaneously. MIL-STD-810G, released in late 2008, Test Method 527, calls for multiple exciter testing.
- The vibration test fixture which is used to attach the DUT to the shaker table must be designed for the frequency range of the vibration test spectrum.
- Generally for smaller fixtures and lower frequency ranges, the designer targets a fixture design which is free of resonances in the test frequency range.
- This becomes more difficult as the DUT gets larger and as the test frequency increases, and in these cases multi-point control strategies can be employed to mitigate some of the resonances which may be present in the future.
- Devices specifically designed to trace or record vibrations are called vibroscopes.

- The fundamentals of vibration analysis can be understood by studying the simple mass–spring–damper model. Indeed, even a complex structure such as an automobile body can be modeled as a "summation" of simple mass–spring–damper models.
- The mass–spring–damper model is an example of a simple harmonic oscillator. The mathematics used to describe its behavior is identical to other simple harmonic oscillators such as the RLC circuit.
- To start the investigation of the mass–spring–damper assume the damping is negligible and that there is no external force applied to the mass .The force applied to the mass by the spring is proportional to the amount the spring is stretched "x" (we will assume the spring is already compressed due to the weight of the mass).
- The proportionality constant, k, is the stiffness of the spring and has units of force/distance .
- Vibrational motion could be understood in terms of conservation of energy. In the above example the spring has been extended by a value of x and therefore some potential energy ($\frac{1}{2}kx^2$) is stored in the spring.
- Once released, the spring tends to return to its un-stretched state (which is the minimum potential energy state) and in the process accelerates the mass. At the point where the spring has reached its un-stretched state all the potential energy that we supplied by stretching it has been transformed into kinetic energy($\frac{1}{2}mv^2$).
- The mass then begins to decelerate because it is now compressing the spring and in the process transferring the kinetic energy back to its potential. Thus oscillation of the spring amounts to the transferring back and forth of the kinetic energy into potential energy.
- In this simple model the mass will continue to oscillate forever at the same magnitude, but in a real system there is always damping that dissipates the energy, eventually bringing it to rest.
- The following are some other points in regards to the forced vibration shown in the frequency response plots.
- At a given frequency ratio, the amplitude of the vibration, X, is directly proportional to the amplitude of the force $F_0$ (e.g. if you double the force, the vibration doubles)
- With little or no damping, the vibration is in phase with the forcing frequency when the frequency ratio $r < 1$ and 180 degrees out of phase when the frequency ratio $r > 1$

whatever the damping is, the vibration is 90 degrees out of phase with the forcing frequency when the frequency ratio r =1, which is very helpful when it comes to determining the natural frequency of the system.

- Resonance is simple to understand if the spring and mass are viewed as energy storage elements – with the mass storing kinetic energy and the spring storing potential energy.
- In other words, if energy is to be efficiently pumped into both the mass and spring the energy source needs to feed the energy in at a rate equal to the natural frequency.
- Applying a force to the mass and spring is similar to pushing a child on swing, a push is needed at the correct moment to make the swing get higher and higher.
- As in the case of the swing, the force applied does not necessarily have to be high to get large motions; the pushes just need to keep adding energy into the system.
- The damper, instead of storing energy, dissipates energy. Since the damping force is proportional to the velocity, the more the motion, the more the damper dissipates the energy. Therefore a point will come when the energy dissipated by the damper will equal the energy being fed in by the force.
- At this point, the system has reached its maximum amplitude and will continue to vibrate at this level as long as the force applied stays the same. If no damping exists, there is nothing to dissipate the energy and therefore theoretically the motion will continue to grow on into infinity.
- The Fourier transform of the square wave generates a frequency spectrum that presents the magnitude of the harmonics that make up the square wave (the phase is also generated, but is typically of less concern and therefore is often not plotted).
- The Fourier transform can also be used to analyze non-periodic functions such as transients and random functions. The Fourier transform is almost always computed using the Fast Fourier Transform (FFT) computer algorithm in combination with a window function.

# MULTIPLE CHOICE QUESTIONS

1. A mass of 1 kg is attached to the end of a spring with a stiffness 0.7 N/mm. The critical damping coefficient of the system is:
(a) 1.40 Ns/m (b) 52.22 Ns/m
(c) 52.92 Ns/m (d) 529.20 Ns/m

2. Two heavy rotating masses are connected by shafts of lengths $l_1$, $l_2$ and $l_3$ and the corresponding diameters are $d_1$, $d_2$ and $d_3$. This system is reduced to a torsionally equivalent system having uniform diameter "$d_1$" of the shaft. The equivalent length of the shaft is:
(a) $\frac{l_1+l_2+l_3}{3}$
(b) $l_1+l_2\left(\frac{d_1}{d_2}\right)^3+l_3\left(\frac{d_1}{d_3}\right)^3$
(c) $l_1+l_2\left(\frac{d_1}{d_2}\right)^4+l_3\left(\frac{d_1}{d_3}\right)^4$
(d) $l_1+l_2+l_3$

3. The equation of free vibrations of a system is $\ddot{x}+36\pi^2 X=0$. Its natural frequency is:
(a) 46 Hz (b) 3 π Hz
(c) 3 Hz (d) 6π Hz

4. Which of the following methods can be used to determine the damping of machine element?
1. Logarithmic method
2. Band-width method
3. Rayleigh method
4. Holzer method
Select the correct answer using the codes given below:
**Codes:**
(a) 1 and 3 (b) 1 and 2
(c) 3 and 4 (d) 1, 3 and 4

5. If $\frac{\omega}{\omega_n}=\sqrt{2}$ where ω is the frequency of excitation and $\omega_n$ is the natural frequency of vibrations, then the transmissibility of vibrations will be:
(a) 0.5 (b) 1.0
(c) 1.5 (d) 2.0

6. A slender shaft supported on two hearings at its ends carries a disc with an eccentricity *e* from the axis of rotation. The critical speed of the shaft is N. If the disc is replaced by a second one of the same weight but mounted with an eccentricity 2*e*, critical speed of the shaft in the second case is:
(a) $\frac{1}{2}$ N (b) $\frac{1}{\sqrt{2}}$ N
(c) N (d) 2N

7. An axial flow fan balanced at one speed often exhibits substantial vibrational effect when operated at other speeds, mainly due to:
(a) primary critical speed effect
(b) secondary critical speed effect
(c) unbalanced parts of the fan
(d) aerodynamic unbalance

8. For a disc mounted shaft to rotate with light side of disc out:
(a) β< 1 (b) β = 1
(c) β> 1 (d) β<< 1
where $\beta=\frac{\omega}{\omega_c}$

9. When shaking force is transmitted through the spring, damping becomes detrimental when the ratio of its frequency to the natural frequency is greater than:
(a) 0.25 (b) 0.50
(c) 1.00 (d) sqrt 2

10. When the mass of a critically damped single degree of freedom system is deflected from its equilibrium position and released, it will:
(a) return to equilibrium position without oscillation
(b) oscillate with increasing time period
(c) oscillate with decreasing amplitude
(d) oscillate with constant amplitude

11. Under logarithmic decrement, the amplitude of successive vibrations are:
(a) constant
(b) in arithmetic progression
(c) in geometric progression
(d) in logarithmic progression

12. The danger of breakage and vibration is maximum:
(a) below critical speed (b) near critical speed
(c) above critical speed (d) none of the above

13. With symbols having the usual meanings, the single degree of freedom system, $m\ddot{x}+c\dot{x}+kx=$ F sin ωt represents:
(a) free vibration with damping
(b) free vibration without damping
(c) forced vibration with damping
(d) forced vibration without damping

14. A simple spring mass vibrating system has a natural frequency of N. If the spring, stiffness is halved and the mass is doubled, then the natural frequency will become:
(a) N/2 (b) 2N
(c) 4N (d) 8N

15. Rotating shafts tend to vibrate violently at whirling speeds because:
(a) the shafts are rotating at very high speeds
(b) bearing centre line coincides with the shaft axis
(c) the system is unbalanced
(d) resonance is caused due to the heavy weight of the rotor.

16. Critical speed of a shaft with a disc supported in between is equal to the natural frequency of the system in:
(a) transverse vibrations
(b) torsional vibrations
(c) longitudinal vibrations
(d) longitudinal vibrations provided the shaft is vertical.

17. In a automobile service station, an automobile is in a lifted up position by means of a hydraulic jack. A person working in the service station gave a tap to one rear wheel and made it rotate by one revolution. The rotation of another rear wheel is:
(a) zero
(b) also one revolution in the same direction
(c) also one revolution but in the opposite direction
(d) unpredictable

18. In the statement "an eccentric mass rotating a 3000 rpm will create X times more unbalanced force than 50% of the same mass rotating at 300 rpm", 'X' stands for:
(a) 10 (b) 50
(c) 100 (d) 200

19. A machine of 100 kg mass has a 20 kg rotor with 0.5 mm eccentricity. The mounting springs have stiffness 85 kN/m and damping is negligible. If the operating speed is $20\pi$ rad/sand the unit is constrained to move vertically, the dynamic amplitude of the machine will be:
(a) $0.170 \times 10^{-4}$ m
(b) $1.000 \times 10^{-4}$ m
(c) $1.274 \times 10^{-4}$ m
(d) $2.540 \times 10^{-4}$ m

20. Match the List I(Force transmissibility) with List II (frequency ratio) and select the correct answer using the codes given below the Lists:

| **List-I (Force transmissibility)** | **Fist-II (Frequency ratio)** |
|---|---|
| A. 1 | 1. $\frac{\omega}{\omega_n} > \sqrt{2}$ |
| B. Less than 1 | 2. $\frac{\omega}{\omega_n} = \sqrt{2}$ |
| C. Greater than 1 | 3. $\frac{\omega}{\omega_n} >> \sqrt{2}$ |
| D. Tending to zero | 4. $\frac{\omega}{\omega_n} < \sqrt{2}$ |

**Codes:**

| | A | B | C | D |
|---|---|---|---|---|
| (a) | 1 | 2 | 3 | 4 |
| (b) | 2 | 1 | 4 | 3 |
| (c) | 2 | 1 | 3 | 4 |
| (d) | 1 | 2 | 4 | 3 |

21. The equation of motion for a single degree of freedom system with viscous damping is: $4\ddot{x}+9\dot{x}+16x=0$. The damping ratio of the system is:
(a) $\frac{9}{128}$ (b) $\frac{9}{16}$
(c) $\frac{9}{8\sqrt{2}}$ (d) $\frac{9}{8}$

22. The critical speed of a rotating shaft depends upon:
(a) mass
(b) stiffness
(c) mass and stiffness
(d) mass, stiffness and eccentricity.

23. Two heavy rotating masses are connected by shafts of length $l_1$, $l_2$ and $l_3$ and the corresponding diameters are $d_1 d_2$ and $d_3$. This system is reduced to a torsionally equivalent system having uniform diameter $d_1$ of the shaft. The equivalent length of the shaft is equal to:
(a) $l_1+l_2+l_3$
(b) $\frac{l_1+l_2+l_3}{3}$
(c) $l_1+l_2\left(\frac{d_1}{d_2}\right)^3+l_3\left(\frac{d_1}{d_3}\right)^3$
(d) $l_1+l_2\left(\frac{d_1}{d_2}\right)^4+l_3\left(\frac{d_1}{d_3}\right)^4$

24. If a mass *'m'* oscillates on a spring having a mass $m_s$ and stiffness *'k'*, then the natural frequency of the system is given by:
(a) $\sqrt{\frac{k}{m+\frac{m_s}{3}}}$ (b) $\sqrt{\frac{k}{\frac{m}{3}+m_s}}$
(c) $\sqrt{\frac{3k}{m+m_s}}$ (d) $\sqrt{\frac{k}{m+m_s}}$

25. Match List-I with List-II and select the correct answer using the codes given below the lists:

| **List-I** | **List-II** |
|---|---|
| A. Node and mode | 1. Geared vibration |
| B. Equivalent inertia | 2. Damped-free vibration |
| C. Log decrement | 3. Forced vibration |
| D. Resonance | 4. Multi-rotor vibration |

**Codes:**

| | A | B | C | D |
|---|---|---|---|---|
| (a) | 1 | 4 | 3 | 2 |
| (b) | 4 | 1 | 2 | 3 |
| (c) | 1 | 4 | 2 | 3 |
| (d) | 4 | 1 | 3 | 2 |

26. The natural frequency of transverse vibration of a massless beam of length L having a mass $m$ attached at its midspan is given by:
(EI is the flexural rigidity of the beam)
(a) $\left(\frac{ml^3}{48EI}\right)^{\frac{1}{2}}$ rad/s (b) $\left(\frac{48ml^3}{EI}\right)^{\frac{1}{2}}$ rad/s
(c) $\left(\frac{48EI}{mL^3}\right)^{\frac{1}{2}}$ rad/s (d) $\left(\frac{3EI}{mL^3}\right)^{\frac{1}{2}}$ rad/s

27. If a spring-mass-dashpot system is subjected to excitation by a constant harmonic force, then at resonance, its amplitude of vibration will be:
(a) Infinity
(b) Inversely proportional to damping
(c) Directly proportional to damping
(d) Decreasing exponentially with time

28. In a forced vibration with viscous damping, maximum amplitude occurs when forced frequency is:
(a) Equal to natural frequency
(b) Slightly less than natural frequency
(c) Slightly greater than natural frequency
(d) Zero

29. The value of the natural frequency obtained by Rayleigh's method:
(a) Is always greater than the actual fundamental frequency
(b) Is always less than the actual fundamental frequency
(c) Depends upon the initial deflection curve chosen and may be greater than or less than the actual fundamental frequency
(d) Is independent of the initial deflection curve chosen.

30. In a multi-rotor system of torsional vibration maximum number of nodes that can occur is:
(a) Two
(b) Equal to the number of rotor plus one
(c) Equal to the number of rotors
(d) Equal to the number of rotors minus one

31. A rotating shaft carries a flywheel which overhangs on the bearing as a cantilever. If this flywheel weight is reduced to half of its original weight, the whirling speed will:
(a) Be double
(b) Increase by $\sqrt{2}$ times
(c) Decrease by $\sqrt{2}$ times
(d) Be half

32. The damping force in forced vibrations with reference to spring force:
(a) leads by 90°
(b) lags by 90°
(c) leads by 180°
(d) lags by 180°

33. Match List-I with List-II and select the correct answer using the codes given below the Lists:

| List-I | List-II |
|---|---|
| A. 6 d.o.f. system | 1. Vibrating beam |
| B. 1d.o.f. system | 2. Vibration absorber |
| C. 2 d.o.f. system | 3. A rigid body in space |
| D. Multi d.o.f. system | 4. Pure rolling of a cylinder |

**Codes:**

| | A | B | C | D |
|---|---|---|---|---|
| (a) | 1 | 2 | 4 | 5 |
| (b) | 1 | 4 | 2 | 3 |
| (c) | 3 | 2 | 4 | 1 |
| (d) | 3 | 4 | 2 | 1 |

34. A shaft carries a weight W at the centre. The CG of the weight is displaced by an amount e from the axis of the rotation. If $y$ is the additional displacement of the CG from the axis of rotation due to the centrifugal force, then the ratio of $y$ to $e$ (where $\omega_c$ is the critical speed of shaft and $\omega$ is the angular speed of shaft) is given by:

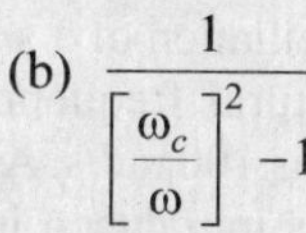

(a) $\frac{1}{\left[\frac{\omega_c}{\omega}\right]^2+1}$ (b) $\frac{1}{\left[\frac{\omega_c}{\omega}\right]^2-1}$
(c) $\left[\frac{\omega_c}{\omega}\right]^2+1$ (d) $\frac{\omega}{\left[\frac{\omega_c}{\omega}\right]^2-1}$

35. When a vehicle travels on a rough road whose undulations can be assumed to be sinusoidal, the resonant conditions of the base-excited vibrations, are determined by the:
(a) mass of the vehicle, stiffness of the suspension spring, speed of the vehicle, wavelength of the roughness curve
(b) speed of the vehicle only
(c) speed of the vehicle and the stiffness of the suspension spring
(d) amplitude of the undulations

36. During torsional vibration of a shaft, the node is characterized by the:
(a) maximum angular velocity
(b) maximum angular displacement
(c) maximum angular acceleration
(d) zero angular displacement

37. A rod of uniform diameter is suspended from one of its ends in vertical plane. The mass of the rod is '$m$' and length T, the natural frequency of this rod in Hz for small amplitude is:
(a) $\frac{1}{2\pi}\sqrt{\frac{g}{l}}$ (b) $\frac{1}{2\pi}\sqrt{\frac{g}{3l}}$
(c) $\frac{1}{2\pi}\sqrt{\frac{2g}{3l}}$ (d) $\frac{1}{2\pi}\sqrt{\frac{3g}{2l}}$

38. The mass moment of inertia of the two motors in a two rotor system arc 100 kg.m$^2$ and 10 kg.m$^2$. The length of the shaft of uniform diameter between the rotors is 110 cm. The distance of node from the rotor of lower moment of inertia is:
(a) 80 cm (b) 90 cm
(c) 100 cm (d) 110 cm

39. A shaft of 50 mm diameter and 1 m length carries a disc which has mass eccentricity equal to 190 microns. The displacement of the shaft at a speed which is 90% of critical speed in microns is:
(a) 810 (b) 900
(c) 800 (d) 820

40. What is the number of nodes in a shalt carrying three rotors?
(a) Zero (b) 2
(c) 3 (d) 4

41. $\frac{\partial^2 u}{\partial t^2} = c^2 \frac{\partial^2 u}{\partial x^2}$ represents the equation for:
(a) Vibration of a stretched string
(b) Motion of a projectile in a gravitational field
(c) Heat flow in thin rod
(d) Oscillation of a simple pendulum

42. The natural frequency of an undamped vibrating system is 100 rad/s. A damper with a damping factor of 0.8 is introduced into the system. The frequency of vibration of the damped system, in rad/s, is:
(a) 60 (b) 75
(c) 80 (d) 100

43. A mass *m* attached to a light spring oscillates with a period of 2 sec. If the mass is increased by 2 kg, the period increases by 1 sec. The value of *m* is:
(a) 1 kg (b) 1.6 kg
(c) 2 kg (d) 2.4 kg

44. High damping reduces the transmissibility if the non-dimensional frequency ratio $\omega/\omega_n$($\omega$ = forcing frequency, $\omega_n$ = natural frequency):
(a) is less than $\sqrt{2}$ (b) is greater than $\sqrt{2}$
(c) is less than $\frac{1}{\sqrt{2}}$ (d) is greater than $\frac{1}{\sqrt{2}}$

45. For lightly damped heavy rotor systems, resonance occurs when the forcing $\omega$ is equal to:
(a) $2\,\omega_{cr}$ (b) $\sqrt{2}\,\omega_{cr}$
(c) $\omega_{cr}$ (d) $\frac{1}{2}\,\omega_{cr}$
where $\omega_{cr}$ is the critical speed.

46. The silencer of an internal combustion engine:
(a) reduces noise
(b) decreases brake specific fuel consumption (BSFC)
(c) increases BSFC
(d) has no effect on its efficiency

47. The deflection of a spring with 20 active turns under a load of 1000 N is 10 mm. The spring is made-into two pieces each of 10 active coils and placed in parallel under the same load. The deflection of this system is:
(a) 20 mm (b) 10 mm
(c) 5 mm (d) 2.5 mm

48. A flexible rotor-shaft system comprises of a 10 kg rotor disc placed in the middle of a massless shaft of diameter 30 mm and length 500 mm between bearings (shaft is being taken massless as the equivalent mass of the shaft is included in the rotor mass) mounted at the ends. The bearings are assumed to simulate simply supported boundary conditions. The shaft is made of steel for which the value of E = 2.1 × 10$^{11}$ Pa. What is the critical speed of rotation of the shaft?
(a) 60 Hz (b) 90 Hz
(c) 135 Hz (d) 180 Hz

49. A vibrating machine is isolated from the floor using springs. If the ratio of excitation frequency of vibration of machine to the natural frequency of the isolation system is equal to 0.5, the transmissibility of ratio of isolation is:
(a) $\frac{1}{2}$ (b) $\frac{3}{4}$
(c) $\frac{4}{3}$ (d) 2

50. For steady flow through an insulated horizontal constant diameter pipe, this property remains constant:
(a) Enthalpy (b) Internal energy
(c) Entropy (d) Volume

51. 100 kJ of energy is transferred from a heat reservoir at 1000 K to a heat reservoir at 500 K. The ambient temperature is 300 K. The loss of available energy due to heat transfer process is:
(a) 20 kJ (b) 30 kJ
(c) 40 kJ (d) 50 kJ

52. A shaft, supported on two bearings at its ends, carries two flywheels 'L' apart. Mass moment of inertia of the two flywheels are $I_a$ and $I_b$ I being the polar moment of inertia of cross-sectional area of the shaft. Distance $l_a$ of the node of torsional vibration of the shaft from the flywheel $I_a$ is given by:
(a) $l_a = \frac{LI_b}{I_a + I_b}$ (b) $l_a = \frac{LI_a}{I_a + I_b}$
(c) $l_a = \frac{LI_b}{I_a + I_b - 1}$ (d) $l_a = \frac{LI_a}{I_a + I_b - 1}$

53. The transmitted force through a mass-spring damper system will be greater than that transmitted through rigid supports for all values of-damping factors, if the frequency ratio $\left(\frac{\omega}{\omega_n}\right)$ is:
(a) more than $\sqrt{2}$ (b) less than $\sqrt{2}$
(c) equal to one (d) less than one

54. In a forced vibrations with viscous damping, maximum amplitude occurs when the forced frequency is:
(a) equal to natural frequency
(b) slightly less than natural frequency
(c) slightly greater than natural frequency
(d) zero.

55. The rotor of a turbine is generally rotated at:
(a) the critical speed
(b) a speed much below the critical speed
(c) a speed much above the critical speed
(d) a speed having no relation to critical speed

56. A reed type tachometer uses the principle of:
(a) torsional vibration (b) longitudinal vibration
(c) transverse vibration (d) damped free vibration

57. A viscous damping system with free vibrations will be critically damped if the damping factor is:
(a) zero (b) less than one
(c) equal to one (d) greater than one

58. In a simple spring mass vibrating system, the natural frequency $\omega_n$ of the system is (k is spring stiffness, $m$ is mass and $m_s$ is springmass):
(a) $\sqrt{\dfrac{k}{m-\dfrac{m_s}{3}}}$ (b) $\sqrt{\dfrac{k}{m+\dfrac{m_s}{3}}}$
(c) $\sqrt{\dfrac{k}{m+3m_s}}$ (d) $\sqrt{\dfrac{k}{m-3m_s}}$

59. Consider the following methods:
1. Energy method
2. Equilibrium method
3. Rayleigh's method.
Which of these methods can be used for determining the natural frequency of the free vibrations?
(a) 1 and 2 (b) 1, 2 and 3
(c) 1 and 3 (d) 2 and 3

60. Consider the following statements:
1. In forced vibrations, the body vibrates under the influence of an applied force.
2. In damped vibrations, amplitude reduces over every cycle, of vibration
3. In torsional vibrations, the disc moves parallel to the axis of shaft.
4. In transverse vibrations, the particles of the shaft moves approximately perpendicular to the axis of the shaft.
Which of these statements are correct?
(a) 1, 2 and 3 (b) 1, 3 and 4
(c) 2, 3 and 4 (d) 1, 2 and 4

61. Whirling speed of shaft is the speed at which:
(a) shaft tends to vibrate in longitudinal direction
(b) torsional vibrations occur
(c) shaft tends to vibrate vigorously in transverse direction
(d) combination of transverse and longitudinal vibration occurs.

62. A shaft has two heavy rotors mounted on it. The transverse natural frequencies, considering each of the rotor separately, are 100 Hz and 200 Hz respectively. The lowest critical speed is:
(a) 5367 rpm (b) 6000 rpm
(c) 9360 rpm (d) 12000 rpm

63. In a system subjected to damped forced vibrations, the ratio of maximum displacement to the static deflection is known as:
(a) Critical damping ratio
(b) Damping factor
(c) Logarithmic decrement
(d) Magnification factor

64. Consider the following statements: Two rotors mounted on a single shaft can be considered to be equivalent to a geared-shaft system having two rotors provided
1. the kinetic energy of the equivalent system is equal to that of the original system.
2. the strain energy of the equivalent system is equal to that of the original system.
3. the shaft diameters of the two systems are equal.
Which of these statements are correct?
(a) 1, 2 and 3 (b) 1 and 2
(c) 2 and 3 (d) 1 and 3

65. A spring-mass suspension has a natural frequency of 40 rad/s. What is the damping ratio required if it is desired to reduce this frequency to 20 rad/s by adding a damper to it?
(a) $\dfrac{\sqrt{3}}{2}$ (b) $\dfrac{1}{2}$
(c) $\dfrac{1}{\sqrt{2}}$ (d) $\dfrac{1}{4}$

66. Transmissibility is unity at two points. Which one of the following is true for these two points?
(a) $\dfrac{\omega}{\omega_n}$ is zero and $\sqrt{3}$ for all values of damping
(b) $\dfrac{\omega}{\omega_n}$ is zero and $\sqrt{2}$ for all values of damping
(c) $\dfrac{\omega}{\omega_n}$ is unity and 2 for all values of damping
(d) $\dfrac{\omega}{\omega_n}$ is unity and $\sqrt{3}$ for all values of damping

67. Suppose two rotors with inertias $i_1$ and $l_2$on shafts of length $l_1$ and $l_2$respectively, are connected by gears such that the speed of the $l_2$ rotor is always G times that of the $l_2$ rotor. This system may, for vibration analysis, he treated as being on one shaft (integral with $i_1$) if:
(a) $l_1$ is changed to $G^2I_1$
(b) $I_2$ is changed to $G^2I_2$
(c) $I$ is changed to $I_1/G^2$
(d) $I_2$ is changed to $I_2/G^2$

68. Two rotors A and B are connected to the two ends of a shaft of uniform diameter. The mass moment of inertia of rotor A about the axis of the shaft is four times that of B. If the length of the shaft is 1 m and C is the position of node for torsional vibrations, then what is the length of AC?
(a) 1/5 m (b) 4/5 m
(c) 1/25 m (d) 16/25 m

69. Which one of the following is realized by hydraulic dashpot shock absorbers?
(a) Viscous damping
(b) Structural damping
(c) Coulomb damping
(d) Spring damping

70. Which one of the following is the correct statement? Transmissibility is defined as the ratio of the:
(a) force applied to the machine to the force transmitted to the foundation
(b) force transmitted to the foundation to the force applied to the machine
(c) force applied to the machine to the vector sum of spring forces
(d) damping forces to the spring forces.

71. Which one of the following is correct for a shaft carrying two rotors at its ends?
(a) It has no node
(b) It has one node
(c) It has two nodes
(d) It has three nodes

72. A shaft has two heavy rotors mounted on it. The transverse natural frequencies, considering each of the rotor separately, are 100 cycles/sec and 200 cycles/sec respectively. The lowest critical speed is:
(a) 5367 rpm (b) 6000 rpm
(c) 9360 rpm (d) 12,000 rpm

73. A shaft has an attached disc at the centre of its length. The disc has its centre of gravity located at a distance of 2 mm from the axis of the shaft. When the shaft is allowed to vibrate in its natural bow-shaded mode, it has a frequency of vibration of 10 radians second. When the shaft is rotated a 300 revolutions per minute, it will whirl with a radius of:
(a) 2 mm (b) 225 mm
(c) 2.50 mm (d) 3.00 mm

74. A uniform cantilever beam undergoes transverse vibrations. The number of natural frequencies associated with the beam is:
(a) 1 (b) 10
(c) 100 (d) infinite

75. Coulomb damping results from which one of the following?
(a) Dry friction between moving parts
(b) Drag between a moving body and the fluid environment
(c) Internal friction within a material
(d) Radiation of energy into the environment107.

76. Consider the following statements:
1. When frequency ratio is $< 2$, the force transmitted to the foundation is more than the exciting force.
2. When frequency ratio is $> 2$, the force transmitted to the foundation increases and the damping is decreased.
3. The analysis of base excited vibrations is similar to that of forced vibrations.

Which of these statements are correct?
(a) 1 and 2
(b) 2 and 5
(c) 1 and 3
(d) 1, 2 and 3

77. Consider the following statements:
1. Critical or whirling speed of the shaft is the speed at which it tends to vibrate violently in the transverse direction.
2. To find the natural frequency of a shaft carrying several loads, the energy method gives approximate results.
3. Dunkerley's method gives accurate results of the natural frequency of a shaft carrying several loads.

Which of these statements is/are correct?
(a) 1 only
(b) 2 and 3
(c) 1 and 3
(d) 1, 2 and 3

78. For a single degree of freedom damped system, transmissibility is less than 1 if frequency ratio is:
(a) Equal to 1 (b) $< 1$
(c) $< \sqrt{2}$ (d) $> \sqrt{2}$

79. For a harmonically excited single degree of freedom viscous damped system, which one of the following is correct?
(a) Inertia force leads damping force by 90° while damping force leads spring force by 90°.
(b) Spring force leads damping force by 90° while damping force leads inertia force by 180°.
(c) Spring force and damping force are in phase, and inertia force leads them by 90°
(d) Spring force and inertia force are in phase, and damping force leads them by 90°.

80. In a viscously damped vibratory system with harmonic excitation, if $\omega_1$ and $\omega_2$ are the half power points, $\omega_n$ is the natural frequency and $\zeta$ is the damping factor, which one of the following is correct?
(a) $\frac{\omega_2 - \omega_1}{\omega_n}$ (b) $\frac{\omega_2 + \omega_1}{\omega_n} = \zeta$
(c) $\frac{\omega_2 - \omega_1}{\omega_n} = \zeta^2$ (d) $\frac{\omega_2 - \omega_1}{\omega_n} = \zeta$

81. Match List-I with List-II regarding a body party submerged in a liquid and select the correct answer using the codes given below the lists:

| List-I | List-II |
|---|---|
| A. Centre of pressure | 1. Point of application of the weight of displaced liquid |
| B. Centre of gravity | 2. Point about which the body starts oscillating when tilted by a small angle |
| C. Centre of buoyancy | 3. Point of application of hydrostatic pressure |
| D. Metacentre | 4. Point of application of the weight of the body |

**Codes:**

| | A | B | C | D |
|---|---|---|---|---|
| (a) | 4 | 3 | 1 | 2 |
| (b) | 4 | 3 | 2 | 1 |
| (c) | 3 | 4 | 1 | 2 |
| (d) | 3 | 4 | 2 | 1 |

82. If a piece of metal having a specific gravity of 13.6 is placed in mercury of specific gravity 13.6, then:
(a) The metal piece will sink to the bottom
(b) The metal piece will simply float over the mercury with no immersion
(c) The metal piece will be immersed in mercury by half
(d) The whole of the metal piece will be immersed with its top surface just at mercury level

83. A bucket of water hangs with a spring balance. If an iron piece is suspended into water from another support without touching the sides of the bucket, the spring balance will show:
(a) An increased reading
(b) A decreased reading
(c) No change in reading
(d) Increased or decreased reading depending on the depth of immersion

84. The least radius of gyration of a ship is 9 m and the metacentric height is 750 mm. The time period of oscillation of the ship is:
(a) 42.41 s (b) 75.4 s
(c) 20.85 s (d) 85 s

85. If the surface tension of water-air interface is 0.073 N/m, the gauge pressure inside a rain drop of 1 mm diameter will be:
(a) 0.146 N/m$^2$
(b) 0.73 N/m$^2$
(c) 146 N/m$^2$
(d) 292 N/m$^2$

86. Newton's law of viscosity depends upon the:
(a) Stress and strain in a fluid
(b) Shear stress, pressure and velocity
(c) Shear stress and rate of strain
(d) Viscosity and shear stress

87. The critical speed of a uniform shaft with a rotor at the centre of the span can be reduced by:
(a) Reducing the shaft length
(b) Reducing the rotor mass
(c) Increasing the rotor mass
(d) Increasing the shaft diameter

88. Match List-I (Surfaces with Orientations) with List-II (Equivalent Emissivity) and select the correct answer using the codes given below the lists:

| List-I (Surfaces with Orientations) | List-II (Equivalent Emissivity) |
|---|---|
| A. Infinite parallel planes | 1. $\epsilon_1$ |
| B. Body 1 completely enclosed by body 2 but body 1 is very small | 2. $\dfrac{1}{\dfrac{1}{\epsilon_1}+\dfrac{1}{\epsilon_2}-1}$ |
| C. Radiation exchange between two small gray bodies | 3. $\dfrac{1}{\dfrac{1}{\epsilon_1}+\left(\dfrac{A_1}{A_2}\right)\left(\dfrac{1}{\epsilon_2}-1\right)}$ |
| D. Two concentric cylinders with large lengths | 4. $\epsilon_1 . \epsilon_2$ |

**Codes:**

| | A | B | C | D |
|---|---|---|---|---|
| (a) | 3 | 1 | 4 | 2 |
| (b) | 2 | 4 | 1 | 3 |
| (c) | 2 | 1 | 4 | 3 |
| (d) | 3 | 4 | 1 | 2 |

89. Two spheres A and B of same material have radii 1 m and 4 m and temperature 4000 K and 2000 K respectively. Which one of the following statements is correct?
The energy radiated by sphere A is:
(a) greater than that of sphere B
(b) less than that of sphere B
(c) equal to that of sphere B
(d) equal to double that of sphere B

90. For an opaque plane surface, the irradiation, radiosity and emissive power are respectively 20, 12 and 10 W/m$^2$. What is the emissivity of the surface?
(a) 0.2 (b) 0.4
(c) 0.8 (d) 1.0

91. Two long parallel surfaces, each of emissivity 0.7, are maintained at different temperatures and accordingly have radiation exchange between them. It is desired to reduce 75% of this radiant heat transfer by inserting thin parallel shields of equal emissivity (0.7) on both sides. What would be the number of shields?
(a) 1 (b) 2
(c) 3 (d) 4

92. The earth receives at its surface radiation from the sun at the rate of 1400 W/m$^2$. The distance of centre of sun from the surface of earth is $1.5 \times 10^{11}$m and the radius of sun is $7.0 \times 10^8$ M. What is approximately the surface temperature of the sun treating the sun as a black body?
(a) 3650 K (b) 4500 K
(c) 5800 K (d) 6150 K

93. A composite plane wall is made up of two different materials of the same thickness and having thermal conductivities of $k_1$ and $k_2$ respectively. The equivalent thermal conductivity of the slab is:
(a) $k_1 + k_2$ (b) $k_1 k_2$
(c) $\frac{k_1 + k_2}{k_1 k_2}$ (d) $\frac{2k_1 k_2}{k_1 + k_2}$

94. A copper wire of radius 0.5 mm is insulated with a sheathing of thickness 1 mm having a thermo-conductivity of 05 W/m.K. The outside surface convective heat transfer coefficient is 10 W/m.K. If the thickness of insulation sheathing is raised by 10 mm, then the electrical current carrying capacity of the wire will:
(a) increase
(b) decrease
(c) remain the same
(d) vary depending upon the electric conductivity of the wire.

95. For the fully developed laminar flow and the transfer in a uniformly heated long circular tube, if the velocity is doubled and the tube diameter is halved, the heat transfer coefficient will be:
(a) double of the original value
(b) half of the original value
(c) same as before
(d) four times of the original value.]

96. For an air conditioning plant above 300 ton, which one of the following system would normally he preferred?
(a) Ammonia reciprocating compressor
(b) Centrifugal Chiller
(c) Absorption refrigeration system
(d) Hermetic compressor

97. Fresh air intake (air change per hour) recommended for ventilation purposes in the air conditioning system of an office building is:
(a) 1/2 (b) 3/2
(c) 9/2 (d) 25/2

98. Air refrigeration cycle is used in:
(a) Commercial refrigerators
(b) Domestic refrigerators
(c) Gas liquefaction
(d) Air-conditioning

99. The flash chamber in a single stage simple vapour compression cycle:
(a) Increase the refrigerating effect
(b) Decreases the refrigerating effect
(c) Increases the work of compression
(d) Has no effect on refrigerating effect

100. Consider the following statements:
In a vapour compression system, a thermometer placed in the liquid line can indicate whether the:
1. Refrigerant flow is too low
2. Water circulation is adequate.
3. Condenser is fouled.
4. Pump is functioning properly.
Of these statement:
(a) 1, 2 and 3 are correct (b) 1, 2 and 4 are correct
(c) 1, 3 and 4 are correct (d) 2, 3 and 4 are correct

101. Match List-I with List-II and select the correct answer using the codes given below the Lists.

| List-I | List-II |
|---|---|
| A. Bell Column refrigeration | 1. Compressor |
| B. Vapour compression refrigeration | 2. Generator |
| C. Absorption refrigeration | 3. Flash chamber |
| D. Jet refrigeration | 4. Expansion cylinder |

**Codes:**

| | A | B | C | D |
|---|---|---|---|---|
| (a) | 1 | 4 | 3 | 2 |
| (b) | 4 | 1 | 3 | 2 |
| (c) | 1 | 4 | 2 | 3 |
| (d) | 4 | 1 | 2 | 3 |

102. The maximum COP for the absorption cycle is given by ($T_c$ = generator temperature $T_c$ = environment temperature, $T_E$ = refrigerated space temperature)
(a) $\frac{T_E(T_G - T_C)}{T_G(T_C - T_E)}$ (b) $\frac{T_G(T_C - T_E)}{T_E(T_G - T_C)}$
(c) $\frac{T_C(T_G - T_E)}{T_G(T_C - T_E)}$ (d) $\frac{T_G(T_C - T_E)}{T_C(T_G - T_E)}$

103. In milk chilling plants, the usual secondary refrigerant is:
(a) Ammonia solution (b) Sodium Silicate
(c) Glycol (d) Brine

104. The desirable combination of properties of a refrigerant include :
(a) High specific heat and low specific volume
(b) High heat transfer coefficient and low latent heat
(c) High thermal conductivity and low freezing point
(d) High specific heat and high boiling point.

105. Which of the following method(s) is/are adopted in the design of air duct system
1. Velocity reduction method
2. Equal friction method
3. Static regain method.

Select the correct answer using the codes given below:

**Codes:**

(a) 1 alone (b) 1 and 2
(c) 2 and 3 (d) 1, 2 and 3

106. To fix the stale point in respect of air-vapour mixtures, three intrinsic properties are needed. Yet, the psychrometric chart requires only two because:
(a) Water vapour is in the superheated state
(b) The chart is for a given pressure
(c) The chart is an approximation to true values
(d) The mixtures can be treated as a perfect gas

107. During sensible cooling of air :
(a) Its wet bulb temperature increases and dew point remains constant
(b) Its wet bulb temperature decreases and the dew point remains constant
(c) Its wet bulb temperature increases and the dew point decreases
(d) It wet bulb temperature decreases and dew point increases.

108. The expression $\dfrac{0.622\,p_v}{p_r - p_v}$ is used todetermine:
(a) Relative humidity (b) Specific humidity
(c) Degree of saturation (d) Partial pressure

109. The effective temperature is a measure of the combined effects of:
(a) Dry bulb temperature and relative humidity
(b) Dry bulb temperature and air motion
(c) Wet bulb temperature and air motion
(d) Dry bulb temperature, relative humidity and air motion.

110. In air-conditioning design for summer months, the condition inside a factory where heavy work in performed as compared to a factory in which light work is performed should have:
(a) Lower dry bulb temperature and lower relative humidity
(b) Lower dry bulb temperature and higher relative humidity
(c) Lower dry bulb temperature and same relative humidity
(d) Same dry bulb temperature and same relative humidity.

111. For low by pass factor a cooling coil, the fin spacing and the number of tube rows will be respectively:
(a) High and high (b) High and low
(c) Low and high (d) Low and low

112. In vapour compression plant, if certain temperature differences are to be maintained in the evaporator and condenser in order to obtain the necessary heat transfer, then the evaporator saturation temperature must be:
(a) Higher than the derived cold-region temperature and the condenser saturation temperature must be lower than the available cooling water temperature by sufficient amounts
(b) Low than the derived cold-region temperature and the condenser saturation temperature must be lower than the available cooling water temperature by sufficient amounts
(c) Lower than the derived cold-region temperature and the condenser saturation temperature must be higher than the available cooling water temperature by sufficient amounts
(d) Higher than the derived cold-region temperature and the condenser saturation temperature must he higher than the available cooling water temperature by sufficient amounts.

113. One ton refrigeration is equivalent to:
(a) 3.5 kW
(b) 50 kJ/s
(c) 1000 J/min
(d) 1000 kJ/min

114. The correct sequence of the given components of a vapour compression refrigerator is:
(a) Evaporator, compressor, condenser and throttle valve
(b) Condenser, throttle valve, evaporator and compressor
(c) Compressor, condenser, throttle valve and evaporator
(d) Throttle valve, evaporator, compressor and condenser

115. The coefficient of performance of a refrigerator working on a reversed Carnot cycle is 4 the ratio of the highest absolute temperature to the lowest absolute temperature is:
(a) 1.2 (b) 1.25
(c) 3.33 (d) 4

116. When a burnt out hermetic compressor is replaced by a new one it is desirable to include in the system a large drier-cum-strainer also. This is to be placed in:
(a) Liquid line
(b) Suction line
(c) Hot gas line
(d) Discharge line

117. A good refrigerant should have:
(a) Large latent heat of vaporization and low operating pressures
(b) Small latent heat of vaporization and high operating pressures
(c) Large latent heat of vaporization and large operating pressures
(d) Small latent heat of vaporization and low operating pressures

118. The most common type of absorption system in use in industrial applications is based on the refrigerant-absorbent combination of:
(a) Air-Water
(b) Lithium bromide-air
(c) Carbon dioxide-Water
(d) Ammonia-Water

119. Solar energy be directly used in:
   (a) Vapour compression refrigeration system
   (b) Vapour absorption refrigeration system
   (c) Air refrigeration system
   (d) Jet refrigeration system

120. The equation $\phi = \frac{p_v}{ps}$ is used to calculate the($p_v$= partial pressure of water vapour in moist air at a given temperature $p_s$ = saturation pressure of water vapour at the same temperature)
   (a) Relative humidity
   (b) Degree of saturation
   (c) Specific humidity
   (d) Absolute humidity

## ANSWERS WITH EXPLANATIONS

1. (c) $\omega_n = \sqrt{\frac{k}{m}} = \sqrt{\frac{0.7\times10^3}{1}} = 26.46$ rad/s

$$c_c = 2\text{m}\,\omega_n = 2\times1\times26.46 = 52.92 \text{ Ns/m}$$

2. (c) Equivalent length,

$$l_e = l_1 + l_2\left(\frac{d_1}{d_2}\right)^4 + l_3\left(\frac{d_1}{d_3}\right)^4$$

3. (c) $f_n = \frac{1}{2\pi}\sqrt{36\pi^2} = 3\text{Hz}$

4. (b) 5. (b)

6. (c) $\omega_n = \omega_c = \sqrt{\frac{k}{m}}$

Critical speed is not a function of eccentricity. Hence critical speed does not change.

7. (b) 8. (c) 9. (b) 10. (a)

11. (b) 12. (c) 13. (c)

14. (a) $\omega_{n1} = \sqrt{\frac{k}{m}}, \omega n_2 = \sqrt{\frac{k}{2}\times\frac{1}{2m}} = \frac{1}{2}\sqrt{\frac{k}{m}} = \frac{1}{2}\omega_{n1} = \frac{\text{N}}{2}$

15. (d) 16. (a) 17. (b)

18. (d) Unbalanced force, $\text{F} = me\omega^2$

$$\omega = \frac{2\pi\text{N}}{60}$$

$$\therefore \quad \text{F} \propto \text{mN}^2$$

$$\frac{\text{F}_1}{\text{F}_2} = \frac{m_1\text{N}_1^2}{m_1\text{N}_2^2} = \frac{m}{\left(\frac{m}{2}\right)}\times\left(\frac{3000}{300}\right) = 2\times100 = 200$$

19. (c) $\omega_n = \sqrt{\frac{k}{\text{M}}} = \sqrt{\frac{85\times10^3}{100}} = 29.15$ rad/s

$$\omega = 20\pi \text{ rad/s}$$

$$\beta = \frac{\omega}{\omega_n} = \frac{20\pi}{29.15} = 2.155$$

$$\mu = \frac{20}{100} = 0.2$$

$$\text{X} = \frac{\mu e\beta^2}{\beta^2 - 1} = \frac{0.2\times0.5\times(2.155)^2\times10^{-3}}{(2.155)^2 - 1}$$

$$= 1.274\times10^{-4}\text{m}$$

20. (b) 21. (b) 22. (c) 23. (d) 24. (a)

25. (c)

26. (c) $k = k = \frac{48\text{EI}}{l^3}$

$$\omega_n = \sqrt{\frac{k}{m}} = \sqrt{\frac{48\text{EI}}{ml^3}}$$

27. (b) $\text{X} = \frac{x_{st}}{\sqrt{(1-\beta^2)+(2\zeta\beta)^2}}$

For $\beta = 1, \text{X} = \frac{x_{st}}{2\zeta} \propto \frac{1}{\zeta}$

28. (b) 29. (a) 30. (d)

31. (b) $k = \frac{3\text{EI}}{\text{L}^3}$

$$\omega_n = \sqrt{\frac{k}{m}} = \sqrt{\frac{3\text{EI}}{m\text{L}^3}} = \sqrt{\frac{3\text{EIg}}{\text{WL}^3}} \propto \sqrt{\frac{1}{\text{W}}}$$

$$\frac{\omega_{n2}}{\omega_{n1}} = \sqrt{\frac{\text{W}_1}{\text{W}_2}} = \sqrt{2}$$

32. (b) 33. (d)

34. (b) $\frac{y}{e} = \frac{\beta^2}{1-\beta^2} = \frac{1}{\left(\frac{\omega_c}{\omega}\right)^2 - 1}$

35. (a) $\beta = \frac{\omega}{\omega_n}, \omega_n = \sqrt{\frac{k}{m}}, \omega = \frac{v}{\lambda}$

where $v$ = vehicle speed,

$\lambda$ = wave length of rod undulations

$$\therefore \quad \beta = f(m, k, v, \lambda)$$

36. (d)

37. (d) The equation of motion is (figure)

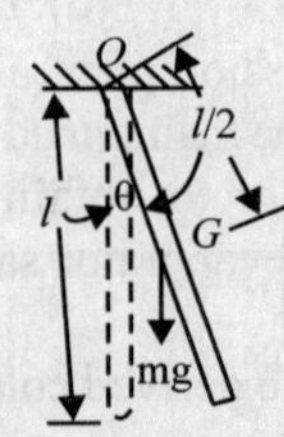


$$\frac{ml^2}{3}\ddot{\theta}\left(\frac{mgl}{2}\right)\theta = 0$$

$$\ddot{\theta}+\frac{3}{2}\frac{g}{l}\theta=0$$

$$f_n=\frac{1}{2\pi}\sqrt{\frac{3g}{2l}}$$

38. (c) $l_2=\left(\frac{J_1}{J_1+J_2}\right)l=\frac{100\times10}{(100+10)}=100$ cm

39. (a) $r=\frac{e\beta^2}{1-\beta^2}=\frac{190\times(0.9)^2}{1-(0.9)^2}=810$ microns

40. (b) 41. (a)

42. (a) $\omega_d=\omega_n\sqrt{1-\zeta^2}=100\sqrt{1-(0.8)^2}$

$= 60$ rad/s

43. (b) $T_1=2\pi\sqrt{\frac{m}{k}}=2$

$$T_2=2\pi\sqrt{\frac{m+2}{k}}=3$$

$$\frac{2}{3}=\sqrt{\frac{m}{m+2}}$$

$m = 1.6$ kg

44. (b) 45. (c) 46. (a)

47. (d) $k_1=\frac{1000}{10}=100$ N/mm

$$k\propto\frac{1}{n}$$

$k_2 = 100\times2 = 200$ N/mm

$k_e = 2\times200 = 400$ N/mm

$\delta=\frac{1000}{400}=2.5$ mm

48. (b) $d = 30$ mm, $l = 500$ mm, $m = 10$ kg,

$E = 2.1\times10^{11}$ Pa

$$k=\frac{48EI}{l^3}=\frac{48\times2.1\times10^{11}\times\pi(30\times10^{-3})^4}{64\times(0.5)^3}$$

$= 3206309$ N/m

$$f_c=\frac{1}{2\pi}\sqrt{\frac{k}{m}}=\frac{1}{2\pi}\sqrt{\frac{3206309}{10}}=90 \text{ Hz}$$

49. (c) $TR=\frac{1}{1-\beta^2}=\frac{1}{1-(0.6)^2}=\frac{4}{3}$

50. (a) 51. (b)

52. (a) $I_a=\left(\frac{I_b}{I_a+I_b}\right)L$

53. (b) $TR>1$ or $\beta<\sqrt{2}$

54. (b) 55. (c) 56. (c) 57. (c) 56. (b)

59. (b) 60. (d) 61. (c)

62. (a) $\frac{1}{\omega_n^2}=\frac{1}{\omega_1^2}+\frac{1}{\omega_2^2}$

$$=\frac{1}{100^2}+\frac{1}{200^2}=\frac{1.25}{10^4}$$

$\omega_n = 89.433$ Hz or 5367 rpm

63. (d) 64. (a)

65. (a) $\omega_d=\omega_n\sqrt{1-\zeta^2}$

$$20=40\sqrt{1-\zeta^2}$$

$$1-\zeta^2=\frac{1}{4}$$

$$\zeta^2=\frac{3}{4},\zeta=\frac{\sqrt{3}}{2}$$

66. (b)

67. (b) $\frac{n_2}{n_1}=G$

$$I_2' = G^2I_2$$

68. (a) $AC=\left(\frac{I_B}{I_A+I_B}\right)l=\left(\frac{I_B}{4I_B+I_B}\right)l$

$$=\frac{l}{5}=\frac{1}{5}\text{ m}$$

69. (a) 70. (b) 71. (b)

72. (a) $\frac{1}{f_n^2}=\frac{1}{f_1^2}+\frac{1}{f_2^2}$

$$\frac{1}{100^2}+\frac{1}{200^2}=\frac{5}{200^2}$$

$$f_n^2=\frac{200^2}{5}, f_n=5367 \text{ rpm}$$

73. (b) $\omega=\frac{2\pi\times300}{600}=10\pi$ rad/s

$$\beta=\frac{\omega}{\omega_n}\frac{10\pi}{10}=\pi$$

$$r=\frac{e\beta^2}{\beta^2-1}=\frac{2\times\pi^2}{\pi^2-1}=225 \text{ mm}$$

74. (d) 75. (a) 76. (a) 77. (a) 78. (d)

79. (c) 80. (a) 81. (c) 82. (d)

83. (c) Buoyant force of equal amount will act on the iron piece and thus spring balance reading will not change.

84. (c) The period of oscillation,

$$T=2\pi\left[\frac{(\text{Radius of gyration})^2}{\text{metacentric height}\times g}\right]^{1/2}$$

$$=2\pi\left[\frac{9^2}{0.75\times0.81}\right]^{1/2}=20.85\text{ s}$$

85. (d) $p = \frac{4\sigma}{d} = \frac{4 \times 0.073}{1 \times 10^{-3}}$

$= 292 \text{ N/m}^2$

86. (c) 87. (c) 88. (c)

89. (c) $\frac{E_A}{E_B} = \left(\frac{A_A}{A_B}\right)\left(\frac{T_A}{T_B}\right)^4$

$= \left(\frac{A_A}{r_B}\right)^2 \left(\frac{T_A}{T_B}\right)^4$

$= \left(\frac{1}{4}\right)^2 \left(\frac{4000}{2000}\right)^4 = 1$

90. (c) Radiosity, $J = \varepsilon E_b + (1-\varepsilon)G$

where G = Irradiation $= 20 \text{ W/m}^2$

$E_b$ = emissive power $= 10 \text{ W/m}^2$

$I = 12 \text{ W/m}^2$

$12 = \varepsilon \times 10 + (1-\varepsilon) \times 20$

$\varepsilon = 0.8$

91. (b) Heat transfer with shields $= \left(\frac{1}{n+1}\right) \times$ Heat transfer without shields

Where $n$ = number of shields

$\frac{1}{n+1} = \frac{1}{4}$

or $n = 3$

92. (c) Temperature of the Sun,

$T_s = \left[\frac{L^2 G_s}{r^2 \sigma}\right]^{1/4}$

where L = mean distance between the Sun and the Earth

$= 1.5 \times 10^{11} \text{ m}$

$r$ = radius of the Sun $= 7 \times 10^8 \text{ m}$

$G_s$ = rate of radiation from the Sun

$= 1400 \text{ W/m}^2$

$\sigma$ = Stefan-Boltzmann constan

$= 5.675 \times 10^{-8} \text{ W/(m}^2\text{.K)}$

$T_s = \left[\frac{(1.5 \times 10^{11})^2 \times 1400}{(7 \times 10^8)^2 \times 5.675 \times 10^{-8}}\right]^{1/4}$

$= 5800 \text{ K}$

$= 900 \text{w/m}_2$

93. (d) 94. (c) 95. (c) 96. (a) 97. (c)
98. (a) 99. (d) 100. (d) 101. (d) 102. (a)
103. (c) 104. (c) 105. (d) 106. (b) 107. (b)
108. (b) 109. (d) 110. (d) 111. (c) 112. (c)
113. (a) 114. (c)

115. (b) $\text{COP} = \frac{T_2}{T_1 - T_2}$

$= \frac{1}{\frac{T_1}{T_2} - 1} = 4$

$4\frac{T_1}{T_2} - 4 = 1$

$\frac{T_1}{T_2} = \frac{5}{4} = 1.25$

116. (d) 117. (a) 118. (d) 119. (b) 120. (a)

❑❑❑

# 13. Materials Science

- Materials science is an interdisciplinary field which deals with the discovery and design of new materials. Though it is a relatively new scientific field that involves studying materials through the materials paradigm its intellectual origins reach back to the emerging fields of chemistry, mineralogy and engineering during the Enlightenment.
- It incorporates elements of physics and chemistry, and is at the forefront of Nano science and nanotechnology research. In recent years, materials science has become more widely known as a specific field of science and engineering.
- It is an important part of forensic engineering (the investigation of materials, products, structures or components that fail or do not operate or function as intended, causing personal injury or damage to property) and failure analysis, the latter being the key to understanding, for example, the cause of various aviation accidents.
- Many of the most pressing scientific problems that are faced today are due to the limitations of the materials that are available and, as a result, breakthroughs in this field are likely to have a significant impact on the future of technology.
- The material of choice of a given era is often a defining point. Phrases such as Stone Age, Bronze Age, Iron Age, and Steel Age are great examples.
- Originally deriving from the manufacture of ceramics and its putative derivative metallurgy, materials science is one of the oldest forms of engineering and applied science.
- Modern materials science evolved directly from metallurgy, which itself evolved from mining and (likely) ceramics and the use of fire. A major breakthrough in the understanding of materials occurred in the late 19th century, when the American scientist Josiah Willard Gibbs demonstrated that the thermodynamic properties related to atomic structure in various phases are related to the physical properties of a material.
- Important elements of modern materials science are a product of the space race: the understanding and engineering of the metallic alloys, and silica and carbon materials, used in the construction of space vehicles enabling the exploration of space.
- Materials science has driven, and been driven by, the development of revolutionary technologies such as plastics, semiconductors, and biomaterials.
- A material is defined as a substance (most often a solid, but other condensed phases can be included) that is intended to be used for certain applications. There are a myriad of materials around us—they can be found in anything from buildings to spacecraft. Materials can generally be divided into two classes: crystalline and non-crystalline.
- The traditional examples of materials are metals, ceramics and polymers.[3] New and advanced materials that are being developed include semiconductors, nanomaterial's, biomaterials, etc.
- The basis of materials science involves studying the structure of materials, and relating them to their properties. Once a materials scientist knows about this structure-property correlation, he/she can then go on to study the relative performance of a material in a certain application.
- The major determinants of the structure of a material and thus of its properties are its constituent chemical elements and the way in which it has been processed into its final form. These characteristics, taken together and related through the laws of thermodynamics and kinetics, govern a material's microstructure, and thus its properties.
- Materials science examines the structure of materials from the atomic scale, all the way up to the macro scale. Characterization is the way materials scientists examine the structure of a material.
- This involves techniques such as diffraction with x-rays, electrons, or neutrons, and various forms of spectroscopy and chemical analysis such as Raman spectroscopy, energy-dispersive spectroscopy (EDS), chromatography, thermal analysis, electron microscope analysis, etc
- Nanostructure deals with objects and structures that are in the 1—100 nm range. In many materials, atoms or molecules agglomerate together to form objects at the Nano scale. This leads to many interesting electrical, magnetic, optical and mechanical properties.
- In describing nanostructures it is necessary to differentiate between the number of dimensions on the Nano scale. Nano textured have one dimension on the Nano scale, i.e., only the thickness of the surface of an object is between 0.1 and 100 nm.
- Nanotubes have two dimensions on the Nano scale, i.e., the diameter of the tube is between 0.1 and 100 nm; its length could be much greater. Finally, spherical nanoparticles have three dimensions on the nano scale, i.e., the particle is between 0.1 and 100 nm in each spatial dimension.

- The terms nanoparticles and ultrafine particles (UFP) often are used synonymously although UFP can reach into the micrometer range. The term 'nanostructure' is often used when referring to magnetic technology. Nano scale structure in biology is often called ultrastructure.
- Materials whose atoms/molecules form constituents in the Nano scale (i.e., they form nanostructure) are called nanomaterial's. Nanomaterial's are subject of intense research in the materials science community due to the unique properties that they exhibit.
- Microstructure is defined as the structure of a prepared surface or thin foil of material as revealed by a microscope above 25× magnification. It deals with objects in from 100 nm to few cm.
- The microstructure of a material (which can be broadly classified into metallic, polymeric, ceramic and composite) can strongly influence physical properties such as strength, toughness, ductility, hardness, corrosion resistance, high/low temperature behavior, wear resistance, and so on. Most of the traditional materials (such as metals and ceramics) are micro-structured.
- The manufacture of a perfect crystal of a material is physically impossible. The microstructure of materials reveals these defects, so that they can be studied.
- Macrostructure is the appearance of a material in the scale millimeters to meters—it is the structure of the material as seen with the naked eye.
- Crystallography is the science that examines the arrangement of atoms in crystalline solids. Crystallography is a useful tool for materials scientists. In single crystals, the effects of the crystalline arrangement of atoms is often easy to see macroscopically, because the natural shapes of crystals reflect the atomic structure.
- In addition, physical properties are often controlled by crystalline defects. The understanding of crystal structures is an important prerequisite for understanding crystallographic defects.
- Mostly, materials do not occur as a single crystal, but in poly-crystalline form . Because of this, the powder diffraction method, which uses diffraction patterns of polycrystalline samples with a large number of crystals, plays an important role in structural determination.
- Most materials have a crystalline structure. But, there are some important materials that do not exhibit regular crystal structure. Polymers display varying degrees of crystallinity, and many are completely non-crystalline.
- Glass as, some ceramics, and many natural materials are amorphous, not possessing any long-range order in their atomic arrangements. The study of polymers combines elements of chemical and statistical thermodynamics to give thermodynamic, as well as mechanical, descriptions of physical properties.
- To obtain a full understanding of the material structure and how it relates to its properties, the materials scientist must study how the different atoms, ions and molecules are arranged and bonded to each other.
- This involves the study and use of quantum chemistry or quantum physics. Solid-state physics, solid state chemistry and physical chemistry are also involved in the study of bonding and structure.
- Synthesis and processing involves the creation of a material with the desired micro/nanostructure. From an engineering standpoint, a material cannot be used in industry if no economical manufacturing method for it has been developed. Thus, the processing of materials is very important to the field of materials science.
- Different materials require different processing/ synthesis techniques. For example, the processing of metals has historically been very important and is studied under the branch of materials science known as physical metallurgy.
- Currently, new techniques are being developed to synthesize nanomaterials such as graphene.
- When a part is subjected to a cyclic stress, also known as stress range (Sr), it has been observed that the failure of the part occurs after a number of stress reversals (N) even if the magnitude of the stress range is below the material's yield strength.
- Generally, higher the range stress, the fewer the number of reversals needed for failure.
- There are four important failure theories: maximum shear stress theory, maximum normal stress theory, maximum strain energy theory, and maximum distortion energy theory.
- Out of these four theories of failure, the maximum normal stress theory is only applicable for brittle materials, and the remaining three theories are applicable for ductile materials.
- Of the latter three, the distortion energy theory provides most accurate results in majority of the stress conditions. The strain energy theory needs the value of Poisson's ratio of the part material, which is often not readily available.

# MULTIPLE CHOICE QUESTIONS

1. Which of the following metal shrinks most from molten state to solid state?
(a) cast iron (b) cast steel
(c) brass (d) admiralty metal

2. Which of the following generally decreases in the steel after quench-hardening
1. Brittleness
2. Percentage elongation
3. Impact strength
(a) 1 and 2 only (b) 2 and 3 only
(c) 1 and 3 only (d) 1, 2 and 3

3. Match List-I (Ingredients) with List-II (Welding functions) and select the correct answer using the codes given below the lists:

| **List-I (Ingredients)** | **List-II (Welding function)** |
|---|---|
| A. Silica | 1. Arc stabilizer |
| B. Potassium silicate | 2. De-oxidizer |
| C. Ferro silicon | 3. Fluxing agent |
| D. Cellulose | 4. Gas forming material |

**Codes:**

| | A | B | C | D |
|---|---|---|---|---|
| (a) | 3 | 4 | 2 | 1 |
| (b) | 2 | 1 | 3 | 4 |
| (c) | 3 | 1 | 2 | 4 |
| (d) | 2 | 4 | 3 | 1 |

4. A carbon steel having Brinell Hardness number 100 should have ultimate tensile strength closer to:
(a) 100 N/mm$^2$ (b) 200 N/mm$^2$
(c) 350 N/mm$^2$ (d) 1000 N/mm$^2$

5. In case carburizing carbon is introduced to form a high carbon layer at the surface. The carbon is introduce in the form of:
(a) graphite flakes (b) pearlite
(c) cementite (d) free carbon

6. Match the following:

| **List-I (Alloying element in steel)** | **List-II (Effect)** |
|---|---|
| A. Lead | 1. Restricts grain growth |
| B. Aluminium | 2. Raises yield point |
| C. Copper | 3. Reduces strength to impact |
| D. Phosphorus | 4. Free machining |

**Codes:**

| | A | B | C | D |
|---|---|---|---|---|
| (a) | 1 | 2 | 3 | 4 |
| (b) | 2 | 3 | 4 | 1 |
| (c) | 3 | 4 | 1 | 2 |
| (d) | 4 | 1 | 2 | 3 |

7. Presence of hydrogen in steel causes:
(a) reduced neutron absorption cross-section
(b) improved weldability
(c) embrittlement
(d) corrosion resistance.

8. The main alloying elements in high speed steel in order of increasing proportion:
(a) Vanadium, Chromium, Tungesten
(b) Tungsten, Titanium, Vanadium
(c) Chromium, Titanium, Vanadium
(d) Tungsten, Chromium, Titanium

9. Dye penetrant method is generally used to locate:
(a) core defects (b) surface defects
(c) superficial defects (d) temporary defects.

10. Herbert cloudburst hardness test is conducted to know:
(a) uniformity of hardness over a surface
(b) softness of non-metallic components
(c) hardness of non-metallic components
(d) hardness at specified depth inside the surface

11. Which of the following statement is true about brittle fracture?
(a) High temperature and low strain rates favour brittle fracture
(b) Many metal with HCP crystal structure commonly show brittle fracture
(c) Brittle fracture is always preceded by noise
(d) Cup and cone formation is characteristic for brittle materials.

12. Which of the following is a point imperfection
1. Vacancy
2. Interstitially
3. Frenkel imperfection
4. Schottky imperfection
(a) 1 and 2 only (b) 2 and 3 only
(c) 2, 3 and 4 only (d) 1, 2, 3 and 4

13. Fillers are added to plastics to:
(a) improve flow
(b) reduce brittleness
(c) facilitate processibility
(d) reduce cost.

14. Quenching is not necessary when hardening is done by:
(a) case carburizing
(b) flame hardening
(c) nitriding
(d) any of the above processes.

15. Specify the sequence correctly:
(a) Grain growth, recrystallization, stress relief
(b) Stress relief, grain growth, recrystallization
(c) Stress relief, recrystallization grain growth
(d) Grain growth, stress relief, recrystallization

16. Small percentage of boron is added to steel to:
(a) increases hardenability
(b) reduce machinability
(c) increases wear resistance
(d) increase endurance strength.

17. Machine tool frame should have:
(a) high rigidity to weight ratio
(b) graphite in the form of nodules
(c) low hardness
(d) high work hardness.

18. Which of the following display properties similar to that of steel?
1. Black-heart cast iron
2. White-heart cast iron
3. Gray cast iron
4. Pig iron
(a) 1 and 2 only (b) 3 and 4 only
(c) 2 and 4 only (d) 1 and 3 only

19. For the pipe fitting like elbow, tee, union etc. which of the following is preferred?
(a) Pig iron
(b) Malleable iron
(c) Spheroidal graphite cast iron
(d) high carbon steel.

20. Addition of which of the following improves machining of copper?
(a) sulphur (b) vanadium
(c) tin (d) zinc

21. Temperature required for full annealing in hyper-eutectoid steel is:
(a) 50°C above upper critical temperature ($AC_3$)
(b) 50°C below upper critical temperature ($AC_3$)
(c) 50°C above lower critical temperature ($AC_1$)
(d) 50°C below lower critical temperature ($AC_1$)

22. Polyamides are characterized by:
(a) flexible chain
(b) rigid chain
(c) amorphous structure
(d) crystalline structure

23. Which of the following would you prefer for checking the hardness of thin sections?
(a) Hebert cloud burst test
(b) Shore's Seleroscope
(c) Knoop hardness test
(d) Vickers hardness test

24. The percentage of phosphorous in phosphor bronze is:
(a) 0.1 (b) 1
(c) 11.1 (d) 98

25. Invar is used or measuring tapes primarily due to its:
(a) non-magnetic properties
(b) high nickel content
(c) low coefficient of thermal expansion
(d) hardenability

26. Which of the following statement is incorrect about duralumin?
(a) it is prone to age hardening
(b) it can he forged
(c) it has good machining properties
(d) it is lighter than pure aluminium.

27. Carriage brass can be:
(a) cold rolled into sheets
(b) drawn into wires
(c) formed into tubes
(d) any of the above.

28. Induction hardening is basically a:
(a) carburising process
(b) surface hardening process
(c) core-hardening process
(d) none of the above.

29. The microstructure composition of pearlite for and $Fe_3C$ diagram consists of:
(a) carbon dissolved in alpha iron having a body-centered cubic structure
(b) carbon dissolved in gama iron having a face-centered cubic structure
(c) a mixture of body-centered alpha iron and face-entered gamma iron
(d) carbon dissolved in body-centered alpha iron and an $F_eFe_3C$.

30. Match List-I with List-II and select the correct answer using the codes given be lists:

| **List-I** **(Steel type)** | **List-II** **(Product)** |
|---|---|
| A. Mild steel | 1. Screw driver |
| B. Tool steel | 2. Commercial beams |
| C. Medium carbon steel | 3. Crane hooks |
| D. High carbon steel | 4. Blanking dies |

**Codes:**

| | **A** | **B** | **C** | **D** |
|---|---|---|---|---|
| (a) | 1 | 4 | 3 | 2 |
| (b) | 2 | 4 | 1 | 3 |
| (c) | 1 | 3 | 4 | 2 |
| (d) | 2 | 4 | 3 | 1 |

31. Which of the following statements are true of annealing of steels?
(1) Steels are heated to 500 to 700°C
(2) Cooling is done slowly and steadily
(3) Internal stresses are relieved
(4) Ductility of steel is reduced.
Select the correct answer using the codes given below:
(a) 2, 3 and 4 (b) 1, 3 and 4
(c) 1, 2 and 4 (d) 1, 2 and 3.

32. Duralumin alloy contains aluminium and copper in the ratio of :

| | **% Al** | **% Cu** |
|---|---|---|
| (a) | 94 | 4 |
| (b) | 90 | 8 |
| (c) | 88 | 10 |
| (d) | 86 | 12 |

33. Eutectic reaction for iron-carbon system occurs at:
(a) 600°C (b) 723°C
(c) 1147°C (d) 1493°C

34. The blade of a power saw is made of:
(a) boron steel (b) high speed steel
(c) stainless steel (d) malleable cast iron

35. Which of the following pairs arc correctly matched?
1. Cellulose nitrate.........Table tenis ball.
2. Phenol furfurol..........Brake linings.
3. Kpoxits .........Jigs and fixtures.
Select the correct answer using the codes given below:
**Codes:**
(a) 1 and 2 (b) 2 and 3
(c) 1 and 3 (d) 1, 2 and 3

36. Quartz is a:
(a) ferroelectric material
(b) ferromagnetic material
(c) piezoelectric material
(d) diamagnetic material.

37. Which of the following pairs are correctly matched?
1. Resilience.......... resistance to deformation
2. Malleability ........... shape change
3. Creep .......... progressive deformation
4. Plasticity ............. permanent deformation
Select the answer using codes given below:
**Codes:**
(a) 2, 3 and 4 (b) 1, 2 and 3
(c) 1, 2 and 4 (d) 1, 3 and 4

38. Consider the following treatments:
1. Normalizing 2. Hardening
3. Martempering 4. Cold working.
Hardness and tensile strength in austenitic stainless steel can be increased by:
(a) 1, 2 and 3 (b) 1 and 3
(c) 2 and 4 (d) 4 alone

39. Killed steels:
(a) have minimum impurity level
(b) have almost zero percentage of phosphorus and sulphur
(c) are produced by LD process
(d) are free from oxygen.

40. Which of following pairs are correctly matched?
1. Silicon steels ......... transformer stamping
2. Duralumin ......... cooking utensils
3. Gun metal .........bearings.
Select the correct answer using the codes given below:
**Codes:**
(a) 1, 2, and 3 (b) 1 and 2
(c) 1 and 3 (d) 2 and 3

41. Which of the following pairs of plastic and their modes of formation are correctly matched?
1. Polythene ............ condensation polymerization
2. Polycarbonate ........... addition polymerization
3. Polystyrene ............addition polymerization
4. Polyamide.........either by addition or by condensation polymerization.
Select the correct answer using the codes given below:
**Codes:**
(a) 1 and 2 (b) 2 and 4
(c) 1 and 4 (d) 3 and 4

42. Cubic boron nitride is used:
(a) as lining material in induction furnaces
(b) for making optical quality glass
(c) for heat treatments
(d) as/for none of the above

43. Match List-1 (materials) With List-II (applications) and select the correct answer using the codes given below the lists:

| **List-I** | **List-II** |
|---|---|
| A. Engineering ceramics | 1. Bearings |
| B. Fiber reinforced | 2. Control plastics rods in nuclear reactors |
| C. Synthetic carbon | 3. Aerospace industry |
| D. Boron | 4. Electrical insulator |

**Codes:**

| | A | B | C | D |
|---|---|---|---|---|
| (a) | 1 | 2 | 3 | 4 |
| (b) | 1 | 4 | 3 | 2 |
| (c) | 2 | 3 | 1 | 4 |
| (d) | 4 | 3 | 1 | 2 |

44. Which of the following pairs are correctly matched?
1. Lead.........screw nutphosphor bronze.
2. Piston.........cast iron.
3. Cam.........EN-31 steel.
4. Lead screw.........wrought iron.
Select the correct answer using the codes given below:
(a) 2, 3 and 4 (b) 1, 3 and 4
(c) 1, 2 and 4 (d) 1, 2 and 3

45. In low carbon steels, presence of small quantities sulphur improves:
(a) weldability (b) formability
(c) machinability (d) hardenability.

46. Consider the following statements: Addition of silicon to cast iron
1. promotes graphite module formation.
2. promotes graphite flake formation.
3. increases the fluidity of the molten metal.
4. improves the ductility of cast iron.
Of these statements:
(a) 1 and 4 are correct (b) 2 and 3 are correct
(c) 1 and 3 are correct (d) 3 and 4 are correct.

47. Match List-I with List-II and select the correct answer using the codes given below the lists:

| List-I (Heat treatment) | List-II (Effect on the properties) |
|---|---|
| A. Annealing | 1. Refined grain structure |
| B. Nitriding | 2. Improves the hardness of the whole mass |
| C. Martempering | 3. Increases surface hardness |
| D. Normalizing | 4. Improves ductility. |

**Codes:**

| | A | B | C | D |
|---|---|---|---|---|
| (a) | 4 | 3 | 2 | 1 |
| (b) | 1 | 3 | 4 | 2 |
| (c) | 4 | 2 | 1 | 3 |
| (d) | 2 | 1 | 3 | 4 |

48. Eutectoid reaction occurs at:
(a) 600°C (b) 723°C
(c) 114°C (d) 1493°C

49. Match List-I with List-II and select the correct answer using the codes give below the lists:

| List-I (Name of material) | List-II (% carbon range) |
|---|---|
| A. Hypo-eutectoid steel | 1. 4.3 – 5.67 |
| B. Hyper-eutectoid steel | 2. 2.0 – 4.3 |
| C. Hypo-eutectic cast iron | 3. 0.8 – 2.0 |
| D. Hyper-eutectic cast iron | 4. 0.008 – 0.8 |

**Codes:**

| | A | B | C | D |
|---|---|---|---|---|
| (a) | 4 | 3 | 2 | 1 |
| (b) | 1 | 3 | 2 | 4 |
| (c) | 4 | 1 | 2 | 3 |
| (d) | 1 | 2 | 3 | 4 |

50. Which one of the following sets of constituents is expected in equilibrium cooling of a hypereutectoid steel from austenitic state?
(a) Ferrite and pearlite
(b) Cementite and pearlite
(c) Ferrite and bainite
(d) Cementite and martensite.

51. Match List-I with List-II and select the correct answer using the codes given below the lists:

| List-I (Alloy) | List-II (Use) |
|---|---|
| A. Low carbon steel | 1. Bearing |
| B. Hadfield mangenese steel | 2. Thermocouple |
| | 3. Wire nails |
| C. Constantan | 4. Bulldozer blades |
| D. Babbit alloy | |

**Codes:**

| | A | B | C | D |
|---|---|---|---|---|
| (a) | 1 | 2 | 3 | 4 |
| (b) | 3 | 4 | 1 | 2 |
| (c) | 3 | 2 | 1 | 4 |
| (d) | 3 | 4 | 2 | 1 |

52. The structure of a polymer is shown in the given figure. This polymer finds special application in:

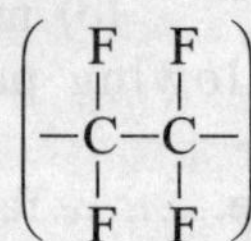


(a) packaging (b) adhesives
(c) bearings (d) fertilizer

53. Addition of magnesium to cast iron increases its:
(a) hardness
(b) ductility and strength in tension
(c) corrosion resistance
(d) creep strength.

54. Which one of the following materials will require the largest size of riser for the same casting?
(a) Aluminium (b) Cast iron
(c) Steel (d) Copper.

55. Consi der the following statements: When a metal or alloy is cold worked:
(a) It is worked below room temperature.
(b) It is worked below recrystallization temperature.
(c) Its hardness and strength increase.
(d) Its hardness increases but strength does not increase.

Of these statements:
(a) 1 and 4 are correct
(b) 1 and 3 are correct
(c) 2 and 3 are correct
(d) 2 and 4 are correct.

56. Which of the following pairs regarding the effect of alloying elements in steel are correctly matched?
1. Molybdenum: Forms abrasion resisting particles.
2. Phosphorus: Improves machinability in free cutting steels.
3. Cobalt: Contributes to red hardness by hardening ferrite.
4. Silicon: Reduces oxidation resistance.

Select the correct answer using the codes given below:
(a) 2, 3 and 4 (b) 1, 3 and 4
(c) 1, 2 and 4 (d) 1, 2 and 3.

57. Machine tool guideways are usually hardened by:
(a) vacuum hardening
(b) martempering
(c) induction hardening
(d) flame hardening.

58. 18/8 stainless steel contains:
(a) 18%, stainless, 8% chromium
(b) 18% chromium, 8% nickel
(c) 18% tungsten, 8% nickel
(d) 18% tungsten, 8% chromium

59. Tin base white metals are used were the bearings are subjected to:
(a) large surface wear
(b) elevated temperatures
(c) light load and pressure
(d) high pressure and load.

60. Alloy steel which is work hardenable and which is used to make the blades of bulldozers, bucket wheel excavators and other earth moving equipment contain iron, carbon and:
(a) chromium (b) silicon
(c) manganese (d) magnesium.

61. Consider the following statements:
Thermosetting plastics are
1. formed by addition polymerisation.
2. formed by condensation polymerisation.
3. softened on heating and hardened on cooling for any number of times.
4. moulded by heating and cooling.
Of these statements:
(a) 1 and 3 are correct (b) 2 and 4 are correct
(c) 1 and 4 are correct (d) 3 and 4 are correct.

62. Match List-I with List-II and select the correct answer

| **List-I** | **List-II (Nature of product)** |
|---|---|
| A. Polyethylene | 1. Adhesive |
| B. Polyurethane | 2. Film |
| C. Cyano-acrylate | 3. Wire |
| D. Nylon | 4. Foam |

**Codes:**

| | A | B | C | D |
|---|---|---|---|---|
| (a) | 2 | 4 | 3 | 1 |
| (b) | 4 | 2 | 3 | 1 |
| (c) | 2 | 4 | 1 | 3 |
| (d) | 4 | 2 | 1 | 3 |

63. Consider the following statements: Fibre reinforced plastics are
1. made of thermosetting resins and glass fibre.
2. made of thermoplastic resins and glass fibre.
3. anisotropic.
4. isotropic.
Of these statements:
(a) 1 and 4 are correct (b) 1 and 3 are correct
(c) 2 and 3 are correct (d) 2 and 4 are correct

64. The highest stress that a material can withstand for a specified length of time without excessive deformation is called:
(a) fatigue strength (b) endurance strength
(c) creep strength (d) creep rupture strength

65. Guideways of lathe beds are hardened by
(a) carburizing
(b) cyaniding
(c) nitriding
(d) flame hardening.

66. A given steel test specimen is studied under metallurgical microscope, magnification used is 100 X. In that different phases are observed. One of them is $Fe_3C$.
The observed phase $Fe_3C$ is also known as:
(a) ferrite (b) cementite
(c) austenite (d) martensite

67. Match List-I with List-II and select the correct answer using the codes given below the lists:

| **List-I** | **List-II** |
|---|---|
| A. Toughness | 1. Moment area method |
| B. Endurance strength | 2. Hardness |
| C. Resistance to abrasion | 3. Energy absorbed before fracture in a tension test |
| D. Deflection in beam | 4. Fatigue loading |

**Codes:**

| | A | B | C | D |
|---|---|---|---|---|
| (a) | 4 | 3 | 1 | 2 |
| (b) | 4 | 3 | 2 | 1 |
| (c) | 3 | 4 | 2 | 1 |
| (d) | 3 | 4 | 1 | 2 |

68. In metals subjected to cold working, strain hardening effect is due to:
(a) slip mechanism
(b) twining mechanism
(c) dislocation mechanism
(d) fracture mechanism.

69. Match List-I with List-II and select the correct answer using the codes are given below the lists:

| **List-I** | **List-II** |
|---|---|
| A. Neoprene | 1. Electric switches |
| B. Bakelite | 2. Adhesive |
| C. Foamed polyurethane | 3. Thermal insulator |
| D. Araldite | 4. Oil seal |

**Codes:**

| | A | B | C | D |
|---|---|---|---|---|
| (a) | 4 | 1 | 2 | 3 |
| (b) | 1 | 4 | 2 | 3 |
| (c) | 4 | 1 | 3 | 2 |
| (d) | 1 | 4 | 3 | 2 |

70. Which one of the following materials is used for car types as a standard material?
(a) Styrene-butadiene rubber (SBR)
(b) Butyl rubber
(c) Nitrile rubber
(d) Any one of the above depending upon the need

71. Which one of the following refractory materials is recommended for steel furnaces containing CaO stages?
(a) Alumina (b) Silica
(c) Magnesia (d) Fireclay

72. Which of the following properties of a solid are dependent on crystal imperfections?
1. Yield stress
2. Melting point
3. Semiconductivity
4. Ductility

Select the correct answer using the codes given below:
(a) 1 and 3
(b) 1, 3 and 4
(c) 2, 3 and 4
(d) 2 and 4

73. Match List-I (Alloying element in steel) with List-II (Property conferred or steel by the element) and select the correct answer using below the lists:

| List-I | List-II |
|---|---|
| A. Nickel | 1. Corrosion resistance |
| B. Chromium | 2. Magnetic permeability |
| C. Tungsten | 3. Heat resistance |
| D. Silicon | 4. Hardenabiliry |

**Codes:**

| | A | B | C | D |
|---|---|---|---|---|
| (a) | 4 | 1 | 3 | 2 |
| (b) | 4 | 1 | 2 | 3 |
| (c) | 1 | 4 | 3 | 2 |
| (d) | 1 | 4 | 2 | 3 |

74. In the basic EOQ model, if demand is 60 per month ordering cost is ₹12 per order holding cost is ₹ 1 per unit per month what is the EOQ?
(a) 12 (b) 144
(c) 24 (d) 28

75. Match List-I (Alloys) with List-II (Applications) and select the correct answer using the codes given below the lists :

| List-I | List-II |
|---|---|
| A. Chromal | 1. Journal bearing |
| B. Babbit alloy | 2. Milling cutter |
| C. Nimonic alloy | 3. Thermocouple wire |
| D. High speed steel | 4. Gas turbine blades |

**Codes:**

| | A | B | C | D |
|---|---|---|---|---|
| (a) | 3 | 1 | 4 | 2 |
| (b) | 3 | 4 | 1 | 2 |
| (c) | 2 | 4 | 1 | 3 |
| (d) | 2 | 1 | 4 | 3 |

76. Which one or the following is correct?
In the basis EOQ model, if lead time increases from 5 to 10 days, the EOQ will:
(a) double
(b) decrease by a factor of two
(c) remain the same
(d) the data is insufficient to find EOQ.

77. Match List-I with List-II and select the correct answer using the codes given below the lists:

| List-I (Material) | List-II (Structure) |
|---|---|
| A. Charcoal | 1. I. F.C.C. |
| B. Graphite | 2. H.C.P. |
| C. Chromium | 3. Amorphous |
| D. Copper | 4. B.CC. |

**Codes:**

| | A | B | C | D |
|---|---|---|---|---|
| (a) | 3 | 2 | 1 | 4 |
| (b) | 3 | 2 | 4 | 1 |
| (c) | 2 | 3 | 4 | 1 |
| (d) | 2 | 3 | 1 | 4 |

78. Consider the following statements: The strength of the fibre reinforced plastic product
1. Depends upon the strength of the fibre alone
2. Depends upon the fibre and plastic
3. Is isotropic
4. Is anisotropic.

Which of these statements are correct?
(a) 1 and 3 (b) 1 and 4
(c) 2 and 3 (d) 2 and 4

79. Match List-I (Crystal structure) with List-II (Atomic packing factor) and select the correct answer using the codes given below the lists:

| List-I | List-II |
|---|---|
| A. Simple cubic | 1. 94% |
| B. Body-centred cubic | 2. 74% |
| C. Face-centred cubic | 3. 52% |
| D. Hexagonal close packed | 4. 68% |

**Codes:**

| | A | B | C | D |
|---|---|---|---|---|
| (a) | 3 | 4 | 2 | 1 |
| (b) | 4 | 3 | 2 | 1 |
| (c) | 3 | 4 | 1 | 2 |
| (d) | 4 | 3 | 1 | 2 |

80. Consider the following pairs of plastics and their distinct characteristics:
1. Acrylics very good transparency to light.
2. Polycarbonate poor impact resistance.
3. PTEF low coefficient of friction.
5. Polypropylene excellent fatigue strength.

Which of these statements are correct?
(a) 2 and 3 (b) 1 and 3
(c) 1 and 4 (d) 2 and 4.

81. Gibb's phase rule is given by (F = number of degrees of freedom, C = number of components, P = number of phases):
(a) F = C + P (b) F=C+P – 2
(c) F=C – P – 2 (d) F=C – P + 2

82. Which of the following are the benefits of inventory control?
1. Improvement in customers relationship.

2. Economy in purchasing
3. Elimination of the possibility of duplicate ordering.

Select the correct answer using the code given below:

(a) 1, 2 and 3 (b) 1 and 2 only
(c) 2 and 3 only (d) 1 and 3 only

83. Match List-I with List-II and select the correct answer using the codes given below the lists:

| **List-I (Material)** | **List-II (Applications)** |
|---|---|
| A. Tungsten carbide | 1. Abrasive wheels |
| B. Silicon nitride | 2. Heating elements |
| C. Aluminium oxide | 3. Pipes for conveying liquid metals |
| D. Silicon carbide | 4. Drawing dies |

**Codes:**

| | A | B | C | D |
|---|---|---|---|---|
| (a) | 3 | 4 | 1 | 2 |
| (b) | 4 | 3 | 2 | 1 |
| (c) | 3 | 4 | 2 | 1 |
| (d) | 4 | 3 | 1 | 2 |

84. Heating the hypoeutectoid steels to 30°C above the upper critical temperature line, soaking at the temperature and then cooling slowly to room temperature to form a pearlite and ferrite structure, is known as:

(a) Hardening (b) Normalizing
(c) Tempering (d) Annealing

85. In a eutectic system, two elements are completely:

(a) insoluble in solid and liquid state
(b) soluble in liquid state
(c) soluble in solid state
(d) insoluble in liquid state.

86. Cast iron is used for machine beds because of its high:

(a) tensile strength (b) endurance strength
(c) damping capacity (d) compressive strength.

87. Cermets are:

(a) metals for high temperature use with ceramic like properties
(b) ceramics with metallic strength and luster
(c) coated tool materials
(d) metal-ceramic composites.

88. Percentages of various alloying elements present in different steel materials are given below:

1. % W ; 4% Cr ; 1% V ; 5% Co ; 0.7% C
2. 8%Mo; 4%Cr; 2%V; 6%W; 0.7%C
3. 27% Cr ; 3% Ni; 5% Mo ; 0.25% C
4. 18% Cr ; 8% Ni ; 0.15 C.

Which of these relate to that of high speed steel?

(a) 1 and 3 (b) 1 and 2
(c) 2 and 3 (d) 2 and 4

89. Pearlite consists of:

(a) 6.67% C and 93.33% ferrite
(b) 12% Fe and 87% cementite
(c) 13% C and 87% ferrite
(d) 13% cementite and 87% ferrite.

90. Addition of vanadium to steel results improvement of:

(a) heat-treatability by quenching
(b) hardenability
(c) fatigue strength
(d) resistance to oxidation at elevated temperature.

91. Atomic packing factor (APF) in the case of copper crystal is:

(a) 0.52 (b) 0.68
(c) 0.74 (d) 1.633

92. During packing solidification, one liquid:

(a) combines with one solid to form a second new solid
(b) solidifies into two different solids
(c) forms one solid
(d) forms one solid and another liquid.

93. Martensite is a super-saturated solution of carbon in:

(a) alpha iron (b) beta iron
(c) gamma iron (d) delta iron.

94. The correct sequence of creep deformation in a creep curve in order of their elongation is:

(a) steady state, transient, accelerated
(b) transient, steady state, accelerated
(c) transient, accelerated, steady state
(d) accelerated, steady state, transient

95. Nodular grey cast iron is obtained from the grey cast iron by adding a small amount of:

(a) Manganese (b) Phosphorus
(c) Magnesium (d) Chromium

96. Which one of the following pairs of axis lengths (a, b, c) and interaxial angles ($\alpha, \beta, \gamma$) represents the tetragonal crystal system?

(a) $a = b = c;\ \alpha = \beta = \gamma = 90°$
(b) $a = b \neq c;\ \alpha = \beta = \gamma = 90°$
(c) $a \neq b \neq c;\ \alpha = \beta = \gamma = 90°$
(d) $a = b = c;\ \alpha = \beta = \gamma \neq 90°$

97. Consider the following quenching media:

1. Oil 2. Water
2. Water + NaOH 4. Brine

The correct sequence of these media in order of increasing hardness of steel undergoing heat treatment is:

(a) 1, 3, 2, 4 (b) 2, 1, 3, 4
(c) 1, 2, 3, 4 (d) 4, 3, 2, 1

98. Which one of the following pairs is correctly matched?

(a) Solid solution strengthening – Increasing density of dislocations
(b) Dispersion hardening – Creating strained region in the crystal
(c) Strain-hardening – Creating particles to resist the movement of dislocations
(d) Precipitation-hardening – Creating particles by decreasing solubility of one phase in another

99. The alloy steel designated as 40 Cr 18 Ni 2 by Bureau of Indian Standards contains:
(a) 0.4% C, 18% Cr and 2% Ni
(b) 4.0% C, 1.8% Cr and 0.2% Ni
(c) 0.4% C, 1.8% Cr and 0.2% Ni
(d) 0.4% C, 1.8% Cr and 0.2 % Ni.

100. Tempering of quenched maritensitic steel is necessary to improve the:
(a) hardness of the metal
(b) surface texture of the metal
(c) corrosion resistance of the metal
(d) ductility of the metal.

101. The molecular weight of vinyl chloride is 62.5. Thus the molecular weight of a polyvinyl chloride with a degree of polymerisation of 20000 is:
(a) $\frac{20000}{62.5}$ (b) $\frac{62.5}{20000}$
(c) $62.5 \times 20000$ (d) 20000

102. Carbide-tipped cutting tools are manufactured by powder-metal technology processes and have a composition of:
(a) Zirconium-Tungsten (35%-65%)
(b) Tungsten carbide-cobalt (90%-10%)
(c) Aluminium oxide-silica (70%-30%)
(d) Nickel-chromium tungsten (30%-15%55%)

103. Match List-I (Name of the element) with List-II (Crystal structure) and select the correct answer using the codes given below the lists:

| List-I | List-II |
|---|---|
| A. Fluorspar | 1. Body-centered cubic |
| B. Alpha-iron | 2. Hexagonal close packed |
| C. Silver | 3. Simple cubic |
| D. Zinc | 4. Face-centered cubic |

**Codes:**

| | A | B | C | D |
|---|---|---|---|---|
| (a) | 3 | 2 | 4 | 1 |
| (b) | 4 | 1 | 3 | 2 |
| (c) | 4 | 2 | 3 | 1 |
| (d) | 3 | 1 | 4 | 2 |

104. Which of the following factors govern solubility of two non-ferrous metals both inliquid state as well as in solid state?
1. Crystal structure
2. Relative size factor
3. Chemical-affinity factor
4. Relative valence factor
Select the correct answer using the codes given below:
(a) 1, 2 and 3 (b) 2, 3 and 4
(c) I and 4 (d) 3 and 4

105. Which of the following are fabricated using engineering plastics?
(1) surface plate
(2) gears
(3) guide way for machine tools
(4) foundry patterns.
Select the correct answer using the codes given below:
**Codes:**
(a) 1, 2 and 3 (b) 1
(c) 2, 3 and 4 (d) 1, 2/3 and 4

106. Consider the following statements]
Polytetrafluorothene is
1. a thermoplastic material
2. having high friction coefficient
3. a thermosetting material
4. having low friction coefficient
5. an electric insulator
6. non sticking to surfaces.
Which of the above statements are correct?
(a) 1, 2 and 5 (b) 2, 3 and 6
(c) 3, 4 and 5 (d) 3, 2 and 5

107. Which of the following fibre materials are used for reinforcement in composite materials:
1. Glass
2. Boron carbide
3. Graphite
Select the correct answer using the codes given below:
**Codes:**
(a) 1 and 2 (b) 1 and 3
(c) 2 and 3 (d) 1, 2 and 3

108. Match List-I (material) with List-II (application) and select the correct answer using the codes given below the lists:

| List-I (Material) | List-II (Application) |
|---|---|
| A. Ceramics chemical | 1. Construction of plants |
| B. Refractories | 2. Columns and pillars |
| C. Stones | 3. Lining of furnaces |
| D. High silica glass | 4. Tiles |

**Codes:**

| | A | B | C | D |
|---|---|---|---|---|
| (a) | 4 | 3 | 2 | 1 |
| (b) | 2 | 1 | 4 | 3 |
| (c) | 4 | 1 | 2 | 3 |
| (d) | 2 | 3 | 4 | 1 |

109. A shop owner with an annual constant demand of 'A' units has ordering costs of ₹ 'P' per order and carrying costs ₹ '*l*' per unit per year. The economic order quantity for a purchasing model having no shortage may be determined from:
(a) $\sqrt{\frac{24P}{Al}}$ (b) $\sqrt{\frac{24AP}{I}}$
(c) $\sqrt{\frac{2AP}{I}}$ (d) $\sqrt{\frac{2AI}{P}}$

110. A furniture company is maintaining a constant work force which can produce 3000 tables per quarter. The annual demand is 12000 units and is distributed seasonally in accordance with the quarterly indexes $Q_1 = 0.80$, $Q_2 = 1.40$, $Q_3 = 1.00$ and $Q_4 = 0.80$. Inventories are accumulated when demand is less than the capacity and are used up during periods of strong demand to supply the total demand. To take into account any seasonal demand the inventories on hand at the beginning of the first quarter should be at least:

(a) 0 (b) 600
(c) 1200 (d) 2400

111. Match List-I (Phase diagram) with List-II (Characteristic) and select the correct answer using the codes given below the lists:

| **List-I (Phase diagram)** | **List-II (Characteristic)** |
|---|---|
| A. Isomorphous system | 1. One liquid decomposes into another liquid and solid |
| B. Eutectic system | 2. One liquid and another solid combine to form a new solid |
| C. Peritectic system | 3. Two metals are corn pletely soluble in liquid state and completely insoluble in solid slate |
| D. Monotectic system | 4. Two metals, soluble in solid and liquid state |

**Codes:**

| | A | B | C | D |
|---|---|---|---|---|
| (a) | 2 | 3 | 4 | 1 |
| (b) | 4 | 1 | 2 | 3 |
| (c) | 2 | 1 | 4 | 3 |
| (d) | 4 | 3 | 2 | 1 |

112. Economic Order Quantity is the quantity at which the cost of carrying is:

(a) minimum
(b) equal to the cost of ordering
(c) less than the cost of ordering
(d) cost of over-stocking.

113. ABC analysis in materials managements is a method of classifying the inventories based on:

(a) The value of annual usage of the items
(b) Economic order quantity
(c) Volume of material consumption
(d) Quantity of materials used.

114. If the annual demand of an item becomes half, ordering cost double, holding cost one-fourth and the unit cost twice, then what is the ratio of the new EOQ and the earlier EOQ?

(a) $\frac{1}{2}$ (b) $\frac{1}{\sqrt{2}}$
(c) $\sqrt{2}$ (d) 2

115. In the ABC method of inventory control. Group A constitutes costly items. What is the usual percentage of such items of the total items?

(a) 10 to 20% (b) 20 to 30%
(c) 30 to 40% (d) 40 to 50%

## ANSWERS WITH EXPLANATIONS

| | | | | |
|---|---|---|---|---|
| 1. (b) | 2. (b) | 3. (c) | 4. (c) | 5. (d) |
| 6. (d) | 7. (c) | 8. (a) | 9. (b) | 10. (a) |
| 11. (b) | 12. (d) | 13. (d) | 14. (d) | 15. (c) |
| 16. (a) | 17. (a) | 18. (a) | 19. (b) | 20. (d) |
| 21. (a) | 22. (d) | 23. (c) | 24. (a) | 25. (c) |
| 26. (c) | 27. (d) | 28. (b) | 29. (d) | 30. (d) |
| 31. (d) | 32. (a) | 33. (b) | 34. (b) | 35. (a) |
| 36. (c) | 37. (d) | 38. (d) | 39. (d) | 40. (c) |
| 41. (d) | 42. (d) | 43. (d) | 44. (b) | 45. (c) |
| 46. (b) | 47. (a) | 48. (d) | 49. (a) | 50. (b) |
| 51. (d) | 52. (c) | 53. (b) | 54. (b) | 55. (c) |
| 56. (a) | 57. (d) | 58. (b) | 59. (d) | 60. (c) |
| 61. (b) | 62. (c) | 63. (b) | 64. (c) | 65. (d) |
| 66. (b) | 67. (c) | 68. (a) | 69. (c) | 70. (a) |
| 71. (b) | 72. (b) | 73. (a) | 74. (a) | 75. (a) |
| 76. (c) | 77. (c) | 78. (d) | 79. (a) | 80. (c) |
| 81. (d) | 82. (c) | 83. (d) | 84. (d) | 85. (b) |
| 86. (c) | 87. (a) | 88. (b) | 89. (d) | 90. (b) |
| 91. (c) | 92. (b) | 93. (a) | 94. (a) | 95. (c) |
| 96. (b) | 97. (a) | 98. (d) | 99. (a) | 100. (d) |

101. (c) Molecular weight,
$M_n$ = Molecular weight of repeating unit, $M_0 \times$ average degree of polymerization, $x = 62.5 \times 20000$

102. (b) 103. (d) 104. (d) 105. (c) 106. (a)
107. (a) 108. (a) 109. (c)

112. (b) Required inventory in the first quarter
$= 0.8 \times 3000 = 24000$
In the second quarter
$= 1.4 \times 3000 = 4200$
In the third quarter
$= 1 \times 3000 = 3000$
In the fourth quarter
$= 0.8 \times 3000 = 2400$
Required quantity at the beginning of first quarter
$= 3000 - 2400 = 600$

111. (d) 112. (b) 113. (a)

114. (d) $\text{EOQ} = \sqrt{\dfrac{2DC_0}{C_c}}$

$$\frac{Q_2^*}{Q_1^*} = \sqrt{\frac{D_2}{D_1} \times \frac{C_{02}}{C_{01}} \times \frac{C_{c1}}{C_{c2}}} = \sqrt{\frac{1}{2} \times \frac{2}{1} \times \frac{4}{1}} = 2$$

115. (a)

❑❑❑

# 14. Metal Forming

- Metal forming is a general term for a large group, that includes a wide variety of manufacturing processes. Metal forming processes are characteristic in that the metal being processed is plastically deformed to shape it into a desired geometry.
- In order to plastically deform a metal, a force must be applied that will exceed the yield strength of the material. When low amounts of stress are applied to a metal it will change its geometry slightly, in correspondence to the force that is exerted. Basically it will compress, stretch, and/or bend a small amount.
- The magnitude of the amount will be directly proportional to the force applied. Also the material will return to its original geometry once the force is released. Think of stretching a rubber band, then releasing it, and having it go back to its original shape. This is called elastic deformation.
- Once the stress on a metal increases past a certain point, it no longer deforms elastically, but starts to undergo plastic deformation. In plastic deformation, the geometric change in the material is no longer directly proportional to stress and geometric changes remain after the stress is released; meaning that the material does not recover its shape.
- The actual level of stress applied to a metal where elastic deformation turns to plastic deformation is called the proportional limit, and is often difficult to determine exactly. The .002 offset convention is usually used to determine the yield point, which is taken for practical purposes as the stress level where plastic deformation, (yielding), begins to occur
- Forming, or metal forming, is the metalworking process of fashioning metal parts and objects through mechanical deformation; the workpiece is reshaped without adding or removing material, and its mass remains unchanged.
- Forming operates on the materials science principle of plastic deformation, where the physical shape of a material is permanently deformed.
- Metal forming tends to have more uniform characteristics across its subprocesses than its contemporary processes, cuttingand joining.
- On the industrial scale, forming is characterized by:
  - Very high required loads and stresses, between 50 and 2500 N/mm$^2$ (7-360 ksi)
  - Large, heavy, and expensive machinery in order to accommodate such high stresses and loads
  - Production runs with many parts, to maximize the economy of production and compensate for the expense of the machine tools
- Forming processes tend to be typified by differences in effective stresses. These categories and descriptions are highly simplified, since the stresses operating at a local level in any given process are very complex and may involve many varieties of stresses operating simultaneously, or it may involve stresses which change over the course of the operation.
- Compressive forming involves those processes where the primary means of plastic deformation is uni- or multiaxial compressive loading.
  - Rolling, where the material is passed through a pair of rollers
  - Extrusion, where the material is pushed through an orifice
  - Die forming, where the material is stamped by a press around or onto a die
  - Forging, where the material is shaped by localized compressive forces
- Tensile forming involves those processes where the primary means of plastic deformation is uni- or multiaxial tensile stress.
  - Stretching, where a tensile load is applied along the longitudinal axis of the work piece
  - Expanding, where the circumference of a hollow body is increased by tangential loading
  - Recessing, where depressions and holes are formed through tensile loading
- Combined tensile and compressive forming
- This category of forming processes involves those operations where the primary means of plastic deformation involves both tensile stresses and compressive loads.
  - Pulling through a die
  - Deep drawing
  - Spinning
  - Flange forming
  - Upset bulging
- This category of forming processes involves those operations where the primary means of plastic deformation is a bending load.

# MULTIPLE CHOICE QUESTIONS

1. Magnetic forming is an example of:
(a) cold forming
(b) hot forming
(c) high energy rate forming
(d) roll forming.

2. Match List-I (Type of Forging) with List-II (Operation) and select the correct answer using the code given below the Lists:

| List-I (Type of Forging) | List-II (Operation) |
|---|---|
| A. Drop Forging | 1. Metal is gripped in the dies and pressure is applied on the heated end |
| B. Press Forging | 2. Squeezing action |
| C. Upset forging | 3. Metal is placed between rollers and pushed |
| D. Roll Forging | 4. Repeated hammer blows |

**Codes:**

| | A | B | C | D |
|---|---|---|---|---|
| (a) | 4 | 1 | 2 | 3 |
| (b) | 3 | 2 | 1 | 4 |
| (c) | 4 | 2 | 1 | 3 |
| (d) | 3 | 1 | 2 | 4 |

3. What are the advantages of powder metallurgy'?
1. Extreme purity product
2. Low labour cost.
3. Low equipment forming
Select the correct answer using the code given below:
(a) 1, 2 and 3 (b) 1 and 2 only
(c) 2 and 3 only (d) 1 and 3 only

4. Which one of the following methods is used for the manufacture of collapsible tooth paste tubes?
(a) impact extrusion (b) direct extrusion
(c) deep drawing (d) piercing.

5. Consider the following steps in forging a connecting rod from bar stock:
1. Blocking 2. Trimming
3. Finishing 4. Edging
Select the correct sequence of these operations using the codes given below:
**Codes:**
(a) 1 –2 –3 –4 (b) 2 –3 –4 –1
(c) 3 –4 –1 –2 (d) 4 –1 –3 –2

6. The extrusion process (es) used for the production of toothpaste tube is/are
1. Tube extrusion 2. Forward extrusion
3. Impact extrusion
Select the correct answer using the codes given below:
**Codes:**
(a) 1 only (b) 1 and 2
(c) 2 and 3 (d) 3 only

7. Cold working produces the following effects:
1. Stresses are set up in metal
2. Grain structure gets distorted
3. Strength and hardness of the metal are decreased
4. Surface finish is reduced
Which of these statements are correct?
(a) 1 and 2 (b) 1, 2 and 3
(c) 3 and 4 (d) 1 and 4.

8. Consider the following statements:
In comparison to hot working, in cold working
1. higher forces are required.
2. no heating is required.
3. less ductility is required.
4. better surface finish is obtained.
Which of the statements given above are correct?
(a) 1, 2 and 3 (b) 2 and 4
(c) 1 and 3 (d) 2, 3 and 4

9. A cylindrical vessel with flat bottom can be deep drawn by:
(a) shallow drawing
(b) single action deep drawing
(c) double action deep drawing
(d) triple action deep drawing.

10. Consider the following statements:
1. Metal forming decreases harmful effects of impurities and improves mechanical strength.
2. Metal working process is a plastic deformation process.
3. Very intricate shapes can be produced by forging process as compared to casting process.
Which of the statements given above are correct?
(a) 1, 2 and 3 (b) 1 and 2 only
(c) 2 and 3 only (d) 1 and 3 only

11. Match List-I (Operations) with List-II (Stresses induced) and select the correct answer using the codes given below the Lists:

| List-I | List-II |
|---|---|
| A. Blanking | 1. Tension |
| B. Stretch forming | 2. Compression |
| C. Coining | 3. Shearing |
| D. Deep drawing | 4. Tension and compression |

**Codes:**

| | A | B | C | D |
|---|---|---|---|---|
| (a) | 2 | 1 | 3 | 4 |
| (b) | 2 | 4 | 3 | 1 |
| (c) | 3 | 4 | 2 | 1 |
| (d) | 3 | 1 | 2 | 4 |

12. Match List-I (Forging operations) with List-II (Descriptions) and select the correct answer using the codes given below the Lists:

| List-I | List-II |
|---|---|
| A. Flattening | 1. Thickness is reduced continuously at different sections along at length |
| B. Drawing | 2. Metal is displaced away from centre, reducing thickness in middle and increasing length |
| C. Fullering | 3. Rod is pulled through a die |
| D. Wire drawing | 4. Pressing a workpiece between two flat dies |

**Codes:**

| | A | B | C | D |
|---|---|---|---|---|
| (a) | 3 | 2 | 1 | 4 |
| (b) | 4 | 1 | 2 | 3 |
| (c) | 3 | 1 | 2 | 4 |
| (d) | 4 | 2 | 1 | 3 |

13. Match List-I (Operation) with List-II (Explanation) and select the correct answer using the codes given below the Lists:

| List-I (Operation) | List-II (Explanation) |
|---|---|
| A. Beading | 1. The edge of the sheet metal is bent into the cavity of a die |
| B. Flanging | 2. The process of punching a hole first and then expanding into a flange |
| C. Hemming | 3. The edge of the sheet metal is folded over itself |
| D. Roll Forming | 4. Bending continuous lengths of sheet metal |
| | 5. The process of bending the edges of sheet metals |

**Codes:**

| | A | B | C | D |
|---|---|---|---|---|
| (a) | 1 | 5 | 3 | 4 |
| (b) | 4 | 2 | 1 | 3 |
| (c) | 1 | 2 | 3 | 4 |
| (d) | 4 | 5 | 1 | 3 |

14. In deciding the clearance between punch and die in press work in shearing, the following rule is helpful:
(a) punch size controls hole size, die size controls blank size
(b) punch size controls both hole size and blank size
(c) die size controls both size and blank size
(d) die size, controls hole size, punch size controls blank.

15. The 'spring back' effect in press working is:
(a) elastic recovery of the sheet metal after removal of the load
(b) regaining the original shape of the sheet metal
(c) release of stored energy in the sheet metal
(d) partial recovery of the sheet metal

16. Which of the following are included in the finishing operations for porous bearing?
1. Infiltration 2. Sizing
3. Heat treatment 4. Coining
Select the correct answer using the code given below:
(a) 1 and 2 (b) 2 and 3
(c) 2 and 4 (d) 1 and 4

17. Which one of the following temperatures is exactly suited to carry out hot working processes?
(a) Room temperature
(b) Temperature of recovery stage
(c) Temperature above recrystallization stage
(d) Temperature of grain growth stage

18. Match List-II (Press-part) with List-II (Function) select the correct answer using the codes given below the lists:

| List-I (Press-part) | List-II (Function) |
|---|---|
| A. Punch plate | 1. Assisting withdrawal of the punch |
| B. Stripper | 2. Advancing the work-piece through correct distance |
| C. Stopper | 3. Ejection of the work-piece from die cavity |
| D. Knock out | 4. Holding the small punch in the proper position |

**Codes:**

| | A | B | C | D |
|---|---|---|---|---|
| (a) | 4 | 3 | 2 | 1 |
| (b) | 2 | 1 | 4 | 3 |
| (c) | 4 | 1 | 2 | 3 |
| (d) | 2 | 3 | 4 | 1 |

19. The process of removing the burrs of flash from a forged component in drop forging is called:
(a) swaging (b) perforating
(c) trimmin ; (d) fettling.

20. Which of the following are the characteristics of extrusion process?
1. Faster speed of production
2. Good surface finish
3. Dimensions can be maintained with close tolerances
4. Mechanical properties of the extruded products are inferior to that of the roiled products.
Select the correct answer using the codes given below:
**Codes:**
(a) 1 and 2 (b) 1, 2 and 3
(c) 3 and 4 (d) 1 and 4.

21. Which of the following are produced by powder metallurgy process
1. Cemented carbide dies
2. Porous bearings
3. Small magnets
4. Parts with intricate shapes

Select the correct answer using the codes given below:

**Codes:**

(a) 1, 2 and 3 (b) 1, 2 and 4
(c) 2, 3 and 4 (d) 1, 3 and 4

22. In part produced by powder metallurgy process, presintering is done to:
(a) increase the toughness of the component
(b) increase the density of the component
(c) facilitate bonding of non-metallic particles
(d) facilitate machining of the part.

23. Which metal forming process is used for manufacture of long steel wire?
(a) deep drawing (b) forging
(c) drawing (d) extrusion.

24. Which one of the following is the correct statement?
(a) extrusion is used for the manufacture of seamless tubes
(b) extrusion is used for reducing the diameter of round bars and tubes by rotating dies which open and close rapidly on the work
(c) extrusion is used to improve fatigue resistance of the metal by setting up compressive stresses on its surface
(d) extrusion comprises pressing the metal inside a chamber to force it out by high pressure through an orifice which is shaped to provide the desired form of the finished part.

25. For calculating the blank diameter D for thin cylindrical shell of outer diameter d and with height of the shall *h*, which one of the following formulae is used when *d* 220*r*, where *r* is the corner radius on the punch?

(a) $D = \sqrt{d^2 + 4dh^2}$

(b) $D = \sqrt{d^2 + 4dh - 0.5r}$

(c) $D = \sqrt{d^2 + 4dh - r}$

(d) $D = \sqrt{d^2 + 4dh - 1.5r}$

26. How are tooth-paste capsules produced?
(a) by boring operation
(b) by tube hiring operation
(c) by impact extrusion
(d) by tube drawing.

27. What is the force required to be exerted by the punch in order to shear out the blank (for a circular disc) of 20 mm diameter and 1.5 mm thickness and having a shear strength equal to 300 MPa?
(a) 9.0 kN (b) 18.0 kN
(c) 28.3 kN (d) 45.0 kN

28. In blanking operation the clearance is provided:
(a) on the punch
(b) on the die
(c) both on the punch and the die
(d) Neither/on the punch nor on the die.

29. Which of the following parts can he made economically be powder metallurgy?
1. gears
2. Automobile cylinders
3. Filters
4. Gun barrels

Select the correct answer using the code given below:

(a) 1 and 2 (b) 1 and 3
(c) 2 and 3 (d) 2 and 4

30. At which temperature is cold working of metals carried out?
(a) At the recrystallization temperature
(b) Below the recrystallization temperature
(c) Above the recrystallization temperature
(d) At any temperature

31. What is the process of making sheet metal components to the contour of a die by making use of an explosive impact known as:
(a) explosive cladding (b) explosive welding
(c) explosive forming (d) explosive joining

32. Consider the following steps involved in conditioning of metal powers in powder metallurgy techniques:
1. Pulverization
2. Blending or mixing
3. Screening
4. rleat Treatment.

Which one of the following is the correct sequence of the above steps?

(a) 1–2–3–4 (b) 2–3–1–4
(c) 4–1–3–2 (d) 4–3–2–1

33. The tooling cost is highest in which one of the following methods of plastic processing?
(a) extrusion
(b) casting
(c) compression molding
(d) injection molding

34. Which one of the following processes necessarily requires mandrel of requisite diameter to form the internal hole?
(a) hydrostatic extrusion
(b) tube drawing
(c) Swaging
(d) wire drawing

35. Which one of the following is the correct relationship between surface velocity of the roils ($V_r$), entrance velocity of work ($V_0$) and exit velocity of work ($V_f$) in rolling?
(a) $V_0 < V_r < V_f$ (b) $V_f < V_r < V_0$
(c) $V_r < V_f < V_0$ (d) $V_0 < V_f < V_r$

36. Which one of the following statements in extrusion processes in not correct?
(a) in forward extrusion, the problem of friction is prevalent because of relative motion between heated metal billet and cylinder wall
(b) in backward extrusion, the problem of friction is completely eliminated
(c) forward cold extrusion is similar to forward hot extrusion forces except extrusion ratios are higher and extrusion pressures are less
(d) cold extrusion forging is similar to impact extrusion except that side walk are much thicker and their height is smaller.

37. In drawing operation if $D_i$ = initial diameter and $D_0$ = outgoing diameter, then what is the degree of drawing equal to?
(a) $\frac{D_i - D_0}{D_i}$ (b) $\frac{D_i^2 - D_0^2}{D_i^2}$
(c) $\frac{D_i^2 - D_0^2}{D_i^2}$ (d) $\sqrt{\frac{D_i^2 - D_0^2}{D_i^2}}$

38. Consider the following statements related to forging:
1. Flash is excess material added to stockwhich flows around, parting line.
2. Flash helps in filling of thin ribs and bosses in upper die.
3. Amount of flash depends upon forging force.
Which of the above statements is/are correct?
(a) 1, 2 and 3 (b) 1 and 2
(c) 1 and 3 (d) 2 and 3

39. In drawing operation, proper lubrication is essential for which of the following reasons.
1. To improve die life
2. To reduce drawing forces
3. To reduce temperature
4. To improve surface finish
Select the correct answer using the code given below:
(a) 1 and 2 only
(b) 1, 3 and 4 only
(c) 3 and 4 only
(d) 1, 2, 3 and 4

40. Which of the following are the characteristics of cold working of metals?
1. Stresses are set up in the metal that remain unless removed by subsequent heat treatment
2. Coarse grains are refined
3. Strength and hardness are increased.
Select the correct answer using the code given below:
(a) 1 and 2 only (b) 1 and 3 only
(c) 2 and 3 only (d) 3 only

41. For punching operation the clearance is provided on which one of the following?
(a) The punch
(b) The die
(c) 50% on the punch 50% on the die
(d) $\frac{1}{3}rd$ on the punch $\frac{2}{3}rd$ on the die

42. Match List-I with List-II and select the correct answer using the code given below the list:

| List-I (Type of Rolling Mill) | List-II (Characteristic) |
|---|---|
| A. Two high non-reversing mills | 1. Middle role rotates by friction |
| B. There high mills | 2. By small working roll, power for rolling is reduced |
| C. Flour high mills | 3. Rolls of equal size are rotated only in one direction |
| D. Cluster mills | 4. Diameter of working roll is very small |

**Codes:**

| | A | B | C | D |
|---|---|---|---|---|
| (a) | 3 | 4 | 2 | 1 |
| (b) | 2 | 1 | 3 | 4 |
| (c) | 2 | 4 | 3 | 1 |
| (d) | 3 | 1 | 2 | 4 |

43. Consider the following statements:
Roll forces in rolling can be reduced by
1. reducing friction
2. using large diameter roller to increase the contact area
3. taking smaller reductions per pass to reduce the contact area.
Which of the statements given above are correct?
(a) 1 and 2 only (b) 2 and 3 only
(c) 1 and 3 only (d) 1, 2 and 3

44. The order of radial clearance between the punch and die for shearing plate of thickness '$t$'(1 mm ≤ 2 mm) is:
(a) 0.05 $t$ (b) 0.15 $t$
(c) 0.20 $t$ (d) 0.25 $t$

45. The force required for piercing a round hole when the die and punch are not provided with any shear is given by:
(a) LST (b) π DS
(c) DLST (d) π DST
Where L = length of die land, D = diameter of hole, T = thickness, S = shear strength

46. Thread rolling is restricted to:
(a) ferrous materials
(b) ductile materials
(c) hard materials
(d) none of the above.

47. A moving mandrel is used in:
(a) wire drawing
(b) tube drawing
(c) metal cutting
(d) forging.

48. In sheet metal work, the cutting force on the tool can he reduced by:
(a) grinding the cutting edges sharp
(b) increasing the hardness of tool
(c) providing shear angle on tool
(d) increasing the hardness of die.

49. Tandem drawing of wires and tubes is necessary because:
(a) it is possible to reduce at one stage
(b) annealing is needed between stages
(c) accuracy in dimension is not possible otherwise
(d) surface finish improves after drawing stage.

50. In order to get uniform thickness of the plate by rolling process, one provides:
(a) camber on the rolls
(b) offset on the rolls
(c) hardening of the rolls
(d) antifriction bearings

51. The blank diameter used in thread rolling will be:
(a) equal to minor diameter of the thread
(b) equal to pitch diameter of the thread
(c) a little large than the minor diameter of the thread
(d) a little large than the pitch diameter of the thread.

52. Which one of the following manufacturing process requires the provision of 'gutters?
(a) closed die forging
(b) centrifugal casting
(c) investment casting
(d) impact extrusion.

53. Match List-I with List-II and select the correct answer using the codes given below the lists:

| List-I (Match Property) | List-II (Related to) |
|---|---|
| A. Malleability | 1. Wire drawing |
| B. Hardness | 2. Impact loads |
| C. Resilience | 3. Cold rolling |
| D. Isotropy | 4. Indentation |
| | 5. Direction |

**Codes:**

| | A | B | C | D |
|---|---|---|---|---|
| (a) | 4 | 2 | 1 | 3 |
| (b) | 3 | 4 | 2 | 5 |
| (c) | 5 | 4 | 2 | 3 |
| (d) | 3 | 2 | 1 | 5 |

54. Match List-I with List-II and select the correct answer using the codes given below the List:

| List-I (Metal forming process) | List-II (A similar process) |
|---|---|
| A. Blanking | 1. Wire drawing |
| B. Coining | 2. Piercing |
| C. Hemming | 3. Embossing |
| D. Cup drawing | 4. Rolling |
| | 5. Deep drawing |

**Codes:**

| | A | B | C | D |
|---|---|---|---|---|
| (a) | 2 | 3 | 4 | 1 |
| (b) | 2 | 3 | 1 | 4 |
| (c) | 3 | 2 | 1 | 5 |
| (d) | 2 | 3 | 1 | 5 |

55. In sheet metal blanking, shear is provided on punches and dies so that :
(a) press load is reduce
(b) good cut edges obtained
(c) warping of sheet is minimized
(d) cut blank are straight

56. For obtaining a cup of diameter 25 mm and height 15 mm by drawing the size of the round blank should be approximately:
(a) 42 mm (b) 44 mm
(c) 46 mm (d) 48 mm

57. Which of the following pairs of process and draft are correctly matched?
1. Rolling ........... 2
2. Extrusion ........... 50
3. Forging .......... 4
Select the correct answer using the codes given below:
(a) 1, 2 and 3
(b) 1 and 2
(c) 1 and 3
(d) 2 and 3

58. The mode of deformation of the metal during spinning is:
(a) bending
(b) stretching
(c) rolling and stretching
(d) bending and stretching.

59. In drop forging, forging is done by dropping:
(a) the work piece at high velocity
(b) the hammer at high velocity
(c) the die with hammer at high velocity
(d) a weight on hammer to produce the requisite impact.

60. Metal extrusion process is generally used for producing:
(a) uniform solid sections
(b) uniform hollow sections
(c) uniform solid and hollow section
(d) varying solid and hollow sections.

61. Match List-I with List-II and select the correct answer

| List-I (Metal formingprocess) | List-II (Associated force) |
|---|---|
| A. Wire drawing | 1. Shear force |
| B. Extrusion | 2. Tensile force |
| C. Blanking | 3. Compressive force |
| D. Bending | 4. Spring back force |

**Codes:**

| | A | B | C | D |
|---|---|---|---|---|
| (a) | 4 | 2 | 1 | 3 |
| (b) | 2 | 1 | 3 | 4 |
| (c) | 2 | 3 | 1 | 4 |
| (d) | 4 | 3 | 2 | 1 |

62. In wire drawing process, the bright shining surface on the wire is obtained if one:
(a) does not use a lubricant
(b) low tooling cost
(c) uses thick paste lubricant
(d) use thin fluid lubricant.

63. Which one of the following is an advantage of forging?
(a) Good surface finish
(b) Low tooling cost
(c) Close tolerance
(d) Improved physical property

64. For 50% penetration of work material, a punch with single shear equal to thickness will:
(a) reduce the punch load to half the value
(b) increase the punch load by half the value
(c) maintain the same punch load
(d) reduce the punch load, to quarter load.

65. A cup 10 cm height and 5 cm diameter is to be made from a sheet metal of 2 mm thickness. The number of deductions necessary will be:
(a) one (b) two
(c) three (d) four

66. Which of the following components can be manufactured by power metallurgy methods?
1. Carbide tool tips
2. Bearings
3. Filters
4. Brake linings.
Select the correct answer using the codes given below:
(a) 1, 3 and 4 (b) 2 and 3
(c) 1, 2 and 4 (d) 1, 2, 3 and 4

67. Which one of the following processes in most commonly used for the forging of bolt heads of hexagonal shape?
(a) closed die drop forging
(b) open die upset forging
(c) close die press forging
(d) open die progressive forging.

68. The bending force required for V-bending, U-bending and Edge-bending will be in the ratio of:
(a) 1 : 2 : 0.5 (b) 2 : 1 : 0.5
(c) 1 : 2 : 1 (d) 1 : 1 : 1

69. In powder metallurgy, the operation carried out to improve the bearing property of a bush is called:
(a) infiltration (b) impregnation
(c) plating (d) heat treatment

70. Consider the following processes for the manufacture of gears:
1. Casting
2. Powder metallurgy
3. Machining from bar stock
4. Closed die forging
The correct sequence in increasing order of bending strength of gear teeth is:
(a) 1, 2, 3, 4 (b) 1, 2, 4, 3
(c) 2, 1, 4, 3 (d) 2, 1, 3, 4

71. Match List-I with List-II and select the correct answer using the codes given below the List:

| List-I | List-II |
|---|---|
| A. Die sinking | 1. Abrasive jet machining |
| B. Deburring | 2. Laser beam machining |
| C. Fine hole drilling (thin materials) | 3. EDM |
| D. Cutting/ sharpening hard materials | 4. Ultrasonic machining |
| | 5. Electro-chemical grinding |

**Codes:**

| | A | B | C | D |
|---|---|---|---|---|
| (a) | 3 | 5 | 4 | 1 |
| (b) | 2 | 4 | 1 | 3 |
| (c) | 3 | 1 | 2 | 5 |
| (d) | 4 | 5 | 1 | 3 |

72. Match List-I with List-II and select the correct answer using the codes given below the Lists:

| List-I | List-II |
|---|---|
| A. Drawing | 1. Soap solution |
| B. Rolling | 2. Camber |
| C. Wire drawing | 3. Pilots |
| D. Sheet metal operations using progressive dies | 4. Crate |
| | 5. Ironing |

**Codes:**

| | A | B | C | D |
|---|---|---|---|---|
| (a) | 2 | 5 | 1 | 4 |
| (b) | 4 | 1 | 5 | 3 |
| (c) | 5 | 2 | 3 | 4 |
| (d) | 5 | 2 | 1 | 3 |

73. Which one of the following metal forming processes is not a high energy rate forming process?
(a) electro-magnetic forming
(b) roll-forming
(c) explosive forming
(d) electro-hydraulic forming.

74. Consider the following operations involved in forging a hexagonal bolt from a round bar stock, whose diameter is equal to the bolt diameter:
1. Flattening
2. Upsetting
3. Swaging
4. Cambering
The correct sequence of these operations is:
(a) 1, 2, 3, 4
(b) 2, 3, 4, 1
(c) 2, 4, 3, 1
(d) 3, 2, 1, 4

75. Which one of the following is the correct temperature range for hot extrusion of aluminium?
(a) 300 – 340°C
(b) 350 – 400°C
(c) 430 – 480°C
(d) 550 – 650°C

76. The correct sequence of the given processes in manufacturing by powder metallurgy is:
(a) blending, compacting sintering and sizing
(b) blending, compacting, sizing and sintering
(c) compacting, sizing, blending and sintering
(d) compacting, blending, sizing and sintering.

77. In the rolling process, roll separating force can be decreased by:
(a) reducing the roll diameter
(b) increasing the roll diameter
(c) providing hack-up rolls
(d) increasing the friction between the rolls and the metal.

78. Consider the following statements:
In forward extrusion process:
(a) the ram and the extruded product travel in the same direction.
(b) the ram and the extruded product travel in the opposite direction.
(c) the speed of travel of the extruded product is same as that of the ram.
(d) the speed of travel of the extruded, product is greater than that of the ram.
Which of these statements are correct?
(a) 1 and 3
(b) 2 and 3
(c) 1 and 4
(d) 2 and 4

79. Which one of the following lubricants is most suitable for drawing mild steel wires:
(a) Sodium stearate
(b) water
(c) lime-water
(d) kerosene

80. Best position of crank for blanking operation in a mechanical press is:
(a) top dead centre
(b) 20 degrees below top dead centre
(c) 20 degrees before bottom dead centre
(d) bottom dead centre.

81. Match List-I (components of a table fan) with List-II (Manufacturing processes) and select the correct answer using the codes given below the lists:

| List-I | List-II |
|---|---|
| A. Base with stand | 1. Stamping and pressing |
| B. Blade | 2. Wire drawing |
| C. Armature coil wire | 3. Turning |
| D. Armature shaft | 4. Casting |

**Codes:**

| | A | B | C | D |
|---|---|---|---|---|
| (a) | 4 | 3 | 2 | 1 |
| (b) | 2 | 1 | 4 | 3 |
| (c) | 2 | 3 | 4 | 1 |
| (d) | 4 | 1 | 2 | 3 |

82. In the forging operation, fullering is done to:
(a) draw out the material
(b) bend the material
(c) upset the material
(d) extrude the material.

83. Which of the following assumptions are correct for cold rolling?
(a) The material is plastic
(b) The arc of contact is circular with a radius greater than the radius of the roil.
(c) Coefficient of friction is constant over the arc of contact and acts in one direction throughout the arc of contact.
Select the correct answer using the code given below:
**Codes:**
(a) 1 and 2 (b) 1 and 3
(c) 2 and 3 (d) 2, 2 and 3

84. A strip is to rolled from a thickness of 30 mm to 15 mm using a two-high mill having rolls of diameter 300 mm. The coefficient of friction for unaided bite should nearly be:
(a) 0.95 (b) 0.5
(c) 0.25 (d) 0.07

85. Which of the following statements are the salient features of hydrostatic extrusion?
(1) It is suitable for soft and ductile material
(2) It is suitable for high-strength super-alloys
(3) The billet is inserted into the extrusion chamber and pressure is applied by a ram to extrude the billet through the die
(4) The billet is inserted into the extrusion chamber where it is surrounded by a suitable liquid. The billet is extruded through the die by applying pressure to the liquid.
Select the correct answer using the code given below:
**Codes:**
(a) 1 and 3 (b) 1 and 4
(c) 2 and 3 (d) 2 and 4

86. Consider the following statements related to piercing and blanking:
   (1) Shear on the punch reduces the maximum cutting force.
   (2) Shear increases the capacity of the press needed.
   (3) Shear increases the life of the punch.
   (4) The total energy needed to make the cut remains unaltered due to provision of shear.
   Which of the above statements are correct?
   (a) land 2 (b) 1 and 4
   (c) 2 and 3 (d) 3 and 4

87. Consider the following steps involved in hammer forging a connecting rod from bar Stock
   1. Blocking 2. Trimming
   3. Finishing 4. Fullering
   5. Edging
   Which of the following is the correct sequence of operations?
   (a) 1, 4, 3, 2 and 5
   (b) 4, 5, 1, 3 and 2
   (c) 5, 4, 3, 2 and 1
   (d) 5, 1, 4, 2 and 3

88. The rate of production of a powder metallurgy part depends on:
   (a) flow rate of powder
   (b) green strength of compact
   (c) apparent density of compact
   (d) compressibility of powder.

89. In rolling a strip between two rolls, the position of the neutral point in the arc of contact' does not depend on:
   (a) amount of reduction
   (b) diameter of the rolls
   (c) coefficient of friction
   (d) material of the rolls.

90. Match List-I (parts) with List-II (Manufacturing processes) and select the correct answer using the codes given below the lists:

| List-I (Parts) | List-II (Manufacturing processes) |
|---|---|
| A. Seamless tubes | 1. Roll forming |
| B. Accurate and smooth tubes | 2. Shot peening |
| C. Surfaces having hardness and fatigue strength | 3. Forging higher |
| | 4. Cold forming |

**Codes:**

| | A | B | C |
|---|---|---|---|
| (a) | 1 | 4 | 2 |
| (b) | 2 | 3 | 1 |
| (c) | 1 | 3 | 2 |
| (d) | 2 | 4 | 1 |

91. Match List-I (Products) with List-II (Processes) and select the correct answer using the codes given below the lists:

| List-I | List-II |
|---|---|
| A. MS angles and channels | 1. Welding |
| B. Carburettors | 2. Forging |
| C. Roof trusses | 3. Casting |
| D. Gear wheels | 4. Rolling |

**Codes:**

| | A | B | C | D |
|---|---|---|---|---|
| (a) | 1 | 2 | 3 | 4 |
| (b) | 4 | 3 | 2 | 1 |
| (c) | 1 | 2 | 4 | 3 |
| (d) | 4 | 3 | 1 | 2 |

92. The forging defect due to hindrance to smooth flow of metal in the component called 'Lap' occurs because:
   (a) the corner radius provided is too long
   (b) the corner radius provided is too small
   (c) draft is not provided
   (d) the shrinkage allowance is inadequate.

93. Magnesium is extruded and not rolled because:
   (a) it has a low melting point
   (b) it has a low density
   (c) its reactivity with roll material high
   (d) it has a dose-packed hexagonal structure.

94. Match List-I (Process) with List-II (Production of parts) and select the correct (answer using the codes given below the lists:

| List-I | List-II |
|---|---|
| A. Rolling | 1. Discrete parts |
| B. Forging | 2. Rod and Wire |
| C. Extrusion | 3. Wide variety of shapes with thin walls |
| D. Drawing | 4. Flat plates and sheets |
| | 5. Solid and hollow parts |

**Codes:**

| | A | B | C | D |
|---|---|---|---|---|
| (a) | 2 | 5 | 3 | 4 |
| (b) | 1 | 2 | 5 | 4 |
| (c) | 4 | 1 | 3 | 2 |
| (d) | 4 | 1 | 5 | 2 |

95. A blank of 30 mm diameter is to be produced out of 10 mm thick sheet on a simple die. If 6% clearance is recommended, then the nominal diameters of die and punch are respectively:
   (a) 30.6 mm and 29.4 mm
   (b) 30.6 mm and 30 mm
   (c) 30 mm and 29.4 mm
   (d) 30 mm and 28.8 mm

96. Rolling very thin strips of mild steel requires:
   (a) large diameter rolls
   (b) small diameter rolls
   (c) high speed rolling
   (d) rolling without a lubricant.

97. Drop forging is used to produce:
(a) small components
(b) large components
(c) identical components in large numbers
(d) medium-size components

98. Consider the following factors:
1. Size and shape that can be produced economically
2. Porosity of the parts produced.
3. Available press capacity
4. High density
Which of the above are limitations of powder metallurgy?
(a) 1, 3 and 4 (b) 2 and 3
(c) 1, 2 and 3 (d) 1 and 2

99. Consider the following characteristics of rolling process:
1. Shows work hardening effect
2. Surface finish is not good
3. Heavy reduction in areas can he obtained
Which of these characteristics are associated with hot rolling?
(a) 1 and 2 (b) 1 and 3
(c) 2 and 3 (d) 1, 2 and 3

100. Match List-I (Products) with List-II (Suitable processes) and select the correct answer using the codes given below the Lists:

| List-I | List-II |
|---|---|
| A. Connecting rods | Welding |
| B. Pressure vessels | Extrusion |
| C. Machine tool beds | Forging |
| D. Collapsible tubes | Casting |

**Codes:**

| | A | B | C | D |
|---|---|---|---|---|
| (a) | 3 | 1 | 4 | 2 |
| (b) | 4 | 1 | 3 | 2 |
| (c) | 3 | 2 | 4 | 1 |
| (d) | 4 | 2 | 3 | 1 |

101. An invicid irrotational flow field of free vortex motion has a circulation constant Ω. The tangential velocity at any point in the flow field is given by $\Omega/r$ where, $r$, is the radial distance from the centre. At the centre, there is a mathematical singularity which can be phiysically substituted by a forced vortex motion ($r = r_c$), the angular velocity E is given by:
(a) $\Omega/(r_c)^2$ (b) $\Omega/r_c$
(c) $\Omega r_c$ (d) $\Omega r_c^2$

102. The normal stress is the same in directions at a point in a fluid only when:
(a) The fluid is frictional
(b) The fluid is frictionless and incompressible
(c) The fluid has zero viscosity and is at rest
(d) One fluid layer has no motion relative to an adjacent layer.

103. Which of the following forces act on a fluid at rest?
1. Gravity force 2. Hydrostatic force
3. Surface tension 4. Viscous force
Select the correct answer using the codes given below:
(a) 1, 2, 3 and 4 (b) 1, 2 and 3
(c) 2, and 4 (d) 1, 3 and 4

104. A stepped cylindrical container is filled with a liquid as shown in the given figure. The container with its axis vertical, is first placed with its larger diameter downward and then upward. The ratio of the forces at the bottom in the two cases will be:

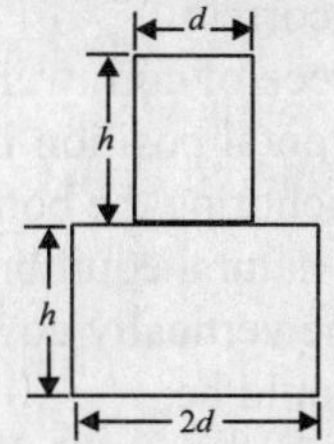


(a) $\frac{1}{2}$ (b) 1
(c) 2 (d) 4

105. A circular annular plate having outer and inner diameters of 1.4 m and 0.6 respectively is immersed in water with its plane making an angle of 60° with the horizontal. The centre of the circular annular plate is 1.85 m below the free surface. The hydrostatic thrust on one side of the plate is:
(a) 1975 N (b) 19.75 N
(c) 11.4 N (d) 22.8 N

106. A house-top water tank is made of fiat plates and is full to the brim. Its height its twice that of any side. The ratio of force on the bottom of the tank to that on any side will be:
(a) 4 (b) 2
(c) 1 (d) 1/2

107. A right-circular cylinder open at the top is filled with liquid of relative density 1.2. It is rotated about its vertical axis at such a speed that half the liquid spills out. The pressure at the centre of the bottom will be:
(a) Zero
(b) One-fourth of the value when the cylinder was full
(c) Half of the value when the cylinder was full
(d) Not determinable from the given data.

108. In the figure shown below, air is contained in the pipe and water is the manometer liquid. The pressure at A' is approximately:

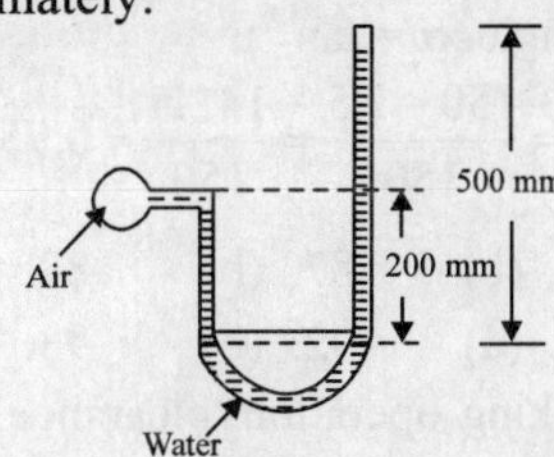


(a) 10.14 m of water absolute
(b) 0.2 m of water
(c) 1.2 of water vacuum
(d) 4901 Pa

109. Consider the following statements:
Filling up a part of the empty hood of a ship with ballasts will:
1. Reduce the metacentric height
2. Lower the position of the centre of gravity
3. Elevate the position of centre of gravity.
4. Elevate the position of centre of buoyancy.
Of these statements:
(a) 1, 3 and 4 are correct
(b) 1 and 2 are correct
(c) 3 and 4 are correct
(d) 2 and 4 are correct

110. A cylindrical piece of cork weighing 'W floats with its axis in horizontal position in a liquid of relative density 4. By anchoring the bottom, the cork piece is made to float at natural equilibrium position with its axis vertical. The vertically downward force exerted by anchoring would be:
(a) 0.5 W (b) W
(c) 2 W (d) 4 W

## ANSWERS WITH EXPLANATIONS

| | | | | |
|---|---|---|---|---|
| 1. (c) | 2. (a) | 3. (b) | 4. (d) | 5. (d) |
| 6. (d) | 7. (a) | 8. (a) | 9. (c) | 10. (a) |
| 11. (c) | 12. (b) | 13. (d) | 14. (d) | 15. (a) |
| 16. (a) | 17. (c) | 18. (a) | 19. (c) | 20. (d) |
| 21. (a) | 22. (c) | 23. (c) | 24. (d) | 25. (a) |
| 26. (c) | | | | |

27. (c) $F = \pi d t \tau = \pi \times 20 \times 1.5 \times 300 = 28.3$ kN

| | | | | |
|---|---|---|---|---|
| 28. (a) | 29. (b) | 30. (b) | 31. (c) | 32. (a) |
| 33. (d) | 34. (a) | 35. (a) | 36. (a) | 37. (c) |
| 38. (c) | 39. (d) | 40. (a) | 41. (b) | 42. (a) |
| 43. (d) | 44. (a) | 45. (d) | 46. (b) | 47. (b) |
| 48. (c) | 49. (a) | 50. (a) | 51. (b) | 52. (a) |
| 53. (b) | 54. (c) | 55. (a) | | |

56. (c) $D = \sqrt{d^2 + 4dh}$

$= \sqrt{25^2 + 4 \times 25 \times 15} = 46$ mm

| | | | | |
|---|---|---|---|---|
| 57. (a) | 58. (d) | 59. (c) | 60. (d) | 61. (c) |
| 62. (d) | 63. (d) | 64. (c) | 65. (c) | 66. (d) |
| 67. (d) | 68. (a) | 69. (a) | 70. (d) | 71. (a) |
| 72. (d) | 73. (b) | 74. (a) | 75. (b) | 76. (a) |
| 77. (c) | 78. (c) | 79. (a) | 80. (c) | 81. (d) |
| 82. (a) | 83. (d) | | | |

84. (a) Bite angle, $\alpha = \tan^{-1}\mu$

$$\cos\alpha = \frac{150 - 7.5}{150} = \frac{142.5}{150} = 0.95$$

| | | | | |
|---|---|---|---|---|
| 85. (c) | 86. (b) | 87. (b) | 88. (d) | 89. (d) |
| 90. (a) | 91. (d) | 92. (b) | 93. (c) | 94. (d) |

95. (c) In banking operation, clearance is provided on punch.

Here clearance $= 6 \times \frac{10}{100} = 0.6 = 0.6$ mm

Punch size = 30 – 0.6 = 29.4 mm

| | | | | |
|---|---|---|---|---|
| 96. (a) | 97. (c) | 98. (c) | 99. (b) | 100. (a) |

101. (a) At the interface of free and forced vortex, tangential velocities are equal.

$$\frac{\Gamma}{2\pi r_c} = \omega r_c$$

or $$\omega = \frac{\Gamma}{2\pi} \times \frac{1}{r_c^2} = \frac{\Omega}{r_c^2}$$

where $\omega = \dfrac{\Gamma}{2\pi}$

102. (b) 103. (b)

104. (d) $F = \rho g A h$

or $F \propto Ah$

For same, $h, F \propto A$

$$\frac{F_2}{F_1} = \frac{A_2}{A_1} = \left(\frac{2d}{d}\right)^2 = 4$$

105. (d) Hydrostatic thrust on inclined plane

$$= \rho g\ A\bar{x}$$

$$= 10^3 \times 9.81 \times \frac{\pi}{4}[(1.4)^2 - (0.6)^2] \times 1.85$$

$$= 22.8 \text{ kN}$$

106. (c) $F_{bottom} = \rho g\ LBh$

$$F_{side} = \frac{1}{2}\rho g\, Lh^2$$

$$\frac{F_{bottom}}{F_{side}} = \frac{2B}{h} = \frac{2B}{2B} = 1$$

107. (a) Let $r$ = radius, $h$ = height of cylinder, $z$ = depth of paraboloid

Volume of water spilled out = Volume of paraboloid of revolution

$$0.5 r\pi^2 h = 0.5\ 5 r\pi^2 z$$

$$z = h$$

Therefore, no water is left in the cylinder at the centre resulting in zero pressure at the centre of bottom.

108. (d) Neglecting static head due to air,

$$P_A = \rho g h_w = 10^3 \times 9.81 \times 500 \times 10^{-3}$$

$$= 4905 \text{ Pa} = 4901 \text{ Pa}$$

109. (d)

110. (d) Relative density of cork = 4

Therefore it will float upto $\frac{1}{4}$*th* of its height in the liquid. Centre of gravity and centre of buoyancy of cork must coincide to make it float in neutral equilibrium. Therefore, the cork must be immersed to its full height. For this purpose, downward force to be applied to cork = buoyant force on cork = 4 W.

❑❑❑

# 15. Metal Casting

- In metalworking, casting involves pouring liquid metal into a mold, which contains a hollow cavity of the desired shape, and then allowing it to cool and solidify.
- The solidified part is also known as a casting, which is ejected or broken out of the mold to complete the process. Casting is most often used for making complex shapes that would be difficult or uneconomical to make by other methods.
- Casting processes have been known for thousands of years, and widely used for sculpture, especially in bronze, jewelry in precious metals, and weapons and tools. Traditional techniques include lost-wax casting, plaster mold casting and sand casting.
- The modern casting process is subdivided into two main categories: expendable and non-expendable casting.
- It is further broken down by the mold material, such as sand or metal, and pouring method, such as gravity, vacuum, or low pressure.
- Sand casting is one of the most popular and simplest types of casting, and has been used for centuries. Sand casting allows for smaller batches than permanent mold casting and at a very reasonable cost.
- Not only does this method allow manufacturers to create products at a low cost, but there are other benefits to sand casting, such as very small-size operations. From castings that fit in the palm of your hand to train beds it can all be done with sand casting.
- Sand casting also allows most metals to be cast depending on the type of sand used for the molds.
- Sand casting requires a lead time of days, or even weeks sometimes, for production at high output rates and is unsurpassed for large-part production. Green (moist) sand has almost no part weight limit, whereas dry sand has a practical part mass limit of 2,300–2,700 kg (5,100–6,000 lb).
- Minimum part weight ranges from 0.075–0.1 kg (0.17–0.22 lb). The sand is bonded together using clays, chemical binders, or polymerized oils (such as motor oil). Sand can be recycled many times in most operations and requires little maintenance.
- Plaster casting is similar to sand casting except that plaster of paris is substituted for sand as a mold material. Generally, the form takes less than a week to prepare, after which a production rate of 1–10 units/hr·mold is achieved, with items as massive as 45 kg (99 lb) and as small as 30 g (1 oz) with very good surface finish and close tolerances.
- Plaster casting is an inexpensive alternative to other molding processes for complex parts due to the low cost of the plaster and its ability to produce near net shape castings. The biggest disadvantage is that it can only be used with low melting point non-ferrous materials, such as aluminium, copper, magnesium, and zinc.
- Shell molding is similar to sand casting, but the molding cavity is formed by a hardened "shell" of sand instead of a flask filled with sand. The sand used is finer than sand casting sand and is mixed with a resin so that it can be heated by the pattern and hardened into a shell around the pattern.
- Because of the resin and finer sand, it gives a much finer surface finish. The process is easily automated and more precise than sand casting. Common metals that are cast include cast iron, aluminium, magnesium, and copper alloys. This process is ideal for complex items that are small to medium sized.
- Investment casting is a process that has been practiced for thousands of years, with the lost-wax process being one of the oldest known metal forming techniques.
- From 5000 years ago, when beeswax formed the pattern, to today's high technology waxes, refractory materials and specialist alloys, the castings ensure high-quality components are produced with the key benefits of accuracy, repeatability, versatility and integrity.
- Investment casting derives its name from the fact that the pattern is invested, or surrounded, with a refractory material. The wax patterns require extreme care for they are not strong enough to withstand forces encountered during the mold making. One advantage of investment casting is that the wax can be reused.
- The process is suitable for repeatable production of net shape components from a variety of different metals and high performance alloys. Although generally used for small castings, this process has been used to produce complete aircraft door frames, with steel castings of up to 300 kg and aluminum castings of up to 30 kg.
- Compared to other casting processes such as die casting or sand casting, it can be an expensive process, however the components that can be produced using investment casting can incorporate intricate contours, and in most cases the components are cast near net shape, so require little or no rework once cast.
- A durable plaster intermediate is often used as a stage toward the production of a bronze sculpture or as a pointing guide for the creation of a carved stone. With the completion of a plaster, the work is more durable

(if stored indoors) than a clay original which must be kept moist to avoid cracking.

- With the low cost plaster at hand, the expensive work of bronze casting or stone carving may be deferred until a patron is found, and as such work is considered to be a technical, rather than artistic process, it may even be deferred beyond the lifetime of the artist.
- In waste molding a simple and thin plaster mold, reinforced by sisal or burlap, is cast over the original clay mixture. When cured, it is then removed from the damp clay, incidentally destroying the fine details in undercuts present in the clay, but which are now captured in the mold.
- The mold may then at any later time (but only once) be used to cast a plaster positive image, identical to the original clay. The surface of this plaster may be further refined and may be painted and waxed to resemble a finished bronze casting.
- This is a class of casting processes that use pattern materials that evaporate during the pour, which means there is no need to remove the pattern material from the mold before casting. The two main processes are lost-foam casting and full-mold casting.
- Lost-foam casting is a type of evaporative-pattern casting process that is similar to investment casting except foam is used for the pattern instead of wax. This process takes advantage of the low boiling point of foam to simplify the investment casting process by removing the need to melt the wax out of the mold.
- Full-mold casting is an evaporative-pattern casting process which is a combination of sand casting and lost-foam casting. It uses an expanded polystyrene foam pattern which is then surrounded by sand, much like sand casting. The metal is then poured directly into the mold, which vaporizes the foam upon contact.
- Non-expendable mold casting differs from expendable processes in that the mold need not be reformed after each production cycle. This technique includes at least four different methods: permanent, die, centrifugal, and continuous casting. This form of casting also results in improved repeatability in parts produced and delivers Near Net Shape results.
- Permanent mold casting is a metal casting process that employs reusable molds ,usually made from metal. The most common process uses gravity to fill the mold, however gas pressure or a vacuum are also used.
- Permanent molds, while lasting more than one casting still have a limited life before wearing out.
- The die casting process forces molten metal under high pressure into mold cavities. Most die castings are made from nonferrous metals, specifically zinc, copper, and aluminum based alloys, but ferrous metal die castings are possible.
- The die casting method is especially suited for applications where many small to medium sized parts are needed with good detail, a fine surface quality and dimensional consistency.
- Semi-solid metal (SSM) casting is a modified die casting process that reduces or eliminates the residual porosity present in most die castings. Rather than using liquid metal as the feed material, SSM casting uses a higher viscosity feed material that is partially solid and partially liquid.
- Used commercially mainly for aluminum and magnesium alloys, SSM castings can be heat treated to the T4, T5 or T6 tempers. The combination of heat treatment, fast cooling rates and minimal porosity provides excellent combinations of strength and ductility.
- Other advantages of SSM casting include the ability to produce complex shaped parts net shape, pressure tightness, tight dimensional tolerances and the ability to cast thin walls
- **Pattern:** An approximate duplicate of the final casting used to form the mold cavity.
- Molding material: The material that is packed around the pattern and then the pattern is removed to leave the cavity where the casting material will be poured.
- **Flask:** The rigid wood or metal frame that holds the molding material.
- **Cope:** The top half of the pattern, flask, mold, or core.
- **Drag:** The bottom half of the pattern, flask, mold, or core.
- **Core:** An insert in the mold that produces internal features in the casting, such as holes.
- **Core print:** The region added to the pattern, core, or mold used to locate and support the core.
- **Mold cavity:** The combined open area of the molding material and core, where the metal is poured to produce the casting.
- **Riser:** An extra void in the mold that fills with molten material to compensate for shrinkage during solidification.
- **Gating system:** The network of connected channels that deliver the molten material to the mold cavities.
- **Pouring cup or pouring basin:** The part of the gating system that receives the molten material from the pouring vessel.
- **Sprue:** The pouring cup attaches to the sprue, which is the vertical part of the gating system. The other end of the sprue attaches to the runners.
- **Runners:** The horizontal portion of the gating system that connects the sprues to the gates.
- **Gates:** The controlled entrances from the runners into the mold cavities.
- **Vents:** Additional channels that provide an escape for gases generated during the pour.
- **Parting line or parting surface:** The interface between the cope and drag halves of the mold, flask, or pattern.
- **Draft:** The taper on the casting or pattern that allow it to be withdrawn from the mold
- **Core box:** The mold or die used to produce the cores.

# MULTIPLE CHOICE QUESTIONS

1. 2000 cc. of air takes 1½ minutes to pass through a standard Specimen of sand (5.08 cm high and 5.08 cm in dia.). The manometer indicates pressure as 5 g/cm$^2$. In this case the permeability number is:
(a) 30 (b) 42
(c) 51 (d) 67

2. Match List-1 (Moulding process) with List-II (Binding agent) and select the correct answer using the codes given below the lists:

| List-I | List-II |
|---|---|
| A. Green sand | 1. Silicate |
| B. Core sand | 2. Organic |
| C. Shell moulding | 3. Clay |
| D. $CO_2$ process | 4. Plaster of Paris |
| | 5. Plastic |

**Codes:**

| | A | B | C | D |
|---|---|---|---|---|
| (a) | 3 | 2 | 5 | 1 |
| (b) | 3 | 2 | 4 | 1 |
| (c) | 2 | 3 | 5 | 4 |
| (d) | 2 | 3 | 4 | 5 |

3. Which of the following are the processes for thermosetting materials?
1. Compression
2. Transfer moulding
3. Injection moulding
4. Extrusion

Select the correct answer using the codes given below:
(a) 1 and 4
(b) 1 and 2
(c) 2 and 3
(d) 2, 3 and 4

4. Directional solidification can be achieved by providing:
(a) chills and chaplets
(b) chaplets and padding
(c) chills and padding
(d) chills, chaplets and padding

5. Which of the following pattern-materials are used in Precision Casting?
1. Plaster of Paris
2. Plastics
3. Anodized aluminium alloy
4. Frozen mercury

Select the correct answer using the codes given below:

**Codes:**
(a) 1 and 2
(b) 2 and 4
(c) 3 and 4
(d) 1 and 3

6. Match List-I (Casting process) with List-II (Applications) and select the correct answer using the codes given below the lists:

| List-I (Casting process) | List-I (Applications) |
|---|---|
| A. Centrifugal casting | 1. Carburettors |
| B. Squeeze casting | 2. Pipes |
| C. Die casting | 3. Wheels for automobiles |
| | 4. gear housings |

**Codes:**

| | A | B | C |
|---|---|---|---|
| (a) | 2 | 3 | 1 |
| (b) | 4 | 1 | 3 |
| (c) | 4 | 3 | 1 |

7. Match List-I (Material to be cast) with List-II (Shrinkage allowance in mm/m) and select the correct answer using the codes given below the lists:

| List-I (Material to be cast) | List-II (Shrinkage allowance in mm/m) |
|---|---|
| A. Grey cast iron | 1. 7 – 10 |
| B. brass | 2. 15 |
| C. Steel | 3. 20 |
| D. Zinc | 4. 24 |

**Codes:**

| | A | B | C | D |
|---|---|---|---|---|
| (a) | 1 | 2 | 3 | 4 |
| (b) | 3 | 4 | 1 | 2 |
| (c) | 1 | 4 | 3 | 2 |
| (d) | 3 | 2 | 1 | 4 |

8. Consider the following statements in respect of fabrication of plastic products:
1. Compression moulding is analogous to hot pressing of powdered metals.
2. Jet moulding is a modification of compression moulding.
3. Injection moulding is analogous to die casting of metals.
4. Transfer moulding is similar to hydraulic extrusion.

Which of these statements are correct?
(a) 1 and 2 (b) 1 and 3
(c) 1, 2 and 4 (d) 2, 3 and 4

9. Which one of the following gating systems is best suited to obtain directional solidification?
(a) top grating (b) part-time grating
(c) bottom grating (d) stepped grating

10. Which of the following are the characteristics of the injection moulding of plastics?
It is the most economical method of mass producing
1. a single item.

2. In most cases finished products are obtained.
3. There is lot of waste of thermoplastic since the
4. Runners and sprues cannot be reused.

Select the correct answer by using the following codes:

(a) 1 and 2
(b) 2 and 3
(c) 1 and 3
(d) 1, 2 and 3

11. Which one of the following processes consists of central sprue to feel metal into the cavities through a number of radial gates?

(a) centrifuging
(b) semi-centrifugal casting
(c) true centrifugal casting
(d) precision casting

12. Match List-I (Name of the casting process) with List-II (Process definition) and select the correct answer using the codes given below the lists:

| List-I (Name of the casting process) | List-II (Process definition) |
|---|---|
| A. Die casting | 1. This process involves use of a mould made of dried silica sand and phenolic resin mixture |
| B. Electroslag casting | 2. In this process, molten metal is forced by pressure into a metal mould |
| C. Centrifugal casting | 3. This process employs a consumable electrode |
| D. Precision casting | 4. This process involves rotating a mould while the metal solidifies |
| | 5. This process produces very smooth, highly accurate castings from both ferrous and non-ferrous alloys |

**Codes:**

| | A | B | C | D |
|---|---|---|---|---|
| (a) | 5 | 4 | 1 | 2 |
| (b) | 2 | 3 | 4 | 5 |
| (c) | 5 | 3 | 4 | 2 |
| (d) | 2 | 4 | 1 | 5 |

13. Match List-I (Casting defects) with List-II (Explanation) and select the correct answer using the codes given below the lists:

| List-I (Casting defects) | List-II (Explanation) |
|---|---|
| A. Metallic projections | I. Consist of rounded or rough projections internal or exposed cavities including blow holes and pin holes |
| B. Cavities | 2. Formed during melting, solidification and moulding |
| C. Inclusions | 3. Includes single folds, laps, scars adhering sand layers and oxide scale |
| D. Discontinuities | 4. Include cracks, cold or hot tearing and cold shuts |
| | 5. Consist of fins, flash or massive projections ions and rough surface |

**Codes:**

| | A | B | C | D |
|---|---|---|---|---|
| (a) | 1 | 5 | 3 | 2 |
| (b) | 1 | 5 | 2 | 4 |
| (c) | 5 | 1 | 2 | 4 |
| (d) | 5 | 1 | 3 | 2 |

14. Which of the following are produced by slush casting?

(a) hollow castings with thick walls
(b) hollow castings with thin walls
(c) thin castings
(d) thick castings

15. Match List-I (Name of the process) with List-II (Advantage) and select the correct answer using the codes given below the lists:

| List-I (Name of the process) | List-II (Advantage) |
|---|---|
| A. Sand casting | 1. Large cylindrical parts with good quality |
| B. Ceramic mold casting | 2. excellent dimensional accuracy and surface finish |
| C. Die casting | 3. Intricate shapes and close tolerance parts |
| D. Centrifugal casting | 4. Almost any metal is cast and there is no limit to size, shape and weight |
| | 5. Good dimensional accuracy, finish and low porosity |

**Codes:**

| | A | B | C | D |
|---|---|---|---|---|
| (a) | 2 | 3 | 5 | 1 |
| (b) | 4 | 1 | 2 | 3 |
| (c) | 2 | 1 | 5 | 3 |
| (d) | 4 | 3 | 2 | 1 |

16. Which one of the following processes consists of central spruces to feed metal into the cavities through a number of radial gates?

(a) centrifuging
(b) semi-centrifugal casting
(c) true centrifugal casting
(d) precision casting

17. The mould in shell moulding process is made up of which of the following?
(a) gypsum + setting agents
(b) green sand + clay
(c) sodium silicate + dried sand
(d) dried silica + phenolic resin

18. Which one of the following statements is not correct?
(a) in injection die moulding, exact amount of material to fill the cylinder is delivered
(b) injection die moulding is generally limited to forming thermoplastic material
(c) thermosetting plastics arc more suitable for extrusion moulding
(d) extrusion moulding process is used for giving shapes, such as rods, tubes, pipes, ropes etc.

19. Which one of the following is the process intermediate to compression and injection moulding?
(a) reaction moulding (b) transfer moulding
(c) pelleting (d) preheating

20. Powder metallurgy process involves which of the following?
1. Converting metals such as iron etc. into powder form.
2. Blending powders of. metals, then compacting and compressing to desired shape at room temperature.
3. Heating the compressed articles to a temperature above melting point of metal.
Select the correct answer using the code given below:
(a) 1, 2 and 3 (b) 1 and 2 only
(c) 2 and 3 only (d) 1 and 3 only

21. Which one of the following statements is correct?
In green sand moulding process, uniform ramming leads to:
(a) less sand expansion type of casting defect
(b) greater dimensional stability of the casting
(c) uniform flow of molten metal into the mould cavity
(d) less chance of gas porosity

22. The most preferred process for casting gas turbine blades is:
(a) die moulding (b) shell moulding
(c) investment moulding (d) sand casting

23. Match List-I with List-II and select the correct answer using the codes given below the lists:

| **List-I (Equipment)** | **List-II (Functions)** |
|---|---|
| A. Hot chamber | 1. Cleaning machine |
| B. Muller | 2. Core making |
| C. Dielectric baker | 3. Die casting |
| D. Sand blasting | 4. Annealing |
| | 5. Mixing |

**Codes:**

| | A | B | C | D |
|---|---|---|---|---|
| (a) | 3 | 5 | 2 | 1 |
| (b) | 4 | 2 | 5 | 3 |
| (c) | 4 | 2 | 3 | 1 |
| (d) | 3 | 5 | 1 | 2 |

24. Which of the materials can be used for making patterns?
1. Aluminium 2. Wax
3. Mercury 4. Lead
Select the correct answer using the codes below:
(a) 1, 3 and 4 (b) 2, 3 and 4
(c) 1, 2 and 4 (d) 1, 2 and 3

25. Directional solidification in castings can be improved by using:
(a) chills and chaplets
(b) chills and padding
(c) chaplets and padding
(d) chills, chaplets and padding.

26. Consider the following ingredients used in moulding:
1. Dry silica sand
2. Clay
3. Phenol formaldehyde
4. Sodium silicate
Those used for shell mould casting include:
(a) 1, 2 and 4 (b) 2, 3 and 4
(c) 1 and 3 (d) 1, 2, 3 and 4

27. Which of the following methods are used for obtaining directional solidification for riser design?
1. Suitable placement of chills.
2. Suitable placement of chaplets.
3. Employing padding.
Select the correct answer:
(a) 1 and 2 (b) 1 and 3
(c) 2 and 3 (d) 1, 2 and 3

28. Misrun is a casting defect which occurs due to:
(a) very high pouring temperature of the metal
(b) insufficient fluidity of the molten metal
(c) absorption of gases by the liquid metal
(d) improper alignment of the mould flasks

29. Which of the following pairs are correctly matched?
1. Pit moulding for large jobs.
2. Investment moulding lost wax process.
3. Plaster moulding mould prepared in gypsum.
(a) 1, 2 and 3 (b) 1 and 2
(c) 1 and 3 (d) 2 and 3

30. Which one of the following pairs is not correctly matched?
(a) Aluminium alloy piston : Pressure die casting
(b) Jewellery : Lost wax process
(c) Large pipes : Centrifugal casting
(d) Large bells : Loam moulding

31. If the melting ratio of a cupola is 10 : 1, then the coke requirement for one ton melt will be:
(a) 0.1 ton (b) 10 tons
(c) 1 ton (d) 11 tons

32. Which one of the following statements is not correct?
(a) The operating characteristic curve of an acceptance sampling plan shows the ability of the plan to distinguish between good and bad lots
(b) No sampling plan can give complete protection against the acceptance of defective products
(c) C chart has straight line limits and U chart has zig-zag limits
(d) Double sampling result in more inspection than single sampling if the incoming quality is very bad

33. Which of the following are the requirements of an ideal gating system?
1. The molten metal should enter the mould cavity with as high a velocity as possible.
2. It should facilitate complete fillings of the mould cavity.
3. It should be able to prevent the absorption of air or gases from the surroundings on the molten metal while flowing through it.

Select the correct answer using the codes given below:
(a) 1, 2 and 3 (b) 1 and 2
(c) 2 and 3 (d) 1 and 3

34. A spherical drop of molten metal of radius 2 mm was found to solidify in 10 seconds. A similar drop of radius 4 mm would solidify in:
(a) 14.14 second
(b) 20 seconds
(c) 18.30 second
(d) 40 seconds

35. In solidification of metal during casting, compensation for solid contraction is:
(a) Provided by the oversize pattern
(b) Achieved by properly placed risers
(c) Obtained by promoting direction solidification
(d) Made by providing chills

36. Match List-I (Types of casting) with List-II (Working principles) and select the correct answer using the codes given below the lists:

| List-I | List-II |
|---|---|
| A. Die casting | 1. Molten metal is forced into the die under pressure |
| B. Centrifugal casting | 2. Axis of rotation does not coincide with axis of mould |
| C. Centrifuging | 3. Metal solidifies when mould is rotating |
| D. Continuous casting | 4. Continuously pouring molten metal into mould |

**Codes:**

| | A | B | C | D |
|---|---|---|---|---|
| (a) | 1 | 3 | 2 | 4 |
| (b) | 4 | 3 | 2 | 1 |
| (c) | 1 | 2 | 3 | 4 |
| (d) | 4 | 2 | 3 | 1 |

37. Match List-I (Process)with List-II (Products/materials) and select the correct answer using the codes given below the lists:

| List-I | List-II |
|---|---|
| A. Die casting | 1. Phenol formaldehyde |
| B. Shell moulding | 2. CI. Pipes |
| C. $CO_2$ moulding | 3. Non-ferrous alloys |
| D. Centrifugal casting | 4. Sodium silicate |

**Codes:**

| | A | B | C | D |
|---|---|---|---|---|
| (a) | 1 | 3 | 4 | 2 |
| (b) | 3 | 1 | 4 | 2 |
| (c) | 3 | 1 | 2 | 4 |
| (d) | 1 | 3 | 2 | 4 |

38. The main purpose of chaplets is:
(a) to ensure directional solidification
(b) to provide efficient venting
(c) for aligning the mould boxes
(d) to support the cores

39. Scab is a:
(a) sand casting defect (b) machining defect
(c) welding defect (d) forging defect

40. The gating ratio 2 : 8 : 1 for copper in gating system design refers to the ratio of areas of:
(a) sprue : runner : ingate (b) runner : ingate : sprue
(c) runner : sprue : ingate (d) ingate : runner : sprue

41. Which one of the following processes produces a casting when pressure forces the molten metal into the mould cavity?
(a) shell moulding (b) investment casting
(c) die casting (d) continuous casting

42. In shell moulding, how can the shell thickness be accurately maintained?
(a) by controlling the time during which the pattern is in contact with mould
(b) by controlling the time during which the pattern is heated.
(c) by maintaining the temperature of the pattern in the range of 175°C – 380°C
(d) By the type of binder used

43. In gating system design, which one of the following is the correct sequence in which choke area, pouring time, pouring basin and sprue sizes are calculated?
(a) choke area - pouring time - pouring basin - sprue
(b) pouring basin - sprue - choke area - pouring time
(c) choke area - sprue - pouring basin - pouring time
(d) pouring basin - pouring time - choke area - sprue

44. In which of the following are metal moulds used?
(a) greensand mould (b) dry sand mould
(c) die casting process (d) loan moulding

45. Which of the following materials are used for making patterns in investment casting method?
1. Wax
2. Rubber
3. Wood
4. Plastic
Select the correct answer using the code given below:
**Code:**
(a) only 1 and 3
(b) only 2 and 3
(c) only 1, 2 and 4
(d) only 2, 3 and 4

46. Shell moulding can be used for:
(a) producing milling cutters
(b) making gold ornaments
(c) producing heavy and thick walled casting
(d) producing thin casting

47. According to Chvorinov's equation, the solidification time of a casting is proportional to:
(a) $v^2$ (b) v
(c) $1/v$ (d) $1/v^2$
where, $v$ = volume of casting

48. A gating ratio of 1 : 2 : 4 is used to design the gating system for magnesium alloy casting. This gating ratio refers to the cross-section areas of the various gating elements as given below:
1. Down sprue
2. Runner bar
3. Ingates
The correct sequence of the above elements in the ratio 1 : 2 : 4 is:
(a) 1, 2 and 3
(b) 1, 3 and 2
(c) 2, 3 and 1
(d) 3, 1 and 2

49. Match List I (Products) with List II (Casting process) and select the correct answer using "the codes given below the lists :

| List-I (Products) | List-II (Casting process) |
|---|---|
| A. Hollow statues | 1. Centrifugal casting |
| B. Dentures | 2. Investment casting |
| C. Aluminium alloy pistons | 3. Slush casting |
| D. Rocker arms | 4. Shell moulding |
| | 5. Gravity die casting |

**Codes:**

| | A | B | C | D |
|---|---|---|---|---|
| (a) | 3 | 1 | 4 | 5 |
| (b) | 1 | 3 | 4 | 5 |
| (c) | 1 | 2 | 3 | 4 |
| (d) | 3 | 2 | 5 | 4 |

50. Match List-I (Type of moulding) with List-II (Mechanism involved) and select the correct answer using the codes given below the lists:

| List-I (Type of moulding) | List-II (Mechanism involved) |
|---|---|
| A. Compression moulding | 1. Mould cavity-must be heated to cure the plastic forced into it |
| B. Injected | 2. Similar to Hydraulic extrusion |
| C. Jet moulding | 3. analogous to hot-pressing of powdered metals |
| D. Extrusion moulding | 4. analogous to die casting of metals |

**Codes:**

| | A | B | C | D |
|---|---|---|---|---|
| (a) | 2 | 4 | 3 | 1 |
| (b) | 3 | 1 | 4 | 2 |
| (c) | 2 | 1 | 3 | 4 |
| (d) | 3 | 4 | 2 | 1 |

51. Match List-I with List-II and select the correct answer using the codes 'given below the lists:

| List-I (Casting process) | List-II (Principle) |
|---|---|
| A. Die casting | 1. The metal solidifies in a rotating mould |
| B. Investment casting | 2. The pattern cluster is repeatedly dipped into a ceramic slurry and dusted with refractory |
| C. Shell moulding | 3. Molten metal is forced by pressure into a metallic mould |
| D. Centrifugal casting | 4. After cooling, the invest is removed from the casting by pressure jetting or vibratory cleaning |

**Codes:**

| | A | B | C | D |
|---|---|---|---|---|
| (a) | 2 | 1 | 3 | 4 |
| (b) | 3 | 4 | 2 | 1 |
| (c) | 2 | 4 | 3 | 1 |
| (d) | 3 | 1 | 2 | 4 |

52. Consider the following statements in respect of investment castings:
1. The pattern or patterns is/are not jointed to a stalk or spure also of wax to form a tree of patterns.
2. The prepared moulds are placed in an oven and, heated gently to dry off the invest and melt out the bulk of wax.

3. The moulds are usually poured by placing the moulds in a vacuum chamber.

Which of the statements given above are correct?

(a) 1 and 2 only (b) 1 and 3 only
(c) 2 and 3 only (d) 1, 2 and 3

53. Which of the following are employed in shell moulding?

1. Resin binder 2. Metal pattern
3. Heating coils

Select the correct answer using the code given below:

(a) 1 and 2 only (b) 1 and 3 only
(c) 2 and 3 only (d) 1, 2 and 3

54. Which one of the following is the correct statement?

In a centrifugal casting method:

(a) no core is used
(b) core may be made of any metal
(c) core is made of sand
(d) core is made of ferrous metal

55. Which cute of the following is the correct statement?

Gate is provided in moulds to:

(a) feed the casting at a constant rate
(b) give passage to gases
(c) compensate for shrinkage
(d) avoid cavities

56. Bottom gating system is sometimes preferred in casting because:

(a) it enables rapid filling of mould cavity
(b) it is easier to provide in the mould
(c) it provides cleaner metal
(d) it reduces splashing and turbulence

57. The pattern adopted for those castings where there are some portions which are structurally weak and are likely to break by the force of ramming are called:

(a) loose piece pattern (b) follow board pattern
(c) skelton pattern (d) single piece pattern

58. Which of the following casting processes does not do not require Central core for producing pipe?

1. Sand casting process
2. Die casting process
3. centrifugal casting process

Select the correct answer using the code given below:

(a) 1 and 2 (b) 2 only
(c) 2 and 3 (d) 3 only

59. Small amount of carbonaceous material sprinkled on the inner surface of mould cavity is called:

(a) backing sand (b) facing sand
(c) green sand (d) dry sand

60. A standard 90°V-notch weir is used to measure discharge. The discharge is $Q_1$ for a height $H_1$ above the sill and $Q_2$ is the discharge for a height $H_2$. If $H_2/H_1$ is 4, then $Q_2/Q_1$ is:

(a) 32 (b) $16\sqrt{2}$
(c) 16 (d) 8

61. A right circular cylinder is filled with a liquid upto its top level. It is rotated about its vertical axis at such a speed that half the liquid spills out, then the pressure at the point of intersection of the axis and bottom surface is:

(a) same as before rotation
(b) half on the value before rotation
(c) quarter of the value before rotation
(d) equal to atmospheric pressure

62. Three immiscible liquids of specific densities ρ, 2ρ and 3ρ are kept in a jar. The height of the liquids in the jar and at the piezometer fitted to the bottom of the air are as shown in the given figure. The ratio H/*h* is:

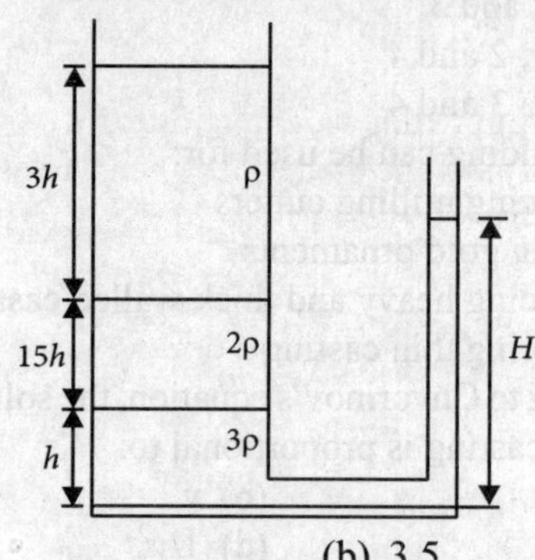


(a) 4 (b) 3.5
(c) 3 (d) 2.5

63. Which one of the following sequences indicates the correct order for flue gas flow in the steam power plant layout?

(a) superheater, economiser, air preheater
(b) economiser, air preheater, superheater
(c) air preheater, economiser, superheater
(d) economiser, superheater, air preheater.

64. Which one of the following statements is not correct?

In a fluidized-bed boiler:

(a) the combustion temperatures are higher than those in the conventional boilers
(b) inferior grade of coal can be used without slagging problems
(c) the formation of NO,, is less than that in the conventional boilers
(d) the volumetric heat release rates are higher than those in the conventional boilers

65. Consider the following statements:

Subcooling in the condenser of a refrigeration system is advisable when:

1. expansion valve is at a higher elevation than condenser.
2. there is a large pressure drop in the line connecting condenser to the expansion valve.
3. the refrigeration effect is to he increased.
4. the compressor work is to he reduced

Which of these statements are correct?

(a) 1 and 2 (h) 1, 3 and 4
(c) 2, 3 and 4 (d) 1, 2 and 3

66. Match List-I (Machines) with List-II (Features) and select the correct answer using the codes given below the lists:

| List-I (Machine) | List-II (Features) |
|---|---|
| A. Steam engine | 1. Velocity compounding |
| B. Impulse turbine | 2. Diagram factor |
| C. Reaction turbine | 3. Continuous pressure drop |
| D. Centrifugal compressore | 4. Isentropic efficiency |

**Codes:**

| | A | B | C | D |
|---|---|---|---|---|
| (a) | 3 | 4 | 2 | 1 |
| (b) | 2 | 1 | 3 | 4 |
| (c) | 2 | 4 | 3 | 1 |
| (d) | 3 | 1 | 2 | 4 |

67. For maximum blade efficiency of a single-stage impulse turbine, the blade speed ratio, ($\alpha$ is the angle made by absolute velocity at inlet) should be:

(a) $\cos 2\alpha$ (b) $\frac{\cos 2\alpha}{2}$

(c) $\frac{\cos\alpha}{2}$ (d) $\frac{2}{\cos\alpha}$

68. The given figure shows the variation of certain steam parameter in case of a simple impulse turbine. The curve A-B-C represents the variation of:

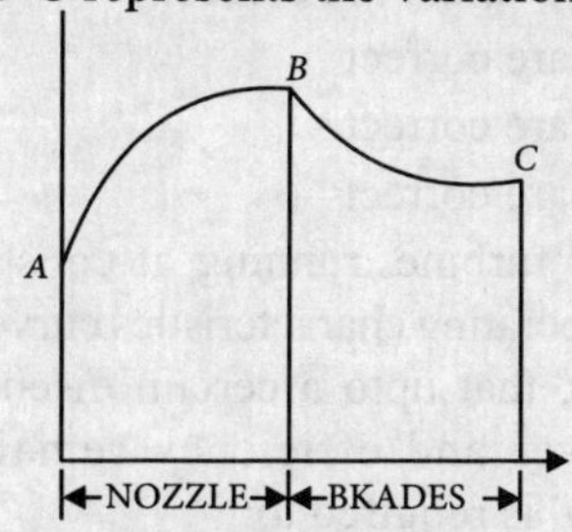


(a) pressure in nozzle and blades
(b) velocity in nozzle and blades
(c) temperature in nozzle and blades
(d) enthalpy in nozzle and blades

69. A solar-absorption refrigeration system has generator temperature of 87°C, evaporator temperature of – 3° C, condenser and absorber temperatures of 27°C each, then its maximum possible COP is:

(a) 10.0 (b) 9.0
(c) 1.80 (d) 1.50

70. The flow in the vaneless space between the impeller exit and diffuser inlet of a centrifugal compressor can be assumed as:

(a) free vortex (b) forced vortex
(c) solid body rotation (d) logarithimic spiral

71. Which of the following statement (s) is/are relevant to critical flow through a steam nozzle?

1. Flow rate through the nozzle is minimum.
2. Flow rate through the nozzle is maximum.
3. Velocity at the throat is supersonic.
4. Velocity at the throat is sonic.

Select the correct answer using the codes given below:

**Codes:**

(a) 1 alone (b) 1 and 3
(c) 2 and 4 (d) 4 alone

72. Which portion of the centrifugal compressor characteristics shown in the figure is difficult to obtain experimentally?

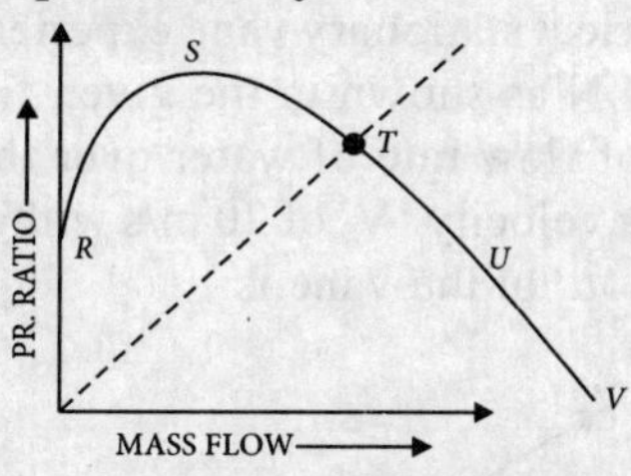


(a) RS (b) ST
(c) TU (d) UV

73. Consider the following statements regarding the axial flow in an air compressor:

1. Surging is a local phenomenon while stalling affects the entire compressor.
2. Stalling is a local phenomenon while surging affects the entire compressor.
3. The pressure ratio of an axial compressor stage is smaller than that of a centrifugal compressor stage.

Of these statements:

(a) 1, 2 and 3 are correct
(b) 1 and 2 are correct
(c) 2 and 3 correct
(d) 1 and 3 correct

74. Match List-I (Expansion device) with List-II (Operation) and select the correct answer using the codes given below the lists:

| List-I (Expansion device) | List-II (Operation |
|---|---|
| A. Float valve | 1. Constant degree of superheat at evaporator exit pressure |
| B. Automatic expansion valve | 2. Constant degree of superheat at evaporator inlet pressure |
| C. Internally equalized thermostatic expansion valve | 3. Constant level of refrigerant in the evaporator |
| D. Extrammaly equalized thermostatic expansion walve | 4. Constant pressure in the evaporator |

**Codes:**

| | A | B | C | D |
|---|---|---|---|---|
| (a) | 1 | 2 | 4 | 3 |
| (b) | 3 | 2 | 4 | 1 |
| (c) | 3 | 4 | 2 | 1 |
| (d) | 1 | 4 | 2 | 3 |

75. Consider the specific speed ranges of the following types of turbines:
1. Francis    2. Kaplan
3. Pelton.
The sequence of their specific speed in increasing order is:
(a) 1, 2, 3    (b) 3, 1, 2
(c) 3, 2, 1    (d) 2, 3, 1

76. A symmetrical stationary vane experiences a force '*F*' of 100 N as shown in the given figure, when the mass of flow rate of water over the vane is 5 kg/s with a velocity 'V' of 20 m/s without friction. The angle 'α' of the vane is:

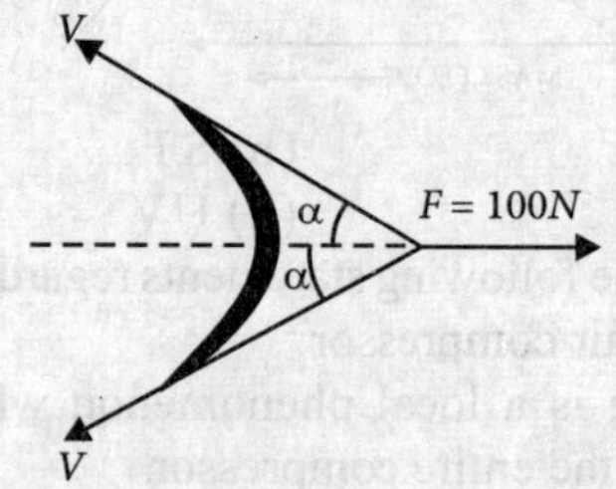


(a) zero    (b) 30°
(c) 45°    (d) 60°.

77. In a fluid coupling, the torque transmitted is 50 kN.m, when the speed of the driving and driven shaft is 900 rpm and 720 rpm respectively. The efficiency of the fluid coupling will be:
(a) 20%    (b) 25%
(c) 80%    (d) 90%.

78. Consider the following statements regarding the fluid coupling:
1. Efficiency increases with increase in speed ratio.
2. Neglecting friction the output torque is equal to input torque.
3. At the same input speed, higher slip requires higher input torque.
Which of these statements are correct?
(a) 1, 2 and 3    (b) 1 and 2
(c) 2 and 3    (d) 1 and 3

79. The level of runner exit is 5 m above the tail race, and atmospheric pressure is 10.3 m. The pressure at the exit of the runner for a divergent draft tube can be:
(a) 5 m    (b) 5.3 m
(c) 10 m    (d) 10.3 m

80. Consider the following statements:
A surge tank provided on the penstock connected to a water turbine
1. helps in reducing the water hammer
2. stores extra water when not needed.
3. provides increased demand of water.
Which of these statements are correct?
(a) 1 and 3.    (b) 2 and 3
(c) 1 and 2    (d) 1, 2 and 3

81. If a reciprocating pump having a mechanical efficiency of 80% delivers water at the rate of 80 kg/s with a head of 30 m, the brake power of the pump is:
(a) 29.4 kW    (b) 20.8 kW
(c) 15.4 kW    (d) 10.8 kW

82. The vertical component of force on a curved surface submerged in a static liquid is equal to the
(a) Weight of liquid column above the C.G. of the curved surface
(b) Weight of liquid above the curved surface
(c) Product of pressure at C.G, multiplied by the area of the curved surface
(d) Product of pressure at C.G, multiplied by the projected area of the curved surface.

83. Consider the following statements pertaining to a centrifugal pump
1. The manometric head is the head developed by the pump.
2. The suction pipe has, generally, a larger diameter as compared to the discharge pipe.
3. The suction pipe is provided with a foot valve and a strainer.
4. The delivery pipe is provided with a foot valve and a strainer.
Of these statements:
(a) 1, 2 and 3 and 4 are correct
(b) 1 and 2 are correct
(c) 2 and 3 are correct
(d) 1 and 3 are correct

84. For a water turbine, running at constant head and speed, the operating characteristics curves in the given figure show, that upto a certain discharge '*q*' both output power and efficiency remain zero. The discharge '*q*' is required to:

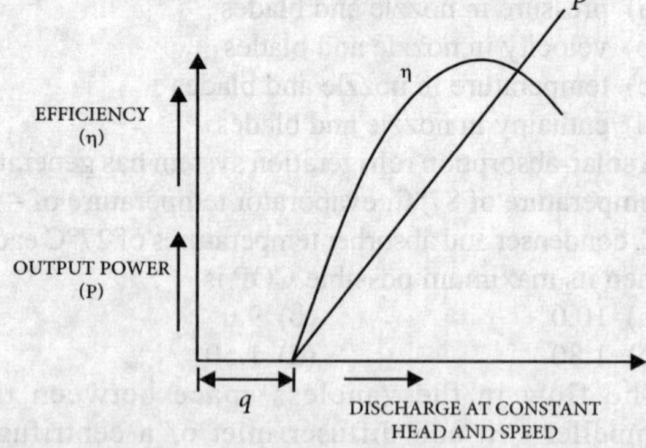


(a) overcome initial inertia
(b) overcome initial friction
(c) keep the hydraulic circuit full
(d) keep the turbine running at no load

85. In fluid machinery, the relationship between saturation temperature and pressure decides the process of:
(a) flow separation    (b) turbulent mixing
(c) cavitation    (d) water hammer

86. A centrifugal blower delivering Qm$^3$/s against a head of H m is driven at half the original speed. The new head and discharge would be:

(a) $H$ and $Q/2$ (b) $\frac{H}{4}$ and $\frac{Q}{2}$

(c) $\frac{H}{2}$ and $\frac{Q}{8}$ (d) $H$ and $\frac{Q}{4}$

87. The maximum number of jets generally employed in an impulse turbine without jet interference is:

(a) 4 (b) 6

(c) 8 (d) 12

88. A hydraulic coupling transmits 1 kW of power at an input speed of 200 rpm, with a slip of 2%. If the input speed is changed to 400 rpm, the power transmitted with the same slip is:

(a) 2 kW (b) 1/2 kW

(c) 4 kW (d) 8 kW

## ANSWERS WITH EXPLANATIONS

1. (d) Permeability number, $P = \frac{Vh}{pAt}$

$V = 2000$ c.c., $t = 1.5$ min, $h = 5.08$ cm, $d = 5.08$ cm, $p = 5$ g/cm$^2$

$$P = \frac{2000 \times 5.08}{5 \times \frac{\pi}{4}(5.08)^2 \times 1.5} = 66.83 = 67$$

2. (b) 3. (a) 4. (c) 5. (a) 6. (a)
7. (a) 8. (b) 9. (b) 10. (a) 11. (c)
12. (b) 13. (c) 14. (b) 15. (d) 16. (c)
17. (d) 18. (c) 19. (d) 20. (a) 21. (d)
22. (c) 23. (a) 24. (c) 25. (b) 26. (c)
27. (b) 28. (b) 29. (a) 30. (d)

31. (b) Melting ratio $= \frac{\text{Weight of coke}}{\text{Weight to melt}}$

Coke required = 10 × 1 = 10 tons

32. (c) 33. (c)

34. (d) Solidification time for a sphere,

$$t \alpha \left(\frac{V}{A}\right)^2$$

$$\frac{V}{A} = \frac{\left(\frac{4}{3}\pi r^3\right)}{4\pi r^2} = \frac{r}{3}$$

$$t \propto r^2$$

$$\frac{t_2}{t_1} = \left(\frac{4}{3}\right)^2 = 4$$

$t_2 = 4 \times 10 = 40$ s

35. (b) 36. (a) 37. (b) 38. (d) 39. (a)
40. (c) 41. (c) 42. (c) 43. (c) 44. (c)
45. (c) 46. (d) 47. (a) 48. (a) 49. (d)
50. (b) 51. (b) 52. (c) 53. (d) 54. (c)
55. (a) 56. (a) 57. (a) 58. (d) 59. (b)

60. (d) $Q \propto H^{3/2}, \frac{Q_2}{Q_1} = \left(\frac{H_2}{H_1}\right)^{3/2} = 4^{3/2} = 8$

61. (d) $\frac{1}{2}.\pi r^2 z = \frac{1}{2}.\pi r^2 h, z = h$

62. (c) $(3\rho h + 3ph + 3\rho h)g = 3\rho gH$

$9\rho gh = 3\ \rho gh$, or $H/h = 3$

63. (a) Sequence of flue gas flow in steam power plant: Superheater → economiser → air preheater

64. (a) The combustion temperatures are lower than those in the conventional boilers. Hence, statement 1 is not correct.

65. (c) 66. (b)

67. (c) For maximum blade efficiency of single-stage impulse turbine, blade speed ratio, $\rho = \frac{\cos\alpha}{2}$

68. (b) Curve A-B-C represents the variation of velocity in nozzle and blades of simple impulse turbine.

69. (d) $COP = \frac{(87+3)}{(87-27)} = \frac{90}{60} = 1.5$

70. (a) The flow in the vaneless space between impeller exit and diffuser inlet of a centrifugal compressor can be assumed as free vortex

71. (c)

72. (a) Portion RS of the centrifugal compressor is difficult to obtain experimentally.

73. (d) 74. (c)

75. (b) The sequence of specific heat of hydraulic turbines in increasing order is Pelton → Francis → Kaplan, i,e 3, 1, 2

76. (d)

77. (c) Efficiency of hydraulic coupling

$$\cos\alpha = \frac{1}{2}, \alpha = 60°$$

$$\frac{N_2}{N_2} = \frac{720}{900} = 0.8 \text{ or } 80\%$$

78. (c) 79. (b) 80. (d) 81. (a) 82. (b)

83. (c)

84. (d) Discharge q is required in a water turbine to keep the turbine running at no load.

85. (c) The relationship between situation temperature and pressure in fluid machinery decides the process of cavitation.

86. (b)

87. (b) Maximum number of jets employed in an impulse turbine without interference = 6

88. (c) $P \propto N^2, P_2 = P_1\left(\frac{N_2}{N_1}\right)^2 = 1 \times \left(\frac{400}{200}\right)^2 = 4\text{kW}$

❑❑❑

# 16. Fabrication Process

- Metal fabrication is the building of metal structures by cutting, bending, and assembling.
- Cutting is done by sawing, shearing, or chiseling torching with hand-held torches and via numerical control (CNC) cutters (using a laser, mill bits, torch, or water jet).
- Bending is done by hammering (manual or powered) or via press brakes and similar tools. Modern metal fabricators utilize press brakes to either coin or air-bend metal sheet into form. CNC-controlled back gauges utilize hard stops to position cut parts in order to place bend lines in the correct position. Off-line programing software now makes programing the CNC-controlled press brakes seamless and very efficient.
- Assembling (joining of the pieces) is done by welding, binding with adhesives, riveting, threaded fasteners, or even yet more bending in the form of a crimped seam. Structural steel and sheet metal are the usual starting materials for fabrication, along with the welding wire, flux, and fasteners that will join the cut pieces. As with other manufacturing processes, both human labor and automation are commonly used.
- The product resulting from fabrication may be called a fabrication. Shops that specialize in this type of metal work are called fab shops. The end products of other common types of metalworking, such as machining, metal stamping, forging, and casting, may be similar in shape and function, but those processes are not classified as fabrication.
- Fabrication shops and machine shops have overlapping capabilities, but fabrication shops generally concentrate on metal preparation and assembly as described above. By comparison, machine shops also cut metal, but they are more concerned with the machining of parts on machine tools. Firms that encompass both fab work and machining are also common.
- Blacksmithing has always involved fabrication, although it was not always called by that name.
- The products produced by welders, which are often referred to as weldments, are an example of fabrication.
- Boilermakers originally specialized in boilers, leading to their trade's name, but the term as used today has a broader meaning.
- Similarly, millwrights originally specialized in setting up grain mills and saw mills, but today they may be called upon for a broad range of fabrication work.
- Ironworkers, also known as steel erectors, also engage in fabrication. Often the fabrications for structural work begin as prefabricated segments in a fab shop, then are moved to the site by truck, rail, or barge, and finally are installed by erectors.
- Metal fabrication is a value added process that involves the construction of machines and structures from various raw materials. A fab shop will bid on a job, usually based on the engineering drawings, and if awarded the contract will build the product.
- Large fab shops will employ a multitude of value added processes in one plant or facility including welding, cutting, forming and machining. These large fab shops offer additional value to their customers by limiting the need for purchasing personnel to locate multiple vendors for different services.
- Metal fabrication jobs usually start with shop drawings including precise measurements then move to the fabrication stage and finally to the installation of the final project. Fabrication shops are employed by contractors, OEMs and VARs. Typical projects include; loose parts, structural frames for buildings and heavy equipment, and hand railings and stairs for buildings.
- Standard raw materials used by metal fabricators are;
  - plate metal
  - formed and expanded metal
  - tube stock,
  - welding wire/welding rod
  - casting
- The raw material has to be cut to size. This is done with a variety of tools.
- The most common way to cut material is by Shearing (metalworking).
- Special band saws designed for cutting metal have hardened blades and a feed mechanism for even cutting. Abrasive cut-off saws, also known as chop saws, are similar to miter saws but with a steel cutting abrasive disk. Cutting torches can cut very large sections of steel with little effort.
- Burn tables are CNC cutting torches, usually natural gas powered. Plasma and laser cutting tables, and Water jet cutters, are also common. Plate steel is loaded on a table and the parts are cut out as programmed.
- The support table is made of a grid of bars that can be replaced. Some very expensive burn tables also include CNC punch capability, with a carousel of different punches and taps. Fabrication of structural steel by plasma and laser cutting introduces robots to move the cutting head in three dimensions around the material to be cut.

- Forming is a process of material deformation. Forming is typically applied to metals. To define the process, a raw material piece is formed by applying force to an object. The force must be great enough to change the shape of the object from its initial shape.
- The process of forming can be controlled with the use of tools such as punches or dies. Machinery can also be used to regulate force magnitude and direction. Proper design and use of tools with machinery creates a repeatable form which can be used to create products for many industries, including jewelry, aerospace, automotive, etc.
- Machining is a trade, in and of itself, although Fab shops will generally entail a limited machining capability including; metal lathes, mills, magnetic based drills along with other portable metal working tools.
- Welding is the main focus of steel fabrication. The formed and machined parts will be assembled and tack welded into place then re-checked for accuracy. A fixture may be used to locate parts for welding if multiple weldments have been ordered.
- The welder then completes welding per the engineering drawings, if welding is detailed, or per his own judgment if no welding details are provided.
- Special precautions may be needed to prevent warping of the weldment due to heat. These may include re-designing the weldment to use less weld, welding in a staggered fashion, using a stout fixture, covering the weldment in sand during cooling, and straightening operations after welding.
- Straightening of warped steel weldments is done with an Oxy-acetylene torch and is somewhat of an art. Heat is selectively applied to the steel in a slow, linear sweep.
- The steel will have a net contraction, upon cooling, in the direction of the sweep. A highly skilled welder can remove significant warpage using this technique.
- Steel weldments are occasionally annealed in a low temperature oven to relieve residual stresses. Such weldments, particularly those employed for engine blocks, may be line-bored after heat treatment.
- The maximum shear stress theory is conservative. For simple unidirectional normal stresses all theories are equivalent, which means all theories will give the same result.
- Maximum Shear stress Theory- This theory postulates that failure will occur if the magnitude of the maximum shear stress in the part exceeds the shear strength of the material determined from uniaxial testing.
- Maximum normal stress theory - This theory postulates that failure will occur if the maximum normal stress in the part exceeds the ultimate tensile stress of the material as determined from uniaxial testing.
- Maximum strain energy theory - This theory postulates that failure will occur when the strain energy per unit volume due to the applied stresses in a part equals the strain energy per unit volume at the yield point in uniaxial testing.
- Maximum distortion energy theory - This theory is also known as shear energy theory or von Mises-Hencky theory. This theory postulates that failure will occur when the distortion energy per unit volume due to the applied stresses in a part equals the distortion energy per unit volume at the yield point in uniaxial testing.
- Fracture mechanics was established by Alan Arnold Griffith and George Rankine Irwin. This important theory is also known as numeric conversion of toughness of material in the case of crack existence.
- Fractology was proposed by Takeo Yokobori because each fracture laws including creep rupture criterion must be combined nonlinearly.
- A material's strength is dependent on its microstructure. The engineering processes to which a material is subjected can alter this microstructure.
- The variety of strengthening mechanisms that alter the strength of a material includes work hardening, solid solution strengthening, precipitation hardening and grain boundary strengthening and can be quantitatively and qualitatively explained.
- Strengthening mechanisms are accompanied by the caveat that some other mechanical properties of the material may degenerate in an attempt to make the material stronger. For example, in grain boundary strengthening, although yield strength is maximized with decreasing grain size, ultimately, very small grain sizes make the material brittle.
- In general, the yield strength of a material is an adequate indicator of the material's mechanical strength. Considered in tandem with the fact that the yield strength is the parameter that predicts plastic deformation in the material, one can make informed decisions on how to increase the strength of a material depending its microstructural properties and the desired end effect.
- Strength is expressed in terms of the limiting values of the compressive stress, tensile stress, and shear stresses that would cause failure. The effects of dynamic loading are probably the most important practical consideration of the strength of materials, especially the problem of fatigue.
- Repeated loading often initiates brittle cracks, which grow until failure occurs. The cracks always start at stress concentrations, especially changes in cross-section of the product, near holes and corners at nominal stress levels far lower than those quoted for the strength of the material.

# MULTIPLE CHOICE QUESTIONS

1. The edge of a steel plate cut by oxygen cutting will get hardened when the carbon content is:
(a) less than 0.1 percent
(b) less than 0.3 percent
(c) more than 0.3 percent
(d) anywhere between 0.1 to 1.0 percent

2. Weld spatter occurs due to any of the following except:
(a) high welding current
(b) too small an electrode
(c) arc
(d) wrong polarity

3. Thick steel plate cut with oxygen normally shows signs of cracking. This tendency for cracking can be minimized by:
(a) slow speed cutting
(b) cutting in two or more stages
(c) preheating the plate
(d) using oxy-acetylene flame

4. Electron beam welding can be carried out in:
(a) open air
(b) a shielding gas environment
(c) a pressurized inert gas chamber
(d) vacuum

5. Which one of the following welding processes uses non-consumable electrodes?
(a) TIG welding
(b) MIG welding
(c) Manual arc welding
(d) Submerged arc welding

6. Match List-I with List-II and Select the correct answer using the codes given below the Lists:

| List-I (Filler) | List-II (Joining process) |
|---|---|
| A. Cu, Zn, Ag alloy | 1. Braze welding |
| B. Cu, Sn alloy | 2. Brazing |
| C. Pb, Sb alloy | 3. Soldering |
| D. Iron oxide and aluminium powder | 4. TIG welding of aluminium. |

**Codes:**

| | A | B | C | D |
|---|---|---|---|---|
| (a) | 4 | 1 | 3 | 2 |
| (b) | 1 | 2 | 4 | 3 |
| (c) | 2 | 1 | 3 | 4 |
| (d) | 2 | 4 | 3 | 1 |

7. Consider the following statements:
MIG welding process uses
1. consumable electrode
2. non-consumable electrode
3. D. C power supply
4. A. C power supply.
Of these statements:
(a) 2 and 4 are correct
(b) 2 and 3 arc correct
(c) 1 and 4 are correct
(d) 1 and 3 are correct

8. In oxy-acetylene gas welding, for complete combustion, the volume of oxygen required per unit of acetylene is:
(a) 1 (b) 1.5
(c) 2 (d) 2.5

9. Small amount of carbonaceous material sprinkled on the inner surface of mould cavity is called:
(a) backing sand (b) facing sand
(c) green sand (d) dry sand

10. The voltage-current characteristics of a DC generator for arc welding is a straight line between an open-circuit voltage of 80 V and short-circuit current of 300 A. The generator settings for maximum arc power will be:
(a) 80 V and 150 A (b) 40 V and 300 A
(c) 40 V and 150 V (d) V and 300 A

11. Which of the following joining processes are best suited for manufacturing pipes to carry gas products?
1. Rivetting 2. Welding
3. Bolts and nuts
Select the correct answer using the codes given below:
**Codes:**
(a) 1 and 2 (b) 1 and 3
(c) 2 alone (d) 1, 2 and 3

12. The correct sequence of the given materials in ascending order of their weldability is:
(a) MS, copper, cast iron, aluminium
(b) Cast iron, MS, aluminium copper
(c) Copper, cast iron, MS, aluminium
(d) Aluminium, copper, cast iron, MS

13. Which one of the following statements is correct?
(a) no flux is used in gas welding of mild steel
(b) borax is the commonly used flux coating on welding electrodes
(c) laser beam welding employs a vacuum chamber and thus avoids use of a shielding method
(d) AC can be used for GTAW process

14. Consider the following processes
1. Gas welding
2. Thermit welding
3. Arc welding
4. Resistance welding
The correct sequence of these processes in increasing order of their welding temperatures is:
(a) 1, 3, 4, 2 (b) 1, 2, 3, 4
(c) 4, 3, 1, 2 (d) 4, 1, 3, 2

15. Which of the following statements is/arc correct in respect of welding of two pieces in upset welding?
   1. The ends to be welded should touch each other before current is switched
   2. The ends to be welded should touch each other after current is switched on.
   3. The two pieces have to be pressed together after desired welding temperature is reached.

   Select the correct answer using the code given below:
   (a) 1 only (b) 1 and 3
   (c) 2 only (d) 2 and 1
16. Arc blow is more common in:
   (a) a.c. welding
   (b) d.c. welding with straight polarity
   (c) d.c. welding with bare electrods
   (d) a.c. welding with bare electrodes.
17. Pinch effect in welding is the result of:
   (a) expansion of gases in the arc
   (b) electromagnetic forces
   (c) electric force
   (d) surface tension of the molten metal
18. In manual arc welding, the equipment should have drooping characteristics in order to maintain the:
   (a) voltage constant when arc length changes
   (b) current constant when arc length changes
   (c) temperature in the arc constant
   (d) weld pool red-hot
19. In are welding D.C. reverse polarity is used to bear greater advantage in:
   (a) overhead welding
   (b) flat welding of lap joints
   (c) edge welding
   (d) flat welding of butt joints
20. Oxyacetylene reducing flame is used while carrying out the welding on:
   (a) mild Steel
   (b) high carbon steel
   (c) grey cast iron
   (d) alloy steels
21. Which one of the following welding techniques in vacuum environment required?
   (a) Ultrasonic welding
   (b) Laser beam welding
   (c) Plasma arc welding
   (d) Electron beam welding
22. Consider the following statements:
   1. In arc welding, 65% to 75% heat is generated the anode.
   2. Duty cycle in case of arc welding is the cycle of complete-welding of work piece from the beginning.
   3. Arc blow is more common with DC welding.

   Which of the statements given above are correct?
   (a) 1, 2 and 3 (b) 1 and 2
   (c) 2 and 3 (d) 1 and 3
23. Hot cracks occur in the weld and fusion zone as the metal solidifies. Which of the following are the causes for hot cracks?
   1. Presence of sulphur and phosphorous for hot cracks.
   2. High carbon or alloy content of the base metal.
   3. Moisture in the joint or electrode.
   4. Joint restraint.

   Select the correct answer using the code given below:
   (a) 1, 2 and 4 (b) 1, 2 and 3
   (c) 3 and 4 (d) 1, 2, 3 and 4
24. In atomic hydrogen welding hydrogen acts as:
   (a) a heating agent
   (b) one of the gases to generate the flame
   (c) an effective shielding gas protecting the weld
   (d) a lubricant to increase the flow characteristics of weld metal.
25. Which of the following are the major characteristics of submerged arc welding?
   1. High welding speeds 2. High deposition rates
   3. Low penetration 4. Low cleanliness

   Select the correct answer using the code given below:
   (a) 2 and 3 (b) 1, 2 and 3
   (c) 3 and 4 (d) 1 and 2
26. Consider the following statements:
   1. In gas welding, the torch should be held at an angle of 30° to 45° from the horizontal plane
   2. In gas welding, the size of the torch depends upon the thickness of metal to be formed
   3. Drag in gas cutting is the time difference between heating of the plate and starting the oxygen gas for cutting.

   Which of the statements given above are correct?
   (a) 1, 2 and 3 (b) 1 and 2
   (c) 2 and 3 (d) 1 and 3
27. In which of the following welding processes, flux is used in the form or granules?
   (a) AC arc welding
   (b) Submerged arc welding
   (c) Argon arc welding
   (d) DC arc welding
28. Which one of the following is not a fusion welding process?
   (a) gas welding
   (b) arc welding
   (c) brazing
   (d) resistance welding
29. Fabrication weldability test is used to determine:
   (a) mechanical properties required for satisfactory performance of welded joint
   (b) susceptibility of welded joint for cracking
   (c) suitability for joint design
   (d) appropriate machining process.

30. Which one of the following welding processes consists of minimum heat effected zone (HAZ)?
(a) Shielded Metal Arc Welding (SWAW)
(b) Laser Beam Welding (L3BW)
(c) Ultrasonic Welding (USW)
(d) Metal Inert Gas Welding MIG)

31. Match List (Welding problems) with List-II (Causes) and select the correct answer using the codes given below the list:

| List-I (Welding problems) | List-II (Causes) |
|---|---|
| A. Spatter | 1. Damp electrodes |
| B. Distortion | 2. Arc blow |
| C. Slag inclusion | 3. Improper cleaning in multipass welding |
| D. Porosity | 4. Poor joint selection |

**Codes:**

| | A | B | C | D |
|---|---|---|---|---|
| (a) | 4 | 2 | 3 | 1 |
| (b) | 4 | 2 | 1 | 3 |
| (c) | 2 | 4 | 1 | 3 |
| (d) | 2 | 4 | 3 | 1 |

32. High speed electron beam of electron beam welding is focused on the weld spot using:
(a) vacuum lens (b) inert gas lens
(c) optical lens (d) magnetic lens

33. In resistance welding, heat is generated due to the resistance between:
(a) electrode and work piece
(b) asperities between touching plates
(c) two dissimilar metals being in contact
(d) interatomic forces.

34. Match List-I (Welding problems) with List-II (Causes) and select the correct answer using the codes given below the list:

| List-I | List-II |
|---|---|
| A. Cracking of weld | 1. Excessive metal stresses |
| B. Cracking of base | 2. High joint metal rigidity |
| C. Porosity | 3. Oxidation |
| D. Inclusions | 4. Excessive $H_2$, $O_2$ $N_2$ in the welding atmosphere |

**Codes:**

| | A | B | C | D |
|---|---|---|---|---|
| (a) | 2 | 1 | 4 | 3 |
| (b) | 3 | 4 | 2 | 1 |
| (c) | 2 | 4 | 2 | 1 |
| (d) | 3 | 1 | 4 | 2 |

35. Consider the following statements:
The size of the heat affected zone (HAZ) will increase with
1. increased starting temperature
2. increased welding speed
3. increased thermal conductivity of the base metal
4. increase in base metal thickness

36. Consider the following statement:
The magnitude of residual stresses in welding depends upon
1. design of welding
2. support and clamping of components
3. welding process used.
Which of the statements given above are correct?
(a) 1 and 2 (b) 1, 2 and 3
(c) 1 and 3 (d) 2 and 3

37. Consider the following statements in respect of oxydiacetylene welding:
1. The joint is not heated to a state of fusion.
2. No pressure is used.
3. Oxygen is stored in steel cylinder at a pressure of 14 MPa
4. When there is an excess of acetylene used, there is decided change in the appearance of flame.
Which of the statements given above are correct?
(a) 1, 2 and 3 (b) 2, 3 and 4
(c) 1, 3 and 4 (d) 1, 2 and 4

38. The coating material of an arc welding electrode contains which of the following?
1. Deoxidising agent.
2. Arc stabilizing agent.
3. Slag forming agent
Select the correct answer using the code given below:
(a) 1, 2 and 3 (b) 1 and 2 only
(c) 2 and 3 only (d) 1 and 3 only

39. In MIG welding, the metal is transferred into the form of which one of the following?
(a) A fine spray of metal
(b) Molten drops
(c) Weld pool
(d) Molecules

40. Consider the following statements in respect of the laser beam welding:
1. It can be used for welding any metal or their combinations because of very high temperature of the focal points.
2. Heat affected zone is very large because of quick heating.
3. High vacuum is required to carry the process.
Which of the statements given above is/are correct?
(a) 1 and 2 only (b) 2 and 3 only
(c) 1only (d) 1, 2 and 3

41. Which of the following effects are possible due to residual stresses in welding?
1. Reduce dimensional stability
2. Weld cracking
3. Effect on fatigue strength
4. Reduction in the creep strength

Select the correct answer using the code given below:

(a) 1 and 2 only (b) 2 and 3 only
(c) 1 and 3 only (d) 1, 2, 3 and 4

42. Assuming a straight line V–I characteristics for a DC welding generator, short-circuit current as 400 A and open circuit voltage as 100 V, which one of the following is the correct voltage and current setting for maximum arc power?

(a) 400 A and 100 V (b) 200 A and 100 V
(c) 400 A and 50 V (d) 200 A and 50 V

43. Open-circuit voltage of 60V and current of 160 A were the welding conditions for arc welding of a certain class of steel strip of thickness 10 mm. For arc welding of 5 mm thick strip of the same steel, the welding voltage and current would be:

(a) 60 V and 80 A (b) 120 V and 160 A
(c) 60 V and 40 A (d) 120 V and 40 A

44. Match List-I (Shielding method) with List-II (Welding process) and select the correct answer using the codes given below the lists:

| List-I | List-II |
|---|---|
| A. Flux coating | 1. Gas metal arc welding |
| B. Flux granules | 2. submerged arc welding |
| C. $CO_2$ | 3. Shielded metal arc welding |
| D. Vacuum | 4. Laser beam welding |
| | 5. Electron beam welding |

**Codes:**

| | A | B | C | D |
|---|---|---|---|---|
| (a) | 1 | 2 | 5 | 3 |
| (b) | 1 | 4 | 2 | 5 |
| (c) | 3 | 5 | 1 | 4 |
| (d) | 3 | 2 | 1 | 5 |

45. Consider the following welding processes:

1. TIG welding
2. Submerged arc welding
3. Electro-slag welding
4. Thermit welding.

Which of these welding processes are used for welding thick pieces of metals?

(a) 1, 2 and 3 (b) 1, 2 and 4
(c) 1, 3 and 4 (d) 2, 3 and 4

46. Match List-I (Welding processes) with List-II (Features) and select the correct answer using the codes given below the Lists:

| List-I | List-II |
|---|---|
| A. Ultrasonic welding | 1. Gas heated to ionized condition for conduction of electric current |
| B. Electron beam welding | 2. High frequency and high intensity vibrations |
| C. Plasma arc welding | 3. Concentrated steam of high-energy Electrons |
| | 4. Exothermal chemical reaction |

**Codes:**

| | A | B | C |
|---|---|---|---|
| (a) | 1 | 2 | 4 |
| (b) | 4 | 3 | 1 |
| (c) | 2 | 1 | 4 |
| (d) | 2 | 3 | 1 |

47. Two plain carbon steel specimens having 0.8% carbon content are weld. If we observe the weldment under Metallurgical Microscope from centre towards either side, the following structures are observed at different zones:

1. Fine Pearlite 2. Coarse Pearlite
3. Martensite

Select the correct sequence using the codes given below:

**Codes:**

(a) 1, 2, 3 (b) 1, 3, 2
(c) 2, 1, 3 (d) 3, 1, 2

48. Match List-I (Welding) with List-II (Application) and select the correct answer using the codes given below the Lists:

| List-I (Welding) | List-II (Application) |
|---|---|
| A. Explosive | 1. Joining thick sheets |
| B. Ultrasonic | 2. Manufacture of heat exchangers |
| C. Thermite | 3. Joining thin sheets or wires of similar/dissimilar metals |
| D. Projection | 4. Joining hydraulic piston rods heat for agricultural Machinery |
| | 5. Joining rails, pipes and thick steel sections |

**Codes:**

| | A | B | C | D |
|---|---|---|---|---|
| (a) | 2 | 5 | 1 | 3 |
| (b) | 4 | 5 | 1 | 3 |
| (c) | 2 | 3 | 5 | 1 |
| (d) | 4 | 3 | 5 | 1 |

49. Preheating before welding is done to:

(a) make the steel softer
(b) burn away oil, grease, etc. from the plate surface
(c) prevent cold cracks
(d) prevent plate distortion

50. Which one of the following is not an electric resistance method of welding?

(a) Electro slag welding (b) Percussion welding
(c) Seam welding (d) Flash welding

51. Which one of the following welding processes consists of similar Heat Affected Zone (HAZ)?

(a) Arc welding
(b) Electron beam welding
(c) MIG welding
(d) Thermite welding

52. Which of the following gases can be used for GMAW as a shielding gas?
1. Argon 2. Oxygen
3. Carbon dioxide
Select the correct answer using the code given below:
(a) 1, 2 and 3 (b) 1 and 2
(c) 2 and 3 (d) 1 and 3

53. In which one of the following welding techniques is vacuum environment required?
(a) Plasma arc welding
(b) Laser beam welding
(c) Electron beam welding
(d) Ultrasonic welding

54. Consider the following welding processes
1. Arc welding 2. MIG welding
3. Laser beam welding 4. Submerged arc welding
Select the correct sequence in increasing order of Heat Affected Zone (HAZ) using the code given below:
(a) 1 – 2–3–4 (b) 1 –4–2–3
(c) 3 – 2 – 4 – 1 (d) 4 – 3 – 2 – 1

55. Consider the following statements in respect of double sampling plan:
1. Average number of pieces inspected is double that of single sampling
2. Average number of pieces inspected is less than that for single sampling
3. Decision to accept or reject the lot is taken only after the inspection of both samples
4. Decision to accept or reject the lot is reached sometimes after one sample and sometimes after two samples.
Which of these statements are correct?
(a) 1, 2 and 3 (b) 2 and 4
(c) 1 and 4 (d) 2 and 3

56. Consider the following fits:
1. I.C engine cylinder and piston
2. Ball bearing outer race and housing
3. Ball bearing inner race and shaft
Which of the above fits are based on the shaft basis system?
(a) 1 and 2 (b) 2 and 3
(c) 1 and 3 (d) 1, 2 and 3

57. Match List I (Quality control concepts) with List II (Quality control techniques) and select the correct answer using the codes given below the lists:

| List-I (Quality control concepts) | List-II (Quality control techniques) |
|---|---|
| A. Tightened and reduced inspection | 1. Dodge roming tables |
| B. Lot tolerance percent defective | 2. Control chart for variables |
| C. Poisson distribution | 3. MIL standards |
| D. Normal distribution | 4. Control chart for number of non-conformities |

**Codes:**

| | A | B | C | D |
|---|---|---|---|---|
| (a) | 2 | 1 | 4 | 3 |
| (b) | 3 | 4 | 1 | 2 |
| (c) | 3 | 1 | 4 | 2 |
| (d) | 2 | 4 | 1 | 3 |

58. Quality control chart for averages was maintained for a imension of the product. After the control was es ablished, it was found that the standard deviation (a) of the process was 1.00 mm. The dimension of the part is 70 ± 2.5 mm. Parts above 725 mm can be reworked but parts below 67.5 mm have to be scrapped. What should be the setting of the process to ensure production of no scrap and to minimize the rework?
(a) 68.5 mm (b) 70 mm
(c) 70.5 mm (d) 725 mm

59. Consider the following statements with respect to control charts for attributes:
1. The lower control limit is non-negative
2. Normal distribution is the order for this data
3. The lower control limit is not significant
4. These charts give the average quality characteristics
Which of the statements given above are correct:
(a) 1, 2 and 3 (b) 2, 3 and 4
(c) 1, 3 and 4 (d) 1, 2 and 4

60. Which one of the following statements is not correct?
(a) The operating characteristic curve of an acceptance sampling plan shows the ability of the plan to distinguish between good and bad lots
(b) No sampling plan can give complete protection against the acceptance of defective products
(c) C chart has straight line limits and U chart has zig-zag limits
(d) Double sampling result in more inspection than single sampling if the incoming quality is very bad

61. Consider the following statements:
A nomenclature $\phi$ 50 H8/p8 denoted that
1. Hole diameter is 50 mm
2. It is a shaft base system
3. 8 indicates fundamental deviation.
Which of the statements given above is/are correct?
(a) 1, 2 and 3 (b) 1 and 2 only
(c) 1 and 3 only (d) 3 only

62. Consider an activity having a duration time $T_{ij}$ E it the earliest occurrence time and L latest occurrence time (see figure given)

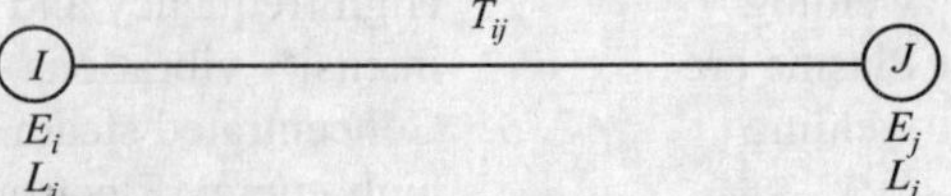


Consider the following statements in this regard:
1. Total float = $L_j – E_i – T_{ij}$

2. Free float = $E_j – E_i t_{ij}$
3. Slack of the tail event = $L_j – E_i$

Of these statements:
(a) 1, 2 and 3 are correct
(b) 1 and 2 are correct
(c) 1 and 3 are correct
(d) 2 and 3 are correct

63. For the network shown in the given Fig. earliest expected completion time of the project is?

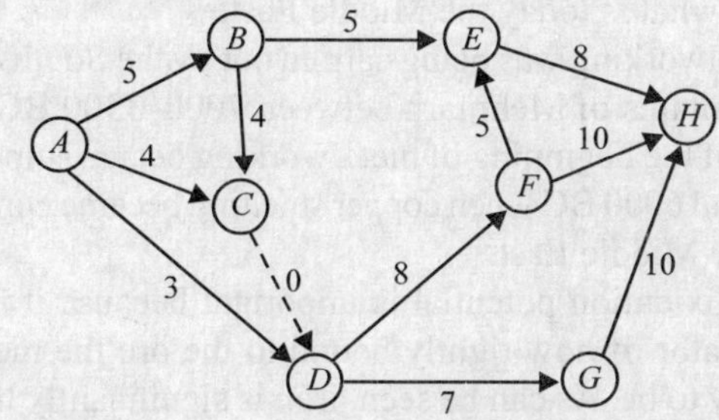


(a) 26 days (b) 27 days
(c) 30 days (d) indeterminable

64. In the network shown below in figure, the critical path is along

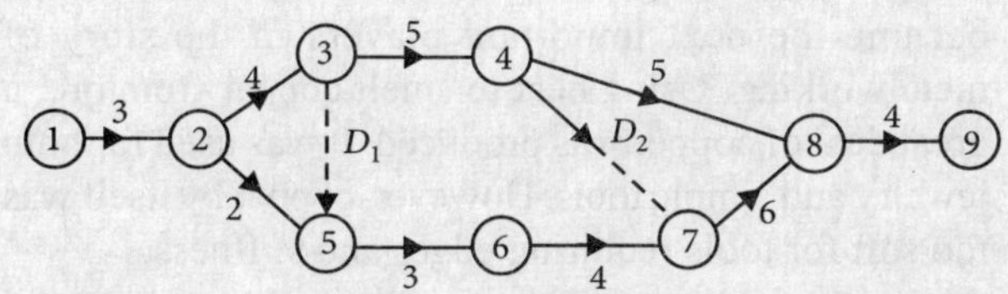


(a) 1 – 2 – 3 – 4 – 8 – 9
(b) 1 – 2 – 3 – 5 – 6 – 7 – 8 – 9
(c) 1 – 2 – 3 – 4 – 7 – 8 – 9
(d) 1 – 2 – 5 – 6 – 7 – 8 – 9

## ANSWERS WITH EXPLANATIONS

1. (c) 2. (d) 3. (a) 4. (d) 5. (a)
6. (c) 7. (d)
8. (c) $C_2H_2 + O_2 = 2CO + H_2$
1 : 1
9. (b)
10. (c) $V = V_0\left(1 - \frac{I}{I_s}\right) = 80\left(1 - \frac{I}{300}\right)$

For V = 40 V

$40 = 80\left(1 - \frac{I}{300}\right)$

I = 150 A

11. (c) 12. (d) 13. (a) 14. (d) 15. (d)
16. (c) 17. (a) 18. (a) 19. (b) 20. (a)
21. (d) 22. (a) 23. (a) 24. (b) 25. (d)
26. (a) 27. (b) 28. (c) 29. (a) 30. (c)
31. (d) 32. (a) 33. (a) 34. (a) 35. (b)
36. (b) 37. (b) 38. (c) 39. (c) 40. (a)
41. (b)

42. (d) $V = V_0\left(1 - \frac{I}{I_s}\right)$

$I_s = 400$ A, $V_0 = 100$ V

$V = 100\left(1 - \frac{I}{400}\right)$

(a) $V - 100\left(1 - \frac{400}{400}\right) = 0 \rightarrow$ invalid

(b) $V = 100\left(1 - \frac{200}{400}\right) = 50V \rightarrow$ invalid

(c) $V = 100\left(1 - \frac{400}{400}\right) = 0 \rightarrow$ invalid

(d) $V = 100\left(1 - \frac{200}{400}\right) = 50V \rightarrow$ valid

43. (a) $V = V_0\left(1 - \frac{I}{I_s}\right)$

$V = 60$ V, $I_3 = 160$ A

$V = 60\left(1 - \frac{I}{600}\right)$

$I \propto t$ and $V_0 \propto \frac{1}{t}$

For 5 mm, $l = \frac{5}{10} \times 160 = 80A$

and $V_0 = 120$ V

$V = 120\left(1 - \frac{80}{160}\right) = 60V$

44. (d) 45. (d) 46. (d) 47. (d) 48. (c)
49. (c) 50. (a) 51. (b) 52. (d) 53. (c)
54. (d) 55. (d) 56. (b) 57. (c)
58. (b) $\sigma = 1.00$ mm

Maximum size = 72.5 mm
Minimum size = 67.5 mm
UCL = 70 + 3σ = 73 mm
LCL = 70 – 3 = 67 mm
The process should be set at 70 mm

59. (c) 60. (c) 61. (c) 62. (a)
63. (c)

Critical Path:
A – B – C – D – F – E – H
Earliest expected completion time = 30 days.

64. (b)

❑❑❑

# 17. Metal Cutting

- Metalworking is the process of working with metals to create individual parts, assemblies, or large-scale structures. The term covers a wide range of work from large ships and bridges to precise engine parts and delicate jewelry. It therefore includes a correspondingly wide range of skills, processes, and tools.
- Metalworking is a science, art, hobby, industry and trade. Its historical roots span cultures, civilizations, and millennia. Metalworking has evolved from the discovery of smelting various ores, producing malleable and ductile metal useful for tools and adornments.
- Modern metalworking processes, though diverse and specialized, can be categorized as forming, cutting, or joining processes. Today's machine shop includes a number of machine tools capable of creating a precise, useful work piece.
- The oldest archaeological evidence of copper mining and working was the discovery of a copper pendant in northern Iraq from 8,700 BC. The earliest substantiated and dated evidence of metalworking in North America was the processing of copper.
- Copper was hammered until brittle then heated so it could be worked some more. This technology is dated to about 4000-5000 BC. The oldest gold artifacts in the world come from the Bulgarian Varna Necropolis and date from 4450 BC.
- Not all metal required fire to obtain it or work it. Isaac Asimov speculated that gold was the "first metal." His reasoning is that gold by its chemistry is found in nature as nuggets of pure gold.
- In other words, gold, as rare as it is, is always found in nature as the metal that it is. There are a few other metals that sometimes occur natively, and as a result of meteors. Almost all other metals are found in ores, a mineral bearing rock, that require heat or some other process to liberate the metal.
- Another feature of gold is that it is workable as it is found, meaning that no technology beyond eyes to find a nugget and a hammer and an anvil to work the metal is needed. Stone hammer and stone anvil will suffice for technology.
- This is the result of gold's properties of malleability and ductility. The earliest tools were stone, bone, wood, and sinew. They sufficed to work gold.
- At some unknown point the connection between heat and the liberation of metals from rock became clear, rocks rich in copper, tin, and lead came into demand. These ores were mined wherever they were recognized. Remnants of such ancient mines have been found all over what is today the Middle East.
- Metalworking was being carried out by the South Asian inhabitants of Mehrgarh between 7000–3300 BC. The end of the beginning of metalworking occurs sometime around 6000 BC when copper smelting became common in the Middle East.
- The oxidation potential is important because it is one indicator of how tightly bound to the ore the metal is likely to be. As can be seen, iron is significantly higher than the other six metals while gold is dramatically lower than the six above it.
- Gold's low oxidation is one of the main reasons that gold is found in nuggets. These nuggets are relatively pure gold and are workable as they are found.
- Copper ore, being relatively abundant, and tin ore became the next important players in the story of metalworking. Using heat to smelt copper from ore, a great deal of copper was produced. It was used for both jewelry and simple tools. However, copper by itself was too soft for tools requiring edges and stiffness.
- At some point tin was added into the molten copper and bronze was born. Bronze is an alloy of copper and tin. Bronze was an important advance because it had the edge-durability and stiffness that pure copper lacked.
- Looking beyond the Middle East, these same advances and materials were being discovered and used the world around.China and Britain jumped into the use of bronze with little time being devoted to copper.
- Japan began the use of bronze and iron almost simultaneously. In the Americas things were different. Although the peoples of the Americas knew of metals, it wasn't until the arrival of Europeans that metal for tools and weapons took off.
- Jewelry and art were the principal uses of metals in the Americas prior to European influence.
- Around the date 2700 BC, production of bronze was common in locales where the necessary materials could be assembled for smelting, heating, and working the metal. Iron was beginning to be smelted. Iron began its emergence as an important metal for tools and weapons. The Iron Age was dawning.
- Metalworking generally is divided into the following categories, forming, cutting, and ,joining. Each of these categories contain various processes.
- Prior to most operations, the metal must be marked out and/or measured, depending on the desired finished product.

- Marking out is the process of transferring a design or pattern to a work piece and is the first step in the handcraft of metalworking. It is performed in many industries or hobbies, although in the repetition industries the need to mark out every individual piece is eliminated.
- In the metal trades area, marking out consists of transferring the engineer's plan to the work piece in preparation for the next step, machining or manufacture.
- Calipers are hand tools designed to precisely measure the distance between two points. Most calipers have two sets of flat, parallel edges used for inner or outer diameter measurements.
- These calipers can be accurate to within one-thousandth of an inch. Different types of calipers have different mechanisms for displaying the distance measured. Where larger objects need to be measured with less precision, a tape measure is often used.
- Plastic deformation involves using heat or pressure to make a workpiece more conductive to mechanical force. Historically, this and casting were done by blacksmiths, though today the process has been industrialized.
- Cutting is a collection of processes wherein material is brought to a specified geometry by removing excess material using various kinds of tooling to leave a finished part that meets specifications.
- The net result of cutting is two products, the waste or excess material, and the finished part. If this were a discussion of woodworking, the waste would be sawdust and excess wood. In cutting metals the waste is chips or swarf and excess metal.
- Chip producing processes most commonly known as machining
- Burning, a set of processes wherein the metal is cut by oxidizing a kerf to separate pieces of metal
- Miscellaneous specialty process, not falling easily into either of the above categories
- Drilling a hole in a metal part is the most common example of a chip producing process. Using an oxy-fuel cutting torch to separate a plate of steel into smaller pieces is an example of burning.
- Chemical milling is an example of a specialty process that removes excess material by the use of etching chemicals and masking chemicals.
- There are many technologies available to cut metal, including:
  - Manual technologies: saw, chisel, shear or snips
  - Machine technologies: turning, milling, drilling, grinding, sawing
  - Welding/burning technologies: burning by laser, oxy-fuel burning, and plasma
  - Erosion technologies: by water jet, electric discharge, or abrasive flow machining.
  - Chemical technologies: Photochemical machining
- Cutting fluid or coolant is used where there is significant friction and heat at the cutting interface between a cutter such as a drill or an end mill and the workpiece.
- Coolant is generally introduced by a spray across the face of the tool and workpiece to decrease friction and temperature at the cutting tool/workpiece interface to prevent excessive tool wear. In practice there are many methods of delivering coolant.
- Milling is the complex shaping of metal or other materials by removing material to form the final shape. It is generally done on a milling machine, a power-driven machine that in its basic form consists of a milling cutter that rotates about the spindle axis and a worktable that can move in multiple directions .
- Turning is a metal cutting process for producing a cylindrical surface with a single point tool. The workpiece is rotated on a spindle and the cutting tool is fed into it radially, axially or both. Producing surfaces perpendicular to the workpiece axis is called facing. Producing surfaces using both radial and axial feeds is called profiling
- Grinding uses an abrasive process to remove material from the workpiece.
- A grinding machine is a machine tool used for producing very fine finishes, making very light cuts, or high precision forms using an abrasive wheel as the cutting device. This wheel can be made up of various sizes and types of stones, diamonds or inorganic materials.
- Filing is combination of grinding and saw tooth cutting using a file. Prior to the development of modern machining equipment it provided a relatively accurate means for the production of small parts, especially those with flat surfaces.
- Broaching is a machining operation used to cut keyways into shafts. Electron beam machining (EBM) is a machining process where high-velocity electrons are directed toward a work piece, creating heat and vaporizing the material. Ultrasonic machining uses ultrasonic vibrations to machine very hard or brittle materials.

# MULTIPLE CHOICE QUESTIONS

1. Tool life is generally specified by:
(a) number of pieces machined
(b) volume of metal removed
(c) actual cutting time
(d) any of the above

2. Tail stock set over method of taper turning is preferred for:
(a) internal tapers (b) small tapers
(c) long slender tapers (d) steep tapers

3. Which of the following statements is incorrect with reference of lathe cutting tools?
(a) The flank of the tool is the surface below and adjacent to the cutting edges
(b) The nose is the comer, or chamfer joining the side cutting and the end cutting edges
(c) The heel is that part which is shaped to produce the cutting edges and face
(d) The base is that surface of the shank which against the support and takes tangent

4. In metal cutting, use of low feeds and high cutting speeds is desired when the objective is:
(a) high metal removal rate
(b) dry machining tool
(c) use of soft cutting tool
(d) surface finish

5. A drill for drilling deep holes in aluminium should have:
(a) high helix angle (b) taper shank
(c) small point angle (d) no lip

6. Gear lapping is:
(a) an operation after heat treatment
(b) an operation prior to heat treatment
(c) an independent operation for gear reconditioning
(d) none of the above

7. Gear burnishing process is for:
(a) removing residual stresses from teeth roots
(b) surface finishing
(c) under-cut gears
(d) cycloidal gears

8. Buffing wheels are made of:
(a) softer metals (b) cotton fabric
(c) carbon (d) graphite

9. In gear hobbing:
(a) only hob rotates
(b) only gear blank rotates
(c) both hob and gear blank rotate
(d) neither hob nor gear blank rotates

10. A surface finish of 0.025 – 0.1 micrometer CLA values is to be produced. Which machining process would you recommend?
(a) Grinding (b) Rough turning
(c) Lapping (d) Honing

11. CLA value for Honing process is:
(a) 6 (b) 0.05 – 3.0
(c) 0.05 – 1.0 (d) 0.025 – 0.1

12. The installation cost of a machine is Rs. 2000. The cost of repairs increases ₹ 40 annual). The scrap value of the machine is ₹ 200. The economic repair life of the machine is nearly:
(a) $5\frac{1}{2}$ years (b) $7\frac{1}{2}$ years
(c) $9\frac{1}{2}$ years (d) $11\frac{1}{2}$ years

13. Which of the following given the correct order of increasing hot hardness of cutting tool materials?
(a) Diamond, Carbide, HSS
(b) Carbide, Diamond, HSS
(c) HSS, Carbide, Diamond
(d) HSS, Diamond, Carbide

14. If the chip-tool contact length is reduced slightly by grinding the tool face, then:
(a) both cutting force and interface temperature would decrease
(b) both cutting force and interface temperature would increase
(c) the cutting force would decrease but the interface temperature would increase
(d) the cutting force would increase but the interface temperature would decrease

15. Tool life in the case of a grinding wheel is the time:
(a) between two successive wheel dressing
(b) taken for the wheel to be balanced
(c) taken between two successive wheel balancing
(d) taken for a wear of 1 mm on its diameter

16. For achieving a specific surface finish in single point turning, the most important factor to be considered is:
(a) depth of cut (b) cutting speed
(c) feed (d) tool rake angle

17. In ASA System, if the tool nomenclature is 8 – 6 – 5 – 5 – 10 – 15 – 2 mm, then the side rake anglewill be:
(a) 5° (b) 6°
(c) 8° (d) 10°

18. Match List-I with List-II and select the correct answer using the codes given below the lists:

| **List-I (Cutting Tool Material)** | **List-II (Major Characteristic Constituent)** |
|---|---|
| A. High speed steel | 1. Carbon |
| B. Satellite | 2. Molybdenum |
| C. Diamond | 3. Nitride |
| D. Coated carbide tool | 4. Columbium |
| | 5. Cobalt |

**Codes:**

| | A | B | C | D |
|---|---|---|---|---|
| (a) | 2 | 1 | 3 | 5 |
| (b) | 2 | 5 | 1 | 3 |
| (c) | 5 | 2 | 4 | 3 |
| (d) | 5 | 4 | 2 | 3 |

19. Consider the following parameters:
    1. Grinding wheel diameter.
    2. Regulating wheel diameter.
    3. Speed of the grinding wheel.
    4. Speed of the regulating wheel
    5. Angle between the axes of grinding and regulating wheels.

    Among these parameters, those which influence the axial feed rate in centreless grinding would include:
    (a) 2, 4 and 5 (b) 1, 2 and 3
    (c) 1, 4 and 5 (d) 3, 4 and 5
20. It is required to cut screw threads of 2 mm pitch on a lathe. The lead screw has a pitch of 6 mm.If the spindle speed is 60 rpm, then the speed of the lead screw will be:
    (a) 10 rpm (b) 20 rpm
    (c) 120 rmp (d) 180 rpm
21. What is the variation of cutting speed with tool life on Log-Log Scale?
    (a) parabolic variation (b) straight line variation
    (c) hyperbolic variation (d) elliptical variation
22. In a miling machine two side milling cutters are mounted with a desired distance between them so mat both sides of the workpiecc can be milled simultaneously. What is this setup called?
    (a) Gang milling (b) Straddle milling
    (c) String milling (d) Side milling
23. The ratio of time of return stroke to time of forward stroke of a shaping machine is 0.6. The stroke is 250 mm and it makes 30 double strokes per minute. What is the overall average speed of operation?
    (a) 3.75 m/min (b) 5.0 m/min
    (c) 7.5 m/min (d) 12 m/min
24. Why does crater wear start at some distance from the tool tip?
    (a) Tool strength is minimum at that region.
    (b) Cutting fluid cannot penetrate that region.
    (c) Tool temperature is maximum in that region
    (d) Stress on rake face is maximum at that region.
25. Which one of the following statements is correct? In the orthogonal cutting system, the cutting edge is:
    (a) perpendicular to shear plane
    (b) perpendicular to direction of tool travel
    (c) perpendicular to direction of depth of cut
    (d) in line with direction of tool travel
26. Which one of the following is not a characteristic of ceramic tools?
    (a) produced by sintering process
    (b) hot hardness up to 1400°C
    (c) exhibit high coefficient of friction with most work materials
    (d) tool tips are highly brittle
27. What is the distance through which the cutter has to move before the full depth of cut is acquired in milling?
    (a) $\sqrt{d(D-d)}$ (b) $\sqrt{D(D-d)}$
    (c) $\sqrt{(D-d)d/2}$ (d) $\sqrt{(D-d)d/2}$

    where D = diameter of the milling cutter and D = depth of cut.
28. Crater wear occurs mainly due to which one of the following?
    (a) adhesion (b) diffusion
    (c) oxidation (d) abrasion
29. In idealized chip formation, built-up edge will break off and remove some of the cutting tool materials, thereby reducing tool life. Which of the following steps prevent built-up edge?
    1. Increasing cutting speed
    2. Increasing feed rate
    3. Increasing ambient workpiece temperature
    4. decreasing rake angle
    5. Reducing friction.

    Select the correct answer using the code given below:
    (a) 1, 2 and 3 (b) 2, 3 and 4
    (c) 1, 3 and 5 (d) 2, 4 and 5
30. Turning operation, the feed could be doubled to increase the metal removal rate. To keep the same level of surface finish, the nose radius of the tool should be:
    (a) halved
    (b) kept unchanged
    (c) doubled
    (d) made four times
31. Match List-I with List-II and select the correct answer using the codes given below the lists:

| **List-I (Machine Tool Cutting Tool)** | **List-II (Part/Characteristics)** |
|---|---|
| A. Screw cutting lathe | 1. Self locking taper |
| B. Drill | 2. Chasing dial |
| C. End mill | 3. Wiper insert |
| D. Grinding wheel | 4. Self releasing taper |
| | 5. Balance weights |

**Codes:**

| | A | B | C | D |
|---|---|---|---|---|
| (a) | 4 | 5 | 3 | 1 |
| (b) | 2 | 1 | 4 | 5 |
| (c) | 4 | 1 | 3 | 5 |
| (d) | 2 | 5 | 4 | 1 |

32. Maximum production of small and slender parts is done by:
    (a) watch maker's lathe
    (b) sliding head stock automatic lathe
    (c) multi-spindle automatic lathe
    (d) capstan lathe

33. Which of the following can be used in dynamometer for measuring cutting forces?
    1. Strain gauge
    2. Peizoelectric transducer
    3. Pneumatic transducer
    4. Hydraulic transducer.

    (a) 1 and 2 (b) 1, 3 and 4
    (c) 2, 3 and 4 (d) 1, 2, 3 and 4
34. Low helix angle drills are preferred for drilling holes in:
    (a) plastics (b) copper
    (c) cast steel (d) carbon steel?
35. Shell reamers are mounted on:
    (a) tool holders (b) armour plates
    (c) arbors (d) shanks
36. A set of eight form relieved milling cutters for each module is provided to enable eating of gears of different:
    (a) materials
    (b) types, e.g., spur, helical, etc.
    (c) number of teeth
    (d) width of gears
37. Which of the machine tools can be used for boring?
    1. Lathe
    2. Drilling machine
    3. Vertical milling machine
    4. Horizontal milling machine

    (a) 1, 2, 3 (b) 1, 3, 4
    (c) 2 and 4 (d) 1, 2 3 4
38. Which Machining of titanium is difficult due to:
    (a) high thermal conductivity of titanium
    (b) chemical reaction between tool and work
    (c) low tool-chip contact area
    (d) none of the above
39. Tool life is generally better when:
    (a) grain size of the metal is large
    (b) grain size of the metal is small
    (c) hard constituents are present in the microstructure of the tool material
    (d) none of the above
40. Ease of machining is primarily judged by:
    (a) life of cutting tool between sharpening
    (b) rigidity of workpiece
    (c) microstructure of tool material
    (d) shape and dimensions of work
41. A 'Dynamometer' is a device used for the measurement of:
    (a) chip thickness ratio
    (b) forces during metal cutting
    (c) wear of the cutting tool
    (d) deflection of the cutting tool
42. The main purpose of boring operation, as compared to drilling is to:
    (a) drill a hole
    (b) finish drilled hole
    (c) correct the hole
    (d) enlarge the existing hole
43. Climb milling is chosen while machining because:
    (a) the chip thickness increases gradually
    (b) it enables the cutter to dig in and start the cut
    (c) the specific power consumption is reduced
    (d) better surface finish can be obtained
44. Internal gears can be made by:
    (a) hobbing
    (b) shaping with pinion cutter
    (c) shaping with rack cutter
    (d) milling
45. A hole of 30 mm diameter is to be produced by reaming. The minimum diameter permissible is 30.00 mm while the maximum diameter permissible is 30.05 mm. In this regard, consider the following statements about the reamer size:
    1. The minimum diameter of the reamer cab be less than 30 mm.
    2. The minimum diameter of the reamer cannot he less than 30 mm.
    3. The maximum diameter of the reamer can be more than 30.05 mm.
    4. The maximum diameter of the reamer must be less than 30.05 mm.

    Of these statements:
    (a) 1 and 4 are correct (b) 1 and 3 are correct
    (c) 2 and 3 are correct (d) 2 and 4 are correct
46. In centreless grinding, the workpiece centre will be:
    (a) above the line joining the two wheel centres
    (b) below the line joining the two wheel centres
    (c) on the line joining the two wheel centres
    (d) at the intersection of the line joining the wheel centres with the work plate plane
47. The following parameters determine the model of continuous chip formation:
    1. True feed
    2. Cutting velocity
    3. Chip thickness
    4. Rake angle of the cutting tool.

    The parameters which govern the value of shear angle would include:
    (a) 1, 2 and 3 (b) 1, 3 and 4
    (c) 1, 2 and 4 (d) 2, 3 and 4
48. What is the correct sequence of the following parameters in order of their maximum to minimum influence on tool life?
    1. Feed rate
    2. Depth of cut
    3. Cutting speed

    Select the correct answer using the codes given below:
    (a) 1, 2, 3 (b) 3, 2, 1
    (c) 2, 3, 1 (d) 3, 1, 2
49. Tool geometry of a single point cutting tool is specified by the following elements:
    1. Back rake angle
    2. Side rake angle

3. End cutting code angle
4. Side cutting code angle
5. Side relief angle
6. End relief angle
7. Nose radius

The correct sequence of these tool elements used for correctly specifying tool geometry is:

(a) 1, 2, 3, 6, 5, 4, 7 (b) 1, 2, 6, 5, 3, 4, 7
(c) 1, 2, 5, 6, 3, 4, 7 (d) 1, 2, 6, 3, 4, 7

50. Consider the following tool materials:
1. Carbide 2. Cermet
3. Ceramic 4. Borazon

The correct sequence of these tool materials in increasing order of the their ability to retain their hot hardness is:

(a) 1, 2, 3, 4 (b) 1, 2, 4, 3
(c) 2, 1, 3, 4 (d) 2, 1, 4, 3

51. The ratio of thrust force to cutting force is nearly 2.5 in:
(a) turning (b) broaching
(c) grinding (d) plain milling

52. Which one of the following operations is carried out at the minimum cutting velocity if the machines are equally rigid and the tool work materials are the same?
(a) Turning (b) Grinding
(c) Boring (d) Milling

53. Given that cutting speed = 9 m/min, the return time to cutting time ratio is = 1 : 2 to the feed rate = 0.3 mm/stroke, the clearance at each of cut = 25 mm and that the plate is fixed 700 mm side along the direction of tool travel, the time required for finishing one flat surface of a plate of size 700 × 300 mm in a shaper, will be:
(a) 10 min (b) 12.5 min
(c) 15 min (d) 20 min

54. Consider the following statements regarding grinding of high carbon steel:
1. Grinding at high speed results in the reduction of chip thickness and cutting forces per grit
2. Aluminium oxide wheels are employed
3. The grinding wheel has to be of open structure.

Of these statements:
(a) 1, 2 and 3 are correct
(b) 1 and 2 are correct
(c) 1 and 3 are correct
(d) 2 and 3 are correct

55. Enlarging an existing circular hole with rotating single point tool is called:
(a) boring (b) drilling
(c) reaming (d) internal turning

56. Consider the following operations:
1. Cutting key ways on shafts
2. Cutting external screw threads
3. Cutting teeth of spur gears
4. Cutting external splines

Those which can be performed with milling cutters would include:
(a) 1 and 2 (b) 2, 3 and 4
(c) 1 and 3 (d) 1, 2, 3 and 4

57. Consider the following machine tools:
1. Hobbing machine
2. Gear shaping machine
3. Broaching machine

The teeth of internal spur gears can be cut in:
(a) 1, 2 and 3 (b) 1 and 2
(c) 1 and 3 (d) 2 and 3

58. In reaming process:
(a) metal removal rate is high
(b) high surface finish is obtained
(c) high form of accuracy is obtained
(d) high dimensional accuracy.

59. The ratio between two consecutive spindle speeds for a six-speed drilling machine using drills of diameter 6.25 to 25 mm size and at cutting velocity of 18 m/min is:
(a) 1.02 (b) 1.32
(c) 1.06 (d) 1.82

60. The angle between the face and the flank of the single point cutting tool is known as:
(a) rake angle (b) clearance angle
(c) lip angle (d) point angle

61. Single point thread cutting tool should ideally have:
(a) zero rake
(b) positive rake
(c) negative rake
(d) normal rake

62. Consider the following statements about nose radius:
1. It improves tool life.
2. It reduces the cutting force.
3. It improves the surface finish.

Of these statements:
(a) 1 and 2 are correct
(b) 2 and 3 are correct
(c) 1 and 3 are correct
(d) 1, 2 and 3 are correct

63. The compositions of some of the alloy steels are as under:
1. 18 W 4 Ct 1 V
2. 12 Mo I W 4 Cr IV
3. 6 Mo 6 W 4 Cr 1 V
4. 18 W 8 Cr IV

The compositions of commonly used high speed steels would include:
(a) 1 and 2 (b) 2 and 3
(c) 1 and 4 (d) 1 and 3

64. The straight grades of cemented carbide cutting tool materials contain:
(a) tungsten carbide only
(b) tungsten carbide and titanium carbide
(c) tungsten carbide and cobalt
(d) tungsten carbide and coal carbide

65. Match List-1 with List-II and select the correct answer using the codes given below the lists:

| List-I (Wear type) | List-II (Associated mechanism) |
|---|---|
| A. Abrasive wear | 1. Galvanic action |
| B. Adhesive wear | 2. Polughing action |
| C. Electrolytic wear | 3. Molecular transfer |
| D. Diffusion wear | 4. Plastic deformation |
| | 5. Metallic bond. |

**Codes:**

| | A | B | C | D |
|---|---|---|---|---|
| (a) | 2 | 5 | 1 | 3 |
| (b) | 5 | 2 | 1 | 3 |
| (c) | 2 | 1 | 3 | 4 |
| (d) | 5 | 2 | 3 | 4 |

66. Crater wear is predominant in:
(a) carbon steel tools
(b) tungsten carbide tools
(c) high speed steel tools
(d) ceramic tools

67. Consider the following work materials:
1. Titanium 2. Mild steel
3. Stainless steel 4. Grey cast iron.
The correct sequence of these materials in terms of increasing order of difficulty in machining is:
(a) 4, 2, 3, 1 (b) 4, 2, 1, 3
(c) 2, 4, 3, 1 (d) 2, 4, 1, 3

68. The primary tool force used in calculating the total power consumption in machining is the:
(a) radial force (b) tangential force
(c) axial force (d) frictional force

69. In the grinding wheel of A 60 G 7 B 23, B stands for:
(a) resinoid bond (b) rubber bond
(c) shellac bond (d) silicate bond

70. Soft material cannot be economically ground due to:
(a) the high temperatures involved
(b) frequent wheel clogging
(c) rapid wheel wear
(d) low workpiece stiffness

71. The effects of setting a boring tool above centre height leads to a/an:
(a) increase in the effective rake angle and a decrease in the effective clearance angle
(b) increase in both effective rake angle and effective clearance angle
(c) decrease in the effective rake angle and an increase in the effective clearance angle
(d) decrease in both effective rank angle and effective clearance angle

72. In a milling operation two side milling cutters are mounted with a desired distance between them so that both sides of a workpiece can he milled simultaneously. This set-up is called:
(a) gang milling (b) straddle milling
(c) string milling (d) side milling

73. Match List-I with List-II and select the correct answer using the codes given below the lists:

| List-I (Product) | List-II (Process of Manufacture) |
|---|---|
| A. Automobile piston in aluminium alloy | 1. Pressure die-casting |
| B. Engine crankshaft spheroidal graphite-iron casting | 2. Gravity die-casting |
| C. Carburettor housing in aluminium alloy | 3. Sand casting |
| D. Cast titanium blades | 4. Precision investment casting |
| | 5. Shell moulding. |

**Codes:**

| | A | B | C | D |
|---|---|---|---|---|
| (a) | 2 | 3 | 1 | 5 |
| (b) | 3 | 2 | 1 | 5 |
| (c) | 2 | 1 | 3 | 4 |
| (d) | 4 | 1 | 2 | 3 |

74. Chip equivalent is increased by:
(a) an increase in side-cutting edge angle of tool
(b) an increase in nose radius and side cutting edge angle of tool
(c) increasing the plant area of cut
(d) increasing the depth of cut

75. Cubic boron nitride:
(a) has a very high hardness which is comparable to that of diamon
(b) has a hardness which is slightly more than that of HSS
(c) is used for making cylinder blocks of aircraft engines
(d) is used for making optical glasses

76. The limit to the maximum hardness of a work material which can be machined with HSS tools even at low speeds is set by which one of the following tool failure mechanisms?
(a) attrition
(b) abrasion
(c) diffusion
(d) plastic deformation under compression

77. A machinist desires to turn a round steel stock of outside diameter 100 mm at 1000 rpm. The material has tensile strength of 75 kg/mm. The depth of cut chosen is 3 mm at a feed rate of 0.3 mm/rev. Which one of the following tool materials will be suitable for machining the component under the specified cutting conditions?
(a) sintered carbides
(b) ceramic
(c) HSS
(d) diansond

78. Notch wear at the outside edge of the depth of cut is due to:
(a) abrasive action of the work hardened chip material
(b) oxidation
(c) slip-stick action of the chip
(d) chipping

79. Which of the following indicate better machinability?
1. Smaller shear angle 2. Higher cutting force
3. Longer tool life 4. Better surface finish.
(a) 1 and 3 (b) 2 and 4
(c) 1 and 2 (d) 3 and 4

80. Small amounts of which one of the following elements/pairs of elements is added to steel to increase its machinability?
(a) nickel
(b) sulphur and phosphorus
(c) silicon
(d) manganese and copper

81. In turning of slender rods, it is necessary to keep the transverse force minimum mainly?
(a) improve the surface finish
(b) increase productivity
(c) improve cutting efficiency
(d) reduce vibrations and chatter

82. Which of the following forces are measured directly by strain gauges or force dynamometers during metal cutting?
1. Force exerted by the tool on the chip acting normally to the tool face
2. Horizontal cutting force exerted by the tool on the workpiece
3. Frictional resistance of the tool against the chip flow acting along the tool face
4. Vertical force which helps in holding the tool in position.
(a) 1 and 3 (b) 2 and 4
(c) 1 and 4 (d) 2 and 4

83. Specific energy requirements in a grinding process are more than those in turning for the same metal removal rate because of the:
(a) specific pressures between wheel and work being high
(b) size effect of the larger contact areas between wheel and work
(c) high cutting velocities
(d) high heat produced during grinding

84. A grinding wheel of 150 mm diameter is rotating at 3000 rpm. The grinding speed is:
(a) 7.5 $\pi$ m/s (b) 15 $\pi$ m/s
(c) 45 $\pi$m/s (d) 450 $\pi$ m/s

85. Grinding wheel is said to be loaded when the:
(a) metal particles get embedded in the wheel surface blocking the interspaces between cutting grains
(b) hounding material comes on the surface and the wheel becomes blunt
(c) workpiece being ground comes to a stop in cylindrical grinding
(d) grinding wheel stops because of very large depth of cut

86. Which of the following statements are correct?
1. A boring machine is suitable for a job shop
2. A jig boring machine is designed specially for doing more accurate work when compared to a vertical milling machine
3. A vertical precision boring machine is suitable for boring holes in cylinder blocks and liners
(a) 1, 2 and 3 (b) 1 and 2
(c) 2 and 3 (d) 1 and 3

87. Consider the following processes for gear manufacture:
1. Milling with form cutter
2. Rack type gear shaper (gear planer)
3. Rotary gear shaper (gear shaper)
4. Gear hobbing.
The correct sequence of these processes in increasing order of accuracy of convolute profile of the gear is:
(a) 3, 2, 4, 1 (b) 2, 3, 4, 1
(c) 3, 2, 1, 4 (d) 2, 3, 1, 4

88. Gear cutting on a milling machine using an involute profile cutter is a:
(a) gear forming process
(b) gear generating process
(c) gear shaping process
(d) highly accurate gear-producing process.

89. For the manufacture of full depth spur gear by hobbing process, the number of teeth to be cut = 30, module = 3 mm and pressure angle = 20°. The radial depth of cut to be employed should be equal to:
(a) 3.75 mm (b) 4.50 mm
(c) 6.00 mm (d) 6.75 mm

90. In orthogonal cutting, the depth of cut is 03 mm at a cutting speed of 2 m/s. If the chip thickness is 0.75 mm, the velocity is:
(a) 133 m/s (b) 2 m/s
(c) 23 m/s (a) 3 m/s

91. Consider the following elements:
1. Nose radius 2. Cutting speed
3. Depth of cut 4. Feed.
The correct sequence of these elements in decreasing order of their influence on tool life is:
(a) 2, 4, 3, 1 (b) 4, 2, 3, 1
(c) 2, 4, 1, 3 (d) 4, 2, 1, 3

92. The rake angle in a twist drill:
(a) varies from minimum near the dead centre to a maximum value at the periphery
(b) is maximum at the dead centre and zero at the periphery
(c) is constant at every point of the cutting edge
(d) is a function of the size of the chisel edge

93. Which one of the following processes does not cause tool wear?
(a) ultrasonic machining

(b) electrochemical machining
(c) electric discharge machining
(d) anode mechanical machining

94. Consider the following forces acting on a finish turning tool:
1. Feed force
2. Thrust force
3. Cutting force.
The correct sequence of the decreasing order of the magnitudes of these forces is:
(a) 1, 2, 3
(b) 2, 3, 1
(c) 3, 1, 2
(d) 3, 2, 1

95. Match List-I (Type of drill) with List-II (Application) and select the correct answer using the codes given below the lists:

| List-I | List-II |
|---|---|
| A. Straight shank | 1. Soft materials |
| B. Taper shank | 2. Deep holes |
| C. Single flute | 3. General purpose |
| D. High helix | 4. Small hole diameter |

**Codes:**

| | A | B | C | D |
|---|---|---|---|---|
| (a) | 3 | 4 | 1 | 2 |
| (b) | 3 | 4 | 2 | 1 |
| (c) | 4 | 3 | 2 | 1 |
| (d) | 4 | 3 | 1 | 2 |

96. Which of the following are the advantages of a hydraulic; shaper over mechanically driven shaper?
1. More strokes per minute can he obtained at a given cutting speed
2. The cutting strokes has a definite stopping point
3. It is simpler in construction
4. Cutting speed is constant throughout most of shecurl.
Select the correct answer using the codes given below:
(a) 1 and 2
(b) 1 and 4
(c) 2 and 4
(d) 1, 3 and 4

97. Consider the following operations:
1. Undercutting
2. Plain turning
3. Taper turning
4. Thread cutting
The correct sequence of these operations in machining a product is:
(a) 2, 3, 4, 1
(b) 3, 2, 4, 1
(c) 2, 3, 1, 4
(d) 3, 2, 1, 4

98. Which one of the following materials is used as the bonding material for grinding wheels?
(a) Silicon carbide
(b) Sodium silicate
(c) Boron carbide
(d) Aluminium oxide

99. Consider the following statements:
In Up milling process,
1. the cutter starts the cut from the machined surface and proceeds upwards
2. the cutter starts the cut from the top surface and proceeds downwards
3. the job is fed in a direction opposite to that of cutter rotation
4. the job is fed in the same direction as that of cutter rotation.
Of these statements:
(a) 1 and 3 are correct
(b) 1 and 4 are correct
(c) 2 and 3 are correct
(d) 2 and 4 are correct

100. Which of the following motions are not needed for spur gear cutting with a hob?
1. Rotary motion of hob
2. Linear axial reciprocatory motion of hob
3. Rotary motion of gear blank
4. Radial advancement of hob.
Select the correct answer using the codes given below:
(a) 1, 2 and 3
(b) 1, 3 and 4
(c) 1, 2 and 4
(d) 2, 3 and 4

101. Match List-I (Gear component) with List-II (Preferred method of manufacturing) and select the correct answer using the codes given below the lists:

| List-I | List-II |
|---|---|
| A. Gear for clocks | 1. Hobbing |
| B. Bakelite gears | 2. Stamping |
| C. Aluminium gears | 3. Powder compacting |
| D. Automobile transmission gears | 4. Sand casting |
| | 5. Extrusion |

**Codes:**

| | A | B | C | D |
|---|---|---|---|---|
| (a) | 2 | 3 | 5 | 1 |
| (b) | 5 | 3 | 4 | 2 |
| (c) | 5 | 1 | 2 | 3 |
| (d) | 2 | 4 | 5 | 3 |

102. A 400 mm long shaft has 100 mm tapered step at the middle with 4° inclined angle. The tailstock offset required to produce this taper on a lathe would be:
(a) 400 sin 4°
(b) 400 sin 2°
(c) 100 sin 4°
(d) 100 sin 2°

103. A single short thread of pitch 2 mm is to be produced on a lathe having a lead screw with a double start thread of pitch 4 mm. The ratio of speeds between the spindle and lead screw for this operation is:
(a) 1 : 2
(b) 2: 1
(c) 1 : 4
(d) 4: 1

104. Mate List-I with List-II and select the correct answer using the codes given below the lists:

| List-I | List-II |
|---|---|
| A. Reaming | 1. Smoothing and squaring surface around the hole for proper seating |
| B. Counter-boring | 2. Sizing and finishing the hole |
| C. Counter-sinking | 3. Enlarging the end of the hole |
| D. Spot facing | 4. Making a conical enlargement at the end of the hole |

**Codes:**

| | A | B | C | D |
|---|---|---|---|---|
| (a) | 3 | 2 | 4 | 1 |
| (b) | 2 | 3 | 1 | 4 |
| (c) | 3 | 2 | 1 | 4 |
| (d) | 2 | 3 | 4 | 1 |

105. Which one of the following pairs of parameters and effects is not correctly matched?
(a) Large wheel diameter...Reduced wheel wear
(b) Large depth of cut...Increased well wear
(c) Large work diameter...Increased well wear
(d) Large well speed... Reduced well wear

106. A component requires a hole which must be within the two limits of 25.03 and 25.04 mm diameter. Which of the following statements about the reamer size are correct?
1. Reamer size cannot be below 25.03 mm
2. Reamer size cannot be above 25.04 mm
3. Reamer size cannot he 25.03 mm
4. Reamer size can be 25.04 mm
Select the correct answer using the code given below:
(a) 1 and 3 (b) 1 and 2
(c) 3 and 4 (d) 2 and 4

107. Consider the following criteria in evaluating machinability:
1. Surface finish 2. Type of chips
3. Tool life 4. Power consumption
In modern high speed CNC machining with coated carbide took, the correct sequence of these criteria in decreasing order of their importance is:
(a) 1, 2, 4, 3 (b) 2, 1, 4, 3
(c) 1, 2, 3, 4 (d) 2, 1, 3, 4

108. In metal cutting operation, the approximate ratio of heat distributed among chip, tool and work, in that order, is:
(a) 80 : 10 : 10
(b) 33 : 33 : 33
(c) 20 : 60 : 10
(d) 10 : 10 : 80

109. The gauge factor of a resistive pick-up of cutting force dynamometer is donned as the ratio of:
(a) applied strain to the resistance of the wire
(b) the proportional change in resistance to the applied strain
(c) the resistance to the applied strain
(d) change in resistance to the applied strain.

110. Poor machinability of centrifugally cast iron pipe is due to:
(a) chilling
(b) segregation
(c) dense structure
(d) highmould rotation speed

111. Consider the following statements:
For precision machining of non-ferrous alloys, diamond is preferred because it has
1. low coefficient of thermal expansion
2. high compression strength
3. high compression strength
4. how fracture toughness
Which of these statements are correct?
(a) 1 and 2 (b) 2 and 4
(c) 2 and 3 (d) 3 and 4

112. The radical force in single-point tool during turning operation varies between:
(a) 0.2 and 0.4 times the main cutting force
(b) 0.4 and 0.6 times the main cutting force
(c) 0.6 and 0.8 times the main cutting force
(d) 0.5 and 0.6 times the main cutting force

113. Which one of the following sets of forces are encountered by a lathe parting/tool while groove cutting?
(a) tangential, radial and axial
(b) tangential and radial
(c) tangential and axial
(d) radial and axial.

114. Match List-I (Machining process) with List-II (Associated medium) and select the correct answer using the codes giver below the lists:

| List-I | List-II |
|---|---|
| A. Ultrasonic machining | 1. Kerosene |
| B. EDM | 2. Abrasive slurry |
| C. ECM | 3. Vacuum |
| D. EBM | 4. Salt solution |

**Codes:**

| | A | B | C | D |
|---|---|---|---|---|
| (a) | 2 | 3 | 4 | 1 |
| (b) | 2 | 1 | 4 | 3 |
| (c) | 4 | 1 | 2 | 3 |
| (d) | 4 | 3 | 2 | 1 |

115. In a single-point turning operation of steel with a cemented carbide tool, Taylor's tool life exponent is 0.25. If the cutting speed is halved, the tool life will increase by:
(a) two times (b) four times
(c) eight times (d) sixteen times

116. Consider the following approaches normally applied for the economic analysis of machining:
1. Maximum production rate
2. Maximum profit criterion
3. minimum cost criterion
The correct sequence in ascending order of optimum cutting speed obtained by these approaches is:
(a) 1, 2, 3 (b) 1, 3, 2
(c) 3, 2, 1 (d) 3, 1, 2

117. Match List-I (ISO classification of carbide tools) with List-II (Applications) and select the correct answer using the codes given below the lists:

| List-I | List-II |
|---|---|
| A. P – 10 | 1. Non-ferrous, roughing cut |
| B. P – 50 | 2. Non-ferrous, finishing cut |
| C. K – 10 | 3. Ferrous material, roughing cut |
| D. K – 50 | 4. Ferrous material, finishing cut |

**Codes:**

| | A | B | C | D |
|---|---|---|---|---|
| (a) | 4 | 3 | 1 | 2 |
| (b) | 3 | 4 | 2 | 1 |
| (c) | 4 | 3 | 2 | 1 |
| (d) | 3 | 4 | 1 | 2 |

## ANSWERS WITH EXPLANATIONS

1. (d) 2. (c) 3. (c) 4. (d) 5. (a)
6. (a) 7. (b) 8. (b) 9. (c) 10. (c)
11. (c)
12. (c) Economic repair life,

$$x = \left[\frac{2(C-S)}{b}\right]^{1/2}$$

$$x = \left[\frac{2(200-200)}{400}\right]^{1/2} = 9.5 \text{ years}$$

13. (c) 14. (c) 15. (a) 16. (c) 17. (b)
18. (b) 19. (a)
20. (b) $\frac{\text{Speed of lead screw}}{\text{Speed of spindle}} = \frac{\text{Pitch of threads}}{\text{Pitch of lead screw}}$

$$\text{Speed of lead screw} = \left(\frac{2\times 60}{6}\right) = 20 \text{ rmp}$$

21. (b) 22. (b)
23. (c) Average speed of operation

$$= \frac{2NL}{10^3} = \frac{30\times 250}{10^3}$$

$$= 7.5 \text{ m/min}$$

24. (c) 25. (b) 26. (c) 27. (C) 28. (b)
29. (c)
30. (d) Surface finish $(R_a)_{max} = \frac{f^2}{8r}$

$$\frac{r^2}{r^1} = \left(\frac{f_2}{f_1}\right)^2 = 2^2 = 4$$

31. (b) 32. (c) 33. (a) 34. (d) 35. (c)
36. (c) 37. (a) 38. (c) 39. (b) 40. (c)
41. (b) 42. (d) 43. (a) 44. (b) 45. (a)
46. (a) 47. (b) 48. (d) 49. (b) 50. (a)
51. (c) 52. (d)
53. (b) Number of strokes,

$$n = \frac{\text{Length of stroke}}{\text{Feed rate}}$$

$$= \frac{30}{0.3} = 100$$

Length of cut, L = 700 + 2 × 25 = 750 mm

$$\text{Cutting time} = \frac{L\times n\times 1.5}{v_c}$$

$$= \frac{0.75\times 100\times 1.5}{9}$$

$$= 12.5 \text{ min}$$

54. (b) 55. (a) 56. (c) 57. (d) 58. (d)
59. (b) $\phi^5 = \frac{25}{6.25} = 4$

$$\phi = 1.32$$

60. (c) 61. (a) 62. (d) 63. (c) 64. (c)
65. (a) 66. (b) 67. (a) 68. (b) 69. (a)
70. (a) 71. (a) 72. (a) 73. (a) 74. (a)
75. (d) 76. (a) 77. (a) 78. (b) 79. (c)
80. (d) 81. (d) 82. (a) 83. (d)
84. (a) Grinding speed $= \frac{\pi DN}{60}$

$$= \frac{\pi\times 0.15\times 3000}{60}$$

$$= 7.5\,\pi \text{ m/s}$$

85. (a) 86. (c) 87. (a) 88. (a) 89. (d)
90. (a) Chip velocity, $v_f$ = Chip thickness ratio × Cutting speed

$$= \frac{0.5}{0.75}\times 2$$

$$= 1.33 \text{ m/s}$$

91. (a) 92. (c) 93. (b)
94. (a) A typical tool life equation for HSS is:

$$vT^{0.13}f^{0.6}d^{0.3}r^{0.1} = C$$

$$\therefore v > f > d > r$$

95. (a) 96. (c) 97. (c) 98. (b) 99. (a)
100. (d) 101. (a)
102. (d) Tailstock offset $= l\sin\left(\frac{\theta}{2}\right) = 100\sin 2°$
103. (c) $\frac{\text{Spindle of fset}}{\text{Lead screw speed}}$

$$= \frac{\text{Pitch of threads to be produceed}}{\text{Number of starts} \times \text{Pitch of threads of lead screw}}$$

$$= \frac{2}{2\times 4} = \frac{1}{4} \text{ or } 1:4$$

104. (d) 105. (c) 106. (b) 107. (c) 108. (a)
109. (b) 110. (a) 111. (a) 112. (a) 113. (a)
114. (b) 115. (d) 116. (c) 117. (d)

❑❑❑

# 18. Tool Engineering

- Tool and die makers are a class of machinists in the manufacturing industries who make jigs, fixtures, dies, molds,machine tools, cutting tools, gauges, and other tools used in manufacturing processes.
- Depending on which area of concentration a particular person works in, he or she may be called by variations on the name, including tool maker(toolmaker), die maker ,mold maker , tool fitter etc.
- Tool and die makers work primarily in tool room environments—sometimes literally in one room but more often in an environment with flexible, semipermeable boundaries from production work.
- They are skilled artisans (craftspeople) who typically learn their trade through a combination of academic coursework and hands-on instruction, with a substantial period of on-the-job training that is functionally an apprenticeship .
- Art and science are thoroughly intermixed in their work, as they also are in engineering. Manufacturing engineers and tool and die makers often work in close consultation as part of a manufacturing engineering team.
- There is often turnover between the careers, as one person may end up working in both at different times of their life, depending on the turns of their particular educational and career path.
- Both careers require some level of talent in both artistic/ artisanal/creative areas and math-and-science areas. Job-shop machinists can be any combination of toolmaker and production machinist.
- Some work only as machine operators, whereas others switch fluidly between tool room tasks and production tasks.
- Tool making typically means making tooling used to produce products. Common tooling includes metal forming rolls, cutting tools , fixtures, or even whole machine tools used to manufacture, hold, or test products during their fabrication. Due to the unique nature of a tool maker's work, it is often necessary to fabricate custom tools or modify standard tools.
- Die making is a subgenre of tool making that focuses on making and maintaining dies. This often includes making punches, dies, steel rule dies, and die sets.
- Precision is key in die making; punches and dies must maintain proper clearance to produce parts accurately, and it is often necessary to have die sets machined with tolerances of less than one thousandth of an inch.
- Although the details of training programs vary, many tool and die makers begin an apprenticeship with an employer, possibly including a mix of classroom training and hands-on experience.
- Some prior qualifications in basic mathematics, science, engineering science or design and technology can be valuable. Many tool and die makers attend a 4- to 5-year apprenticeship program to achieve the status of a journeyman tool and die maker.
- Today's employment relationships often differ in name and detail from the traditional arrangement of an apprenticeship, and the terms "apprentice" and "journeyman" are not always used, but the idea of a period of years of on-the-job training leading to mastery of the field still applies.
- The standard differentiation of jigs from fixtures is that a jig is what mounts onto a workpiece, whereas a fixture has the workpiece placed on it, into it, or next to it.
- The terms are sometimes used interchangeably. A jig and fixture maker needs to know how to use an assortment of machines to build these devices such as having skills in welding and in some cases the knowledge of wood working equipment, of course with the tool room machining skills.
- They are often advised by an engineer in building the devices. A wide knowledge of various materials is needed beyond wood and metal such as plastics. They also can create, design and build without engineering plans/blueprints.
- Jig/fixture makers gain hands on practical experience while monitoring and making alterations as the manufacturing process is constantly improved and reviewed with/by engineering. They also can be required to make these adjustments without engineering help, depending on the size of the company.
- Some Jigs and fixtures require electronic and pneumatic actuation, which will involve knowledge/training in these fields as well.
- Properly built jigs and fixtures reduce waste by insuring perfectly fitting parts. Jigs and fixtures can be as big as a car or be held in hand.
- Production needs dictate form and function. Jigs, fixtures and gages are needed to maintain quality standards for repeated low and high volume production demands.

# MULTIPLE CHOICE QUESTIONS

1. Which of the following drive systems is used in computer numerically controlled machine tools?
(a) Stepper motor
(b) Amorphous structure
(c) Thyristor controlled DC motor
(d) Servo controlled pneumatic drives

2. Feed gear box for a screw cutting is designed on the basis of:
(a) geometric progression
(b) arithmetic progression
(c) harmonic progression
(d) none

3. A 'block' of information in N.C machine program means:
(a) one row on tape
(b) a word comprising several rows on tape
(c) one complete instruction
(d) one complete program for a job

4. The floating position of the holding fixture in a rotary transfer device is used to:
(a) improve the accuracy of location
(b) reduce the tendency to over-index
(c) reduce the cycle time
(d) improve upon the acceleration and deceleration characteristics

5. When supported on three points, out of the 12 degrees of freedom the number of degrees of freedom arrested in a body is:
(a) 3 (b) 4
(c) 5 (d) 6

6. A diamond locating pin is used in jigs and fixtures because:
(a) diamond is very hard and wear-resistant
(b) it occupies very little space
(c) it helps-assembly with tolerance on centre
(d) is has along life

7. In a single spindle automatic lathe two tools are mounted on the turret one form tool on the front slide and the other, a parting tool, on the rear slide. The parting tool operation is much longer than form tool operation and they operate simultaneously (overlap). The number of cams required for this job is:
(a) one (b) two
(c) three (d) four

8. Feed drives in CNC milling machines are provided by:
(a) synchronous motors
(b) induction motors
(c) stepper motors
(d) servo-motors

9. In a transfer line:
(a) all the machine tools must be automatic
(b) the work stations must form a closed-loop
(c) the cycle time if total time taken by all the machining operations
(d) all the machine tools must he of conventional and general purpose type.

10. Consider the following statements regarding fixtures employed for holding workpiece during machining.
1. The location is based on the 3 – 2 – 1 principle
2. The numbers refer to the pins employed in three mutually perpendicular planes to arrest all the degrees of freedom
3. Fixture also provides tool guidance.
Of these statements:
(a) 1, 2 and 3 are correct
(b) 2 and 3 are correct
(c) 1 and 3 are correct
(d) 1 and 2 are correct

11. Two jigs are under consideration for a drilling operation to make a particular part.Jig A costs ₹ 800 and has operating cost of ₹ 0.10 per part. Jig B costs ₹ 1200 and has operating cost of ₹ 0.08 per part. The quantity of parts to be manufactured at which either jig will prove equally costly is:
(a) 8000 (b) 15000
(c) 20000 (d) 23000

12. Consider the following features:
1. All spindles operate simultaneously
2. One piece is complete each time the tools are withdrawn and the spindles are indexed
3. The tool slide indexes or revolves with the spindle carrier.
Which of these features are characteristics of a multispindle automatic machine used for bar work?
(a) 1, 2 and 3 (b) 1 and 2
(c) 2 and 3 (d) 1 and 3

13. Consider the following mechanisms:
1. Geneva gearing
2. Rack and pinion
3. Ratchet and pawl
Which of these mechanisms are used to index the work table or a transfer machine?
(a) 1 and 2 (b) 2 and 3
(c) 1 and 3 (d) 1, 2 and 3

14. Machining centre is:
(a) an automatic tool changing unit
(b) a group of automatic machine tools
(c) a next logical step beyond NC machine
(d) an NC machine tool

15. Consider the following operations and time required on a multispindle automatic machine to produce a particular job:
1. Turning — 1.2 minutes
2. Drilling — 1.6 minutes

3. Forming — 0.2 minute
4. Parting — 0.6 minute

The time required to make one piece (cycle time) will be:
(a) 0.6 minute (b) 1.6 minutes
(c) 3.6 minutes (d) 0.9 minute

16. Which of the following mechanisms are suitable for indexing the table of rotary transfer line?
1. Rack and pinion
2. Ratchet and pawl
3. Lead screw
4. Geneva mechanism

Select the correct answer by using the codes given below:
**Codes:**
(a) 1, 2 and 3 (b) 2, 3 and 4
(c) 1, 3 and 4 (d) 1, 2 and 4

17. Consider the following statements related to Turret lathe:
1. Turret is mounted directly on the saddle
2. Turret is mounted on an auxiliary slide
3. Much heavier and larger jobs than Capstan lathe can be produced

Which of the above statements is/are correct?
(a) 1 and 3 (b) 2 and 3
(c) 1 only (d) 2 only

18. Swiss type screw machines have:
(a) turrets
(b) radial slides
(c) spindle carriers
(d) tool DOMS

19. In a multi-spindle automatic machine, on which one of the following factors does the cycle time for each operation depend?
(a) shortest single-operation
(b) shortest multi-operations
(c) longest single-operation
(d) longest multi-operations

20. Which of the following statements is true for the case of a transfer line?
(a) The work stations must form a closed-loop
(b) The cycle time is total time taken by all the machining operations
(c) All the machine tools must be automatic
(d) All the machine tools must be of conventional and general purpose type

21. In a mechanical shaper, the length of stroke is increased by:
(a) increasing the centre distance of bull gear and crank pin
(b) decreasing the centre distance of bull gear and crank pin
(c) increasing the length of the ram
(d) decreasing the length of the slot in the slotted lever

22. While cutting helical gears on a non-differential gear hobber, the feed change gear ratio is:
(a) independent of index change gear ratio
(b) dependent on speed change gear ratio
(c) interrelated to index change gear ratio
(d) independent of speed and index change gear ratio

23. Consider the following characteristics:
1. Multiple operations can he performed
2. Operator's fatigue is greatly reduced
3. Ideally suited for batch production
4. A breakdown in one machine does not affect the flow of products
5. Can accommodate modifications in design of components, within certain limits.

The characteristics which can he attributed to special purpose machines would include
(a) 1, 3 and 4
(b) 1, 2 and 4
(c) 2, 3 and 5
(d) 1, 2 and 5

24. Match List-I with List-II and select the correct answer using the codes given below the lists:

| List-I (A function connected with NC m/c tool) | List-II (Associate parameter) |
|---|---|
| A. interpolation | 1. Tape preparation |
| B. Parity check | 2. Canned cycle |
| C. Preparatory function | 3. Drilling |
| D. Point-to-point | 4. Controlling |
| | 5. Turning |

**Codes:**

| | A | B | C | D |
|---|---|---|---|---|
| (a) | 4 | 1 | 2 | 3 |
| (b) | 4 | 1 | 2 | 5 |
| (c) | 5 | 1 | 3 | 2 |
| (d) | 1 | 4 | 3 | 2 |

25. Consider the following characteristics of production jobs:
1. Processing of parts frequently in small lots
2. Need to accommodate design changes of products
3. Low rate of metal removal
4. Need for holding close tolerances

The characteristics which favour the choice of numerically controlled machines would include:
(a) 1, 2 and 3
(b) 2, 3 and 4
(c) 1, 3 and 4
(d) 1, 2 and 4

26. In APT language, the cutter motion in incremental coordinate mode is addressed as:
(a) GO/TO/ (b) GO/TO
(c) GO DLTA/ (d) GO FWD7

27. Match List-I with List-II and select the correct answer using the codes given below the lists:

| List-I (Task) | List-II (Recommendation) |
|---|---|
| A. Three components in a straight line should work in one loading | 1. Clamp with a floating pad |
| B. Unloading of clamp element from jig is essential | 2. Quick action |
| C. Clamping of rough surface | 3. Cam clamp |
| D. Need for heavy clamping force | 4. Equalizing clamp |
| | 5. Strap clamp |

**Codes:**

| | A | B | C | D |
|---|---|---|---|---|
| (a) | 5 | 2 | 3 | 4 |
| (b) | 4 | 2 | 1 | 5 |
| (c) | 1 | 4 | 2 | 3 |
| (d) | 4 | 1 | 5 | 3 |

28. If the diameter of the hole is subject to considerable variation, then for locating in jigs and fixtures, the pressure type of locator used is:
(a) conical locator (b) cylindrical locator
(c) diamond pin locator (d) vee locator

29. In manual programming and tape preparation for an NC drilling machine, the spindle speed was coded as S 684 (using the magic-three code). The spindle speed in rpm will be:
(a) 684 (b) 68.4
(c) 840 (d) 6840

30. Which of the following pairs are correctly matched?
1. CNC machine ........ Post processor.
2. Machining centre .......... Tool magazine
3. DNC ......... FMS
(a) 1, 2 and 3 (b) 1 and 2
(c) 1 and 3 (d) 2 and 3

31. Which of the following is/are the advantage (*s*) of numerical control of machine tools?
1. Reduced lead time
2. Consistently good quality
3. Elaborate fixtures are not required
(a) 2 and 3 (b) 1 and 2
(c) 1 alone (d) 1 and 3

32. Consider the following statements:
The cutter setting block in a milling fixture
1. sets the cutting tool with respect to two of its surface
2. limits the total travel required by the cutter during machining
3. takes location from the location scheme of component.

Out of these statements:
(a) 1, 2 and 3 are correct
(b) 1 and 2 are correct
(c) 2 and 3 are correct
(d) 1 and 3 are correct

33. The type of quick return mechanism employed mostly in shaping machines is:
(a) DC reversible motor
(b) Fast and loose pulleys
(c) Whitworth motion
(d) Slotted link mechanism

34. Which of the following arc valid statements for point-to-point motion of the tool in APT language?
1. GO/TO/....... 2. GODLTA/.........
3. GO/TO.......
Select the correct answer using the codes given below:
(a) 1 and 2 (b) 2 and 3
(c) 1 and 3 (d) 1, 2 and 3

35. Match List-I with List-II and select the correct answer using the codes given below the lists:

| List-I (Track numbers on paper tape) | List-II (Holes on those tracks represent |
|---|---|
| A. Track nos. 1 to 4 | 1. Alphabets |
| B. Track no. 5 | 2. Numerals |
| C. Track nos. 6 and 7 | 3. End of block |
| D. track no. 8 | 4. Block number |
| | 5. Parity check |

**Codes:**

| | A | B | C | D |
|---|---|---|---|---|
| (a) | 2 | 5 | 1 | 3 |
| (b) | 1 | 4 | 2 | 5 |
| (c) | 2 | 4 | 1 | 3 |
| (d) | 1 | 5 | 2 | 3 |

36. One of the pins in a dual pin locator of a jig or fixture is shaped as a "diamond pin locator" because:
(a) diamond pin does not wear fast
(b) it is easy to clamp
(c) any variation between the centres of the hole is taken care of
(d) it will be easy to machine afterwards when the locator is worn out.

37. In tape preparation for an NC machine tool the code S 624 would represent spindle speeds of:
(a) 624 rpm, 240 rpm and 246 rpm
(b) 624 rpm and 240 rpm
(c) 624 rpm and 246 rpm
(d) 240 rpm and 246 rpm

38. Which of the following are the rules of programming NC machine tools in APT language?
1. Only capital letters are used
2. A period is placed at the end of each statement
3. Insertion of space does not affect the APT word.

Select the correct answer using the codes given below:

(a) 1 and 2 (b) 2 and 3
(c) 1 and 3 (d) 1 alone

39. Transfer machines can be defined as:
(a) material processing machines
(b) material handling machines
(c) material processing and material handling machines
(d) component feeders for automatic assembly

40. Consider the following statements regarding numerically controlled machine tools:
1. They reduce non-productive time
2. They reduce fixturing
3. They reduce maintenance cost.

Which of these statements are correct?
(a) 1, 2 and 3 (b) 1 and 2
(c) 2 and 3 (d) 1 and 3

41. Diamond pin location is used in a fixture because:
(a) it does not wear out
(b) it takes care of any variation in centre distance between two holes
(c) it is easy to clamp the part on diamond pins
(d) it is easy to manufacture

42. Consider the following characteristics of a robot:
1. The tip of the robot arm moves from one point to another with its in between path not being defined.
2. It can be used for drilling holes at different points in a workpiece.
3. It can be used for V butt joint welding between two points.
4. The memory capacity required for its control unit is low.

Which of these are the characteristics associated with a point-to-point robot?
(a) 1 and 2 (b) 1, 3 and 4
(c) 1, 2 and 4 (d) 2, 3 and 4

43. Match List-I (Components used in jigs and fixtures) with List-II (Their functions) and select the correct answer using the codes given below the lists:

| List-I | List-II |
|---|---|
| A. Jack pin | 1. To guide the drill hit during machining |
| B. V-locator | 2. For easy removal of the work-piece from the jig or fixture after the machining operation is over |
| C. Bushes | 3. To locate the circular or semicircular objects in a jig or fixture |
| D. Ejectors | 4. To locate workpieces whose dimensions are subject to variations |

**Codes:**

| | A | B | C | D |
|---|---|---|---|---|
| (a) | 3 | 4 | 1 | 2 |
| (b) | 3 | 4 | 2 | 1 |
| (c) | 4 | 3 | 1 | 2 |
| (d) | 4 | 3 | 2 | 1 |

44. The indexing of the turret in a single-spindle automatic lathe is done using:
(a) Geneva mechanism
(b) Ratchet and Pawl mechanism
(c) Rack and pinion mechanism
(d) Whitworth mechanism

45. Which one of the following sets of elements are quick-acting clamping elements for fixtures?
(a) Wedge and Cam
(b) Cam and Toggle
(c) Toggle and Wedge
(d) Wedge, Cam and Toggle

46 Match List-I (NC machine tool systems) with List-II (Features) and select the correct answer using the codes given below the lists:

| List-I | List-II |
|---|---|
| A. NC system | 1. It has an integrated automatic tool changing unit and a component indexing device |
| B. CNC system | 2. A number of machine tools arc controlled by a computer. No tape reader, the part programme is transmitted directly to the machine tool from the computer memory |
| C. DNC system | 3. The controller consists of soft-wired computer and hard-wired logic system.Graphic display of tool path is also possible |
| D. Machining centre | 4. The instruction on tape is prepared inbinary decimal form and operated by a series, of coded instructions |

**Codes:**

| | A | B | C | D |
|---|---|---|---|---|
| (a) | 4 | 2 | 3 | 1 |
| (b) | 1 | 3 | 2 | 4 |
| (c) | 4 | 3 | 2 | 1 |
| (d) | 1 | 2 | 3 | 4 |

47. In a machine tool gear box, the smallest and largest spindles are 100 rpm and 1120 rpm respectively. If there are 8 speeds in all, the fourth speed will be:
(a) 400 rpm (b) 280 rpm
(c) 800 rpm (d) 535 rpm

48. In a CNC machine tool, encoder is used to sense and control:
(a) table position (b) table velocity
(c) spindle speed (d) coolant flow

49. Which one of the following mechanisms is employed for indexing of turret in an automatic lathe?
(a) Whitworth
(b) Rack and pinion
(c) Ratchet and Pawl
(d) Geneva wheel

50. If the earliest starting time for an activity is 8 weeks, the latest finish time is 37 weeks and the duration time of the activity is 11 weeks, then the total float is equal to:
(a) 18 weeks (b) 14 weeks
(c) 56 weeks (d) 40 weeks

51. Match List-I (An element of jigs and fixtures) with List-II (Association system) and select the correct answer using the codes given below the lists:

| **List-I (An element of jigs and fixtures)** | **List-II (Association system)** |
|---|---|
| A. Bush | 1. Milling fixture |
| B. Setting block | 2. Turning fixture |
| C. Diamond pin | 3. Radial location |
| D. V-block | 4. Cylindrical location |
| | 5. Drill jigs |

**Codes:**

| | A | B | C | D |
|---|---|---|---|---|
| (a) | 5 | 4 | 3 | 1 |
| (b) | 3 | 1 | 2 | 4 |
| (c) | 5 | 1 | 3 | 4 |
| (d) | 3 | 4 | 2 | 1 |

52. Which one of the following is the most significant property to be considered in the selection of material for the manufacture of locating pins and drill jig bushes used in jigs and fixtures?
(a) wear resistance (b) elasticity
(c) shear strength (d) tensile strength

53. Consider the following alignment tests on machine tools:
1. Straightness 2. Flatness
3. Run out 4. Parallelism
Which of the above alignment tests on machine tools are common to both lathe and shaper?
(a) 1 and 2 (b) 2 and 3
(c) 3 and 4 (d) 1 and 4

54. Which item best describes a CAM technology?
(a) Geometric modelling (b) Documentation
(c) Drafting (d) Numerical control

55. Flexible manufacturing allows for:
(a) tool design and production
(b) automated design
(c) quick and inexpensive product
(d) quality control.

56. Which one of the following is the third basic component of robots besides power supply and control (memory) console?
(a) software
(b) coaxial cable
(c) mechanical unit arm
(d) microcomputer

57. What are the main components of an NC machine?
1. part program 2. machine control unit
3. servo meter
Select the correct answer using the code given below:
(a) 1, 2 and 3 (b) 1 and 2 only
(c) 2 and 3 only (d) 1 and 3 only

58. According to the principle of location in jigs and fixtures, how many degrees of freedom are to be eliminated to have a body fixed in space?
(a) 3 (b) 4
(c) 5 (d) 6

59. Which of the following are the rules of programming NC machine tools in APT language?
1. Only capital letters are used
2. A period is placed at the end of each statement
3. Insertion of space does not affect the APT word.
Select the correct answer using the codes given below:
(a) 1 and 2 (b) 2 and 3
(c) 1 and 3 (d) 1 alone

60. A “block” of information in NC machine program means:
(a) one row on tape
(b) a word comprising several rows on tape
(c) one complete instruction
(d) one complete program for a job

61. The floating position of the holding fixture in a rotary transfer device is used to:
(a) improve the accuracy of location
(b) reduce the tendency to over-index
(c) reduce the cycle time
(d) improve upon the acceleration and deceleration characteristics

62. Consider the following statements regarding numerically controlled machine tools:
1. They reduce non-productive time
2. They reduce fixturing
3. They reduce maintenance cost
Which of these statements are correct?
(a) 1, 2 and 3
(b) 1 and 2
(c) 2 and 3
(d) 1 and 3

63. In computer aided drafting practice, an arc is denned by:
(a) two end points only
(b) centre and radius
(c) radius and one end point
(d) two end points and centre.

64. With reference to NC machines, which of the following statements is wrong:
(a) Both closed-loop and open-loop control systems are used
(b) Paper tapes, floppy tapes and cassettes are used for data storage
(c) Digitizers may be used as interactive input devices
(d) Post processor is an item of hardware.

65. In a point-to-point type of NC system:
(a) control of position and velocity of the tool is essential
(b) control of only position of the tool is sufficient
(c) control of only velocity of the tool is sufficient
(d) neither position nor velocity need be controlled

66. In an NC machining operation, the tool has to be moved from point (5, 4) to point (7, 2) along a circular path with centre at (5, 2). Befoit starting the operation, the tool is at (5, 4). The correct G and M code for this motion is:
(a) N010 G03 X 7.0 Y2.0 15.0 J2.0
(b) N010 G02 X 7.0 Y2.0 15.0 J2.0
(c) N010 G01 X 7.0 Y2.0 15.0 J2.0
(d) N010 G00X 7.0 Y2.0 15.0 J2.0

67. In finish machining of an island on a casting with CNC milling machine, an end mill with 10 mm diameter is employed. The corner points of the island arc represented by (0, 0), (0, 30), (50, 30) and (50, 0). By applying cutter radius right compensation, the trajectory of the cutter will be:
(a) (– 5, 0),(– 5, 35), (55, 35), (55, –5), (–5, –5)
(b) (0, –5), (55, – 5), (55, 35), (– 5, 35), (–5, –5)
(c) (5, 5), (5, 25), (45, 25), (45, 5), (5, 5)
(d) (5, 5), (45, 5), (45, 25), (5, 25), (5, 5)

67. In finish machining of an island on a casting with CNC milling machine, an end mill with 10 mm diameter is employed. The corner points of the island arc represented by (0, 0), (0, 30), (50, 30) and (50, 0). By applying cutter radius right compensation, the trajectory of the cutter will be:
(a) (– 5, 0),(– 5, 35), (55, 35), (55, –5), (–5, –5)
(b) (0, –5), (55, – 5), (55, 35), (– 5, 35), (–5, –5)
(c) (5, 5), (5, 25), (45, 25), (45, 5), (5, 5)
(d) (5, 5), (45, 5), (45, 25), (5, 25), (5, 5)

68. The product is assembled from parts A and B. The probability of defective parts A and B are 0.1 and 0.2 respectively. Then the probability of the assembly of A and B to be non-defective is:
(a) 0.7 (b) 0.72
(c) 0.8 (d) 0.85

69. Which of the following conditions are necessary of applying linear programming
1. There must be a well defined objective function
2. The decision variables should be interrelated and non-negative
3. The resources must be in limited supply.
(a) 1 and 2 only (b) 1 and 3 only
(c) 2 and 3 only (d) 1, 2 and 3

70. Dummy activities are used to:
(a) determine critical path
(b) determine project completion time
(c) maintain the required flow in a network
(d) facilitate computations of stack

71. Consider the following statements:
1. an optimum solution.
2. an initial feasible solution.
3. Vogel's approximate solution.
Of these statements:
(a) 1 alone is correct
(b) alone is 2 correct
(c) 3 alone is correct
(d) 2 and 3 are correct

72. Consider the following statements:
Linear programming model can be applied to
1. line balancing problem
2. transportation problem
3. project management
Of these statements:
(a) 1, 2 and 3 are correct
(b) 1 and 2 are correct
(c) 2 and 3 are correct
(d) 1 and 3 are correct

73. In a 6 × 6 transportation problem, degeneracy would arise, it the number of filled slots were:
(a) equal to thirty six
(b) more than twelve
(c) 2 and 3 twelve
(d) less then eleven

74. For a M/M/T: ∞ /FCFS queue, the probability of the queue size being greater than N is given by λ= mean arrival rate and μ= mean service rate):
(a) $\left(\frac{\lambda}{\mu}\right)^N$ (b) $\left(\frac{\mu}{\lambda}\right)^N$
(c) $(\mu\lambda)^N$ (d) $\mu\lambda^N$

75. Earliest finish time can be regarded as:
(a) EST + duration of activity
(b) EST – duration of activity
(c) LFT + duration of activity
(d) LET – duration of activity

76. In the forging operation, fullering is done to:
(a) draw out the material
(b) bend the material
(c) upset the material
(d) extrude the material.

77. Which of the following assumptions are correct for cold rolling?
(a) The material is plastic
(b) The arc of contact is circular with a radius greater than the radius of the roil.
(c) Coefficient of friction is constant over the arc of contact and acts in one direction throughout the arc of contact.
Select the correct answer using the code given below:
**Codes:**
(a) 1 and 2 (b) 1 and 3
(c) 2 and 3 (d) 2, 2 and 3

78. A PERT network has three activities on critical path with mean time 3, 8 and 6, and standard deviation 1, 2 and 3 respectively. The probability that the project will be completed in 20 days is:
(a) 0.50 (b) 0.79
(c) 0.84 (d) 0.95

79. The software package used for computer simulation is known as:
(a) GPSS
(b) HTPM
(c) CRAFT
(d) COMSOAL

80. Match List I with List II and select the correct answer using the codes given below the lists:

| **List-I** | **List-II** |
|---|---|
| A. Linear programming problem | 1. Travelling salesman |
| B. Queuing problem | 2. Saddle point |
| C. Dynamic problem | 3. Product mix |
| D. Game theory problem | 4. Normal distribution |

**Codes:**

| | A | B | C | D |
|---|---|---|---|---|
| (a) | 3 | 4 | 1 | 2 |
| (b) | 4 | 3 | 1 | 2 |
| (c) | 3 | 4 | 1 | 2 |
| (d) | 4 | 3 | 2 | 1 |

81. A simple table for a linear programming problem is given below:

| 5 | 2 | 3 | 0 | 0 | 0 | | |
|---|---|---|---|---|---|---|---|
| $X_1$ | $X_2$ | $X_3$ | $X_4$ | $X_5$ | $X_6$ | Z | |
| $X_4$ | 1 | 2 | 2 | 1 | 0 | 0 | 8 |
| $X_5$ | 3 | 4 | 1 | 0 | 1 | 1 | 7 |
| $X_6$ | 2 | 3 | 4 | 0 | 0 | 1 | 10 |

Which one of the following correctly indicates the combination of entering and leaving variable?
(a) $X_1$ and $X_4$
(b) $X_2$ and $X_6$
(c) $X_2$ and $X_5$
(d) $X_3$ and $X_4$

82. A feasible solution to the linear programming problem should:
(a) satisfy the problem constraints
(b) optimize the objective function
(c) satisfy the problem constraints and non-negativity restrictions
(d) satisfy the non-negativity restrictions

83. If the arrival takes place every 10 minutes with a service time 4 minutes per unit then the mean arrival rate, mean service at and the probability that one would have to wait will be respectively:
(a) 10, 4 and 0.25
(b) 0.1, 0.25 and 0.4
(c) 10, 0.4 and 0.25
(d) 0.1, 0.25 and 0.1

84. In a M/M/I queuing system, expected waiting time of a unit that actually waits is given y?
(a) 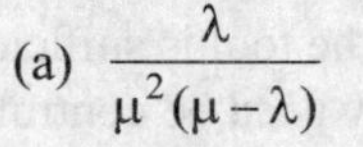 $\frac{\lambda}{\mu^2(\mu-\lambda)}$ (b) $\frac{\lambda}{\mu-\lambda}$
(c) $\frac{1}{\mu-\lambda}$ (d) $\frac{\lambda}{\mu^2(\mu-\lambda)}$

85. In a connected network of '*n*' arcs (roads) joining '*m*' verticals (towns), a selection of roads is taken up for resurfacing based on a minimum spanning tree of the network as being the least cost solution. This spanning tree will contain:
(a) *m* arcs
(b) (*m* + 1) arcs
(c) (*m*– 1) arcs
(d) (*m* + *n*– 1) arcs

86. For the PERT network shown in the given figure, the probability of completing the project in 27 days is?

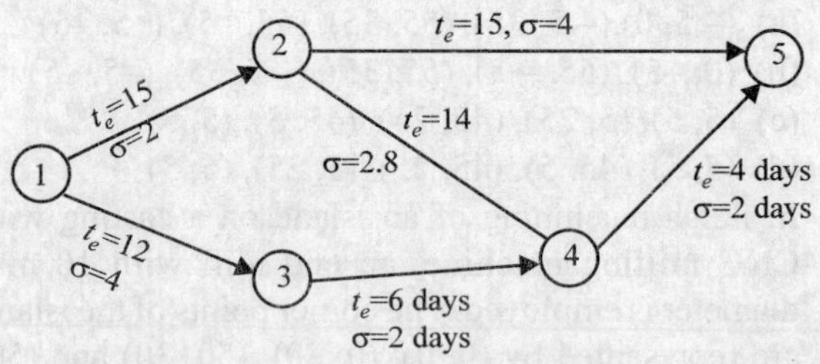


(a) 0.841 (b) 0.919
(c) 0.964 (d) 0.977

87. In CPM the cost slope is determined by:
(a) $\frac{\text{Crash cost}}{\text{Normal cost}}$
(b) $\frac{\text{Crash cost} - \text{Normal cost}}{\text{Normal time} - \text{crash time}}$
(c) $\frac{\text{Normal cost}}{\text{Crash cost}}$
(d) $\frac{\text{Normal cost} - \text{Crash cost}}{\text{Normal time} - \text{crash time}}$

88. Match List with List-II and select the correct answer using the codes given below the lists:

| **List-I (O.R. technique)** | **List-II (Application** |
|---|---|
| A. Linear programming | 1. Warehouse location decision |
| B. Transportation | 2. Machine allocation decision |
| C. Assignment | 3. Product mix decision |
| D. Queuing theory | 4. Project management decision |
| | 5. Number of servers decision |

**Codes:**

| | A | B | C | D |
|---|---|---|---|---|
| (a) | 1 | 2 | 3 | 5 |
| (b) | 3 | 1 | 2 | 5 |
| (c) | 1 | 3 | 2 | 5 |
| (d) | 3 | 2 | 1 | 4 |

89. Match List-I with List-II and select the correct answer using the codes given below the list:

| **List-I** | **List-II** |
|---|---|
| A. Linear programming | 1. Ritchie |
| B. Dynamic programming | 2. Dantzig |
| C. C programming | 3. Bell |
| D. Integer Programming | 4. Gomory |

**Codes:**

| | A | B | C | D |
|---|---|---|---|---|
| (a) | 2 | 1 | 4 | 3 |
| (b) | 1 | 2 | 3 | 4 |
| (c) | 2 | 3 | 1 | 4 |
| (d) | 2 | 3 | 4 | 1 |

90. The solution in a transportation model (of dimension $m \times n$) is said to be degenerate it has?
(a) exactly $(m + n - 1)$ allocations
(b) fewer than $(m + n - 1)$ allocations
(c) more than $(m + n - 1)$ allocations
(d) $(m \times n)$ allocations

91. A Solution is not a basic feasible solution in a transportation problem if after allocations:
(a) there is not closed loop
(b) there is a closed loop
(c) total number of allocations is one less than the sum of number of sources and destinations
(d) there is degeneracy.

92. Which one of the following subroutines does, a computer implementations liner programming by the simplex method use?
(a) Finding a root of a polynomial
(b) Finding the determinant of a matrix
(c) Finding the Eigen values of matrix
(d) Solving a system of linear equations

93. If the arrival rate of units is X and the service rate is $u$ for a waiting line system having '$m$' number of service stations, then the probability of services unit being turned out in the time interval, $(t + \nabla t)$:
(a) Zero
(b) $\mu.\nabla.t$
(c) $m\,\mu.\nabla.t$
(d) $n\,\mu.\nabla t$

94. Which of the following are the guidelines for the construction of a network diagram?
1. Each activity is represented by one and only one arrow in the network
2. Two activities can be identified by the same beginning and end events
3. Dangling must be avoided in a network diagram
4. Dummy activity consumes no time or resource.

Select the correct answer using the codes given below:
(a) 1, 2 and 3
(b) 1, 3 and 4
(c) 1, 2 and 4
(d) 2, 3 and 4

95. A strip is to rolled from a thickness of 30 mm to 15 mm using a two-high mill having rolls of diameter 300 mm. The coefficient of friction for unaided bite should nearly be:
(a) 0.95
(b) 0.5
(c) 0.25
(d) 0.07

96. Consider the following aspects:
1. Speed
2. Decision making
3. Accuracy
4. Cost savings.

The advantages of computers include:
(a) 1, 2 and 3
(b) 2 and 4
(c) 1, 3 and 4
(d) 1, 2, 3 and 4

97. When there are '$m$' rows and '$n$' columns in a transposition problem, degeneracy is said to occur when the number of allocations is:
(a) less than $(m + n - 1)$
(b) greater than $(m + n - 1)$
(c) equal to $(m - n - 1)$
(d) less than $(m - n - 1)$

98. Consider the following linear programming problem:
Max, $Z = 2A + 3B$, Subject to $A + B \leq 10$, $4A + 6B \leq 30$, $2A + B \leq 17$, $A, B \geq 0$
What can one say about the solution?
(a) It may contain alternative optima
(b) The solution will unbounded
(c) The solution will be degenerate
(d) It cannot be solved by simplex method

99. Consider two queueing disciplines in a single server queue. Case 1 has a first come first served discipline and case 2 has a last come first served discipline. If the average waiting times in the two cases are $W_1$ and $W_2$ respectively, then which one of the following inferences would be true?
(a) $W_1 > W_2$
(b) $W_1 < W_2$
(c) $W_1 = W_2$
(d) Data insufficient to draw any tangible inference

100. In a single server queue customers are served a at rate of μ. If W and $W_q$ represent the mean waiting time in the system and mean waiting time in the queue respectively, then W will be equal to?
(a) $W_q - \mu$ (b) $W_q + \mu$
(c) $W_q + 1/\mu$, (d) $W_q - 1/\mu$

101. A horizontal beam is carrying uniformly distributed load supported with equal overhangs as shown in the given figure

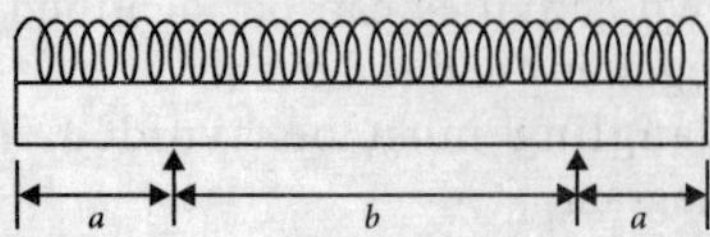


The resultant bending moment at the mid-span shall be zero if *a/b* is:
(a) 3/4 (b) 2/3
(c) 1/2 (d) 1/3

102. Two identical springs labelled as 1 and 2 are arranged in series and subjected to force F as shown in the given figure.

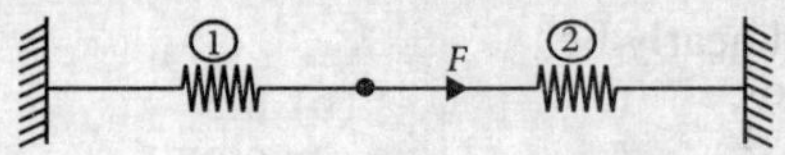


Assume that each spring constant is K. The strain energy stored in spring 1 is:
(a) $F^2/2K$ (b) $F^2/4K$
(c) $F^2/8K$ (d) $F^2/16K$

103. The given figure (all dimensions are in mm) shows an I-section of the beam

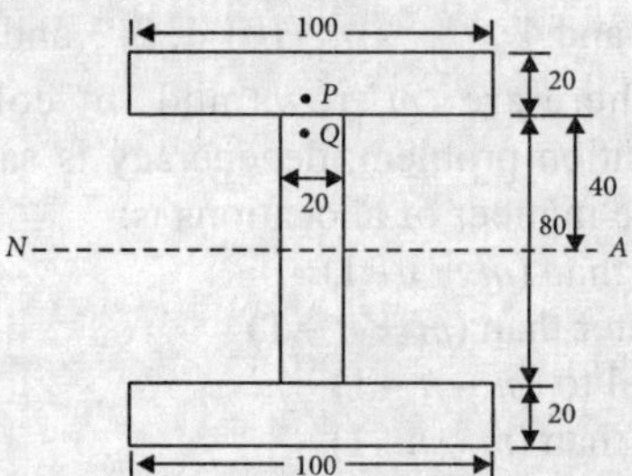


The shear stress at point P (very close to the bottom of the flange) is 12 MPa. The stress at point Q in the web (very close to the flange) is:
(a) indeterminable due to incomplete data
(b) 60 MPa
(c) 18 MPa
(d) 12 MPa

104. The given figure shows the Klein's construction for acceleration of the slider-crank mechanism. Which one of the following quadrilaterals represents the required acceleration diagram?

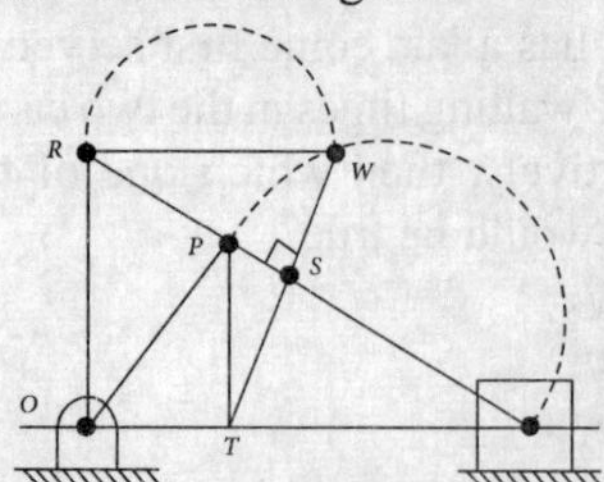


(a) ORST (b) OPST
(c) ORWT (d) ORPT

105. Match List-I (Methods) with List-II (Applications) and select the correct answer using the codes given below the lists:

| List I | List II |
|---|---|
| A. Break even analysis | 1. To provide different facility at different locations |
| B. Transportation | 2. To take action from among the paths with uncertainty. |
| C. Assignment problem | 3. To choose between different methods of Manufacture |
| D. Decision tree | 4. To determine the location of the additional plant |

**Codes:**

| | A | B | C | D |
|---|---|---|---|---|
| (a) | 4 | 3 | 1 | 2 |
| (b) | 3 | 4 | 1 | 2 |
| (c) | 3 | 4 | 2 | 1 |
| (d) | 4 | 3 | 2 | 1 |

106. A variable which has no physical meaning, but is used to obtain an initial basic feasible solution to the linear programming problem is referred to as:
(a) Basic variable
(b) Non-basic variable
(c) Artificial variable
(d) Basis

107. In transportation problem, the materials are transported from 3 plants to 5 warehouses. The basis feasible solution must contain exactly, which one of the following allocated cells?
(a) 3 (b) 5
(c) 7 (d) 8

108. The assignments algorithm is applicable to which of the following combined situations for the purpose of improving productivity?
1. Identification of-sales force-market.
2. Scheduling of operator-market
3. Fixing machine – location

Select the correct answer using the codes given below:

**Codes:**
(a) 1, 2 and 3 (b) 1 and 3
(c) 2 and 3 (d) 1 and 2

109. For A M/M/I: ∞ /FCFS queue, the mean array rate is equal to 10 per hour and the mean service rate is 15 per hour The expected queue length is:
(a) 1.33 (b) 1.53
(c) 2.75 (d) 3.20

110. In a transportation problem North-West corner rule would yield:
(a) An optimum solution
(b) An initial feasible solution
(c) A Vogel's approximate solution
(d) A minimum cost solution

111. In the solution of a linear programming problem by simple method, if during an iteration, all ratios of right-hand side $b_i$ to the coefficients of entering variable a are found to be negative, it implies that the problem has:
(a) Infinite number of solution
(b) Infeasible solution
(c) Degeneracy
(d) Unbound solution

112. Consider the following statements regarding the characteristics of the standard from of a linear programming problem:
1. All the constraints are expressed in the form of equations
2. The right hand side of each constraints equation is non-negative
3. All the decision variables are non-negative

Which of these statements are correct?
(a) 1, 2 and 3 (b) 1 and 2
(c) 2 and 3 (d) 1 and 3

113. The average time between two arrivals of customers at a counter in a ready-made store is 4 min. The average time of the counter clerk to serve the customer is 3 min. The arrivals are distributed as per Poisson distribution and the services art exponential distribution. The probability that a customer arriving at the counter to wait, is:
(a) Zero (b) 0.25
(c) 2 and 3 (d) 0.75

114. Time estimates of an activity in a PERT network are:
Optimistic time $t_0$ = 9 days pessimistic time $t_p$ = 21 days and most likely time $t_e$ = days.
The time approximates probability of completion of this activity in 13 days is:
(a) 16% (b) 34%
(c) 50% (d) 84%

115. Match List-I (Scientist) with List-II (Research work) and select the correct answer using the codes given below the lists:

| **List-I** | **List-II** |
|---|---|
| A. Schewart | 1. Less function in quality |
| B. Taguchi | 2. Queuing model. |
| C. Erlang | 3. Zero defect |
| | 4. Control charts |

**Codes:**

| | **A** | **B** | **C** |
|---|---|---|---|
| (a) | 3 | 1 | 2 |
| (b) | 4 | 3 | 1 |
| (c) | 4 | 1 | 2 |
| (d) | 3 | 4 | 1 |

116. Which one of the following statements is not correct?
(a) Assignment model is a special case of a liner programming problem
(b) In queuing model, Poisson arrivals and exponential services are assumed
(c) In transportation problems, the non-square matrix is made square by adding a dummy row or a dummy columns
(d) In linear programming problems, dual of a dual is a primal.

117. Consider the following statements:
1. A linear problem with three variables and two constraints can be solved by graphical method
2. For solutions of a linear programming problem with mixed constraints, Big-M-method can be employed
3. In the solutions process of a linear programming problem using Big-M-method which an artificial variable leaves the basis, the column of the artificial-variable can be removed from all subsequent tables.

Which of these statements are correct?
(a) 1, 2 and 3 (b) 1 and 2
(c) 1 and 3 (d) 2 and 3

118. Arrivals at a telephone booth arc considered to be Poisson with an average time of 10 minutes between one arrival and the next. The length of a phone call is assumed to be distributed exponentially with mean of 3 minutes. The probability that a person arriving at the hook will have to wait, is:
(a) 0.043 (b) 0.300
(c) 0.429 (d) 0.700

119. Dummy activities are used in a network to:
(a) facilitate computation of slacks
(b) satisfy precedence requirements
(c) determine project completion time
(d) avoid use of resources.

120. If the earliest starting time for an activity is 8 weeks, the latest finish time is 37 weeks and the duration time of the activity is 11 weeks, then the total float is equal to:
(a) 18 weeks (b) 14 weeks
(c) 56 weeks (d) 40 weeks

## ANSWERS WITH EXPLANATIONS

1. (d) 2. (a) 3. (c) 4. (a) 5. (d)
6. (c) 7. (a) 8. (d) 9. (c) 10. (d)
11. (c) Let $x$ = quantity of parts to be manufactured

$$800 + 0.10 \times x = 1200 + 0.08 \times x \; 0.02x = 400$$

$$x = 20{,}000$$

12. (a) 13. (d) 14. (b)
15. (c) Cycle time = 1.2 + 1.6 + 0.2 + 0.6 = 3.6 min
16. (a) 17. (c) 18. (c) 19. (c) 20. (a)

21. (a) 22. (c) 23. (c) 24. (a) 25. (d)
26. (c) 27. (d) 28. (a) 29. (a) 30. (a)
31. (b) 32. (b) 33. (d) 34. (c) 35. (a)
36. (c)
37. (d) The spindle speed function is programmed in rpm and should be expressed by a 3 digit coded number. Thus 6 represents three digits in rpm and these should start with 24. Thus, it could be 240 and 246.
38. (c) 39. (b) 40. (b) 41. (b) 42. (c)
43. (c) 44. (a) 45. (a) 46. (a)
47. (b) $\phi^{8-1} = \frac{1120}{100} \phi = 11.2$

$\phi = 1.412$

$N_1 = 100$ rpm, $N_2 = 100 \times 1.412$

$= 0.141.2$ rpm

$N_3 = 141.2 \times 1.412 = 200$

$N_4 = 280$ rpm

48. (a) 49. (d)
50. (a) Total Float, $FT = [(TL)_j - (TE)_i] - t_{ij}$

$Z = (37 - 8) - 11 = 18$ weeks

51. (c) 52. (c) 53. (b) 54. (d) 55. (c)
56. (c) 57. (a) 58. (d) 59. (c) 60. (c)
61. (a) 62. (b) 63. (d) 64. (d) 65. (b)
66. (b) 67. (b) 67. (b)
68. (b) P (A) to be non-defective = 1 – 0.1 = 0.9

P (B) to be non-defective = 1 – 0.2 = 0.8

P (AB) to be non-defective = P (A) × P (B) = 0.9 × 0.8 = 0.72

69. (d) 70. (c) 71. (b) 72. (b)
73. (d) Degeneracy would arise if the number of filled slots are less than $m + n - 1$, *i.e.,* $6 + 6 - 1 = 11$
74. (a) 75. (a) 76. (a) 77. (d)
78. (b) Standard derivation, $\sigma = 1_2 + 2_2 + 3_2 = 3.7416$

$T_m = 3 + 8 + 6 = 17$ days

$T_s = 20$ days

Probability factor, $z = \frac{T_s - T_m}{\sigma} = 0.802$

For z = 0.802, area under the normal distribution curve = 0.7881 = 0.79

79. (b) 80. (a)
81. (c) Minimum value of z = 7 corresponding to X = 5 and maximum value of variable is X = 2 and leaving variable is X 5
82. (a) 83. (b) 84. (a) 85. (b) 86. (a)

1 → 2: $t_e$=15, σ=2
1 → 3: $t_e$=12, σ=4
2 → 5: $t_e$=15, σ=4
2 → 4: $t_e$=14, σ=2.8
3 → 4: $t_e$=6 days, σ=2 days
4 → 5: $t_e$=4 days, σ=2 days

Critical path: 1 – 2 – 4 – 5

Critical time = 23 days

Standard deviation,

$$\sigma = \sqrt{2^2 + (2.8) + 2^2}$$

$$= 3.98$$

$$z = \frac{27 - 23}{3.98} = 1$$

For z = 1, area under the normal distribution curve = 0.8413

Probability of completing the project = 0.841

87. (b) 88. (b) 89. (c) 90. (b) 91. (a)
92. (d) 93. (b) 94. (b)
95. (a) Bite angle, $\alpha = \tan^{-1}\mu$

$$\cos\alpha = \frac{150 - 7.5}{150}$$

$$= \frac{142.5}{150} = 0.95$$

96. (c) 97. (a) 98. (a) 99. (b) 100. (c)
101. (c) 102. (b) 103. (b)
104. (b) OPST is the acceleration diagram in Klein's construction.
105. (b) 106. (a) 107. (c) 108. (c)
109. (a) $\lambda = 10$, $\mu = 15$,

$$\rho = \frac{\lambda}{\mu} = \frac{10}{15} = \frac{2}{3}$$

Expected queue length $= \frac{\rho^2}{1-\rho} = \frac{(4/9)}{(1-2/3)} = 1.33$

110. (b) 111. (b) 112. (a) 113. (d) 114. (a)
115. (b) 116. (d) 117. (d)
118. (d) $\rho = \frac{\lambda}{\mu} = \frac{3}{10} = 0.3$

Probability of waiting = 1 – ρ = 1 – 0.3 = 0.7

119. (d)
120. (a) Total Float, $FT = [(TL)_j - (TE)_i] - t_{ij}$

$Z = (37 - 8) - 11 = 18$ weeks

❑❑❑

# 19. Metrology and Inspection

- Metrology is the science of measurement. Metrology includes all theoretical and practical aspects of measurement.
- Metrology is defined by the International Bureau of Weights and Measures (BIPM) as "the science of measurement, embracing both experimental and theoretical determinations at any level of uncertainty in any field of science and technology.
- Metrology is a very broad field and may be divided into three basic activities, though there is considerable overlap between the activities:
- Realization of these units of measurement in practice
- Application of chains of traceability linking measurements made in practice to reference standards.
- Metrology also has three basic subfields, all of which make use of the three basic activities, though in varying proportions:
  – Scientific or fundamental metrology
  – Applied, technical or industrial metrology
  – Legal metrology
- Scientific or fundamental metrology concerns the establishment of quantity systems, unit systems, units of measurement, the development of new measurement methods, realisation of measurement standards and the transfer of traceability from these standards to users in society.
- The BIPM maintains a database of the metrological calibration and measurement capabilities of various institutes around the world. These institutes, whose activities are peer-reviewed, provide the top-level reference points for metrological traceability.
- In the area of measurement the BIPM has identified nine metrology areas including length, mass and time.
- Applied, technical or industrial metrology concerns the application of measurement science to manufacturing and other processes and their use in society, ensuring the suitability of measurement instruments, their calibration and quality control of measurements.
- Although the emphasis in this area of metrology is on the measurements themselves, traceability of the calibration of the measurement devices is necessary to ensure confidence in the measurements.
- Legal metrology "concerns activities which result from statutory requirements and concern measurement, units of measurement, measuring instruments and methods of measurement and which are performed by competent bodies."
- Such statutory requirements might arise from, amongst others, the needs for protection of health, public safety, the environment, enabling taxation, protection of consumers and fair trade.
- The OIML was set up to assist in harmonising such regulations across national boundaries to ensure that legal requirements do not inhibit trade. In Europe WELMEC was established to promote cooperation on the field of legal metrology.
- A core concept in metrology is metrological traceability defined by the Joint Committee for Guides in Metrology as "property of a measurement result whereby the result can be related to a reference through a documented unbroken chain of calibrations, each contributing to the measurement uncertainty".
- Metrological traceability permits comparison of measurements, whether the result is compared to the previous result in the same laboratory, a measurement result a year ago, or to the result of a measurement performed anywhere else in the world.
- Traceability is most often obtained by calibration, establishing the relation between the indication of a measuring instrument and the value of a measurement standard. These standards are usually coordinated by national metrological institutes.
- Traceability is used to extend measurement from a method that works in one regime to a different method that works in a different regime, by calibrating the two using an overlapping range where both work.
- Traceability, accuracy, precision, systematic bias, evaluation of measurement uncertainty are critical parts of a quality management system.
- Mistakes can make measurements and counts incorrect. Even if there are no mistakes, nearly all measurements are still inexact. The term 'error' is reserved for that inexactness, also called measurement uncertainty. Among the few exact measurements are:
- The absence of the quantity being measured, such as a voltmeter with its leads shorted together: the meter should read zero exactly.
- Measurement of an accepted constant under qualifying conditions, such as the triple point of pure water: the thermometer should read 273.16 Kelvin (0.01 degrees Celsius, 32.018 degrees Fahrenheit) when qualified equipment is used correctly.
- Self-checking ratio metric measurements, such as a potentiometer: the ratio in between steps is independently adjusted and verified to be beyond influential inexactness.

- All other measurements either have to be checked to be sufficiently correct or left to chance. Metrology is the science that establishes the correctness of specific measurement situations.
- This is done by anticipating and allowing for both mistakes and error. The precise distinction between measurement error and mistakes is not settled and varies by country.
- Calibration is the process where metrology is applied to measurement equipment and processes to ensure conformity with a known standard of measurement, usually traceable to a national standards board.
- Metrology laboratories are places where both metrology and calibration work are performed. Calibration laboratories generally specialize in calibration work only.
- Both metrology and calibration laboratories must isolate the work performed from influences that might affect the work. Temperature, humidity, vibration, electrical power supply, radiated energy and other influences are often controlled.
- Generally, it is the rate of change or instability that is more detrimental than whatever value prevails.
- Calibration technicians execute calibration work. In large organizations, the work is further divided into three groups.
- Metrology technicians perform investigation work in addition to calibrations. They also apply proven principles to known situations and evaluate unexpected or contradictory results.
- Specific education in metrology was formerly limited to sub-professional work. Most of the branches of the US Military train 'enlisted-grade' technicians to meet their specific needs.
- Large industrial organizations also develop people who demonstrate aptitude in testing functions.
- Mythologists are people who perform metrology work at and above the technician levels.
- The metrology and calibration work described above is always accompanied by documentation. The documentation can be divided into two types: one related to the task, and the other related the administrative program.
- Task documentation includes calibration procedures and the collected data. Administrative program documentation includes equipment identification data, 'calibration certificates', calibration time interval information and 'as-found' or 'out-of-tolerance' notifications.
- Standards are objects or ideas that are designated as being authoritative for some accepted reason. Whatever value they possess is useful for comparison to unknowns for the purpose of establishing or confirming an assigned value based on the standard.
- The design of this comparison process for measurements is metrology. The execution of measurement comparisons for the purpose of establishing the relationship between a standard and some other measuring device is calibration.
- The ideal standard is independently reproducible without uncertainty. This is what the creators of the "metre" length standard were attempting to do in the 19th century when they defined a metre as one ten-millionth of the distance from the equator to one of the Earth's poles.
- It was later learned that the Earth's surface is an unreliable basis for a standard, as the Earth is not spherical and it is constantly changing in shape. But the special alloy metre bars that were created and accepted in that time period standardized international length measurement until the 1950s.
- Careful calibrations allowed tolerances as small as 10 parts per million to be distributed and reproduced in metrology laboratories worldwide, regardless of whether the rest of the metric system was implemented and in spite of the shortfalls of the metre's original basis.
- Currently, five independent units of measure are internationally recognized:temperature interval, linear distance, electrical current, frequency and mass. Any measurement can be based on one or more of these measurement units.
- To supplement these five, two units of angle measurement that are also independent are recognized. For example, Ohm's law is a widely known concept in electrical study. Of the three units of measure involved, only current (ampere) is an independent unit. Voltage and resistance units are dependent on current units, as defined by Ohm's law.
- In industrial metrology, several issues beyond accuracy constrain the usability of metrology methods. These include:
- The speed with which measurements can be accomplished on parts or surfaces in the process of manufacturing, which must match the takt time of the production line.
- The completeness with which the manufactured part can be measured such as described in high-definition metrology,
- The ability of the measurement mechanism to operate reliably in a manufacturing plant environment considering temperature, vibration, dust, and a host of other potential hostile factors
- The ability of the measurement results, as they are presented, to be assimilated by the manufacturing operators or automation in time to effectively control the manufacturing process variables.

# MULTIPLE CHOICE QUESTIONS

1. Process capability of machine is definas the capability of the machine to:
(a) produce definite volume of work per minute
(b) produce definite number of operations
(c) produce a job at a definite spectrum of speed
(d) hold a definite spectrum of tolerances and surface finish.

2. Interchangeability can be achieved by:
(a) standardization
(b) better process planning
(c) simplification
(d) better product planning.

3. Which one of the following step would lead to interchangeability?
(a) quality control (b) process planning
(c) operator training (d) product design.

4. Match List-I with List-II and select the correct answer using the codes given below the lists:

| List-I (Measuring device) | List-II (Parameter measured) |
|---|---|
| (A) Diffraction grating | 1. Smaller angular deviations on long flat surfaces |
| (B) Optical flat | 2. On-line measurement of moving parts |
| (C) Auto collimators | 3. Measurement of gear pitch |
| (D) Laser scan micrometer | 4. Surface texture using interferometry |
| | 5. Measurement of very small displacements |

**Codes:**

| | A | B | C | D |
|---|---|---|---|---|
| (a) | 5 | 4 | 2 | 1 |
| (b) | 3 | 5 | 1 | 2 |
| (c) | 3 | 5 | 4 | 1 |
| (d) | 5 | 4 | 1 | 2 |

5. Which one of the following tolerances set on inner diameter and outer diameter respectively of headed jig bush for press fit it correct?
(a) G7h6 (b) F7 n6
(c) H7 h6 (d) F7 j6

6. Match List-I with List-II and select the correct answer using the codes given below the lists:

| List-I | List-II |
|---|---|
| (A) Control charts for variables | 1. Binomial distribution |
| (B) Control chart non-conformities | 2. Beta for number of distribution |
| (C) Control chart for fraction rejected | 3. Normal distribution |
| (D) Activity time distribution in PERT | 4. Poisson distribution |
| | 5. Exponential distribution |

**Codes:**

| | A | B | C | D |
|---|---|---|---|---|
| (a) | 3 | 4 | 1 | 5 |
| (b) | 5 | 4 | 3 | 1 |
| (c) | 4 | 3 | 1 | 2 |
| (d) | 3 | 4 | 1 | 2 |

7. Match List-I withList-II and select the correct answer using the codes given below the lists:

| List-I | List-II |
|---|---|
| (A) OC curve | 1. Acceptance sampling |
| (B) AOQL | 2. Dodge rooming table |
| (C) Binomial distribution | 3. P-charts |
| (D) Normal curve | 4. Control charts for variables |

**Codes:**

| | A | B | C | D |
|---|---|---|---|---|
| (a) | 1 | 2 | 3 | 4 |
| (b) | 1 | 3 | 2 | 4 |
| (c) | 4 | 2 | 3 | 1 |
| (d) | 4 | 3 | 2 | 1 |

8. A 60-foot gear when hobbed on a differential hobber with a two-start hob, the index change gear ratio is governed by which one of the following kinematic balance equations?
(a) 1 revolution of gear blank = 1/60 of hob revolutions
(b) 1 revolution of gear blank = 1/60 of hob revolutions
(c) 1 revolution of hob = 2/6() of hob revolutions
(d) 1 revolution of hob = 1/60 of blank revolutions.

9. Match List-I (Limits in normal distribution) with List-II (Population covered) and select the correct answer using the codes given below the lists:

| List-I (Limits in normal distribution | List-II (Population covered) |
|---|---|
| (A) ± 3 σ | 1. 03413 |
| (B) ± 2σ | 2. 06826 |
| (C) ± 1σ | 3. 0.9973 |
| | 4. 0.9545 |

**Codes:**

| | A | B | C |
|---|---|---|---|
| (a) | 3 | 4 | 2 |
| (b) | 3 | 2 | 4 |
| (c) | 4 | 2 | 3 |
| (d) | 4 | 3 | 2 |

10. In the tolerance specification 25 D 6, the letter D represents:
(a) Grade of tolerance
(b) upper deviation
(c) lower deviation
(d) type of fit.

11. Repetitive fast speed activities can be effectively analyzed by taking photograph at:
(a) low speed and screening at low speed
(b) high speed and screening at high speed
(c) high speed and screening at low speed
(d) low speed and screening at high speed.

12. The tolerance specified by the designer for the diameter of a shaft is 20.00 ± 0.025 mm. The shafts produced by three different machines A, B and C have mean diameters of 19.99 mm, 20.00 mm and 20.01 mm respectively, with same standard deviation. What will be the percentage rejection for the shafts produced by machines A, B and C?
(a) same for the machine A, B and C since the standard deviation is same for the three machines
(b) least for machine A
(c) least for machine B
(d) least for machine C.

13. A control chart is established with limits of ±2 standard errors for use in monitoring samples of size $n = 20$. Assume the process to be in control. What is the likelihood of a sample mean falling outside the control limits?
(a) 97.7% (b) 95.3%
(c) 4.5% (d) 23%

14. Which of the following is an interference fit?
(a) push fit
(b) running fit
(c) sliding fit
(d) shrink lit

15. The M and E-system in metrology are related to measurement of:
(a) screw threads
(b) flatness
(c) angularity
(d) surface finish

16. Consider the following advantages:
1. Rapid process
2. Work with keyways can be ground
3. No work holding device is required.
Which of these are the advantages of centreless grinding?
(a) 1, 2 and 3 (b) 1 and 2
(c) 2 and 3 (d) 1 and 3

17. What is the dominant direction of the tool marks or scratches in a surface texture having a directional quality, called?
(a) primary texture
(b) secondary texture
(c) lay
(d) flaw

18. Which one of the following is not the characteristics of acceptance sampling?
(a) this is widely suitable in mass production
(b) it causes less fatigue to inspectors
(c) this is much economical
(d) it gives definite assurance for the conformation of the specifications for all the pieces.

19. The span of control refers to the:
(a) total amount of control which can he exercised by the supervisor
(b) total number of persons which report to any one supervisor
(c) delegation of authority by the supervisor to this subordinates
(d) delegation of responsibility by the supervisor to his subordinates.

20. Match List-1 (Trend/Defect) with List-II (Chart) and select the correct answer using the codes given below the lists:

| List-I (Trend/Defect) | List-II (Chart) |
|---|---|
| (A) Trend | 1. R-Chart |
| (B) Dispersion | 2. C-Chart |
| (C) Number of defects | 3. $\overline{X}$ -Chart |
| (D) Number of defectives | 4. *np*-Chart |
| | 5. *u*-Chart |

**Codes:**

| | A | B | C | D |
|---|---|---|---|---|
| (a) | 5 | 3 | 2 | 4 |
| (b) | 3 | 1 | 4 | 2 |
| (c) | 3 | 1 | 2 | 4 |
| (d) | 3 | 4 | 5 | 2 |

21. Consider the following statements in respect of double sampling plan:
1. Average number of pieces inspected is double that of single sampling
2. Average number of pieces inspected is less than that for single sampling
3. Decision to accept or reject the lot is taken only after the inspection of both samples
4. Decision to accept or reject the lot is reached sometimes after one sample and sometimes after two samples.
Which of these statements are correct?
(a) 1, 2 and 3 (b) 2 and 4
(c) 1 and 4 (d) 2 and 3

22. Consider the following fits:
1. I.C engine cylinder and piston
2. Ball bearing outer race and housing
3. Ball bearing inner race and shaft
Which of the above fits are based on the shaft basis system?
(a) 1 and 2
(b) 2 and 3
(c) 1 and 3
(d) 1, 2 and 3

23. Match List I (Quality control concepts) with List II (Quality control techniques) and select the correct answer using the codes given below the lists:

| **List-I (Quality control concepts)** | **List-II (Quality control techniques)** |
|---|---|
| (A) Tightened and reduced inspection | 1. Dodge roming tables |
| (B) Lot tolerance percent defective | 2. Control chart for variables |
| (C) Poisson distribution | 3. MIL standards |
| (D) Normal distribution | 4. Control chart for number of non-conformities |

**Codes:**

| | A | B | C | D |
|---|---|---|---|---|
| (a) | 2 | 1 | 4 | 3 |
| (b) | 3 | 4 | 1 | 2 |
| (c) | 3 | 1 | 4 | 2 |
| (d) | 2 | 4 | 1 | 3 |

24. Quality control chart for averages was maintained for a dimension of the product. After the control was established, it was found that the standard deviation (a) of the process was 1.00 mm. The dimension of the part is 70 ± 2.5 mm. Parts above 725 mm can be reworked but parts below 67.5 mm have to be scrapped. What should be the setting of the process to ensure production of no scrap and to minimize the rework?

(a) 68.5 mm (b) 70 mm
(c) 70.5 mm (d) 725 mm

25. Consider the following statements with respect to control charts for attributes:
1. The lower control limit is non-negative
2. Normal distribution is the order for this data
3. The lower control limit is not significant
4. These charts give the average quality characteristics

Which of the statements given above are correct.
(a) 1, 2 and 3
(b) 2, 3 and 4
(c) 1, 3 and 4
(d) 1, 2 and 4

26. Which one of the following statements is not correct?
(a) The operating characteristic curve of an acceptance sampling plan shows the ability of the plan to distinguish between good and bad lots
(b) No sampling plan can give complete protection against the acceptance of defective products
(c) C chart has straight line limits and U chart has zig-zag limits
(d) Double sampling result in more inspection than single sampling if the incoming quality is very bad.

27. Consider the following statements:
A nomenclature ϕ 50 H8/p8 denoted that
1. Hole diameter is 50 mm
2. It is a shaft base system
3. 8 indicates fundamental deviation.

Which of the statements given above is/are correct?
(a) 1, 2 and 3
(b) 1 and 2 only
(c) 1 and 3 only
(d) 3 only

28. What symbol is used to indicate surface roughness?
(a) = (b) $\sqrt{}$
(c) $^{0.1}\sqrt{}$ (d) Δ

29. What term is used to designate the direction of the pre-dominant surface pattern produced by machining operation?
(a) roughness (b) lay
(c) waviness (d) cut-off

30. Which one of the following tolerances set on inner diameter and outer diameter respectively of headed jig bush for press fit is correct?
(a) G7h6 (b) F7h6
(c) H7 h6 (d) F7J6

31. A fit is specified as 215 H 8/e8. The tolerance value for a nominal diameter of 25 mm in IT8 is 33 microns and fundamental deviation for the shaft is –40 microns. The maximum clearance of the fit in micron is:
(a) – 7 (b) 7
(c) 73 (d) 106

32. Match List-1 (instruments) with List-II (measurement) and select the correct answer by using the codes given below the lists:

| **List-I (Instrument)** | **List-II (Measurement)** |
|---|---|
| (A) Pitot-tube | 1. R.P.M. of a shaft |
| (B) McLeod gauge | 2. Displacement |
| (C) Planimeter | 3. Flow velocity |
| (D) LVDT | 4. Vacuum |
| | 5. Surface finish |
| | 6. Area |

**Codes:**

| | A | B | C | D |
|---|---|---|---|---|
| (a) | 4 | 3 | 6 | 2 |
| (b) | 4 | 3 | 2 | 6 |
| (c) | 3 | 4 | 2 | 6 |
| (d) | 3 | 4 | 6 | 2 |

33. A slot is to be milled centrally on a block with a dimension of 40 ± 0.05 mm. A milling cutter is 20 mm width is located with reference to the side of the block within ± 0.02 mm. The maximum offset in mm between the centre line of the slot and the block is:
(a) ±0.070 (b) 0.070
(c) ±0.020 (d) 0.045

34. In the specification of dimension and fits, allowance is:
(a) equal to bilateral tolerance
(b) equal to unilateral tolerance
(c) independent of tolerance
(d) equal to the difference between maximum and maximum dimension specified by the tolerance.

35. Ideal surface roughness, as measured by the maximum height of unevenness, is best achieved when the material is removed by:
(a) an end mill
(b) a grinding wheel
(c) a tool with zero nose radius
(d) a ball mill.

36. Auto collimator is used to check:
(a) roughness
(b) flatness
(c) angle
(d) automobile balance

37. Cold working produces the following effects:
1. Stresses are set up in metal
2. Grain structure gets distorted
3. Strength and hardness of the metal are decreased
4. Surface finish is reduced
Which of these statements are correct?
(a) 1 and 2 (b) 1, 2 and 3
(c) 3 and 4 (d) 1 and 4.

38. Three blocks $B_1$, $B_2$ and $B_3$ are to inserted in cannel of width S maintaining a minimum gap of width T = 0.125 m, as shown in figure. For = 18.75 ± 0.08 ; Q = 25.00 ± 0.12 ; R = 28.125 ± 0.1 and S = 72.35 + X, (where all dimensions are in mm), the tolerance X is:
(a) + 0.38 (b) – 0.38
(c) + 0.05 (d) – 0.05

39. Match List-I (Measuring instruments) with List-II (Applications) and select the correct answer by using the codes given below the lists:

| **List-I (Measuring instruments)** | **List-II (Applications)** |
|---|---|
| (A) Talysurf | 1. T-slots |
| (B) Telescopic gauge | 2. Flatness |
| (C) Transfer calipers | 3. Internal diameter |
| (D) Autocollimator | 4. Roughness |

**Codes:**

| | A | B | C | D |
|---|---|---|---|---|
| (a) | 3 | 4 | 2 | 1 |
| (b) | 4 | 3 | 1 | 2 |
| (c) | 4 | 3 | 2 | 1 |
| (d) | 3 | 4 | 1 | 2 |

40. Two shafts A and B have their diameters specified as 100 ± 0.1 mm and 0.1 ± 0.0001 mm respectively. Which of the following statements (*s*) is/are true?
(a) tolerance in the dimension is greater in shaft A
(b) the relative error in the dimension is greater in shaft A
(c) tolerance in the dimension is greater in shaft B
(d) the relative error in the dimension is same for shaft A and shaft B.

41. Allowance in limits and fits refers to:
(a) maximum clearance between shaft and hole
(b) minimum clearance between shaft and hole
(c) difference between maximum and minimum size of hole
(d) difference between maximum- and minimum size of shaft.

42. Process capability of a machine is defined as the capability of the machine to
(a) produce a definite volume of work per minute
(b) perform definite number of operations
(c) produce job at a definite spectrum of speed
(d) hold a definite spectrum of tolerances and surface finish.

43. Interchangeably can be achieved by:
(a) standardization
(b) better process planning
(c) simplification
(d) better product planning.

44. A manufacturer of rivets claims that the failure load in shear of his product is 500 ± 25 N. This specification implies that
(a) no rivet is weaker than 475 N and stronger than 525 N
(b) the standard deviation of strength of random sample of rivets is 25 N
(c) there is an equal probability of failure strength to be either 475 N or 525 N
(d) there is approximately two-to-one chance that the strength of a rivet lies between 475 N or 525 N.

45. A shaft (diameter 20 + 0.15 – 0.15 mm) and a hole (diameter 20 σ mm) when assembled would yield:
(a) transition fit
(b) interference fit
(c) clearance fit
(d) none

46. Which one of the following is the correct statement? In cost estimation at the break even point, the cost production is:
(a) greater than the sales
(b) less than the sales
(c) equal to total sales
(d) profit sales

47. For a manual operation of study the total processing standard time using a chronometer, following observations were made:

| | |
|---|---|
| Processing time | : 16 minutes |
| Rating of the worker | : 120% |
| Personal allowance | : 0.6 minutes |
| Basic fatigue allowance | : 1.92 minutes |
| Unavoidable delay allowance | : 1.08 minutes |

What is the standard operation time for the operation?
(a) 16 minutes (b) 17.92 minutes
(c) 21.52 minutes (d) None of the above

48. Match List-I with List-II and select the correct answer using the code given below the lists:

| List-I (Type of Job) | List-II (Appropriate Method-study Technique) |
|---|---|
| A. Complete sequence of operations | 1. Flow diagram |
| B. Factory layout : movement of materials | 2. Flow process chart |
| C. Factory layout:movement of workers | 3. Multiple activity chart |
| D. Gang work | 4. String diagram |

**Codes:**

| | A | B | C | D |
|---|---|---|---|---|
| (a) | 4 | 3 | 2 | 1 |
| (b) | 2 | 1 | 4 | 3 |
| (c) | 4 | 1 | 2 | 3 |
| (d) | 2 | 3 | 4 | 1 |

49. What is a chart that shows the step-by-step procedure used and the inter-relationship between anyone or more persons, forms or products when the procedure involves movement from place to place, called:
(a) multi activity chart
(b) simo chart
(c) flow process chart - man analysis
(d) process chart - combined analysis

50. For a manual operation observed time data are given below:

| | | |
|---|---|---|
| Recorded time | : | 15 minute |
| Rating of the worker | : | 80% |
| Personal allowance | : | 0.6 minute |
| Basic fatigue allowance | : | 0.8 minute |
| Contingency work allowance | : | 12 minute |
| Unavoidable delay allowance | : | 11 minute |

What is the standard time for the operation?
(a) 16.4 minute (b) 175 minute
(c) 185 minute (d) None of the above

51. The following data is available form time study on a job: Observed time = 0.75 min., rating = 110% relaxation allowance = 10% personal allowance = 3%, delay allowance = 2%.
All allowances are expressed in % of normal time.
What is the approximate standard time for this job?
(a) 0.95 minutes
(b) 0.625 minutes
(c) 0.825 minutes
(d) 0.74 minutes

52. Match List-I with List-II and select the correct answer using the code given below the lists:

| List-I (Technique) | List-II (Suitable for) |
|---|---|
| A. Time study | 1. Short-cycle nonrepetitive jobs |
| B. Work sampling | 2. Manual operations |
| C. Analytical estimation | 3. Short-cycle repetitive jobs |
| D. MTM | 4. Long-cycle jobs/ heterogeneous operations/operations involving team work |

**Codes:**

| | A | B | C | D |
|---|---|---|---|---|
| (a) | 2 | 4 | 1 | 3 |
| (b) | 3 | 1 | 4 | 2 |
| (c) | 2 | 1 | 4 | 3 |
| (d) | 3 | 4 | 1 | 2 |

53. A sum of ₹ 500/-Paid as wages for erecting a machine should be debited to:
(a) machinery account (b) suspense account
(c) wages account (d) repair account

54. Which of the following plans guarantees minimum wage to a workers and bonus based on fixed percentage of time saved:
(a) Gantt plan (b) Halsey plan
(c) Rowan plan (d) Bedaux plan.

55. In Bedaux skill and effort rating, a normal worker is rated at:
(a) B (b) 60 B
(c) 100B (d) 144B

56. The essential condition for the decompression of an activity is:
(a) The project time should change due to decompression
(b) After decompression the time of an activity invariably exceeds its normal time
(c) An activity could be decompressed to the maximum extent of its normal time
(d) None of the above.

57. A diagram showing the path followed by men and materials while performing a task is known as:
(a) String Diagram (b) Flow Process Chart
(c) Travel Chart (d) Flow Diagram

58. Match List-I with List-II and select the correct answer using the codes given below the lists:

**List-I**
A. A man is doing one productive work
B. A load is moving from one place to another
C. A hand is not accomplishing anything and is waiting
D. A hand is holding and object

**List-II**

1. 2. 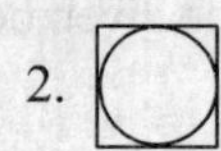

3. 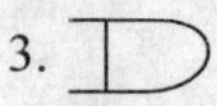 4.

5. 

**Codes:**

| | A | B | C | D |
|---|---|---|---|---|
| (a) | 1 | 4 | 3 | 5 |
| (b) | 1 | 3 | 4 | 5 |
| (c) | 3 | 2 | 1 | 4 |
| (d) | 3 | 4 | 5 | 2 |

59. The following data pertain to a worker:
Base rate = ₹ 20 per hour
Time taken for completing the job = 2 hours.
Standard time = 3 hours.
Under Halsey plan, the total earning of the worker is:
(a) ₹ 36.67 (b) ₹ 40.67
(c) ₹ 46.67 (d) ₹ 5657

60. For the maintenance section of an industry, the most suitable incentive plan would be:
(a) piece rate system
(b) group incentive plane
(c) bonus plan
(d) profit sharing plan.

61. Consider the following objective:
1. To train the individual regarding motion economy
2. To assist in research projects in the field of work study
3. To help in the collection of motion time data
The objectives of Micromotion study would include:
(a) 1, 2 and 3 (b) 1 and 2
(c) 2 and 3 (d) 1 and 3

62. Consider the following steps:
1. Method time measurement
2. Work sampling
3. Work factor system.
PMTS (predetermined motion time systems) in work study would include:
(a) 1, 2 and 3 (b) 1, 3 and 4
(c) 1, 2 and 4 (d) 1, 2 and 3

63. Earning in Rowan system

$$= R \times T_a + \frac{T_s - T_a}{T_s} T_a R,$$

Earning in 50 % Halsey plan = $R \times T_a + p\,(T_s - T_a)$ R, where R = hourly rate, $T_a$ actual completion time of tank, $T_s$ = standard time of task, $p$ = percentage allowed. Both Rowan system and 50% Halsey plane will provided the same bearing when the actual time is:
(a) equal to standard time
(b) half the standard time
(c) one-quarter of standard time
(d) twice the standard time.

64. In time study, the rating factor is applied to determine:
(a) standard time of job
(b) merit rating of the worker
(c) fixation of incentive rate
(d) normal time of job.

65. Work study is mainly aimed at:
(a) determining the most efficient method of performing a job
(b) establishing the minimum time of completion
(c) developing the standard method and standard time of a job
(d) economizing the motions involved on the part of the worker while performing a job.

66. Consider the following factors:
1. Adequate incentive
2. Ease of administration
3. Flexibility
4. Guaranteed basic pay
5. Higher wages
6. Simplicity
Among these, the factors which are to be considered while developing a good wage incentive plan would include:
(a) 1, 2, 3 and 5 (b) 2, 3, 4 and 5
(c) 1, 2, 4 and 6 (d) 1, 2, 5 and 6

67. Match List-I with List-II and select the correct answer

| **List-I (Object)** | **List-II (Tool)** |
|---|---|
| A. Improving utilization of supervisory staff | 1. Micromotion study |
| B. Improving plant layout | 2. Work sampling |
| C. Improving work layout | 3. Flow process chamber |
| D. Improving highly repetitive hand movements | 4. Chronocyclegraph. |

**Codes:**

| | A | B | C | D |
|---|---|---|---|---|
| (a) | 2 | 3 | 1 | 4 |
| (b) | 3 | 2 | 1 | 4 |
| (c) | 2 | 3 | 4 | 1 |
| (d) | 3 | 2 | 4 | 1 |

68. Determination of standard time in complex job system is best done through:
(a) stop watch time study
(b) analysis of micromotion
(c) group timing techniques
(d) analysis of standard data system.

69. Procedure of modifying work content to give more meaning and enjoyment to the job by involving employees in planning, organization and control of their work, is termed as:
(a) job enlargement
(b) job enrichment
(c) job rotation
(d) job evaluation

70. Given that E = Earnings, R = Rate per hour, T = worked in hours, S = Standard time on the basis of date in hours. Rowan wage incentive plan is:

(a) $E = RT + \left(\frac{S-T}{S}\right)R$

(b) $E = RT + (S - T)\,R$

(c) $E = RT + 0.4\,(s - T)\,R$

(d) $E = RT + \left(\frac{S-T}{S}\right)RT$

71. Consider the following conditions:
1. Minimum wages should he guaranteed
2. Providing incentive to group efficiency performance
3. A differential price rate should exist
4. All standards should he based on optimum standard of production
5. Those essential for an incentive plan include.
(a) 1 and 4
(b) 1 and 2
(c) 3 and 4
(d) 2 and 3

72. Two alternative methods can produce a product first method has fixed cost of ₹ 2000 and variable cost of ₹ 20 piece. The second method has fixed cost of ₹ 1500 and a variable cost of ₹ 30. The break evenquantity between the two alternatives is:
(a) 25 (b) 50
(c) 75 (d) 100

73. If one state occurred four times in hundred observations while using the work-sampling technique, then the precision of the study using a 95% confidence level will be:
(a) 90%
(b) 92%
(c) 95%
(d) 98%

74. Process I requires 20 units of fixed cost and 3 units of variable costs per piece, while process II required 50 units of fixed costs and I units of variable cost per piece. For a company producing 10 pieces per day:
(a) process I should be chosen
(b) process II should he chosen
(c) either of the two processes should he chosen
(d) a combination of process 1 and process II should be chosen

75. Match List-I (Charts) with List-II (Details) and select the correct answer using the codes given below the lists:

| List-I | List-II |
|---|---|
| A. Multiple activity | 1. Work factor chart system |
| B. SIMO chart | 2. Movement of material |
| C. String diagram | 3. Motion analysis |
| D. MTM | 4. Working an idle time of two or more men/machines |

**Codes:**

| | A | B | C | D |
|---|---|---|---|---|
| (a) | 4 | 3 | 2 | 1 |
| (b) | 3 | 4 | 2 | 1 |
| (c) | 4 | 3 | 1 | 2 |
| (d) | 3 | 4 | 1 | 2 |

76. The standard time of an operation has been calculated as 10 min. The worker was rated at 80%. If the relaxation and other allowances were 25%, then the observed time would be:
(a) 12.5 min (b) 10 min
(c) 8 min (d) 6.5 min

77. MTM is a work measurement technique by:
(a) Stopwatch study
(b) Work sampling study
(c) Predetermined motion time system
(d) Past data comparison

78. The management is interested to know the percentage of idle time of an equipment. The trial study should that percentage of idle time would be 20%. The number of random observations necessary for 95% level of confidence and + 5% accuracy is:
(a) 6400 (b) 1600
(c) 460 (d) 160

79. Last year, a manufacturer produced 15000 products which were sold for Rs. 300 each. At that volume, the fixed costs were Rs. 15.2 lacs and the total variable costs were Rs. 21 lacs. The break even quantity of product would be:
(a) 4000 (b) 7800
(c) 8400 (d) 9500

80. Match List-I (Study) with List-II (Related factors) and select the correct answer using the codes given below the lists:

| List-I (Study) | List-II (Related Factors) |
|---|---|
| A. Job enrichment | 1. Gilbreth's principle |
| B. Job evaluation | 2. Movement of limbs by work factor system |
| C. Method study | 3. Herzberg Motivators |
| D. Time study | 4. Jacques time-span of discretion |

**Codes:**

| | A | B | C | D |
|---|---|---|---|---|
| (a) | 2 | 1 | 4 | 3 |
| (b) | 3 | 4 | 1 | 2 |
| (c) | 3 | 4 | 1 | 2 |
| (d) | 4 | 1 | 2 | 3 |

81. If a the total investment is ₹ 500000 for a target production, the income for the current year is ₹ 300000 and total operating cost is ₹ 100000; what is the economic yield?
(a) 10% (b) 30 %
(c) 20 % (d) 40 %

82. Which one of the following statements is not correct?
(a) work sampling is a technique of work measurement
(b) method study is a technique aimed at evolving improved methods
(c) synthetic data is not a technique covered under pre-determined motion time systems
(d) 'select' is the first step of method study

83. A time standard for a date entry clerk is to be set. A job is rated at 120 percent, it takes 30 seconds to enter each record and the allowances are 15%. What is the normal time?
(a) 25 seconds (b) 30 seconds
(c) 36 seconds (d) 40 seconds

84. Which one of the following pairs is correctly matched?
(a) Work space design : Ergonomics
(b) Motion economy : Tetra-technology
(c) Method study : Milestone chart
(d) Time study : Clinograph

85. An equipment has been purchased for Rs. 120 and is estimated to have 10 years life and a scrap value of Rs. 20/- at the end of life. The book value of the equipment at the end of sixth year then the interest rate is 5% (using declining balance methods) will be:
(a) Rs. 40.95 (b) Rs. 51.25
(c) 55.00 (d) Rs. 59.25

## ANSWERS WITH EXPLANATIONS

1. (d) 2. (a) 3. (a) 4. (d) 5. (c)
6. (d) 7. (d) 8. (c) 9. (a) 10. (c)
11. (c) 12. (a) 13. (b) 14. (d) 15. (a)
16. (b) 17. (c) 18. (d) 19. (d) 20. (c)
21. (d) 22. (b) 23. (c)
24. (b) $\sigma = 1.00$ mm
Maximum size = 72.5 mm
Minimum size = 67.5 mm
UCL = 70 + 3σ = 73 mm
LCL = 70 – 3 = 67 mm
The process should be set at 70 mm
25. (c) 26. (c) 27. (c) 28. (c) 29. (c)
30. (c)
31. (d) Minimum clearance of fit
= 33 + 40 + 33 = 106 microns
32. (d) 33. (c) 34. (c) 35. (d) 36. (b)
37. (a)
38. (d) Tolerance build up,
$$P + Q + R + T = (18.75 \pm 0.08) + (25.00 \pm 0.12) + (28.125 \pm 0.10) + 0.125$$
$$= 72.000 \pm 0.30$$
$$72.35 + X = 72.00 \pm 0.30$$
$$X = 72.30 - 72.35 = -0.05 \text{ mm}$$
39. (b) 40. (a) 41. (c) 42. (d) 43. (a)
44. (a) 45. (c) 46. (c) 47. (d) 48. (b)
49. (a)
50. (d) Standard time
$$= 15\left[0.8\left\{1 + \frac{0.6+0.8+1.2+1.1}{15}\right\}\right]$$
$$= 1.5\,[0.8\,(1 + 0.2467)] = 14.96 \text{ min}$$
51. (a) Standard time = 0.75 [(1.10) + 0.1 + 0.03 + 0.02]
= 0.75 [1.1 × 1.15] = 0.95 min
52. (d) 53. (a) 54. (c) 55. (b) 56. (c)
57. (b) 58. (a)
59. (c) Under Halsey plan,
$$W = HA + (S - A)\frac{H}{3}$$
$$= 20 \times 2 + (3-2) \times \frac{20}{3} = \text{Rs. } 46.67$$
60. (c) 61. (d) 62. (d) 63. (b) 64. (b)
65. (a) 66. (c) 67. (c) 68. (a) 69. (b)
70. (d) 71. (b)
72. (b) $200 + 20x = 1500 + 30x$
$x = 50$
73. (d) $$S_p = K\sqrt{\frac{p(1-p)}{N}}$$
K = 2 for 95% confidence level
$$S \times 0.04 = 2\sqrt{\frac{0.04 \times 0.96}{100}} = 0.0392$$
S = 0.98 or 98%
74. (a) $P_1 = 20 + 30x = 20 + 3 \times 10 = 50$ units
$P_2 = 50 + 1x = 50 + 1 \times 10 = 60$ units
Process 1 is cheaper
75. (a)
76. (b) Observed time
$$= \frac{\text{Standard time} \times 10}{\text{Rating of worker} \times (100 + \%\text{ allowance})}$$
$$= \frac{10 \times 100}{0.8 \times (100 + 25)} = 10 \text{ min.}$$
77. (c)
78. (a) $$S_p = K\sqrt{\frac{(1-p)}{N}}$$
$$0.05 \times 0.2 = 2\sqrt{\frac{0.2 \times 0.8}{N}}$$
N = 6400
79. (d) $$300\,Q = \left(\frac{15.2 + 21Q}{15000}\right) \times 10^5$$
Q = 9500
80. (b)
81. (d) Profit = Income – operating cost
= 300,000 – 100,000 = 200,000
$$\text{Economic yield} = \frac{200,000}{500,000} \times 100 = 40\%$$
82. (d) 83. (c) 85. (a)
85. (d) Rate of depreciation, $p = 1 - \left(\frac{S}{C}\right)^{\frac{1}{N}}$
$$= 1 - \left(\frac{20}{120}\right)^{\frac{1}{10}} = 0.164$$
Book value of the end of 6 years
= C (1 – p) N = 120 (1 – 0.164) × 6
= Rs. 40.95

❑❑❑

# 20. Production Planning

- Production planning is the planning of production and manufacturing processes in a company or industry. It utilizes the resource allocation of activities of employees, materials and production capacity, in order to serve different customers.
- Different types of production methods, such as single item manufacturing, batch production, mass production, continuous production etc. have their own type of production planning.
- Production planning can be combined with production control into production planning and control, or it can be combined and or integrated into enterprise resource planning.
- Production planning is used in companies in several different industries, including agriculture, industry, amusement industry, etc.
- Production planning is a plan for the future production, in which the facilities needed are determined and arranged. A production planning is made periodically for a specific time period, called the planning horizon. It can comprise the following activities:
- Determination of the required product mix and factory load to satisfy customers needs.
- Matching the required level of production to the existing resources.
- Scheduling and choosing the actual work to be started in the manufacturing facility"
- Setting up and delivering production orders to production facilities.
- In order to develop production plans, the production planner or production planning department needs to work closely together with the marketing department and sales department. They can provide sales forecasts, or a listing of customer orders."
- The "work is usually selected from a variety of product types which may require different resources and serve different customers.
- Therefore, the selection must optimize customer-independent performance measures such as cycle time and customer-dependent performance measures such as on-time delivery."
- A critical factors in production planning is "the accurate estimation of the productive capacity of available resources, yet this is one of the most difficult tasks to perform well."
- Production planning should always take "into account material availability, resource availability and knowledge of future demand."
- Modern production planning methods and tools have been developed since late 19th century. Under Scientific Management, the work for each man or each machine is mapped out in advance .The origin of production planning back goes another century.
- Advanced planning and scheduling refers to a manufacturing management process by which raw materials and production capacity are optimally allocated to meet demand. APS is especially well-suited to environments where simpler planning methods cannot adequately address complex trade-offs between competing priorities.
- Production scheduling is intrinsically very difficult due to the factorial dependence of the size of the solution space on the number of items/products to be manufactured.
- Capacity planning is the process of determining the production capacity needed by an organization to meet changing demands for its products. In the context of capacity planning, design capacity is the maximum amount of work that an organization is capable of completing in a given period.
- Effective capacity is the maximum amount of work that an organization is capable of completing in a given period due to constraints such as quality problems, delays, material handling, etc. The phrase is also used in business computing as a synonym for capacity management.
- A master production schedule (MPS) is a plan for individual commodities to produce in each time period such as production, staffing, inventory, etc. It is usually linked to manufacturing where the plan indicates when and how much of each product will be demanded.
- This plan quantifies significant processes, parts, and other resources in order to optimize production, to identify bottlenecks, and to anticipate needs and completed goods. Since an MPS drives much factory activity, its accuracy and viability dramatically affect profitability. Typical MPS's are created by software with user tweaking.
- Material requirements planning (MRP) is a production planning, scheduling, and inventory control system used to manage manufacturing processes. Most MRP systems are software-based, while it is possible to conduct MRP by hand as well.

- Manufacturing resource planning (MRP II) is defined as a method for the effective planning of all resources of a manufacturing company. Ideally, it addresses operational planning in units, financial planning, and has a simulation capability to answer "what-if" questions and extension of closed-loop MRP.
- Scheduling is the process of arranging, controlling and optimizing work and workloads in a production process or manufacturing process. Scheduling is used to allocate plant and machinery resources, plan human resources, plan production processes and purchase materials.
- A workflow consists of an orchestrated and repeatable pattern of business activity enabled by the systematic organization of resources into processes that transform materials, provide services, or process information. It can be depicted as a sequence of operations, declared as work of a person or group, an organization of staff, or one or more simple or complex mechanisms.
- Employee scheduling software automates the process of creating and maintaining a schedule. Such software will usually track vacation time, sick time, compensation time, and alert when there are conflicts. As scheduling data is accumulated over time, it may be extracted for payroll or to analyze past activity.
- Enterprise resource planning (ERP) is a business management software—usually a suite of integrated applications—that a company can use to collect, store, manage and interpret data from many business activities, including:
  - – Product planning. cost
  - – Manufacturing or service delivery
  - – Marketing and sales
  - – Inventory management
  - – Shipping and payment
- Inventory Control is the supervision of supply, storage and accessibility of items in order to ensure an adequate supply without excessive oversupply.
- Product Planning is the on going process of identifying and articulating market requirements that define a product's feature set. Product planning serves as the basis for decisions about price, distribution and promotion. Product planning is the process of creating a product idea and following through on it until the product is introduced to the market.
- Project planning is part of project management, which relates to the use of schedules such as Gantt charts to plan and subsequently report progress within the project environment.
- Process planning is concerned with determining the sequence of individual manufacturing operations needed to produce a given part or product. The resulting operation sequence is documented on a form typically referred to as a route sheet containing a listing of the production operations and associated machine tools for a work part or assembly.
- Process planning in manufacturing also refers to the planning of use of blanks, spare parts, packaging material, user instructions (manuals) etc.
- Sales and operations planning is an integrated business management process developed in the 1980s by Oliver Wight through which the executive/leadership team continually achieves focus, alignment and synchronization among all functions of the organization.
- The S&OP planning includes an updated forecast that leads to a sales plan, production plan, inventory plan, customer lead time (backlog) plan, new product development plan, strategic initiative plan and resulting financial plan.
- Strategy is a high level plan to achieve one or more goals under conditions of uncertainty.
- Strategy is important because the resources available to achieve these goals are usually limited. Strategy generally involves setting goals, determining actions to achieve the goals, and mobilizing resources to execute the actions.

# MULTIPLE CHOICE QUESTIONS

1. For transporting materials over long distance with greater speed, which one of the following devices is most suitable?
(a) motor vehicle
(b) industrial vehicle
(c) belt conveyor
(d) roller conveyor

2. Match List-I (Equipment) with List-II (Typical situations) and select the correct answer using the codes given below the lists:

| **List-I (Equipment)** | **List-II (Typical situations)** |
|---|---|
| A. Conveyor | 1. Driverless vehicle with varying path |
| B. Cranes | 2. Vertical movement of materials |
| C. Industrial trucks | 3. Varying paths of movement |
| D. Lifts | 4. Movement of intermittent load |
| | 5. Fixed route movement |

**Codes:**

| | A | B | C | D |
|---|---|---|---|---|
| (a) | 1 | 3 | 2 | 4 |
| (b) | 5 | 4 | 3 | 2 |
| (c) | 1 | 4 | 3 | 2 |
| (d) | 5 | 3 | 2 | 4 |

3. Johnson's rule is applicable for planning a job shop for:
(a) *n* machines and 2 jobs
(b) 2 machines and *n* jobs
(c) *n* machines and *n* jobs
(d) 1 machine and *n* jobs

4. A work shift is for 8 hours duration; 30 minutes lunch break and two 15 minutes (each) tea breaks are allowed per shift. If products are to go out after assembly at the rate of 60 per shift, and total assembly time content for a product is 42 minutes, then minimum number of work stations needed is:
(a) 8 (b) 12
(c) 6 (d) 5

5. The layout of ship-building industry should be:
(a) process layout
(b) group layout
(c) fixed location layout
(d) product layout

6. Motions of limbs are through
1. Elbow 2. Finger
3. Hip 4. Shoulder
5. Wrist.
What is the correct sequence in descending order of motion in terms of time and fatigue involved?
(a) 3 – 4 – 1 – 5 – 2 (b) 2 – 5 – 1 – 4 – 3
(c) 5 – 2 – 3 – 1 – 4 (d) 4 – 3 – 2 – 1 – 5

7. Which of the following are the characteristics of job order production?
(a) high degree of production control is required
(b) division of labour is effective
(c) detailed schedule is needed for each component
(d) a flexible layout is preferred
Select the correct answer using the codes given below:
**Codes:**
(a) 1,3 and 4 (b) 2 and 4
(c) 1 and 3 (d) 3 and 4

8. Which one of the following is the correct definition of critical ratio in scheduling?
(a) demand time/supply lead time
(b) supply lead time/demand time
(c) demand time/manufacturing lead time
(d) manufacturing lead time/demand time

9. Several sequencing rules can be used to sequence jobs. The performance of these rules can be studied using several performance measures. Consider the following sequencing rules: SPT (Shortest Processing Time)EDD (Expected Due Date)and the following performance measures:
MFT (Mean Flow Time)
ML (Mean Lateness)
Which one of the following is not correct?
(a) SPT minimizes MFT (b) EDD minimizes MFT
(c) EDD minimizes ML (d) SPT minimizes ML

10. Which of the following factors necessitate a change in schedule?
1. Change in Board of Directors
2. Capacity modification
3. Lack of capital
4. Unexpected rush orders
Select the correct answer using the codes given below:
(a) 2,3 and 4 (b) 1,2 and 5
(c) 2,4 and 5 (d) 1,3 and 4

11. Consider the following statements:
A process layout
1. has machines of same functions arranged in a place
2. is suitable for batch production
3. has machines of different functions arranged according to processing sequence
4. is suitable for mass production.
Of these statements:
(a) 1 and 2 are correct (b) 3 and 4 are correct
(c) 2 and 3 are correct (d) 1 and 4 are correct

12. The layout suitable for the low demand and high variety products is:
(a) group layout (b) process layout
(c) product layout (d) static layout

13. Which one of the following pairs is not correctly matched?
(a) Job production ... Process layout
(b) Mass production ... Product layout
(c) Job production ... Special purpose
(d) Job production ... Production purpose

14. Dispatching function of production planning and control refers to:
(a) dispatch of finished goods on order
(b) movement of in-process material from shop to shop
(c) authorizing a production work order to be launched
(d) dispatch of bills and invoices to the customer

15. Match List-I with List-II and select the correct answer using the codes given below the lists:

| List-I | List-II |
|---|---|
| A. Just-In-Time inventory and Procurement Techniques | 1. Intermittent Production |
| B. Work-In-Process likely to be low compared to Output | 2. Repetitive Production |
| C. Scheduling Typically Most Complex process | 3. Continuous Production |
| D. Flexible Manufacturing Cell | 4. Job Production |

**Codes:**

| | A | B | C | D |
|---|---|---|---|---|
| (a) | 2 | 3 | 4 | 1 |
| (b) | 3 | 2 | 1 | 4 |
| (c) | 2 | 3 | 1 | 4 |
| (d) | 3 | 2 | 4 | 1 |

16. Consider the following advantages:
1. Very flexible
2. Simple to understand
3. Detailed operation can be visualized

Which of these are the advantages of master scheduling?
(a) 1 and 2 (b) 1 and 3
(c) 2 and 3 (d) 1, 2 and 3

17. A set of requirement for a product layout in an industry is:
(a) general purpose machine and skilled labour
(b) special purpose machine and skilled labour
(c) general purpose machine and unskilled labour
(d) special purpose machine and semi-skilled labour

18. Match List-I (Types of layout) with List-II (Uses) and select the correct answer using the codes given below the Lists:

| List-I | List-II |
|---|---|
| A. Product Layout | 1. Where a large quantity of products is to be produced |
| B. Process Layout | 2. Where a large variety of products is manufactured |
| C. Combined Layout | 3. Where item is being made in different types of sizes |
| D. Fixed Position Layout | 4. Where too heavy or huge item is used as raw material |

**Codes:**

| | A | B | C | D |
|---|---|---|---|---|
| (a) | 1 | 2 | 3 | 4 |
| (b) | 2 | 1 | 4 | 3 |
| (c) | 1 | 2 | 4 | 3 |
| (d) | 2 | 1 | 3 | 4 |

19. In which one of the following types of industrial activities, the problem of loading and scheduling becomes more difficult?
(a) Single-product continuous
(b) Multi-product continuous
(c) Batch production
(d) Continuous or process production

20. The correct sequence of factors in order of decreasing importance for location of a thermal power plant is:
(a) load, coal, water (b) coal, water, load
(c) water, load, coal (d) water, coal, load

21. For economic manufacture, the total annual cost is given as $12M\left(P+\frac{D}{Q}\right)$; where
1. M is number of parts made per month
2. P is processing cost per part.

Which one of the following is represented by D/Q in the above expression?
(a) setting up cost (b) profit per part
(c) bonus (d) setting up cost/part

22. Consider the following statements:
In designing a plant layout, a "Product Layout" should be preferred if
1. the variety of the products is low
2. the variety of the products is very large
3. the quantity of production is very small in each variety
4. the quantity of production is very large in each variety
5. the in-process inspection is maximum
6. the in-process inspection is minimum.

Which of the statements given above are correct?
(a) 1,3 and 6 (b) 1,4 and 5
(c) 2,3 and 5 (d) 1,4 and 6

23. Consider the following:
1. Simplified production planning and control systems
2. Reduced material handling
3. Flexibility of equipment and personnel.

The advantages of flow-line layout in manufacturing operation are:

(a) 1,2 and 3 (b) 1 and 2
(c) 2 and 3 (d) 1 and 3

24. Which of the following activities pertain to a master production schedule.
 1. Sizing and timing of specific items, production lot
 2. Sequencing of individual orders of jobs
 3. Short term allocation of resources to individual operations
 4. Product design

 Select the correct answer using the code given below:

 (a) 1, 2 and 4 (b) 2, 3 and 4
 (c) 1, 3 and 4 (d) 1, 2 and 3.

25. Which one of the following forecasting techniques is not suited for making forecasts for planning production schedules in the short range?
 (a) moving average
 (b) exponential smoothing method
 (c) regression analysis
 (d) delphi method.

26. Consider the following statements:
 Queuing Theory is used for
 1. inventory problems
 2. traffic congestion studies
 3. job-shop scheduling.

 Which of the statements given above are correct?

 (a) 1, 2 and 3 (b) 1 and 2
 (c) 2 and 3 (d) 1 and 3

27. Which one of the following expressions given the rate depreciation by the straight line method? (C = initial cost, S = scrap value, N = life in years).
 (a) D = (C – S)/N
 (b) D = (C + S)/N
 (c) D = C – S
 (d) D = C + S

28. On which of the following factors does selection of material handling equipment depend?
 1. Cost
 2. Material characteristics
 3. Type of productions
 4. Equipment's available and their characteristics

 Select the correct answer using the code given below:

 (a) 1, 2, 3, and 4
 (b) 2 and 3
 (c) 1, 3 and 4
 (d) 1, 2 and 4

29. Which of the following factors influence a plant layout?
 1. Type of industry
 2. Type of machines
 3. Type of products
 4. Volume of production

 Select the correct answer using the code given below:

 (a) 2 and 3 (b) 1, 2 and 4
 (c) 1, 3 and 4 (d) 1 and 4

30. Maximum problems in scheduling are encountered in:
 (a) job type production
 (b) batch production
 (c) mass production
 (d) flow type production.

31. A factory is producing 100 bolts and nuts per hour on a machine. Its material cost is ₹ 375, labour cost is ₹ 245 and the direct expense is ₹ 80. The factory on cost is 150% of the total labour cost. What is the total factory cost?
 (a) ₹ 1067.50
 (b) ₹ 367.50
 (c) ₹ 320.25
 (d) ₹ 1387.75.

32. Which of the following form the overhead expenses?
 1. Factory expenses
 2. Material expenses
 3. Administrative expenses
 4. Sales and distribution expenses.

 Select the correct answer using the code given below:

 (a) 1, 2 and 3 (b) 1, 3 and 4
 (c) 1 and 2 (d) 3 and 4

33. If the objective is to project the trend and seasonal variations in forecasting demand, then which is the appropriate model?
 (a) simple moving average
 (b) time series decomposition
 (c) weighted moving average
 (d) double exponential smoothing.

34. Which one of the following is not an advantage of a product layout?
 (a) reduced martial handling
 (b) better utilization of machines and men
 (c) less floor area is occupied by the material in transit and for temporary storage
 (d) less capital investment.

35. Which one of the following factors does not affect the plant location decision:
 (a) organization's objectives
 (b) resources
 (c) socio-economic environment
 (d) organizational structure.

36. Which one of the following is the basic objective of a good plant layout?
 (a) new plant construction
 (b) better use of labour
 (c) improvement in production process as a whole
 (d) to meet customer's expectations.

37. Match List-1 (Material to be Handled) with List-II (Appropriate Material Handling Equipment) and select the correct answer using the code given below the lists:

| List-I (Material to Handled) | List-II (Appropriate be Material Handling Equipment) |
|---|---|
| A. Large Castings | 1. Screw Conveyor |
| B. Granular Material | 2. Belt Conveyor |
| C. Auto Engine Block | 3. Overhead Crane |
| D. Small Engine Parts | 4. Roller Conveyor |

**Codes:**

| | A | B | C | D |
|---|---|---|---|---|
| (a) | 2 | 1 | 4 | 3 |
| (b) | 3 | 4 | 1 | 2 |
| (c) | 2 | 4 | 1 | 3 |
| (d) | 3 | 1 | 4 | 2 |

38. Which one of the following systems combines microelectronics and mechanical engine to bring economics of scale to batch production?
(a) job-shop production
(b) group technology
(c) flexible manufacturing
(d) production.

39. Match List-I with List-II and select the correct answer using the code given below the lists:

| List-I (Plant Layout) | List-II (Characteristic Use) |
|---|---|
| A. Fixed Position | 1. Avoids back tracking |
| B. Functional Layout | 2. Ship building |
| C. Product Layout | 3. Machines performing similar operations are grouped together |
| D. Process Layout | 4. Helps in reducing total production time |

**Codes:**

| | A | B | C | D |
|---|---|---|---|---|
| (a) | 2 | 4 | 3 | 1 |
| (b) | 1 | 3 | 4 | 2 |
| (c) | 1 | 4 | 3 | 2 |
| (d) | 2 | 3 | 4 | 1 |

40. In case of mutually exclusive projects, which one is the most suitable criterion for evaluation of projects?
(a) Net Present Value
(b) Payback Period
(c) Internal Rate of Return
(d) Rate of Return

41. In a low volume production, the dispatching function is not concerned with issuing of which one of the following?
(a) Work tickets
(b) Requisition of raw materials, parts and components
(c) Route sheets to production supervisor
(d) Requisition of tools and facilities

42. Which of the following are the objectives of scheduling?
1. Reducing average waiting time of a batch
2. To meet the deadline of order fulfillment
3. To improve quality of products
4. To increase facility utilization

Select the correct answer using the code given below:
(a) 1, 2 and 4 (b) 2, 3 and 4
(c) 1, 2 and 3 (d) 1 and 3 only

43. Which of the following are needed as the input data for materials requirement planning?
1. Weekly production schedule
2. Bill of material
3. Supplier lead time
4. Market forecast.

Select the correct answer using the code given below:
(a) 1, 2 and 3 (b) 2, 3, and 4
(c) 1 and 4 (d) 1, 2, 3 and 4

44. Consider the following statements:
Method study is carried out to achieve
1. the most effective use of plant and equipment
2. the most effective use of human efforts
3. evaluation of human work.

Which of the statements given above are correct?
(a) 1 and 3 only (b) 2 and 3 only
(c) 1 and 2 only (d) 1, 2 and 3

45. Match List-I with List-II and select the correct answer using the code given below the lists:

| List-I (Purpose of Transportation) | List-II (Device) |
|---|---|
| A. Coal from the pit to surface | 1. Bucket elevator |
| B. Lump and powder material in bulk transportation to storage | 2. Belt conveyor |
| C. Stacking components in store | 3. Fork lift truck |
| D. Heavy material transportation in machine shop | 4. Crane |

**Codes:**

| | A | B | C | D |
|---|---|---|---|---|
| (a) | 3 | 4 | 1 | 2 |
| (b) | 1 | 2 | 3 | 4 |
| (c) | 3 | 2 | 1 | 4 |
| (d) | 1 | 4 | 3 | 2 |

46. Consider the following statements:
1. The manufacturing equipment used in batch production is general-purpose but designed for higher rates of production
2. The machine tools used in batch manufacture are

not combined with specially designed jigs and fixtures.

Which of the statements given above is/are correct?
(a) 1 only
(b) 2 only
(c) Both 1 and 2
(d) Neither 1 nor 2

47. Which one of the following is not a necessary information input to Material Requirements Planning?
(a) Inventory on hand
(b) Bill of materials
(c) Sequence of operations on a job
(d) Master production schedule (MPS).

48. Break-even analysis can be used for which of the following?
1. Profit analysis
2. Production method cost comparison.

Select the correct answer using the code given below:
(a) 1 only (b) 2 only
(c) Both 1 and 2 (d) Neither 1 nor 2

49. The factory overhead rate is 125% and direct labour cost for a job is ₹ 900. What is the factory overhead charge?
(a) ₹ 360 (b) ₹ 720
(c) ₹ 1125 (d) ₹ 2250

50. A certain part is produced in a batch size of 50 units and requires a sequence of 8 operations in the plant. The average set-up time and average non-operation time per operation are3 hours and 7 hours, respectively. The average operative time per machine per part is 6 minutes. What is the manufacturing lead time?
(a) 100 hours (b) 120 hours
(c) 150 hours (d) 180 hours

51. Consider the following statements:
1. In product-flow layout, the arrangement of facilities within the plant is relatively inflexible.
2. Process layout is typical in job shops and batch production.

Which of the statements given above is/are correct?
(a) 1 only
(b) 2 only
(c) Both 1 and 2
(d) Neither 1 nor 2

52. A factory producing 150 electric bulbs a day, involves direct material cost of ₹ 250, direct labour cost of ₹ 200 and factory overheads of ₹ 225. Assuming a profit of 10% of the selling price, and selling on-cost 30% of the factory cost, what is the selling price of one electric bulb?
(a) ₹ 6.50 (b) ₹ 12.50
(c) ₹ 18.50 (d) ₹ 21.00

53. Consider the following statements in respect of operations planning:
1. Aggregate planning addresses the supply side of the firm's ability to meet the demand
2. The purpose of Master Productions Scheduling (MPS) is to meet the demand for individual products in the product group

Which of the statements given above is/are correct?
(a) 1 only
(b) 2 only
(c) Both 1 and 2
(d) Neither 1 nor 2

54. Consider the following steps in a line balancing problem:
1. Apply an assignment heuristic to assign tasks to each work station
2. Identify the precedence requirements
3. Calculate the required minimum number of work stations.

Which one of the following is the correct sequence of the above steps?
(a) 2 – 3 – 1 (b) 1 – 2 – 3
(c) 2 – 1 – 3 (d) 1 – 3 – 2

55. Which of the following is/are advantage(s) of cellular manufacture?
1. Lower work-in-progress inventories
2. Fewer tooling changes

Select the correct answer using the code given below:
(a) 1 only (b) 2 only
(c) Both 1 and 2 (d) Neither 1 nor 2

56. The constant factor in case of R 10 series of preferred number *i* is:
(a) 1.6 (b) 1.25
(c) 1.12 (d) 1.03

57. Which grade symbol represents surface roughness of broaching?
(a) $N_{12}$ (b) $N_3$
(c) $N_4$ (d) $N_1$

58. The minimum attractive rate return is different for various types of projects. All of the following factors will affect the minimum attractive rate of return for a new project except:
(a) the amount of capital that is available in the retained earnings
(b) the interest paid on capital, which is obtained through debt financing
(c) the rates used be the lending institutions or other firms
(d) none of the above.

59. A piece of equipment has been purchased by the city for ₹ 10,000 with an anticipated salvage at ₹ 500 after 8 years. Which of the depreciation models will yield the greatest reduction in the book value of the equipment?
(a) straight line depreciation
(b) sum-of-years digits depreciation
(c) declining balance depreciation
(d) declining balance depreciation is switched to straight line.

60. Which one of the following correctly explains process capability?
(a) Maximum capacity of the machine
(b) Mean value of the measured variable
(c) Lead time of the process
(d) Maximum deviation of the measured variables of the components

61. A dealer sells a radio set at ₹ 900 and makes 80% profit on his investment. It he can sell it at ₹ 200 more, his profit as percentage of investment will be:
(a) 160
(b) 180
(c) 100
(d) 120

62. Match List-I with List-II and select the correct answer using the code given below the lists:

| List-I (Contribution) | List-II (Contributor) |
|---|---|
| A. Specialization of Labour in Manufacturing | 1. Henry Gantt |
| B. Scheduling techniques | 2. George Dantzig |
| C. Linear Programming | 3. Adam Smith |
| D. Quality and Productivity Applications from Japan | 4. W.E. Deming |

**Codes:**

| | A | B | C | D |
|---|---|---|---|---|
| (a) | 3 | 4 | 2 | 1 |
| (b) | 2 | 1 | 3 | 4 |
| (c) | 4 | 3 | 1 | 2 |
| (d) | 2 | 4 | 3 | 1 |

63. In thermal power plants, coal is transferred from bucker to the other places by:
(a) hoists (b) conveyors
(c) cranes (d) lifts

64. Production scheduling is simpler, and high volume of output and high labour efficiency are achieved in the case of:
(a) fixed position layout
(b) process layout
(c) product layout
(d) a combination of line process layout

65. Consider the following features/characteristics:
1. Need for greater variety of skills in labour
2. Intermittent flow of materials and parts
3. Preference for flexible layout
The characteristics of job order layout would include:
(a) 1, 2 and 3
(b) 1 and 2
(c) 2 and 3
(d) 1 and 3

66. Air cargo movements fall under:
(a) fixed path system
(b) continuous system
(c) intermittent system
(d) variable path system

67. Match List-1 with List-II and select the correct answer using the codes given below the lists:

| List-I (Equipment) | List-II (Application) |
|---|---|
| A. Hoist | 1. For moving over a fixed route |
| B. Conveyor | 2. For transporting material over a varying path |
| C. Fork truck | 3. For vertically raising or lowering material in a fixed location |
| D. Elevators | 4. For overhead lifting of loads in fixed area |
| | 5. For moving persons up or down |

**Codes:**

| | A | B | C | D |
|---|---|---|---|---|
| (a) | 4 | 2 | 3 | 5 |
| (b) | 2 | 3 | 4 | 5 |
| (c) | 4 | 1 | 2 | 3 |
| (d) | 2 | 1 | 4 | 3 |

68. Consider the following situations that would warrant a study of the layout:
1. Change in the work force
2. Change in production volume
3. Change in product design
4. Competition in the market
The situation (s) that would lead to a change in the layout-would include:
(a) 1, 2, 3 and 4
(b) 1, 3 and 4
(c) 3 alone
(d) 2 alone

69. Match List-I with List-II and select the correct answer using the codes given below the lists:

| List-I (Products) | List-II (Factors for site selection) |
|---|---|
| A. Aluminium | 1. Transporation Cost |
| B. Photographic Material | 2. Skilled Labour |
| C. Cement | 3. Abundance of power |
| D. Jigs and Fixtures | 4. Climatic Conditions |

**Codes:**

| | A | B | C | D |
|---|---|---|---|---|
| (a) | 2 | 4 | 1 | 3 |
| (b) | 3 | 4 | 1 | 2 |
| (c) | 1 | 2 | 4 | 3 |
| (d) | 4 | 3 | 1 | 2 |

70. A device used for lifting of lowering objects suspended from a hook at the end of retractable chains or cable is called:
(a) hoist (b) jib crane
(c) portable elevator (d) chain conveyor

71. Production cost refers to prime cost plus:
(a) factory overheads
(b) factory and administration overheads
(c) factory, administration and sales overheads
(d) factory, administration and sales overheads and profit.

72. For a small scale industry, the fixed cost per month is ₹ 5000. The variable cost per product is ₹ 20 and sales price is ₹ 30 per piece. The break-even production per month will be:
(a) 300 (b) 460
(c) 500 (d) 10000

73. Which one of the following methods can be used for forecasting the sales potential of a new product?
(a) Time Series Analysis
(b) Jury of Executive Opinion Method
(c) Sales Force Composite Method
(d) Direct Survey Method

74. Which of the following charts are used for plant layout design?
1. Operation process chart
2. Man machine chart
3. Correlation chart
4. Travel chart
Select the correct answer using the codes given below:
(a) 1, 2, 3 and 4 (b) 1, 2 and 4
(c) 1, 3 and 4 (d) 2 and 3

75. In manufacturing management, the term "Despatching" is used to describe:
(a) despatch of sales order
(b) despatch of factory mail
(c) despatch of finished product to the user
(d) despatch of work orders through shop floor.

76. Which of the following factors are to be considered for production scheduling?
1. Sales forecast
2. Component design
3. Route sheet
4. Time standards
Select the correct answer using the codes given below:
**Codes:**
(a) 1, 2 and 3 (b) 1, 2 and 4
(c) 1, 3 and 4 (d) 2, 3 and 4

77. A device for lifting or lowering objects suspended from a hook at the end of a retractable chain or cable is called:
(a) hoist
(b) jib crane
(c) chain conveyor
(d) elevator

78. Which one of the following software packages is used for plant layout?
(a) SIMSCRIPT
(b) DYNAMO
(c) CRAFT
(d) MRP

79. The routing function in a production system design is concerned with:
(a) manpower utilization
(b) machine un-utilization
(c) quality assurance of the product
(d) optimising material flow through the plan

80. Match List-I (type of Products) with. List-II (type of layout) and select the correct answer.

| **List-I** | **List-II** |
|---|---|
| A. Ball Bearings | 1. Process Layout. |
| B. Tools and Gauges | 2. Product Layout |
| C. Large Boilers | 3. Combination of Product and Process layout |
| D. Motor cycle assembly | 4. Fixed Position Layout. |

**Codes:**

| | A | B | C | D |
|---|---|---|---|---|
| (a) | 1 | 3 | 4 | 2 |
| (b) | 3 | 1 | 4 | 2 |
| (c) | 1 | 2 | 4 | 3 |
| (d) | 3 | 1 | 2 | 4 |

81. Which of the following are the principles of material handling?
1. Keep all handling to the minimum
2. Move as few pieces as possible in one unit
3. Move the heaviest weight to the least distance
4. Select only efficient handling equipment
Select the correct answer using the codes given below:
(a) 1, 2, 3 and 4
(b) 1, 3 and 4
(c) 1, 2 and 3
(d) 2 and 4

82. Match List-I with List-II and select the correct answer using the codes given below the Lists.

| **List-I (Topic)** | **List-II (Method of solving)** |
|---|---|
| A. Forecasting | 1. North-West corner Method |
| B. Linear Programming | 2. Rowan Plan |
| C. Wage Incentive | 3. Method of penalty |
| D. Work Measurement | 4. Time seriesAnalysis |
| | 5. Work FactorSystem |

**Codes:**

| | A | B | C | D |
|---|---|---|---|---|
| (a) | 4 | 3 | 1 | 5 |
| (b) | 4 | 1 | 5 | 3 |
| (c) | 4 | 3 | 2 | 5 |
| (d) | 3 | 1 | 2 | 4 |

83. Given
T = underlying trend,
C = cyclic variations within the trend
S = seasonal variation within the trend and
R = residual, remaining or random variation, as per the time series analysis of salesforecasting, the demand will be a function of
(a) T and C
(b) R and S
(c) T, C and S
(d) T, C, S and R

84. A production line is said to be balanced when:
(a) there are equal number of machines at each work station
(b) there are equal number of operators at each work station
(c) the waiting time for service at each station is the same
(d) the operation time at each station is the same.

85. Consider the data given in the following table:

| Production plan Period | Demand | Regular Prod. | Overtime Prod. | Others |
|---|---|---|---|---|
| 1 | 500 | 500 | ... | ... |
| 2 | 650 | 650 | 150 | ... |
| 3 | 800 | 650 | 150 | ... |
| 4 | 900 | 650 | 150 | ? |

Give the fact that production in regular and overtime is limited to 650 and 150 respectively, the balance demand of 100 units in the 4th period can be met by:
(a) using overtime in period 2
(b) using regular production in period 1
(c) subcontracting
(d) using any of the steps indicated in (a), (b) and (c)

86. Based on the given graph figure, the economic range of batch sizes to be preferred for general purpose machine (GP). NC machine (NC) and special purpose (SP) will be:

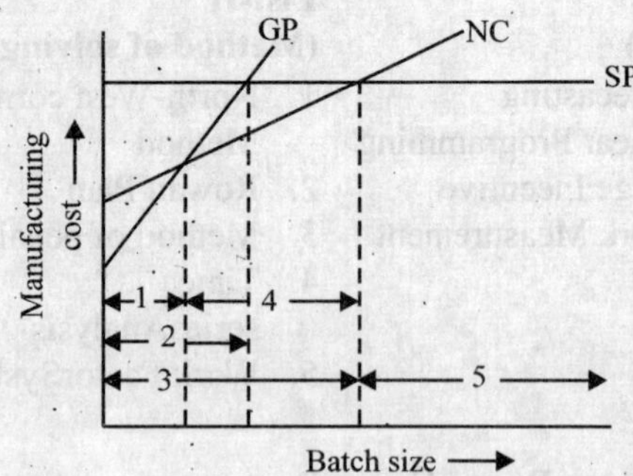


Codes:

| | GP | NC | SP |
|---|---|---|---|
| (a) | 2 | 5 | 4 |
| (b) | 1 | 4 | 5 |
| (c) | 3 | 2 | 4 |
| (d) | 1 | 4 | 2 |

87. Details of cost for make or buy decision are shown in the given graph figure. A discount is offered for a volume of purchase above 'V'. Which one of the following ranges would lead to the economic decision?

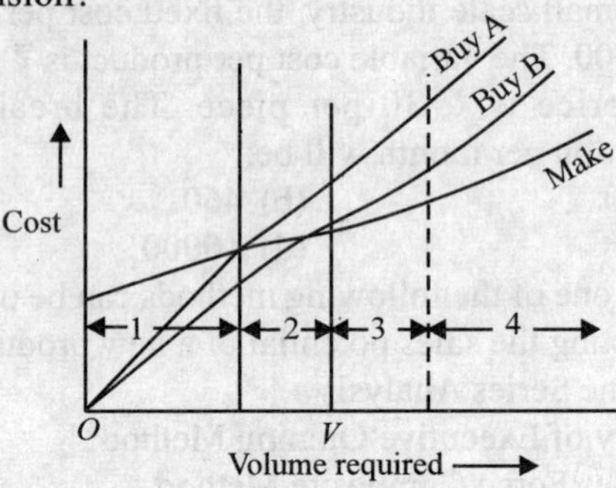


| | Buy A, B | Make |
|---|---|---|
| (a) | 1 and 2 | 3 and 4 |
| (b) | 1and 3 | 2 and 4 |
| (c) | 2 and 4 | 1 and 3 |
| (d) | 1 and 4 | 2 and 3 |

88. What term is used to designate the direction of the pre-dominant surface pattern produced by machining operation?
(a) roughness
(b) lay
(c) waviness
(d) cut-off

89. Which one of the following is a qualitative technique of demand forecasting?
(a) correlation and regression analysis
(b) moving average method
(c) delphi technique
(d) exponential smoothing.

90. Match List-I (Methods) with List-II (Problems) and select the correct answer using the codes given below the lists.

| List-I | List-II |
|---|---|
| A. Moving Average | 1. Assembly |
| B. Line Balancing | 2. Purchase |
| C. Economic Batch Size | 3. Forecasting |
| D. Johnson alogorithm | 4. Sequencing |

Codes:

| | A | B | C | D |
|---|---|---|---|---|
| (a) | 1 | 3 | 2 | 4 |
| (b) | 1 | 3 | 4 | 2 |
| (c) | 3 | 1 | 4 | 2 |
| (d) | 3 | 1 | 2 | 4 |

91. Consider the following statements:
Dispatching
1. Is the action of operations, planning and control
2. Releases work to the operating divisions
3. Convey instructions to the shop floor.
Of these statements:
(a) 1, 2 and 3 are correct
(b) 1 and 2 are correct

(c) 2 and 3 are correct
(d) 1 and 3 are correct

92. Which of the following are the benefits of assembly line balancing?
1. It minimises the in-process inventory
2. It reduces the work content
3. It smoothens the production flow
4. It maintains the required rate of output

Select the correct answer using the codes given below:

**Codes:**
(a) 1, 2 and 3 (b) 2, 3 and 4
(c) 1, 3 and 4 (d) 1, 2 and 4

93. The characteristic life-cycle of a product consists of four periods. The rate of consumption increases rapidly at the beginning of the:
(a) incubation period (b) growth period
(c) maturity period (d) decline period

94. Which one of the following tolerances set on inner diameter and outer diameter respectively of headed jig bush for press fit is correct?
(a) G7h6 (b) F7h6
(c) H7 h6 (d) F7J6

95. Which of the following input data are needed for MRP?
1. Master production schedule
2. Inventory position
3. Machine capacity
4. Bill of materials

Select the correct answer using the codes given below:
(a) 1, 2 and 3 (b) 2, 3 and 4
(c) 1, 2 and 4 (d) 1, 3 and 4

96. The type of layout suitable for use of the concept, principles and approaches of 'group technology' is:
(a) Product layout (b) Job-shop layout
(c) Fixed position layout (d) Cellular layout

97. A linkage is shown below in the figure in which links *ABC* and *DEF* are ternary links whereas *AF*, *BE* and *CD* are binary links.

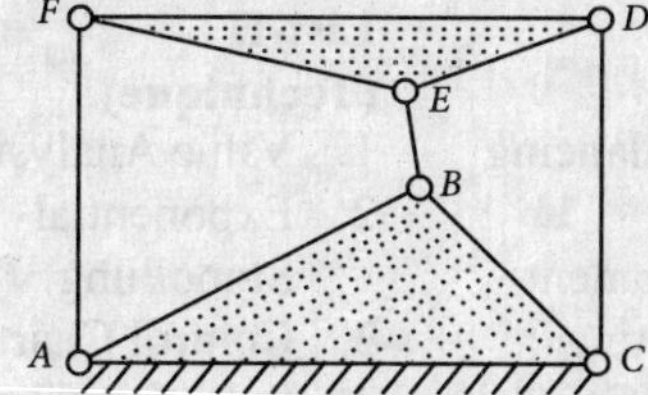


The degrees of freedom of the linkage when link ABC is fixed are:
(a) 0 (b) 1
(c) 2 (d) 3

98. A operations consultant for an automatic car wash wishes to plan for enough capacity to handle 60 cars hour. Each car will have wash time of 2 minutes, but there is to be a 20 per cent allowance for setup, delays and payment transactions. The installation capacity of car wash stalls should be:
(a) 3 (b) 4
(c) 5 (d) 6

99. A company intends to use exponential smoothing technique for making a forecast for one of its products. The previous year's forecast has been 78 units and the actual demand for the corresponding period turned out to be 73 units. If the value of the smoothering constant a is 0.2, the forecast for the next period will be:
(a) 73 units (b) 75 units
(c) 77 units (d) 78 units

100. Which one of following statements is correct in relation to production, planning and control? Expediting initiates the execution of production plans, whereas dispatching maintains them and sees them through to their successful completion:
(a) Dispatching initiates the execution of production plans, whereas expediting maintains
(b) Them and sees through to their successful completion
(c) Both dispatching and expediting initiate the execution of production plans
(d) Both dispatching and expediting maintain the production plans and see them through to their successful completion.

101. Consider the following statements regarding plant location and plant layout:
1. Qualitative factor analysis is a method of evaluating a potential location without applying quantitative values to the decision criteria
2. The three determinants of the type of layout are type of product, type of process and the volume of production
3. An appliance manufacturing plant where products are made on assembly lines would be classified as job shop type of layout.

Which of these statements is/are correct?
(a) 1, 2 and 3 (b) 1 and 2
(c) 2 alone (d) 3 alone

102. Routing in production planning and control refers to be:
(a) balancing of load on machines
(b) authorization of work to be performed
(c) progress or work performed
(d) sequence of operations to be performed

103. A production system has a product type of layout in which there are four machines laid in series. Each machine does a separate operation. Every product needs all the four operations to be carried out. The designed capacity of each of the four machines is 200, 175, 160 and 210 products per day. The system capacity would be:
(a) 210 products per day
(b) 200 products per day
(c) 175 products per day
(d) 160 products per day

104. In production, planning and control, the document which authorizes the start of an operation on the shop floor is the:
(a) Dispatch order (b) Route plan
(c) Loading chart (d) Schedule

105. During manufacture of cement, the handling of limestone is done by:
(a) belt conveyor
(b) bucket conveyor
(c) overhead came
(d) fork-lift crane.

106. Which one of the following combinations is valid for product layout?
(a) general purpose machine and skilled labour
(b) general purpose machine and unskilled labour
(c) special purpose machine and semi-skilled labour
(d) special purpose machine and skilled labour

107. Dispatching function of production, planning and control is:
(a) the dispatch of finished goods on order
(b) the movement of in-process material form shop to shop
(c) authorizing a production work order to be launched
(d) the dispatch of bills and invoice to the customers.

108. Match List-I (Files in MRP) with List II (Inputs required) and select the correct answer using the codes given below the lists:

| **List-I (Files in MRP)** | **List-II (Inputs required)** |
|---|---|
| A. Master Production Schedule | 1. Scheduled Receipts |
| B. Bills of Materials | 2. Unit Costs and Discounts |
| C. Inventory Records | 3. Production Capacity |
| | 4. Product Structure |

**Codes:**

| | A | B | C |
|---|---|---|---|
| (a) | 4 | 1 | 3 |
| (b) | 3 | 4 | 2 |
| (c) | 3 | 4 | 1 |
| (d) | 4 | 3 | 1 |

109. The proper sequence of activities for material requirement planning are:
(a) master production schedule, capacity planning, MRP and order release
(b) order release, master production schedule, MRP and capacity planning
(c) master production schedule, order release, capacity planning and MRP
(d) capacity planning, master production schedule, MRP and order release.

110. Which one of the following is true in respect of production control for continuous or assembly line production?
(a) control is achieved by PERT network
(b) Johnson algorithm is used for sequencing
(c) control is on one work centre only
(d) control is on flow of identical components through several operations.

111. Which one of the following is the preferred logical sequence in the development of a new product?
(a) technical feasibility, social acceptability and economic viability
(b) social acceptability, economic viability and technical feasibility
(c) economic viability, social acceptability and technical feasibility
(d) technical feasibility, economic viability and social acceptability.

112. Which one of the following methods can be used for forecasting when a demand pattern is consistently increasing or decreasing?
(a) regression analysis
(b) moving average
(c) variance analysis
(d) weighted moving average.

113. For a product, the forecast for the month of January was 500 units. The actual demand turned out to he 450 units. What is the forecast for the month of February using exponential smoothing method with a smoothing coefficient = 0.1?
(a) 455
(b) 495
(c) 500
(d) 545

114. Match List-I (Activity) with List-II (Technique) and select the correct answer using the code given below the lists:

| **List-I (Activity)** | **List-II (Technique)** |
|---|---|
| A. Line Balancing | 1. Value Analysis |
| B. Product Development | 2. Exponential Smoothing |
| C. Forecasting | 3. Control Chart |
| D. Quality Control | 4. Selective Control |
| | 5. Rank positive Matrix |

**Codes:**

| | A | B | C | D |
|---|---|---|---|---|
| (a) | 2 | 1 | 4 | 3 |
| (b) | 5 | 3 | 2 | 1 |
| (c) | 2 | 3 | 4 | 1 |
| (d) | 5 | 1 | 2 | 3 |

115. What are the key functions of a master schedule?
1. To generate material and capacity requirements
2. To maintain valid priorities
3. An effective capacity utilization

4. Planning the quantity and timing of output over the intermediate time horizons.

Select the correct answer using the code given below:

(a) 1, 2 and 3 (b) 2, 3 and 4
(c) 1, 3 and 4 (d) 1, 2 and 4

116. Match List-1 (Production Control Function) with List-II (Explanation) and-select the correct answer using the code given below the lists:

| List-I (Production Control Function) | List-II (Explanation) |
|---|---|
| A. Bill of Materials (BOM) | 1. A technique for determining the quantity and timing of dependent demand items |
| B. Capacity Resource Planning (CRP) | 2. A technique for determining personal and equipment capacities needed to meet the production objectives |
| C. Material Requirement Planning(MRP) | 3. Specific what end items are to be |
| D. Master Production Schedule (MPS) | 4. The part number and quantity required per assembly |

**Codes:**

| | A | B | C | D |
|---|---|---|---|---|
| (a) | 4 | 1 | 2 | 3 |
| (b) | 3 | 2 | 1 | 4 |
| (c) | 4 | 2 | 1 | 3 |
| (d) | 3 | 1 | 2 | 4 |

117. Which one of the following forecasting techniques is most suitable for making long range forecasts?

(a) Time series analysis
(b) Regression analysis
(c) Exponential smoothing
(d) Market surveys

118. The double slider-crank chain is shown in the diagram its three possible inversions. The link shown hatched is the fixed link.

1. 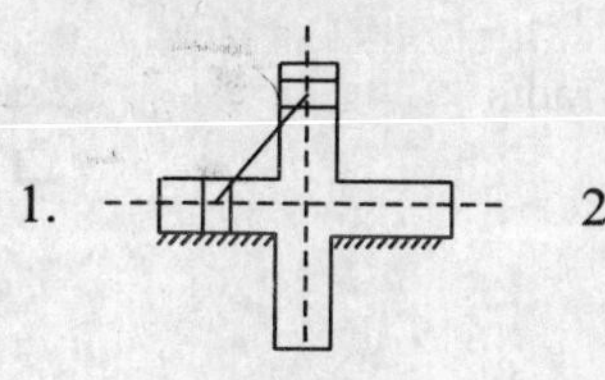

2. 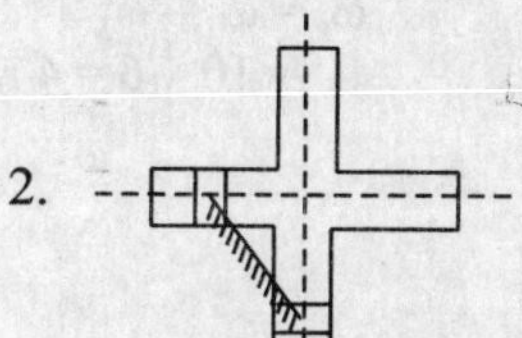

3. 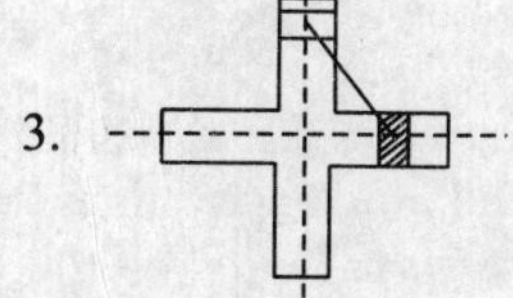

Which one of the following statement is correct?

(a) Inversion (1) is for ellipse trammel and inversion (2) is for Oldham coupling.
(b) Inversion (1) is for ellipse trammel and inversion (3) is for Oldham coupling.
(c) Inversion (2) is for ellipse trammel and inversion (3) is for Oldham coupling.
(d) Inversion (3) is for ellipse trammel and inversion (2) is for Oldham coupling.

119. ABCD is a four bar mechanism, in which AD is the fixed link, and link BC is in the form of a circular disc with centre P. In which one of the following cases P will be the instantaneous centre of the disc?

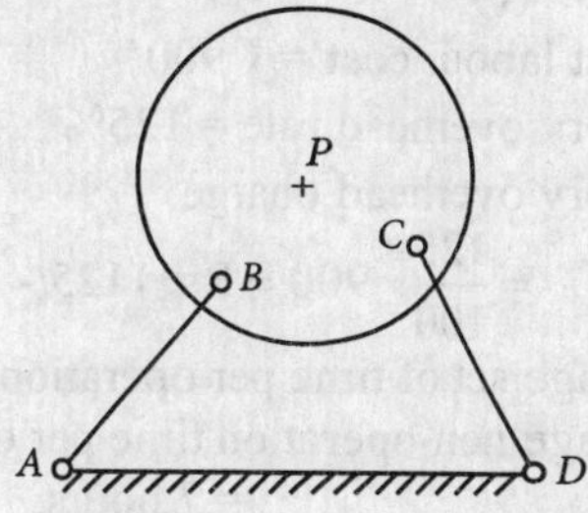


(a) If it lies on the perpendicular bisector of line BC.
(b) If it lies on the intersection of the perpendicular bisectors of BC and AD.
(c) If it lies on the intersection of the perpendicular bisectors of AB and CD.
(d) If it lies on the intersection of the extensions of AB and CD.

120. In the diagram given below, the magnitude of absolute angular velocity of link 2 is 10 radians per second while that of link 3 is 6 radians per second. What is the angular velocity of link 3 relative to 2?

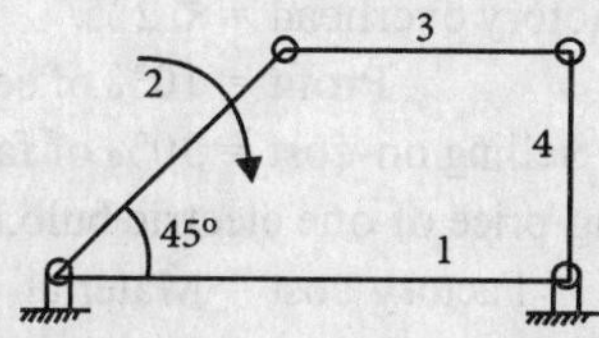


(a) 6 radians per second (b) 16 radians per second
(c) 4 radians per second (d) 14 radians per second

## ANSWERS WITH EXPLANATIONS

1. (c) 2. (b) 3. (b)

4. (c) Time for one work shift = 8 × 60 = 480 min

Actual time available for work

$$= 480 - (30 + 2 \times 15) = 420 \text{ min}$$

$$\text{Time required per product, } = \frac{420}{60} = 7 \text{ min}$$

Minimum number of work stations needed

$$= \frac{\text{Assembly time content}}{\text{Time required product}}$$

$$= \frac{42}{7} = 6 \text{ min}$$

5. (c) 6. (b) 7. (c) 8. (c) 9. (d)
10. (c) 11. (a) 12. (b) 13. (a) 14. (c)
15. (a) 16. (a) 17. (a) 18. (a) 19. (c)
20. (d) 21. (d) 22. (d) 23. (a) 24. (c)
25. (a) 26. (c) 27. (a) 28. (d) 29. (c)
30. (b)

31. (a) Total factory cost = Material cost + Labour cost + Direct expenses + on cost
$= 3.75 + 245 + 80 + 1.5 \times 245$

32. (b) 33. (c) 34. (d) 35. (d) 36. (c)
37. (d) 38. (c) 39. (d) 40. (d) 41. (b)
42. (a) 43. (d) 44. (b) 45. (b) 46. (a)
47. (c) 48. (c)

49. (c) Direct labour cost = ₹ 900/-
Factory overhead rate = 125%
Factory overhead charge
$= \frac{125}{100} \times 900 =$ Rs. 1125/-

50. (b) Average set of time per operation = 3 hours
Average non-operation time per operation = 7 hours.
Number of operation = 8
Average operative time per machine per part = 6 min
Batch size = 50

$$\text{Lead time} = 8(3+7) + \frac{8 \times 6 \times 50}{60}$$
$= 80 + 40 = 120$ hours.

51. (c)

52. (a) Production of electric bulbs per day = 150
Direct material cost = ₹ 250/
Direct labour cost = ₹ 200/
Factory overhead = ₹ 225/
Profit = 10% of selling price
Selling on-cost = 30% of factory cost.
Selling price of one electric bulb,
Factory cost = Material cost + Labour cost + overheds
$= 250 + 200 + 225$
= ₹ 675/-
Selling on cost = $0.3 \times 675$
= ₹ 202.5/
Total Cost = $675 + 202.5$
= ₹ 877.5/

Let $x$ = selling price per electric bulb.
$$x = \frac{1}{150} \times 877.5 + 0.1x$$
$0.9x = 5.85$
$x =$ ₹ 6.50

53. (c) 54. (c) 55. (c)

56. (b) Constant factor in ₹ 10 series
$= (10)^{1/10}$
$= 1.25$

57. (b) 58. (d) 59. (d) 60. (d)

61. (d) Let principle value of radio = ₹ X
$900 = X(1 + 0.8)$
$X = 500$
Net profit = 900 + 200
$= 500(1 + y)$
$$y = \frac{1100}{500} = 1.2 \text{ or } 120\%$$

62. (c) 63. (b) 64. (c) 65. (a) 66. (a)
67. (c) 68. (c) 69. (c) 70. (a) 71. (a)

72. (c) $5000 + 20 \times 500 = 30X$
$X = 500$

73. (d) 74. (b) 75. (d) 76. (d) 77. (a)
78. (c) 79. (b) 80. (c) 81. (b) 82. (c)
83. (d) 84. (d) 85. (d)

86. (b) GP = 1, NC = 4, SP = S

87. (a) 88. (c) 89. (c) 90. (d) 91. (c)
92. (c) 93. (b) 94. (c) 95. (c) 96. (a)

97. (a) Degrees of freedom, $F = 3(N-1) - 2P_1 - P_2$,
where $P_1 = 1/2\,(2N_2 + 3N_3)$.
Number of binary links, $N_2 = 3$,
Number of ternary links, $N_3 = 2$
$P_1 = 1/2\,.\,(2 \times 3 + 3 \times 2) = 6$,
$N = 5$, $P_2 = 0$
$F = 3(5-1) - 2 \times 6 = 0$

98. (a) 99. (c) 100. (b) 101. (a) 102. (d)
103. (d) 104. (d) 105. (b) 106. (c) 107. (c)
108. (c) 109. (d) 110. (d) 111. (c) 112. (a)
113. (b) 114. (d) 115. (c) 116. (c) 117. (d)

118. (a) For elliptical trammel, link 4 is fixed and for Oldham's coupling, link 2 is fixed.

119. (d) *P* will be the instantaneous centre when it lies on the intersection of links *AB* and *DC*.

120. (c) Relative angular velocity.
$\omega_r = \omega_2 - \omega_3$
$= 10 - 6 = 4$ rad/s

❑❑❑